ENCYCLOPEDIA OF

Group Processes & Intergroup Relations

Editorial Board

2

ENCYCLOPEDIA OF
Group Processes
& Intergroup Relations

JOHN M. LEVINE | MICHAEL A. HOGG | editors

University of Pittsburgh   *Claremont Graduate University*

Los Angeles | London | New Delhi
Singapore | Washington DC

A SAGE Reference Publication

For information:

SAGE Publications, Inc.
2455 Teller Road
Thousand Oaks, California 91320
E-mail: order@sagepub.com

SAGE Publications Ltd.
1 Oliver's Yard
55 City Road
London EC1Y 1SP
United Kingdom

SAGE Publications India Pvt. Ltd.
B 1/I 1 Mohan Cooperative Industrial Area
Mathura Road, New Delhi 110 044
India

SAGE Publications Asia-Pacific Pte. Ltd.
33 Pekin Street #02-01
Far East Square
Singapore 048763

Printed in the United States of America

Library of Congress Cataloging-in-Publication Data

Encyclopedia of group processes and intergroup relations/John M. Levine, Michael A. Hogg, editors.
　　p. cm.
Includes bibliographical references and index.
ISBN 978-1-4129-4208-9 (cloth)
　　1. Social groups—Encyclopedias. 2. Intergroup relations—Encyclopedias. I. Levine, John M. II. Hogg, Michael A., 1954-

HM716.E53 2010
302.303—dc22　　　　　　　　2009026419

This book is printed on acid-free paper.

09　10　11　12　13　10　9　8　7　6　5　4　3　2　1

Publisher:	Rolf A. Janke
Acquisitions Editor:	Michael Carmichael
Editorial Assistant:	Michele Thompson
Developmental Editors:	Diana E. Axelsen, Carole A. Maurer
Reference Systems Manager:	Leticia Gutierrez
Reference Systems Coordinator:	Laura Notton
Production Editor:	Kate Schroeder
Copy Editors:	Bonnie Freeman, Jamie Robinson
Typesetter:	C&M Digitals (P) Ltd.
Proofreaders:	Kris Bergstad, Sandy Zilka Livingston, Penny Sippel
Indexer:	Joan Shapiro
Cover Designer:	Candice Harman
Marketing Manager:	Amberlyn McKay

Contents

Volume 2

List of Entries   *vii*

Entries

K	507	S	723
L	511	T	897
M	549	U	941
N	591	V	947
O	613	W	953
P	635	X	959
R	675		

Index   963

List of Entries

Action Research
Affect Control Theory
Affirmative Action
Ageism
Allport, Gordon
Ambivalent Sexism
Anticonformity
Anti-Semitism
Apartheid
Asch, Solomon
Assimilation and Acculturation
Attachment Theory
Attitudes Toward Women Scale
Attribution Biases
Authoritarian Personality
Aversive Racism

Banality of Evil
Black Sheep Effect
Boundary Spanning
Brainstorming
Bystander Effect

Categorization
Charismatic Leadership
Children: Stereotypes and Prejudice
Children's Groups
Civil Rights Legislation
Civil Rights Movement
Cliques
Coalitions
Cognitive Consistency
Collaboration Technology
Collective Guilt
Collective Induction
Collective Movements and Protest
Collective Self

Collectivism/Individualism
Common-Identity/Common-Bond Groups
Common Ingroup Identity Model
Common Knowledge Effect
Commons Dilemma
Communication Networks
Compliance
Computer-Mediated Communication
Computer Simulation
Conformity
Conservatism
Conspiracy Theories
Contingency Theories of Leadership
Cooperation and Competition
Cooperative Learning
Cross-Categorization
Crowding
Crowds
Cults
Culture
Culture of Honor

Decategorization
Dehumanization/Infrahumanization
Deindividuation
Delphi Technique
Depersonalization
Desegregation
Deutsch, Morton
Deviance
Discrimination
Distributive Justice
Diversity
Dogmatism
Dominance Hierarchies
Dyads
Dynamical Systems Approach

Emergent Norm Theory
Entitativity
Escalation of Commitment
Essentialism
Ethnicity
Ethnocentrism
Ethnolinguistic Vitality
Eugenics
Evolutionary Psychology
Experimentation
Extended Contact Effect

Fads and Fashions
False Consensus Effect
Families
Faultlines
Feminism
Festinger, Leon
Free Riding
Frustration-Aggression Hypothesis

Gangs
Gender and Behavior
Gender Roles
Genocide
Graduated Reciprocation in Tension Reduction
   (GRIT)
Great Person Theory of Leadership
Group Boundaries
Group Cohesiveness
Group Composition
Group Development
Group Dissolution
Group Ecology
Group Emotions
Group Formation
Group Learning
Group Memory
Group Mind
Group Motivation
Group Performance
Group Polarization
Group Position Theory
Group Potency
Group Problem Solving and Decision Making
Group Socialization
Group Structure
Group Task
Groupthink

Hate Crimes
Hidden Profile Task
Holocaust
Homophily
Homophobia

Identification and Commitment
Identity Control Theory
Ideology
Idiosyncrasy Credit
Illusion of Group Effectivity
Illusory Correlation
Immigration
Implicit Association Test (IAT)
Implicit Prejudice
Inclusion/Exclusion
Informational Influence
Ingroup Allocation Bias
Initiation Rites
Innovation
Institutionalized Bias
Interactionist Theories of Leadership
Interaction Process Analysis
Interdependence Theory
Intergroup Anxiety
Intergroup Contact Theory
Intergroup Emotions Theory
Intergroup Empathy
Intergroup Violence
Interindividual–Intergroup Discontinuity
Islamophobia

J-Curve Hypothesis
Jigsaw Classroom Technique
Job Design
Juries
Justice
Just World Hypothesis

Köhler Effect

Language and Intergroup Relations
Leader Categorization Theory
Leader-Member Exchange (LMX) Theory
Leadership
Legitimation
Leniency Contract
Levels of Analysis
Lewin, Kurt

Linguistic Category Model (LCM)
Linguistic Intergroup Bias (LIB)
Looking-Glass Self
Loyalty

Mediation
Mergers
Minimal Group Effect
Minority Coping Strategies
Minority Groups in Society
Minority Influence
Modern Forms of Prejudice
Modern Racism
Modern Sexism
Moscovici, Serge
Multiculturalism
Multiple Identities
Mutual Intergroup Differentiation Model

Nationalism and Patriotism
Need for Belonging
Need for Closure
Need for Power
Negotiation and Bargaining
Normative Influence
Norms

Obedience to Authority
Opinion Deviance
Optimal Distinctiveness
Organizations
Ostracism
Outgroup Homogeneity Effect

Path–Goal Theory of Leadership
Perceived Group Variability
Personality Theories of Leadership
Personnel Turnover
Pluralistic Ignorance
Power
Power–Dependence Theory
Prejudice
Prisoner's Dilemma
Procedural Justice
Process Consultation
Process Gain and Loss
Protestant Work Ethic

Racial Ambivalence Theory
Racism

Realistic Group Conflict Theory
Reference Groups
Referent Informational Influence Theory
Relational Cohesion Theory
Relational Model of Authority in Groups
Relative Deprivation
Research Methods and Issues
Reverse Discrimination
Right Wing Authoritarianism
Ringelmann Effect
Roles
Role Transitions
Romance of Leadership
Rumor

Scapegoating
Schisms
Self-Categorization Theory
Self-Esteem
Self-Fulfilling Prophecy
Self-Managing Teams
Self-Stereotyping
Sensitivity Training Groups
Sexism
Sexual Harassment
Shared Mental Models
Sherif, Muzafer
Slavery
Social Class
Social Comparison Theory
Social Compensation
Social Darwinism
Social Decision Schemes
Social Deviance
Social Dilemmas
Social Dominance Theory
Social Entrainment
Social Exchange in Networks and Groups
Social Facilitation
Social Identity Model of Deindividuation Effects
Social Identity Theory
Social Identity Theory of Leadership
Social Impact Theory
Social Loafing
Socially Shared Cognition
Social Mobility
Social Networks
Social Relations Model
Social Representations

Socioemotional and Task Behavior
Sociometer Model
Sociometric Choice
Sports Teams
Stanford Prison Experiment
Status
Status Characteristics/Expectation States Theory
Status Construction Theory
Stepladder Technique
Stereotype Threat
Stereotyping
Stigma
Subjective Group Dynamics
Subtyping
Sucker Effect
Support Groups
Survey Methods
Symbolic Interactionism
Symbolic Racism
SYMLOG
System Justification Theory
System Theory

Tajfel, Henri
Team Building

Team Negotiation
Team Performance Assessment
Team Reflexivity
Teams
Territoriality
Terrorism
Terror Management Theory
Therapy Groups
Tokenism
Transactional Leadership Theories
Transactive Memory Systems
Transformational Leadership Theories
Trust

Ultimate Attribution Error
Uncertainty-Identity Theory

Vertical Dyad Linkage Model
Virtual/Internet Groups

Weightism
Work Teams

Xenophobia

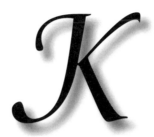

KÖHLER EFFECT

The *Köhler effect* is a kind of group motivation gain effect—an instance where a person works harder as a member of a group than when working individually. In the Köhler effect, that person is, to some degree, a "weak link" for the group—that is, if he or she fails to do well, the group will not do well. There are many tasks where a bad performance by a single member can ensure a bad group performance; social psychologists refer to these as *conjunctive group tasks*. For example, a mountain-climbing team that is tethered together cannot climb any faster than the slowest climber in the group. The Köhler effect is the finding that incapable members—the "weak links"—tend to exert extra effort, especially at such conjunctive tasks; for example, a slow climber should climb harder and faster when tethered to faster climbers than when climbing alone.

Because there is a great deal of research that shows the opposite pattern—group motivation losses, often referred to as *social loafing*—some scholars have suggested that members of performance groups or teams may be generally less strongly motivated than individual performers. But the Köhler effect, like other motivation gain effects, shows that this is untrue—under the right conditions, members of performance groups can be exceptionally motivated workers. Because many important tasks are carried out by groups (more and more often in modern organizational work teams),

many people—in industry, in business, in sports, and in government—are naturally very interested in better understanding such effects. This entry examines several aspects of the Köhler effect, such as its history, why it occurs, and when it occurs.

Historical Context

The Köhler effect was first discovered by German industrial psychologist Otto Köhler in the 1920s. He was interested in how differences in group members' abilities affected group performance. He asked members of a Berlin rowing club to perform a hard persistence task—to do standing curls with a heavy weight (44kg per rower) until they were so exhausted they could not go on. Sometimes they did this alone; other times they did it in two- or three-person groups. When they worked in groups, they held a single weighted bar. The bar was twice as heavy for dyads; three times as heavy for triads. This group task was conjunctive; as soon as any group member quit, the rest of the group could not continue very long. Köhler found that the groups persisted longer than their weakest members had persisted as individuals. This surprising motivation gain was biggest when the members of the groups were moderately different in ability. If the difference in ability was very small, or it if was very big, the motivation gain was not as large.

These provocative findings were largely forgotten for more than 60 years, until a 1989 article by Erich Witte rekindled research interest.

Since Witte's article, Köhler's motivation gain effect has been replicated repeatedly, not only for physical persistence tasks, like those used originally by Köhler, but for several other tasks (e.g., simple computations, visual attention tasks).

Causes of the Köhler Effect

Much research suggests that the Köhler effect may have at least two causes, one rooted in the process of social comparison, the other rooted in the effects of individual members being indispensable to the group. First, simply learning that others are performing better than you, can often be sufficient to boost your efforts. Such upward social comparisons can lead you to set a higher performance goal to try to compete with those others, or it may simply remind you of some of the stigmas that attach to those who are less capable. This process occurs in groups where you are less capable than your fellow group members, but it can also occur when the others with whom you compare yourself are not actually working with you.

Second, knowing that your work group is depending on you to perform well can also boost your efforts, if you care about how well the group does or about how the rest of the group will evaluate you. Although both processes seem to contribute independently to the overall Köhler effect, certain characteristics of the group performance situation and of the group members can affect their relative importance. For example:

The motivation gain is larger when the group's task is conjunctive, and the least capable members' efforts are highly indispensable, than when the group's task is additive (e.g., a group tug of war), where every members' efforts matter to some degree and, hence, the least capable members are not uniquely indispensable.

As Köhler showed in his original work, the motivation gain is largest when members' abilities are moderately different (vs. about the same or very different). This appears mostly to be due to the social comparison mechanism; for example, we stop comparing ourselves with others if they are too much more capable than we are because we see the task of matching or competing with them as unachievable.

The indispensability mechanism appears to be relatively more important to females, whereas the social comparison mechanism appears to be relatively more important to males. It has been suggested that these gender differences reflect more general gender differences in levels of concern for others and for relationships (stronger in females) versus for social status and dominance (stronger in males).

Certain aspects of the work group setting seem to facilitate both causal mechanisms. For example, the Köhler effect is stronger when group members are able constantly to monitor one another's level of performance, compared to when monitoring is difficult or impossible. Such monitoring makes it easier to make upward social comparisons, and for incapable group members to be reminded that they are indeed "weak links" in the group's chain. Likewise, the effect is stronger when group members are physically in one another's presence than when they are not (e.g., as in so-called virtual work teams, becoming ever more popular in the Internet age). Such physical presence seems to enhance concerns with how we are likely to be evaluated by others, either because we are not as capable as they are (upward social comparison) or because we may be holding the group back (indispensability).

Other Group Research

Otto Köhler's original interest was in how group composition would affect group member performance. And he showed that the relative abilities of group members were critical for the motivation gain effect that now bears his name. In more recent research, other aspects of group composition have also been shown to affect the Köhler effect. For example, an incapable male working at a physical-strength task produces a much larger Köhler effect when his more capable partner is a female than when this partner is another male. Apparently, it is more embarrassing to males to be outperformed by a woman than by a man, at least at a task that requires physical strength.

And when social comparison is possible, the Köhler effect is larger when one's more capable dyad partner is a member of an *outgroup* (a group to which one does not belong) than when he or she is a member of one's *ingroup*. Apparently, it is more embarrassing to be bested by someone in a "competing" group than by someone who is not. Both of these aspects of group composition appear to alter the social comparison mechanism, but some aspects of group composition also alter the indispensability mechanism. For example, if your more capable partner rejects or ostracizes you, you tend to become less concerned about the fact that your efforts are indispensable to the group.

The Köhler effect is in some ways like another well-documented group motivation gain—the *social compensation effect*. In both phenomena, being indispensable to the group's success prompts higher levels of effort. In social compensation, that higher level of effort comes from a relatively capable group member who believes that the others in the group either cannot or will not work hard enough for the group to succeed. Conversely, the higher level of effort in the Köhler effect comes from a relatively *in*capable group member.

Another interesting difference between the two phenomena is the emotional reactions of the people working extra hard. For social compensation, if the rewards of group success are shared equally in the group, then the capable and hard-working group member is likely to feel exploited, and hence upset, when he or she works harder than others but receives no more reward than those others. The tables are turned, however, for the incapable and hard-working group member in the Köhler effect. He or she has to worry about a more capable partner feeling frustrated by being "held back" by a less capable partner. In general, however, when the incapable group member works hard in the Köhler effect, his or her emotional reactions are more likely to be positive (e.g., relief, pride)

than are those of the capable member who works hard in the social compensation effect.

Norbert L. Kerr

See also Group Composition; Group Motivation; Group Performance; Group Task; Social Comparison Theory; Social Compensation; Social Facilitation; Social Loafing; Work Teams

Further Readings

Hertel, G., Kerr, N. L., & Messé, L. A. (2000). Motivation gains in performance groups: Paradigmatic and theoretical developments on the Köhler effect. *Journal of Personality and Social Psychology, 79*(4), 580–601.

Kerr, N. L., Messé, L. A., Seok, D., Sambolec, E. J., Lount, R. B., Jr., & Park, E. S. (2007). Psychological mechanisms underlying the Köhler motivation gain. *Personality and Social Psychology Bulletin, 33*(6), 828–841.

Köhler, O. (1926). Kraftleistungen bei Einzel- und Gruppenabeit [Physical performance in individual and group situations]. *Industrielle Psychotechnik, 3,* 274–282.

Stroebe, W., Diehl, M., & Abakoumkin, G. (1996). Social compensation and the Köhler effect: Toward a theoretical explanation of motivation gains in group productivity. In E. Witte & J. Davis (Eds.), *Understanding group behavior: Consensual action by small groups* (Vol. 2, pp. 37–65). Mahwah, NJ: Lawrence Erlbaum.

Weber, B., & Hertel, G. (2007). Motivation gains of inferior group members: A meta-analytical review. *Journal of Personality and Social Psychology, 93*(6), 973–993.

Witte, E. H. (1989). Köhler rediscovered: The anti-Ringelmann effect. *European Journal of Social Psychology, 19,* 147–154.

LANGUAGE AND INTERGROUP RELATIONS

Language is a tool people use to realize goals in groups. These goals can manifest in socially constructive ways such as democracy, cooperation, and altruism, but they can also manifest in socially destructive ways such as totalitarianism, hate speech, and genocide. The ways in which these social structures and behaviors evolve depends on the relations between groups, and it depends on language. Language can also be a defining attribute of a group that distinguishes it from other groups.

This entry describes some of the ways in which language is used to manage social distance, and reviews research on language and prejudice. Then, it discusses relationships between language and power, with reference to gender, status hierarchy formation in small groups, and linguistic devices used to mask acts of power. Finally, it describes some relations between language and social cognition.

Language and the Management of Social Distance

People use language to socially approach or distance themselves from others. For example, we can mimic the idioms others use ("Dude, that is rad") or approach their accents by changing our pronunciation, speech rate and/or volume, lexical diversity, and so on. These linguistic approach moves are referred to as *speech accommodation*. We can also keep our accents, phrases, or language unaltered when talking with others to maintain social distance, or even intensify our use of these forms to further increase social distance. These maintenance and withdrawal moves are referred to as *speech divergence.*

Originally, sociolinguists thought that such shifts were dictated by social situations. More formal situations, for example, might lead one to use more "correct" pronunciation than less formal situations. This idea was overturned, however, when Howard Giles proposed his speech accommodation theory, now called communication accommodation theory. According to this theory, people are motivated to use accommodating language when they want to express similarity and attraction, and they do so when they believe their interaction partner has legitimate social status. Conversely, when people believe the social status of others is low or illegitimate, they are likely to use divergent language.

In a now classic demonstration, Richard Bourhis and Howard Giles asked Welsh second-language learners, who were highly committed to their Welsh identity, to participate in a study on second-language learning. In one experimental condition, an English experimenter who employed received pronunciation (i.e., nonregional accented English) challenged participants' reasons for studying Welsh: "Why study a dying language with a dismal future?" These participants answered in a broader Welsh accent, used more Welsh terms in their replies, and referred to their Welsh identity more often than those not so provoked. The Welsh speakers' divergent replies can be understood as attempts to maintain their ethnic heritage in the face of a threat from what they considered to be the illegitimately high-status English.

There is now a wealth of evidence that such linguistic shifts are driven by motivations and perceptions of status relations between groups. In the case of intergenerational relations, the elderly commonly experience patronizing speech from younger generations. Mary Lee Hummert and Ellen Ryan have shown that nonaccommodating language follows from negative stereotypes of the elderly (e.g., as lacking intelligence and basic competence); this then increases the likelihood that the elderly will further enact behaviors that confirm this stereotype (e.g., being helpless and confused), which, in turn, has a negative consequence for elderly cognitive functioning, health, and self-esteem. The bitter twist to this phenomenon is that these outcomes can then reinforce the original stereotype, producing a cycle of negative intergenerational relations that is difficult to prevent.

In the case of policing, evidence suggests that police officers who use accommodating language—who are polite, listen, and show respect—are more trusted, are viewed as more competent, instill greater satisfaction in civilians, and are more likely to gain compliance than are nonaccommodating officers. This has proven to be the case in the United States, Taiwan, South Africa, and China.

In these three examples, and indeed many others, it is evident that the management of linguistic distance affects the nature of relations between groups. An important conclusion here is that accommodating language is not just a path to ameliorating tensions between groups; it is also a path to producing positive and socially constructive relations between groups.

Language and Prejudice

Hate Speech: The Case of Ethnophaulisms

People are creative in their use of disparaging terms to refer to one another: *wetback, frog, mick, limey*. These ethnic slurs are *ethnophaulisms*, a term derived from the Greek words meaning "a national group" and "to disparage." Ethnophaulisms can take many forms: derisive adjectives, metaphors (e.g., *Italian perfume* for garlic),

derisive verb forms (e.g., *to gyp, to go Dutch*), proverbs (e.g., *beware of the Hun in the sun*), children's stories, and ethnic jokes. Ethnophaulisms are a form of hate speech that is typically applied to ethnic and especially immigrant groups.

Brian Mullen's research shows that ethnophaulisms vary in complexity (some groups have many ethnophaulisms that refer to many qualities, some relatively few), and they vary in terms of the degree of negativity, although they are typically quite negative. A number of variables have an impact on ethnophaulisms. The smaller the immigrant group, the less complex the ethnophaulisms. So, for example, in the United States, there is one ethnophaulism for Pakistanis (*paki*), whereas five have been identified for Greeks (*asshole-bandit, greaseball, grikola, johnny,* and *marble-head*). Groups with low-complexity ethnophaulisms also tend to have more negative representations, and both complexity and the negative valence are associated with the degree of familiarity of the group within a culture (in terms of representations in books and songs) and the degree of foreignness of the group (in terms of linguistic difference, facial appearance, and complexion). Smaller, less familiar, and more foreign groups have more negative and less complex ethnophaulisms applied to them.

Ethnophaulisms have been linked with various indicators of social exclusion. Groups with less complex ethnophaulisms were more likely to have lower immigration quotas from the 1920s through to the 1960s, and they were proportionately less likely to become naturalized U.S. citizens from the early 1900s to 1930. Research has shown that less complex ethnophaulisms are associated with lower rates of intermarriage and employment in more hazardous occupations. More negative ethnophaulisms are associated with greater ethnically segregated housing. Most disturbingly, rates of suicide among immigrants are higher than rates of suicide of people in the immigrants' home country, and the more negative the ethnophaulisms for any given group, the higher the rate of suicide.

Language Attitudes

In the United States, people of British heritage are often delighted to find that their accent, while often misunderstood, confers social prestige that implies that the user is sophisticated, cultured, and intelligent. Extra service in stores, opportunities to persuade, and the receipt of glowing admiration— *Oh, I just love your accent!*—are not uncommon. For immigrants in other ethnic groups, less flattering evaluations are the norm. These evaluations of ethnic accents and accompanying discrimination are language attitudes—evaluations of speakers based not on individual personality or skills, but on stereotypes.

Language attitudes became a focus for study when Wallace Lambert devised the matched guise technique. In this experimental situation, bilingual speakers were recorded speaking in one of two languages or accents. Research participants were then informed that these speakers were different people and asked to evaluate the speakers' personalities. The first study to use this method was published in 1960 and presented French- and Anglo-Canadian respondents with tapes of four French-English bilinguals to evaluate on 14 traits (e.g., height, good looks, leadership, intelligence). Both French- and Anglo-Canadian research participants rated the English guise speakers higher than French guise speakers on almost all attributes. For Anglo participants, the only exception was sense of humor, and for French participants, the only exceptions were religiousness and kindness. Even so, the French-Canadian participants rated the English guise speaker much more strongly on good looks, leadership, intelligence, self-confidence, and character.

Subsequent research showed quite different patterns. For example, around the same time, research in Israel revealed a pattern of mutual downgrading among Palestinian and Israeli respondents. Later research in the U.K. revealed a pattern where the English were rated high on status variables (wealth, intelligence) but low on solidarity variables (friendliness, warmth), whereas the reverse was true for the Scots. While this area of research has yielded inconsistent patterns, these and other patterns of language attitudes ultimately became interpretable using the ethnolinguistic identity theory developed by Giles and his colleagues. The fundamental idea of ethnolinguistic identity theory is that groups vary in status factors (e.g., economically and historically), demographic factors (e.g., numbers of group members and rates of birth), and institutional factors (e.g., representation of groups in government and educational contexts), and the higher the group scores on these factors, the higher the group is said to be in vitality. High-vitality groups tend toward competitive social relations with others and thus upgrade the ingroup relative to outgroup in language attitudes, whereas groups lower in vitality either avoid direct comparison with dominant groups or actually identify more strongly with the high-vitality outgroup.

Language and Power

Sik Hung Ng and Jim Bradac have described five ways in which the relationships between language and power can be understood, and these can be grouped under two general headings. First, there is the idea of power behind language. In this case, language is incidental in comparison to the power that the individual or group is thought to possess. So, the perceived power of language ebbs and flows with the power of the group, and this is reflected in people's attitudes toward a particular variety of language.

The first study conducted on the language attitudes associated with French-Canadian speakers suggested a very negative appraisal. Since the 1960s, however, there has been a linguistic revival of French language and culture in Quebec, and with this increase in cultural power, there has been an accompanying elevation of perceived prestige of the language. Language can also be used to reveal the power of a speaker. "Everybody freeze! This is a hold up!" conveys to listeners that the speaker has the power that comes from having a loaded gun.

Language itself can serve as a source of power— the power *of* language. People can use language to create power where they had none, to depoliticize acts of power that others might find distasteful, and to construct or express social arrangements.

Power Behind Language

There is a large body of research on powerful and powerless language styles. Powerless language is characterized by the relatively frequent use of hedges (e.g., "sort of," "maybe"), disclaimers (e.g., "I'm no expert, but . . ."), and tag questions (e.g., "That's interesting, isn't it?"). Research has shown that the absence of these features—powerful language—is typically associated with the belief that the speaker is credible, intelligent, competent, and knowledgeable. The obvious expectation here is that people who use powerful language are more likely to be influential. There is evidence to support this, but there is also evidence that women who use powerless language with men are more likely to be persuasive than those who use powerful language, despite the negative evaluations of powerless language users.

Other research has focused on the evaluation of language as spoken or written by men and women. This work shows a gender-linked language effect. Feminine language (e.g., greater use of questions) is typically seen as being more aesthetically pleasing and intellectual but less dynamic than male language (e.g., greater use of directives). Interestingly, when given samples of male and female written language, even when people are unable to discern the gender of the writer, samples written by women are evaluated as nice and sweet and those by men as strong and active.

Power of Language

Language conveys the material power of users, and it can be used to create power. A common situation is group-based decision making. People often find themselves in ad hoc situations with relative strangers and a task at hand. This is the case in juries, committees, and interdepartmental discussion groups at work. In these situations, people will typically create a psychological group with a consensually established status hierarchy with or without much knowledge of each other. Robert Bales, in the 1950s and 60s, showed that people who took more speaking turns, independent of the content, were more likely to emerge as influential in the discussion.

Subsequent research has demonstrated that the content of what is said is important. Research by Scott Reid and Sik Hung Ng has suggested, consistent with expectation states theory, that groups form these status hierarchies very quickly. Use of proactive language early in the discussion (i.e., offers of task suggestions, disagreement, and replies to questions) suggests that an individual has some expertise at the task and creates *performance expectations*. These early expectations suggest status difference in the group, and these status distinctions determine who gets to speak. Reid and Ng reasoned that if this is the case, then it should be evident in the pattern of interruptions within the group. Indeed, those who emerged as high in status were more likely to have successful rather than unsuccessful interruptions when using proactive language. When those same high-status group members used reactive language (i.e., requested information or agreed with others' suggestions), they were more likely to have unsuccessful than successful interruptions. This suggests that the ability to gain turns in the group depends on what others in the group are willing to concede. Those presumed to have status are granted the right to speak if they are proactive, but they are blocked in their attempts to interrupt if what they say is reactive, and thus inconsistent with that status.

Language is also used to depoliticize acts of power. There are a number of techniques available to power users to maintain their power. When taking an unpopular action, leaders may employ the *passive voice transformation*. So, instead of saying "I expelled the illegal aliens from the country," the speaker might choose to say "The illegal aliens did not have the correct paperwork." The passive voice transformation can effectively remove the actor from the act of power, and this can decrease the degree to which such actors are seen as responsible for their actions.

A second device is *permutation*. One might say, "Employers always quarrel with unions," or "Unions always quarrel with employers." Clearly, the entity at the beginning of the sentence is assumed to have been the party responsible for the action. A third device is *generalization*. A speaker may say, "John punched Chris," "John hurt Chris," or "John is an aggressive person." Each sentence may be a reasonable description of the same behavior, but the sentences produce different impressions.

Over time, language can be used to routinize social relations, whereby powerful language consistently used over time may blend into the social landscape. In the case of English and many other languages, there are, as a matter of convention, masculine generics: "One small step for a man, one giant leap for mankind." Of course, these words are intended to speak for all of humanity, not just men. Nonetheless, the use of masculine generics means that women may be rendered less visible and of secondary importance to men because of the way in which language is structured. Indeed, there is evidence that people who hear these masculine generics do not mentally picture women.

Language and Social Cognition

Gün Semin and Klaus Fiedler have shown that we can choose four linguistic forms to describe any behavior. These forms vary in abstraction, but all could potentially be used to describe the same behavior. Starting at the most concrete level, we can use *descriptive action verbs* (e.g., *find, run, kiss*), *interpretive action verbs* (e.g., *help, offend, loot*), *state verbs* (e.g., *believe, love, hate*), or *adjectives* (e.g., *honest, helpful, aggressive*), with the latter language forms considered increasingly abstract.

Ann Maass and others have shown that people tend to describe positive ingroup and negative outgroup behaviors in relatively abstract language, but negative ingroup and positive outgroup behaviors in relatively concrete language. This *linguistic intergroup bias* is particularly likely to manifest when groups are socially competitive (e.g., environmentalists vs. hunters), are of a similar social standing, and share a history of competition or conflict (e.g., rival Italian cities). It is believed that such language use effectively diffuses or maintains stereotypes. In other words, language is a contributor to stereotypes, and thus prejudice.

Other work that more directly investigates stereotyping has focused attention on the degree to which people discuss and maintain *stereotype consistent* (SC) and *stereotype inconsistent* (SI) information. Although SI information is novel and potentially surprising, which would lead one to erroneously think it memorable, SC information is more likely to persist in communication chains. Research suggests that some stereotype content is more communicable because it serves psychological functions. Stereotypes that accurately describe properties that distinguish groups from one another and that fulfill identity-enhancing functions are those that are more likely to be communicated interpersonally, and therefore most likely to survive and prosper.

Scott A. Reid and Grace L. Anderson

See also Ethnolinguistic Vitality; Identification and Commitment; Linguistic Intergroup Bias (LIB); Power; Prejudice; Social Identity Theory; Stereotyping

Further Readings

Giles, H., & Coupland, N. (1991). *Language: Contexts and consequences.* Milton Keynes, UK: Open University Press.

Harwood, J., & Giles, H. (Eds.). (2005). *Intergroup communication: Multiple perspectives.* New York: Peter Lang.

Maass, A. (1999). Linguistic intergroup bias: Stereotype perpetuation through language. *Advances in Experimental Social Psychology, 31*, 79–121.

Ng, S. H., & Bradac, J. J. (1993). *Power in language: Verbal communication and social influence.* Newbury Park, CA: Sage.

Reid, S. A., & Ng, S. H. (1999). Language, power, and intergroup relations. *Journal of Social Issues, 55*, 119–139.

Reid, S. A., & Ng, S. H. (2006). The dynamics of intragroup differentiation in an intergroup social context. *Human Communication Research, 32*, 504–525.

Robinson, W. P., & Giles, H. (Eds.). (2001). *The new handbook of language and social psychology.* Chichester, UK: John Wiley.

LEADER CATEGORIZATION THEORY

Leader categorization theory (LCT), originally proposed by Robert Lord, places emphasis on the cognitive and perceptual processes underlying workplace leadership. It proposes that subordinates, through socialization and past experiences with leaders, develop *implicit leadership theories* (ILTs), that is, cognitive representations in the form of prototypes that specify the traits and abilities that characterize an "ideal" workplace leader. ILTs represent preexisting cognitive structures or prototypes that are stored in memory and come into play when subordinates communicate with leaders. In other words, when subordinates interact with someone in a leadership position, this activates their ILT from memory, and then they can evaluate the person's leadership qualities against their ILT. This entry describes leader categorization theory and related research.

ILTs do not represent objective realities inherent in the leader, but rather, are perceptual abstractions, summary labels that subordinates use to categorize individuals in leadership positions. ILTs are, therefore, subjective and reflect each person's assumptions of what characteristics and traits make an ideal workplace leader.

ILTs tend to form around a number of common factors, such as sensitivity, dedication, charisma, attractiveness, intelligence, strength, tyranny, and masculinity. Each person's ILT represents a belief that an ideal workplace leader will have certain amounts of each of these factors. While people can vary in terms of their ILT profile, each person's ILT tends to be relatively robust, and it does not change markedly over time. In addition, while ILTs tend to be relatively consistent within the same culture, they can vary quite considerably between different cultures—especially between individualist (e.g., United States, United Kingdom, Australia) and collectivist (e.g., India, China, Japan) countries. Thus, national culture plays a role in shaping the prototype of an ideal workplace leader. This has many implications for leaders who manage subordinates from different cultures (as is becoming increasingly common with globalization), as these subordinates may have different ILTs concerning what constitutes an "ideal" leader.

The subordinate's perception of the leader is determined by two processes. First, leadership can be *recognized* from the qualities and behaviors revealed through interactions between the leader and subordinate (e.g., the way the leader behaves leads to attributions concerning his or her leadership qualities). Second, leadership can be *inferred* from the outcomes of events determined by the leader (e.g., the performance of the leader can give clues concerning the qualities of the leader).

Leader categorization theory is a recognition-based approach to leadership. A person is evaluated as a leader on the basis of the perceived match between the behavior and character of the leader and those of the perceiver's ILT prototype. ILTs are the benchmark subordinates use to form an impression of their actual leader. Subordinates are assumed to engage in an "ILT vs. actual manager" matching process, and any discrepancies identified are subsequently thought to affect the overall impression that the subordinate forms of the leader.

In other words, when subordinates interact with a leader, they evaluate that leader against their own personal ILT profile. The better the leader matches the subordinate's ILT, the more positive will be the subordinate's judgment of the leader. Since subordinates might have differences in their ILTs, the perception of the qualities of the same leader might vary among members of the same work group.

Research Evidence

Some research has suggested that ILTs can act as a source of bias in leadership measurement. This is because subordinates might rely on their ILT prototype when they complete leadership questionnaires designed to evaluate their actual leader's behavior. In other words, individuals may simply regenerate their ILT prototype of an ideal leader when rating an actual leader, without paying sufficient attention to the value of the leader's behaviors and traits.

In support of the central tenet of leader categorization theory, however, research concerning the matching hypothesis shows that the more subordinates rate their actual manager as being close to their ILT prototype on several dimensions, the more likely the subordinate will be to report higher job satisfaction and general satisfaction with the leader. However, it might not be the case that every subordinate engages in the matching process in the same way. It is likely that there are many individual factors (such as personality) and situational factors (such as the degree of leader–subordinate interdependence) that might determine the extent to which subordinates evaluate their leader by comparing him or her to the ideal leader in their ILTs.

Leader categorization theory provides a different way to examine workplace leadership compared to other approaches. It does not focus on the style of leadership or the relationship between the leader and subordinate; instead, it focuses on the *perception* of leadership that results when subordinates compare the leader's traits and characteristics against their personal ILT prototype of an ideal leader.

The theory has many important implications for leadership development and training. It shows that leaders need to understand how their subordinates perceive their leadership qualities—through their actions and from the outcomes of their performance. Also, leaders need to understand that each subordinate will evaluate their leadership ability by comparing them against his or her individual ILT prototype. Since subordinates are likely to vary in terms of their ILT prototype of an ideal leader, leaders need to be aware that their behavior might be interpreted differently by different subordinates.

Robin Martin

See also Categorization; Leadership

Further Readings

Lord, R. G., Foti, R. J., & Phillips, J. S. (1982). A theory of leadership categorization. In J. G. Hunt, U. Sekaran, & C. Schriesheim (Eds.), *Leadership: Beyond establishment views* (pp. 104–121). Carbondale: Southern Illinois University Press.

Lord, R. G., & Hall, R. (2003). Identity, leadership categorization, and leadership schema. In D. van Knippenberg & M. A. Hogg (Eds.), *Leadership and power: Identity processes in groups and organizations* (pp. 48–64). London: Sage.

Lord, R. G., & Maher, K. J. (1993). *Leadership and information processing. Linking perceptions and performance.* London: Routledge.

LEADER-MEMBER EXCHANGE (LMX) THEORY

Leader-member exchange (LMX) *theory* is rooted in the idea that leaders and followers exchange benefits, and that their relationships are at the heart of the leadership process. Social scientists have long attempted to understand how people relate to each other, beginning with explorations of costs and rewards, interpersonal behavior, and human relationships. A number of theories have used the lens of interpersonal relationships to understand leadership, including Edwin Hollander's focus on idiosyncrasy credits, Tom Tyler's notion of procedural justice, Dave Messick's delineation of psychological exchanges, and James MacGregor Burns's conceptualization of transforming and transactional leadership. Most notably, George Graen and his colleagues constructed the formal leader-member exchange theory, which began by elaborating on the nature of the leader–follower relationship and its outcomes, and later created a model for effective leadership. This entry traces the background of these ideas and discusses the Graen theory in some detail.

Historical Context

Starting with their early work on learning, psychologists have recognized that rewards and punishments have a strong influence on behavior. At the end of the 19th century, Edward Thorndike at Harvard University published research on learning in cats, done in William James's basement in Cambridge, Massachusetts, which established "the law of effect"—the idea that reward stamps behavior in and punishment stamps behavior out, as Thorndike put it.

A great deal has been made of this basic idea that behavior is under the control of outcomes, specifically rewards and punishments, or more generally, benefits and costs. In social psychology, George Homans developed the idea that interpersonal behavior is an exchange where one individual's behavior provides costs or benefits to another person. Influence happens as a result of rewards and costs people can provide for each other.

Related work by John Thibaut and Harold Kelley developed the idea that each person in a relationship derives an *outcome level* (OL) based on the average degree of rewards minus costs that he or she obtains through the interaction exchanges in the relationship. Furthermore, they argued that the outcome level is evaluated against a *comparison level* (CL), based on all the outcomes a person knows about through his or her own and other people's relationship histories. The CL provides a baseline, or an expectation, of what level of outcome a person will or should get in a relationship. When the OL exceeds the CL, the relationship is satisfying. If the OL is less than the CL, people are dissatisfied and are likely to leave the relationship, depending on the available alternatives.

Hollander's Idea

The idea that people in relationships engage in some kind of exchange, and that each must provide satisfactory outcomes for the other if the relationship is to continue, has been important in Edwin Hollander's exchange theory of leadership. The leader provides "adequate role behavior directed toward the group's goal attainment," and followers accord the leader "status, recognition, and esteem." In effect, the followers give the leader legitimacy, which obliges them to follow the suggestions and directives of the leader. The key concept in Hollander's approach is the highly influential idea of *idiosyncrasy credit*. Leaders have varying amounts of credit given to them by followers, based fundamentally on individual leaders' competence and conformity to group norms. Credit is essentially legitimacy. It is the resource leaders need to provide direction for the group.

The legitimacy that followers give in exchange for leader competence and conformity is called idiosyncrasy credit, because although credit is built up partially on the basis of conformity, followers expect that leaders will use their credit to innovate— and that might mean not conforming. A leader who deviates, or acts idiosyncratically, may simply spend the credit, or if his or her initiatives lead the group to a better place, to more rewards, the deviation may actually build up credits rather than depleting them.

An example of using idiosyncrasy credit is U.S. President Richard Nixon's opening a peace initiative with China in 1972. The United States had shunned all public communication with "Red China" for more than 20 years. Conservative Republicans had been loudest in their condemnation of the "Chinese Communists" and their opposition to recognizing its government. When Nixon traveled to China, fellow Republicans swallowed their opposition and waited to see how the initiative would play out. A Democratic president, lacking credit with the political right, would have been pilloried. Nixon's diplomacy deviated from the group norm but ended up building credit with his followers for further innovations.

Hollander defines the legitimacy given to leaders by followers as the basis for leaders' ability to induce their followers to voluntarily comply with their directives for change. A leader without legitimacy will not be followed. According to Tom Tyler, the legitimacy of a leader or authority depends very heavily on the leader's using fair procedures in making decisions, that is, on *procedural justice*. Procedural justice provides a benefit, but it is a psychological rather than a tangible benefit. Through treating the follower fairly, the leader signals that the follower is a valuable member of the group. By being fair and unbiased, by listening to the follower's ideas and viewpoints, and by treating the follower with dignity, the leader confirms the follower's good standing in the group. In return, the follower accords the leader increased legitimacy, and more readily complies with his or her commands and suggestions.

Related Research

The distinction between psychological and tangible exchanges between leaders and followers is highlighted in James MacGregor Burns's concepts of transactional and transformational leadership. *Transactional leadership* involves the tangible exchange of benefits—as illustrated by the politician who promises no new taxes in exchange for election to office or the manager who offers an extra vacation day for employees who meet a lofty quota. In contrast, Burns's concept of *transformational* or *transforming leadership* contends that leaders empower followers to achieve fundamental change through the exchange of psychological benefits that raise both the followers' and the leaders' levels of motivation and morality.

David Messick further delineates the mutually beneficial exchange of psychological benefits between leaders and followers in his *social exchange model* of leadership. People follow leaders because they get something valuable from them, and leaders in turn benefit from their followers. For example, leaders give their followers vision and direction in return for focus and self-direction from the followers. In addition, leaders give their followers protection and security, achievement and effectiveness, inclusion and belonging, and pride and self-respect. Followers reciprocate these benefits with gratitude and loyalty, commitment and effort, cooperation and sacrifice, and respect and obedience.

The Graen Team's Work

The principal theory that makes the individual leader-member dyadic relationship the fundamental component of the leadership process is George Graen and his colleagues' *leader-member exchange* (LMX) theory. LMX theory has evolved through a number of stages. Originally, it was termed the *vertical-dyad linkage* (VDL) theory, and at that point, researchers examined the vertical linkages, or relationships, leaders created with their followers.

They found that followers with positive, high-quality relationships consisting of mutual respect, trust, and obligation become part of the leader's ingroup. Followers in the ingroup become trusted assistants going above and beyond their job descriptions for their leader. In return, the leader does more for ingroup than outgroup members and gives ingroup members more information and influence.

VDL theory subsequently became leader-member exchange theory, and the focus shifted to examining the nature of these relationships and the organizational outcomes associated with the quality of leader–follower relationships. At this stage, researchers noted that these dyadic relationships occur through a role-making process, and they identified a number of characteristics and behaviors of both leaders and followers that have an impact on the development of these relationships. For example, the quality of these relationships is influenced by the value agreement between leaders and followers, communication patterns and frequency, interaction patterns, and influence tactics, as well as by followers' optimism, dependability, and efficacy. High-quality relationships between leaders and followers are associated with a great variety of positive outcomes, including organizational performance, job satisfaction, and career progress.

The next stage in the evolution of LMX theory has shifted the focus from a descriptive approach to a prescriptive approach, emphasizing the development of effective dyadic partnerships in the leadership-making model. Thus, the focus has shifted from examining how leaders differentiate among followers to highlighting how leaders can develop effective relationships with all group members. There also has been a shift from a hierarchical leader–follower approach to viewing leadership as a partnership of group members. This model suggests that leadership making occurs progressively over three phases. The first phase, termed the *stranger* phase, is characterized by rule-bound, formal interactions focused on purely contractual exchanges; leaders give followers what they need to do their job, and followers do only the basic requirements of their job. This phase is akin to the transactional model of leadership and is characterized by low-quality exchanges and self-interested motivations.

When one of the dyad members makes an offer for improved relations, the relationship can move to the second phase, *acquaintance*, which is characterized by increased social exchanges such as sharing information and resources of both a personal and work nature. Finally, the relationship can mature to the third phase, *mature partnership*, which includes even greater social exchanges such as respect, trust, and obligations. This final stage is marked by high-quality dyadic exchanges, with a shift in focus from self-interest to the interests of the group; thus, the relationship at this stage can be considered transformational in nature.

Crystal L. Hoyt and George R. Goethals

See also Charismatic Leadership; Contingency Theories of Leadership; Great Person Theory of Leadership; Idiosyncrasy Credit; Interactionist Theories of Leadership; Leadership; Path–Goal Theory of Leadership; Personality Theories of Leadership; Procedural Justice; Relational Model of Authority in Groups; Social Exchange in Networks and Groups; Social Identity Theory of Leadership; Transactional Leadership Theories; Transformational Leadership Theories; Vertical Dyad Linkage Model

Further Readings

Burns, J. M. (2003). *Transforming leadership: A new pursuit of happiness.* New York: Atlantic Monthly Press.

Graen, G., & Uhl-Bien, M. (1995). Relationship-based approach to leadership: Development of leader-member exchange (LMX) theory of leadership over 25 years: Applying a multi-level multi-domain perspective. *The Leadership Quarterly, 6,* 219–247.

Hollander, E. P. (1993). Legitimacy, power, and influence: A perspective on relational features of leadership. In M. M. Chemers & R. Ayman (Eds.), *Leadership theory and research: Perspectives and directions* (pp. 29–48). San Diego, CA: Academic Press.

Messick, D. M. (2005). On the psychological exchange between leaders and followers. In D. M. Messick & R. M. Kramer (Eds.), *The psychology of leadership: New perspectives and research* (pp. 81–96). Mahwah, NJ: Lawrence Erlbaum.

Thibaut, J. W., & Kelley, H. H. (1959). *The social psychology of groups.* New York: John Wiley.

Tyler, T. R., & Lind, E. A. (1992). A relational model of authority in groups. *Advances in experimental social psychology* (Vol. 25, pp. 115–191). San Diego, CA: Academic Press.

LEADERSHIP

We are consumed with interest in leaders. We animatedly gossip about "the boss"; airport bookshops bulge with leadership books; current affairs dissect the actions of leaders; and much of the organizational and management sciences is a study of leadership and the role of the CEO (chief executive officer). This is not surprising. Our leaders have enormous influence over us—they make decisions for us and shape the course of our lives and even the type of people we are, and so we focus on how effective they are; how we elect, appoint, and depose them; and whether they lead for good or for evil. This entry defines leadership, and then describes the major organizational and social psychological theories of leadership.

Defining Leadership

Leadership is a process where an individual, or clique, is able to influence others, as a group or as group members, to internalize a collective vision, and mobilize them toward attaining that vision. Effective leadership transforms people's goals and ambitions, even their identity, and replaces self-oriented behavior with group-oriented behavior. The exercise of power over people to force them, through rewards and punishments, to merely comply with commands and bend to one's will is not leadership.

One important distinction is between effective/ineffective leadership and good/bad leadership. The effectiveness of leadership is largely a matter of fact (the leader can or cannot change attitudes and motivate action), whereas the difference between good and bad leadership is largely a subjective judgment hinging on whether the leader has attributes we applaud, uses means we approve of, and sets and achieves goals we value. Leadership research focuses on leadership effectiveness rather than the moral quality of the means and ends of leadership.

Personality Attributes of Great Leaders

Although leadership is a group process (leaders require followers), leadership research has a long history of focusing on the personality attributes of leaders that make them great leaders. The 19th-century belief that leaders are born not made is no longer in vogue—research has failed to find "great leader" genes. However, the idea that some of us have personalities, however acquired, that predispose us to lead effectively in all or most situations, whereas others do not, has attracted enormous research attention. For example, modern transformational theories of leadership (see below) capture this idea with the concept of charisma—a charismatic personality or leadership style is critically important for leaders to be able to transform group goals and practices. James Meindl talks about "the romance of leadership" to capture our obsession with charisma as a basis of effective leadership.

A definitive review published in 2002 concluded that three of the "Big Five" personality dimensions identified by personality research are associated with effective leadership: They are extraversion/surgency, intellect/openness to experience, and conscientiousness. Overall, however, many leadership theorists believe that personality perspectives on leadership do not allow us very reliably to differentiate between effective and ineffective leaders.

What Do Effective Leaders Do?

One reaction to a focus on stable personality correlates of effective leadership was a somewhat extreme stance that we can all lead effectively if the situation is right. Research shows this to be only partially true—some people still appear to be more effective across a range of situations. A less extreme reaction to personality perspectives is to focus on leadership behaviors: Maybe some *behaviors* are more effective for leadership than others. One reliable distinction that has emerged over and over again in many different guises is between a leadership style that pays more attention to the group task and getting things done (task-oriented leadership), and one that pays attention to relationships among group members (socioemotional leadership). Most groups require both types of leadership and people who are capable of being both task focused and socioemotionally focused tend to be the most effective.

Contingency Theories

However, different situations and different group activities call for different emphases on the task or on relationships—in which case the relative effectiveness of task-oriented and relationship-oriented leaders may be contingent on properties of the leadership situation. This idea is reflected in Fred Fiedler's *contingency theory* of leadership. Very popular in the 1970s, one strength of this theory was that Fiedler had a way to measure leadership style—the Least Preferred Coworker (LPC) Scale, according to which people who rate their least preferred coworker favorably are relationship oriented, while those who rate their least preferred coworker unfavorably are task oriented—and to classify how well structured situations were. Generally, relationship-oriented leadership was most effective unless the group task was very poorly structured or very well structured, when a task-oriented style was more effective.

Another contingency perspective is *normative decision theory*. Leaders can choose to make decisions autocratically (subordinate input is not sought), consultatively (subordinate input is sought, but the leader retains authority to make the final decision), or as a genuine group decision (leader and subordinates are equal partners in shared decision making). The efficacy of these strategies is contingent on the quality of leader–subordinate relationships (which influences how committed and supportive subordinates are), and on task clarity and structure (which influences the leader's need for subordinate input). Autocratic leadership is fast and effective if leader–subordinate relationships are good and the task is well structured. When the task is less clear, consultative leadership is best, and when leader–subordinate relations are poor, group decision making is best.

A third contingency theory is *path–goal theory*. It assumes that a leader's main function is to motivate followers by clarifying the paths that will help them attain their goals—leaders do this by directing task-related activities (structuring) or by addressing followers' personal and emotional needs (consideration). Structuring is most effective when followers are unclear about their goals and how to reach them, and consideration is most effective when the task is boring or uncomfortable. Structuring can be viewed as meddling and micromanagement when tasks are well understood, and consideration can be considered distracting and unnecessary when followers are already engaged and motivated.

A fourth contingency theory is *situational leadership theory*. A distinction is drawn between directive and supportive behavior that produces four leadership behaviors: telling (high directive, low supportive), selling (high directive, high supportive), participating (low directive, high supportive), and delegating (low directive, low supportive). Effective leaders need to tailor their behavior to the situational demands of subordinates' level of task ability and task willingness—for example, telling is best suited to low-ability followers, and participating to highly motivated followers.

Transactional Leadership

Another way to view leadership is as a transaction between leaders and followers—the leader does something benefiting followers, and followers in turn allow the leader to lead. Underpinning this idea is an assumption that leadership is a process of exchange, similar to contractual relations in economic life that are based on good faith. Leaders transact with followers to get things done, setting expectations and goals and providing recognition and rewards for task completion. There also is an equity dimension to the leader–follower relationship. Because effective leaders play a greater role in steering groups to their goals than do followers, followers may reinstate equity by rewarding the leader with social approval, praise, prestige, status, and power—the trappings of effective leadership.

An early transactional approach is Edwin Hollander's analysis of *idiosyncrasy credit*. Leaders who initially conform to group norms, and therefore serve the group well, lay the groundwork for a transaction in which they are subsequently rewarded by the group by being allowed to be idiosyncratic and innovative—key features of effective leadership.

Another well-known transactional leadership theory is the *vertical dyad linkage* (VDL) *model*. Leaders develop different exchange relationships with specific subordinates, in which the subordinate can either be treated as a close and valued "ingroup" member with the leader or in a more remote manner as an "outgroup" member who is separate from the leader.

This model quickly evolved into the now better-known *leader-member exchange* (LMX) *theory* in which the dichotomous ingroup/outgroup transaction was replaced by a continuum of quality of exchange relationships ranging from ones that are based on mutual trust, respect, and obligation (high-quality LMX relationships), to ones that are mechanically based on the terms of the formal employment contract between leader and subordinate (low-quality LMX relationships). Effective leadership hinges on high-quality LMX relationships. High-quality relationships motivate subordinates to internalize the group's and the leader's goals, whereas low-quality relationships lead subordinates to simply comply with the leader's goals, without internalizing them as their own. However, from a leader's point of view high-quality relationships are labor intensive; so over time leaders tend to develop them with only a small subset of group members and develop low-quality relationships with the rest of the group.

Transformational Leadership and Charisma

Typically, effective leaders are innovative and able to mobilize followers to buy and implement their new vision for the group—they are transformational. Transformational leadership is characterized by (a) careful attention to followers' needs, abilities, and aspirations; (b) challenging followers' basic thinking, assumptions, and practices; and (c) exercise of charisma and inspiration. Charisma is critical for transformational leadership (there is much talk about charismatic or visionary leaders and leadership), which has engaged a debate among scholars about (a) whether this is a return to older personality perspectives on leadership and (b) how one can distinguish between charisma in the service of evil (e.g., Slobodan Milosevic) and charisma in the service of good (e.g., Nelson Mandela).

Transformational leadership and transactional leadership are foci on leadership, but both are also leadership styles that can be contrasted to other leadership styles. Transformational leaders inspire followers to adopt a vision, whereas transactional leaders appeal more to followers' individual self-interest. A third leadership style—laissez-faire (noninterfering) leadership, which involves not making choices or decisions, and not rewarding others or shaping their behavior—has recently been added to transactional and transformational leadership. The components of transactional and transformational leadership are measured by the Multifactor Leadership Questionnaire (MLQ), which has been extraordinarily widely used and is the leadership questionnaire of choice of the organizational and management research communities.

Perceptions, Schemas, and Stereotypes of Leaders

There are a number of perspectives on leadership that focus on the causes and consequences for leadership of our cognitive representations of what makes an effective leader. According to Robert Lord's *leader categorization theory*, we have stereotypical expectations (schemas) and implicit theories about the attributes an effective leader should have in general, or in specific leadership situations. Once we categorize someone as a leader we automatically engage the relevant leadership schema—the better the match between the leader's actual characteristics and the leadership schema, the more favorable are our evaluations of the leader and his or her leadership, and the more likely we are to follow his or her lead.

There are two other ways in which stereotypical expectations (schemas, implicit theories) might affect leadership. According to *status characteristics theory*, in a task-oriented group our evaluations of effective leadership rest on whether we believe the leader has the attributes to perform the group task, called *specific status characteristics*, and whether the leader is a member of a high-status group in society generally and therefore possesses attributes that are valued in society, called *diffuse status characteristics*. Influence, or leadership, is an additive function of perceived group task competence and perceived societal status.

Role congruity theory focuses primarily on gender and leadership. The argument is that social stereotypes of women typically do not match well with schemas of effective leadership, and thus in many leadership situations women find it difficult to be endorsed, by both males and females, as effective leaders. There is a lack of congruity between the attributes of the leadership role and the stereotypical attributes of women.

Social Identity and Leadership

A number of approaches to leadership assign followers a key role—as noted above for transactional theories and schema-based approaches. Other perspectives have argued that "followership" is critical to good leadership, as effective followers can guide leaders in the "right" direction—helping to contain any tendency for corrupt or ineffective leadership.

One aspect of leadership that is often underemphasized is its identity function—groups furnish members with a sense of identity, and people look to groups and their leaders to fulfill this function. This idea has been pursued by Michael Hogg's *social identity theory of leadership*. According to the social identity theory of leadership, a key function of leadership is to forge, transform, and consolidate one's identity as a group member—one's social identity. The implication of this is that if membership in a group is important to you, particularly to your sense of self, you are more likely to be influenced by a leader who matches your understanding of what the group stands for (a leader who is *prototypical* of the group) than one who does not. Effective leadership in such groups rests significantly on the leader's being perceived by followers as being prototypical—even to the extent that general attributes of good leadership decline in importance. One reason leaders who are prototypical members of subjectively important groups can be effective is that followers believe that because their identity and that of the group are closely matched, these leaders treat members fairly and must be acting in the best interest of the group—they are therefore trusted and allowed to be innovative.

For the social identity theory of leadership, and in line with James Meindl's "romance of leadership," charisma is an attributional consequence of effective leadership, not a cause—people unduly attribute leadership behavior to the leader's dispositions rather than situational or contextual factors. Charisma constructed in this way further facilitates leadership.

Overall effective leaders are, or learn to be, what Steven Reicher has termed "entrepreneurs of identity"—they are adept at being able to maintain the group's perception that they are highly prototypical of the group. They can do this in different ways: talk up prototypical aspects of their behavior and talk down nonprototypical aspects, characterize as marginal those members who do not share their prototype of the group, vilify and cast as deviant those who are contending for leadership,

identify as relevant comparison outgroups those that are most favorable to their own prototypicality, and engage in a discourse to raise or lower the salience of the group for its members (raising salience benefits more prototypical leaders, lowering salience benefits nonprototypical leaders). Nonprototypical leaders engage in group-oriented behaviors to strengthen their membership credentials.

Although leadership can be a matter of weaving a collection of individuals into a group with a single identity and vision, more often than not it is matter of transcending intergroup divisions that can sometimes be deep and conflictual—for example, the challenge of providing national leadership in Iraq to Sunnis, Shi'ites, and Kurds. The challenge of successful intergroup leadership is the wider challenge of building social harmony and a common purpose and identity out of conflict among groups. A key issue is that intergroup leaders are often viewed as representing one group more than the other; they are outgroup leaders to one subgroup, and thus suffer compromised effectiveness. To overcome this problem, intergroup leaders need to build a common ingroup identity that does not threaten the identity of subgroups—a careful balancing of the superordinate identity and associated vision with recognition of the integrity and valued contribution of subgroup identities.

Trust and the Group Value Model

A key dimension of leadership is trust. Can we trust our leaders; if we are to follow their lead surely we should trust them? One important basis of trust is shared group membership, and so we tend to trust leaders who we view as being "one of us"—prototypical members of a group we identify with.

We are also more likely to trust our leaders if they treat us fairly and with respect. According to Tom Tyler's *group value model* and his *relational model of authority in groups*, fairness and justice perceptions are critical to group life. Trust in leadership is particularly influenced by members' perceptions that leaders have used fair procedures (procedural justice) in their dealings with them. Distributive justice (the fairness of resource allocations within the group) is important, but procedural justice is more important. One reason for this is that procedural justice serves a social identity function—it conveys a favorable social evaluation of followers as group members. The respect for group members conveyed by procedural fairness builds member identification and thus feeds into cooperative and compliant behavior. As members identify more strongly with the group, they care more that the leader is procedurally fair, and care less that the leader is distributively fair. This asymmetry arises because with increasing identification, instrumental outcome-oriented considerations (distributive justice) become less important relative to intragroup relational and membership considerations (procedural justice).

One ramification of this analysis is that leadership can be an effective structural solution to social dilemmas. Social dilemmas are crises of trust in which people fail to make short-term personal sacrifices for the longer term greater good of the group as a whole—instead they pursue their own short-term selfish interests. Social dilemmas are notoriously difficult to resolve. However, enhancing a sense of common social identity can build trust that resolves the dilemma. Leadership plays an often critical role in this process precisely because a leader can transform selfish individual goals into shared group goals by building a sense of common identity, shared fate, interindividual trust, and custodianship of the collective good.

Michael A. Hogg

See also Charismatic Leadership; Contingency Theories of Leadership; Great Person Theory of Leadership; Interactionist Theories of Leadership; Leader Categorization Theory; Leader-Member Exchange (LMX) Theory; Path–Goal Theory of Leadership; Personality Theories of Leadership; Relational Model of Authority in Groups; Romance of Leadership; Social Identity Theory of Leadership; Socioemotional and Task Behavior; Status; Status Characteristics/Expectation States Theory; Transactional Leadership Theories; Transformational Leadership Theories; Vertical Dyad Linkage Model

Further Readings

Chemers, M. M. (2001). Leadership effectiveness: An integrative review. In M. A. Hogg & R. S. Tindale (Eds.), *Blackwell handbook of social psychology: Group processes* (pp. 376–399). Oxford, UK: Blackwell.

Hogg, M. A. (2007). Social psychology of leadership. In A. W. Kruglanski & E. T. Higgins (Eds.), *Social psychology: Handbook of basic principles* (2nd ed., pp. 716–733). New York: Guilford.

Hogg, M. A. (2010). Influence and leadership. In S. T. Fiske, D. T. Gilbert, & G. Lindzey (Eds.), *The handbook of social psychology* (5th ed.). New York: John Wiley.

Judge, T. A., Bono, J. E., Ilies, R., & Gerhardt, M. W. (2002). Personality and leadership: A qualitative and quantitative review. *Journal of Applied Psychology, 87*, 765–780.

Kellerman, B. (2004). *Bad leadership: What it is, how it happens, why it matters.* Cambridge, MA: Harvard Business School Press.

Northouse, P. G. (2007). *Leadership: Theory and practice* (4th ed.). Thousand Oaks, CA: Sage.

Riggio, R. E., Chaleff, I., & Lipman-Blumen, J. (Eds.). (2008). *The art of followership: How great followers create great leaders and organizations.* San Francisco: Jossey-Bass.

van Knippenberg, D., van Knippenberg, B., De Cremer, D., & Hogg, M. A. (2004). Leadership, self, and identity: A review and research agenda. *The Leadership Quarterly, 15*, 825–856.

Yukl, G. (2006). *Leadership in organizations* (6th ed.). Upper Saddle River, NJ: Prentice Hall.

LEGITIMATION

When something is legitimated, such as an employment practice in an organization (e.g., a family leave policy) or a particular person in a managerial position, this means that its existence and prevalence is taken for granted by a "social audience" (i.e., real other people or the presence of others implied by social norms and ideologies). Thus, *legitimation* refers to the taken-for-granted support of an aspect of social life (e.g., acts, individuals, a position, or a structure of positions) by real or implied other people. Questions of legitimacy repeatedly arise in studies pertaining to political and organizational structures, status relations in and between groups, and inequality.

The early 20th-century sociologist Max Weber noted that people feel obligated to obey the norms or rules associated with a legitimated object (e.g., the rules of an authority structure in an organization), even when they personally disagree with them. This taken-for-granted aspect of social life often becomes seen as what is right. For example, a person in a managerial position is perceived to be legitimate when there is a real or perceived consensus that this person is the appropriate person for the job. Subordinates, then, obey the manager's commands, even when they personally disagree with him or her.

Many things can be legitimated. For example, a particular act, such as a manager firing a subordinate or an individual holding a position (e.g., floor supervisor), or a structure of positions in groups or organizations, or intergroup status relations in a society become legitimated through a social process. This process involves people assuming that other people in general accept the object for what it is and, often over time, for what it should be.

Scholars who study legitimacy processes in groups focus on how the legitimacy of groups' status hierarchies emerges and how authorities acquire legitimacy in the eyes of their subordinates in organizations. Status hierarchies develop in groups (e.g., committees, task forces, gangs), where some members are seen as more worthy and esteemed than other members. Scholars also investigate the consequences of the legitimacy of status hierarchies in groups and status relations among groups, as well as the conditions under which these legitimate orders become inefficient and perpetuate inequality within groups, organizations, and society. They also examine the consequences of the legitimacy of authorities for interaction in organizations.

Emergence of Legitimation

Legitimacy theories argue that low- and high-status members in a group expect that those with highly valued states of social characteristics (e.g., men in regard to the social characteristic gender, and Whites in terms of race) will occupy highly valued positions within the group because this is what they perceive to be typical around them (e.g., in groups within occupational, political, and religious structures). Consequently, when these individuals become high-status members within a group, low- and high-status members tend to react to this as if it should have happened this way because they, in fact, expected this to happen. Thus, low-status members express deferential behaviors such as esteem, respect, and honor

(communicated verbally or nonverbally) toward high-status members. This interaction creates a process where everyone believes that everyone else supports the person who is more worthy and who gets more influence (this process is called *endorsement* of the group status hierarchy). If no one challenges this deference, members will continue to act as if this should happen, and the hierarchy will become implicitly legitimate.

Sometimes, members who do not possess the more highly valued states of social characteristics still become high-status members because they possess specific skills that are relevant to the group's task (e.g., a Black member who is a legal expert working on a legal task). These people are at a disadvantage, however, in trying to gain legitimacy in their positions, because it is not typical or usual for people like them to occupy high-status positions. As a result, although they are influential, they face more obstacles in becoming legitimated in their positions. Members' endorsement (i.e., support) for these people's leadership is weaker, as are expectations for compliance with their directives.

Researchers also examine how individuals in authority positions acquire legitimacy. Previous studies have shown that individuals in authority positions are more likely to be legitimated when their appointments are based on qualifications and past achievements and are designated by someone at the top of the authority structure. Authorities also acquire legitimacy based on the ways they interact with subordinates—two specific ways are the use of fair procedures when making decisions and the benevolent use of power. Authorities use fair procedures when they make decisions that are seen as unbiased, respectful, and consistent across individuals and that take into consideration the subordinates' views.

An authority's use of fair procedures and treatment ensures that subordinates feel respected within their group, which in turn increases subordinates' feelings of self-worth. Many social psychologists assume that individuals are motivated by and desire positive social identities from their standing in a group and the value of their group. The use of fair procedures signals to the subordinates that they are respected within their group. Therefore, when an authority uses fair procedures to make decisions and treats subordinates fairly, the legitimacy of that authority is enhanced. For example, when a floor supervisor acts respectfully toward assembly-line workers and treats them all consistently, those workers are more likely to see that supervisor as legitimate.

An authority also gains legitimacy by providing resources to subordinates that benefit their welfare. Authorities typically have more resources than subordinates, and therefore have opportunities to contribute to subordinates' welfare by distributing rewards that assist their subordinates in being successful in their jobs. For example, authorities often have access to valuable knowledge, skills, training, and strategic information that is useful to subordinates. They may also offer guidance, assistance, and advice to enhance and facilitate subordinates' work, and may be able to benefit subordinates in other ways, such as by allowing extra time for lunch, giving credit to subordinates for successful outcomes, providing bonuses, and upgrading offices.

When authorities provide rewards that contribute to the *collective* interest of subordinates, this creates obligations between the authority and the subordinates. Repeated successful exchanges (exchanges of rewards and cooperation) between authorities and their subordinates are likely to stimulate perceptions of trust and fairness and feelings of social obligation, leading to perceptions of the legitimacy of authorities. Taken together, using fair procedures in decision making and distributing valued rewards fairly among subordinates contribute to a collective sense of the legitimacy of an authority. That is, subordinates perceive that other subordinates support the authority (i.e., give the authority their endorsement) and this, in turn, perpetuates the authority's legitimacy.

Scholars recognize that women and minorities, in many contexts, are at a disadvantage in acquiring legitimacy compared to their White male counterparts. Women and minorities are more likely to receive fewer resources, support, and positive evaluations from their superiors, which is referred to as *lack of authorization*. As a result, they have fewer opportunities to benefit their subordinates and to create the joint obligations needed to gain legitimacy.

Consequences of Legitimation

Researchers show how the legitimacy of groups' status hierarchies can lead to the maintenance and persistence of inequality. Group members who possess more highly valued states of social characteristics are likely to be more assertive and influential in decision making than members who are status disadvantaged. Yet, this consequence often leads to inefficient decision making because the members who are in fact most competent are not always those who are most influential. Also, group members who actually may not be as competent at the group's task may still receive deferential behavior from other group members that, in effect, maintains the status quo. These patterns of deference are backed by the threat of informal sanctions from group members, creating a context where valuable opinions by status-disadvantaged members are ignored and poor decisions are made.

In addition, studies show that women and minorities who become high-status members in groups because they possess specific skills needed by the group are more likely to face resistance from others when they become "too directive." This resistance faced by members with status disadvantages is a reflection of a problem of the legitimation of the group's status structure. As a consequence of their lack of legitimacy, women and minorities are more limited in the range of their behaviors accepted by the other group members.

In regard to authorities, legitimacy is undoubtedly a key factor in predicting their success with their subordinates. Subordinates who perceive their boss as legitimate are more likely to comply and defer to his or her requests. Also, legitimated authorities are perceived as more effective and influential by their subordinates than authorities without legitimacy. They also have more leeway in the directives (e.g., work assignments, evaluations, and/or demands of performance) subordinates accept from them, even though these directives must fall within the scope of their authority. Legitimacy, then, obligates the subordinates to obey the authority's commands, and this *social* obligation is enforced through informal sanctions by the subordinates and through formal sanctions by those from above.

When authorities are not legitimated, subordinates are more likely to go over their heads or form coalitions with each other to resolve conflicts than when authorities are legitimated. Notably, research shows that the benefits of legitimacy are greater for women and minorities in authority positions, in that they are less likely to receive cooperation and deference unless they are legitimated in their positions. Yet, ironically, they have the most difficulty in acquiring legitimacy.

In addition to reporting the findings of their studies on the emergence and consequences of legitimation, scholars also note that not all legitimated aspects of social life remain so. New practices, procedures, and ways of doing things emerge as the legitimacy of old ones is challenged. For example, status hierarchies in groups may become delegitimated when an authority external to the group negatively evaluates the leader's work and, in effect, questions the leader's right to his or her high status position. Research also suggests that when members of status-disadvantaged groups within society believe that their group's position is illegitimate and unstable, and that a different social order is possible, they are likely to engage in intergroup competition that directly challenges the legitimacy of current intergroup status relations.

The arguments above show that legitimation of certain aspects of social life can lead to negative consequences. The acceptance of widespread consensual beliefs in the larger society, such as status beliefs associated with social characteristics and cultural beliefs about intergroup status differences within a society, fosters nonoptimal decisions and practices and also fuels the reproduction of inequality in and between groups. Thus scholars in intergroup relations examine how dominant groups with high status and power in a society continue to impose the dominant value system that benefits these groups and, in turn, uphold the legitimacy of the status quo (i.e., the existing status differences between groups). However, legitimation of other social aspects can lead to positive consequences. The legitimacy of authority relations in organizations, for example, can foster stability and cooperation in interaction among organizational members. Whether legitimacy is bad or good in a particular context, however, it is a fundamental process that is basic to social organization.

Cathryn Johnson

See also Power; Procedural Justice; Social Identity Theory; Status; Status Characteristics/Expectation States Theory

See also Charismatic Leadership; Contingency Theories of Leadership; Great Person Theories of Leadership; Interactionist Theories of Leadership; Leader-Member Exchange (LMX) Theory; Path–Goal Theory of Leadership; Personality Theories of Leadership; Power; Procedural Justice; Relational Model of Authority in Groups; Romance of Leadership; Social Identity Theory; Social Identity Theory of Leadership; Status Characteristics/Expectation States Theory; Transactional Leadership Theories; Transformational Leadership Theories; Vertical Dyad Linkage Model

Further Readings

Berger, J., Ridgeway, C. L., Fiske, M. H., & Norman, R. Z. (1998). The legitimation and delegitimation of power and prestige orders. *American Sociological Review, 63,* 379–405.

Johnson, C., Dowd, T. J., & Ridgeway, C. L. (2006). Legitimacy as a social process. *Annual Review of Sociology, 32,* 53–78.

Jost, J. T., & Majors, B. (Eds.). (2001). *The psychology of legitimacy: Emerging perspectives on ideology, justice, and intergroup relations.* Cambridge, UK: Cambridge University Press.

Suchman, M. (1995). Managing legitimacy: Strategic and institutional approaches. *Academy of Management Review, 20,* 571–610.

Weber, M. (1968). *Economy and society* (G. Roth & C. Wittich, Eds.). Berkeley: University of California Press. (Original work published 1918)

Zelditch, M., Jr. (2001). Processes of legitimation: Recent developments and new directions. *Social Psychology Quarterly, 64,* 4–17.

Zelditch, M., Jr., & Walker, H. A. (1984). Legitimacy and the stability of authority. *Advances in Group Processes, 1,* 1–25.

LENIENCY CONTRACT

The *leniency contract* is an influential model of minority influence. It is designed to identify factors that affect the likelihood that a minority group will be able to persuade the majority to adopt its point of view. The essence of the contract is that majority members agree to hear a minority view they might otherwise dismiss out of hand—thus, the term *leniency*—on the implicit condition that the viewpoint is provided by a member of the ingroup, and with the proviso that the majority will not be expected to change. In some cases, despite this understanding, the minority does influence the majority. This entry describes the theoretical background that gives rise to the leniency contract, and then considers elements of the contract in detail and summarizes some research that bears on its validity.

Theoretical Context

Typically, the majority can bring considerable pressure on errant members to act in ways that most other group members consider appropriate. The majority can sanction members' beliefs and actions in many ways, including physical punishment and social ostracism, so it is natural that we think of the effects of the majority on the minority when we think of ways groups influence people.

Even so, the influence of the minority on the majority bears consideration. Think of the early Christian church: In the beginning, it had little power. Its members were ignored or ostracized and sometimes put to death for their beliefs. By the 3rd century, however, Emperor Constantine had become a Christian, and the Christian church was the unofficial religion of Imperial Rome.

How did this change occur? Social psychologists have been actively studying how minorities exert influence, trying to understand how groups with no power to enforce their views can prevail. According to many thoughtful researchers, this issue is important because minority groups are responsible for most creative and innovative social changes.

To understand the power of minorities, we must acknowledge the importance of our group memberships, which we value because they help us define ourselves and present ourselves to others. I am a teacher, a runner, a Democrat; she is a nurse, a black belt, a Steelers fan—our group identities help us create a picture of ourselves and present ourselves to the outside world.

In early minority influence research, individuals' membership in the majority or minority was recognized, but the significance of these groups as a source of self-identity was underappreciated. Today, the importance of group membership in explaining minority influence is better understood.

Elements of the Leniency Contract

The leniency contract was created to identify the conditions under which the minority's message will have an immediate influence on majority group members' focal attitudes (the beliefs that are the target of persuasion), a delayed influence on focal attitudes, an indirect influence (i.e., an influence on attitudes related but not identical to the focus of the minority's message), or no influence at all. All these outcomes are found in minority influence research. Prior to the leniency contract, no theory could account for all of them.

The contract leans on social identity theory and the elaboration likelihood model to generate predictions. It uses information concerning the ingroup or outgroup status of the minority and the strength of its persuasive message. Minority status can be based on number, demographic features (race, sex, ethnicity), or the relative deviance of a position. In most research on minority-based persuasion, the factors of number and opinion deviance are combined, in that a small numerical minority advocates a deviant opinion. The leniency contract was devised to pinpoint the psychological processes that occur when a minority source voices a position at odds with established majority views.

The contract holds that the majority's first response to a persuasive message coming from a minority source is to determine the source's ingroup or outgroup status. If the source is an outgroup, their standing must be established: Is the outgroup favored or despised? If the group is despised, its message will be dismissed outright, unless it represents a severe threat to the ingroup. In that case, the majority might bolster its position to overcome the threat presented by the outgroup. If the outgroup is favored, its message may be influential if the topic is one in which the majority believe the minority source possesses great expertise. This influence is not the result of much thought, so minority influence in this circumstance will be temporary and easily undone.

A different set of decision processes occurs when the minority source is part of the ingroup (that is, part of the majority group, but voicing a position that is at variance with the position of most of the other group members). First, the minority's message is considered carefully or elaborated. Elaboration involves determining if the message threatens the group's continued existence. If so, then to preserve the group, the majority will attempt to bring the deviant ingroup minority back into the fold. If this attempt proves unsuccessful, the ingroup minority is recast as an outgroup.

If the ingroup minority's message is not deemed threatening to the group's existence, a second elaboration phase begins. In this situation, the quality of the minority's message determines the outcome. Weak or uninvolving messages will have transitory effects, if any, on indirect attitudes (beliefs that are associated with the topic of the persuasive message but not identical to it).

Consider, for example, a persuasive message on the right to choose abortion that is contrary to the general beliefs of the majority. The message might not change anyone's mind about abortion, but it might affect views regarding contraception. Messages from minority sources will not affect focal attitudes because majority members are hesitant to be associated with the minority's position, which may attract considerable flak. However, indirect attitude change may ensue—but it will not persist if the persuasive message is not strong and compelling.

If the ingroup's message is strong, however, a number of interesting effects will occur. The message will be viewed positively; it also might result in a more positive evaluation of the minority and very likely will cause immediate indirect attitude change. Immediate focal change will not occur. So, for example, a message in favor of a woman's right to choose abortion that is delivered by an ingroup minority to the anti-abortion majority may result in a more positive majority view of contraception, even though the minority's prochoice message never mentioned contraception. This indirect attitude-change effect, which only occurs in response to an ingroup minority's message, is one of the most remarkable features of minority influence research.

Related Research

Research consistent with these predictions was presented in 1997 by Eusebio Alvaro and William Crano, who prepared a strong counterattitudinal message, attributed to an ingroup minority, which advocated disallowing gays in the military. This position was contrary to the group's established attitude. The message had no effect on the group's attitudes toward gays in the military, but that it had a powerful effect on their attitudes toward gun control. Earlier research had established that these two attitudes were strongly related, although participants were only dimly aware of this.

When the same message was attributed to an outgroup minority or presented as the majority's position, no attitude change was evident in those receiving the message. The leniency contract holds that indirect change in group members' response to a minority ingroup's counterattitudinal message occurs because of the implicit rules of conduct that guide behavior in groups. To placate the rebellious ingroup minority while maintaining group integrity, which is vital if the group is a source of social identity, the majority will consider the ingroup minority position leniently, with no disapproval of the messenger.

Ordinarily, such open-minded responses facilitate attitude change, but the leniency contract holds that this tolerant orientation is adopted because of the quid pro quo that is part of all contracts, namely, that in payment for a lenient reception of deviant (i.e., minority) views, no change will ensue. It is as if the majority were to say, "We will allow you to speak your piece, courteously and with little critique. In turn, we will not change." This contractual system placates the minority while simultaneously maintaining the stability of the majority group's belief structure. The contract need not be explicit or even conscious. It is a convention that fosters group preservation while allowing considerable ingroup attitudinal variation on noncritical issues.

This is not to suggest that the minority is an impotent change agent. When the majority openmindedly considers a counterattitudinal message without condemning the source, it creates considerable pressure to change. Although focal change is precluded by the leniency contract, the reality of the pressure cannot be denied. The leniency model holds that this pressure to change spreads to other, closely related attitudes, and this is why ingroup minorities produce immediate changes on related attitudes.

Such changes can have substantial, if delayed, effects on focal attitudes. Strong minority-induced indirect attitude change will bring about delayed focal attitude change because attitudes are linked in a cognitive network. Thus, a large change in one attitude will affect related attitudes. This delayed focal change pattern is common in the minority influence literature. The leniency contract supplies a plausible explanation of this pattern, while also explaining immediate direct change, or no change at all.

William D. Crano

See also Anticonformity; Categorization; Idiosyncrasy Credit; Informational Influence; Innovation; Minority Influence; Opinion Deviance; Social Identity Theory

Further Readings

Alvaro, E. M., & Crano, W. D. (1997). Indirect minority influence. Evidence for leniency in source evaluation and counterargumentation. *Journal of Personality and Social Psychology, 72,* 949–965.

Crano, W. D., & Chen, X. (1998). The leniency contract and persistence of majority and minority influence. *Journal of Personality and Social Psychology, 74,* 1437–1450.

Crano, W. D., & Seyranian, V. (2008). Majority and minority influence. *Social and Personality Psychology Compass, 1,* 572–589.

Martin, R., Hewstone, M., Martin, P. Y., & Gardikiotis, A. (2008). Persuasion from minority and majority groups. In W. D. Crano & R. Prislin (Eds.), *Attitudes and attitude change* (pp. 361–384). New York: Psychology Press.

LEVELS OF ANALYSIS

Although groups necessarily contain individuals and have some relation to the larger institutional, cultural, and societal forces around them, group processes occur at the group level of analysis rather than at the individual or societal level. Likewise, intergroup processes are those that occur between groups, rather than between individuals or within a group, institution, culture, or society. And yet it seems clear that both group and intergroup processes may be affected by factors at other levels of analysis. For example, the way in which a work group operates may be affected by the characteristics of the individuals who make up the group (e.g., their cooperative or competitive nature), as well as by the characteristics of the institution within which the group exists (e.g., its pay and promotion structure). Thus, a full understanding of group and intergroup processes requires attention to multiple *levels of analysis.* This entry describes those levels and their interrelationships.

Multiple Levels of Analysis

The eight levels of analysis relevant to group and intergroup processes vary from macro to micro (see Figure 1). In between the macro and micro levels lies the intermediate, meso level of analysis. In his 1996 book, *How to Think Like a Social Scientist,* Thomas F. Pettigrew argued that the meso level operates as a link between the macro and micro levels of analysis. This may be why social psychologists are often most interested in examining group and intergroup processes at the meso level. Some historians of the field, such as Rob Farr, have suggested that social psychology is a marriage of the sociological and psychological perspectives. This suggests that social psychologists give special attention to the meso level because it may be the level where sociological and psychological phenomena meet.

Although it is typically referred to only in science fiction, the most macro level of analysis possible for the study of group and intergroup processes is the *interglobal* level. When researchers examine people's attitudes toward space exploration and the existence of extraterrestrial life, they are examining the potential intergroup relation between beings on our globe and those on another. In practice, the most macro level of analysis studied is the *intraglobal* level. Research on people's concern for the effects of the warming of the earth's atmosphere is an environmental concern at the intraglobal level of analysis. At this level of analysis, global warming's differential impact on societies, as well as on plants, humans, and other animals, is put aside to emphasize the ways in which global warming affects everyone and everything everywhere on this planet.

Psychological approaches to group and intergroup processes often emphasize the intraglobal level of analysis. Because a good deal of psychology presumes that people operate in much the same way, regardless of how they vary at less macro levels

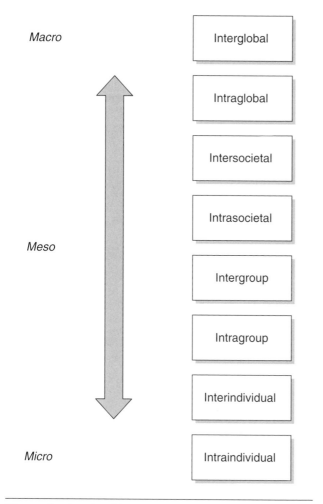

Macro — Interglobal

Intraglobal

Intersocietal

Intrasocietal

Meso — Intergroup

Intragroup

Interindividual

Micro — Intraindividual

Figure 1 Levels of Analysis

Source: Author.

of analysis, psychology is able to propose universal theories that aim to explain people at the most macro, global level. This perspective is often referred to as the *psychic unity of humankind.*

The *intersocietal* level of analysis operates at one step less macro than the intraglobal level. At the intersocietal level, attention is given to the similarities and differences between societies in norms; values; practices; and social, political, and economic structures. Recent political rhetoric about a purported clash of civilizations between "the West" and "Islam" claims that countries around the world can be characterized as either Western or Islamic. These two broad types of societies are presumed to be very different from each other. The clash of civilizations rhetoric also suggests that the two societies are locked in mortal combat, with each society seeking to impose its agenda on the other.

This level of analysis is most common in historical, political, and economic studies, where there is concern for empires, continents, and geographical regions. For example, historical studies of the Roman Empire's relations to competing empires, such as those of Carthage, Macedon, and Egypt, focus on the intersocietal level of analysis. Although social psychologists may wish to use their research to comment on group and intergroup processes at the intersocietal level, psychologists rarely study the relations between large-scale societal-level groupings. However, there are exceptions. During the cold war, a number of peace and political psychologists examined people's attitudes toward a potential nuclear war between "the West" and the "Russian bloc."

A clash of civilizations may also be examined at an *intrasocietal* level of analysis. The notion that two civilizations are in conflict necessarily presumes that each civilization is a coherent entity within which individuals and (ethnic, religious, and economic) groups are unified enough to see themselves as part of two opposing societies in the world. Thus, at the intrasocietal level, one may examine the degree to which individuals and groups view themselves and their interests as connected to that of other Westerners or Muslims. For example, research at the intrasocietal level might assess to what degree people from around the world viewed the September 11th attacks on the World Trade Center in New York as an attack on "the West." Or, it might examine the degree to which the notion of a clash of Western and Islamic societies leads Sunni, Shiite, and other Muslims to view themselves as a coherent category of likeminded people whose interests are aligned against those of "the West."

The intrasocietal level of analysis is most common in sociology, anthropology, economics, and political science, although it is also the focus of some social psychological research. For example, studies of the degree to which people from different countries in Europe identify themselves as European (rather than, for example, British, French, or Spanish) and participate in European politics examine the intrasocietal level of analysis.

The *intergroup* level of analysis is often pursued by social psychologists, who have a long-standing concern about how ethnic, gender, religious, and other groups within societies relate to each other.

Many sociologists and political scientists, and some anthropologists and economists, also study intergroup relations within complex societies made up of many groups. Unlike other social scientists, however, social psychologists tend to focus on the intergroup level to the near exclusion of the intrasocietal level within which intergroup relations typically operate. Thus, social psychologists that examine phenomena at the intergroup level pay special attention to the relation that a specific ingroup has to one specific outgroup. How the members of this ingroup compare themselves to, compete against, or act toward members of the outgroup are of particular interest.

Intragroup processes were studied widely by social psychologists in the first half of the 20th century. Topics such as conformity, compliance, and group polarization all focus on the ways in which interactions within groups affect individuals differently from interactions within society or between individuals. Based in the group dynamics tradition of research, championed by influential figure Kurt Lewin, social psychological work at the intragroup level of analysis examined individuals' interactions within small, co-acting groups. Based in a different tradition, called symbolic interactionism, microsociology also focused on the group-level processes present in small co-acting collections of individuals, such as families, clubs, and work groups. This differentiates microsociology from most of the rest of sociology, which tends to focus on more macro levels, such as the intergroup or intrasocietal level.

Although they operate at more micro levels than group or intergroup processes, the *interindividual* and *intraindividual* levels of analysis are relevant to such processes. For example, interindividual differences in the motive to gain power, achieve, or affiliate with others help determine to what degree individuals work toward group goals that facilitate or impede their individual motives. Thus, a good deal of social psychological work on group and intergroup processes takes the interindividual level of analysis into account. Not surprisingly, however, most research combines examination of the interindividual level with a focus on the more macro levels of analysis at which group and intergroup processes occur.

In a similar way, research may also take account of similarities and differences in the way that individuals think, feel, and act over time or across situations. This represents the intraindividual level of analysis. For example, research on the commitment of individual workers to a political campaign might examine how consistently these workers come to work and perform their duties over the course of a month during the campaign.

Relations Among Levels

Nested

It may be apparent from the above that each level is contained (or nested) within the more macro levels above it. For example, phenomena at the intergroup level necessarily occur within the societies within which multiple groups exist. And, differences between individuals necessarily occur within the groups to which these individuals belong. Indeed, part of the way in which individuals know that they differ from others is by comparing themselves to other members of their reference group.

Early social psychological work on group dynamics was concerned with the way in which individuals being nested within small- and large-scale groups affected them. Today, advanced statistical techniques, such as multilevel modeling, enable researchers to carefully examine nested levels of analysis. For example, many studies of students' self-concepts now examine students not only as individuals but also as nested within classrooms, which are nested within schools, which are nested within neighborhoods, which are nested within countries, which are nested within one globe.

Independent

Although the levels of analysis are nested within one another, what occurs at one level is not necessarily associated with what occurs at another level. Thus, phenomena at each level of analysis can operate independently of phenomena at other levels. This is part of the reason that it is important to be clear about which level of analysis is being examined in a given piece of research. For example, studies of the association between economic prosperity and satisfaction with life show somewhat different patterns at the interindividual level of analysis than at the intersocietal level. Although being richer than other individuals within your country does not seem to bring much life satisfaction, people in rich countries tend to be much more satisfied than those in poor countries. Without an understanding that the former finding is specific to the interindividual level of analysis, whereas the latter finding is specific to the intersocietal level, one might be perplexed by the apparent inconsistency of these results.

Interactive

That group and intergroup processes may operate independently at different levels of analysis also raises the possibility that there is an interaction between different levels of analysis. Contemporary multilevel modeling statistics enable researchers to examine such interactions, although these complex analyses remain relatively rare. It is clear, however, that a full understanding of group and intergroup processes requires examination of the multiple levels of analysis relevant to the process of interest. If this examination can analyze the ways in which individual-level phenomena interact with group- and societal-level phenomena to determine the process of interest, then the examination will begin to approach the complexity of life as it is lived. As we are all, at one and the same time, individuals, members of many groups, and members of at least one society, research methods that account for this multilevel reality will be best positioned to analyze it.

Colin Wayne Leach

See also Group Performance; Group Structure; Organizations; Research Methods and Issues

Further Readings

Bolger, N., Davis, A., & Eshkol, R. (2003). Diary methods: Capturing life as it is lived. *Annual Review of Psychology, 54,* 579–616.

Farr, R. (1996). *The roots of modern social psychology 1872–1954.* Oxford, UK: Blackwell.

Kenny, D. A., Kashy, D. A., & Bolger, N. (1998). Data analysis in social psychology. In D. T. Gilbert, S. T. Fiske, & G. Lindzey (Eds.), *The handbook of social psychology* (Vol. 1, pp. 233–265). Boston: McGraw-Hill.

Leach, C. W., & Vliek, M. L. W. (2008). Group membership as a "frame of reference" for interpersonal comparison. *Social Psychology and Personality Compass, 2*(1), 539–554.

Pettigrew, T. F. (1996). *How to think like a social scientist.* Addison-Wesley.

Raudenbush, S. W., & Bryk, A. S. (2002). *Hierarchical linear models: Applications and data analysis methods* (2nd ed.). Thousand Oaks, CA: Sage.

LEWIN, KURT (1890–1947)

Kurt Lewin is remembered as a "practical theorist" and considered the intellectual father of the modern discipline of social psychology. Born in 1890 in a German village that is now part of Poland, Lewin was educated in Germany and served as an infantry soldier during World War I. His experience growing up as a Jew in an authoritarian society rampant with anti-Semitism shaped his view of human behavior and his focus on group processes. Trained in philosophy and experimental psychology, and influenced by the German Gestalt theorists, Lewin did his pioneering work in the development of *field theory,* a framework for understanding human behavior that focuses on how an individual conceptualizes and responds to physical and social environments. Field theory provides a paradigm for understanding and conducting studies of group processes and intergroup relations.

Lewin is known as the practical theorist because he linked the study of applied problems to theory. He saw theory as essential for understanding practical social problems, and he viewed the conduct of empirical studies of applied problems as essential for the development of theory. He was vitally concerned with the central social and political issues of his era, in particular the role of democracy in promoting effective interpersonal relations and group dynamics. His maxim was that "there is nothing so practical as a good theory," and he was as concerned with the problems faced by world as he was with developing theory to explain human behavior.

Lewin's Paradigm Shift in Social Psychology

Lewin epitomizes Thomas Kuhn's description of a scientific revolutionary. He was acutely aware of the gaps in our understanding of human behavior and our ability to predict and change relations among people. In 1914, shortly after he completed his PhD, World War I began. As his biographer and daughter, Miriam Lewin, has written, he had a "strong revulsion" to militarism, but joined the military and served in an artillery unit. He was seriously wounded and spent nearly a year recovering in a hospital. Although we do not know precisely how his time on the front lines of this conflict between groups affected his outlook, it is not surprising that his subsequent theorizing and empirical studies focused on intergroup relations. His experience was exacerbated by the discrimination he experienced as a Jew, which in 1934 led him to flee Nazi Germany and immigrate to the United States.

No doubt, other psychologists and social theorists were similarly affected by the tumultuous events of the first part of the 20th century. What made Lewin unique and led to his enormous influence on modern thinking about group behavior is that he developed a broad theoretical framework that was linked to experimental methods. In Kuhnian terms, he created a paradigm that enabled us to think differently about human behavior and gave us the tools to study the complexity of social interaction. He was committed to developing psychology as a science but also mindful of the ways in which a science of the mind had to differ from physical science. His lasting contribution was reframing how we think about groups and the relationship of individuals to groups.

Lewin's Field Theory

The fundamental postulate of Lewin's field theory was that human behavior should be understood as a function of the interaction between an individual and his or her psychological understanding of the physical and social environment. He used mathematical symbols to explicate his theory, and summarized the essence of field theory in this formula: $B = f(P, E)$. Behavior (B) was broadly construed (including action, thinking, and valuing) and person (P) and environment (E) were dynamically related. Together, the person and the environment form the *life space*. Understanding the structure and influences on the life space became the focus of Lewin's work.

The mathematical language used by Lewin (which was drawn from topological geometry) has not survived, but his perspective on how behavior is influenced by a person's perception of the environment continues to be a central influence on social psychology and, in particular, on the study of group processes. In its time, his approach was revolutionary and led to a host of discoveries about how human behavior is influenced by culture, education, and small group dynamics. Today, Lewin's approach is well represented in modern cognitive social psychology and in a variety of applications of psychology to group and societal problems.

Lewin's theorizing also spawned new ways of viewing collective behavior. In some ways it was more sociological than psychological, as it led to ascribing to groups the same kind of life space analysis that was used to analyze individual behavior. Thus, a group or institution could be seen not simply as the sum of the individuals or other units who make up the group, but as an entity that could be quite different. Groups could, for example, have their own norms, and the dynamic processes of the group were not necessarily predictable from understanding the life space of individuals.

Lewin the Empiricist

Integral to his theorizing about person–environment relationships was his commitment and approach to empirical research and, in particular, to experimentation. He pioneered the integration of laboratory and field research. Lewin created a science of studying group behavior that has persisted for more than half a century. He was a master of taking the most complex social phenomena and creating paradigms to study them in simple ways. Two of his research efforts, both conducted after he came to the United States, illustrate his theoretical–methodological approach to the study of group processes and dynamics.

In the late 1930s, Lewin and his students conducted a series of studies to investigate the impact of different ways of organizing groups. Initially, his focus was to understand the impact of democratic versus authoritarian group leadership, operationalized in terms of whether the leader engaged the group in decision making or directed them without explanation; later, he studied what he called laissez-faire leadership, in which a group was allowed to function without direction from a leader. He studied the problem by conducting a series of experiments in which different leadership styles were tried with groups of young boys. He demonstrated that distinctive "group atmospheres" could be created with each leadership style. The democratic style was the most effective, and the authoritarian style yielded the most aggression among the boys.

In a later program of research, conducted during World War II, he studied ways to change food preferences to mitigate the impact of rationing and food shortages. It began as a study of food habits and "channels" of influence in decision making, and evolved into a series of studies of group decision making. Parallel to his studies of democratic and authoritarian leadership, his food habit studies experimentally compared lecturing and group discussion methods as approaches to changing behavior. Groups of women were exposed to different presentations and discussions of food preferences. He demonstrated that the way in which the group was engaged predicted behavior change. Active involvement in group discussion led to significantly more change in participants than did passive listening to a lecture.

Lewin's Action Research

One of Lewin's lasting contributions was his development of *action research*. It was based on his view that social problems should be central to the concerns of psychologists and that, to understand a phenomenon, one had to try to change it. Through action research, he promoted the systematic study of social problems and their solution. He saw it as a spiral process of data collection, theorizing, and assessment. Action research was, for Lewin, rooted in principles of group dynamics. He proposed that change occurred by phases: unfreezing, moving, and refreezing. His goals, democratized by engaging researchers and practitioners, were to create knowledge, intervention principles, and support for those who carry out organizational and institutional change. One outcome of this work was the creation of the National Training Laboratory for Group Development (now known as the NTL Institute), dedicated to improving organizational effectiveness and the development of sensitivity training.

The Legacy of Kurt Lewin

Lewin, through both his theoretical work and his approach to empirical studies of behavior, left a rich legacy. He changed our conception of individual behavior and identified how, while experiences may shape a person, the key to understanding behavior is to understand a person's life space—how individuals perceive the world, and how changes in the environment affect their perceptions and behavior. The range of Lewin's work is extraordinary, in terms of both the issues he investigated and his efforts to integrate theory and method. When Kurt Lewin died in 1947, at the age of 57, he headed the MIT Center for Group Dynamics; after his death, the center moved to the University of Michigan. His students and research colleagues went on to become central figures in psychology and applied social science. His legacy is evident today, as it is difficult to view any topic in group processes and dynamics without seeing the influence of Lewinian thinking.

Leonard Saxe

See also Action Research; Anti-Semitism; Culture; Group Performance; Group Problem Solving and Decision Making; Minority Groups in Society; Organizations; Research Methods and Issues; Sensitivity Training Groups

Further Readings

Gold, M. (Ed.). (1999). *The complete social scientist.* Washington, DC: American Psychological Association.

Lewin, K. (1948). *Resolving social conflicts.* New York: Harper & Row.

Lewin, K. (1951). *Field theory in social science: Selected theoretical papers* (D. Cartwright, Ed.). Chicago: University of Chicago Press.

Lewin, M. (1992). The impact of Kurt Lewin's life on the place of social issues in his work. *Journal of Social Issues, 48*(2), 15–29.

Marrow, A. J. (1969). *The practical theorist: The life and work of Kurt Lewin.* New York: Basic Books.

LINGUISTIC CATEGORY MODEL (LCM)

The *linguistic category model* (LCM), which classifies predicates on a scale from abstract to concrete, is a tool for systematic analysis of language. It has been used extensively to analyze not only communication in experimental settings but also newspaper editorials and transcripts of current and historical court cases. The availability of the LCM opens novel ways of analyzing written and spoken language in communication by clarifying the processes driving linguistic choices in formulating messages and the impact of these messages on recipients. This entry begins by explaining the language processes underlying the model, and then discusses how the model works and some research applications.

Using Language to Describe People

What types of words are available to describe others, their interactions, and their makeup? What types of words do people use when they are describing something that happens to a member of their ingroup or of an outgroup? Is there a systematic difference in how people communicate an event that happens to their ingroups or outgroups? Do such differences in the language they use provide any insights into their motives and their thought processes?

To answer such questions, we have to know something about the general properties of the language we use to describe ourselves, others, interactions between people, and people's makeup and to use this knowledge to examine how people represent social events when they communicate about them.

There are three different types of words or lexical categories that serve these purposes, namely, verbs, adjectives, and nouns. With verbs, we can describe not only the interactions between two or more people but also the types of feelings or states people have regarding others. Thus, we can describe an event, such as somebody's fist traveling rapidly in space only to connect hard with another person's chin, with "Jack punched Homer," or "Jack hurt Homer" describing the action. It is also possible to describe the very same event with the feelings or emotions that drove the action, as in "Jack hates Homer." Alternatively, we can represent the same event with "Jack is aggressive" or "Jack is a bully," respectively with an adjective or a noun. These lexical categories exhaust the possible range of word options that we have to represent interpersonal events, that is, terms by which we can capture what happened, what the psychological states

were in such events, and the features of those involved in a social event.

While we have only three groups of lexical possibilities (verbs, adjectives, and nouns), the range of events that we can cover with the multitude of distinct words that we can find in each category is virtually limitless. When we are talking about social events, we can access a lexicon, which contains virtually thousands of verbs, adjectives, and nouns. This vast range permits us to capture the nuances of each event with considerable flexibility. Are there some general features of this linguistic domain that allow us to systematically examine such language use? The linguistic category model provides such a handle.

How the Model Works

In the LCM, verbs are classified into two broad groups, namely, verbs of state and verbs of action. *State verbs* (SV) are verbs that refer to invisible states, such as *respect, hate, dislike,* and *love,* identifying specific affective or mental states that a person feels or experiences toward another (e.g., "Jack hates Homer"). *Action verbs* (AV) are verbs describing activities with a clear beginning and end.

These verbs have been subdivided into three separate categories with distinct characteristics. Verbs in the first category, *descriptive action verbs* (DAV), have the unusual quality of mapping the action directly and retaining an unambiguous perceptual feature of the action. Examples would be *lick, kick,* and *pick,* involving, respectively, references to very specific actions involving the mouth, foot, and hand. Generally, these terms have no evaluative meaning but can acquire such meaning in specific contexts (e.g., "Jack *pushed* Homer under an oncoming bus" or "Jack *pushed* Homer away from an oncoming bus which Homer had not seen").

The second action verb category is *interpretive action verbs* (IAV). These also refer to actions with a clear beginning and end; however, these verbs subsume a large range of different actions. For instance, *cheat* is a verb that can refer to a wide range of different behaviors, as can the verb *help.* The direct perceptual correspondence between verb and action is lost in this category.

The third category, *state action verbs* (SAV), contains verbs that refer to the affective consequences of actions (e.g., *amaze, thrill, stun,* and *surprise)* but conceal the nature of the action that led to the emotion. Nevertheless, these verbs describe emotional consequences (e.g., "Homer *bored* me to death") in ways that allow the reasons to be easily specified (e.g., "with his lecture"). There is a difference in this respect between SAV and SV, since with SV it is perfectly possible to say, "I like him very much, but I really cannot explain why."

The final category describes attributes of people. This category includes *adjectives* (ADJ), which describe qualifiers of people such as *friendly, aggressive,* and *helpful,* as well as *nouns* (NOUN) such as *thief, father,* and *athlete.*

Features and Applications

One distinctive way in which these categories vary systematically is along the abstractness–concreteness dimension, with DAV being the most concrete category, IAV next, followed by SAV, SV, and finally, ADJ and NOUN as the most abstract categories. Abstractness–concreteness has been operationalized in terms of different inferential features in which these terms vary. These features are measured by asking people to respond to a set of questions about simple subject-verb-object sentences in which verb types and adjectives are varied.

These questions are (1) How enduring is the characteristic describing the sentence subject? (2) How easy/difficult is it to confirm and disconfirm statements constructed with these verbs or adjectives? (3) What is the temporal duration of the interpersonal event depicted by these terms? (4) How informative is the sentence about situational pressures or circumstances? and (5) What is the likelihood of the event reoccurring at a future point in time? These variables have been shown to form an abstractness–concreteness dimension on which the categories of the LCM are ordered systematically.

Thus, DAV is the most concrete category and, when used in sentence form (e.g., "Bill *punched* David"), does not describe an enduring characteristic of a person. Rather, the event these verbs describe is easy to confirm and of short duration, is highly informative about the situation, and is less likely to occur at a future point in time. If the same event is represented by an adjective (e.g.,

"Bill is *aggressive*"), the most abstract term, then the responses on all these variables are at the other end of the scale compared to DAV, with IAV, SAV, and SV falling in between. Finally, it should be noted that abstractness–concreteness is a generic dimension on which the linguistic categories can be represented—that is, it constitutes a property that runs across all words in the interpersonal domain.

One of the chief uses of the LCM is in examinations of strategic category use in communication. A prominent example is the *linguistic intergroup bias* (LIB). The question this research addresses is why and how people shape specific linguistic features of their communicative acts in the context of communicating stereotypes. How do people use different linguistic categories strategically and in particular how do they do so in the context of stereotyping? The LIB involves a tendency for individuals to describe positive ingroup and negative outgroup behaviors in relatively abstract terms. The choice of abstract words (e.g., ADJ) implies that the behavior is attributable to internal factors, that is, to the actor's stable characteristics.

Conversely, negative ingroup and positive outgroup behaviors are found to be typically described in relatively concrete terms. Concrete terms imply situational specificity, and hence an external attribution of the behavior. In this context, the systematic investigation of strategic language use reveals two things. First, these differences in abstractness and concreteness reveal possible psychological processes driving biased language use. One possible mechanism underlying the LIB is motivational, based on the desire to see the ingroup as more positive than the outgroup. Thus, abstract descriptions of positive ingroup behaviors and of negative outgroup behaviors portray the ingroup in favorable terms and the outgroup in unfavorable terms, implying that these behaviors are due to enduring characteristics. In contrast, concrete descriptions of negative ingroup behaviors minimize their significance as evidence for corresponding group characteristics, as do concrete depictions of positive outgroup behaviors. In other words, those linguistic (and conceptual) tendencies serve to protect the perception that the ingroup is superior to the outgroup. Second, the analysis of strategic language use informs us also about how stereotypes are transmitted in communication and recent research shows that systematic differences in language use shape the inferences of receivers to such messages.

The LCM has been shown not to be restricted to Indo-Germanic languages, but to be applicable across diverse linguistic communities, including Japanese, Chinese, and Turkish.

Gün R. Semin

See also Ethnocentrism; Language and Intergroup Relations; Linguistic Intergroup Bias (LIB); Prejudice; Stereotyping

Further Readings

Maass, A., Salvi, D., Arcuri, L., & Semin, G. (1989). Language use in intergroup contexts: The linguistic intergroup bias. *Journal of Personality and Social Psychology, 57,* 981–993.

Semin, G. R. (2000). Agenda 2000: Communication. Language as an implementational device for cognition. *European Journal of Social Psychology, 30,* 595–612.

Semin, G. R., & Fiedler, K. (1988). The cognitive functions of linguistic categories in describing persons: Social cognition and language. *Journal of Personality and Social Psychology, 54,* 558–568.

Semin, G. R., & Fiedler, K. (1991). The linguistic category model, its bases, applications and range. In W. Stroebe & M. Hewstone (Eds.), *European review of social psychology* (Vol. 2, pp. 1–30). Chichester, UK: John Wiley.

See www.cratylus.org (resources) for a detailed coding manual of the LCM.

Linguistic Intergroup Bias (LIB)

Linguistic intergroup bias (LIB) is the tendency of speakers to describe the actions of individuals at different abstraction levels depending on the actor's group membership and the valence of the action. For example, imagine that you are watching your favorite basketball team and one of the players makes a slam dunk. A few minutes later, a member of the opposing team also dunks the ball. Would you describe these two actions in exactly the same way? What if the player's action was negative, such as committing a foul? Researchers have

discovered that in addition to directly expressing our thoughts and feelings about other individuals (e.g., by labeling them as heroes or villains), we can use more subtle ways to convey our opinions, such as varying the verb tense we use in describing their behavior, choosing active versus passive voice, or shifting the abstraction level.

LIB is an example of the latter strategy. Positive ingroup behavior is described more abstractly (e.g., "I always told you that he is fantastic!") than positive outgroup behavior (e.g., "Look, he managed to shoot a basket!"). In contrast, negative ingroup behavior is described more concretely (e.g., "Oh no, he pushed him accidentally!") than negative outgroup behavior (e.g., "What a dirty player he is!"). Whereas a concrete description implies a single event with little or no consequence for future situations, abstract language suggests stable behavior that is likely to be repeated in the future. In this subtle way, the LIB leads to ingroup favoritism and outgroup discrimination.

This entry describes the theoretical context of LIB and examines its measurement, underlying mechanisms, and applications.

The Linguistic Category Model

The assumptions of the LIB are based on Semin and Fiedler's *linguistic category model* (LCM), which postulates an abstraction continuum with four different levels. For example, you can describe the same situation in the following ways: (1) the basketball player *hits* his opponent during the game, (2) the basketball player *hurts* his opponent during the game, (3) the basketball player *hates* his opponent, and (4) the basketball player is *aggressive*.

All four statements are accurate descriptions of the observed situation, yet they differ in abstraction. At the concrete end of the abstraction continuum are *descriptive action verbs* (e.g., *hit*), which provide an objective description of a single observable behavior. Descriptive action verbs are typically defined by at least one invariant physical feature of the action (e.g., one person *hits* another) and refer to a specific object (e.g., the opponent) and situation (e.g., the game).

Interpretative action verbs (e.g., *hurt*) represent the second abstraction level. They likewise refer to an observable behavior, but, in contrast to descriptive action verbs, they describe a more general class of behaviors. For instance, there are many different ways to hurt somebody, such as by hitting or by kicking the person, or by attacking him or her verbally. As a consequence, interpretative action verbs generally go beyond mere description, allowing different interpretations of a given situation.

State verbs (e.g., *hate*) represent the next abstraction level. They describe a lasting emotional or mental state, are interpretative and evaluative, and are independent of the specific action and context, but they maintain a reference to a specific object. In the example above, the basketball player hates his opponent outside the specific game and can express his feelings in many different ways.

Finally, at the abstract pole of the continuum are adjectives (e.g., *aggressive*). They are not only independent of the situation but also of the object of the action. They describe abstract characteristics and offer a wide range of interpretations. In the example cited above, the aggressiveness of the basketball player is directed at his opponent in this specific game and also represents an enduring characteristic of the player that generalizes across targets and situations.

Measuring the LIB

The LIB, namely that ingroup and outgroup behaviors are described at different abstraction levels depending on the valence of the behavior, has been assessed by the cued sentence completion procedure and by the multiple-choice method. In both cases, study participants are presented with cartoons showing a member of their own group or another group acting in either a socially desirable or undesirable way. The participants' task is to describe the scene.

In the cued sentence completion procedure, participants are instructed to complete a sentence such as, "A member of team Y . . ." in their own words. Responses are then scored for abstraction by independent raters on a continuum ranging from 1 to 4, with higher values reflecting higher levels of abstraction. In the multiple-choice method, four descriptions are presented, constructed according to the four classes of the linguistic category model, and participants are asked to choose one. In recent years, additional methods have been developed to measure the LIB, but comparable language biases have been obtained in a wide variety of intergroup

settings independent of the specific measure used to assess the LIB.

Underlying Mechanisms

Two different mechanisms have been proposed to explain the LIB, involving either motivation or cognition. The motivational approach assumes that ingroup protective motives operate in the LIB. Social identity theory postulates that one's self-concept is, in part, defined by one's group membership, so that positive evaluations of one's group lead to a positive self-concept and negative evaluations lead to a negative self-concept. According to this perspective, the LIB can be used as a subtle means to enhance or protect one's social identity. Describing positive behavior of one's own group and negative behavior of an opposing group in abstract terms implies that the behavior in question is typical for the group and stable over time. In contrast, describing negative ingroup and positive outgroup behavior in a more concrete way suggests that the behavior is atypical and unlikely to be repeated in the future. Such language-based favoritism of the ingroup relative to the outgroup contributes to a positive evaluation of one's own group and, hence, to a positive social identity.

The social cognitive approach assumes that the LIB is driven by differential expectancies about ingroup and outgroup members. Regardless of its valence, behavior consistent with prior expectancies about a group is considered to reflect typical and stable action tendencies and is therefore described in relatively abstract terms. In contrast, behavior inconsistent with prior expectancies is considered atypical and hence is described in a more concrete way.

In many intergroup settings, the two explanations lead to the same predictions, because in general people expect more positive and fewer negative behaviors from their own group than from other groups. Therefore, experimental studies were conducted to identify the actual mechanism underlying the LIB. To test the two accounts against one another, some researchers investigated individuals in intergroup settings for expectancies involving stereotypes, that is, beliefs that associate a given social group and its members with specific traits or behaviors.

For instance, gender stereotypes are beliefs about the differential behaviors that men and women are expected to perform. If ingroup protective motives underlie the LIB, men and women should describe positive behaviors of their own gender (he/she is assertive; he/she is helpful) and negative behaviors of the opposite gender (he/she is rude; he/she is dependent on others) more abstractly than in the reversed cases, regardless of whether the behavior is viewed as typical of males or of females. In contrast, if the differential expectancy explanation is correct, people should describe role-congruent behaviors (he is assertive/rude; she is helpful/dependent on others) more abstractly than role-incongruent behaviors (he helps someone/asks for advice; she expresses her opinion/insults someone) regardless of whether the behavior is positive or negative.

Research has generally shown that in intergroup settings (such as those involving gender relations) in which stereotypical expectancies prevail, the differential expectancy approach offers the most convincing account because people share very similar expectancies about typical behaviors of different groups independent of their own group membership. In contrast, the motivational approach plays an important role in competitive or hostile intergroup settings. Under highly competitive circumstances, such as conflicting interests of hunters and environmentalists or hostile relations between nations in times of war, ingroup protective motives come to the fore, and positive ingroup behaviors as well as negative outgroup behaviors are described at a higher abstraction level.

Thus, there is support for both explanations, with cognitive processes being predominant when socially shared expectancies exist, as in the case of stereotypes, and motivational processes becoming relevant when the ingroup is threatened by highly competitive conditions. The two processes can operate both independently and additively. In order to distinguish between the two mechanisms, the term *linguistic intergroup bias* (LIB) is now used to describe differences in abstraction level evoked by ingroup protective motives. In contrast, language biases produced by differential expectancies are now labeled by the term *linguistic expectancy bias* (LEB). Empirical evidence for both mechanisms has been found in a wide range of intergroup settings.

Interaction of Speaker Goals and Recipient Inferences

When people say something to someone else, their message is influenced by their individual motives, beliefs about the world, and communication goals. As described in the preceding paragraph, the LIB can satisfy self-enhancing motivations by causing one's own group to appear in a more favorable light, and the LEB can serve as a vehicle to express one's beliefs or expectancies. Moreover, irrespective of whether biased language use is intended or unconscious, it is likely to have an impact on the recipient of the message. Describing actions more concretely suggests a situational explanation, whereas describing actions more abstractly implies that the behavior occurs more frequently and reflects enduring characteristics of the actor.

Mass communication is a domain in which a single message can have an impact on thousands of people. Let's consider the two headlines: "Our secretary of state will not attend the peace talks" and "Rebels' boycott of peace talks continues." In both cases the peace talks do not take place, but the inferred reasons can be very different for the secretary of state and the rebels. The concrete description ("Our secretary of state *will not attend* the peace talks") suggests that the behavioral episode is an isolated event that can be attributed to many different causes and contextual factors not necessarily linked to the secretary of state's personal characteristics or psychological states. Describing the case in abstract terms ("Rebels' *boycott* of peace talks continues"), however, implies that the act of not attending the peace talks reflects an enduring negative characteristic of the rebels, such as hostility or aggressiveness.

By this subtle means, the recipient of the message forms a very different impression of the same situation depending on the level of abstraction in the language used by the speaker. This interplay between what the speaker says and what the recipient infers contributes to ingroup favoritism and outgroup discrimination (in the case of LIB) as well as to the maintenance and perpetuation of stereotypes (in the case of LEB).

Christiane Schoel and Anne Maass

See also Language and Intergroup Relations; Linguistic Category Model (LCM); Social Identity Theory; Stereotyping

Further Readings

Maass, A. (1999). Linguistic intergroup bias: Stereotype perpetuation through language. In M. P. Zanna (Ed.), *Advances in experimental social psychology* (Vol. 31, pp. 79–121). New York: Academic Press.

Maass, A., Milesi, A., Zabbini, S., & Stahlberg, D. (1995). The linguistic intergroup bias: Differential expectancies or ingroup protection? *Journal of Personality and Social Psychology, 68,* 116–126.

Maass, A., Salvi, D., Arcuri, L., & Semin, G. R. (1989). Language use in intergroup contexts: The linguistic intergroup bias. *Journal of Personality and Social Psychology, 57,* 981–993.

Semin, G. R., & Fiedler, K. (1991). The linguistic category model, its bases, applications and range. In W. Stroebe & M. Hewstone (Eds.), *European review of social psychology* (Vol. 2, pp. 1–30). Chichester, UK: John Wiley.

Wigboldus, D. H. J., & Douglas, K. (2007). Language, stereotypes, and intergroup relations. In K. Fiedler (Ed.), *Social communication* (pp. 79–106). New York: Psychology Press.

Wigboldus, D. H. J., Semin, G. R., & Spears, R. (2000). How do we communicate stereotypes? Linguistic bases and inferential consequences. *Journal of Personality and Social Psychology, 78,* 5–18.

LOOKING-GLASS SELF

The *looking-glass self* is a concept introduced by Charles Horton Cooley in 1902. Cooley was working to develop a theory of self as essentially social, and he used the image of a mirror to capture the idea of people imagining what they look like to others, then incorporating what they imagine into their own self-concept. This concept of self as a product of interaction with environment, and reflection based upon that interaction, has come to occupy a pivotal role in both psychology and sociology. Group interaction studies, a strain of sociology known as symbolic interactionism, and studies of both empathy and prejudice have all relied heavily on its core idea that people develop a self-concept based on their emotional reactions to what they believe others are thinking about them.

Cooley described three components or "principal elements" of the looking-glass self: "the imagination of our appearance to the other person; the imagination of his judgment of that appearance; and some sort of self-feeling, such as pride or mortification." He developed the concept through careful observation of his own children, particularly his third child, a daughter, "M," whom he systematically observed from shortly after her birth until she was almost 3 years old. Cooley was particularly struck by the development in children's speech of the personal pronouns *I, me,* and *mine,* which he reasoned could come only from children's awareness of others and of themselves in contrast to others, and thus as distinct from others.

For example, he worked extensively with what he called *appropriation,* which refers to children's taking and owning of things. Cooley observed that children begin appropriative processes with attempts to control the things closest to them, including their own bodies, and then move outward to the people in their vicinity, just as infants exert their social power to attract attention. From this observation, he reasoned that people's sense of self emerges from relations with their immediate group (loved ones, caregivers, mothers) in particular, and continues to develop as they relate to an increasingly wide set of acquaintances. As children learn what they can and cannot control, they begin to define themselves in terms of the images they see others assigning to them; thus they begin to manipulate those around them, beginning with the ones who are easiest to control.

Adults, he reasoned, are not that much different; their imaginations are merely more complex and specific, and their manipulations of others more subtle. The process of imagining others' perceptions and judgments and reconciling them with what one knows becomes a dynamic process of building self-concept. It includes reflection, but it puts emotional responses and feelings at the center of the development of self-concept. The self is inextricable from society, "twin-born," as Cooley called it, because it emerges in interaction and becomes meaningful only in contrast to the society that is not of self.

This idea furthered the work of William James, and encompassed more than the processes involved in the concept of the looking-glass self. However, despite this and other major contributions to sociological thought (including the idea of the primary group), Cooley is today best known for the concept of the looking-glass self, if only because it captured the imaginations of so many. His use of a couplet by Ralph Waldo Emerson was often repeated, and even mistakenly attributed to Cooley:

> *Each to each a looking-glass*
> *Reflects the other that doth pass.*

Critics of Cooley point out that when carried to its furthest dimension, the concept of the looking-glass self makes the developing human appear to be passive, dependent upon others for approval, and constantly changing to fit his or her environment. Cooley argued, however, that the self-image also encompasses a more stable, autonomous image, one that resists the easy influence of rare or extraordinary events, and that is more heavily relied upon by the person of substantial character. In Cooley's conceptualization, children learn how to sympathize with others through their primary groups (caregivers and family members). Through early processes of appropriation and attribution of images, eventually children come to fuse their individuality to that common whole, and develop the kind of respect for the feelings of others that Cooley argued would make them mature members of society. Ultimately, they apply that sense of empathy to increasingly wider circles of acquaintances.

Some have pointed out that it is ironic that Cooley himself would be aghast at the idea of a person whose self-image had been entirely created by the impressions of others. But his colorful and dramatic use of the image of mirrors, and of the rhyme, so engaged the thinkers of his era that it ensured his fame for ensuing generations. With the concept of the looking-glass self, he had shown the way society and its values were taken in by individuals and internalized by their own mental processes.

His analysis continues to have great appeal to a wide swath of sociology, psychology, and group behavior studies. Relying on and expanding on Cooley's work, many branches of thought in many areas have flowered in the time since. For example, social identity theory, a foundational concept in the study of group processes and intergroup relations, holds that in interactions within and between groups, an individual calls on more than one identity. These identities start with the self, alone, but move outward in concentric circles to include identities called upon in personal interactions, and then, in wider circles, in increasingly larger groups. People can thus be expected to behave differently in personal interactions and in different groups. They will also act differently within groups, depending on several factors, among them the extent to which they consider the group an ingroup, that is, a group to which they feel they belong. Finally, people can behave differently depending on the roles they assume, or tend to assume, within those groups—for example, leaders versus followers.

Ideas such as the relative nature of concepts of self and the notion of concentric circles, with an individual's relationships moving from personal and family relationships outward into more impersonal groups, draw heavily on Cooley's work. Social identity theory has also expanded to encompass ideas of national identity. How people come to see their own nation in relation to other nations or groups is an evolving image that may or may not be unified. It is certainly collective, however, and important in the shaping of national opinions and actions.

Symbolic interactionism, a branch of sociology with its genesis in the theorizing of the philosopher George Herbert Mead and its dissemination in a book with that title by Herbert Blumer, builds upon Cooley's idea by saying that we impute meaning to things around us, including other people, based upon our idea of what others are thinking. In taking the role of the other, especially the generalized other, we develop a sense of self in interaction, which can then be understood as dynamic and influenced by those with whom we are interacting. It is generally accepted that Mead built upon the work of Cooley, with Cooley providing the mechanism by which the mind internalizes and appropriates the values and views of society, whereas Mead's elaboration shows how society is in turn influenced and changed by the values of the individuals within it.

Cooley's looking-glass self, with its emphasis on individual reflection and the emotional aspects of developing one's identity, has strongly influenced all of symbolic interactionism, but was especially instrumental in the ensuing development of what is now known as the *sociology of emotions*. This branch of sociology studies how social situations affect emotions, the cultural rules and norms that we learn about what emotions we can or should express and when it is appropriate to do so, how emotions shape action and interaction, and the collective emotions that maintain or alter social structures. Cooley called the feelings intrinsic to the looking-glass self "social sentiments," and his focus on the cultural shaping of reflection and interpretation laid the foundation for the later work of C. Wright Mills, Erving Goffman, and Arlie Russell Hochschild.

Cooley's concept of the looking-glass self stressed the role of the child's attribution of others' images, the first stages of empathy in the development of the child's understanding. Empathy studies have furthered Cooley's work by taking his description of the child's development of empathy, of seeing others' perspectives and reacting accordingly, and building on it. These scholars have stressed the role empathy can play in improving relations among, between, and within groups. Cooley considered increasing empathy for wider and more distantly related groups to be the essence of human progress; therefore, studying the nature, essence, and origin of empathy should be a worthy pursuit in and of itself. Empathy is now divided into two kinds, *cognitive* and *emotional,* with emotional empathy further divided into *parallel* (feeling what others feel) and *reactive* (reacting to what others feel). Cooley's work in noticing that children's development of self is based on their immediate observation of others and others' reaction to them, and the role of emotion in developing this sense of self, was instrumental in the development of this field.

Perhaps one of the most profound manifestations of Cooley's description of a dynamic, evolving sense of self, a self based upon the way one's self-image interrelates with the images of one's acquaintances, lies in the field of the study of prejudice. Prejudice was well known to be both deeply ingrained in human consciousness, and enormously destructive as a social force, by the time third-grade teacher Jane Elliott did the class exercises in 1968 that ultimately became the 1985 Frontline program "A Class Divided." In her social experiment, based on a lesson on prejudice given to a class of children in Iowa the day after the assassination of Dr. Martin Luther King, Jr., she divided her students into a brown-eyed group and a blue-eyed group. She discriminated against each group in turn, and observed the children doing the same, even as their test scores rose and fell accordingly.

This established the role of prejudice in developing not only one's sense of community and one's role in it, but also a view of one's own abilities and, presumably as a result of that, one's test scores and success or failure in quantitative measurements of skills and abilities. By artificially establishing groups, rules, and social norms that reinforced prejudice, Elliott's experiment proved quite directly that images of oneself, attributed to members of one's community or social group and based on their reactions, can undermine one's self-esteem so dramatically as to influence one's measurable performance levels on tests in such basic areas as math and reading. Test scores would presumably be based on one's skills and abilities, which by other theories should be independent of the influence of the vagaries of one's day-to-day emotional variation. Prejudice, in other words, by undermining our self-image at its very heart, can influence and undermine us so thoroughly as to affect every aspect of our performance in society.

Cooley relied on the image of the mirror, or looking glass, to express the idea that the image we create of ourselves is primarily the product of other images: the images we imagine that others have of us. The dramatic image of the looking glass attracted many thinkers of his time, partly because he carefully captured the process by which we internalize society's values as part of our very core. It was also popular because it captured the way a society, particularly the small town, Midwest America of which he was a part, was displaying increasing absorption with appearance and the impressions of others. For this, the concept of the looking-glass self, and the shallow obsession with appearance that it represented, were roundly criticized. The concept survived, however, due to its utility in accurately portraying both the development of the self-concept of the child and the interrelationship of the society and the human perception that tries to make sense of it.

Jennifer L. Dunn

See also Collective Self; Multiple Identities; Roles; Social Identity Theory; Symbolic Interactionism

Further Readings

Cooley, C. H. (1930). *Sociological theory and social research*. New York: Henry Holt.

Cooley, C. H. (1964). *Human nature and the social order*. New York: Schocken. (Original work published 1902)

Cooley, C. H. (1998). The social self—the meaning of "I." In H. J. Schubert (Ed.), *Charles Horton Cooley: On self and social organization* (pp. 155–175). Chicago: University of Chicago Press. (Original work published 1902)

Franks, D. D., & Gecas, V. (1992). Autonomy and conformity in Cooley's self-theory: The looking-glass self and beyond. *Symbolic Interaction, 15*(1), 49–68.

Gutman, R. (1958). Cooley: A perspective. *American Sociological Review, 23*(3), 251–256.

Jandy, E. C. (1942). *Charles Horton Cooley: His life and social theory*. New York: Dryden.

Mead, G. H. (1930). Cooley's contribution to American social thought. *American Journal of Sociology, 35*(5), 693–706.

LOYALTY

Loyalty is a term used to describe an individual's orientation toward something or someone, where that orientation is characterized by faithful adherence, devotion, allegiance, commitment, and a merging or overlap between the individual's interests and those of the target of the loyalty. Loyalty can be extended to individuals, such as leaders, partners, spouses, friends, coworkers, or family, or it can be extended to groups or categories, such as companies, religions, volunteer organizations, professional societies, or countries. Loyalty can also occur with respect to ideals or principles, such as justice, fairness, freedom, honesty, equality, honor, and truth. This entry looks at these different kinds of loyalty and discusses related dilemmas and future research directions.

Loyalty to Groups

There have been different operationalizations of loyalty across relatively few scientific examinations. For example, group loyalty is sometimes equated by researchers with group commitment. Other researchers do not formally define or operationalize group loyalty but infer it based on the observation of biased evaluations. Despite these differences, there is an underlying similarity in much of the research on group loyalty, which is that loyalty is an adherence or faithfulness to a group, even in the face of countervailing pressure or when personal sacrifice must be made. That is, loyalty can be inferred when an individual chooses to remain in a group even when the individual would benefit more personally by leaving it.

Likewise, loyalty to a group can also be inferred when an individual leaves the group even when the individual would gain more by staying in it. Of course, loyalty is not always inferred based on decisions to remain in or leave groups. Individuals may defend their current groups from attack or criticism, and loyalty is inferred when doing so would endanger the defenders. Essentially, then, loyalty is putting the interests and image of the group ahead of personal interests.

Social psychological research examining group loyalty includes investigations of cooperation versus competition in social dilemma paradigms. In a typical social dilemma paradigm, individuals are consumers of a shared resource and must decide between individual self-interest and the collective good. In the short term, a strategy of maximizing personal outcomes may be beneficial to individuals. Over time, however, this strategy proves to be disastrous. By contrast, placing group concerns above personal interests can extend the life of the resource and optimize outcomes for everyone involved. Roderick Kramer and Marilynn Brewer have shown that identification with a group predicts whether individuals will exercise personal restraint in the use of a common resource and assign greater weight to group outcomes than to personal outcomes.

Social psychologists Bozena Zdaniuk and John M. Levine examined group loyalty by creating laboratory groups in which members were randomly assigned (a) to identify weakly or strongly with the group, and (b) to have few or many resources, relative to other group members. Group members were asked to make a decision about whether to remain in or leave the group. If they remained in the group, their resources would be divided among all group members. If they left the group, however, they would take their individual resources, leaving the remaining group members to divide what they had left among themselves.

For participants with many resources, it was considered loyalty to stay in the group because if they stayed, their many resources would raise the average payoff within the group (even though it would mean a personal sacrifice). By contrast, for participants with few resources, it was considered loyalty to leave the group because if they left, the average potential payoff within the group would be raised (but at a personal cost to the one who left the group). They found that, regardless of the level of resources, those who identified more strongly with the group were more likely to stay in the group than those whose identification with the group was weak.

Related research by Mark van Vugt and Claire Hart also has demonstrated that strength of identification with a group is a robust predictor of group loyalty, or choosing to stay in a group even at a personal cost. In addition, they found evidence that loyalty behavior was strongly correlated with positive group perceptions. Thus, it may be the case that identification with a group leads to greater liking for the group, as well as a consequent desire to remain even when attractive alternative options exist.

Loyalty is also an important topic in organizational research. In this arena, loyalty is conceptualized in a similar manner, namely, as the willingness to forgo more attractive work alternatives and stay with a company, organization, or union. Loyalty is also inferred when observing "organizational citizenship behaviors," which are discretionary acts that benefit the organization. By definition, these behaviors are not required and received no immediate tangible compensation.

Loyalty to Relationships and Individuals

Close relationships can be thought of as a type of group—an intimacy group—in which two people are similar, interdependent, and often goal oriented. In relationship research, the concept of loyalty has many similarities to the analogous concept in group research. That is, during difficult times in a relationship, or when attractive alternative partners are available, remaining in the relationship constitutes loyalty.

Caryl Rusbult, Isabella Zembrodt, and Lawanna Gunn have proposed four responses to relationship dissatisfaction. These vary along the dimensions of constructive versus destructive responses and active versus passive responses. The active destructive response is called *exit,* which is separation or leaving the relationship. The active constructive response, *voice,* is discussing problems and working toward solutions. The passive destructive response, called *neglect,* refers to ignoring the partner, treating the partner badly either emotionally or physically, and refusing to discuss problems. Finally, the passive constructive response is called *loyalty,* which is waiting optimistically for the relationship to be mended and problems to be solved.

Rusbult and her colleagues have found that this type of loyalty increases as a function of relationship satisfaction and the magnitude of tangible and emotional investments in the relationship but decreases as a function of the quality of alternative partners. Thus the concept of relationship loyalty differs slightly from the concept of group loyalty, which involves staying in the group even when better alternatives are available.

As a conceptual subset of relationship research, social scientists who study organizational dynamics also examine loyalty to leaders or superordinates. This type of loyalty is typically conceptualized as subordinates' public expressions of support for superordinates and their policies. Loyalty in subordinate–superordinate dyads has been shown to be distinct from organizational loyalty.

Loyalty to Principles

Loyalty to principles, like the various forms of loyalty discussed above, is inferred when an individual behaves according to a ideal or standard even when there is pressure to do otherwise, or when adhering to a principle requires a cost or sacrifice on the part of the individual. Organizational whistleblowing is a quintessential example of loyalty to moral principles over loyalty to an organization.

Related Constructs

As discussed above, identification with a group is a strong predictor of group loyalty. That is, the stronger an individual identifies with his or her ingroup, the more that person can be expected to be loyal to the group.

Apart from strength of ingroup identification, other social processes are likely to yield group and relationship loyalty. Groups may exert normative influence on members to remain loyal. For example, the motto of the U.S. Marine Corps is *semper fidelis,* often shortened to *semper fi,* which means "always faithful" in Latin. Such a motto makes loyalty cognitively accessible and thus influential on behavior. Religious groups sometimes publicly shame or shun those who fall away from or leave their faith, and such acts serve the function of communicating to remaining adherents that a similar fate awaits them if they choose disloyalty.

Another process likely to yield loyalty is being the recipient of trust and loyalty. Over time and through experience with an organization, group, or relationship partner, individuals may see that others are willing to trust them, defend them, and stay with them even when they could do otherwise. This creates a sense of obligation, and reciprocal loyalty can be expected.

Dissonance-based justification processes are also likely to be involved in the creation of loyalty. In a classic effort-justification experiment by Elliot Aronson and Judson Mills, participants had to earn membership in a group by performing a mild or severe initiation. Those who performed the more embarrassing tasks (i.e., the severe initiation) rated the group more favorably than did those who completed relatively mild tasks to gain entry to the group. If individuals can be induced to sacrifice freely for a group or relationship, they will justify that behavior by endorsing it and by coming to like the group more. Group or relationship loyalty is then a likely consequence.

Although loyalty is typically considered a beneficial behavioral orientation toward a group or partner, it can also be maladaptive in some circumstances. As a consequence of expressed or implied loyalty, individuals may feel pressure to engage in unethical, immoral, or destructive behaviors. For example, loyal employees may feel obligated to lie and cover up corporate wrongdoings. Many members of Jim Jones's Peoples Temple cult were so loyal that they took their own lives by drinking the famous cyanide-laced Flavor Aid. The extent of true loyalty is unclear in this case, however, because those who resisted suicide were shot or injected with cyanide.

Loyalty Dilemmas

Individuals may experience extreme psychological conflict if they have to choose between competing loyalties, where outcomes are in a zero-sum-like arrangement. For instance, if a child of divorced parents is asked by both parents to spend a holiday with them, the child is forced to choose between pleasing one parent and necessarily hurting the other. Likewise, individuals may simultaneously belong to two groups that have conflicting values or behavioral expectations. In such cases, total loyalty to each group is not possible. If an individual's fraternity or sorority expects group members to engage in behaviors that are prohibited by his or her religious group, for example, the individual must make a choice regarding the relative importance of each group loyalty. Immigrants or exiles may also feel a sharp sense of conflict between loyalty to their country of origin and loyalty to their new host country.

Of course, many loyalty dilemmas occur not between competing groups or relationships, but instead between a group or relationship and some principle or ideal, as in the case of organizational whistleblowing or of soldiers who must decide whether to be loyal to a superior and follow illegal orders or to be loyal to the law and refuse to follow orders. Although there has been empirical research examining group and relationship loyalty, very little research, if any, has been conducted on the approach–avoid dynamics of competing loyalties.

Whereas loyalty conceptually represents an intriguing behavioral phenomenon, namely, the willingness to incur personal costs to protect, preserve, or benefit a relationship or group, it is relatively understudied. Further research is needed not only to refine the operationalization of loyalty, but also to develop a broader understanding of when loyalty is likely to arise, what other constructs are associated with it, and what various cognitive, affective, and behavioral consequences arise as a function of it.

Jared B. Kenworthy

See also Cooperation and Competition; Identification and Commitment

Further Readings

Aronson, E., & Mills, J. (1959). The effect of severity of initiation on liking for a group. *Journal of Abnormal and Social Psychology, 59*, 177–181.

James, K., & Cropanzano, R. (1994). Dispositional group loyalty and individual action for the benefit of an ingroup: Experimental and correlational evidence. *Organizational Behavior and Human Decision Processes, 60*, 179–205.

Kramer, R. M., & Brewer, M. B. (1984). Effects of group identity on resource use in a simulated commons dilemma. *Journal of Personality and Social Psychology, 46*, 1044–1057.

Rusbult, C., Zembrodt, I., & Gunn, L. (1982). Exit, voice, loyalty, and neglect: Responses to dissatisfaction in romantic involvements. *Journal of Personality and Social Psychology, 43*, 1230–1242.

van Vugt, M., & Hart, C. (2004). Social identity as social glue: The origins of group loyalty. *Journal of Personality and Social Psychology, 86*, 585–598.

Zdaniuk, B., & Levine, J. M. (2001). Group loyalty: Impact of members' identification and contributions. *Journal of Experimental Social Psychology, 37*, 502–509.

MEDIATION

Mediation is a process whereby a person becomes involved in a dispute or decision between two or more others and attempts to affect the outcome. This person, the *mediator*—also known as the *third party* and sometimes referred to as the *neutral*, depending on the context—has no authority to dictate the outcome but rather exercises influence to affect an outcome. Mediation is a special case of negotiation in which the mediator helps the disputants, or *negotiators*, reach an agreement that they might otherwise not reach on their own. It preserves the voluntary, joint-decision features of negotiation: The disputants retain the right to accept or reject any suggestion made by the mediator. As such, mediation is a form of assisted negotiation, and it is helpful to understand negotiation as a precursor to understanding mediation.

There are many interesting aspects of mediation that reflect the complex social, cognitive, and emotional processes of how people think, feel, and act toward members of their own and other groups. Additional complexity derives from the fact that mediation often occurs in the context of complex social, organizational, institutional, political, and legal systems that have constraints and historical underpinnings. Mediation always involves communication processes, both verbal and nonverbal. A mediator, for example, might say to the parties, "Let me make the following suggestion to you about how to settle your problem" and may distribute his or her visual attention equally between the parties while making that statement.

Another view of mediation is that it is a role in a specific setting: "I am the mediator in today's pretrial court proceeding." Mediation can also be a career choice, such as divorce or labor mediation, that entails specialized training and professional credentials and is guided by formal rules and regulations. Seen broadly, mediation occurs every day, informally, anytime someone attempts to influence the outcome of a decision being made by others. This entry looks at the history of mediation, describes the mediation process, and discusses its effectiveness.

Background and History

Mediation appears to occur everywhere, among all peoples, in all societies and cultures. It is a universal, within and between cultures and within and between groups, organizations, and nations. The primatologist Frans de Waal has reported that even chimpanzees and other nonhuman primates mediate their disputes. Among humans, mediation has been important for quite some time. The earliest known writing, about 4,500 years ago, includes a stone carving that describes a Sumerian ruler in Mesopotamia who helped avert a war and develop an agreement between neighboring groups in a dispute over land and water. Indeed, mediation is arguably the oldest and most common form of dispute resolution.

The 1960s and 1970s saw a revolution of mediation in U.S. society, stimulated by passage of state and federal laws. For example, public employees earned the right to bargain collectively, which led to the advent of state agencies such as the public employment relations boards and the public employment relations commissions that provide mediation, often as a required step in the event of a labor contract dispute. The landmark 1964 Civil Rights Act provided, in Article X, for the creation of the Community Relations Service of the U.S. Department of Justice. This organization provides mediation in community disputes that relate to discriminatory practices based on race, color, or national origin.

The 1970s also saw the advent of community mediation centers, such as the Conflict Resolution Center in Chicago, which provide mediation services in a variety of disputes and are often associated with the courts. Family mediation has increased, as well as divorce mediation, which is required for all divorces in some states. And public resource mediation of environmental disputes has grown. This growth reflects U.S. chief justice Warren E. Burger's comments in the 1970s that the existing judicial system was too costly and inefficient, which encouraged the use of alternative methods of dispute resolution, such as mediation, especially in disputes involving divorce, child custody, adoptions, personal injury, landlord and tenant cases, and probate of estates. It is not surprising that law schools, and business schools as well, offer courses in alternative dispute resolution, including negotiation and mediation training. Middle and high schools often offer mediation training and programs in peer mediation, and many colleges and universities now include mediation training and programs for residence hall and other disputes.

Mediators are guided and aided by professional societies. For example, the document *Model Standards of Conduct for Mediators* was prepared jointly in the 1990s by the American Arbitration Association, the American Bar Association, and the Society of Professionals in Dispute Resolution. Regional organizations, such as the Southern California Mediation Association (SCMA), provide guidance and support to professional mediators and to the legal community. For example, the SCMA filed in 2003 an amicus curiae brief with the California Supreme Court in a case (*Rojas v. Superior Court*) that led to a seminal decision affecting mediation confidentiality in California.

In international disputes, the use of mediation by organizations such as the Organization of African Unity, the Organization of American States, the International Committee of the Red Cross, and many other nonstate organizations has also increased. Moreover, representatives of organized religion often play a role in mediating international disputes, as the Vatican did in the early 1980s in the dispute between Chile and Argentina over property rights in the Beagle Channel.

The Study of Mediation

Researchers have studied what mediators do, when they do it and why, and with what effect. In addressing these issues, researchers often consider differences between contexts of mediation. Following a distinction made by the political scientist Saadia Touval, many researchers distinguish between contractual mediation and emergent mediation.

The Context of Mediation: Contractual and Emergent

Contractual mediation occurs within a set of rules and guidelines that have been previously established by the community. It is usually done by a professional who has received formal training and is available for more than one case. Labor mediation, divorce mediation, community mediation, and any mediation that occurs in the courts are examples. The term *neutral* is often used to describe mediators in such cases because neutrality is a key source of mediator influence in these contexts.

In *emergent mediation*, the mediator typically has an ongoing relationship with the disputants and is an interested party who emerges from the organization or system in which the dispute has occurred. Examples include a dispute between two coworkers in a business and another coworker who steps in to help as a mediator or a dispute between two nations over the location of a common border and a third nation that offers to mediate.

What Do Mediators Do?

A good deal of research on mediation deals with descriptions and taxonomies of mediator behavior. The mediation literature offers many typologies and distinguishing factors of mediator interventions. The social psychologist Ken Kressel developed an early influential framework that classifies mediator behavior into three categories: (1) behavior that addresses the substance of the issues (e.g., making an outcome suggestion to the parties or putting pressure on the parties to make concessions), (2) behavior that affects the context of negotiation (e.g., attempting to restructure the agenda of issues in discussions), and (3) behavior that lays the foundation for later success (e.g., developing rapport with parties or meeting with the parties separately in a caucus). The ability of mediators to control communications and modify information exchange is seen as a key element.

Other work has adapted research on social power and influence to mediation. For example, some scholars note that mediator behavior can reflect the use of rewards (carrots) and punishment (sticks), as well as the application of information in solving the disputants' problem (problem solving). Social psychologist Peter Carnevale developed a series of studies suggesting that a perceptual factor (the mediator's estimate of the likelihood of a win–win agreement) and a motivational factor (the mediator's concern for the parties' needs and interests) together predict the occurrence of different forms of mediator behavior.

Contingent Effectiveness of Mediation

Mediator behavior can be adaptive, that is, mediators often act with *contingency*, in the sense that they first attempt to understand the problem they face and then try one thing or another to achieve their goals. In one study, an analysis of actual transcripts of a labor negotiation revealed that labor mediators adopted a more forceful style of intervention when the disputing parties became more intransigent. Other evidence indicates that mediators become more forceful when time pressure increases.

Many studies have also revealed that disputants adapt to mediation, which indicates that mediator behavior is contingently effective. In an early study by social psychologist Dean Pruitt, negotiators were especially receptive to a third party's suggestion if they simultaneously had impression management concerns and a strong need to reach agreement. This situation is referred to as the *face-saving function* of mediation.

There is evidence that mediation is more effective when conflict is moderate rather than intense

and when the parties are highly motivated to reach settlement, as they are in a *hurting stalemate*, an intolerable impasse so painful or costly that the parties search for a way out. Mediation also is more effective when the issues do not involve general principles and when the parties are relatively equal in power.

There is evidence that direct, forceful mediator behavior is effective when the conflict between disputants is so intense that they are unable to engage in problem solving. However, such intervention is counterproductive when the disputants are capable of engaging in problem solving. In a study of divorce mediation, agreement was more likely to be reached if the mediator interrupted the disputants when their discussion became hostile and refrained from interrupting when their discussion was friendlier.

The traditional view that mediator bias is totally incompatible with success has been challenged by several authors, who note that a biased mediator is sometimes the only one available to mediate the conflict and is often the person with the greatest influence over the party that most needs to change. There is evidence, which may apply mainly to emergent mediation contexts, that a mediator who is seen as biased in favor of the opponent at the outset of mediation is seen in a very favorable light if that mediator acts clearly in an evenhanded manner during the mediation and is seen even more favorably than a mediator who was initially perceived as completely impartial.

Mediation has also been shown to be more effective when arbitration is a next step. *Arbitration* is a procedure in which the intermediary listens to the arguments of both sides and makes a decision for the disputants. One exciting avenue for future work is the development and assessment of hybrid forms of third-party roles in disputes, such as combinations of mediation and arbitration.

Peter J. Carnevale

See also Cooperation and Competition; Distributive Justice; Negotiation and Bargaining; Procedural Justice; Relative Deprivation; Team Negotiation; Trust

Further Readings

Bercovitch, J. (Ed.). (2002). *Studies in international mediation: Essays in honor of Jeffrey Z. Rubin.* London: Palgrave-MacMillan.

Carnevale, P. J., & De Dreu, C. K. W. (Eds.). (2006). *Methods of negotiation research*. Leiden, The Netherlands: Martinus Nijhoff.

Carnevale, P. J., & Pruitt, D. G. (1992). Negotiation and mediation. *Annual Review of Psychology, 43*, 531–582.

de Waal, F. B. M. (1989). *Peacemaking among primates*. Cambridge, MA: Harvard University Press.

Donohue, W. A. (1991). *Communication, marital dispute and divorce mediation*. Hillsdale, NJ: Lawrence Erlbaum.

Kressel, K., & Pruitt, D. G. (Eds.). (1989). *Mediation research: The process and effectiveness of third-party intervention*. San Francisco: Jossey-Bass.

Moore, C. (2003). *The mediation process: Practical strategies for resolving conflict* (3rd ed.). San Francisco: Jossey-Bass.

Rojas v. Superior Court for the State of California, County of Los Angeles, 33 Cal. 4th 407 (2004).

Touval, S., & Zartman, I. W. (1985). *International mediation in theory and practice*. Boulder, CO: Westview Press.

MERGERS

Mergers are now commonplace in the corporate world as organizations seek to enhance their competitiveness and effectiveness in an increasingly complex and globalized corporate environment. A *merger* takes place when two previously separate organizations combine to form a single organizational entity. Over the past two decades in particular, numerous mergers have occurred. In both media reports and scientific papers, negative employee reactions to mergers are frequently reported. Moreover, although they are typically justified in terms of sound business assumptions, it is not unusual for mergers to be less successful than anticipated in business terms. Indeed, they may ultimately be dissolved. Hence, it is now widely accepted that mergers may be less successful than expected and that they may in fact fail because of the "us-versus-them" dynamics engendered by the situation.

Most organizational changes create stress and job insecurity, but organizational mergers represent a particularly stressful kind of change, given the large-scale nature of this change and the fact that employees must relinquish an identity that was previously important to them and shift their allegiance to the newly merged organization. To account for the fact that between 60% and 70% of mergers fail to achieve their economic aims, commentators have proposed that relying on a strictly economic point of view is unlikely to provide insights into why mergers so often fail. Researchers have proposed that there is a considerable amount of unexplained variance in predicting why mergers fail or succeed and that various noneconomic factors need to be taken into consideration to account for what goes on during organizational mergers.

A number of psychological approaches have been proposed to explain employees' reactions to organizational mergers. Studies using a stress and coping approach have focused on variables such as employees' appraisals or subjective judgments of the merger situation and the coping strategies used to deal with it. Researchers who have studied mergers from the perspective of job characteristics have stressed that after a merger, jobs should be designed in a way that sustains or increases employees' job satisfaction and commitment during this change. To design jobs in this way, management should directly involve employees in the job redesign process, train them to adjust to this change, and provide a clear rationale for the change. Such strategies should facilitate employees' support for and adjustment to the merger and hence minimize resistance and conflicts.

Other approaches have focused more directly on the conflict and the rivalries that may develop between employees from the merging organizations. The goal of such approaches is to understand the processes by which two merging organizations come to fit together and form a new superordinate entity. The acculturation perspective on mergers, for instance, focuses on the intergroup dimension of the merger by proposing that the successful integration of both organizations into an overarching, merged entity depends on the degree of fit between the values and the practices endorsed by the management of the two merging organizations. From this perspective, when employees feel threatened by a merger and fear losing their accustomed way of doing things, acculturation stress and conflict will result, a state referred to as *culture clash*.

An intergroup approach goes further in an effort to clarify the conflict that may emerge during mergers. Mergers involve the imposition of a new superordinate identity on employees, at the same time as they require the employees to relinquish their premerger organizational identity. For this reason, mergers are likely to trigger the social identification processes that are central to intergroup theories. Because employees of the two organizations will be motivated to establish an optimal position for their own group in the new organization, a merger may engender competitive and antagonistic intergroup relations. Case studies of mergers suggest that these negative us-versus-them dynamics and responses may well undermine the success of the merger.

A social identity perspective focuses on identification and recategorization processes as key factors that need to be considered in an effort to understand intergroup conflict in response to an organizational merger. *Social identity*, which can be defined as that part of the individual self-concept that derives from memberships in social groups, is a fundamental psychological variable that shapes individuals' feelings and behaviors. Organizational identity, as one specific type of social identity, represents an important basis for self-definition.

Because the self is defined in terms of the group membership, a social identity perspective assumes that people are motivated to favor their ingroup over the outgroup. This self-enhancement motive means that group members are motivated to acquire or to maintain a positive social identity for their ingroup. People seek to belong to groups that compare well with others. That is, to the extent that one's ingroup is perceived as better than the outgroup, a person's social identity becomes more positive. For this reason, people seek to belong to high-status groups. The desire for a positive social identity means that whereas members of a low-status group are motivated to acquire a more positive social identity, members of a high-status group are motivated to maintain such an identity, which involves maintaining both their membership in the group and its continued existence.

The nature of an organizational merger challenges employees' organizational identity, which is likely to result in antagonistic and conflictual intergroup perceptions and behaviors. In fact, the merger situation implies a direct confrontation between the two organizations as they both seek to optimize their position and standing in the new organization. Furthermore, like many other intergroup contexts, mergers often involve organizations that differ in status—that is, one organization is likely to be more productive, resourceful, and competitive than the other. During a merger, such differences are likely to be accentuated. This means that members of the lower-status group are confronted with the reality of their disadvantaged position in the new intergroup structure. In contrast, members of the higher-status group are motivated to ensure their dominant position in the merged organization and, as a consequence, to impose their own premerger identity on the new, merged organization. Doing so will directly threaten the survival of the lower-status group's identity within the new organization. Hence, members of the lower-status group should be particularly threatened by a merger situation, a finding that has emerged in a number of studies. Nevertheless, if they see that the merger situation will improve or enhance their social identity (e.g., through open boundaries, in the new organization, between the lower- and higher-status premerger organizations), then responses of the members of the lower-status group to the merger will be more positive.

The temporal dynamics that emerge during the course of a merger and that influence intergroup relations are also important for understanding the impact and success of organizational mergers. The temporal dimension is important given that intergroup relations are likely to change as the merger evolves, which will influence how employees will come to identify (or not) with the new, merged organization. Longitudinal merger research has revealed interesting trends over time. There is evidence that just before a merger, employees are motivated to perceive continuity between their premerger organizational identity and the anticipated identity that will define the new, merged organization.

The intergroup tensions between the groups and the us-versus-them dynamics become more marked as the merger becomes a reality. At this point, the specific differences between the premerger organizations become salient, and status differences have tangible implications for members of each premerger organization. Increasingly, longitudinal merger research is revealing that identification with the new, merged organization is likely to decrease from the premerger implementation or anticipation stage to the stage when the merger is implemented.

In fact, over time, employees' views of the anticipated new organizational identity are likely to be revised, particularly because during the implementation stage, the threatening aspects of the merger are likely to become more salient and hence an issue of concern for employees. A merger is an important change that is likely to trigger feelings of uncertainty and threat because of its unstable nature and the risks that it potentially poses to employees' work conditions and social benefits. In addition, the fact that a merger poses a potential threat to one's identity can be felt more specifically. Such feelings of threat are important to address within organizations undergoing mergers because they are likely to undermine efforts to build both a sense of identification with the new, merged organization and the view that the new, merged organization represents one united social group.

Organizational mergers require employees from the two premerger organizations not only to identify with a new social group but also to manage different organizational allegiances, namely, their identity as a member of their premerger organization and the developing identification with the new, merged organization. In investigating how employees attempt to reconcile these different social identities, researchers have found that employees from the lower- and higher-status premerger organizations differ in how they come to see these identities fitting with each other rather than being in opposition to one another. In fact, merger research has shown that these two identities are more difficult to reconcile for members of the lower-status premerger organization, whose premerger organizational identity is more likely to be erased in the context of the new, merged organization. In contrast, members of the higher-status premerger organization are more likely to see these organizational identities as compatible and as continuous, given that the new, merged organizational identity is likely to retain more of the features (e.g., name, logo) of the higher-status premerger organization.

One solution to reconciling these potentially conflicting social identities involves developing a new, merged organizational identity that is complex and inclusive of the specific premerger organizations that constitute it. Such a superordinate organizational identity accounts for the specific characteristics of each premerger organization and also recognizes the unique contributions of each organization to the new superordinate whole. Some commentators have suggested that keeping positive features from both premerger groups, rather than trying to erase all preexisting organizational characteristics or retaining only the features of the higher-status premerger organization, is key to facilitating positive intergroup relations during a merger and establishing a productive and successful new, merged organization. In fact, research has demonstrated that the more employees identify with their new, merged organization and come to recognize that the new, merged organization represents one united group, the more positive the consequences, whether these consequences are intrapersonal in nature (e.g., higher job satisfaction, well-being) or involve entire groups (e.g., lower ingroup bias).

Deborah J. Terry and Catherine E. Amiot

See also Categorization; Common Ingroup Identity Model; Cooperation and Competition; Group Boundaries; Identification and Commitment; Intergroup Contact Theory; Multiple Identities; Social Identity Theory

Further Readings

Amiot, C. E., Terry, D. J., & Callan, V. J. (2007). Status, fairness, and social identification during an intergroup merger. *British Journal of Social Psychology, 46,* 557–577.

Cartwright, S., & Cooper, C. L. (1992). *Mergers and acquisitions: The human factor.* Oxford, UK: Butterworth/Heinemann.

Haunschild, P. R., Moreland, R. L., & Murrell, A. J. (1994). Sources of resistance to mergers between groups. *Journal of Applied Social Psychology, 24,* 1150–1178.

Marks, M. L., & Mirvis, P. H. (1998). *Joining forces: Making one plus one equal three in mergers, acquisitions and alliances.* San Francisco: Jossey-Bass.

Seo, M.-G., & Hill, N. S. (2005). Understanding the human side of merger and acquisition: An integrative framework. *Journal of Applied Behavioral Science, 41,* 422–443.

Terry, D. J., Carey, C. J., & Callan, V. J. (2001). Employee adjustment to an organizational merger: An intergroup perspective. *Personality and Social Psychology Bulletin, 27,* 267–280.

MINIMAL GROUP EFFECT

Intergroup discrimination is a feature of most modern societies, and the question of why individuals seem to favor their own groups over other groups, as expressed in phenomena such as prejudice and discrimination, is one that has interested researchers in many disciplines for many years. There have been many accounts of the motivations for prejudice and discrimination, some focusing on aspects of the individual and some focusing on the role of conflict between groups over resources. It was in attempting to investigate why prejudice and discrimination occur that Henri Tajfel and Michael Billig developed the *minimal group paradigm* (MGP) and first observed the minimal group effect. The *minimal group effect* refers to the fact that individuals will express ingroup favoritism even when there is minimal ingroup affiliation, no interaction among group members, anonymity of group members, no conflicts of interest, and no previous hostility between the groups. Thus, it appears that the mere perception of belonging to two distinct groups—*social categorization*—is sufficient to trigger intergroup discrimination.

History and Background

Tajfel and his colleagues developed the MGP to establish the baseline conditions for intergroup discrimination. The idea was to strip two groups of the features identified as important in triggering group discrimination, such as interaction among group members, group history, and conflict between the groups, to create minimal social categories. Then, different features of intergroup relations would be added cumulatively to determine at which point intergroup discrimination occurs.

In the MGP, individuals are classified as members of two mutually exclusive groups, ostensibly on the basis of some rather arbitrary performance criterion (e.g., overestimators vs. underestimators of dots projected on a screen, fans of the painters Klee and Kandinsky) or by a completely random procedure such as a coin toss. Thus, the groups are truly minimal: They have no content, there is no interaction among group members, group membership is completely anonymous, and the groups have no history or future outside the laboratory.

After being informed of their group membership, participants are asked to allocate points to members of their own group (the *ingroup*) and/or members of the other group (the *outgroup*). In some studies, these points represent actual outcomes, such as money or course credit, but in other studies, the points are meaningless. At no point during the experiment can participants allocate points to themselves, which rules out self-interest as an explanation for point allocation.

In order for researchers to assess responses in the MGP, participants are asked to make their allocation decisions using a series of matrices. These matrices, known as *Tajfel matrices*, contain pairs of numbers that represent points to be allocated to a member of the ingroup and a member of the outgroup. The targets of the allocation decision are identified only by group membership and an identification code. Participants are asked to choose the pair of numbers that represents the points that they wish to allocate to the ingroup member and the outgroup member.

There are three types of Tajfel matrices, which are presented twice to participants on separate pages of a booklet, and responses on these matrices represent four basic strategies of intergroup behavior. *Parity–fairness* is a strategy that awards equal points to ingroup and outgroup recipients. *Maximum ingroup profit* is a strategy that awards the highest absolute number of points to the ingroup, regardless of the points awarded to the outgroup. *Maximum joint profit* is a strategy that maximizes the total number of points distributed to both the ingroup and the outgroup. Finally, *maximum differentiation* is a strategy that maximizes the difference in points awarded to the two recipients, with the difference favoring the ingroup but sacrificing absolute ingroup profit. Thus, the strategy of intergroup differentiation is in competition with strategies based on more "rational" principles, such as being fair or obtaining maximum benefit for all.

One might expect that participants placed in this situation, in which group membership is arbitrary and meaningless, would allocate points on a random basis or allocate the points in a fair manner. However, this was not what was found. Rather, participants tended to give more points to members of the ingroup than to members of the outgroup. Indeed, participants preferred the maximum differentiation strategy, even though it meant fewer absolute points for the ingroup compared with the maximum ingroup profit strategy. This striking finding, published in 1971, was contrary to predictions based on traditional theories of intergroup relations but has been found to be an extremely reliable effect.

The explanation of the minimal group effect was an important part of the development by Tajfel and John Turner of *social identity theory*. Drawing on the results of the minimal group studies and Tajfel's earlier work on categorization, Tajfel and Turner suggested that the process of making salient us-and-them distinctions changes the way people see themselves. When social categories are salient, individuals see themselves in terms of their social identity (rather than their personal identity) and are motivated to attain a positive social identity. Thus, the motivating principle underlying competitive intergroup behavior is seen as a desire for a positive and secure self-concept.

One way to achieve a positive social identity is through intergroup differentiation—favoring your own group relative to other groups. Social identity theory is often interpreted as stating that discrimination and ingroup favoritism are an inevitable consequence of categorization. However, although social categorization is a necessary precondition for discrimination, it is not sufficient—people must identify with the category and see it as part of their self-concept in order for discrimination to occur.

Early research on the social identity approach was dominated by studies using the MGP. One reason is that the MGP made it possible to manipulate the variables thought to be important in intergroup relations, such as status, legitimacy of status differentials, and permeability of group boundaries, and to test their independent effects on individual and collective behavior. However, this approach led to criticisms that the results of minimal group research might not be valid in broader, "real-world" contexts. Nevertheless, subsequent research that has used real-world groups and conflicts has borne out many of the insights obtained in minimal group research, demonstrating the power of social identity theory.

One point to note about the minimal group effect is that it is more reliable when participants are distributing positive outcomes, such as ostensible salary increases, to members of the ingroup and the outgroup than when they are distributing negative outcomes, such as ostensible salary cuts. This phenomenon has been called the *positive–negative asymmetry effect*. The presence of the positive–negative asymmetry effect suggests that the MGP may be better suited to the assessment of ingroup favoritism than to outgroup derogation.

Debate

The use of the MGP as a tool to study intergroup relations has been a topic of considerable debate. The MGP has obvious strengths: It eliminates the impact of external factors such as group history and prior bonds, and it reduces the cost and time associated with the use of real groups. However, the MGP is not without its critics.

One major criticism is that the minimal group effect is due simply to demand characteristics associated with the paradigm. That is, when a participant receives the information that there are two groups, one to which she or he belongs and one to which she or he does not belong, and is asked to allocate money to anonymous members of these groups, the participant may believe that intergroup differentiation is the only logical response to such a situation or is the response that is expected by the experimenter. However, studies by social identity researchers have demonstrated that demand characteristics are not solely responsible for the minimal group effect.

Another criticism of the MGP rests on the criterion used to categorize individuals into the two groups. Early studies categorized participants into groups on the basis of preferences (e.g., for the painter Klee or Kandinsky) or on the basis of performance (e.g., overestimators or underestimators). Thus, it is possible that participants perceive similarity with other group members, and this similarity underpins intergroup discrimination, as opposed to mere categorization into "us" and "them." However, other research, in which arbitrary assignment to groups is used, such as a coin toss, has found the same minimal group effect.

Jacob Rabbie and his colleagues have argued that the minimal group effect results from mutual interdependence among individuals for the achievement of particular needs. The *behavioral interaction model* suggests that although participants cannot allocate points directly to themselves, they can benefit indirectly through beliefs about reciprocity. That is, if participants allocate points to fellow ingroup members, they may believe that they will be allocated points *by* fellow ingroup members. However, research has generally found greater support for the explanations of the minimal group effect offered by social identity theory, based on identification and the need for a positive social identity, than for the explanations given by the behavioral interaction model.

In sum, several explanations other than social identity theory have been given for the minimal group effect. However, research has not supported alternative explanations based on conformity to cultural norms, the type of criterion used to categorize respondents, the unfamiliar character of the MGP, demand characteristics within the MGP, expected discrimination from outgroup members, or implied interdependence among participants.

Despite criticisms, the MGP remains an important tool for researchers interested in studying intergroup relations. Recent research has incorporated additional features designed to improve the external validity of the paradigm, such as placing the groups within a social context (e.g., branches within an organization) and by placing values on the points allocated in the matrices (e.g., salary increases and decreases). The minimal group effect is not merely an historical or experimental artifact but continues to be demonstrated and to influence current thinking on intergroup relations.

Joanne R. Smith

See also Categorization; Discrimination; Identification and Commitment; Ingroup Allocation Bias; Self-Categorization Theory; Social Identity Theory; Tajfel, Henri

Further Readings

Bourhis, R. Y., Sachdev, I., & Gagnon, A. (1994). Intergroup research with the Tajfel matrices: Methodological notes. In M. P. Zanna & J. M. Holmes (Eds.), *The psychology of prejudice: The Ontario symposium on personality and social psychology* (Vol. 7, pp. 209–232). Hillsdale, NJ: Lawrence Erlbaum.

Mummendey, A., & Otten, S. (1998). Positive-negative asymmetry in social discrimination. *European Review of Social Psychology, 9,* 107–143.

Rabbie, J. M., Schot, J. C., & Visser, L. (1989). Social identity theory: A conceptual and empirical critique from the perspective of a behavioural interaction model. *European Journal of Social Psychology, 19,* 171–202.

Tajfel, H., Billig, M. G., Bundy, R. P., & Flament, C. (1971). Social categorization and intergroup behaviour. *European Journal of Social Psychology, 1,* 149–178.

Tajfel, H., & Turner, J. C. (1979). An integrative theory of intergroup conflict. In W. G. Austin & S. Worchel (Eds.), *The social psychology of intergroup relations* (pp. 33–47). Monterey, CA: Brooks-Cole.

MINORITY COPING STRATEGIES

Social groups such as ethnic and religious groups vary in a variety of ways, including whether they represent a numerical minority or majority within a culture and whether they are valued (high status) or devalued (low status) within that culture. In this entry, the term *minority* is used to refer to a social group or social identity that is devalued or stigmatized rather than numerically underrepresented. *Minority coping* refers to strategies that members of devalued groups use to manage emotion, thought, behavior, and their environment in order to deal with stress associated with possessing a devalued social identity.

Being (or being perceived to be) a member of a devalued minority group is often stressful. Members of minority groups are targets of negative stereotypes, social exclusion, prejudice, and discrimination, all of which can lead individuals to conclude that their social identity as a group member is devalued by society. Members of minority groups also often have poorer educational and occupational outcomes, less access to adequate housing and health care, and worse physical and mental health compared with members of socially valued groups. Some scholars believe that as a result of their negative experiences, members of devalued minority groups inevitably suffer negative psychological effects, such as low self-esteem. Research does not support this view. Although there is ample evidence that membership in a devalued minority group has many negative effects, it does not uniformly or invariably lead to negative psychological outcomes. Indeed, members of some devalued minority groups (e.g., Black Americans) report higher self-esteem than do members of advantaged majority groups (e.g., White Americans).

This entry addresses theory and research about the ways that members of minority groups cope with their predicament. Perspectives on coping with social devaluation are discussed first, followed by a review of specific coping strategies. The entry concludes with a discussion of factors that influence the type of coping strategies that individuals employ and the effectiveness of coping.

Coping With Minority-Related Stressors

Individuals differ in how they respond to membership in a devalued minority group. Responses differ depending on how individuals appraise their situation—for example, how much they perceive their identity to be threatened in a given situation. Stress appraisals can lead people to experience involuntary responses such as increased anxiety, increased blood pressure, vigilance for threat-related stimuli, decreased working memory capacity, and impaired performance on intellectually demanding tasks. Stress appraisals also lead to coping. *Coping* refers to voluntary attempts to regulate emotion, thought, behavior, and the environment. Coping is distinct from its outcomes—just because people engage in efforts to cope with a stressor does not mean their efforts are successful.

People who are targets of negative stereotypes, prejudice, and discrimination engage in a wide variety of cognitive and behavioral coping strategies. Classic texts such as Erving Goffman's *Stigma: Notes on the Management of Spoiled Identity* and Gordon Allport's *The Nature of Prejudice* discuss some forms of coping used by targets of stigma and prejudice. Although scholars use different labels, several core dimensions of coping have been identified. One key distinction is between problem-focused and emotion-focused coping. Problem-focused (or active) coping efforts are geared toward changing the problematic relationship between the person and the environment that is causing stress. For example, members of devalued minority groups may attempt to eliminate the stress associated with their group membership by changing themselves (e.g., attempting to shed a devalued identity), changing aspects of the situation that is generating stress (e.g., avoiding environments where

discrimination is likely), or changing others or the social context (e.g., confronting people who discriminate). Emotion-focused coping efforts are geared toward regulating negative or stress-related emotions rather than changing the problem that is causing the stress. An example of emotion-focused coping is lessening the sting of rejection by de-emphasizing the importance of a domain from which one is excluded.

In the next section, research examining minority coping strategies is organized according to the broad distinction between problem-focused and emotion-focused coping. The distinction is often blurred, however, because a single coping strategy may serve multiple functions. In addition, people typically use multiple coping strategies rather than a single strategy.

Problem-Focused Minority Coping

Problem-focused coping strategies attempt to create an environment in which stressors (e.g., prejudice and discrimination) associated with minority group membership are reduced or absent. Some problem-focused coping efforts target the self to reduce the likelihood of experiencing the negative effects associated with membership in a devalued minority group. One example of a self-directed coping strategy is trying to *shed the identity* that is producing stress, such as by leaving the devalued minority group or attempting to shed the attribute that qualifies one for membership in a minority group. There are many examples of people attempting to cope with a devalued identity in this way. Overweight individuals, for example, spend millions of dollars each year on diet books and diet programs in order to be slim. People who regard themselves as physically unattractive spend millions of dollars on plastic surgery, and people who are addicted to drugs spend millions of dollars on therapy. This coping strategy of identity elimination, of course, is available only to individuals who have (or perceive themselves to have) control over shedding their stigma.

Another coping strategy is to attempt to *conceal* or disguise a minority identity from others in order to "pass" as a member of a more highly valued group. This strategy may enable people to protect themselves from personally experiencing discrimination and prejudice and allow them to preserve jobs or relationships with others who would reject them if their true identity were known. Concealment, however, does not protect people from observing that others like themselves are rejected. Further, coping by concealment can be psychologically costly. Concealment prevents individuals from receiving social support from other minority group members. Concealing an identity also can make people feel inauthentic and untrue to themselves. In addition, attempting to conceal an aspect of the self can lead, ironically, to increased intrusive thoughts about precisely the thing one is trying to conceal. This development in turn can lead to increased stress and poorer mental and physical health. The coping strategy of concealment is available primarily to individuals whose stigmatizing social identity is not readily visible.

A third self-directed strategy used to cope with a devalued social identity is attempting to *compensate* for a devalued identity, such as by working harder, preparing more, or persisting longer in domains in which one is negatively stereotyped so as to improve one's likelihood of obtaining desired goals. People may also compensate by behaving in ways designed to disprove negative stereotypes of their group. Although the extra effort involved in compensation can help a person achieve desired outcomes, it can also backfire. Trying extra hard to overcome negative group stereotypes can lead to increased stress, impair working memory, and, ironically, cause poorer intellectual performance.

Problem-focused coping efforts also can be targeted at others or the larger social context. For example, members of devalued minority groups may cope by seeking to change others' negative attitudes toward their group through education or confrontation. They may try to prevent others from acting on prejudice or may engage in collective action to combat discrimination and change laws. Confrontational strategies aim to communicate discontent to others, thereby reducing the likelihood that threats to identity will reoccur. Confrontation can range from simply expressing displeasure with a discriminatory comment to participating in action to produce social change. Directly confronting perpetrators of discrimination has been shown to produce feelings of guilt in the perpetrator and reduce the likelihood that he or she will subsequently discriminate. Nevertheless, confronting discrimination is a relatively uncommon coping strategy. Research has shown that minority individuals who claim they are victims of discrimination are perceived to be hypersensitive or troublemaking, even when it is very clear that they are in fact discriminated against. Thus members of minorities are afraid of being socially derogated and mistreated for complaining about discrimination.

Problem-focused coping efforts also can attempt to structure situations so as to avoid encountering minority-related stressors. For example, individuals may avoid situations in which they might be exposed to prejudice and discrimination or will be the sole member of their group. Overweight people, for example, may avoid places such as the beach or health club, which are especially likely to expose them to censure, and ethnic minority groups stereotyped as less intelligent may avoid academic settings. Members of minority groups also may selectively affiliate with members of their own group, thereby gaining a respite from prejudice. Complete segregation within one's minority group, however, may cut people off from many important life domains.

Emotion-Focused Coping

Emotion-focused forms of coping attempt to minimize negative affect associated with minority-related stressors and protect individual and collective self-esteem. Several forms of emotion-focused coping with minority-related stressors have been identified. One is altering one's identification with the minority group by either strengthening or weakening it. Identification refers to the extent to which individuals value a social group to which they belong and integrate that group into their self-concept. Perceiving discrimination against the ingroup has been shown to lead to increased group identification among individuals already highly identified with their group but to decreased group identification among those not highly identified with their minority group initially. In general, members of lower-status minority ethnic groups (such as African Americans and Latinos) report being more highly identified with their ingroup (i.e., say that their group is more important to them) than do members of higher-status majority groups (such as Whites). When under stress, minority individuals may increase identification with their group because it provides them with social support resources such as a sense of belonging, emotional support to cope with discrimination, and a positive conceptualization of the ingroup to contrast with the negative views present in the dominant culture. Hence selective affiliation with the ingroup may allow minority groups to reject negative stereotypes of their group that are present in the larger society. High identification with the ingroup often relates to positive outcomes such as greater self-esteem.

Another form of coping with devalued minority status is to selectively engage in social comparisons, that is, to compare one's own situation with that of other members of one's minority group rather than with the situation of members of dominant groups who have higher status and better outcomes. Comparing oneself to minority, rather than majority, group members can protect self-esteem and diminish negative affect in part because disparities between oneself and others are less likely to be noticed. However, socially comparing solely with minority group members can maintain the status quo by preventing minority individuals from becoming aware of inequalities in society between their own group and other groups.

Another coping strategy minority individuals may use is to attribute negative outcomes to discrimination based on minority status rather than to internal, stable features of the self, such as a lack of ability. In general, attributing negative events to external causes protects self-esteem better than does attributing negative events to internal causes. Attributing rejection to another person's prejudice is a more external attribution than attributing rejection to one's own shortcomings. Research has shown that blaming negative outcomes on prejudice instead of oneself can be an effective way of buffering self-esteem in the face of rejection if there are clear cues in the situation that prejudice was present. Attributing outcomes to prejudice in the absence of clear cues is not protective of self-esteem. Furthermore, since group membership is an aspect of the self, attributing negative outcomes to discrimination is not as protective of self-esteem as is making an attribution to a cause completely external to the self. There are also other downsides to attributing negative outcomes to discrimination. Doing so can dampen individuals' awareness of their own strengths and shortcomings and hence hinder accurate self-knowledge.

In addition, individuals who attribute negative outcomes to discrimination are often perceived negatively by others as complainers who fail to take responsibility for their own outcomes.

Members of minority groups also may cope with their situation by psychologically disengaging from domains in which they and other group members fare poorly. Psychological disengagement refers to separating one's self-esteem from a particular evaluative domain such that one's self-views are not affected by performance in that domain. For example, members of minority groups that are stereotyped to be less intelligent may disengage from academic situations by devaluing the importance of academic performance or by discounting the validity of academic performance evaluations. Through disengagement, minority individuals may preserve their self-esteem when they receive negative evaluations by deeming those evaluations insignificant. Although psychological disengagement can protect against threats to self-esteem, it may be a difficult strategy to employ when the culture highly values a domain in which one's group fares poorly. Disengagement may also reduce individuals' motivation to succeed in domains vital to success in broader society.

Moderators of Coping

How a person copes with membership in a devalued minority group is shaped by characteristics of the person, situation, group, and larger sociocultural context. Individual factors that influence how a person copes with minority-related stressors include (a) the person's goals in a particular situation (for example, whether his or her goal is to feel good about the self or to get along with others), (b) the extent to which a person is identified with the minority group, (c) the extent to which a person expects to be a target of discrimination based on his or her group membership, (d) the extent to which the person internalizes society's negative views of the group, and (e) the person's beliefs about the stability and legitimacy of group status differences and the permeability of group boundaries. Situational factors that influence how people cope include the extent to which negative stereotypes and prejudice are blatant or subtle in the situation and whether members of the ingroup or outgroups are present. For example, minorities are more likely to blame negative outcomes on discrimination when they are alone or with members of their own group than when they are with members of a dominant outgroup. Characteristics of the minority group also may influence coping. Minority groups differ in the extent to which membership is readily visible to others, perceived as under a person's control, and associated with a recognizable group identity. Concealment is not an option for individuals whose group membership is readily visible to others but is frequently used by those whose membership is not visible. Individuals who perceive they have some control over or can change their group membership are more likely to cope through self-focused efforts than are those who perceive no control over their group membership. Members of groups that are *entitative*, or have a recognizable group identity, are more likely to identify with ingroup members, attribute negative outcome to prejudice, seek out similar others for affiliation, and engage in collective efforts on behalf of their group than are those whose group has a less recognizable group identity.

Conclusion

Members of devalued minority groups engage in varied efforts to regulate their emotion, cognition, behavior, and the environment. Coping efforts are influenced by characteristics of the person, the situation, the group, and the social context. Research on coping portrays members of devalued minority groups as active, motivated agents rather than passive victims. Current research does not point to a single minority coping strategy that is most effective. Rather, certain strategies are more appropriate depending on the person's goals and the particular situation encountered. Further, coping strategies that are successful in achieving one desired outcome (e.g., decreasing negative affect) may lead to other undesired outcomes (e.g., social isolation). Because prejudice and discrimination are social problems, the most effective strategies for coping are likely to be those that are directed toward changing the sociocultural context that fosters stereotyping, prejudice, and discrimination.

Brenda Major and Dina Eliezer

See also Ageism; Collective Movements and Protest; Collective Self; Discrimination; Homophobia; Identification and Commitment; Minority Groups in Society; Prejudice; Racism; Sexism; Social Identity Theory; Stereotype Threat; Stereotyping

Further Readings

Allport, G. W. (1979). *The nature of prejudice.* Cambridge, MA: Perseus Books. (Original work published 1954)

Crocker, J., & Major, B. (1989). Social stigma and self-esteem: The self-protective properties of stigma. *Psychological Review, 96,* 608–630.

Goffman, E. (1963). *Stigma: Notes on the management of spoiled identity.* Englewood Cliffs, NJ: Prentice Hall.

Link, B. G., Mirotznik, J., & Cullin, F. T. (1991). The effectiveness of stigma coping orientations: Can negative consequences of mental illness labeling be avoided? *Journal of Health and Social Behavior, 32,* 302–320.

Major, B., & Gramzow, R. (1999). Abortion as stigma: Cognitive and emotional implications of concealment. *Journal of Personality and Social Psychology, 77,* 735–745.

Major, B., Quinton, W. J., & McCoy, S. K. (2002). Antecedents and consequences of attributions to discrimination: Theoretical and empirical advances. In M. P. Zanna (Ed.), *Advances in experimental social psychology* (Vol. 34, pp. 251–330). San Diego, CA: Academic Press.

Major, B., Spencer, S., Schmader, T., Wolfe, C., & Crocker, J. (1998). Coping with negative stereotypes about intellectual performance: The role of psychological disengagement. *Personality & Social Psychology Bulletin, 24*(1), 34–50.

Miller, C., & Kaiser, C. (2001). A theoretical perspective on coping with stigma. *Journal of Social Issues, 57,* 73–92.

Miller, C. T., & Major, B. (2000). Coping with stigma and prejudice. In T. F. Heatherton, R. E. Kleck, M. R. Hebl, & J. G. Hull (Eds.), *The social psychology of stigma* (pp. 243–272). New York: Guilford.

Miller, C. T., Rothblum, E. D., Felicio, D., & Brand, P. (1995). Compensating for stigma: Obese and nonobese women's reactions to being visible. *Personality and Social Psychology Bulletin, 21,* 1093–1106.

Tajfel, H., & Turner, J. C. (1986). The social identity theory of intergroup behavior. In S. Worchel & W. G. Austin (Eds.), *Psychology of intergroup relations* (pp. 7–24). Chicago: Nelson Hall.

MINORITY GROUPS IN SOCIETY

Minorities are social groups whose members have less control over their fate than do members of dominant segments of society, who commonly hold minorities in low regard. Thus, minorities are defined with respect to their position within a society's hierarchy in terms of (a) power or control that group members have over their lives, (b) status or prestige afforded to group membership, or (c) both.

Frequently, minority groups are smaller than other groups in the society. African Americans in the United States and the French-speaking citizens of Canada are examples of numerically small minorities. Minorities, however, may be comparable in size to the rest of the society, as is the case with women in most societies. Or they can be more numerous than the rest of the society, as, for example, were Blacks in South Africa or Shiites in Iraq during Saddam Hussein's regime. Size in itself does not make a group a minority. Rather, it is the group's social position. Some groups with relatively few members may hold power or be high in status. Numerically small groups that exert disproportional power over the rest of the society (e.g., top military, political, or business leaders) or that enjoy high status (e.g., aristocracy in some European countries) constitute a separate social category that can be termed *elites*.

Salient characteristics shared by members of a minority group can be social, psychological, or physical. Thus, we may talk about racial, ethnic, gender, and religious minorities, as illustrated by the aforementioned examples. In addition, minority position may stem from political orientation (e.g., Libertarians), sexual orientation (e.g., gays), mental health (e.g., people with schizophrenia), physical health (e.g., AIDS patients), or physical disability (e.g., deaf people). For a minority to become a distinguishable social entity, most of its members must become aware of characteristics that distinguish them from the rest of the society and perceive that they are treated in the same, typically negative, manner by the dominant members of the society.

Disparity in power that distinguishes minorities from majorities leads to disparities in the distribution of positive and negative societal outcomes.

Minority groups get a smaller share of benefits but a larger share of social and economic burdens. For example, members of minority groups have less access to education, health care, and well-paid jobs than do members of the dominant segments of a society. At the same time, they are more likely to be unemployed, in poorer health, and incarcerated. It is not uncommon for a minority group to be kept apart (e.g., Jewish ghettos) or even directly persecuted (e.g., the Holocaust).

Minorities as Targets: The Dominant Group's Reactions

In addition to these tangible disparities, there are important intangible burdens of being in a minority. These have been documented in social-psychological research on dominant groups' reactions toward minorities. Members of dominant groups tend to perceive minorities in a uniform, stereotypical way. Although characteristics believed to be associated with membership in a minority group need not always be negative, they tend overall to portray minorities as inferior. Minorities tend to be stigmatized, and membership in a minority group becomes a discrediting attribute. Minorities are suspected of being "less worthy until proven otherwise."

Negative views of minorities tend to be perpetuated through the process called *stereotype confirmation*. Members of the dominant group who enter interactions with minority members frequently hold negative expectations about the outcomes of such interactions. In a form of self-fulfilling prophecy, prejudiced individuals' expectations lead them to behave in a way that causes minority members to confirm their expectations. This is especially likely in social contexts that emphasize power and status differences (e.g., police interrogations, job interviews). For example, stereotypical expectations about minority members' violence may cause a police officer to treat a minority member aggressively. In response, the member may become violent, thus confirming the stereotype and feeding the vicious cycle of minority derogation.

Stereotype threat is another mechanism that may perpetuate negative stereotypes. Being aware that their negative behaviors, including their failures, are explained in terms of their group membership, minorities may develop the fear that their performance on achievement tasks will confirm the stereotype. For example, being aware that they are stereotyped as inferior in mathematics, women taking a math test may become concerned that they may confirm the stereotype. Preoccupied with this concern, minority members end up underperforming and, therefore, confirming the stereotype.

Negative stereotypes and prejudice against minorities serve several purposes. Discrediting, for example, immigrants or gays makes those who devalue minorities feel superior. In addition to this symbolic benefit, those who devalue minorities may reap tangible benefits from doing so. Because of their group's historically privileged position, members of the dominant group often have a sense of entitlement to scarce resources in a society (e.g., jobs, education). When they perceive minorities as a competitive threat to what they believe "belongs" to them, members of the dominant group derogate minorities, especially if dominant-group members value hierarchical relations among groups in a society (*high social dominance orientation*). Their reactions justify their privileged positions and a view of existing power and status arrangements as fair. Interestingly, this system justification tendency need not be unique to members of the dominant group. Paradoxically, it sometimes may be observed among minority members who, in an apparent defiance of self-interest, may defend the status quo in the power hierarchy.

Tokenism is another mechanism that perpetuates the status quo. Members of the dominant group may admit very few, very qualified minority members (*tokens*) to positions that dominant-group members usually occupy, while denying access to all other members of the minority. Because they tend to perceive tokenism as a legitimate meritocracy, the dominant group members can use it to justify existing inequality. Although they are less likely to perceive tokenism as legitimate, minority members, including successful tokens, are less likely to challenge existing inequality through a collective action when positions of power are open to tokens than when they are completely closed to minorities.

Minorities as Agents: Identity Protection Strategies

In spite of many disadvantages associated with their position, minority members can and do have a positive view of themselves and their group. However, being targets of largely negative reactions, minorities need to protect their sense of worth. Strategies they use to protect their sense of personal worth (self-esteem) and value of group membership (social identity) range from disengagement from the dominant segments of a society to reinterpretation and restructuring of their mutual interactions.

In a form of *disengagement*, minorities learn to discount as irrelevant the negative feedback they repeatedly receive. For example, minority students failing in schools learn to attribute their failing to prejudice. Attribution of the failure to external factors rather than dispositions protects minority members' sense of self-worth, at least temporarily. However, its long-term effect may be detrimental in that it may undermine students' motivation and a sense of self-efficacy, ultimately resulting in helplessness.

Minority members who discount stereotypically negative feedback as irrelevant still need a point of reference to evaluate themselves. They find it in their own group. In addition to protecting their sense of self-worth, this ingroup comparison strengthens minority members' identification with the group. In turn, increased identification may further increase investments in the group and discounting of the dominant group, thus creating a self-sustaining cycle of reactions.

Withdrawing from the dominant culture is not the only way minorities can protect themselves against derogation. A strategy that allows them to remain engaged but protected is to be selective about dimensions of social comparison. For example, members of the Latino minority in the United States may emphasize their group's family orientation, a dimension valued by the dominant group, too. This strategic choice of a comparison dimension allows them to compare favorably with the dominant group and to be different on their own terms and not the terms imposed by the dominant group.

When the context narrows the choice of comparison dimensions to those on which a minority group is negatively stereotyped, minority members may protect themselves through downward comparison to another (typically minority) group that fares even worse on the salient dimension. For example, members of an older wave of immigrants may compare their achievements with those of "new arrivals." Although useful in protecting the older immigrant group's social identity, this strategy may be an obstacle to forging coalitions among minority groups that the older group needs in order to improve its position in society.

In a direct defiance of the stereotype imposed by the dominant group, members of a minority group may *reevaluate* the stereotyped dimension, replacing the imposed negative interpretation with a new, favorable interpretation. An illustration of this strategy is the "Black is beautiful" motto espoused by African Americans. By celebrating their distinct characteristics, they turn what used to be marks of stigma into badges of honor.

Reevaluation of the stereotyped dimension, more than any other identity-protective strategy, may be a double-edged sword in intergroup relations. It may be a first step in changing the dominant group's view of the minority and improving intergroup relations, but it also may exacerbate intergroup conflict. Improvement is more likely when the reevaluated characteristic contributes to realization of common goals shared by both minority and dominant groups.

When they feel threatened, members of minority groups may attempt to conceal their identity. For example, hiding their identity may well be the best survival strategy for gays in a homophobic environment or for Christians in present-day Iraq, as it was for Jews in Europe during the Nazi era. Although protective, this strategy is highly taxing because it requires that minority members hide who they are while trying to act what they pretend to be. Thus, there may be time limits to how long this strategy can be successfully employed.

Rules of Engagement: Minority Group and Dominant Group Perspectives

Although negative stereotypes about minorities are pervasive, they are not harbored by all members of the dominant group. However, even if their reactions are positive at the explicit, conscious level, dominant group members may have negative reactions at the implicit, unconscious level. When this is true, dominant members' interactions with minorities will be anxiety provoking. Every encounter with minority members puts to the test the dominant members' unbiased, nonprejudiced self-image. Tensions arising from such concerns tend to make their reactions toward minority members extreme (overly negative or overly positive) and highly variable.

Minority members, on the other hand, learn to anticipate negative reactions from the dominant group. As a result, they tend to be vigilant for signs of prejudice. Their "on guard" interaction style is a form of preemptive strike against possible prejudice and discrimination. Dominant group members' anxiety and minority group members' sensitivity make their interactions challenging, even when both sides enter them with the best of intentions.

One challenge that dominant and minority groups face in a pluralistic society is coming to an agreement about the value of their respective identities, customs, and cultures. The two most frequently advocated solutions are minority assimilation and multicultural integration. Assimilation occurs when minority members abandon their group values to adopt those of the dominant group. In contrast, integration occurs when minority members retain their group values and incorporate them into the larger society. The pros and cons of these two forms of intergroup relations are hotly debated in pluralistic societies, especially those with a large influx of immigrants. For example, members of the dominant groups in the United States and the European Union advocate assimilationist policies that require minorities to adopt a common identity as defined by the dominant group. In contrast, minorities prefer policies that allow them to integrate into the larger society by adopting a common identity that incorporates rather than negates their culture of origin.

These differential preferences have important implications for interventions aimed at improving intergroup relations. Most likely to succeed are those interventions that encourage members of the minority and dominant groups to work together toward common goals whose realization requires the distinct strengths of each group. This approach creates positive interdependence between groups such that each group benefits from the other group's distinct qualities. Groups with complementary strengths and common goals are likely to develop mutual appreciation and therefore improve their relationships.

Social Change Strategies:
Minority Influence and Social Movements

Active minorities strive not only to protect themselves but also to reverse their position in society, from powerless and stigmatized to powerful and valued. As many historic examples illustrate, successful minorities try to engineer social change by altering existing power and status arrangements in a society. For example, the civil rights movement and the women's movement in the United States changed significantly the positions of African Americans and women in U.S. society. This is not to say that every minority-instigated change improves the human condition. Minority advocacy may fall anywhere along the ideological spectrum. Regardless of their agenda, however, all minorities advocating social change succeed when they sway dominant views so that many of their central tenets become commonplace, mainstream positions.

Given the disregard associated with being in a minority, active minorities advocating change must first address their targets' fear of being associated with a minority. This may be achieved by casting themselves as, for example, innovators or advocates of positions reflective of the zeitgeist. Emphasizing a common higher-order identity or values that they share with the targets increases the likelihood that the minority message is heard rather than immediately dismissed as deviant. For example, in their plea for acceptance, gays in Ireland emphasized "traditional Irish tolerance," evoking ethnicity and a core value they shared with their targets.

Minorities also must offer strong, cogent arguments for their position. Consistently repeating these arguments attracts their targets' attention. By persisting in their advocacy, especially in the face of possible punitive reactions, minorities demonstrate that they are certain of their position and committed to social change. This strategy may force their targets to think about the merits of the minority's request for change. If targets cognitively elaborate the minority's request and if the request is supported by strong arguments, targets may start questioning their view of the minority. Although they are not likely to accept immediately the minority's core requests, the targets' relatively open-minded consideration of the minority advocacy is likely to change the targets' position on related issues. Over time, these changes on related issues may accumulate to put pressure on the targets to accept minority's core requests. The targets' eventual conversion represents a genuine, privately accepted change in its position.

Minorities are likely to adopt a collective strategy of social change to the extent that their members perceive that the only way to improve their condition is by acting together as a group. This typically happens when individual paths to social mobility are blocked. Once a large number of minority members joins forces to improve collectively their position in a society, they become a social movement. Social-psychological research shows that in addition to complex political, sociological, and organizational factors, identity factors play an important role in social movements. It is not identification with the minority group per se that turns minority members into activists. Rather, it is identification with a minority movement that underlies minority members' activism. Thus, a first challenge in minority groups' quest for change is to articulate their plight as a movement.

Successful minorities improve their position within a society, and in doing so, they change the society as a whole. If social change is framed in zero-sum terms such that minority gains are also the dominant group's losses, it likely will destabilize society. If, however, social change is framed in non–zero-sum terms of increased mutual acceptance and benefits, the overall increased integration may strengthen society.

Conclusion

Minorities are social groups low in power and status that receive a smaller share of social goods but a larger share of social burdens than the dominant group. Negative stereotypes and prejudice against minorities serve to boost the dominant group members' sense of superiority and justify inequality between groups. To protect their sense of personal worth and value of their group membership, minorities use strategies that range from disengagement from the dominant segments of a society to reinterpretation and restructuring of their mutual interactions. These interactions are most likely to be mutually satisfactory in the context of collaborative efforts toward shared goals whose realization requires that minority and dominant groups pull together their distinct but complementary strengths. Although minorities may exert social influence under a highly constrained set of conditions, they nonetheless may sway dominant views to effect social change. Their chances for success increase when they adopt a collective strategy of social change through a social movement. Clearly, in spite of or perhaps because of their position of low power and victimization in a society, minority groups can often serve as agents of social change.

Radmila Prislin

See also Assimilation and Acculturation; Collective Movements and Protest; Minority Coping Strategies; Minority Influence; Multiculturalism; Self-Fulfilling Prophecy; Social Comparison Theory; Social Dominance Theory; Social Identity Theory; Stereotype Threat; Stigma; Tokenism

Further Readings

De Dreu, C. K. W., & De Vries, N. K. (2001). *Group consensus and minority influence: Implications for innovation.* Oxford, UK: Blackwell.

Dovidio, J. F., Gaertner, S. L., & Saguy, T. (2007). Another view of "we": Majority and minority group perspectives on a common ingroup identity. *European Review of Social Psychology, 18,* 296–330.

Prislin, R., & Christensen, P. N. (2005). Social change in the aftermath of successful minority influence. *European Review of Social Psychology, 16,* 43–73.

Simon, B., & Klandermans, B. (2001). Politicized collective identity: A social psychological analysis. *American Psychologist, 56,* 319–331.

Steele, C. M., Spencer, S. J., & Aronson, J. (2002). Contending with group image: The psychology of stereotype and social identity threat. In M. Zanna (Ed.), *Advances in experimental social psychology* (Vol. 34, pp. 379–440). San Diego, CA: Academic Press.

Tajfel, H. (1981). *Human groups and social categories: Studies in social psychology* (especially The social psychology of minorities, pp. 309–343). Cambridge, UK: Cambridge University Press.

MINORITY INFLUENCE

Minority influence is the impact that minority groups have on majorities, an area relatively unexplored by social scientists until the 1970s. Most prior research addressed the obvious impact that majorities have on the minority. Then French psychologist Serge Moscovici challenged this orthodox approach by reminding psychologists of the enormous power that minority groups sometimes wield. Think of the women's movement, the struggle for racial equality waged by African Americans, Freud's psychoanalytic circle of adherents, Galileo's scientific advances, even the early Christian Church, and the (positive and negative) reactions they stimulated. All these groups or individuals began as feeble minorities, as voices in the wilderness, but over time emerged as powerful forces.

Moscovici maintained that the source of creativity, innovation, and social progress is the minority. He argued that if we are to understand how society changes, how innovations are adopted, then we had better understand the ways minorities wield their influence. This entry provides a historical context, defines some important terms, and then explores the growing body of research on minorities and their impact.

Background

For many years in psychology, social influence research was much like a broad one-way street. Researchers focused on the impact of the powerful on the powerless, the strong on the weak, the expert on the uninformed, the majority on the minority. It was obvious that the powerful majority could exert tremendous pressure on the minority to do its bidding. This orientation assumed that most people wanted to belong to the majority group, an assumption borne out in considerable research. Threats of ostracism or expulsion from one's social group are taken very seriously. They are a major source of the majority's persuasive strength.

The stress on majority influence in social psychology was long-standing. It was encouraged by Solomon Asch's famous line of judgment studies and carried forward by Carl Hovland's persuasion experiments of the 1950s. Most influence studies focused on factors that affected the success (or failure) of the majority to induce the minority to do its bidding—or at least to agree publicly with the majority's position.

Definition of Minority Group

Minorities have been defined in a number of ways, along a number of dimensions, the most important of which are number, power, and normativeness. The simplest and most widely used dimension in research on minorities is number. The group with the most members is the majority, and those with fewer members constitute minority groups.

Power matters as well. The majority typically has considerably more clout than the minority. It has the muscle to reward or punish, to include or ostracize, and it uses this power to get its way and to maintain its superior position. Sometimes power and number are not synonymous. Before the end of White rule in South Africa, for example, the Black population was considered to be the minority, even though Blacks vastly outnumbered the White ruling class. The White power structure, however, wielded sufficient control to maintain its superior position. In this case, number did not define the minority, whereas a lack of power certainly did.

Finally, there is the normative dimension. Typically, the majority defines what is right or wrong, proper or improper. It is unusual for leaders of a victorious army to prosecute their soldiers for war crimes. Usually, it is the soldiers of the losing side who are defined as criminals—as those who violated the norms of good conduct, as defined by the winners (the majority). As such, the majority often views the minority as holding improper or illegitimate positions relative to the majority's definition of what is good and proper.

Putting all this together, we can define the typical minority group as one that is less numerous, wields less power, and holds counternormative beliefs relative to a larger, more powerful, and norm-defining comparison group, the majority. Sometimes, a group can be in the minority even if it does not satisfy all these criteria. For example, in many counties of the pre-Civil War South, Blacks far outnumbered Whites. Yet given their lack of power, Blacks clearly were the minority group, despite their numeric superiority. Further, their behavior often was branded as quaint, improper, or demonic (depending on the orientation of the perceiver) because it was contrary to standards defined by the majority as proper, appropriate, or godly.

Research Studies

The early research on minority influence was concerned with determining whether the minority actually could affect the perceptions or attitudes of the majority. Because this had not been established, it was a necessary first step to jump-start this area of investigation. In an early representative study, Moscovici and his colleagues had groups of six judges view a series of 36 colored slides and report their perceptions of the color of each slide immediately after it was presented. The slides were uniformly blue, but two of the six judges (a minority) reported them as being green on each of the trials. Of course, these two judges were confederates of the experimenter. Over the course of the judgments, this two-person minority affected the estimates of the other participants. The effect was not great—about 9% of the time, the naive participants agreed with the confederates—but it did show that the minority could influence the majority, even when the correct judgment was clearly obvious.

The two-person minority could not impose its will on the four-person majority, so how did it have any influence? Perhaps the consistent minority was viewed as confident, certain, or brave, and thus worthy of respect. A second study bolstered this possibility. It showed that when the minority respondents were not absolutely consistent—that is, when they responded "green" on only 24 of the 36 judgment trials, their impact on majority respondents' judgments evaporated. They had no effect at all.

From this research, social psychologists deduced two important facts: First, the minority *can* affect the majority, even when the majority's view is clearly correct; second, unless the minority is unanimous and unequivocal, it is unlikely to have much of an effect. These results are difficult to understand from a rational perspective, but a number of useful theories have been devoted to capturing this understanding.

Moscovici's theoretical explanation for minority influence effects was based on majority group members' curiosity. When members of their own group advocate a position at odds with the majority's view, the members of the majority respond, "Why do they think that?" They focus on the minority's position and try to make sense of it. In so doing, some might be persuaded by the minority. There is a problem, however, with agreeing with the minority, because it forces the person who has been persuaded to move from the safe, majority camp to that of the minority, an uncomfortable spot sometimes. As such, immediate agreement with the minority is most often resisted. However, as time goes by, the minority's arguments sometimes are accepted. Somehow, the threat of being associated with the minority dissipates, and minority influence becomes evident, even though it is delayed.

An interesting alternative to this explanation was proposed by Charlan Nemeth, whose theory on the workings of the minority still claims adherents today. She argued that being exposed to a minority viewpoint caused the majority group member to think divergently—to consider a wide range of possible solutions to the problem that was posed by minority dissent. On the other hand, being exposed to the majority viewpoint caused the deviant member to think convergently—to focus on the specific solution or perception suggested by the majority and to ignore other possibilities. Viewed in this way, minority dissent may be seen as stimulating creative thinking and problem solving, whereas the majority fosters conservative, rote, well-learned responses.

The implications of Nemeth's ideas are interesting and anticipate the results found in the minority influence literature. First, her theory, like Moscovici's, suggests that minority influence, if it occurs, should come about after some amount of cognitive work. That is, it will not happen immediately but will be delayed. In addition, if the minority's unexpected position causes divergent thinking in majority group members, then it seems likely that it might have an effect on beliefs that are associated with, but not identical to, the topic under consideration.

So if a liberal Episcopal priest argues for a liberalization of abortion policy to a group of conservative Roman Catholic bishops, it is not likely that they would adopt his or her position. However, Nemeth's research suggests that the bishops might become slightly more liberal on the issue of contraception, a practice that is related to abortion, in that both have to do with reproduction. This example seems far-fetched. Conservative bishops would probably never be swayed by the dissident

position of a liberal Episcopal priest, especially on issues of abortion and contraception.

What really would happen? At best, they would simply disregard the priest's position and view it as unworthy of their consideration. Who is this person to tell us what to believe? This response is common when the majority reacts to an outgroup minority's deviant views. To put it another way, the majority members would not see a dissident priest as part of their group—this person is an outsider, and what he or she has to say about these issues is not only false but irrelevant.

Factors That Affect Response to Minority Groups

This likely response introduces another important feature of minority influence research that was neglected in early studies, namely, the membership group of the minority dissident. In many circumstances, the minority may not belong to the group it is trying to influence. This is important because we use our membership groups to help us identify who we are. As such, we are more sensitive to disagreements with members of our own group (the ingroup) than to disagreements with members of other groups (outgroups).

We can safely ignore the rants of outgroup members unless they are threatening the ingroup, in which case they have to be engaged and discredited. However, disagreement with members of the ingroup is unexpected and uncomfortable—they are, after all, just like us. In those circumstances, we carefully consider what they have to say. When the disagreement does not threaten the very existence of the group in which we share a common membership, and from which we derive our social identity, we will consider the ingroup dissidents' position.

Response to the dissident position depends on a number of factors. One of the most important of these is the strength of their message. Obviously, if the position is weak and unconvincing, it is not going to be influential. Out of politeness, the majority might acknowledge the importance of the ingroup minority's position, and certainly its right to raise the issue, but in the end, the majority will not concede to the minority.

Much the same outcome is apparent when the minority's message is strong and cogent. The change the minority seeks through its persuasive presentation rarely occurs—at least not immediately. However, as time passes, some researchers have found that the initial rejection of the minority's position later gives way to acceptance. How this happens can tell us much about the ways minority influence works and has been the focus of considerable debate.

When confronted with a dissident ingroup communication, the majority will process the information carefully and with little defensiveness. This course allows the minority the chance to vent and to attempt to alleviate a perceived injustice. However, the majority is unlikely to accept the minority's position, for to do so might destabilize the group, resulting in a shift in the power structure in the group and generally threaten the status quo.

So a convention is set up that allows the relatively free exchange of ideas between ingroup minorities and the majority, but with the implicit understanding that no change will occur. This would seem a recipe for consistent minority failure, but there is more to it than this. Considerable research has shown that as a result of their open-minded processing of the ingroup minority's information, majority attitudes and beliefs that are related to (but not identical with) the focus of the minority's position might be affected.

For example, if the minority were arguing for the elimination of capital punishment, a practice of which the majority approves, the minority's position might have no immediate effect on majority group members' attitudes. However, if the ingroup minority's message is strong and persuasive, it is probable that the majority will move to a more lenient position on attitudes that are related to capital punishment, such as beliefs regarding punishment on noncapital offenses. Indirect attitude change of this nature is a common feature of much research on minority influence. It is an extremely intriguing feature of minority influence because the change on related attitudes can occur even if those particular attitudes are never even mentioned in the minority's persuasive appeal.

This is not to suggest that the minority can never persuade the majority on the issue that is the focus of the minority's complaint. Rather, the influence is not immediate. It is conceivable that the minority will prevail on the focal issue; however, it will not prevail immediately. Many studies in the minority influence literature reveal a clear minority influence

effect after a delay of some time. It also should be said that there are plenty of studies in this literature that *do not* show this delayed effect.

What accounts for this irregular pattern of results? Why should the minority sometimes cause delayed focal change and sometimes fail to do so? There are many possible explanations for this apparent irregularity, but the one that seems most probable is derived from the *leniency contract*. This explanation begins with some easily accepted propositions. First, attitudes are not held in isolation but rather are linked in people's minds. People's beliefs regarding global warming, for example, probably are linked to their attitudes regarding conservation. This set of linkages may be viewed structurally, with some attitudes more closely linked than others. Changing one element of the attitude structure may unbalance the structure. People do not like imbalance, and so this unpleasant state will be redressed somehow.

If an element of the structure (an attitude or a belief) is changed, but not too drastically, the inertia of the overall belief system might be sufficient to undo the change as time goes on. Thus, the changed belief will revert to its original position. However, if the change is drastic, this simple reversion is not likely. In that case, the change will pressure the entire structure to adjust to the newly revised belief, and the attitudes that are most likely to change to accommodate this new belief are the ones that were the focus of the original persuasive communication.

In terms of minority influence effects, this explanation, which was proposed and supported in research by William Crano and Xin Chen, illustrates how the process works. First, the ingroup minority proposes a position that is contrary to the general opinion of the majority. The minority's message, however, is strong and compelling and thus is difficult to ignore or brush off. In reaction, the majority refuses to budge on the focal issue; however, it does modify its position on beliefs related to the focal issue. A few weeks later, those who have shown the greatest change on the related attitudes have readjusted their attitudes on the focal issue as well. The attitude change the minority was seeking takes time, but it does occur. However, a different pattern is evident among those in the majority who showed rather little indirect change. For these individuals, the small changes in indirect attitudes apparently were not sufficient to unbalance the overall system of beliefs. Thus, when these participants return later, their focal attitude remains unchanged, and the indirect attitude change that was observed has returned to the original position. The work of the minority was undone by the inertia of the overall belief structure.

How Minority Groups Bring About Change

So how does the minority bring the majority to its way of thinking? First, it establishes its identity with the group it is attempting to influence. The minority must convince the majority that they are one and the same, that they all share the same identity. This is more difficult in some instances than in others, but failure to establish this connection seriously reduces the likelihood that the minority will prevail. Then, the minority must present its case as persuasively as possible. A strong and compelling message is essential.

Further, the minority must never deviate from its position. Compromise or a break in the unanimity of the minority is a recipe for failure. Having presented its case, the minority should not expect immediate results but rather attend to changes on issues related to the thrust of its message and endeavor to enhance these changes as well. Doing so will facilitate a delayed change on the central issue.

Obviously, this is not a quick or easy process, but it is essential if the minority hopes to influence the majority to adopt its position. On some issues, the first step is the hardest—how can a disadvantaged minority "prove" that its members are part and parcel of the majority? Often, they adopt a higher-order identification. In the civil rights movement in the United States, the minority gained traction when it shifted the terms of identity. Sure, members argued, we are of different races, but we share the common bond of being Americans. This took some time to sell, but when enough of the majority accepted this simple fact, progress toward racial equality was facilitated. Minority influence is not immediate, and the process is not easy, but it can be done and may indeed be, as Moscovici suggested, a major source of creativity, social progress, and innovation.

William D. Crano

See also Anticonformity; Asch, Solomon; Conformity; Leniency Contract; Minority Coping Strategies; Moscovici, Serge; Opinion Deviance; Social Deviance

Further Readings

Crano, W. D., & Chen, X. (1998). The leniency contract and persistence of majority and minority influence. *Journal of Personality and Social Psychology, 74,* 1437–1450.

Crano, W. D., & Hannula-Bral, K. (1994). Context/comparison model of social influence: Majority and minority influence in the formation of a novel response norm. *Journal of Experimental Social Psychology, 30,* 247–276.

Hovland, C. I., Janis, I. L., & Kelley, H. H. (1953). *Communication and persuasion.* New Haven, CT: Yale University Press.

Martin, R., Hewstone, M., Martin, P. Y., & Gardikiotis, A. (2008). Persuasion from majority and minority groups. In W. D. Crano & R. Prislin (Eds.), *Attitude and attitude change* (pp. 361–384). New York: Psychology Press.

Moscovici, S. (1976). *Social change and social influence.* London: Academic Press.

Nemeth, C. J. (1985). Differential contributions of majority and minority influence. *Psychological Review, 93,* 23–32.

MODERN FORMS OF PREJUDICE

Significant improvements in intergroup relations during the past century have been spurred by heightened awareness of the problem of prejudice and its inherent injustice, legal prohibitions against discrimination, changing norms, and individuals' adoption of less prejudiced personal attitudes. Nonetheless, an undercurrent of internalized bias remains for many people. Individuals who may not outwardly express traditional forms of prejudice may harbor internal prejudices. Theories of modern prejudice seek to provide a psychological account of this incongruity. This entry reviews the historical context of prejudice, discusses a number of forms of modern prejudice, and looks at tools for detecting these less overt attitudes.

History and Background

Many societies proudly profess that they are founded on principles of democracy and fairness, although prejudice is often a deeply ingrained part of their history and practices. For example, Gunnar Myrdal wrote of the "ever-raging conflict" in U.S society in his 1944 book, *An American Dilemma*. On one hand are general principles of fairness, Christian precepts, and equality; on the other hand are the realities of individual and group motivations, needs, and habits that foster prejudice.

Historically, individuals' prejudices have been encouraged and legitimized with the support not only of norms and customs but of laws. Such widespread sanctioning of inequality helped to keep any conflict people might experience over their prejudices at bay. Prejudice was expressed in unabashed and uncensored ways during these times, yielding consequences ranging from open verbal disparagement and segregation to lynching and genocide. Such overt prejudice is often referred to as "old-fashioned" prejudice.

After World War II and the Nazis' attempt to exterminate the Jewish people, many started to see prejudice in a different light and to entertain the idea that it might be wrong and illegitimate. In 1954, Gordon Allport published his eminent book, *The Nature of Prejudice*. Allport treated prejudice as a social problem and, among many other contributions, described the concept of "prejudice with compunction." Specifically, Allport contended that most people experience compunction or remorse in connection with their prejudices because they realize at an intellectual level that prejudice is wrong.

In U.S. society, important movements soon followed Allport's publication that further reinforced the idea that individual and institutionalized prejudice was unethical and immoral. The U.S. civil rights movement (1955–1968) especially encouraged greater egalitarianism and reductions in prejudice. The "American dilemma" about which Myrdal had written became a salient reality for many people as the conflict between their self-image as decent and fair people and their continuing prejudice toward certain groups became more apparent.

With changing laws (e.g., desegregation) and social norms, people's outwardly expressed attitudes eventually became less prejudiced. For example, surveys showed that 68% of White people supported racially segregated schools in 1942, compared with 4% in 1995. In fact, this decline was so marked that the researchers claimed that racial stereotypes in the United States were fading. Researchers also noted declines in negative beliefs related to women and, to some extent, in prejudice toward gay men and lesbians.

Despite the evidence suggesting prejudice is becoming a thing of the past, the story is not quite that straightforward. Researchers found that negative stereotypes were not fading but rather changing in content and that prejudice was decreasing in outward expressions only. More subtle measures uncovered biased behavior in many forms. For example, an influential review article published in 1980 summarized many studies of subtle bias conducted around that time. These experiments showed that White people in the United States treated Black people in the United States more negatively than they treated Whites in helping situations (i.e., were less likely to give help to Blacks than to Whites), in interpersonal aggression studies, and in their nonverbal communication.

This phenomenon is certainly not confined to the United States. Similar findings are widely reported between nationals and immigrant groups in many European countries and, more recently, between nationals and immigrant groups in Canada. Researchers began to wonder whether people were complying with egalitarian and nonprejudiced ideology when they were obviously under surveillance but had not truly internalized the motivation to respond without prejudice and whether they had actually reduced their prejudiced feelings and beliefs. Researchers suggested that prejudice remained solidly entrenched beneath a veneer of professed egalitarianism.

Against this backdrop, researchers proposed a variety of theories, starting in the mid-1980s, that sought to describe and explain these modern forms of prejudice. The predominant theories of modern forms of prejudice are modern/symbolic racism, aversive racism, racial ambivalence, and prejudice with compunction.

Conceptualizations of Modern Prejudice

An element of intrapersonal conflict is inherent in the various conceptualizations of modern prejudice.

That is, modern forms of prejudice are distinct from old-fashioned, blatant prejudice in that people experience a conflict between forces that encourage them to appear to others and perhaps even to themselves as if they are nonprejudiced and forces that encourage negative outgroup evaluations and behavior. This conflict may be consciously recognized, or people may be unaware of their conflicting tendencies and resulting coping responses. This is in contrast to old-fashioned prejudice, in which people are at liberty to openly express their inwardly felt biases.

What is common to each conceptualization of modern prejudice is that certain factors discourage an individual from holding and expressing prejudices while, simultaneously, other factors act to sustain prejudice. Although the various forms of modern prejudice are conceptually and empirically distinct, the same people may vacillate at different times in their lives or across situations in the form of modern prejudice that they exhibit.

Modern/Symbolic Prejudice

The *theory of symbolic racism* (which is very similar to another theory, called the *modern racism theory*) describes a form of prejudice thought to apply mostly to the prejudice of right-wing White conservatives in the United States toward Black people. According to this form of prejudice, people adhere to abstract principles of justice and so do not want to be seen as prejudiced, which leads them to avoid expressions of outright bigotry. At the same time, symbolic racists experience anti-Black feelings that they acquired in preadult life through socialization. These feelings are not necessarily consciously recognized and are experienced as racial anxiety and antagonism. In addition, symbolic racists adhere strongly to traditional conservative values, including individualism (the idea that hard work brings success), and believe that Blacks violate such values.

The theory of symbolic racism maintains that negative feelings toward Blacks are justified and rationalized in a political belief system with the tenets that (a) discrimination toward Blacks is largely a thing of the past, (b) Blacks' lack of progress stems from their unwillingness to work hard enough, (c) Blacks are making too many demands and want results too fast, and (d) what Blacks get outweighs what they deserve.

Aversive Racism

The *theory of aversive racism* describes a form of prejudice toward Blacks that many White people in the United States with liberal ideologies and strong egalitarian values are thought to hold. Given their strong desire to treat all people as equals, aversive racists desire to maintain a nonprejudiced image in the eyes of others and also in how they see themselves. Aversive racists therefore do not consciously act in obviously unfavorable or discriminatory ways toward Blacks. However, aversive racists have unacknowledged prejudiced tendencies related to negative feelings toward Blacks in the form of discomfort, uneasiness, disgust, and sometimes fear.

Three primary factors play a role in fostering and sustaining aversive racists' prejudiced tendencies. The first is the human need to simplify the complex social world by categorizing and stereotyping people. Second, motivational factors such as the need for self-esteem and superior status encourage racial bias. Third, sociocultural factors such as learning negative societal stereotypes at an early age and unfavorable media depictions of Blacks foster aversive racists' negative feelings toward Blacks.

The theory of aversive racism maintains that people engage in nondiscriminatory behavior and do not show their negative racial bias when social norms clearly dictate what would be appropriate behavior and when it is not possible to rationalize prejudicial biases. However, aversive racists will treat Blacks unfavorably when the normative structure is not salient or is ambiguous or when a negative response can be rationalized as unrelated to race.

Consider an example. A well-known finding in social psychology called the *bystander effect* indicates that people are much less likely to help someone (e.g., someone who has dropped a large stack of papers) if other bystanders are present who might also offer their aid. Applying this effect to aversive racism theory, researchers demonstrated that Whites showed the traditional bystander effect when the person who needed help was also White. More important, when the person who needed help was Black, White participants not only helped less when bystanders were present than when bystanders were absent, but Whites were less than half as likely to help a Black person than a White person when bystanders were present.

Presumably, norms clearly dictated helping regardless of victim race when there were no bystanders present, so equal help was given to Blacks and Whites. With other bystanders, the excuse "I thought someone else would help" becomes possible. This nonracial rationalization results not only in less help for Whites and Blacks alike (i.e., the bystander effect) but in especially low rates of helping for Blacks. Aversive racists differ from modern/symbolic racists inasmuch as they do not deny the existence of prejudice and discrimination but seek to attribute their discriminatory actions to factors other than prejudice.

Ambivalent Racism Theory

The theory of racial ambivalence maintains that many White people in the United States are socialized to hold two conflicting value orientations that have conflicting implications for their attitudes toward and responses in relation to Black people. One value orientation is humanitarianism–egalitarianism, which has the ideal of social justice and concern for others' well-being at its core. This value orientation encourages sympathetic reactions and attitudes among Whites toward Blacks, given their plight as a disadvantaged and mistreated minority group. The other value orientation is individualism, which involves adherence to elements of the Protestant work ethic, including personal freedom, self-reliance, discipline, dedication to work, and achievement. This orientation feeds anti-Black prejudices because people attribute negative behaviors that are stereotypically associated with Blacks (e.g., crime and unemployment) to personal weaknesses rather than to situational factors.

Awareness of one's simultaneous tendencies toward pro- and anti-Black attitudes is experienced as psychological ambivalence. Individuals are motivated to alleviate the discomfort produced by their ambivalent attitudes and do so by amplifying their positive or negative responses toward Blacks, thereby discrediting whichever attitudinal inclination is not being acted on. For example, Whites may evaluate a Black criminal particularly harshly and link a multitude of personal faults to the criminal, thereby discrediting the relevance of their pro-Black attitudes to their evaluations.

Prejudice With Compunction

The three forms of modern prejudice discussed thus far all posit that prejudice is maintained through rationalization and justification processes. People are either unwilling or unable to recognize their racial biases, so they persist unchallenged. Borrowing from Allport's classic notion of *prejudice with compunction*, other researchers have argued that people may become aware of their racial biases, feel guilty about their inherent inconsistency with egalitarian principles and nonprejudiced personal motivations, and attempt to change their prejudiced ways. This conceptualization is rooted in Patricia Devine's distinction between the automatic and controlled components of stereotyping and prejudice. Devine argued that, due to a lifetime of socialization and a multitude of factors that encourage intergroup stereotyping and prejudice, cultural group-based associations come to be automatically activated among most people.

For example, most Whites learn early in life the stereotype that Blacks are unintelligent. This association becomes strong through repeated activation until it can be activated automatically (i.e., with little conscious attention, awareness, or intent). In contrast, people's low-prejudice attitudes often come to mind only with the operation of controlled processes, which require conscious attention, awareness, and intention for their activation. The result is that people may apply their automatically activated associations to intergroup situations before they have had the input of their low-prejudice attitudes. Thus, much like a bad habit, stereotypes and biased evaluations of various groups may determine impressions, judgments, and behaviors before people can consciously take their low-prejudiced attitudes into account.

However, researchers have also found that many people become aware that they are responding in ways that are more prejudiced than their personal standards suggest are appropriate. For example, a White woman may find herself clutching her purse when passing a Black pedestrian on the street and then may realize that her behavior is inappropriate. Much research has shown that people experience guilty feelings when they realize that they have responded with prejudice despite their personal low-prejudiced standards. Studies have also shown that such guilt often instigates attempts to learn how to control and change patterns of prejudiced responding or to de-automatize the "prejudice habit" through self-regulation.

Beyond White–Black Prejudice

Although modern prejudice has been studied in large part in the White–Black U.S. context, the theories can be applied to other intergroup prejudices within and outside the United States. Some research has indicated that the tenets of symbolic racism also apply to modern prejudice toward women in the United States and to modern prejudice in Europe. For example, although there are norms against discrimination and overt racism in the Netherlands, symbolic and aversive racism have been reported as distinct phenomena among Dutch residents toward ethnic immigrants. Symbolic racism is expressed toward Asians and West Indians in Britain, and aversive racism toward Asians has been studied in Canada. Prejudice with compunction has been studied in connection with women and gays in the United States, and it has been applied in other countries also.

Tools for Measuring Modern Prejudice

Explicit measures such as surveys and opinion polls rely on individuals' willingness and ability to accurately report their attitudes and beliefs. Modern forms of prejudice cannot be assessed directly with such obvious questions about intergroup attitudes because of people's desire to maintain a nonprejudiced image. Thus, a variety of indirect means for assessing modern prejudice have been devised.

Symbolic racism is assessed according to extent of agreement with political attitudinal items such as "Blacks are getting too demanding in their push for equal rights." The aversive form of racism cannot be measured with any sort of explicit opinion or attitudinal items, because people sincerely embrace nonprejudiced attitudes. However, it can be assessed indirectly through behavioral responses when norms for nonprejudiced responding are ambiguous or racial bias can be justified in nonprejudiced ways—such as in the helping research described earlier. Ambivalent racism can be assessed by measuring pro- and anti-Black attitudes related to egalitarianism and individualism, respectively.

Finally, because prejudice with compunction involves an awareness of the discrepancy between how one actually responds in biased ways and how one personally believes one should respond, it can be assessed more directly. Specifically, the *Should–Would Discrepancy Scale* asks individuals to consider various situations and indicate how they would respond in the situations and how they should respond. For instance, Whites may report that they find themselves feeling uncomfortable around Blacks even though they believe that they should not and such discrepancies lead to feelings of guilt.

Regardless of the form of modern prejudice, all entail negative feelings and beliefs that can be assessed with implicit measures. Relying on computer-based reaction-time methods, these measures tap into the automatic activation of associations and attitudes in ways that largely cannot be altered or inhibited. One such measure involves stereotype or evaluative priming. For example, a stereotype-priming task involves the rapid (and sometimes subliminal) presentation of group exemplars (e.g., a picture of a Black person) followed by targets (e.g., the word *lazy*). Reaction times to targets are measured, and bias is indicated when responses to stereotypic words are faster when the prime is a member of the stereotyped group compared with when it is not. The well-known *Implicit Association Test* measures the ease with which people can associate category exemplars (e.g., Blacks vs. Whites) with evaluative concepts (e.g., positive vs. negative words). Bias is calculated by the difference in reaction times between evaluatively congruent pairs (e.g., Blacks and poison) and evaluatively incongruent pairs (e.g., Blacks and paradise).

The *Weapons Identification Task* assesses speed and errors when individuals are asked to quickly identify whether various targets (typically Black and White males) are holding guns or neutral objects. The typical finding is that White people are faster to identify Blacks holding guns than Whites holding guns, and White people are more likely to erroneously decide that Blacks are holding guns than they are to reach the same decision for Whites. These implicit measures and similar others all bypass people's consciously held intergroup attitudes to reveal biases that may be deeply rooted in the subconscious.

Conclusion

Theories of modern forms of prejudice provide explanations for the incongruities between many individuals' nonprejudiced outward expressions and internalized feelings of bias. The new measurement techniques that tap these internal and often unconscious biases enable researchers to explore the impact of these internalized biases on behavior and the extent to which they are amenable to change. Understanding the psychological underpinnings of modern forms of prejudice, combined with skillful measurement techniques, provides a framework and the tools for developing and evaluating interventions for the reduction of prejudice and discrimination.

Margo Monteith and Anna Woodcock

See also Ambivalent Sexism; Aversive Racism; Conservatism; Implicit Association Test (IAT); Implicit Prejudice; Modern Racism; Modern Sexism; Prejudice; Protestant Work Ethic; Racial Ambivalence Theory; Racism; Stereotyping; Symbolic Racism

Further Readings

Allport, G. W. (1954). *The nature of prejudice.* New York: Addison-Wesley.

Crosby, F., Bromley, S., & Saxe, L. (1980). Recent unobtrusive studies of Black and White discrimination and prejudice: A literature review. *Psychological Bulletin, 87,* 546–563.

Devine, P. G. (1989). Stereotypes and prejudice: Their automatic and controlled components. *Journal of Personality and Social Psychology, 56,* 5–18.

Devine, P. G., & Elliot, A. J. (1995). Are racial stereotypes *really* fading? The Princeton trilogy revisited. *Personality and Social Psychology Bulletin, 21,* 1139–1150.

Dovidio, J. F. (2001). On the nature of contemporary prejudice: The third wave. *Journal of Social Issues, 57,* 826–849.

Dovidio, J. F., & Gaertner, S. L. (1986). *Prejudice, discrimination, and racism.* San Diego, CA: Academic Press.

Fazio, R. H., & Olson, M. A. (2003). Implicit measures in social cognition research: Their meaning and use. *Annual Review of Psychology, 54,* 297–327.

Monteith, M. J., & Mark, A. Y. (2005). Changing one's prejudice ways: Awareness, affect, and self-regulation. *European Review of Social Psychology, 16,* 113–154.

MODERN RACISM

Modern racism is a form of prejudice against African Americans that developed in the United States after the civil rights movement of the 1950s and 1960s. It is characterized by beliefs that racism is not a continuing problem, that African Americans should put forth their own efforts to overcome their situation in society without special assistance, and that African Americans are too demanding and have gotten more than they deserve. At the roots of modern racism are basic beliefs that Blacks violate cherished U.S. values. The idea that the quality of prejudice toward Blacks can shift over time has spawned important generalizations of the theory to other groups, such as women (see the entry titled "Modern Sexism"), recent immigrant groups (including Asians and Latinos in North America and Turks in Europe), the obese, and gays, among others.

The term *modern racism* was introduced in 1981 by John McConahay in the literature on group processes and intergroup relations, but the theory behind it had emerged in 1971 with the name *symbolic racism.* Because modern racism theory was derivative of symbolic racism theory, the two positions were originally closely aligned conceptually and, in fact, difficult to distinguish substantively. However, in recent years, developments in symbolic racism (e.g., concerning the origins of the attitudes) have distinguished the positions more clearly. This entry examines modern racism and relevant criticisms, describes measurement tools, and contrasts the concept with related theories.

The Nature and Origins of Modern Racism

Modern racism is among the most widespread forms of verbally expressed negative racial attitudes in the United States today. It is thought to have replaced, to a substantial degree, older and more blatant forms of prejudice, characterized by beliefs that Blacks are a biologically inferior race and that institutionalized segregation and formal discrimination against Blacks are appropriate social policies. The civil rights movement made these old-fashioned beliefs largely socially unacceptable, and although old-fashioned racism still exists in the United States, it largely has been replaced by modern racist beliefs.

Modern racism is also one of the most powerful influencers of racial politics in the United States today. It powerfully predicts voting against political candidates who are Black or sympathetic toward Blacks and voting on policies designed to assist Blacks, such as affirmative action and school integration programs. It also strongly influences policies that do not directly mention Blacks but disproportionately impact the African American community, including those involving welfare, unemployment, crime, and the death penalty. It predicts these political attitudes better than conservatism, education, identification as a Democrat or Republican, and, most important, personal interests in the outcomes of a vote.

One important characteristic of modern racism is the assumption that it is learned during socialization. In other words, people acquire modern racist attitudes through their parents, their peers, and the media. Emerging research suggests that modern racism is acquired as early as adolescence (earlier than other political attitudes, such as conservatism) and that it is stable throughout the life span.

As a theoretical construct, modern racism is not tied to threats to a White person's interests or personal experiences with African Americans. This is a point of some confusion: Some concepts such as *symbolic threat*, which seem to be similar to modern racism, assert that prejudiced beliefs are rooted in threats that Blacks pose to Whites' worldview. To be clear, the theory of modern racism was designed from the beginning to demonstrate the opposite, namely, that powerful negative racial attitudes can be rooted in constructs other than threat, fear, or personal interests.

Theoretical Criticisms

Naturally, a construct as popular as modern racism has received considerable critical attention in the literature. These criticisms have helped shape our understanding of the modern racism construct. One major criticism is that the construct of modern racism really is not racism at all. Conservatives have suggested that modern racism actually captures core nonracial principles behind conservatism (such as opposition to excessive government intervention and that the mention of Blacks is incidental

for the construct, with the conclusion that racism is not an important political force today. Although strong evidence exists for an important link between raw negative racial attitudes and modern racism attitudes, this controversy is yet unresolved.

A second major criticism takes the exact opposite position, suggesting that modern racism really is racism, but not a particularly "modern" form of racism. These critics say that it is the same thing as old-fashioned racism but put in more socially acceptable terms. As they see it, regardless of the language used, modern racism serves the same function of rationalizing continuing discrimination against Blacks. However, although blatant prejudice toward Blacks and modern racism have some connection, they still act independently in predicting political attitudes. A person does not have to hold deep-seated blatantly racist views to react in a punitive manner on perceiving that Blacks (or any group) undermine cherished values. Nevertheless, this controversy, too, is an ongoing one.

The Modern Racism Scale

Modern racism is probably most well known through the *Modern Racism Scale*, which is among the most commonly used methods for identifying modern racism. The original intent of the scale was to create a theoretically driven and more indirect measure of racism relative to old-fashioned, or blatant, forms of racism. The scale is typically administered using paper-and-pencil surveys or through telephone interviewing. The items capture the themes described earlier, such as agreement with the statement "It's really a matter of some people not trying hard enough; if Blacks would only try harder, they could be just as well off as Whites." The original scale (developed in 1986) has since been updated with the *Symbolic Racism 2000 Scale*.

Some psychologists have criticized the Modern Racism Scale, suggesting that it does not capture racism but instead individuals' sensitivity to giving politically correct responses about race and their motivations to appear unprejudiced. Although the Modern Racism Scale may not be a true pipeline to people's negative racial attitudes and other measures should be considered, the scale and its variants have proven to be useful theoretical tools for understanding many race-related processes.

Relations to Other Forms of Racism

Modern racism has many similarities to other concepts in use in the social sciences. It is essentially identical to symbolic racism and *racial resentment* and is related to concepts such as *subtle prejudice*, *racial ambivalence*, and *aversive racism*. Although these latter theories have their own unique perspectives, they all share the perceptions that the nature of racist expression has changed over time, that current expressions do not appear as much like racism as older expressions did, and that these newer expressions nevertheless contain a certain quality of racism.

Because modern racism is measured by means of survey methodology and requires deliberate responses, it is considered an explicit assessment of prejudice. It can be contrasted with implicit assessments of prejudice, such as the *Implicit Association Test*, which measures how easily negative versus positive concepts are associated with African American representations (such as names or faces) because negative concepts operate at an unconscious or automatic level. Although there appears to be some relationship between modern racism and implicit measures of negative racial bias, the evidence is mixed. What seems certain is that modern racism is better at predicting voting behavior and policy preferences, whereas implicit measures are better at predicting nonverbal and subtle behaviors in Whites' interactions with Blacks. The exact theoretical relationship between modern racism and implicit associations remains a point of controversy.

Conclusion

Despite the controversies surrounding the theory of modern racism and its relatives (most notably symbolic racism), what is agreed even by the theory's harshest critics is that modern racist beliefs represent some of the most powerful attitudes underlying current U.S. racial politics. The precise nature of modern racism, however, is an important lingering question.

P. J. Henry

See also Ambivalent Sexism; Aversive Racism; Conservatism; Implicit Association Test (IAT); Implicit Prejudice; Modern Forms of Prejudice; Modern Sexism; Prejudice; Protestant Work Ethic; Racial Ambivalence Theory; Racism; Stereotyping; Symbolic Racism

Further Readings

Dovidio, J. F., Kawakami, K., & Gaertner, S. L. (2002). Implicit and explicit prejudice and interracial interaction. *Journal of Personality and Social Psychology, 82*, 62–68.

Fazio, R. H., Jackson, J. R., Dunton, B. C., & Williams, C. J. (1995). Variability in automatic activation as an unobtrusive measure of racial attitudes: A bona fide pipeline? *Journal of Personality and Social Psychology, 69*, 1013–1027.

Henry, P. J., & Sears, D. O. (2002). The Symbolic Racism 2000 Scale. *Political Psychology, 23*, 253–283.

McConahay, J. B. (1986). Modern racism, ambivalence, and the Modern Racism Scale. In J. Dovidio & S. Gaertner (Eds.), *Prejudice, discrimination, and racism* (pp. 91–126). Orlando, FL: Academic Press.

McConahay, J. B., Hardee, B. B., & Batts, V. (1981). Has racism declined in America? It depends on who is asking and what is asked. *Journal of Conflict Resolution, 25*, 563–579.

Sears, D. O., & Henry, P. J. (2005). Over thirty years later: A contemporary look at symbolic racism. *Advances in Experimental Social Psychology, 37*, 95–150.

Sears, D. O., Sidanius, J., & Bobo, L. (Eds.). (2000). *Racialized politics: The debate about racism in America.* Chicago: University of Chicago Press.

Sniderman, P. M., & Tetlock, P. E. (1986). Symbolic racism: Problems of motive attributions in political analysis. *Journal of Social Issues, 42*, 129–150.

MODERN SEXISM

Sexism consists of attitudes, beliefs, behaviors, and practices at the individual, institutional, and societal level that involve negative evaluations of people or promote unequal treatment based on gender. *Modern sexism*, which represents current manifestations of sexism, includes both older, overt forms of sexism and more subtle and less often recognized expressions. By definition, sexism can be directed against both women and men. However, most psychological research focuses on antifemale sexism.

Although gender relations have, as a consequence of cultural, political, and social movements, shifted away from considerable inequality to emerging egalitarianism, particularly in economically wealthier countries, egalitarian norms have not resulted in full gender equality. On a societal level, this is reflected, for instance, by the frequency of interpersonal violence against women, the ongoing gender-specific division of labor, and the overrepresentation of men in decision-making positions. On an individual level, women report more experiences with interpersonal forms of sexism than do men, with women reporting about one to two sexist incidents per week traceable to traditional gender stereotypes (e.g., expectations about women's and men's behaviors and expressions of traditional gender stereotypes) and unwanted sexual attention (e.g., staring at body parts or unwanted sexual touching).

Rather than appearing in blatant forms of sexist behaviors or open endorsement of sexist beliefs, sexism has changed its appearance to covert and subtle manifestations. Modern sexism is expressed by a new language and new strategies. These changes are reflected in researchers' development of concepts that mirror contemporary forms of sexism. The most important developments during the past 15 years have been the concepts of modern sexist behaviors, modern sexist and neosexist beliefs, and the concept of ambivalent sexist beliefs, which will be outlined below. Characteristics of current manifestations of sexist behaviors are described, and then current manifestations of sexist beliefs are discussed.

Modern Sexist Behaviors

Modern sexist behaviors consist of blatant, subtle, and covert sexist behaviors. *Blatant sexist behaviors* still exist and consist of unequal and harmful treatment of women in family life, employment, politics, and religion, as well as quid pro quo sexual harassment and interpersonal violence. *Subtle sexist behaviors* can be intentional or unintentional and may be difficult to detect because many individuals do not perceive this type of sexist behavior as serious and harmful. Examples of subtle sexist behaviors are condescending chivalry (women are paternalistically protected but treated as subordinates), "friendly" harassment (sexually oriented behaviors that appear harmless, such as flattery), and subjective objectification (women are treated as property or sex objects). Finally, *covert sexist behaviors* are conscious, intentional attempts to undermine women; they are hidden and therefore difficult to document. Examples of covert sexist behavior are *tokenism* (hiring a few representative women to prevent complaints about excluding all women) and *containment* and *manipulation* (e.g., undermining a woman's position to discourage her advancement into higher positions). Several of the sexist behaviors described above can be considered as forms of *backlash* against increasing gender equality.

There is some disagreement about whether certain behaviors are forms of modern sexism. However, it can be argued that those behaviors, even when unintentional, are sexist because of their negative consequences and implications for women on both an individual and a macro level. For instance, sexist jokes can elicit negative emotional responses in women, and patronizing acts by powerful men can negatively affect low-power female recipients' performance. On a macro level, paternalistic behaviors can lead to conceiving of women as incompetent for high-status positions, thus maintaining gender inequality.

Modern Sexist Beliefs

Modern sexism is expressed not only in behaviors but also in beliefs. These include modern sexist, neosexist, and ambivalent sexist beliefs. All of them reflect contemporary forms of prejudice against women but do not match the mental prototype of what most people think to be sexist. Hence, the sexist nature of these beliefs is not as obvious as the sexist nature of blatant and old-fashioned sexist beliefs. These beliefs are problematic because they provide justification for the status quo and undermine the desirability or need to address gender inequality.

Modern Sexist and Neosexist Beliefs

The concepts of modern sexism and neosexism have been developed to assess "hidden" prejudice against women. Both concepts derive from research that was done on modern and symbolic racism. Modern sexism manifests itself in terms of downplaying the existence of discrimination against women and resentment of complaints about sexism and efforts to assist women. In theory, neosexism represents a conflict between egalitarian values and negative feelings toward women. Both of these beliefs represent resistance to efforts addressing the problem of sexism and imply an inclination to maintain current gender relations.

Modern and neosexist beliefs can be regarded as legitimizing ideologies that provide moral and intellectual justification for existing social arrangements and distributions. For instance, one prominent theory that helps explain endorsement of these beliefs is *system justification theory*. System justification theorists argue that people are motivated to give a positive evaluation not only to themselves and their groups but also to the superordinate societal system. People want to believe that social outcomes and arrangements are fair, legitimate, and deserved. Believing otherwise would imply that people might be treated unfairly and that the world is not a predictable place. As a consequence, members of both advantaged and disadvantaged groups (e.g., men and women, respectively) show a tendency to justify existing status hierarchies, even when those hierarchies disadvantage their own group.

Methodologically, the *Modern Sexism Scale* primarily measures perceptions of discrimination, and the *Neosexism Scale* focuses mostly on the resentment of complaints about sexism and efforts to assist women. Endorsement of modern and neosexist beliefs in these measures is distinct from endorsement of traditional gender roles, but the two attitudes have several similar characteristics, such as negative reactions toward affirmative action, negative evaluations of feminists and feminism, greater use of sexist language, and lesser likelihood of judging particular incidents as sexual harassment.

Ambivalent Sexist Beliefs

Ambivalent sexism is another expression of contemporary sexism. It describes how women can be oppressed and loved at the same time. According to this theory, sexism emerges within the context of patriarchal structures and heterosexual interdependencies between women and men. Ambivalent sexism is composed of *hostile* and *benevolent sexism*. Hostile sexist beliefs include perceptions of women as seeking control over men through sexuality or feminist ideology. Hostile sexist beliefs are hidden by their benevolent counterparts: Benevolent sexism appears subjectively positive. It includes the belief that women should be protected and taken care of by men, characterizes women as wonderful, pure creatures, and may flatter women. However, it also reinforces patriarchy by portraying women as childlike, incompetent, needing men to protect them, and therefore best suited for low-status positions.

Integration and Implications

Sexism against women is still prevalent all over the world, but it has changed its appearance, at least in economically wealthier countries. Modern sexist behaviors include covert and subtle sexist behaviors that are not easily detected, as well as the continuation of more blatant, obvious sexist beliefs. Modern sexist beliefs include those beliefs (e.g., denial of discrimination and negativity toward attempts for change) that legitimize and maintain the status quo, as well as ambivalent beliefs that combine beliefs that appear benevolent but still maintain gender inequality with hostile beliefs directed at women who challenge inequality and men's dominance. Whereas people are likely to identify hostile sexism and endorsement of traditional gender roles as sexist, they often do not identify other current manifestations of sexism (e.g., paternalism or denial of discrimination) as serious or harmful because these expressions of sexism do not match the mental prototype of sexism.

As a consequence, changing modern sexist behaviors and beliefs is a difficult task. Therefore, new types of interventions for both women and men are necessary to change the beliefs and motivations that underlie modern sexism. Research on reduction of sexist beliefs shows that drawing attention to the frequency of sexist behaviors and the harm of ostensibly "positive" sexism is a promising way to decrease endorsement of modern and benevolent sexist beliefs. However, sexism will decline only through changes on multiple levels. That is, besides changes in beliefs, attitudes, and behaviors at individual levels, changes in roles and opportunities at the societal level are necessary.

Janet K. Swim and Julia C. Becker

See also Affirmative Action; Ambivalent Sexism; Aversive Racism; Feminism; Gender Roles; Implicit Prejudice; Modern Forms of Prejudice; Modern Racism; Prejudice; Racial Ambivalence Theory; Sexism; Stereotyping; Symbolic Racism; System Justification Theory

Further Readings

Benokraitis, N. V., & Feagin, J. R. (1995). *Modern sexism: Blatant, subtle, and covert discrimination* (2nd ed.). Englewood-Cliffs, NJ: Prentice Hall.

Swim, J. K., Aikin, K. J., Hall, W. S., & Hunter, B. A. (1995). Sexism and racism: Old-fashioned and modern prejudices. *Journal of Personality and Social Psychology, 68,* 199–214.

Swim, J. K., Becker, J., Pruitt, E. R., & Lee, E. (2009). Sexism reloaded: Worldwide evidence for its endorsement, expression, and emergence in multiple contexts. In H. Landrine & N. Russo (Eds.), *Handbook of diversity in feminist psychology.* Washington, DC: American Psychological Association.

Swim, J. K., & Hyers, L. L. (2008). Sexism. In T. Nelson (Ed.), *Handbook of prejudice* (pp. 407–430). New York: Psychology Press.

MOSCOVICI, SERGE (1925–)

Serge Moscovici is a leading European social psychologist. Born in 1925 in Romania, he immigrated after World War II to France, where he studied psychology and philosophy. Along with Henri Tajfel, Moscovici played a crucial role in the development of European social psychology. He provided intellectual guidance and organizational leadership that helped to channel U.S. efforts to revitalize social psychology in postwar western Europe. Moscovici is one of the founders and the first president of the European Association of Experimental Social Psychology, established in 1966.

In the 1970s, Moscovici was at the forefront of a quest for social psychology with a distinctly European flavor. The goal was to replace then-prevailing U.S. ideas with theoretical models that would reflect European cultural and historical complexity. Moscovici's criticism of U.S. individualistic thought and his innovative work, which emphasized the role of social and cultural factors in psychological phenomena, helped establish what came to be known as *European social psychology*. Although more a mosaic of orientations than a homogeneous school of thought, European social psychology is generally characterized by its emphasis on the social dimension of human psychological functioning.

This emphasis on studying psychological phenomena in the social and cultural context is evident in Moscovici's entire body of work, which includes several lines of research. They are tied together by a common theme of a social psychology of knowledge. Examining the role of social factors in the development, maintenance, and change of knowledge, Moscovici developed two influential theories—a *theory of minority influence* and a *theory of social representations*—both discussed in this entry.

Minority Influence

Moscovici's theory of minority influence emerged from his criticism of the U.S. approach to social influence, which equated influence with conformity. He rejected the assumption underlying much of U.S. research at the time that influence can be reduced to change that individuals or minorities undergo under pressure from a group. Moscovici argued that influence also included change in the opposite direction. From innovators in science to revolutionaries in politics, history abounds with examples of minorities that prevailed in their opposition to a majority.

According to Moscovici's "genetic" model of minority influence, numerical minorities create conflict within a group at two levels: At the cognitive level, they question the established (majority) worldview; at the social level, they threaten interpersonal relationships. Initially, people try to resolve the conflict by attributing the minority position to undesirable psychological characteristics (e.g., deviance, insanity, naïveté). However, if the minority continues to advocate its position consistently, conveying commitment and certainty, its behavioral style may convince the majority to reconsider its initial reaction and adopt the minority position as a valid alternative.

In a revision of his initial model, Moscovici placed less emphasis on behavioral style and elaborated on the ways that people resolve conflict caused by the dissenting minority. According to his conflict theory, the dissenting minority triggers a validation process through which people try to understand the minority position and examine their own position. This thorough examination of the minority position may cause people to convert. However, to avoid being associated with a minority, they are likely to keep their conversion private. In contrast, when exposed to majority influence, people are primarily concerned with potentially negative consequences of their deviation from the majority. They engage in the comparison process, through which they try to fit in with the majority. Because people change their views without close examination of the majority position, their change is superficial in that it represents public compliance and not private acceptance of the majority position.

Moscovici's theorizing that minorities, like majorities, can exert influence revitalized research on social influence in the early 1970s. Moreover, his ideas continue to stimulate research today.

Social Representations

The original impetus for the development of the theory of social representations was Moscovici's attempt to understand how ordinary people gain ownership of scientific knowledge and how they transform scientific knowledge into public knowledge. Moscovici's concept of social representations has its intellectual roots in Emile Durkheim's collectivistic approach to social behavior, which, in turn, was influenced by Wilhelm Wundt's *Völkerpsychologie*. Social representations could be understood as a form of public (common) knowledge grounded in group membership. As a result, people have different social representations depending on groups to which they belong.

The theory of social representations postulates that people need a common frame of reference to orient themselves in the world and to communicate with others. Social representations provide such a reference. They emerge in the process of social interaction as people try to make what is unfamiliar and unknown into something familiar and known. This process of making sense of the world is constructive in that it involves anchoring or classifying the unfamiliar into already existing categories. Situating the unfamiliar within existing categories removes the threat of the unknown and enables people to name it. People are then able to objectify the unknown, thinking about it not as an abstraction but rather as something real. In doing so, they create social reality. Social representations, therefore, do not mirror reality. Instead, they create it.

Social representations are both the outcome and the process of social construction. On one hand, they emerge as the outcome of the process of social interaction. On the other hand, they shape how people think, communicate, and relate during social interaction. Being a group-specific means of understanding the world, social representations also are a form of social identification. This becomes especially important when competing representations from different groups clash. The resultant conflict may stimulate innovation—an idea that Moscovici elaborated in his theory of minority influence.

Since its inception in the 1960s, the theory of social representations has generated research and dialogue not only among social psychologists but also among sociologists, anthropologists, and other social scientists. Its focus on a dialectic (two-way) relationship between individuals and social groups resonates well with the European orientation in social sciences. Not surprisingly, Moscovici's theory of social representations has been most influential in Europe; it has also gained popularity in a few Latin American countries.

In addition to his work on minority influence and social representations, Moscovici has made significant contributions to research and theorizing on several other topics, including crowding, conspiracy and collective decisions, psychology of language, history of psychology, and philosophy of science. In recognition of his intellectual contributions and leadership in the development of the discipline, Moscovici has received numerous professional and civic awards. Among other honors, he was awarded the highest decoration in France, the *Légion d'Honneur* (Legion of Honor); the International Balzan Prize; the American Psychological Association Wundt-James Prize; and many honorary doctorates. Moscovici is currently director of the European Laboratory of Social Psychology at the Maison des sciences de l'homme, in Paris.

Radmila Prislin

See also Conformity; Innovation; Minority Influence; Socially Shared Cognition; Social Representation

Further Readings

Moscovici, S. (1985). Innovation and minority influence. In S. Moscovici, G. Mugny, & E. Van Avermaaet (Eds.), *Perspective on minority influence* (pp. 9–51). Cambridge, UK: Cambridge University Press.

Moscovici, S. (1997). *Chronique de années egarées* [Chronicle of stray years]. Paris: Stock.

Moscovici, S. (2000). *Social representations: Explorations in social psychology*. New York: New York University Press.

MULTICULTURALISM

Multiculturalism as discussed in this entry refers to policies that support the preservation and egalitarian treatment of intergroup differences and distinct minority and majority group identities within a unified state. People of diverse cultural and linguistic groups have had contact with one another throughout known human history. However, contact now takes place in the context of rapid globalization, involving the movement of hundreds of millions of people around the world and the global expansion of communications, transportation, and trade. A major challenge confronting humankind at local, national, regional, and international levels is how to better manage intergroup contact, as well as cultural diversity.

Multiculturalism stands in contrast to *assimilation*, which is defined as the melting away of intergroup differences through market forces, government policy, or both, to create a more homogeneous society. The impact of *globalization* in many ways reinforces assimilationist trends, so lifestyles around the world become in important ways more similar. Just as diversity is decreasing among plants and animals, so is it decreasing among human cultures and languages. When Columbus landed in the western hemisphere, there were about 15,000 living languages in the world; today, only about 6,000 survive. Hundreds of languages have one or just a few speakers and are on the verge of extinction. Most people in the world today speak one of only about 10 major languages (e.g., Mandarin Chinese, English, Spanish), representing a decline in diversity that is associated with assimilation.

Multiculturalism and assimilation are topics for social-psychological investigation because they are supported by assumptions about intergroup behavior. The original assumptions supporting multiculturalism were promoted in Canada, a historically immigrant-receiving country with a population one tenth the size of the U.S. population. Then prime minister Pierre Trudeau, in a speech on national unity to the House of Commons in 1971, argued that individual identity is both the base from which respect for others develops and the base for national unity. Although the origins of multiculturalism as an official government policy are Canadian, multiculturalism has gained broader international attention in the United States, in the European Union, and well beyond.

This entry assesses the five core assumptions that underpin policies of multiculturalism: (1) a cultural free market, (2) heritage culture retention, (3) ingroup confidence and outgroup acceptance, (4) ingroup affiliation and outgroup bias, and (5) minority and majority endorsement of multiculturalism and intergroup attitudes.

Cultural Free Market

The foundational assumption of multiculturalism is that the cultural marketplace is one where (a) individuals freely select their cultural identities and (b) relations between cultural groups are egalitarian. While cultural groups do not have equal power, they are assumed to have equal merit. Cultural groups may compete in a free and open "market"; the government should not disrupt market forces by designating an official culture.

This assumption has been criticized for promoting a form of relativism that threatens both harmonious intergroup relations and social justice. If all cultures and cultural practices are given equal merit, it may be challenging or even impossible for a state body to resolve conflicts between cultural groups. Applying live-and-let-live ethics to minority groups that practice forced marriage or honor killings or otherwise relegate women to second-class status has already presented enormous challenges. The Nazi-led Holocaust is frequently brought forth as the most provocative case of the harm that can result from applying a free-market ideology to the cultural marketplace. Indeed, a cultural free market appears to be unrealistic.

Heritage-Culture Retention

This assumption is that all cultural groups are motivated to preserve the culture passed down to them by their parents. Empirical evidence testing this assumption is divided. Studies led by John Berry and K. G. O'Bryan in 1977 and 1975, respectively, generally support this assumption, at least in samples of majority culture members in Canada. However, the perspective of minority group members is mixed, and this is particularly true for minorities that are physically different from the majority groups (e.g., because of skin and hair color).

More recent studies in the United States, published by Wallace E. Lambert and Donald M. Taylor in 1990, show that some minorities—working-class Blacks, Poles, Arabs, Albanians, Puerto Ricans, and Mexican Americans—hold positive feelings toward their heritage cultures. Among minorities living in Europe, however, the trends are more difficult to generalize. The complexity of the European situation is important because the number of minorities in Europe has been increasing rapidly, resulting in millions of South Asians living in the United Kingdom, North Africans in France, Turks in Germany, and so on. About 20 million Muslims now live in the European Union.

One reason some cultural groups may not be motivated to retain their heritage culture is fear of discrimination. Maintaining heritage culture may involve public displays and avowals of one's heritage, practices that increase one's visibility as a cultural minority. This visibility, some minorities fear, may expose them to discrimination they would not otherwise experience. Such fears are not unfounded. Thomas Pettigrew surveyed western Europeans and reported in 1998 that discrimination against immigrants persists. It can be argued that members of minorities who choose not to preserve their heritage culture are rationally protecting their interests.

Ingroup Confidence and Outgroup Acceptance

Multiculturalism is assumed to foster a positive, strong, and secure heritage identity, which in turn leads to acceptance of other groups. The logic of this assumption supports a rational view of human beings. Presumably, people have no rational reason to hold biases against outgroups so long as their ingroup identity is secure. Outgroup bias is treated as the rational outcome of an insecure ingroup identity.

However, there are numerous examples of groups that take pride in their identity yet hold extremely biased views of, and implement aggressive practices against, outgroups. Nazis, the Ku Klux Klan, and some religious fundamentalists are a few examples that challenge the assumption that ingroup security fosters outgroup acceptance. They display intense feelings of ingroup superiority and outgroup contempt, refuting the assumption that love of one's ingroup fosters acceptance of outgroups.

This critique of the ingroup-confidence–outgroup-acceptance assumption begins from an *irrationalist* view of human beings. The argument made is that unacknowledged feelings of intense insecurity drive group members to publicly proclaim their superiority. Shocking displays of ingroup pride mask hidden insecurities. The debate over whether public displays of group pride are authentic or part of a system of defenses has not been resolved by empirical testing and hence currently depends on the theoretical commitment of the interpreter.

Ingroup Affiliation and Outgroup Bias

An optimistic interpretation of the multiculturalism hypothesis is that love for one's ingroup does *not* lead to hate for outgroups. This hypothesis has been controversial. The writings of Sigmund Freud, for instance, could be interpreted as implying that love for one's own group would inevitably be counterbalanced with hate for outsiders. This counterbalancing is thought to hold groups such as the family together. Social identity theorists, too, have weighed in on this hypothesis. One interpretation of social identity theory is that the more people identify with their ingroup, the less favorably they look on other groups. Charles Negy and colleagues reported in 2003 that among Whites and Latinos, the more positive regard they reported for their own groups, the more negative views they reported having against other groups (ethnocentrism).

These results, like those of many previous studies, support social identity theory predictions and refute this aspect of the multiculturalism hypothesis. However, Black people in the United States did not fit this pattern. They displayed no correlation between ethnic identity and ethnocentrism. They also reported higher self-esteem and ethnic identity than did Whites or Latinos. Thus, one factor that may moderate the relationship between ingroup affiliation and outgroup bias is the relative perceived status of each group, which is shaped by historical and cultural experiences.

Minority and Majority Endorsement of Multiculturalism and Intergroup Attitudes

In countries where multiculturalism is official policy, the focus is on promoting minority rather than majority group heritage cultures and languages. This practice deserves careful scrutiny. The intended, if unstated, goal is often to instill pride and security in ethnic minority groups so that their attitudes toward outgroups are positive. Outgroups may be other ethnic minorities or the majority group.

However, how does this strategy address discrimination on the part of the majority against minorities? If multiculturalist policy is based on the assumption that outgroup bias results from insecurity and lack of pride in the ingroup, then to alleviate majority-led discrimination, it follows that the majority group rather than minority groups should be the target of multiculturalist policies. Increasing majority group pride and affiliation should presumably increase the majority's acceptance of minority groups. It could be argued, however, that majority groups already enjoy high security and affiliation: To the extent that majority groups are intolerant of others, the hypothesis of ingroup confidence and outgroup acceptance fails. Indeed, if we control for education, majority group members are not any more tolerant of outgroups than are minority group members. Along these lines, research by Maykel Verkuyten shows that majority groups tend to favor multiculturalism much less than do minority groups.

One might also consider the personal and group functions of multiculturalist and assimilationist orientations. For example, maintaining the salience of cultural differences can be important for minority groups to mobilize for social action.

Assimilation, which represents a colorblind approach, may support the status quo by limiting group-based initiatives.

Policy Issues

The practical question of how states can best manage cultural diversity will likely persist and become more urgent in the next few decades, as globalization accelerates and intergroup contact increases. Finding adequate policy solutions requires developing and testing theories of how members of different groups are likely to respond. Thus, at the core of sound policy making is an understanding of human psychology and, most important, intergroup dynamics.

Multiculturalism has emerged as an attractive alternative to assimilation, and minorities generally look on this policy as more democratic and morally superior. Yet further theory building and empirical work are needed to address some of the shortcomings discussed in this entry. The notion of a culture-free market appears to be unrealistic because in everyday life, groups are not granted equal merit. The heritage-culture retention assumption is falsified by those ethnic minorities that choose to abandon their heritage culture. The relationship between how one feels about one's ingroup versus one's outgroups is not consistent across samples. There is also the complex question of which groups should be targeted in esteem- and confidence-building efforts: the majority, the minority, or both. Perhaps the largest challenge to multiculturalism is the question of how diverse groups can develop and maintain a core shared set of values.

Controlled laboratory experiments offer a crucial but partial picture. Such studies can be complemented with field-based analysis of events such as the formation and expansion of the European Union, which represents the most recent large-scale attempt to unify diverse groups. In the North American context, the largest field experiment in recent history is being carried out, involving the integration of an estimated 40 million to 50 million Latinos, their cultures anchored in Spanish-speaking enclaves in Florida, California, Texas, New Mexico, and some other states. These developments ensure that debates about multiculturalism will remain center stage in national and global contexts.

Naomi Lee and Fathali M. Moghaddam

See also Assimilation and Acculturation; Diversity; Ethnocentrism; Group Boundaries; Immigration; Intergroup Contact Theory; Social Identity Theory

Further Readings

Beunker, J. D., & Ratner, L. A. (Eds.). (2005). *Multiculturalism in the United States: A comparative guide to acculturation and ethnicity*. Westport, CT: Greenwood Press.

Kymlicka, W., & He, B. (Eds.). (2005). *Multiculturalism in Asia*. New York: Oxford University Press.

Lambert, W. E., & Taylor, D. M. (1990). *Coping with cultural and racial diversity in urban America*. New York: Praeger.

Máiz, R., & Requejo, F. (Eds.). (2005). *Democracy, nationalism, and multiculturalism*. London: Frank Cass.

Moghaddam, F. M. (2008). *Multiculturalism and intergroup relations: Psychological implications for democracy in global context*. Washington, DC: American Psychological Association.

Parekh, B. (2006). *Rethinking multiculturalism*. New York: Palgrave/Macmillan.

MULTIPLE IDENTITIES

In large and complex societies, individuals are differentiated or subdivided along many meaningful social dimensions, including gender and sexual orientation, life stage (e.g., student, worker, retiree), economic sector (e.g., technology, service, academics, professional), religion, political ideology, and recreational preferences. Each of these divisions provides a basis for shared identity and group membership that may become an important source of social identification. Further, most of these differentiations are crosscutting in the sense that individuals may share a common ingroup membership on one dimension but belong to different categories on another dimension. Hence, having multiple group memberships reduces the likelihood that one's social world can be reduced to a single ingroup-versus-outgroup distinction. The fact that people have multiple, crosscutting social identities has important implications for ingroup identification and intergroup relations. This entry looks at the various ways in which people perceive their multiple identities and then examines the impact of these perceptions on their level of tolerance for those different from themselves.

Social Identity Complexity

The objective relationship between any two bases of categorization can take different forms. Within a given domain, groups may be hierarchically nested; that is, some groups may be completely embedded in others (e.g., all Catholics are Christians). In this case, an individual who belongs to one of the subgroups also belongs to the more inclusive, superordinate category, and an individual who is a member of the outgroup at the subgroup level is an ingroup member at the superordinate level. Antagonism between subgroups (e.g., Protestants and Catholics) may be reduced if members of both subgroups also identify with the common superordinate ingroup.

Membership in groups that are defined on different dimensions of categorization (e.g., religion or occupation or nationality) may be related to different degrees. Some categorizations may be completely uncorrelated. Knowing, for example, that people are Muslim does not tell us whether they are male or female because religion and gender memberships are uncorrelated. In other cases, group memberships may be correlated to some extent (e.g., gender and occupation; nationality and religion). In that case, ingroup members in one category (e.g., corporate executives) are also likely to be ingroup members in the other (e.g., males). Nonetheless, the groups overlap only partially because some members of the occupational group are of a different gender.

When there is extensive overlap between ingroups defined by different dimensions of categorization (i.e., the categories are highly correlated), identification is relatively simple—the individuals who constitute the ingroup versus outgroups are the same for either categorization. When ingroups defined by different dimensions of categorization overlap only partially, however, the implications for social identification become more complex. In this case, some of those who are fellow ingroup members on one dimension are simultaneously outgroup members on the other. Consider the case of a woman who is a corporate executive. When the social context emphasizes professional identity (e.g., a management conference), she is likely to perceive a male colleague as an ingroup member. Nonetheless, she may be aware that in different circumstances (circumstances that emphasize her identity as a woman), that same colleague is an outgroup member.

How do individuals construct their social identities in relation to such multiple, nonconvergent ingroup memberships? Sonia Roccas and Marilynn Brewer developed the concept of *social identity complexity* to refer to a person's *subjective* representation of his or her multiple identities. More specifically, individuals with low social identity complexity see their ingroups as highly overlapping and convergent whereas those with high complexity see their different ingroups as distinct and crosscutting membership groups.

Bicultural Identity Patterns

Individuals who are bicultural provide an illustration of the different ways that multiple identities may be combined. The prototypic case here is the member of an immigrant group or an ethnic enclave whose societal group membership (country of residence or citizenship) and ethnic or national group membership represent distinct cultures and partially overlapping group memberships. One form of bicultural adaptation is to locate one's ingroup identity at the intersection of the ethnic and societal categories and thus form a blended (hyphenated) bicultural identity (e.g., African American, Turkish Dutch). In this model, the ingroup is defined exclusively as those who share both ethnic heritage and residence in the host society. The two identities have been combined into a single, convergent social identity.

The second, more complex form of biculturalism is *intercultural identity*, which acknowledges multiple cultural identities simultaneously and combines and integrates membership, values, and norms of both groups. This conceptualization equates biculturalism with the acquisition of a more inclusive, complex group identity than that represented by any component cultural identity alone. With this representation, the cultural ingroup is expanded to include all fellow countrymen (regardless of their ethnic identity) *and* all members of the same ethnic group (regardless of the country in which they reside).

Individual Differences in Social Identity Complexity

As illustrated by the bicultural identity example, two individuals who belong to the same multiple social groups may differ in how they combine their ingroup identities. An individual may perceive his or her ingroups as having highly overlapping sets of members, such that a set of group memberships may even form a single, exclusive, compound category (e.g., White Catholic Republican doctors). This would be described as a *simple* identity structure. The opposite end of the continuum would be characterized by an individual who recognizes that his or her ingroup memberships are composed of distinct and only partially overlapping member sets. This would be described as a *complex* identity structure (e.g., Whites *and* Catholics *and* Republicans *and* doctors). With a complex representation, the individual recognizes that each of his or her group memberships incorporates a different set of people as ingroup members and that the combined representation is the *sum* of all these group identities—more inclusive than any one ingroup identity considered alone.

For instance, a woman who is both White and Christian may think of her religious ingroup as composed primarily of White people (even though, objectively, there are many non-White Christians). Conversely, she may think of her racial ingroup as largely Christian (despite the fact that, objectively, there are many Whites who embrace other religions). In contrast, another White female Christian may be very aware of the fact that many Christians are non-White (i.e., do not share her racial identity) and that many Whites are not Christians in their religious affiliation. The difference between these two cases is whether the individual *perceives* her ingroups as highly overlapping (convergent) or as only partially overlapping (crosscutting). Roccas and Brewer define social identity complexity in terms of such differences in perceived overlap of multiple ingroups.

Research on social identity complexity indicates that high complexity is associated with liberal ideology, universalistic values, openness, and experience with diversity. Further, stress and threat influence social identity complexity. Under conditions of felt threat, individuals tend to reduce complexity and see their multiple ingroups as more convergent.

Multiple Identities and Intergroup Tolerance

Roccas and Brewer also speculated that social identity complexity (as represented by perceived overlap among ingroup memberships) would be associated with tolerance for outgroups in general. Social identity complexity is based on awareness of cross-categorization in one's own social group memberships and those of others. A simple (convergent) social identity is likely to be accompanied by the perception that any individual who is an outgroup member on one dimension is also an outgroup member on all others. In contrast, if individuals are aware that their multiple ingroups do not completely overlap, then they are also aware that outgroup members on one dimension may be ingroup members on others.

For both cognitive and motivational reasons, a complex representation of one's multiple ingroup identities should influence intergroup attitudes and behavior in ways that reduce bias and discrimination. Multiple group memberships reduce the importance of any one social identity for satisfying an individual's need for belonging and self-definition, reducing the motivational base for ingroup bias and outgroup prejudice.

Results of survey research on the correlates of social identity complexity confirm that social identity complexity is associated with both tolerance-related policy preferences and feelings toward outgroups. The degree of perceived overlap among a respondent's multiple ingroups proved to be significantly correlated with attitudes toward affirmative action, multiculturalism, and feelings toward outgroups, after controlling for age, education, and ideology. Holding the number and diversity of ingroups constant, individuals who perceive low overlap among their ingroups are more accepting of multicultural policies, have more positive feelings toward ethnic and religious outgroups, and show less implicit racial prejudice than do individuals who see their multiple ingroups as highly overlapping and convergent.

In sum, then, the way in which individuals think about their own multiple ingroup identities affects the inclusiveness of their social world and their tolerance for difference and diversity. Promoting multiple social identities with awareness of crosscutting memberships provides an effective formula for reducing intergroup prejudice.

Marilynn B. Brewer

See also Collective Self; Common Ingroup Identity Model; Cross-Categorization; Prejudice; Social Identity Theory

Further Readings

Amiot, C. E., de la Sablonniere, R., Terry, D. J., & Smith, J. R. (2007). Integration of social identities in the self: Toward a cognitive-developmental model. *Personality and Social Psychology Review, 11,* 364–388.

Brewer, M. B., & Pierce, K. P. (2005). Social identity complexity and outgroup tolerance. *Personality and Social Psychology Bulletin, 31,* 428–437.

Crisp, R., & Hewstone, M. (Eds.). (2006). *Multiple social categorization: Processes, models and applications.* Hove, UK: Psychology Press.

LaFromboise, T., Coleman, H. L. K., & Gerton, J. (1993). Psychological impact of biculturalism: Evidence and theory. *Psychological Bulletin, 114,* 395–412.

Roccas, S., and Brewer, M. B. (2002). Social identity complexity. *Personality and Social Psychology Review, 6,* 88–106.

MUTUAL INTERGROUP DIFFERENTIATION MODEL

The *mutual intergroup differentiation model,* proposed by Miles Hewstone and Rupert Brown, is an extension of the *intergroup contact hypothesis,* the proposition that contact between members of different groups will reduce intergroup prejudice. The model states that contact between members of different groups will be most likely to result in positive intergroup relations when those involved embrace their respective group memberships and acknowledge the differences that exist between the groups.

The model draws on *social identity theory,* which proposes that we are motivated to hold a positive perception of groups we belong to and that we tend to favor our own group over other groups to achieve this. It is argued that each group can view itself positively during the intergroup encounter by considering itself to be superior on *different* dimensions from the other group.

The model is important for our understanding of group processes and intergroup relations because it identifies a key moderator of intergroup contact, highlighting *when* contact is most likely to improve intergroup attitudes. The theoretical and empirical background of the model, evidence for and drawbacks of the model, and recent developments that extend and clarify the model are outlined in this entry.

Background of the Model

The contact hypothesis has generated an extensive body of research over the past 50 years that has, by and large, demonstrated that high-quality contact between members of different groups can reduce intergroup prejudice. The contact hypothesis has, however, a notable limitation: It fails to specify how the effects of contact would generalize beyond the immediate contact situation to other situations and from the individuals involved in the contact to the entire outgroup. Accordingly, research has shown that although participants who engage in cooperative contact with outgroup members develop more positive attitudes toward the specific outgroup members involved in the contact, their attitudes toward *other* outgroup members and the outgroup *in general* often remain unchanged.

To identify how and when the positive effects of contact are likely to generalize from individuals involved in the contact to the entire outgroup, researchers have drawn on social identity theory. According to this theory, when an individual's membership in a given group becomes salient, this membership becomes incorporated into the individual's self-concept, resulting in a social identity rather than an individual identity. We are motivated to hold a positive social identity, so when our group membership is salient, we have a tendency to show a preference for groups we belong to over groups we do not belong to; in other words, we show ingroup bias. The social identity approach has led to the emergence of three diverging perspectives with regard to when the positive aspects of the contact situation result in more positive attitudes toward the outgroup *in general*.

Given that we tend to show intergroup bias when our group membership is salient, the *decategorization* approach proposes that intergroup contact is most likely to reduce prejudice when those involved focus on one another's individual characteristics rather than their respective group memberships. It is acknowledged that, in the short term, information acquired about individual category members is not directly generalized to the entire outgroup. However, the long-term effect of such interactions is a decrease in category-based processing in general and therefore reduced intergroup prejudice.

The *recategorization* approach, also known as the *common ingroup identity model*, also proposes that group boundaries are eliminated but argues that, rather than removal of category boundaries altogether, the categories are altered so that both groups are included in one superordinate group. This transforms group members' cognitive representations from two groups (us and them) to one inclusive group (we). In this situation, former ingroup and outgroup members now share a new ingroup membership, and so former outgroup members no longer pose a threat to a positive social identity. Thus, ingroup bias associated with the original groups is reduced or eliminated.

There are, however, some difficulties with these two approaches to intergroup contact. First, if group memberships are completely eliminated, individual-to-group generalization is unlikely because the connection between individual outgroup members and the group to which they belong is broken. One may like an outgroup member, but if that person is not recognized as being an outgroup member, attitudes toward the outgroup in general are unlikely to become more positive. Second, group membership is often an important aspect of an individual's identity. To ignore its existence or to impose on individuals a superordinate category may result in strong resistance from group members, particularly when the two groups differ in size, power, or status.

Evidence Supporting the Model

The mutual intergroup differentiation model provides an alternative solution to the issue of contact generalization that circumvents the problems presented by the decategorization and recategorization approaches. It contends that the positive effect of contact between ingroup and outgroup members generalizes to the entire outgroup only when the group memberships of those involved remain psychologically salient during contact. The model acknowledges that group members seek a positively distinct social identity by elevating their group compared with other groups. It is, however, possible for both groups to maintain a positively distinct social identity by distinguishing themselves from the other group on *different* sets of traits. In sum, if there is mutual recognition of one another's superiorities and inferiorities, positive intergroup contact is possible. Supporting the model, research has shown that although positive contact with an outgroup member leads to more positive attitudes toward that individual, it leads to more positive attitudes toward the outgroup in general only when those involved acknowledged their respective group memberships at some point during the interaction.

The mutual intergroup differentiation approach is not, however, without its dangers. First, although intergroup contact with category salience may be more likely to generalize to the outgroup, if that contact is negative rather than positive, it could lead to an increase in generalized prejudice toward a group. Second, an overemphasis on group membership may lead to an increase in intergroup anxiety, the negative emotional reaction that may arise as a result of negative expectations about encounters with members of other groups. In turn, this anxiety may lead to an increase in stereotyping and prejudice. This creates something of a dilemma: Decategorized contact, in which the focus is on personal characteristics, is likely to induce positive feelings and therefore liking of individual outgroup members, whereas making category membership salient may reinforce stereotypes and result in anxiety. But it is contact that is intergroup rather than interpersonal in nature that is most likely to generalize to the outgroup as a whole.

Recent Developments

The decategorization and recategorization approaches have recently been integrated with the mutual intergroup differentiation approach to overcome their respective limitations. Rather than seeing decategorization and mutual intergroup differentiation as mutually exclusive, researchers now argue that interpersonal (decategorized) and intergroup (category-based) contact should be viewed as orthogonal dimensions, which together can create highly effective conditions of outgroup contact. Specifically, outgroup contact will be most effective when contact is both highly intergroup and highly interpersonal. In contrast, contact that is low on either or both intergroup and interpersonal dimensions is likely to be less successful at generalizing the effect of contact to outgroup attitudes. That is, high intimacy but low group salience will fail to generalize, whereas high salience but low personalization is likely to result in heightened intergroup anxiety. Research has shown that having an encounter with outgroup members who disclose personal information but who are also perceived as typical of their group is associated with more positive outgroup attitudes than is contact with outgroup members who are typical but do not disclose personal information or with outgroup members who disclose personal information but are atypical.

Conclusion

The mutual intergroup differentiation model has made two important contributions to our knowledge of group processes and intergroup relations. First, it highlights category salience as an important moderator of intergroup contact, enabling the development of more effective contact interventions. Second, by generating a vigorous debate between the diverging perspectives of mutual intergroup differentiation, decategorization, and recategorization, it has provided a more sophisticated understanding of when intergroup contact will be most effective, recognizing the combined benefits of interpersonal and intergroup contact.

Rhiannon N. Turner and Miles Hewstone

See also Categorization; Common Ingroup Identity Model; Decategorization; Desegregation; Intergroup Anxiety; Intergroup Contact Theory; Prejudice; Social Identity Theory

Further Readings

Brewer, M. B., & Miller, N. (1984). Beyond the contact hypothesis: Theoretical perspectives on segregation. In

N. Miller & M. B. Brewer (Eds.), *Groups in contact: The psychology of desegregation* (pp. 281–302). Orlando, FL: Academic Press.

Brown, R., & Hewstone, H. (2005). An integrative theory of intergroup contact. In M. P. Zanna (Ed.), *Advances in experimental social psychology* (Vol. 37, pp. 255–343). San Diego, CA: Academic Press.

Gaertner, S. L., & Dovidio, J. F. (2000). *Reducing intergroup bias: The common ingroup identity model.* New York: Psychology Press.

Hewstone, M., & Brown, R. (1986). Contact is not enough: An intergroup perspective on the 'contact hypothesis.' In M. Hewstone & R. Brown (Eds.), *Contact and conflict in intergroup encounters* (pp. 1–44). Oxford, UK: Blackwell.

NATIONALISM AND PATRIOTISM

Nationalism and patriotism, which are different aspects of national identification, are group phenomena of both theoretical and applied importance. Whereas *patriotism* represents attachment to one's country, *nationalism* refers to the tendency to favor one's own country over others. National identification can facilitate cooperation and cohesion within one's country but at the same time engender conflict directed at other national groups. This entry illustrates the relevance of patriotism and nationalism in present societies and discusses their functions for individuals and groups, as well as the conditions determining whether and when identification with one's own country translates into the relative devaluation or derogation of other countries and their members.

Distinguishing Patriotism and Nationalism

Patriotism and nationalism refer to phenomena that can be encountered frequently and in various guises. In extreme situations such as interstate wars, but also during international sports competitions, it is quite obvious that belonging to a certain country has a strong impact on people's emotions, perceptions, and behaviors. In our everyday life as well, national categories are constantly present: To a large extent, politics is founded on national institutions and aims at pursuing the interests of one's country. Politicians often appeal to feelings of pride,

and newspapers subtly reinforce national categories by giving priority to domestic over foreign affairs.

Patriotism and *nationalism* are terms that have been used differently, regarding both their valence and their specific meaning, in different historical periods. Scientific disciplines such as history, political science, and psychology also exhibit differences as to the level of analysis—nations, social groups, or individuals—implied by these terms. In contemporary social psychology, *patriotism* and *nationalism* commonly refer to the individual level.

Patriotism, paralleling the concept of social identity, denotes the identification with, and feelings of attachment and commitment to, one's country and the people perceived as belonging to it. Hence, patriotism is defined by how closely an individual feels linked with his or her national group. Typical items used in scales measuring individuals' levels of patriotism are "I love my country" or "The fact that I am [a U.S. citizen] is an important part of my identity."

Nationalism, in contrast, usually denotes a tendency of individuals to support national interests of their country to the relative disadvantage of other countries and to see their own country as superior to other countries. One example is consumer nationalism, a tendency of consumers to favor goods and services produced in their own country or by domestic companies over "foreign" goods and services. Typical items for measuring individuals' levels of nationalism are "In view of [the United States'] moral and material superiority, it is only right that we should have the biggest say in deciding United Nations policy" and "The important thing for the [U.S.] foreign aid program is to see to it that [the United States] gains a political advantage."

Regarding patriotism, researchers have distinguished between different forms, such as between blind and constructive patriotism or between iconoclastic, symbolic, instinctive, environmental, capitalistic, and nationalistic-symbolic patriotism. In principle, these differentiations capture (a) to which degree patriotism encompasses an active and critical versus a passive and uncritical orientation toward one's country and its authorities and (b) to which degree patriotism is based on certain features of one's country, that is, how national identity is defined in terms of normative content. Often, there is a societal consensus, or at least a consensus between large groups within society, about which features are (and should be) constitutive of one's national identity. These can include, for example, national symbols such as the flag, a certain ethnicity, a particular ideology, endorsement of democratic aspects such as political institutions or basic rights of citizens, certain cultural or religious characteristics, or fundamental beliefs of group members about the country's situation vis-à-vis other countries.

Although both concepts refer to identification with one's country and national identity (i.e., social identity based on a national category), patriotism is an *intra*group phenomenon that exclusively relates to one's own country, whereas nationalism is an *inter*group phenomenon, a comparative orientation toward one's own and other countries. Despite this conceptual difference, however, both constructs are often closely interrelated: Under certain conditions, patriotic feelings can easily lead to nationalistic feelings of superiority of one's own country. Accordingly, many scholars have argued that patriotism is primary and nationalism can be considered a potential consequence of patriotism.

Functions of Patriotism and Nationalism

Why are people patriotic, and why do they feel closely attached to their countries? First of all, belonging to a national group has instrumental benefits by providing access to education, economic resources, social security, health care, and so on. Although these benefits can provide a basis,

patriotism is also (and maybe primarily) rooted in symbolic issues. As with other social categories, identification with one's country can provide people with self-esteem and meaning. For the individual, it can reduce uncertainty relating to self-concept (e.g., Who am I? What did and can I achieve?), and it can help fulfill the fundamental need to belong to social entities. Moreover, close attachment to one's country can affirm relevant cultural worldviews linked to national entities. From an existentialist perspective, the belief in the rightness of the cultural values and standards of one's group helps individuals handle the threat implied by the awareness of their mortality.

At the group level, patriotism serves important functions of unity, cohesiveness, and mobilization, which together enable group existence. Because groups with members who do not show any patriotic feelings will have a higher probability of ultimate disintegration, groups establish political or cultural mechanisms that stabilize and reinforce such feelings. In other words, attachment to one's own group is evolutionarily adaptive.

Although evolutionary functions can explain why people are patriotic, these functions are also relevant to people's tendencies to differentiate their own national group from others. Because human survival strongly depends on cooperation, people need to rely on markers indicating whether a potential interaction partner can be trusted and expected to cooperate or not. Belongingness to an ingroup or an outgroup is such a marker. Clear group boundaries and, hence, in the case of national identifications, the combination of both patriotism and nationalism provide a good balance between the need to belong and the need to be distinct, thereby enhancing trust, cooperation, and feelings of security.

Moreover, nationalism helps ensure a positive self-concept by providing positive comparison outcomes in relation to other countries. The resulting positive distinctiveness of the one's own country serves people's striving for positively valued identities and, thereby, reduces uncertainty and buffers self-esteem.

Consequences of Patriotism and Nationalism

On a normative level, lay people, but also scholars in social psychology, come to different conclusions as to whether patriotism should be seen as a vice or a virtue. Whereas, for example, the former German president Johannes Rau was careful to emphasize that he was happy rather than proud to be a German, in the United States, there has been probably not a single presidential candidate who did not stress being proud to be an American.

In light of the above-mentioned multiple functions that patriotism fulfills for individuals and groups, one can argue that patriotism is quite healthy and positive. It relates to feelings of security, trust, and solidarity with one's fellow group members as well as commitment to one's group, and by satisfying the fundamental need to belong, it can exert positive effects on well-being and health. Yet the picture changes when one focuses on the implications for intergroup relations. As will be argued further, patriotism can easily translate into nationalism and derogation of national outgroups.

Nationalism is much more consensually considered a negative and undesirable phenomenon that may sometimes even lead to dehumanization of outgroups and international conflict. It correlates with negative attitudes toward outgroups and support for the use of military force for dominative purposes. Yet nationalism may also be seen as positive under certain conditions, such as when a country is illegitimately oppressed by another country and strives for liberation. Comparing one's own country with other countries and questioning the legitimacy of status and power differentials is necessary to motivate collective action and social change.

For example, beliefs about being as good as or even better than the so-called developed countries can help people from poor states in Africa to claim more voice and rights on the international stage. It is therefore important not to confuse scientific and normative aspects of patriotism and nationalism and instead take into account moderators that lead to different (positive and negative) consequences of both constructs.

Conceptualizing patriotism as identification with a country and nationalism as a potential consequence of national identification raises the questions of how closely and in which way the two constructs are correlated and, especially, how far high degrees of patriotism straightforwardly translate into nationalism and derogation of national outgroups. More generally stated, this question refers to the conditions under which ingroup love turns into outgroup hate. Clearly, such an interrelation is not a firm

given but rather contingent on characteristics of the context and the groups involved and on the processes leading to the conclusion that their own group is positively distinct from others. Therefore, it is not surprising that studies have revealed, on average, only moderate correlations between patriotism and nationalism.

As said before, nationalism implies an intergroup comparison between one's own country and other countries, whereby the former is typically seen as superior to the latter. However, such superiority can be obtained in two ways: by an above-average positive view of one's own country or by an explicitly negative evaluation of other national groups. The latter case is more probable when the national identity is insecure rather than secure, when there is intergroup competition for power or resources, and/or when the groups involved are, as clearly applies for national groups, political entities. In that case, especially in hierarchically organized social systems, the risk is high that political leaders will fuel distrust and hostility against outgroups.

Moreover, pride in one's own country need not necessarily be based on intergroup comparisons. Research has shown that the link between attachment to one's own country and negative evaluations of other countries depends on whether people focus on intergroup comparisons or on temporal comparisons at the intragroup level. For example, thinking of how one's own country has developed economically or politically during the past 10 years can enhance national pride without simultaneously fueling negative international attitudes. If, however, the focus is on how one's own country developed in comparison with other countries, feelings of pride imply that other countries are seen as inferior.

Threats to one's own country's safety, welfare, and positive regard are powerful contextual conditions that can affect both patriotism and nationalism. Such threats can be symbolic (affecting personal values or worldviews), materialistic (e.g., competition for limited tangible resources), or physical (such as in wartime or in the context of terrorist attacks). The tragic terrorist attacks on September 11, 2001, provided a very strong example for the impact of being reminded of one's own and one's fellow country members' mortality: U.S. citizens' feelings of belonging, commitment, and loyalty to the nation strongly increased, as did the relevance of national symbols (e.g., the U.S. flag).

Yet even under threatening conditions such as in the aftermath of September 11, 2001, the link between attachment and loyalty to the own national group and intolerance toward other groups need not necessarily be strong. It rather depends on how the country as an entity is defined: If it is conceptualized as having a strong common "essence," obtained from a small set of shared and well-defined norms and common characteristics of its members, patriotism and nationalism tend to go together. If, however, the country is defined by the need to address common problems and objectives requiring cooperation and coordination, being loyal toward one's own country need not translate into resenting those who are different.

In a similar vein, societies characterized by increasing numbers of immigrants and an increasing degree of cultural diversity differ in the extent to which they perceive diversity as a valuable and constitutive element of their identity. Although in Canada or New Zealand, for example, cultural diversity is recognized as an important aspect of the country's identity, in other countries it is perceived as a threat to the clarity or stability of national identity. In these cases, high levels of patriotism can lead to within-nation differentiation and, possibly, discrimination against national minorities. The debate over how immigrants should acculturate often has, as a starting point, the proviso that some basic features of the host country (such as its language) need to be adopted. Some characteristics of immigrants and their culture are not tolerated by many host society members (e.g., Muslim women wearing headscarves at their workplace in modern western European countries).

National Identifications as Social Identity: What Is Unique?

In which ways does identification with one's country differ from other social identifications? In fact, the functions of patriotism and nationalism summarized earlier are to a large extent general and not specific to national groups. Both phenomena are in line with *social identity theory*, which assumes that people strive for a meaningful and positive self-concept, which they derive in part from their memberships in social groups. By taking pride in one's groups and by positively distinguishing them from other groups, one can ensure a positive self-concept.

Yet there are some unique characteristics of a country as compared with other social groups. First, a country is a very large social category, which implies that its meaning is much more determined by formalized norms (e.g., a constitution) and value systems than by the quality of intragroup interactions. Moreover, as alluded to in the beginning of this entry, nationality is a feature that becomes relevant quite often in people's lives: when traveling abroad, following the news about international economic and political alliances, or following international sports competitions. Hence, this social category is highly accessible; that is, people will often define themselves and others in terms of their national affiliation. In addition, national groups are quite impermeable: It is often difficult, or at least dependent on substantive administrative efforts, to become the citizen of another country.

Probably the most distinctive aspect of countries, however, is that they are political entities. As such, their meaning has a clear ideological loading, and their functioning can be strongly determined by political leaders, an element that can be especially strong in hierarchically structured societies. People typically have a need to define the meaning and the core features constitutive of their country. However, in times of globalization, multiculturalism, and rapid social changes, this is a difficult, controversial, and highly ideologically loaded issue.

Implications

Both patriotism and nationalism are phenomena with great societal relevance. Both are aspects of identification with one's country: Although patriotism is defined by the relation of the individual to his or her country, nationalism is comparative in nature and implies that one's own country is evaluated more favorably than other countries. Although researchers have tried to clearly distinguish healthy patriotism from dangerous nationalism, it would be an oversimplification to see the outcomes of patriotism as positive and those of nationalism as bad. Moreover, a strong link between patriotism and nationalism is not a firm given; these concepts can be distinguished phenomenologically and psychologically. Under certain circumstances, such as a physical or economic threat between countries, however, patriotism and nationalism go hand in hand, and the connection is often fueled by political leaders.

Of course, these social-psychological concepts can offer only some pieces for the multidisciplinary undertaking of understanding national and international problems such as terrorism, warfare, security politics, and international unions. Also, there is still much to learn about patriotism and nationalism. Among other questions, it would be interesting to systematically compare patriotism, nationalism, and their moderators across cultures and political systems and to monitor in longitudinal studies whether and how these two phenomena change in rapidly changing societies.

Sabine Otten and J. Christopher Cohrs

See also Collective Self; Discrimination; Essentialism; Identification and Commitment; Optimal Distinctiveness; Realistic Group Conflict Theory; Social Identity Theory; Xenophobia

Further Readings

Bar-Tal, D., & Staub, E. (Eds.). (1997). *Patriotism: In the lives of individuals and nations.* Chicago: Nelson-Hall.

Billig, M. (1995). *Banal nationalism.* London: Sage.

Blank, T., & Schmidt, P. (Eds.). (2003). National identity in Europe [Special issue]. *Political Psychology, 24*(2).

Brewer, M. B. (2001). Ingroup identification and intergroup conflict: When does ingroup love become outgroup hate? In R. D. Ashmore, L. Jussim, & D. Wilder (Eds.), *Social identity, intergroup conflict, and conflict resolution* (pp. 17–41). New York: Oxford University Press.

Druckman, D. (1994). Nationalism, patriotism, and group loyalty: A social psychological perspective. *Mershon International Studies Review, 38,* 43–68.

Esses, V. M., Dovidio, J. F., Semenya, A. H., & Jackson, L. M. (2005). Attitudes toward immigrants and immigration: The role of national and international identity. In D. Abrams, M. A. Hogg, & J. M. Marques (Eds.), *The social psychology of inclusion and exclusion* (pp. 317–337). New York: Psychology Press.

Kosterman, R., & Feshbach, S. (1989). Toward a measure of patriotic and nationalistic attitudes. *Political Psychology, 10,* 257–274.

Li, Q., & Brewer, M. B. (2004). What does it mean to be American? Patriotism, nationalism, and the American identity after 9/11. *Political Psychology, 25,* 727–739.

Mummendey, A., Klink, A., & Brown, R. (2001). Nationalism and patriotism: National identification and out-group rejection. *British Journal of Social Psychology, 40,* 159–172.

Schatz, R. T., & Lavine, H. (2007). Waving the flag: National symbolism, social identity, and political engagement. *Political Psychology, 28,* 329–355.

Sullivan, J. L., Fried, A., & Dietz, M. G. (1992). Patriotism, politics, and the presidential election of 1988. *American Journal of Political Science, 36,* 200–234.

NEED FOR BELONGING

The *need for belonging* refers to the motivation to feel connected to and accepted by other people. While this need can operate at the interpersonal level (interactions between two people), humans are also motivated to feel included in groups. For most people, satisfying the need to belong is not difficult. However, for those who fail to gain acceptance, the consequences can be quite negative.

Background and Psychological Bases

The need to belong has been viewed as a critical motivation since the early 1900s. For example, Sigmund Freud highlighted the important psychological benefits of contact between people in groups. A few years later, Abraham Maslow, in his famous hierarchy of human needs, argued that only two other basic needs have greater priority than the need to belong: physiological and security needs. In recent years, the need to belong has been incorporated in many psychological theories.

To the extent that the need to belong is innate, it should be manifested from a very early age. Research on John Bowlby's *attachment theory* provides evidence that infants experience a strong need to feel connected to their caregivers. This need is met in very young children who develop secure bonds with their caregivers. Such children have higher social competence (they are more socially adept) and fewer problems developing relationships with other people later on in life than do children who fail to develop secure bonds with their caregivers. These latter children often experience anxiety and lack of trust in their later social relationships. Thus, meeting the need to belong as an infant is important not only for a child's early survival but also for his or her later social development.

The need to belong probably functions below conscious awareness. However, there are also conscious processes that lead people to affiliate and collaborate with others. These include the desire to compare one's opinions, abilities, and emotional reactions to those of others and the motivation to achieve collective goals (e.g., winning a basketball game).

Research on the need to belong tends to focus on what happens when people feel that they do not belong to (are excluded from) important groups. Rejection produces a host of problems. In terms of physical health, exclusion from groups is associated with increased risk for heart attacks, reduced blood pressure regulation, and increased insomnia. In terms of psychological effects, feeling that one does not belong is associated with negative feelings about oneself, anxiety, and lowered self-esteem. People who fail to meet the need to belong over an extended time are at risk for depression and have a reduced life expectancy.

According to Mark Leary's *sociometer model*, self-esteem reflects one's perceived belongingness in important relationships and groups. High self-esteem signifies that a person is meeting this need, whereas low self-esteem signifies that he or she is failing to do so. Therefore, people with low self-esteem should be motivated to increase their level of belongingness. Research on the sociometer model has found that people do indeed seek to establish social bonds when their self-esteem has been lowered, supporting the idea that self-esteem is an internal index of one's success in meeting the need to belong.

Other theories propose different mechanisms underlying the need to belong. According to *uncertainty-identity theory*, people who feel uncertain about themselves, their future, or their place in the world are motivated to increase their identification with groups—suggesting that one's level of uncertainty is the basis of the desire to belong. According to *terror management theory*, the need to belong is stimulated by an existential fear of death. By identifying with groups, people obtain a sense of symbolic immortality. While these theories disagree about the psychological mechanism underlying the need to belong (self-esteem, uncertainty, fear of death), they all assume that people possess a social monitoring system that alerts them to their level of belongingness and initiates actions to increase this belongingness when it falls below a critical level.

Group Processes

In groups, people can coordinate their actions and cooperate to achieve goals that individuals acting alone cannot achieve. Groups also serve another important function: They provide people with a lens through which to understand the world. Stated differently, people construct and construe the world on the basis of the beliefs and values of their group. When people are excluded or made to feel that they do not belong to important groups, their ability to understand the world is reduced, which in turn produces anxiety and decreased self-confidence.

Failing to satisfy the need to belong can have a number of consequences for how people behave in groups. For example, research has shown that people who have been excluded from valued groups are more likely to derogate (put down, make fun of) those who are different from themselves, adopt ingroup stereotypes that make them feel like typical group members, and punish people who break group rules.

So far, we have focused on how people respond to being excluded. But it is also important to consider why this exclusion occurs in the first place. Normal group functioning hinges on the willingness of members to follow the norms (rules for behavior) of the group. When members do not follow these norms, the entire group is likely to suffer. Therefore, groups develop methods to motivate their members to follow norms. One powerful method for motivating normative behavior is the use (or threat) of exclusion, which capitalizes on members' need to belong to the group.

In all groups, exclusion of one sort or another is used to punish those who deviate from established rules for proper behavior. An example is prison sentences for those found guilty of committing crimes. Prison is a tool to socially isolate people who violate important norms. Even within prison, exclusion can be used in a punitive way. One of the worst things that can happen to a prisoner is to be placed in the "hole"—put in social isolation. Even on playgrounds, children use social exclusion as a punishment. For example, in the game of dodge ball, children who are slow or uncoordinated are hit with the ball and banished from the group activity until the game is over. Another familiar example involves being chosen last for an athletic team. Being chosen last signifies that one is not really wanted in the group. Those so designated feel excluded and suffer reduced self-esteem as a result.

The need to belong is an important human motive, which has important implications for group processes. This motive is likely to have evolutionary roots, although personal self-interest plays an important role as well—people are motivated to belong to groups in order to achieve individual goals. Groups need people to follow norms and use exclusion to punish members who fail to do so.

Zachary P. Hohman and Jason E. Rivera

See also Attachment Theory; Conformity; Deviance; Identification and Commitment; Inclusion/Exclusion; Ostracism; Social Comparison Theory; Sociometer Model; Uncertainty-Identity Theory

Further Readings

Abrams, D., Hogg, M. A., & Marques, J. M. (Eds.). (2005). *The social psychology of inclusion and exclusion.* New York: Psychology Press.

Baumeister, R. F., & Leary, M. R. (1995). The need to belong: Desire for interpersonal attachment as a fundamental human motivation. *Psychological Bulletin, 117,* 497–529.

Bowlby, J. (1969). *Attachment and loss: Attachment.* Harmondsworth, UK: Penguin.

Hogg, M. A. (2007). Uncertainty-identity theory. In M. P. Zanna (Ed.), *Advances in experimental social psychology* (Vol. 39, pp. 69–126). San Diego, CA: Academic Press.

Leary, M. R., & Baumeister, R. F. (2000). The nature and function of self-esteem: Sociometer theory. In M. P. Zanna (Ed.), *Advances in experimental social psychology* (Vol. 32, pp. 1–62). San Diego, CA: Academic Press.

Levine, J. M., & Kerr, N. L. (2007). Inclusion and exclusion: Implications for group processes. In A. W. Kruglanski & T. E. Higgins (Eds.), *Social psychology: Handbook of basic principles* (2nd ed., pp. 759–784). New York: Guilford Press.

Williams, K. D., Forgas, J. P., & Hippel, W. V. (Eds.). (2005). *The social outcast: Ostracism, social exclusion, and bullying.* New York: Psychology Press.

NEED FOR CLOSURE

Why do some people seem to thrive on uncertainty and ambiguity whereas other people seem to jump to conclusions and seek quick answers? The answer to this question may lie in people's need for closure. *Need for closure* (also known as *need for cognitive closure*) refers to an individual's desire to have any answer on a given topic rather than to have confusion and ambiguity. This can be contrasted with *need for specific closure*, which refers to an individual's desire to have a particular answer on a given topic.

Need for closure has been found to influence many aspects of our behavior, from information processing to group behavior, and it has been studied in many diverse fields, including political attitudes, organizational change, judgments in criminal investigations, susceptibility to delusions, attitude change, intergroup behavior, and consumer behavior.

History and Background

The notion that individuals may differ in their motivations toward gaining and using knowledge has been of interest to theorists in personality and social psychology for many years. Early theorists emphasized psychodynamic aspects, linking openness to new experiences to the successful completion of early stages of development or linking closed-mindedness to the prejudiced personality. In recent years, however, theorists such as Arie Kruglanski, the social psychologist most closely associated with research in this area, have emphasized the motivational aspects of need for closure and the myriad ways in which need for closure influences human behavior.

Need for closure is seen as an individual difference that varies across individuals and across situations. Individual differences in need for closure may emerge because of cultural values and norms, such as in societies where closure is valued highly, or because of family dynamics and socialization processes. However, situational factors that influence the perceived benefits of closure, such as freeing the individual from further information processing, or the perceived costs of closure, such as concern about making the incorrect decision, will influence need for closure. For example, need for closure may be heightened in circumstances in which action or quick decisions are required, such as when group members must work together to complete a task within a deadline or when an individual is suffering from mental fatigue or is engaged in a particularly dull task.

Two tendencies are seen to underpin need for closure: a tendency toward urgency in judgments and decision making, or *seizing*, and a tendency toward permanency in judgments and decision making, or *freezing*. Need for closure may express itself in certain ways, such as a desire for definite order and structure, feeling uncomfortable with ambiguity, a desire for urgency in judgment and decision making, a desire for stable and predictable information, and an unwillingness to have one's knowledge challenged or confronted.

Individuals with a high need for closure may be more likely to jump to conclusions because they seek quick closure by relying on early cues and the first answer available. In addition, a person high in need for closure may exhibit rigidity of thought and a reluctance to consider alternative views. Indeed, such individuals may react negatively to having their sense of closure or order threatened by other people or other opinions. In contrast, individuals with a low need for closure (or a high need to avoid closure) may enjoy the freedom associated with ambiguity and uncertainty, express more flexibility in their ideas, and engage in more creative acts. However, a person with a low need for closure may prefer to suspend judgment on issues and may be reluctant to commit to definite opinion or judgment.

Studying Need for Closure

Need for closure is mainly considered to be an individual difference in disposition but one that can be strengthened or weakened by situational factors. Thus, it is possible to study need for closure by assessing dispositional need for closure or by using well-established experimental manipulations of situational need for closure. Dispositional need for closure is assessed with the Need for Closure Scale (NFCS), developed by Donna Webster and Arie Kruglanski. The NFCS is a multi-item scale that assesses five dimensions considered to underlie need for closure: preference for order, preference for predictability, decisiveness, discomfort with ambiguity, and closed-mindedness. In addition, a number of situational factors are known to strengthen need for closure, such as time pressure, environmental noise, mental fatigue, a dull task, or the request for a judgment. Research across a number of domains has revealed that either measuring differences or manipulating differences in need for closure leads to identical effects.

Areas of Research

Need for closure has a broad influence on the way knowledge is constructed and used and, as a result, influences a wide range of intrapersonal, interpersonal, and group processes.

Information Processing

It has been argued that individuals with a high need for closure have a tendency to seize and freeze on early information. As a result, need for closure is associated with a narrow information search and decreased information processing prior to judgment. In addition, individuals with a high need for closure may generate fewer alternative hypotheses to a problem before reaching a decision. However, such individuals may actually be quicker to attain high levels of confidence in their judgments. Need for closure is associated with a tendency to use cognitive shortcuts to find solutions and a reliance on early or preexisting cues, such as stereotypes, to make judgments. These information processing biases express themselves in phenomena such as primacy effects in impression formation (impressions are more heavily influenced by initial information), anchoring effects in judgments (once made, judgments seem to be anchored and are slow and difficult to change), and correspondence biases (the tendency to map people's behavior onto underlying personality dispositions).

Interpersonal Behavior

Need for closure also influences a number of interpersonal behaviors. For example, people with a high need for closure may display lower levels of *perspective taking* and *empathic concern* for interaction partners. In addition, people with a high need for closure may use more abstract concepts in communication, which can create greater interpersonal distance between communicators and decrease liking for one another. Finally, research on negotiation behavior has found that people with a high need for closure make smaller concessions, engage in less systematic processing, and base their negotiation behavior on stereotypes about their opponents.

Political Attitudes

One of the areas in which the role of need for closure has been studied extensively is the domain of political attitudes. Need for closure has been found to be associated with conservative ideologies, the endorsement of right-wing political attitudes, and membership in right-wing organizations. Indeed, in an extensive review of the literature, John Jost and his colleagues argued that conservative political ideologies—those that support a social order that is hierarchical, stable, and predictable—are more likely to satisfy a psychological need to avoid uncertainty and ambiguity. However, it should be noted that the desire for permanent and stable information suggests that need for closure should be associated with a preference to maintain the status quo, regardless of whether it is right wing or left wing. Research by Agnieszka Golec has found that the way in which high need for closure is expressed does depend on the political and cultural context and what is classified as the traditional position and what is classified as the modern position.

Group Behavior

Individuals with a high need for closure desire firm and definite knowledge about social reality. Groups offer a shared social reality, which, for individuals high in need for closure, should prompt engagement in a range of intragroup and intergroup behaviors. Individuals high in need for closure are more likely to desire consensus and opinion uniformity within a group and to react negatively to people who undermine the shared social reality of the group by deviating in their opinions or by violating group norms. A high need for closure may also foster positive liking for the group and hostility toward other groups because the group is the source of firm knowledge about social reality. Moreover, individuals high in need for closure show a preference for autocratic and hierarchical group processes and strong leaders because such processes provide structure and predictability. Finally, people high in need for closure may show a greater tendency to be task oriented and cooperative in problem-solving groups in order to achieve group goals.

Joanne R. Smith

See also Conservatism; Dogmatism; Uncertainty-Identity Theory

Further Readings

Golec de Zavala, A., & Van Bergh, A. (2007). Need for cognitive closure and conservative political beliefs: Differential mediation by personal worldviews. *Political Psychology, 28,* 587–608.

Jost, J. T., Glaser, J., Kruglanski, A. W., & Sulloway, F. J. (2003). Political conservatism as motivated social cognition. *Psychological Bulletin, 129,* 339–375.

Kruglanski, A. W., Pierro, A., Mannetti, L., & De Grada, E. (2006). Groups as epistemic providers: Need for closure and the unfolding of group-centrism. *Psychological Review, 113,* 84–100.

Kruglanski, A. W., & Webster, D. M. (1996). Motivated closing of the mind: "Seizing" and "freezing." *Psychological Review, 103,* 263–283.

Roets, A., & Van Hiel, A. (2007). Separating ability from need: Clarifying the dimensional structure of the Need for Closure Scale. *Personality and Social Psychology Bulletin, 33,* 266–280.

NEED FOR POWER

Individuals differ from one another in the extent to which they are motivated to control the environment and influence others. Some individuals actively seek opportunities to influence everyday situations, events, and people, whereas other individuals are more prone to be affected by circumstances and others. This personality tendency is known as *need for power* or *dominance*. It has implications for the ways individuals process information, how they perceive others, the goals they pursue, and ultimately for the ways society is organized in terms of distribution of resources.

The motivation to attain power reflects a desire to influence others and have an impact over the environment. Individuals who seek power network more, become more visible, define group agendas, and build alliances. They often attain leadership positions and are able to create a team spirit. Longitudinal research that assessed the future careers of university students found that those students who were high in need for power chose professions in which they could exert influence over others, such as teaching, psychology, clergy, business, management, and journalism. The desire for power in some individuals is an important ingredient in groups and in society because it acts as the glue that coordinates interindividual behavior and facilitates group action. This entry looks at how dominance is conveyed and measured, then examines how it is expressed in social interactions.

Dominance is conveyed by verbal and nonverbal cues. The nonverbal behavior of dominant individuals displays comfort and relaxation. These individuals make more use of the space that surrounds them, including reducing the physical distance to others. When interacting with others, they speak more, are louder, interrupt others more, use fewer hesitations, and have a more varied speech code. They also touch others more. In dyadic interactions, dominant individuals exhibit equal amounts of looking the interaction partner in the eyes while listening and looking while speaking. Submissive individuals, in contrast, look more while listening than while speaking. These individuals assume more constricted body positions and expressions of tension or fear.

Dominance is usually assessed through self-report measures in which individuals are asked to estimate, using rating scales, how much they possess of several traits, such as being forceful or domineering. However, the power motive can be measured in more subtle ways. One implicit measure of power motivation uses projective tests that display pictures of interpersonal scenes. Participants are asked to describe the scenes. Their descriptions are then content analyzed regarding the extent to which they reflect dynamics linked to prestige, control, or influence.

Gender differences in dominance are complex. Studies that used implicit measures of need for power (i.e., projective tests) did not find significant differences between men and women. For both gender groups, need for power was associated with behavioral indicators of a desire for prestige and getting formal social power in society. Nevertheless, differences were found in the ways dominant men and women behaved. Dominant men displayed more incidences of negative impulsive behavior such as drinking, aggression, gambling, or sexual exploitation, compared with their female counterparts. In addition, studies examining nonverbal behavior found more gestures of dominance in men than in women. For example, in dyadic interactions, men usually exhibit the gaze pattern that is typical for dominant individuals, whereas women display the subordinate gaze pattern.

These differences in overt dominance between men and women are substantiated by differences in levels of testosterone, a steroid hormone responsible for physical masculine attributes and for aggressive behavior in nonhuman animals. Men produce significantly higher levels of testosterone than women do. Furthermore, men who have high levels of baseline (rest level) testosterone exhibit more dominant behavior, especially involving aggression, than other men do.

Although dominance is a relatively stable attribute of the person, research shows that there is context-specific variability in the behavioral expression of dominance. When people interact with one another, one person's level of dominance is affected by the level of dominance of the other person. If one person acts in submissive ways, the other person tends to act in dominant ways, and vice versa. This tendency for complementarity in dominance occurs both on a moment-to-moment basis, without the person's awareness, and in more structured, long-term relationships. In other words, individuals adapt their level of dominance to that of their interaction partners; and they also actively seek to establish relationships with those who are complementary to them in need for power. An individual who has a high motivation to attain power tends to surround himself or herself with others who are more submissive and can validate his or her dominant position.

The extent to which a person is dominant affects how he or she makes judgments and decisions. Compared with nondominant individuals, dominant individuals rely more on their gut feelings and the subjective experiences that arise while thinking. For example, when it is easy to generate arguments in favor of a topic (e.g., when asked to generate a few arguments regarding introducing biometric ID cards), dominant individuals, but not subordinate individuals, will express a more positive attitude toward the topic compared with when it is difficult to generate arguments in favor of the topic (e.g., when asked to generate many arguments). Merely manipulating the number of arguments that individuals are asked to generate affects more the attitudes of dominant than of subordinate individuals.

Individuals with a high need for power tend to respond in similar ways to individuals who are given an actual power position. In both cases, they enjoy a sense of entitlement, are prone to use others for their own ends, have difficulty in taking the perspective of others, and pay little attention to others' needs. Need for power also affects the ways individuals perceive others and is often linked with a tendency to rely on stereotypes rather than on individuating attributes of other people.

However, dominance can be associated with social responsibility, as shown by the behavior of many world leaders. The desire to influence others may serve the attainment of personal goals, ideals, and advantages for the self, or it may serve the attainment of group goals and ideologies that are deemed relevant by the individual. For example, high need for power is frequently found in religious leaders and political or social activists. Whether the behavior of dominant individuals is guided by social responsibility or by the desire to attain selfish ends depends, to a great extent, on the values of the individual. This occurs because dominant individuals respond in line with activated constructs, including values and worldviews. Nevertheless, when survival tendencies are activated, dominance creates the conditions for a fiery pursuit of self-serving goals.

Finally, asymmetries in dominance impact society at large. Legitimized social positions, such as occupational positions, differ in the extent to which they have an impact on others. Compared with low-power positions, high-power positions have a greater impact on how economic and social resources are distributed, as well as the development of social norms and ideologies. Individuals who are motivated to achieve power tend to occupy higher-power positions in the social structure and thereby have more influence on groups and society at large.

The tendency for powerful positions to be occupied by dominant individuals reinforces the status quo and contributes to maintaining social inequality. This occurs because dominant individuals tend to focus on their needs and the needs of their groups. Furthermore, dominance is linked to an asymmetric participation of individuals in the development of social norms and the distribution of resources. As such, dominance is a central mechanism for maintaining social inequality.

Ana Guinote

See also Dominance Hierarchies; Gender and Behavior; Leadership; Power

Further Readings

Jackson, D. N. (1967). *Personality research from a manual.* New York: Research Psychologists Press.

Winter, D. G. (1973). *The power motive.* New York: Free Press.

NEGOTIATION AND BARGAINING

Negotiation and *bargaining* refer to a communication process between two or more parties to reach agreement or strike a bargain. People frequently negotiate, and many of these negotiations can be solved in a mutually beneficial, integrative way. Unfortunately, individual negotiators often forgo such integrative agreements because they fail to be truly concerned about both their own and their counterpart's needs and interests and because they are bounded in their rationality. The negotiation context, however, drives concern for both self and other and motivates negotiators to deliberately process information in a systematic way. Thus, when time pressure is mild, when power differences are weak or nonexistent, when negotiators are accountable, and when cooperative incentives are being emphasized, mutually beneficial, integrative agreements are quite likely to emerge. This entry begins with some general parameters and descriptions of negotiation and then discusses the main theories that have been developed in this area.

What Is Negotiation?

In a negotiation, parties may be individuals, as in the bargaining between a buyer and a seller of a Volvo 240 DL Estate, or between a boss and an employee about training and development opportunities or career goals and expectations. Alternatively, parties may be groups of people, as in the negotiation between prison guards and inmates about certain privileges or between the boards of two large companies about the terms of a merger.

When groups become larger or when issues require specific expertise, representatives may be engaged to do the negotiation. Examples of such representative negotiation include labor negotiations between union representatives and representatives from management and peace negotiations between representatives from the Israeli government and the Palestinian authorities.

The above examples should not be taken as if negotiation is confined to rather formal and infrequent encounters in business and diplomacy. Quite to the contrary, and although often not recognized as such, negotiation is a basic aspect of most interpersonal and intergroup encounters. When settling in for a long air trip, we negotiate with our neighboring passenger about who gets what part of the shared armrest. We do not speak to each other about who gets what, but through nonverbal (and gentle) pushing and withdrawing, we coordinate into a mutually comfortably position. Likewise, driving down a narrow road may lead us to negotiate with an upcoming driver about who goes first and in what way. But we do not get out of our cars to talk and discuss. We remain behind the steering wheel and limit ourselves to shaking our heads, blinking our eyes, pointing our fingers, and if all this really doesn't work, we finally but reluctantly may use the horn and headlights.

Neither should the above examples be taken as suggesting that negotiation is about one single issue, such as the price of the Volvo, peace between Israel and the Palestine Liberation Organization, or what part of the armrest you get during the flight from Reykjavik to Johannesburg. Far more often, negotiations involve several issues. In the case of the Volvo, one may negotiate the price of the car but also talk about delivery, tune-up cost, and warranty. Labor negotiations usually include discussions about salary increases, vacation, pension plans, and training and development. Israel and the Palestine Liberation Organization talk about Jerusalem, the settlements, the borders, Gaza, and issues concerning trade and security. And even in the case of the armrest negotiation, we may also deal with leg space and whether we are going to have long conversations or instead do some undisturbed reading. In short, negotiations often are about multiple issues, and in case they are not, parties can bring new issues to the table or break up issues into several smaller ones.

Negotiating about several issues at the same time may have interesting advantages. Mary Parker Follett, a pioneering scholar of negotiation, tells the story of two sisters quarreling over an orange. After a while, they decide to split the orange into two equal parts. One sister squeezes her part, throws away the peel, and drinks the juice. The other squeezes hers, throws away the juice, and processes the peel to flavor a cake she is baking. Clearly, had these sisters talked about the juice and the peel, they could have reached a more mutually beneficial agreement (the entire peel to the one sister and all the juice to the other) than they reached by quarreling over one single issue—the orange.

Or consider Roger Fisher and William Ury, founding fathers of the Harvard Project on Negotiation, who tell the story of the Camp David negotiations between Israel and Egypt in 1977. Since the Yom Kippur War in 1973, Israel had occupied the Sinai Desert, which Egypt wanted back. Instead of dividing the desert in more or less equal parts, it was decided that Egypt would get back the desert so that it could satisfy its historical claims and restore its reputation in the Arab world. But, critically, Egypt would keep the desert demilitarized so that Israel's need for safety and security was satisfied. Put differently, both parties achieved a much better deal by talking about historical claims and reputation as well as about the need for security and safety rather than focusing on the single surface issue of who gets what part of the Sinai Desert.

Integrative Agreements

Agreements that take advantage of the fact that several issues are involved that are not all equally important to all parties are called *integrative agreements*. In integrative agreements, parties trade unilaterally important issues (important to one party, unimportant to the other—e.g., the peel, reputation among Arab neighbors) for bilaterally important issues (important to both parties—e.g., juice, security). Reaching integrative agreements—as opposed to simple split-the-difference compromises or victory-to-one settlements—has a number of critically important consequences.

First, integrative agreements tend to be relatively stable and to reduce the likelihood of renewed conflict between the parties. Second, integrative agreements generate positive feelings of happiness, satisfaction, and pride and instill a sense of self-efficacy, allowing parties to approach new conflicts and negotiation in a more coolheaded and optimistic manner. Third, integrative agreements are implemented better—parties are more committed to their part of the bargain and more motivated to do the things they promised to.

Fourth, integrative agreements create more value to both parties than does any other type of agreement and thereby foster economic prosperity and wealth. Fifth, and last, integrative agreements foster mutual understanding, trust, and respect and create a sense of collective success. Thus, integrative agreements create stability, harmony, and economic prosperity; failure to reach (integrative) agreements creates frustration, conflict, distrust, and weakened social ties and hurts economic progress.

The Nash Equilibrium

Partly because reaching integrative agreements is vital to societal functioning, many scholars in psychology, economics, and political sciences have tried to understand when and why negotiators do or do not achieve integrative agreements. Much of this work traces back to the early 1950s, when John Nash, as a postdoctoral fellow at the Princeton Institute for Advanced Studies, published an article in which he proposed that many bargaining problems are best solved when individual parties follow their self-interest in a strict rational manner: They would choose those behaviors that maximized their personal outcomes and avoid those behaviors that would not do so. This would result in the achievement of a so-called *Nash equilibrium*, that is, a solution in which neither party could do better without the opposing party's doing worse. Most of the time, integrative agreements are Nash equilibria, and according to Nash's analysis, rational pursuit of self-interest leads parties to uncover these optimal and mutually beneficial agreements.

Nash provided a mathematical analysis based on assumptions about human behavior. Soon after its publication, Sidney Siegel and Lawrence Fouraker, Harold Kelley, and Dean Pruitt set out to experimentally test his theory. These authors created two-person negotiation tasks in which each party was shown a chart depicting several issues (e.g., the price of the car, delivery time, method of payment) and for each issue, several levels of agreement (e.g., for price, 5,000, 4,500, 3,000, etc.; for delivery time, 1 week, 2 weeks, 3 weeks, etc.; for method of payment, cash, credit card, bank transfer, etc.). Each party was also shown the payoff he or she would receive for a particular agreement. Thus, for price, the seller would see that 5,000 yielded greater payoff (e.g.,

100 points) than 4,000 (e.g., 75 points), and the buyer would see that 5,000 yielded lower payoff (e.g., 0 points) than 4,000 (e.g., 25 points).

Furthermore, the task was set up so that what was valuable to one party was less valuable to the other, and vice versa. For example, whereas the buyer could earn between 0 and 100 on price, the seller would earn only between 0 and 50, and on delivery the buyer could earn only between 0 and 50 whereas the seller could earn between 0 and 100. Thus, by trading the less important issue for the more important one, buyer and seller were able to earn more personally and collectively (100 to each = 200 together) than by splitting the difference on both issues (25 + 50 to each = 150 together).

Put differently, these authors created a task with integrative potential, allowing parties to integrate interests and achieve mutually beneficial agreements. But because each side was shown only his or her own payoffs and not those of the counterpart, negotiators could not immediately see the optimal, integrative outcome; through negotiation, exchange of information, and communication, they had to uncover this possibility. Nevertheless, according to Nash, rational, self-interested negotiators should be able to reach this optimally integrative agreement.

The integrative negotiation task has been used in literally hundreds of studies, and time and time again, results have shown that individuals have great difficulty achieving integrative agreements. This could mean that Nash was wrong and that rationally self-interested individuals do not achieve Nash equilibrium. Alternatively, his theory may have been correct, but the underlying assumptions were not. Indeed, most of the negotiation literature has been devoted to understanding the psychological mechanisms behind (not) achieving integrative agreements. A large part of this work is predominantly concerned with external conditions, such as time pressure and power differentials that motivate individuals toward certain behavioral strategies. These works thus question whether individuals are always and only motivated by self-interest or perhaps also, or even more, by other concerns, such as fairness, reputation, concern for the other and the relationship, and so on.

Another large part of the literature is predominantly concerned with the cognitive processes that prohibit or facilitate the discovery of mutually beneficial, integrative agreements. The cognitive approach thus questions whether humans are rational or, instead, bounded in their rationality. The cognitive approach focuses more on such issues as reasoning errors and reliance on more or less inaccurate rules of thumb, how people see the negotiation and the opponent, and so on. The remainder of this chapter presents some of the key findings within each of these approaches.

Structural-Motivational Approaches

The structural-motivational approach heavily relies on the notion that negotiators simultaneously face a *cooperative incentive* to reach agreement with their counterpart (i.e., agreement is better than no agreement) and a *competitive incentive* to do well personally. Whereas the cooperative incentives motivate negotiators to make and reciprocate concessions, to lower their demands, and to openly and accurately exchange information, the competitive incentives motivate them to withhold and retract concessions, to remain tough in their demands, and to deceive and mislead their counterpart. By implication, if cooperative incentives become relatively more important and available than competitive incentives, negotiators will engage in more cooperative behavior and are less likely to reach a mutually hurting stalemate.

Cooperative incentives gain or lose prominence relative to competitive incentives because of aspects of the negotiation setting. *Power and bargaining strength* are one good example. When a negotiator receives an interesting offer from an outsider, this circumstance may fuel the competitive incentive to increase personal outcomes from the negotiation. Thus, when during the negotiation about the price of the Volvo 240 your neighbor sends you a text message offering to pay 4,500, it is unlikely that you will settle with your current negotiation partner for anything less than 4,500. Or when an employee knows the director controls not only the budget for training and development but also whether annual bonuses are being paid, the employee may be more willing to give in and offer to follow work-relevant courses during holiday season. Put differently, when their bargaining strength and power increase, negotiators generally become reluctant to make and reciprocate concessions, and when one's power and bargaining strength are less than that of one's counterpart, one's motivation to cooperate and concede increases.

Another good example of a factor influencing the balance between cooperative and competitive incentives is *time pressure*. Time pressure may emerge because the goods (e.g., fish or fruits) that are being negotiated may deteriorate or because an external or self-imposed deadline is approaching (e.g., the market closes at 5 p.m.; the divorce papers are being filed and take effect soon). Time pressure focuses parties on agreement and the consequences of failing to avoid impasse; it shifts the focus to the cooperative aspect of the negotiation and, in general, fosters concession making and cooperative exchange.

It was noted earlier that negotiators often operate on behalf of some constituents. In such representative negotiation, negotiators need to take into consideration not only their own and their counterpart's needs and desires but those of these constituents as well. Such accountability to constituents is another prominent factor influencing the focus on cooperative rather than competitive incentives in the negotiation. Research has shown, for example, that negotiators tend to comply with their constituents' desires—when the constituents want a tough game, representatives negotiate more competitively than when their constituents want an agreement no matter what. It is interesting that there is quite some evidence that when constituent goals and desires are unknown or unclear, negotiators tend to assume they should compete rather than cooperate. The mere fact that an individual represents one or more others generally increases toughness and competitive behavior.

Dual Concern Theory

These factors—bargaining strength, time pressure, and accountability to constituents—all affect the extent to which negotiators care for their own outcomes, and these factors lead negotiators to resist making concessions. Other variables have been shown to influence the extent to which negotiators care for the outcomes of their counterpart. For example, when negotiators are friends, they may be particularly concerned about the outcomes their counterpart gets, so as not to jeopardize their friendship. Or when negotiators expect to work with the counterpart in the future, they are more motivated to search for an agreement that satisfies their counterpart. And to give one final example, when some external party, such as a manager of one's constituent, refers to one's counterpart as *partner*, negotiators are more likely to be concerned about the other's needs and interests than when the counterpart is systematically referred to as *opponent*.

Dual concern theory, developed by Dean Pruitt and Jeffrey Rubin, summarizes these tendencies among negotiators to be concerned with their own outcomes and, independently, to be concerned with their partner's outcomes. When concern for one's own outcomes is high (e.g., there is high bargaining strength) and concern for the other's outcomes is low (e.g., one does not expect to work together in the future), negotiators are expected to engage in tough, competitive behavior aimed at dominating the partner. They are reluctant to make concessions and fail to listen to the other's demands and needs. When concern for one's own outcomes is low (e.g., there is high time pressure) and concern for the other's outcomes is high (e.g., the other is considered a friend), negotiators are expected to engage in conciliatory, cooperative behavior aimed at submitting to the partner. They are willing to make (unilateral) concessions and carefully listen to the other's demands and needs. When parties engage in mutual forcing—when they each have high concern for their own outcomes and low concern for their partner's—the negotiation is likely to end in a mutually hurting stalemate, and integrative agreements are unlikely. Likewise, when parties engage in mutual yielding—when they each have a low concern for their own outcomes and high concern for the partner's—the negotiation is likely to end in a quick, middle-of-the-road compromise. Again, integrative agreements are unlikely. In fact, the theory predicts that integrative agreements come about when the parties each have a high concern for both their own and the other's outcomes. On one hand, they resist making concessions because doing so hurts personal interests. On the other hand, they want to make concessions because doing so helps the other's interests. This dilemma leads negotiators to search for creative solutions that integrate both their own and each other's interests optimally.

Dual concern theory has received strong support in numerous studies. It thus appears that a pure and rational focus on self-interest does not lead to integrative agreements. Instead, to achieve integrative agreements, negotiators need to combine a concern for their own interests with a concern for those of their partner. Any structural factor that promotes a negotiator's concern for his or her own outcomes will thus promote toughness when the negotiator has a low concern for the other's outcomes, but it will promote a problem-solving approach toward integrative agreements when the negotiator has high concern for the other's outcomes.

Bounded Rationality and the Cognitive Underpinnings of Negotiation

Dual concern theory mainly concerns the role of selfishness and prosocial motivation and is rather silent on the cognitive underpinnings of integrative negotiation. But recall that in Nash's theorizing, it was assumed that negotiators are fully rational and able to see and process all available information optimally. This assumption is problematic, and research has shown time and time again that individual negotiators cannot process all relevant information—they are bounded in their rationality because their cognitive ability is limited and because not all relevant information is or can be made available.

Also, negotiators may try to mislead and deceive each other, and thus some of the available information is deliberately inaccurate and cannot be trusted. To deal with the cognitively taxing task, negotiators have been shown to rely on cognitive heuristics—shortcuts that help them make fast and satisfactory judgments and decisions. Thus, negotiators may infer their counterpart's intentions on the basis of stereotypic information—if the other is sharply dressed as a businessperson, one may be more likely to infer shrewdness and toughness than if the other is wearing jeans and a college sweatshirt.

Max Bazerman and Maggie Neale developed the *behavioral decision approach*, which encompasses a great variety of these cognitive shortcuts and how they affect the achievement of integrative agreements. One prominent example is the so-called *fixed-pie assumption*—at the outset, negotiators tend to assume that what is important to them (e.g., juice) is equally important to the other party, and what is irrelevant to them (e.g., peel) is equally irrelevant to the other. Given such a fixed-pie assumption, it makes no sense searching for integrative agreements; all we need to do is claim value and try to get the biggest share of the pie (or orange). And this is indeed what has been found many times: A large majority of negotiators, novices and experts alike, tend to begin with a fixed-pie assumption, and if they do, they search for victory or, when fairness concerns prevail, 50–50 compromises. Only when negotiators realize during negotiation that their fixed-pie assumption is erroneous do they start searching for integrative agreements.

Recent studies have invoked the notion that negotiators may switch between more shallow and automatic information processing—in which case they rely heavily on cognitive heuristics—and more deliberate and systematic information processing. Under systematic information processing, the influence of cognitive heuristics is attenuated, and negotiators are more likely to reach integrative agreements. This work also shows that negotiators engage in more systematic information processing when they have low rather than high power, when time pressures are mild rather than intense, or when they are held accountable. Put differently, there are quite a number of structural, context-related variables that can lead negotiators away from their basic tendency to rely on cognitive heuristics that inhibit mutually beneficial, integrative agreements.

Carsten K. W. De Dreu

See also Coalitions; Cooperation and Competition; Distributive Justice; Group Problem Solving and Decision Making; Prisoner's Dilemma; Team Negotiation

Further Readings

De Dreu, C. K. W., Beersma, B., Steinel, W., & Van Kleef, G. A. (2007). The psychology of negotiation: Principles and basic processes. In A. W. Kruglanski & E. T. Higgins (Eds.), *Handbook of basic principles in social psychology* (2nd ed., pp. 608–629). New York: Guilford Press.

Lewicki, R. J., Saunders, D. M., Minton, J. W., & Barry, B. (2005). *Negotiation.* New York: McGraw-Hill.

Thompson, L. L., & Brett, J. M. (Eds.). (2006). *The social psychology of negotiation.* New York: Psychology Press.

NORMATIVE INFLUENCE

Normative influence is one of the two main ways in which people influence one another in group interaction. It is a form of influence in which pressure is exerted to cause someone to conform to the expectations and preferences of others. The expectations and preferences of others function as a reference group norm that conveys how individuals ought to behave or what decision they ought to make. Although normative reference groups may exist outside the immediate group setting (e.g., religious norms), more frequently the source of the influence is a norm established or detected among those people who are physically present in the group interaction.

It is instructive to contrast normative influence with the other major form of influence within groups. *Informational influence* refers to changing individual behavior by incorporating information about issues as evidence about reality. In contrast to normative influence, which is social in nature, informational influence is primarily intellectual, centering on the issues being considered by the group rather than the preferences of people within or outside the group. Having different bases, the two forms of influence differ in the motives and conditions that produce them, their distinctive interaction behaviors, and their consequences on group process. This entry looks at the conditions for and consequences of normative influence.

Conditions Promoting Normative Influence

Normative influence focuses on the values and preferences of other people regarding the issues and tasks facing a group. It is a people-centered form of influence, and susceptibility to it reflects one or more of several underlying motives: to be accepted by others, to promote interpersonal harmony, and to use other people's behaviors as yardsticks to gauge the effectiveness of one's judgments and behaviors. Therefore, conditions that call attention to the preferences of others for resolving intragroup issues will foster normative influence. Conversely, conditions that emphasize the importance of the group's decision and its factually correct resolution will favor the use of informational influence.

Chief among conditions determining whether normative or informational influence prevails is the type of issue (judgmental versus intellectual) discussed by the group. *Judgmental issues* are matters of preference and values, such as judgments of right and wrong. They are not issues capable of resolution by the application of facts, such as whether some event or state exists. Judgmental issues are resolved by appealing to the normative preferences of group members (e.g., numerical majority or high-status members) or to outside authorities (e.g., the Bible). But even *intellectual issues*, which rely on the gathering and consideration of facts (e.g., "What is the repair record of Toyotas?"), will provoke normative influence if they are information poor, a condition in which relevant information is lacking among group members. In such circumstances, the group will resort to normative influence as a criterion for correctness.

Aside from the nature of the issue under discussion, there are other conditions that foster normative influence; these include the goal of the group interaction, the personal orientation of group members, and the style of interaction. If a group considers its goal is to maintain harmony and cohesion, that is, if relations within the group are important, normative influence is likely to be enhanced. This would be a likely outcome in enduring groups, compared with groups convened only for specific, short-term tasks. If a group meets repeatedly, there is more opportunity to get to know one another and more pressure to maintain harmony for the sake of group continuance, conditions that favor normative influence.

Similarly, individuals with strong personal dispositions toward interpersonal harmony and the welfare of others (*communal orientation*) would be more likely to take the preferences of other group members into account than those inclined toward finding the correct solution of the issues facing the group (*task completion* or *agentic orientation*). Does the individual (or group as a whole) want to reach a mutually satisfying decision or a factually correct one?

Finally, if a group takes early and frequent votes on an issue, it is more likely to engage in normative than in informational influence. Taking an early public vote focuses attention on member preferences rather than the facts of the issue, and discussion will be driven by the decision preferences of members and defending their votes rather than by thorough discussion of relevant facts. This distinction in the style of group discussion is referred to as *verdict-driven* versus *evidence-driven style*.

Forms of Argumentation

Normative and informational influences take distinctive forms. In the former, group members argue on the basis of decision preferences of numerical or prestigious majorities in the group (e.g., "Most of us think Toyotas are better cars" or "Group members who know about cars prefer Toyotas") or outside the group (e.g., "Toyota sells more cars"). Arguments are framed in terms of a particular decision alternative and supported by their internal (to the group) or external normative support. In informational influence, on the other hand, arguments are phrased in terms of observable facts and reasoning that support a particular decision alternative (or that disprove other alternatives), such as "Toyotas have the best gas mileage figures in the industry" or "Fords have a lower life expectancy." Thus, the style of normative influence practiced in groups is consistent with the motive to compare one's decision to that of others to foster group consensus and/or to resolve an issue in the absence of hard evidence.

Consequences of Normative Influence

Generally, predominant use of normative influence in group discussions can lead to quicker decisions, especially when agreement is reached by a vote other than unanimity. In issues that inherently require social agreement, such as judgmental issues or intellective issues for which little information is available, normative influence is indeed natural. But in issues with a factually correct solution, and where information is available to the group, normative influence inhibits accurate and creative solutions. It places emphasis on satisfaction with the outcome rather than the best solution to the issue.

In the real world of decision making—for example, political decisions—there are many striking instances in which, in retrospect, poor decisions were based on the pursuit of mutual satisfaction with the decision outcome rather than on incorporating the best available information. Predominant use of normative influence can retard the sharing of critical information possessed by group members, particularly those in the group's numerical minority. Normative influence is a powerful tool of the majority, whereas the minority's best strategy is to use informational influence on the majority. The critical contribution of a group minority is to provide the majority with fresh and novel information to improve decision making. The group conflict that is ostensibly avoided by normative influence can actually be productive in many instances, especially for intellective issues.

Normative influence facilitates agreement and reduces conflict, but it also reduces the breadth and depth of information being shared during discussion. It encourages members to think about the issue in simpler, superficial ways. This is called *heuristic reasoning*, which refers to use of simple rules and a narrow set of information to make decisions—for example, "What do most people think?" Informational influence, however, enables systematic reasoning, a thought process whereby group members consider a broad range of relevant information, think about it in depth, and elaborate on the meaning of facts—for example, "Toyotas cost more than Fords but need fewer repairs and get better gas mileage, so they must be precision engineered and cost less in the long run."

Normative influence can be satisfying, useful, and economical. Were it not, it would not be as widely practiced in groups. It is satisfying because it is a direct way to achieve consensus, and please the most people, among parties who differ in their decision preferences. It is useful because sometimes we do not have relevant information to make a well-considered decision or sometimes the issue is one that does not lend itself well to factual resolution—think of religious and moral issues. It is economical because it is simpler to find out what others prefer than to explore the bases of those preferences. In groups composed of experts in different fields that are relevant to an issue (e.g., marketing, finance, engineering, design, and aesthetics), using normative influence makes sense if one assumes that each person's decision preference is based on systematic consideration of the facts in his or her domain.

But normative influence can compromise competent decisions by restricting the systematic use of a broad range of relevant information, considered in depth, and with the novel input of group minorities. These are the very components of creative decision making and require open sharing of information.

Martin F. Kaplan

See also Anticonformity; Conformity; Group Polarization; Group Problem Solving and Decision Making; Inclusion/Exclusion; Innovation; Minority Influence

Further Readings

Deutsch, M., & Gerard, H. B. (1955). A study of normative and informational social influences upon individual judgment. *Journal of Abnormal and Social Psychology, 51,* 629–636.

Kaplan, M. F., & Wilke, H. (2001). Cognitive and social motivation in group decision making. In J. P. Forgas, K. D. Williams, & L. Wheeler (Eds.), *The social mind: Cognitive and motivational aspects of interpersonal behavior* (pp. 406–428). Cambridge, UK: Cambridge University Press.

Wilke, H., & Kaplan, M. F. (2001). Task creativity and social creativity in decision-making groups. In C. M. Allgood & M. Selart (Eds.), *Decision making: Social and creative dimensions* (pp. 35–51). Dordrecht, the Netherlands: Kluwer.

NORMS

Norms are social standards that describe and prescribe behavior. Norms serve as guides for one's own behavior, help establish expectations about how others will act, and therefore promote greater coordination in social interactions. Norms may be descriptive in the sense that they specify the frequency and pervasiveness of some behavior. Norms may be prescriptive in the sense that they specify the behaviors that a person ought or ought not to perform. According to some theorists, the possibility of informal punishments and sanctions for failures to comply with prescriptive norms is a defining characteristic of a norm.

This entry examines the distinctions between norms that are primarily descriptive in nature and those that are more prescriptive. Although norms are often thought of as social standards, individuals may internalize the prescription of social norms and formulate their own personal norms to guide their behavior. Certain social norms (the norm of reciprocity and fairness norms) are so universal that they have been singled out for special attention because their influence is seen in such a wide variety of social situations. Finally, characteristics that are related to when and why norms are most likely to emerge will be discussed.

Social Norms

The distinction between social norms that summarize how people behave and norms that specify how people ought to behave is reflected in the defining characteristics of descriptive and prescriptive norms.

Descriptive Norms

Descriptive norms are inferred by individuals from their day-to-day observations of their own behavior and the behavior of others. Descriptive norms reflect the frequency and pervasiveness of a given behavior; they may be thought of as summary statements about how people behave. These descriptive norms may be global and apply quite broadly across a wide variety of circumstances (e.g., using the title Mr. or Ms. to address a higher-status person), or they may be situational and apply to a more restricted set of circumstances (e.g., cheering at athletic events).

Global norms are useful when a person must determine his or her standing in terms of some ability, accuracy of some attitudinal position, or appropriateness of some behavior. For example, assume you are introduced to a stranger and say, "It is nice to meet you, Dr. Johnson." If Dr. Johnson replies, "Oh, you can call me Chris," you may infer that Dr. Johnson considers you to be a social equal. Although a global norm suggests that one shows respect to higher-status others by using a formal title, the norm also suggests that the use of first names is appropriate when speaking to an equal, and Dr. Johnson's reply has clarified your standing.

Situational norms play a similar role but are more dependent on the particular setting or context and more limited in their application. A situational norm defines how people act in a specific setting: Patrons are quiet in a library. When in novel situations, people will often use the actions of others to help decide on the appropriate course of action. The benefit provided by descriptive norms is that understanding and being able to predict how others are likely to act allows people to coordinate their actions for smoother interactions. When social norms are widely shared and the advantages of social coordination are recognized, certain behaviors (e.g., queuing behavior, shaking hands when introduced to a stranger, passing to the right when approaching a person on a sidewalk) are performed almost mindlessly because they are so deeply ingrained within the members of a culture.

In addition, people filling a particular social role (e.g., leader, teacher, emergency responder) may come to define and understand their responsibilities by identifying the specific norms that are associated with that role. For example, the norms of being a leader include maintaining order within the group, promoting the interests of the group, and distributing resources among group members fairly. These norms may then be considered role prescriptions that would apply to anyone occupying that particular social position.

It should be made explicit that just because many others are behaving in a particular way does not necessarily mean that the course of action is correct or the best way to act. Furthermore, some normative beliefs may be inaccurate and yet may still be used as guides for behavior. For example, many college students believe that the frequency of binge drinking on campus is far greater than it actually is, setting the stage for students to overindulge in the mistaken belief that "everyone is doing it."

Prescriptive Norms

Prescriptive norms shift the emphasis from the question of "what is" to the question of "what ought to be." Prescriptive norms (sometimes called *injunctive norms*) specify what one should do as well as what one should not do. These prescriptive norms are informal standards of behavior that have evolved over time or within a given situation, and they are expected to be followed and obeyed to promote smooth social interactions. Violations of prescriptive norms may lead to expressions of disapproval from others who observe the transgression. The disapproval after the violation of a prescriptive norm may involve the administration of an informal social sanction, such as frowning or shaking of the head, comments to let the transgressor know that the norm violation was observed, explicit calls for some corrective action, social rejection, or overt retaliation for the offense. Because norms reflect informal standards, there are no formal institutional reactions to norm violations, but informal sanctioning systems will often emerge over time that establish how others might appropriately respond to norm violations. The sanctioning systems, therefore, come to be governed by their own prescriptive norms. According to some definitions, the presence of a sanctioning system is a necessary condition for an observed behavioral standard to be considered a prescriptive norm.

Although the notion of a social norm implies that a group endorses a particular standard of behavior, this does not necessarily mean that each individual within the group must accept that standard to the same degree. A given norm will influence an individual's actions most strongly if others respected by the individual endorse that norm as it applies to a particular behavior. This distinction is seen in the notion of subjective norms incorporated into the *theory of reasoned action* as one of the factors that affects a person's intentions about how to behave.

According to this approach, people consider what they believe to be the normative beliefs of others and then decide how motivated they are to meet those normative expectations. For example, a teenager will consider the normative standards that his parents, neighbors, teachers, and friends might hold about a particular behavior (e.g., voting in an election, premarital sex) when trying to decide how to act. The teenager will also consider how much he or she cares about meeting the standards and normative beliefs of these other people. One implication of this approach is that the normative standards of those who are not considered to be particularly important to an individual (e.g., a neighbor) will exert relatively little influence on behavior. However, if others close to the individual (e.g., best friend, parents) have strong feelings for or against compliance with some social norm, the normative beliefs of these important others will play a greater role in influencing the person's behavior.

If prescriptive norms and their associated informal sanctioning systems are found to be insufficient to ensure compliance with social standards of behavior, formal standards may be instituted within the legal system to accomplish these goals. The legal system specifies the expected standards of behavior that are to be displayed by those within the system (e.g., laws enacted by legislative actions), the mechanisms by which violations are identified (e.g., law enforcement agencies), procedures that determine whether sanctions are required (e.g., the judicial system), and the nature of those sanctions (e.g., fines, imprisonment). Within the current discussion, these arrangements might be considered to be legal norms.

Personal Norms

Personal norms are internalized standards that have been adopted as guides for one's own behavior. At a descriptive level, personal norms are roughly equivalent to one's habits—behaviors that an individual does on a regular basis (e.g., brushing teeth, buckling seat belts). Personal norms at this level reflect a routine pattern of behavior that serves to simplify life: I have no need to think about whether I am going to brush my teeth—it is just something that I do. Personal norms may also include a component

analogous to prescriptive norms, and deviations from one's personal norms can lead to a sense of guilt for failing to live up to one's own personal standards. For example, if a person believes that citizens should exercise their right to vote and has internalized this belief as a personal standard for behavior, failure to make it to the polls on election day will make the person feel guilty.

Once they are internalized, the individual follows these personal norms even when no social sanctions would be possible (e.g., when a person is alone or when in a large group so that no one else can monitor the person's behavior). If a person has fully accepted and internalized the social norm of commitment as a personal norm, that person will follow through with a promise to contribute to a friend's favorite charity even though the friend would never be able to determine whether the contribution had really been made. The normative pressure to make the contribution is driven by the person's desire to avoid feelings of guilt and pangs of conscience that would arise if the person deviated from the prescriptions of the commitment norm.

Roles of Norms in Social Behavior

Social and personal norms play important directive roles in social behavior, but it is important to note that norms do not cause behavior. Instead, norms guide an individual's course of action by either offering information about what most people do in similar situations (serving the descriptive function) or reminding the individual what important others expect him or her to do (serving the prescriptive function), with some risk of social sanction if the person fails to comply with the social standards. It is also important to recognize that the existence of a norm per se does not necessarily mean that it will play any role in guiding one's action; according to the *focus theory of normative conduct*, an individual's attention must be focused on a particular norm in order to activate its influence potential.

For example, social norms associated with environmental issues (e.g., recycling) may not have any impact on a person's behavior until some event calls attention to the need for pro-environmental action (e.g., seeing someone throw an aluminum can in the trash). The individual has a norm-based potential for pro-environmental action, but for that norm to be used as a guide for behavior, some situational cue must be present to focus the individual's attention on an existing norm.

Although some norms may emerge that satisfy the specific needs of a group or of a particular situation, there is a class of *general interaction norms* that apply to a broad spectrum of social situations and may be particularly accessible for easy activation. Two examples of general interaction norms are the *norm of reciprocity* and *fairness norms*.

Norm of Reciprocity

The norm of reciprocity is one of the most prevalent social norms and one that is easy to understand. If someone does a favor for another, the recipient will feel a certain social (normative) pressure to return the favor, due to the norm of reciprocity. There have been suggestions that there are evolutionary roots for this norm, with instances of helping and cooperation being based in part on what is called *reciprocal altruism*: If I help you when you are in need, I believe—because of my belief in the norm of reciprocity—that you will help me when I need assistance, and we will both be better off in the long run because of our compliance with this social rule. Returning favors fulfills norm-based social expectations, but an inability to reciprocate will result in the person who had received the favor feeling a continuing sense of obligation until the social debt can be repaid.

The norm of reciprocity is particularly important in casual relationships in which those involved are primarily concerned with their immediate outcomes and with making sure that no one has taken advantage of them. The strength and pervasiveness of the norm of reciprocity are so great that those who fail to reciprocate may be punished for their failure to meet this social obligation. In extreme cases, those failing to reciprocate may even be expelled from a group if they do not live up to this normative standard.

Fairness Norms

There are also fairness norms that govern how we deal with others. If social organizations are to keep themselves going by protecting the advantages gained by cooperative actions, each member of the organization must feel that the benefits of being a part of the group outweigh the personal costs incurred for being in the group. For example, assume a Little League association requires parents to staff the concession stand during games. Parents may prefer not to serve in this role, but the league would have to cease operation if the stand were not open. The consequence of no one's helping would be the loss of a valuable resource (i.e., the league), but most parents recognize that the benefits of giving their children an opportunity to play ball outweigh the time spent working in the concession stand.

Two closely related fairness norms provide the basis for how the duties required by the group will be assigned. The *equal division norm* and the *equity norm* are the most frequently applied standards for the fair allocation of both benefits to be received and costs to be shared. Application of the equal division rule results in each group member's receiving an equal share of a reward (e.g., all children can play in the league) or making an equal contribution to the group's common need (i.e., each parent must work one game). The equal division scheme is easily applied and is seen as producing a fair outcome in many situations. However, imagine how parents who have only one child might feel while working in the concession stand with parents who have three children, all of whom are playing in the league.

Treating everyone the same when there are clear differences in benefits to be gained may not be perceived as fair. In such cases, the equity norm may be more appropriate. According to the equity norm, the relationship between what a person contributes to the group and what that person receives in return should be proportional to the relationship between the contributions and returns for others in the group. An equitable arrangement in the case described above might involve the parents of an only child working one game in the concession stand and the parents of three children working three games.

Additional Characteristics of Norms

Social norms emerge from the experiences of people in a group because the norms serve some beneficial function for the group and, more specifically, for the individuals within a group. Norms are most likely to emerge in groups in which members share common values and attitudes and generally agree on how people ought to act. Because social norms are social constructions based largely on the beliefs and behaviors of others, norms are most likely to emerge when powerful members of a group have, by their public behavior and pronouncements, given their support to a particular course of action. People often use powerful others as sources of information about how one ought to behave, and powerful others are in strong positions to offer reinforcements for compliance with norms and for punishment of transgressions.

In other cases, a given behavior may come to be accepted as part of a prescriptive norm with little justification: The mere fact that the majority of people behave in a uniform manner (i.e., the descriptive feature of norms) may be taken as sufficient evidence for a prescriptive social norm to arise and to be seen as "the way things ought to be." Finally, there is a conditional nature to social norms that recognizes that people do not behave in blind obedience to norms in all situations. For example, most people strongly endorse a norm stating "Thou shalt not kill," but many people believe that there are circumstances under which taking the life of another is acceptable (e.g., self-defense). The degree of conditionality represents a measure of the generality of the norm; in this regard, norms can be seen as socially agreed on standards of behavior that are subject to modifications by the group as changing circumstances warrant.

David A. Schroeder

See also Emergent Norm Theory; Group Socialization; Normative Influence; Reference Groups; Roles

Further Readings

Bicchieri, C. (2006). *The grammar of society: The nature and dynamics of social norms.* New York: Cambridge University Press.

Cialdini, R. B., & Trost, M. R. (1995). Social influence: Social norms, conformity, and compliance. In D. Gilbert, S. Fiske, & G. Lindzey (Eds.), *The handbook of social psychology* (5th ed., pp. 151–192). New York: McGraw-Hill.

Ellickson, R. C. (1991). *Order without law: How neighbors settle disputes.* Cambridge, MA: Harvard University Press.

Hechter, M., & Opp, K. (2001). *Social norms.* New York: Russell Sage.

Miller, D. T., & Prentice, D. A. (1996). The construction of social norms and standards. In E. T. Higgins & A. W. Kruglanski (Eds.), *Social psychology: Handbook of basic principles* (pp. 799–829). New York: Guilford Press.

Posner, E. A. (2000). *Law and social norms.* Cambridge, MA: Harvard University Press.

OBEDIENCE TO AUTHORITY

Obedience to authority refers to the act of following orders or instructions from someone in a position of authority. Psychologists are particularly interested in situations in which people obey orders to perform an act they believe to be wrong. Much of the research on obedience to authority has been conducted with an eye to understanding morally questionable acts, and the findings have been used to explain atrocious events such as the Holocaust. However, the research also has implications for everyday situations, such as following questionable orders from physicians or airline pilots.

Background

The first systematic effort by a social psychologist to study obedience to authority was conducted by Stanley Milgram in the early 1960s. Milgram's obedience studies are arguably the most well-known research in social psychology, both within the field and among the general public. The obedience studies were conducted between August 1961 and May 1962. With one exception, all the studies were carried out on the campus of Yale University. Participants were members of the community recruited through newspaper ads and direct mail solicitations. All of Milgram's participants were between the ages of 20 and 50, and in all but one version of the study, they were men. Participants believed at the outset that they would be participating in a "scientific study of memory and learning."

The basic experimental procedure involved three individuals: the participant, a confederate pretending to be another participant, and the experimenter. The experimenter explained to the participant and confederate that they would be randomly assigned to either the role of learner or the role of teacher. He further explained that the study was concerned with the effect of punishment on learning and that electric shocks would be used as the punishment in the experiment. The drawing was rigged so that the real participant was always the teacher and the confederate was always the learner.

The experiment was conducted in two rooms separated by a thin wall. On one side of the wall, the learner was strapped into a chair. Electrodes supposedly connected to a shock generator in the adjacent room were attached to his arm. A speaker allowed the learner to hear the teacher's instructions from the other room, but the learner could respond only by pressing one of four buttons within reach of his strapped-in hands. With the real participant watching, the learner mentioned that he had a heart condition and that he was worried about the effect of the electric shocks.

The participant–teacher was then seated on the other side of the wall in front of a large machine the experimenter identified as a shock generator. Thirty switches spanned the front of the machine, each identified with the amount of voltage it supposedly delivered. The voltage labels started at 15 volts (V) and continued in 15-V increments to 450 V. Labels on the machine identified the shocks as increasingly severe, ranging from *Slight Shock* to *Danger: Severe Shock*. The 450-V lever was labeled simply with three red Xs.

The teacher read a list of 25 word pairs (e.g., blue-girl) for the learner to memorize. The teacher then tested the learner by providing the first word in the pair and four possible options for the second word. The learner gave his response to each test item by pressing one of the four switches, which lit up a corresponding light on the teacher's side of the wall. If the learner got the test item incorrect, the teacher was instructed to deliver an electric shock. The teacher was told to give a 15-V shock for the first wrong answer and to increase the intensity by 15 V for each successive wrong answer until the learner had memorized all 25 word pairs. In reality, the learner received no shocks. But he deliberately gave many wrong answers, forcing the teacher to deliver increasingly severe shocks. After pressing the 75-V lever, the participant heard the learner grunt in pain (actually, a prerecorded sound) through the wall. After the 150-V punishment, the participant heard the learner cry out that his heart was bothering him and that he wanted to be released. The learner gave increasingly loud protests after each successive punishment, including screams of pain and demands to be released.

After the 300-V shock, the learner refused to answer, which the experimenter said should be considered a wrong answer. After 330 V, despite intense screams earlier in the procedure, the learner no longer made a sound when shocked. Whenever the participant expressed a reluctance to go on, the experimenter instructed him to continue, using a sequence of four prods: *Please continue* or *Continue, The experiment requires that you continue, It is absolutely essential that you continue,* and *You have no other choice, you must continue.* The prod sequence started anew after each shock. If a participant refused to continue the procedure after receiving the fourth prod, the experimenter ended the session. Otherwise, the experiment continued until the participant had pressed the highest shock lever (450 V) three times.

The key measure was the point at which the participant-teacher refused to continue. That is, how long would the participant obey the experimenter's orders despite the obvious suffering of the learner? People hearing about the obedience studies for the first time typically assume that virtually every participant will stop long before reaching the

end of the shock generator. However, Milgram found surprisingly high rates of obedience. In the basic procedure described here, 65% of the participant–teachers continued to press the levers all the way to the end of the procedure. Milgram argued from these findings that whether a person engages in seemingly brutal behavior is often not a function of the individual's character. Rather, in certain situations, good people can be made to do bad things.

Milgram explored some of the causes of obedience by changing features of the procedure in subsequent studies. For example, he found obedience decreased when the learner was physically closer to the teacher, such as in the same room. Obedience also decreased when the experimenter was in another room and delivered his orders over the phone. Participants were less likely to obey orders from a confederate posing as another participant than orders from the experimenter. But conducting the study in an office building with no apparent affiliation to Yale University did not significantly reduce compliance. In the one study for which he recruited women, Milgram found that they behaved very similarly to men.

Explaining the Effect

Most people find the high rates of obedience in Milgram's studies surprising and disturbing. Before conducting the research, Milgram described the procedures to a large number of people, including a group of psychiatrists, and asked them to predict the results. Everyone agreed that finding even one participant who went to the end of the shock generator would be extremely unlikely. The gap between this expectation and the actual results is often held up as an example of what social psychologists call the *fundamental attribution error*. That is, when explaining the causes of another person's behavior, people typically fail to fully appreciate the role situational forces play.

Individuals hearing about Milgram's research for the first time are often tempted to attribute the obedient participants' behavior to personal characteristics, such as a sadistic personality or a lack of conscience. But Milgram demonstrated that following the experimenter's orders was the normative response. What people fail to recognize are the features of the situation that made it difficult for

Milgram's participants to do anything but obey the orders.

What are these situational features? Milgram emphasized the power of the authority figure in this setting. He argued that people are raised to respect and follow orders from authority figures, such as parents, teachers, or police officers. The authority figure does not need to be forceful or charismatic but must simply be seen as legitimate. In the obedience studies, participants granted the experimenter this authority by virtue of his association with the experiment, the university, and perhaps even science. Observers have pointed out that Milgram's experimenter also may have been seen as an expert. Because the experimenter presumably knew all about the dangers of the shock generator and apparently was not concerned, participants may have deferred to his judgment and continued to deliver shocks.

Psychologists have identified other features in Milgram's procedures that most likely contributed to the high rates of obedience. One of these is the incremental nature of the task. As indicated previously, all participants began with the lowest level of shock—15 V—and worked their way toward the 450-V lever in 15-V increments. Researchers find that step-by-step progression of this sort is an effective tactic for changing attitudes and behaviors in other settings. Among the processes that come into play in such situations are the need for consistency and a change in the way people think of themselves as they move through the steps.

In most cases, pressing the next lever on the shock generator is different from pressing the last lever only in degree. If a participant pressed the 170-V lever, there is no apparent reason he should not press the 185-V lever. Consistent with this reasoning, investigators can identify in Milgram's data a few places in the procedure at which participants were most likely to refuse to continue. Each of these stopping points corresponds to a qualitative change in the task. For example, the most common point for participants to refuse the experimenter's orders is after pressing the 150-V lever. This is the first time participants hear the learner's protests through the wall and his demands to be released. Continuing to give shocks at this point is a noticeably different act than it was earlier. Similarly, refusals increase when the learner refuses to answer and when the learner turns suddenly silent.

Another explanation for the high rates of obedience in Milgram's research concerns the novelty of the situation and the behavior of the experimenter. Most likely, participants had little prior experience with psychology experiments or machinery like the shock generator. When they first heard the learner's protests, participants probably began to search for information about how they should respond. In most versions of Milgram's procedures, the experimenter provided the only source of information, and he assured participants that nothing was wrong and that they should continue the test. Thus, it was not entirely unreasonable for participants to conclude under these circumstances that continuing the procedure was the right thing to do. Results consistent with this interpretation come from one of Milgram's studies. Before being asked to press the levers themselves, participants in one study saw two other "teachers" refuse to continue. Obedience declined significantly in this version of the procedure.

The experimental situation also provided Milgram's participants an easy opportunity to diffuse personal responsibility for any harm that came to the learner. Research in a number of areas finds that people are often motivated to assign responsibility for undesirable acts to someone else. Moreover, removing the burden of personal responsibility typically increases the chances that people will act in socially inappropriate ways. Although they were the ones pressing the levers, participants in the obedience studies frequently attributed responsibility for continuing the procedure to the experimenter. In the participants' eyes, they were just following orders. Indeed, when participants asked about responsibility, the experimenter was instructed to say that he himself was responsible for any harm that came to the learner.

Ethical Concerns

Milgram's obedience studies played an important role in stimulating debate among psychologists about the treatment of human participants in research. Critics pointed to the potential harm to Milgram's participants. Many participants experienced intense stress as they wrestled with what to do while listening to the learner's apparent suffering. Psychologists also worried about the long-term psychological consequences of going through such an experience.

Milgram was not unaware of or insensitive to these concerns. All participants were debriefed about the study immediately after the session, and obedient participants were assured that their behavior was normal and that their conflicted feelings were shared by other participants. Moreover, follow-up questionnaires found 84% of participants were glad they had been part of the study, and the vast majority agreed that more experiments of this kind should be conducted. Nonetheless, the obedience studies are clearly out of bounds by today's standards. No study using Milgram's full procedures has been published since the 1970s.

Implications and Remaining Questions

Milgram's obedience studies continue to generate discussions inside and outside psychology, largely because of their implications for understanding the worst of human behaviors: atrocities, massacres, and genocide. Milgram often drew parallels between his participants' behavior and the obedience witnessed in Nazi Germany during the Holocaust. However, other psychologists urge caution when making the leap from findings of controlled laboratory studies like Milgram's to complex social behaviors like those involved in the Holocaust. Nonetheless, laboratory studies on obedience provide valuable insights into some of the conditions that lead people to act in seemingly uncharacteristic and sometimes horrific ways.

Researchers have also applied findings from the obedience studies to other important concerns. Investigations into airline crashes suggest crew members are often reluctant to challenge a flight captain's judgment, even when they believe a captain's instructions are in error. Similarly, medical personnel may follow a physician's orders, such as administering an unusual dose of medicine, even when they believe the action might harm the patient. Milgram's results have also been used to explain why followers of a cult leader sometimes obey orders to act in harmful or self-destructive ways.

One persistent question about Milgram's research is whether the results would be replicated if the studies were conducted today. Ethical concerns prevent researchers from unequivocally answering the question, but a recent partial replication of Milgram's procedure provides some insight. The investigator noted that most of the participants who refused to continue in Milgram's basic procedure did so after hearing the learner's first verbal protests at the 150-V mark. If participants made it past this point, there was a nearly 80% chance that they would continue to the end of the shock generator. Thus, the researcher avoided many of the ethical objections to Milgram's investigations by stopping the procedure after 150 V. The study, conducted in 2006, found rates of obedience that were similar to those that Milgram had found 45 years earlier.

Jerry M. Burger

See also Banality of Evil; Genocide; Holocaust; Just World Hypothesis; Leadership; Norms; Power; Roles; Stanford Prison Experiment

Further Readings

Blass, T. (Ed.). (2000). *Obedience to authority: Current perspectives on the Milgram paradigm.* Mahwah, NJ: Lawrence Erlbaum.

Blass, T. (2004). *The man who shocked the world: The life and legacy of Stanley Milgram.* New York: Basic Books.

Burger, J. M. (2008). Replicating Milgram: Would people still obey today? *American Psychologist, 64*(1), 1–11.

Milgram, S. (1974). *Obedience to authority: An experimental view.* New York: Harper & Row.

Miller, A. G. (2004). What can the Milgram obedience experiments tell us about the Holocaust? Generalizing from the social psychology laboratory. In A. G. Miller (Ed.), *The social psychology of good and evil* (pp. 193–239). New York: Guilford.

Miller, A. G., Collins, B. E., & Brief, D. E. (Eds.). (1995). Perspectives on obedience to authority: The legacy of the Milgram experiments [Special issue]. *Journal of Social Issues, 51*(3).

OPINION DEVIANCE

Deviance can be loosely defined as any conduct that diverges from normative expectations. These expectations may originate from observations of what most people *actually* do or say in specific situations or from socially transmitted propositions that are internalized by individuals and stipulate what, in general, people *ought* to do or say. For the present purposes, the important point is that people who fail to meet these expectations often attract disapproval from other people. Such disapproval may translate into negative evaluations of the deviants or even their expulsion from their group.

Consensus in Small Groups

Social psychology is typically concerned with the impact of deviance on people who behave in normatively appropriate ways and with the conditions that shape their reactions toward deviants. Most of what is known about opinion deviance stems from traditional social-psychological literature on small-group processes. Small groups are typically conceived of as social units composed of 3 to 15 interacting individuals who are attached to one another by reciprocal positive affective ties (e.g., friendship), who interdependently achieve common goals, who share a common fate, and who perceive themselves as a more or less tangible entity. Perhaps the clearest way to understand the impact of opinion deviance is to ask why people join face-to-face groups in the first place.

Consider what happens when we enter a new social environment (e.g., a new school, a new job, a new neighborhood). Would we affiliate with anyone at random? Would we affiliate with people who have opinions and attitudes different from ours and who might therefore contribute a richer, more diversified, and, hence, more accurate understanding of the world? Or would we affiliate with people who, from the outset, are likely to agree with our own views, while we overtly or tacitly avoid those who have different opinions? Provided that everyone is equally available (for instance, in terms of geographical proximity), the last of the three alternatives is most likely.

Clearly, we do not see everyone as an equally attractive candidate for affiliation. We usually prefer to affiliate with people who espouse the same attitudes and beliefs as we do. These people strengthen our convictions and increase the likelihood that we can achieve our goals as group members. This is also why, once groups are formed, their members devote a significant amount of time and energy to establishing group norms, reinforcing group consensus, and preventing group deviance.

Social Reality, Group Locomotion, and Group Influence

The foregoing ideas underlie Leon Festinger's classic 1950 *theory of informal social communication.* In this theory, Festinger stressed the paramount role of consensus in groups. In many situations, he argued, we validate our perceptions by means of objective reality checks, through clues that are immediately accessible to our senses (e.g., boiling water burns the skin; hitting a drum makes a noise). However, perhaps our most important and meaningful beliefs (e.g., whether the death penalty is right, whether God exists, whether abortion is acceptable) cannot be validated by direct evidence. Yet, if we could not validate such beliefs, we would experience a permanent state of uncertainty, with associated anxiety, perhaps even helplessness. The solution is to find an alternative process of validation, and this process is to check our beliefs against the opinions of others (i.e., social consensus).

According to Festinger, the stronger the social consensus for our beliefs, the more confident we are about their accuracy. Therefore, we are motivated to compare our beliefs, not with those of a representative sample of other individuals, but rather with those of a biased sample of individuals who are likely to agree with us. The theory of *informal social communication* thus proposes that group consensus helps fulfill a *social reality function*, allowing group members to gain a sense of validity for their beliefs through selective affiliation with those who share similar beliefs. Associated with this function, there is also a *locomotion function of consensus*, allowing group members to cooperate in order to reach goals that they could not accomplish in isolation. Consensus thus operates as a psychosocial source of subjective validity, as well as a means to accomplish one's aspirations. Clearly, the emergence of opinion deviance in such a context represents a psychological threat because it generates uncertainty and jeopardizes goal achievement.

Research shows that uniformity among group members is facilitated by two forces operating in the group. These are what Morton Deutsch and Harold Gerard termed *informational influence* and *normative influence*. Informational influence is directly related to the social reality function of consensus and the motivation to avoid uncertainty.

It occurs when we accept information provided by other people as objective and trustworthy evidence about reality. In contrast, normative influence is associated with the desire to be liked and to avoid disapproval by relevant others. It occurs when we comply with their opinions or behavior, not because we agree with them or believe they are telling us the truth, but rather because we wish them to view us in positive ways. These two forms of influence facilitate group uniformity. On one hand, they are based on motivations that lead group members to express similar opinions and to display similar behavior. On the other hand, their operation reinforces such motivations, thus reducing the likelihood that group members will deviate from the group's normative views or behavior. However, they are not always enough to prevent divergence on the part of some group members. How do other members react when such divergence occurs?

Deviance and Strategies to Restore Group Uniformity

A classic study conducted by Stanley Schachter, in 1951, illustrates the typical social-psychological experiment designed to study reactions of group members to opinion deviance. In that study, groups of several university students participated in a discussion. Unknown to the other participants, three group members were confederates instructed to play either a *modal* role (involving full and consistent agreement with the modal opinion of the group), a *deviant* role (involving full and consistent disagreement with the modal opinion), or a *slider* role (involving initial disagreement followed by gradual movement to agreement). The issue under discussion was the best strategy to handle a case of juvenile delinquency. Schachter varied whether the group was high or low in cohesiveness and whether the case was relevant or irrelevant to the group's purpose. During the discussion, he observed the amount of communication participants directed to each confederate. Results indicated that the most overall communication was directed to the deviant, the next most to the slider, and the least to the mode. Moreover, communication to the deviant tended to increase over time in most conditions, whereas communication to the mode remained constant, and communication to

the slider went down. After the discussion, participants were asked to evaluate the confederates. In general, the deviant received more rejection than the slider or the mode, who were liked about equally, and the deviant was generally rejected more when the group was cohesive and the discussion topic was relevant to the group's purpose. From the participants' standpoint, the slider had been "socialized" to accept the group's views and hence was treated like a regular member (the mode). The deviant, however, was harming the group's social reality and locomotion and therefore was rejected.

Inclusive and Exclusive Reactions to Deviants

As suggested by John Levine and his colleagues, groups may deal with deviants in a variety of ways, depending on the relative power of the normative members and the deviants in the group. Some of these involve *inclusive* attempts to reintegrate the deviants into the group, whereas others involve *exclusive* reactions, in which the group redefines its boundaries by expelling the deviants.

Schachter's communication data illustrate a particular type of inclusive reaction, *attempted influence*. The normative members of the group directed their communication to deviants in a persuasive attempt to lead the deviants back to the group's modal opinion. Often, this communication pressure is effective, either because the deviants are truly persuaded by the group consensus or because they wish to avoid disapproval or a marginal status. It is interesting that persuasive efforts toward deviants do not depend on the need for a fully consensual agreement. Other studies show that communication pressures are also strong when the group must reach a majority, rather than a fully consensual, opinion. Cross-cultural research conducted by Schachter and colleagues in Belgium, France, Germany, the Netherlands, Norway, Sweden, and the United Kingdom obtained results similar to those found in the United States.

Research has also established several factors that increase group members' motivation to exert communication pressures on deviants. For example, motivation to persuade deviants increases with the interpersonal similarity among group members, with their interdependence for rewards, with their desire to be in the group, with deviants' perceived responsiveness to communication pressures, with the strength of situational demands for consensus, and with the amount of outside threat to the group.

It is interesting that some of the above factors also have been shown to affect the propensity to abandon persuasive efforts and to engage in exclusive reactions toward the deviants through redefinition of the group's boundaries. This latter reaction occurs when, in spite of communication pressures directed toward them, deviants persist in their position, thus making it clear that communication is ineffective. In this case, deviants may be deprecated, marginalized, punished, stigmatized, or even expelled from the group. This process is more likely to occur when, for example, a consensual agreement has to be reached quickly.

Expelling deviants can be beneficial to the group for reasons beyond social reality and group locomotion. To illustrate, in 1984, Patrick Lauderdale and colleagues conducted a partial replication of Schachter's experiment in which the future existence of a discussion group containing a deviant confederate either was or was not threatened by an external authority. At the end of the discussion, participants learned that their group had to be reduced in size and were asked to evaluate other members in terms of whether they should stay or leave. As might be expected on the basis of Schachter's findings, participants evaluated the deviant confederate unfavorably compared with the other members and ranked this person first to be excluded. In addition, negative evaluation of and desire to exclude the deviant were stronger when the continuity of the group was threatened than when it was not. More important, when the group's existence was threatened, the more strongly that majority members advocated the expulsion of the deviant, the stronger the solidarity (i.e., cohesiveness) they expressed toward each other. This result suggests that a group's redefinition of its boundaries in the face of deviance can have positive consequences beyond the removal of a disruptive person, in this case an increase in cohesiveness among normative members.

Most of the research on reaction to deviants has focused on influence pressures and redefinition of group boundaries. However, two types of inclusive responses to deviants deserve mention, namely

compromise and *minority influence*. Compromise refers to opinion convergence, in which deviants and normative members shift toward each other's position. Compromise is more likely when normative members are not certain about the validity of their position, such as in newly formed groups that have not yet defined their beliefs and values.

Minority influence, in which deviants cause normative members to move to their position, can be produced by both high-status and low-status deviants. The former kind of influence is illustrated by Edwin Hollander's work on *idiosyncrasy credits*, which demonstrates that members taking deviant positions can produce innovation in a group only after they acquire legitimacy and status by showing initial conformity to the group's norms. The latter kind of influence is illustrated by Serge Moscovici's and Gabriel Mugny's work showing that deviants without legitimacy or status can produce innovation if they generate uncertainty in normative members by using certain kinds of behavioral style. This can involve expressing their position in a consistent and committed way, demonstrating its coherence and situational adequacy, and showing flexibility by shifting from a prior extreme position to a more moderate one. Consistency and commitment to their position increase the deviants' salience. Once they are salient, deviants must demonstrate that their position is coherent and adequate and therefore should be attributed externally rather than to their personal dispositions. If this demonstration is successful, deviants create uncertainty as to the validity of the modal group position, which encourages normative members to accept their innovative views. In showing flexibility, deviants facilitate movement toward those views.

In brief, the kind of strategy groups adopt to deal with deviance depends on a number of factors, including the particular context in which deviance emerges (e.g., whether a quick decision has to be reached, whether the group is under threat), the internal characteristics of the group (e.g., whether members are similar to one another, whether they like each other and the group as a whole), the magnitude of deviance (e.g., the amount of discrepancy between the deviant position and the modal position), the relative power of the majority and the deviants (based, for example, on their expertise and status), and the deviants' response to the pressures for compliance (e.g., whether they consistently defend their point of view and show some sensitivity to the majority's reaction). The topic of reaction to deviance, although an old one in social psychology, continues to stimulate new theoretical and empirical work, as illustrated by current research on the *black sheep effect* and *subjective group dynamics*, which are discussed in other entries.

José M. Marques

See also Black Sheep Effect; Conformity; Group Socialization; Informational Influence; Leadership; Minority Influence; Normative Influence; Subjective Group Dynamics

Further Readings

Festinger, L. (1950). Informal social communication. *Psychological Review*, 57, 271–282.

Levine, J. M. (1989). Reaction to opinion deviance in small groups. In P. B. Paulus (Ed.), *Psychology of group influence* (pp. 187–231). Hillsdale, NJ: Lawrence Erlbaum.

Levine, J. M., & Kerr, N. L. (2007). Inclusion and exclusion: Implications for group processes. In A. E. Kruglanski & E. T. Higgins (Eds.), *Social psychology: Handbook of basic principles* (2nd ed., pp. 759–784). New York: Guilford.

Moscovici, S. (1976). *Social influence and social change.* London: Academic Press.

Schachter, S. (1951). Deviation, rejection, and communication. *Journal of Abnormal and Social Psychology*, 46, 190–207.

Turner, J. C. (1991). *Social influence.* Milton Keynes, UK: Open University Press.

OPTIMAL DISTINCTIVENESS

"Everyone needs to belong." "Everyone needs to be unique." That fact that both these statements are true is the basis for Marilynn Brewer's theory of optimal distinctiveness, which helps to explain why we join social groups and become so attached to the social categories of which we are part. *Optimal distinctiveness theory* is about social identity, that is, how we come to define ourselves in terms of our social group memberships. Secure inclusion in a distinctive ingroup serves human needs for belonging and differentiation. The upside of achieving optimal social identity is that secure group identity enhances well-being and motivates positive social behavior. The downside is that insecure group identity motivates exclusion, intolerance, and possibly intergroup hatred. This entry begins with a fuller description of optimal distinctiveness theory and then examines how it affects self-identity and intergroup relations.

Definition and Background

For group membership to satisfy an individual's need for meaning and coherence, the clarity of the boundary that separates ingroup membership from nonmembership becomes particularly important. This calls attention to the importance of the *distinctiveness* of social categories as a factor in group identification. Optimal distinctiveness theory provides a model of the psychological motives underlying the preference for distinctive social identities.

According to the optimal distinctiveness model, social identities derive from a fundamental tension between two competing social needs—the need for inclusion on one hand and a countervailing need for uniqueness and individuation on the other. People seek social inclusion to alleviate or avoid the isolation, vulnerability, or stigmatization that may arise from being highly individuated. Researchers studying the effects of *tokenism* and *solo status* have generally found that individuals are both uncomfortable and cognitively disadvantaged in situations in which they feel too dissimilar from others, or too much like "outsiders." On the other hand, too much similarity, or excessive deindividuation, provides no basis for self-definition, and hence individuals are also uncomfortable in situations in which they lack distinctiveness. Being "just a number" in a large, undifferentiated mass of people is just as unpleasant as being too alone.

Because of these opposing social needs, social identities are selected to achieve a balance between needs for inclusion and for differentiation in a given social context. Optimal identities are those that satisfy the need for inclusion *within* one's own group and simultaneously serve the need for differentiation through distinctions *between* one's own group and other groups. In effect, optimal social identities involve *shared distinctiveness*. (Think of adolescents' trends in clothes and hairstyles: Each teenager is anxious to be as much like others of their age group as possible, while at the same time differentiating themselves from the older generation.) To satisfy both needs, individuals will select group identities that are inclusive enough that they have a sense of being part of a larger collective but exclusive enough that they provide some basis for distinctiveness from others.

Importance and Implications

Optimal distinctiveness theory has direct implications for self-concept at the individual level and for intergroup relations at the group level. Research testing the basic assumption of optimal distinctiveness theory has demonstrated that individuals adapt their self-image to maintain or restore optimal identities, prefer membership in groups that are relatively small and distinctive, and defend or restore group boundaries if distinctiveness is threatened.

Optimal Identity and Self-Stereotyping

If individuals are motivated to sustain identification with optimally distinct social groups, then the self-concept should be adapted to fit the normative requirements of such group memberships. Achieving optimal social identities should be associated with a secure and stable self-concept in which one's own characteristics are congruent with being a good and typical group member. Conversely, if optimal identity is challenged or threatened, the individual should react to restore congruence between the self-concept and the group representation. Optimal identity can be restored either by adjusting individual self-concept to be more consistent with the group norms or by shifting social identification to a group that is more congruent with the self.

Self-stereotyping is one mechanism for matching the self-concept to characteristics that are distinctively representative of particular group memberships. People stereotype themselves and others in terms of salient social categorizations, and this stereotyping leads to an enhanced perceptual similarity between self and one's own group members and an enhanced contrast between one's own group and other groups. Results of experimental studies have demonstrated that threatening an individual's standing in the group—that is,

giving the person feedback that indicates that he or she is on the margins of the ingroup—results in increased levels of *self-stereotyping*. Adopting the traits that are considered to be stereotypical of the ingroup and considering them to be more self-descriptive align the self more closely with the ingroup and make a person appear more representative of the group. Thus, enhanced self-stereotyping (assimilation to ingroup characteristics and norms) is one mechanism for restoring a loss of inclusiveness.

Because enhancing ingroup similarity also enhances contrast between the ingroup and outgroups, self-stereotyping also serves to preserve or restore ingroup distinctiveness. Consistent with the assumptions of optimal distinctiveness theory, research has found that members of distinctive minority groups exhibit more self-stereotyping than members of large majority groups. In addition, people tend to self-stereotype more when the distinctiveness of their group has been challenged.

Identification With Minority Groups

Optimal distinctiveness theory accounts for the pervasive finding that social identification and ingroup favoritism are greater for members of minority groups than for majority group members. Further, when individuals belong to multiple social categories, they prefer to be associated with their smaller, distinctive group memberships rather than larger, majority ingroups. This group size effect has been obtained in both laboratory and field studies, despite the fact that minority status is often associated with other social disadvantages. Experimental evidence indicates that when the need for differentiation is activated, individuals value minority category membership more than membership in majority groups, regardless of other status differentials between ingroup and outgroup.

Because they are distinctive and clearly bounded, minority groups meet their members' needs for optimal social identity more effectively than majority groups do. This helps account for the finding that identification and attachment to minority ingroups is often quite high, even when such groups are socially disadvantaged or stigmatized. In fact, evidence suggests that strong social identification provides a psychological buffer that protects self-esteem among members of groups that are devalued or negatively stereotyped by majority group members. Thus, group identity may play a particularly important role in enhancing self-worth and subjective well-being for individuals who have stigmatizing characteristics or belong to disadvantaged social categories.

In effect, some of the potential negative effects of belonging to a social minority may be offset by the identity value of secure inclusion in a distinctive social group. Results of survey research have revealed a positive relationship between strength of ethnic identity and self-worth among minority group members, and some experimental studies have demonstrated that individuals' self-esteem can be enhanced by their being classified in a distinctive, minority social category.

Defending Group Distinctions

Finally, because distinctive group identities are so important to one's sense of self, people are very motivated to maintain group boundaries—to protect the distinctiveness of their groups by enhancing differences with other groups and limiting membership to "people like us." When individuals are told that their ingroup characteristics are very similar to everyone else in a larger, more inclusive category, ingroup distinctiveness and clarity are threatened. Individuals react to such information by reasserting the distinctive features of their group, enhancing intragroup similarity and solidarity, and becoming more stringent about the standards for inclusion in the ingroup.

For instance, when students in a particular university have been given survey data that suggest that they are "very typical of college students everywhere," they increase the number of traits that members must have to be "good representatives" of their university and reduce the number of people who are included as "true" ingroup members. Thus, threats to distinctiveness lead members to define the ingroup in a more exclusionary way.

Being restrictive and excluding others from the group may serve an important function for group members' own sense of belonging. In effect, exclusion may be one way that individuals are able to enhance their own feelings of group inclusion. In fact, those who are the *least* secure in their membership status (e.g., new members of a group or marginalized members) are sometimes the most

likely to adhere to the group's standards and discriminate against members of other groups. For example, new pledges to a sorority are often more likely than the more senior sorority members to wear clothing with sorority letters and to attend functions held by the sorority. Ironically, these noncentral group members may be even more likely than those who truly embody the group attributes to notice and punish others for violating the norms and standards of the group.

When given the power, marginal group members may also be more discriminating in determining who should belong in the group and who should be excluded—for example, when it comes time to decide on the next group of new pledges. In experimental studies, it has been demonstrated that when individuals are made to feel that they are marginal (atypical) group members, they become more stringent about requirements for group membership and more likely to exclude strangers from their group.

When the clarity of the distinction between ingroup and outgroups is threatened, highly identified ingroup members also respond by becoming more competitive in dealings with outgroup members. Ingroup favoritism in the allocation of rewards or resources to ingroup and outgroup members becomes one way to restore the differentiation between ingroup and outgroup. Under these circumstances, a cooperative exchange that would benefit both the ingroup and the outgroup may be rejected in favor of a competitive option in which the overall benefit is less but the ingroup gets more than the outgroup. Ensuring that the ingroup gets more in comparison with the outgroup not only enhances the status of the ingroup relative to the outgroup but also increases intergroup distance. Thus, preserving the distinctiveness of the ingroup may motivate intergroup discrimination and bias.

Marilynn B. Brewer

See also Inclusion/Exclusion; Need for Belonging; Self-Categorization Theory; Social Identity Theory

Further Readings

Brewer, M. B. (1991). The social self: On being the same and different at the same time. *Personality and Social Psychology Bulletin, 17,* 475–482.

Brewer, M. B. (2003). Optimal distinctiveness, social identity, and the self. In M. Leary & J. Tangney (Eds.), *Handbook of self and identity* (pp. 480–491). New York: Guilford.

Pickett, C., Bonner, B., & Coleman, J. (2002). Motivated self-stereotyping: Heightened assimilation and differentiation needs result in increased levels of positive and negative self-stereotyping. *Journal of Personality and Social Psychology, 82,* 543–562.

Pickett, C., & Brewer, M. B. (2005). The role of exclusion in maintaining in-group inclusion. In D. Abrams, M. Hogg, & J. Marques (Eds.), *Social psychology of inclusion and exclusion* (pp. 89–112). New York: Psychology Press.

ORGANIZATIONS

An *organization* is a social structure created by individuals to support the collaborative pursuit of specified goals. Organizations can be found in a variety of shapes and sizes, ranging from very large, formal, bureaucratic forms in government to very small, informal, and decentralized collectives in cyberspace. Organizations serve as the building blocks of modern society and offer the possibility for individuals to accomplish things they could never accomplish in isolation. Whatever their shape or size, all organizations must address a number of common issues in order to work effectively. This entry discusses the issues that organizations and work groups experience in defining shared objectives, selecting and training members, developing systems for control and coordination, interacting with the environment, and providing leadership. It concludes with an overview of recent trends with respect to groups in organizations and the methods researchers use to examine these and other organizational issues.

Defining Objectives

Although having a shared objective is part of the definition of an organization, many organizations struggle to develop *clear* shared objectives. Research on goal setting has shown that, at the individual level, the specificity and difficulty of goals are very influential in performance, as is the individual's level of commitment to achieving the goal. At the organizational level, however, setting clear and specific goals is extremely difficult, and most members do not agree on what the organization's overall goals are, much less the relative priority of goals for the subunits in the organization. Classic organizational theorists Richard Cyert and James March proposed that organizations deal with this by setting a general *aspiration level*, which is adjusted through experience with the environment. Modern managers implement this idea through programs such as *management by objectives*. This approach emphasizes participatively set objectives that are tangible, verifiable, and measurable. Managers at all levels participate in setting objectives for each organizational unit, which are aligned with the overall organizational objectives. The approach facilitates goal commitment through the participation of managers at all levels.

One way that organizations attempt to keep members aligned with and focused on objectives is to base employee rewards on attainment of them. *Pay for performance* and *bonus programs* have become increasingly popular in organizations, with rewards based on how many objectives were met and how well they were met. Although this form of feedback is effective in many situations, some have argued that overreliance on such systems can bring about dysfunctional consequences. Pay for performance systems can breed dishonesty or encourage employees to focus only on specified goals while overlooking other activities that would also be beneficial to the organization. Research on internal motivation suggests that instead of relying solely on monetary rewards, it is important for management to give employees meaningful work, knowledge of results, and autonomy in making decisions about how work is done. High internal motivation leads workers to strive to do good work even in the absence of significant external rewards and to complete tasks for the good of the organization even when those tasks are not formally part of their job.

Selection and Training of Members

Individuals joining an organization are generally expected to enact a certain *role*. A role is defined by a set of expected behavior patterns, which can include individual tasks and responsibilities as well as the ways in which work relates to that of others in the organization. Roles and role systems are key defining features of organizations. Identifying roles and finding the right people to fill various roles in an organization occupy a lot of the time and energy of management in formal organizations. In more informal or fluid organizations, such as the volunteer organizations that work on Wikipedia or Linux, roles are defined and filled through more of a self-selection process.

As an individual joins an organization and comes to occupy a role, others in the organization attempt to influence the new individual's behavior so that it will conform to the norms and social values of the organization. Just as people living together in a nation share an identifiable national culture, people working together in an organization develop a shared *organizational culture*. Organizational culture refers to a system of shared meaning developed and perpetuated by members that distinguishes the organization from other organizations. Different organizational cultures involve different rituals and social norms for how to dress, how to speak, what hours to keep, and so on. Organizational cultures vary in terms of their strength, or how intensely held and widely shared the members' beliefs are. Over time, new members are socialized to behave in ways that conform to the culture of the organization or else are forced out.

Because of this tendency of organizations to bring about conformity in behavior, there is some debate among scholars regarding the costs and benefits of membership turnover. Some research has demonstrated that membership change can be costly to an organization or group because it creates social disruption as well as a loss in knowledge and historical information about the organization's or group's work. Airline mishaps are much more common during a crew's first flight together, and long-standing research and development groups exhibit productivity declines with the loss or gain of members, both serving as examples of the costs of membership change. Other researchers argue that there can be benefits associated with membership change, in the form of new and more creative ideas as well as the possibility of breaking old and dysfunctional patterns. They point out that long-standing management teams in organizations frequently fall into ruts that they break out of only when new members are brought in to shake things up.

Control and Coordination of Member Contributions

Once an organization has identified its objectives and the people to carry out those objectives, it must go about organizing people to complete the work. This involves decisions about how to control individuals' work as well as how to coordinate individual contributions so that they lead to the accomplishment of organizational objectives.

Early work on the topic of organizational structure conducted by theorists such as Max Weber and Frederick Taylor followed an approach best described as *machine theory*. The organization is viewed as a machine that can follow precise specifications for turning inputs, such as people and materials, into outputs. Work done in this tradition assumes that tasks can be broken down into elemental parts, which can be assigned to individuals and then coordinated in such a way as to achieve maximum efficiency and uniformity with no duplication of function. In so doing, command is centralized, and supervision is provided in the optimal ratio of worker to manager, such that the manager can adequately control all subordinates. In the middle of the 20th century, theorists such as James March and Herbert Simon began to observe an increasing number of situations in which rules could not anticipate all the possible contingencies an organization faced, and in such circumstances, control was best decentralized and local, with decisions made by workers who were closest to the problems and had the best information. Today's organizations generally use a mix of the two approaches, with some decisions centralized at the top and others made by workers themselves.

The particular form an organization takes to coordinate and control member inputs is partially a function of the interdependence required among different subunits. James Thompson developed a framework to describe the different types of interdependence characterizing work. Standard factory piecework falls into what Thompson termed *pooled interdependence* because individual workers are responsible for a whole piece of work, and the total output of the workers is added together to represent the output for the organization. Classic assembly lines, such as those devised by Henry Ford at the beginning of the 20th century, reflect a *sequential interdependence*, in which the output of one worker becomes the input of another. However, much of the production in today's knowledge work economy requires a more complex level of coordination, what Thompson termed *reciprocal interdependence*, in which workers both make use of and contribute to the work of others, often in iterative fashion. Software engineering, product development, and biomedical research all require this more complex approach to coordination.

The interdependence requirements of work inform the ways in which the organization is broken into smaller units. Most organizations are broken down into subunits, such as departments, projects, or teams. These smaller work groups are the major building blocks of organizations because they tend to be more effective for providing the supervision and social support that employees need. These units can be grouped by function, such as marketing, operations, and accounting. However, when highly interdependent work among units is necessary, organizations frequently create product- or client-based groups or teams to facilitate the reciprocal interdependence necessary among the different functions. Although traditionally these units were created and headed by a manager who made most of the decisions about how work was conducted, more and more organizations are decentralizing this control to teams, which manage themselves.

Creating small groups within an organization not only helps management attend to the technical needs of task interdependence but also enables managers to attend to the social and emotional needs of employees, which promotes good performance. The emergence of the team idea in organizations can be traced back to the late 1920s and early 1930s and the now-classic Hawthorne studies. These involved a series of research activities designed to examine in depth what happened to a group of workers under various conditions. After much analysis, the researchers agreed that the most significant factor was building a sense of group identity, a feeling of social support and cohesion that came with increased worker interaction. Other researchers focused on helping to solve some problems at the Harwood Manufacturing Company, in rural Virginia, by designing group-based interventions to increase worker involvement and participation in organizational improvements, with impressive results. Since that time, much research has been done, in both field and laboratory settings, on the use of teams as an approach to organizational design. Beyond their initial use in manufacturing and service provision, teams have become a major engine of the growing knowledge economy, in which new ideas in many sectors, including business, medicine, and scientific research, are the product of the collaboration of team members who have different backgrounds and expertise.

Although initially managers were concerned that teams left to their own devices would underperform, researchers have found that team members often hold higher standards for one another's behavior than managers could contemplate enforcing, delivering tough sanctions to members who are perceived as not working hard enough. In addition, teams that are trained together and remain intact can evolve very effective systems of coordinating the knowledge and resources they hold through the development of *transactive memory systems*, which can operate much more efficiently than more formal role systems.

Interaction With Environment

Although the decisions an organization makes internally with respect to motivating and coordinating work are important to its success, other organizations in the environment can be just as, if not more, important. Far from existing in a vacuum, organizations exist in an environment populated by other organizations and entities with which they must interact. These other organizations assert a strong influence in determining an organization's success in attaining its goals. These other entities might be competitors, suppliers, customers, or partners. Sometimes the same external entity might occupy multiple roles; a customer for one product, a competitor on another, and a supplier on yet another. Those who adopt the *open-systems view* of organizational boundaries argue that it can be difficult at times to delineate exactly where the boundaries of an organization end and the "environment" begins. In addition to the multifaceted relationships organizations have with each other, the relationships among the people who make up any organization can be similarly multifaceted. As more and more organizations are made up of contract, temporary, or even volunteer employees, more of these individuals are affiliated with multiple organizations, making the boundaries among them less easily discerned.

Although organizational boundaries may be loose at times with respect to employment relationships, the marketplace is very clear about which entity absorbs the financial impact of its activities, creating serious competitive dynamics among organizations. Competition can be very motivating, but it can also fuel some of the negative intergroup dynamics discussed elsewhere in this volume. Members of groups that are in competition with one another exhibit cognitive biases, in which members overestimate their own group's abilities and underestimate those of competitors. Group members also generate stereotypes of the outgroup and judge outgroup members' actions more harshly and with more negative attributions than their own. In addition to the negative social impact such dynamics can generate, they can ultimately have a negative impact on an organization's survival, because biased interpretations of events can lead to a failure to recognize when a change in organizational strategy is needed.

Many organizational researchers concern themselves with understanding how organizations adapt to changes in their environment. One view, known as the *population ecology* tradition, maintains that organizations do not make large adaptations but simply die out, and new organizations form to take their place. An alternative view is that organizations can make even radical adaptations to stay afloat in a competitive environment. Research on *organizational learning* is concerned with the ways in which organizations adapt to the environment and improve their processes to enhance their performance. The changes that organizations make can vary in their level of difficulty to implement, with some consisting of *single-loop learning*, or changes that are made without altering underlying practices and routines, and others consisting of *double-loop learning*, which involves change in fundamental organizational policies and practices. Some researchers of organizational learning examine how organizations progress through learning curves by accumulating gradual improvements over time and incorporating the learning in the form of new routines, structures, and technologies. Most agree that learning is difficult for organizations: Research and experience both demonstrate that it is challenging to get a group of workers to understand and endorse a new set of goals or processes and to change their behavior accordingly in a coordinated fashion.

Leadership

Over time, the understanding of leadership reflected in research has shifted away from an understanding of leadership in terms of who a leader *is* and toward an understanding of what leaders *do*. Traditionally, research on leadership has focused on the kinds of people that were the most likely to emerge as leaders, identifying various personality and behavioral traits that correlated with leadership emergence. In the 1960s and 1970s, researchers began to explore contingency models of leadership, acknowledging the importance of the match between the person and the situation. Even more recent are the behavioral theories of leadership, the most comprehensive based on the Ohio State studies, which narrowed a thousand dimensions of leadership behavior down to two: *initiating structure* and *consideration*. Along with this more behavioral approach, researchers have explored different styles leaders can employ for carrying out these functions, with *charismatic* and *transformational* leadership among the more widely researched styles.

Leadership scholars generally agree that basic intelligence, courage, and interpersonal skill are all necessary ingredients for effectively carrying out leadership functions and are not easily learned. Beyond these basic components, most writers on the topic argue that leadership skills can be acquired through training and experience. Business and professional schools have launched many courses on leadership on the basis of this premise and strive to teach the best approaches for developing leadership.

In addition to the question of whether leaders are born or made, leadership scholars debate whether leadership is the domain of a single individual or can be shared. Successful top management teams, and groups such as the conductorless Orpheus Chamber Orchestra, are heralded as examples of how leadership can be exercised by a collective. Research has explored the conditions that promote the success of a team to lead an organization, finding that these conditions are similar to those needed for groups and organizations to succeed in general—a clear purpose, the right people, and the right strategy for coordinating members' work.

Recent Trends in Teams and Organizations

Although traditional conceptions of an organization have involved notions of people working face-to-face in a shared organizational space, both globalization and the Internet have stretched the notion of what it means to be an organization. Thanks to technology, goods are purchased, services are rendered, and payments exchanged, all without tangible evidence of human involvement.

Although a growing number of organizations exist entirely on the Internet, even traditional organizations are increasingly convening work groups or teams that are "virtual." In addition, as opposed to belonging to one group or department, organization members may be participants in multiple groups within the organization simultaneously, a phenomenon that poses new challenges for the development of group identity and the coordination of work. Both of these trends enhance the core difficulties that organizations experience.

Distributed Teams

Distributed, or virtual, teams are composed of members who reside in different physical locations and who carry out their work with few or no face-to-face meetings. Distributed teams can vary in the degree to which members are distributed. Some teams might simply be split in half, with members at two different locations, and other teams might have members who are each at their own unique location. In addition to degree of distribution, distributed teams can also vary with respect to how much *asynchrony* characterizes their communications. Synchronous communications consist of face-to-face meetings, conference calls, or video conferences, whereas asynchronous communications occur through e-mail, voice messages, or threaded online discussions. As increasing numbers of organizations have had experience with distributed teams, it has become clear that electronic communication among members is not a panacea. Distributed teams do relatively well with innovation tasks for which ideas and solutions

need to be generated, for example, but generally underperform face-to-face teams on decision-making tasks. Although decision support systems can improve performance slightly, decisions made from afar still tend to take more time, involve less exchange of information, and result in less participant satisfaction with the outcome than is the case with face-to-face teams.

Temporary Project Teams and Multiple Team Membership

A separate but related trend in organizations involves membership on temporary or multiple simultaneous teams. Although classic research on the conditions necessary for team success point to the benefits of stable, bounded teams that stay intact long enough for members to develop a solid base of trust and cohesion, organizational structures are becoming more dynamic and flexible and hence create the opposite conditions for many teams. An increasing number of organizations are structured around projects, involving teams that work on a temporary basis. Although some of these temporary teams work well, others struggle, and researchers are only beginning to understand the conditions necessary for effective temporary teams. It is also increasingly the case in project-based organizations that individuals divide their time among multiple teams simultaneously, leveraging their expertise in different areas as it is needed. In such a situation, the employment relationship as traditionally conceived is turned on its head: Instead of managers carefully devising roles and coordinating role systems, individual employees craft their own jobs through involvement in different projects and bear much of the responsibility for coordination.

Both these trends pose challenges in the areas that are challenging to organizations more generally: how to define and prioritize among competing objectives, select individuals and socialize them in such a diverse environment, coordinate work, interface among projects, and provide a unity of leadership when many leaders are involved. Although working in a distributed manner and on multiple projects can be tolerated well in some circumstances, allowing individuals and teams to experience increased autonomy and learning and enriched social networks, other circumstances lead to individual stress and team disintegration. Ongoing research is investigating the conditions that allow such systems to operate effectively.

Studying Organizations

The issues discussed so far require an eclectic set of research tools. Some phenomena are observable only in field settings, and so their investigation requires a variety of field research methods, including observations, interviews, and surveys. Such research requires a high degree of cooperation from an organizational sponsor, as well as a broad base of participation from organizational members. Conducting a quantitative field study necessitates a relatively large sample size (frequently upwards of 200 respondents) to ensure a broad cross section of the organization and enough intact groups for analysis. Researchers dealing with quantitative data from multiple organizational groups often must use advanced statistical techniques to account for the lack of independence of members of the same group, or clusters of individuals within organizational departments or units, because such nonindependence of observations violates the assumptions of traditional regression models. Locating good measures of performance in field research can also be a challenge because most organizations do not maintain systematic evaluations of performance. In addition to collecting survey or observational data, some researchers in organizations conduct *quasi-experiments*, for example, by introducing interventions to alter the behavior of experimental groups, which is then compared with the behavior of control groups that did not receive the intervention.

As an alternative to field research, some organizational researchers isolate variables of interest in an organizational setting but then study them in the more controlled conditions of a laboratory. These researchers typically use traditional experimental techniques commonly employed by researchers in other traditions of psychology, manipulating specific independent variables to observe their effects on dependent variables.

Regardless of the methods used, organizational research is a fascinating and dynamic endeavor, one that requires continuous innovation in methods and theories. Organizational researchers can be found in traditional sociology and psychology departments, as well as in economics, business, medicine, law, computer science, and public policy, among other academic programs. The diversity of approaches to organizational research is very useful given the diversity of organizations themselves.

Anita Williams Woolley

See also Action Research; Boundary Spanning; Culture; Group Performance; Identification and Commitment; Job Design; Leadership; Personnel Turnover; Roles; Self-Managing Teams; Transactive Memory Systems; Virtual/Internet Groups; Work Teams

Further Readings

Argote, L. (1999). *Organizational learning: Creating, retaining, and transferring knowledge.* Norwell, MA: Kluwer Academic.

Argyris, C. (1999). *On organizational learning.* Malden, MA: Blackwell.

Barker, J. R. (1993). Tightening the iron cage: Concertive control in self-managing teams. *Administrative Science Quarterly, 38*(3), 408–437.

Cyert, R. M., & March, J. G. (1963). *A behavioral theory of the firm.* Englewood Cliffs, NJ: Prentice Hall.

March, J. G., & Simon, H. A. (1958). *Organizations.* New York: John Wiley

Hackman, J. R., & Oldham, G. R. (1980). *Work redesign.* Reading, MA: Addison-Wesley.

Katz, D., & Kahn, R. L. (1966). *The social psychology of organizations.* New York: John Wiley.

Locke, E. A., & Latham, G. P. (1990). *A theory of goal setting & task performance.* Englewood Cliffs, NJ: Prentice Hall.

Thompson, J. D. (1967). *Organizations in action.* New York: McGraw-Hill.

Wageman, R., Nunes, D. A., Burruss, J. A., & Hackman, J. R. (2008). *Senior leadership teams: What it takes to make them great.* Boston: Harvard Business School Press.

OSTRACISM

Ostracism occurs when someone is ignored and excluded by others. According to Kipling Williams and his colleagues, the act of ostracism is an adaptive response that occurs within groups as a reaction to burdensome members who threaten the group's strength or safety. Ostracism can allow the ostracized individual to correct his or her behavior or seek out other groups to join, thereby ensuring the individual's survival. Although considered largely a group phenomenon, ostracism can also occur within dyadic relationships, where it is commonly known as *the silent treatment*.

Since the mid-1990s, researchers have conducted hundreds of experiments assessing the impact of ostracism (and the related phenomenon of rejection) on an individual's physiological responses, cognitions, emotions, and behaviors. A variety of paradigms have been used to manipulate ostracism and to measure its outcomes, resulting in converging evidence that even the slightest hint of ostracism is detected quickly and causes immediate pain, distress, an embodied feeling of coldness, threatened needs (belonging, self-esteem, control, and meaningful existence), and negative emotion. The evidence then diverges into different (sometimes paradoxical) behavioral responses.

Often, behavioral responses to ostracism appear to facilitate future inclusion in a group. For instance, ostracized individuals have been observed to pay closer attention to social information and to better interpret nonverbal social signals related to acceptance and liking (e.g., distinguishing between genuine and nongenuine smiles). Further, ostracized individuals are more likely to mimic (consciously and nonconsciously) others, to conform to unanimous but incorrect majorities, to comply with costly requests, and to behave in ways that make them appear more socially acceptable.

However, researchers have also observed ostracized individuals to feel emotionally numb and to be cognitively impaired (on complex tasks) or to retaliate and aggress toward nonresponsible others. When ostracism appears to be permanent or heavily thwarts a sense of control, the emotional system appears to shut down, self-regulation is impaired, and antisocial responses increase. Current thinking is that when future inclusion is unlikely, desires to control one's social environment and force others to acknowledge one's existence can trump desires to be liked, resulting in fewer prosocial actions (e.g., less volunteering, fewer donations, less cooperation), increased retaliation (e.g., noise blasts), and aggression.

Methods to Experimentally Induce Ostracism

Ostracism research employs a variety of research methods, or paradigms. Whereas a robust and consistent response (e.g., pain, distress, negative emotion) occurs to all manipulations of ostracism, the variations noted above (emotional numbness, prosocial vs. antisocial responses) may reflect differences among the paradigms that are not yet fully understood.

Ball Tossing

The ball-tossing paradigm is a face-to-face interaction among individuals who are typically waiting for an experimenter. The ball-tossing emerges, apparently spontaneously, when someone (a confederate) notices a ball, picks it up, and begins throwing it to the other participants. Only one participant is, in fact, naïve to the situation; the other two (both confederates) follow an inclusion or ostracism script. Once each person has had a chance to catch and throw the ball a few times, participants randomly assigned to the ostracism condition are never again thrown the ball, nor are they even looked at or responded to. The confederates continue playing enthusiastically for another few minutes. In the inclusion condition, participants receive the ball just as often as anyone else.

Cyberball

In the cyberball paradigm, participants are led to believe they are tossing a virtual ball with other alleged players via computers connected to the Internet. The cover story for the study is that the researchers are interested in the effects of mental visualization on a subsequent task, and the participants are told that a good way to warm up is to engage in a mental visualization exercise. The participants are told to use the cyberball experience as a means to visualize the other alleged players, trying to imagine (for example) where those players are, what they look like, and so on. Actually, the computer software controls participants' levels of inclusion or ostracism. The researcher programs the software to direct the course and speed of the ball-toss game, the frequency of inclusion, player information, and iconic representations of every player. Ostracism is manipulated by how often the ball is thrown to a participant. Typically, the ostracized participant receives one or two throws at the beginning, but after that, the other players throw the ball exclusively to one another. Inclusion occurs when a participant receives the ball just as often as anyone else. Typically, the game proceeds for 20 to 40 throws.

Life Alone

The life-alone prognosis paradigm involves a manipulation of ostracism in which participants respond to a personality questionnaire, receive accurate feedback about their levels of introversion and extroversion, and then are given one of three additional forms of feedback. The participants in these studies are generally young individuals whose lives are mostly still ahead of them. In the accepted, high-belonging condition, participants are told that they are the type of person who has rewarding relationships throughout life, a long and stable marriage, and enduring friendships with people who care about them. In the rejected, low-belonging condition, participants are told that they are the type of person who ends up alone later in life, and that although they have friends and relationships now, by the time they are in their mid-20s, most of these will disappear. Finally, in a negative-feedback control condition, participants are told that they will endure a lifetime of accidents and injuries. The purpose of this condition is to distinguish the effects specific to ostracism from those associated with negative outcomes in general.

Get Acquainted

This paradigm involves the use of a small group of actual participants engaged in a get-acquainted discussion. They are given examples of topics to discuss (e.g., movies, college majors) and take turns talking within the group setting. After this discussion, they are separated and asked to identify the person in the group with whom they would most like to work on an upcoming task. A few minutes later, they are told by the researcher that either everyone wanted to work with them (inclusion) or that no one wanted to work with them (rejection).

Additional Paradigms

Researchers have also employed manipulations that involved conversations (i.e., face-to-face, chat room, or cell phone text messages), role-playing, scenario descriptions of rejection and social exclusion, relived or imagined rejection experiences, daily diary entries, and virtual reality worlds.

Responses to Ostracism

Reflexive Reactions to Ostracism: Pain and Distress

Reflexive reactions to ostracism are relatively insensitive to individual differences or situational context. Thus, they appear to be triggered prior to cognitive appraisals. Reflexive measures include retrospective self-reports ("how were you feeling *during* the experience?"), online affective measures ("turn a dial to indicate your current feelings of positivity/negativity"), and physiological responses (blood pressure, dorsal anterior cingulate cortex activation). For self-reports, participants are typically asked immediately after an episode of ostracism how they felt *during* that episode. These measures contrast with *reflective* measures that ask participants at a later point (between 5 and 45 minutes after an episode of ostracism) how they are feeling *right now*. The "during" measures assess ostracism's immediate or reflexive impact; the "right now" measures assess ostracism's impact after the initiation of cognitive, emotional, and behavioral coping mechanisms. The evidence suggests that the immediate or reflexive reactions to ostracism are painful and are not moderated by individual differences or situational factors.

Exceptions to unmoderated distress to ostracism appear to occur when the ostracism is more ambiguous. Less severe or more ambiguous manipulations of ostracism allow individual differences (e.g., social anxiety, loneliness, rejection sensitivity) and situational constraints (e.g., ostracism from ingroup vs. outgroup members) to moderate even immediate reactions. Partial ostracism is another way in which the ostracism experience is more ambiguous. Partial ostracism involves less exclusion than does complete ostracism and simultaneously provides the individual with a glimmer of hope for inclusion. Partial ostracism often involves "out-of-the-loop experiences," in which individuals are included in some, but not all, aspects of group activity. These experiences also appear to engage cognitive appraisals that are sensitive to individual differences among ostracized individuals and situational variations involving, for example, who is ostracizing whom, and why.

Reflective Responses to Ostracism: Threatened Needs and Coping

The available evidence suggests that the reflexive pain or distress signal is quickly followed by appraisals and coping mechanisms that direct the individual toward thoughts and feelings that alleviate the pain or fortify thwarted needs. In contrast to reflexive responses, reflective responses to ostracism are sensitive to situational factors and individual differences. Thus, one can repair damage to belonging or self-esteem needs by trying to behave in ways that will meet the group's approval, joining a new group, or even thinking about strong social ties in other realms of one's life. Repairing damage to control and existence needs, however, might involve exerting social control over others, provoking recognition from others, and even being aggressive toward others. Individual differences can also moderate a broad collection of coping responses to ostracism. Social anxiety, for instance, moderates reflective responses to ostracism and also affects the rate of recovery. Socially anxious individuals, when ostracized, are more likely to ruminate about and thereby prolong the negative impact of ostracism, and to experience threats to self-regulation, than are individuals who are less socially anxious.

Conclusion

Research on ostracism, social exclusion, and rejection has proliferated in the past decade, and the field of social psychology has benefited from a considerable amount of theory and empirical evidence about these processes and their impact. Clearly, even for brief episodes with minimal mundane realism, ostracism plunges people into a temporary state of misery, pain, distress, sadness, and anger. It is also clear that exposures to short episodes of ostracism, social exclusion, and rejection lead to robust behavioral consequences, many of which can be characterized as potentially dysfunctional to the individual's well-being, such as becoming socially susceptible to influence, eager for social attention, antisocial and hostile, or

cognitively impaired. Future research needs to address the role of personality variables and situational contexts that steer individuals down different behavioral paths. Other factors, such as whether individuals perceive the ostracism to be targeted at them as individuals or at their group memberships, also merit attention as researchers begin to consider ostracism on a larger scale, as when particular cultures, religions, and political ideologies are the sources (or targets) of ostracism.

Kipling D. Williams and
Adrienne R. Carter-Sowell

See also Cliques; Deviance; Discrimination; Inclusion/Exclusion; Power; Sociometric Choice; Stigma

Further Readings

Eisenberger, N. I., Lieberman, M. D., & Williams, K. D. (2003). Does rejection hurt? An fMRI study of social exclusion. *Science, 302,* 290–292.

Williams, K. D. (2001). *Ostracism: The power of silence.* New York: Guilford Press.

Williams, K. D. (2007). Ostracism. *Annual Review of Psychology, 58,* 425–452.

Williams, K. D., Forgas, J. P., & von Hippel, W. (Eds). (2005). *The social outcast: Ostracism, social exclusion, rejection, and bullying.* New York: Psychology Press.

OUTGROUP HOMOGENEITY EFFECT

"They all look the same to me." This kind of statement about an outgroup is often heard. The tendency to perceive outgroups as more homogeneous, or less variable, than ingroups is called the *outgroup homogeneity effect.* This entry describes how the outgroup homogeneity effect was first experimentally demonstrated, reviews evidence examining the robustness of the effect, and discusses some factors that influence the magnitude of the effect.

Background Research

In some of the first work on the outgroup homogeneity effect, men and women were asked to rate men and women on positive and negative dimensions that were stereotypically masculine or feminine. Results showed that over and above any overall ingroup preference (i.e., rating one's own group more positively than the outgroup), participants judged the outgroup more stereotypically than the ingroup. More specifically, when participants were asked what percentage of each group had attributes that were consistent with the group's stereotype and what percentage had attributes that were inconsistent with that stereotype, they reported that the outgroup had relatively more consistent group members and fewer inconsistent group members than did the ingroup. These results represent strong support for the outgroup homogeneity effect because ratings were collected from both groups, and the effect was found for the men's ratings and for the women's ratings. In addition, the effect was found on positive as well as on negative stereotypic attributes, indicating that it is independent of any tendency to see the outgroup as having relatively more members who are consistent with only negative attributes. And finally, the use of gender groups permits one to conclude that the effect exists even when familiarity is high for both the ingroup and the outgroup.

The outgroup homogeneity effect has been replicated with a wide variety of social groups in addition to gender-defined groups: sororities, experimentally created groups, and groups defined by age, nationality, and ethnicity. A meta-analysis of the effect across published studies concluded that the outgroup homogeneity effect is a small but nevertheless robust effect. In addition, it appears that the effect is smaller with experimentally created groups than with real groups.

One interesting research development has been the identification of two different forms of perceived group variability and, therefore, of the outgroup homogeneity effect. The first component of perceived variability is the degree to which a group is seen as having a relatively large number of people who confirm the stereotype, compared with the proportion of those who do not. This component, referred to as *perceived stereotypicality*, was originally examined when outgroup homogeneity was demonstrated with groups defined by gender, as described above. The other component is the *perceived dispersion* of a group, that is, the extent to which group members vary around what is perceived to be the group mean on an attribute dimension. To make clear this distinction, imagine that one person sees a group on average more stereotypically than another person does. It might still be the case that they both agree on the actual variability within the group around the group average. Stereotypicality refers to the extremity of the group mean on stereotypic attributes. Dispersion refers to the perceived variability around that group mean. It has been demonstrated that these two components of perceived group variability need not be highly related to each other. However, outgroup homogeneity has been shown for both components, although it appears to be larger for perceived stereotypicality than for perceived dispersion.

Causes and Consequences of the Outgroup Homogeneity Effect

To explain the outgroup homogeneity effect (why it occurs and what makes it stronger or weaker), researchers have asked participants to verbalize their thoughts while making group ratings. When reflecting on impressions of their ingroup, participants made frequent references to the self and to specific subgroups of the ingroup. When considering the outgroup, mentions of the self or of specific subgroups were notably scarce. From this and related results, it has been argued that the outgroup homogeneity effect is mainly due to the fact that people hold a much more complex representation of the groups to which they belong than of those to which they do not belong.

A difference in familiarity between ingroups and outgroups has been cited as a factor causing the outgroup homogeneity effect, and this seems a reasonable explanation in part. However, the fact that the effect has been shown with groups defined by gender suggests that there are other factors that are also responsible for the effect, because one is likely to be as familiar with the gender outgroup as with the gender ingroup. In experimental contexts, it has also been demonstrated that manipulations of familiarity (i.e., getting to know more group members) did not have a major impact on the magnitude of the outgroup homogeneity effect.

There have also been explanations of outgroup homogeneity that are more motivational in nature, suggesting that, to some extent, one is simultaneously motivated to be a part of one's ingroup and to be distinct or unique as an individual. This means that although one values one's ingroup membership, one nevertheless also values a unique and distinctive identity. As a result, one may attribute these same desires to other ingroup members and hence come to see the ingroup as more diverse and variable than the outgroup.

Some have argued that the outgroup homogeneity effect is moderated by the size and status of the ingroup relative to the outgroup. What is clear is that smaller groups and perhaps lower-status groups are sometimes judged to be more homogeneous. And this effect of size and status on perceived variability may mean that participants who come from minority groups may see the outgroup as *less* homogeneous than the ingroup. However, strictly speaking, this difference in perceived variability is not attributable to perceiving the outgroup as less homogeneous than the ingroup, because in this case the outgroup–ingroup distinction is confounded with group size or status. We can think of this simply as a group size or status effect on perceived variability: Everyone agrees that smaller and low-status groups are more homogeneous, and this perception does not depend on whether the perceiver is a member of those groups.

Regarding the consequences of the outgroup homogeneity effect, research has shown that outgroup stereotypes are more likely to be applied to members of the outgroup than ingroup stereotypes are to be applied to members of the ingroup. In general, group stereotypes are more potent, in that they have a greater influence on the judgment of individual group members, the less the perceived variability of the group.

Charles M. Judd and Nicolas Kervyn

See also Categorization; Optimal Distinctiveness; Perceived Group Variability; Social Identity Theory; Stereotyping

Further Readings

Linville, P. W., Fischer, G. W., & Salovey, P. (1989). Perceived distributions of the characteristics of in-group and out-group members: Empirical and a computer simulation. *Journal of Personality and Social Psychology, 57,* 165–188.

Mullen, B., & Hu, L. (1989). Perceptions of in-group and out-group variability: A meta-analytic integration. *Basic and Applied Social Psychology, 10,* 233–252.

Park, B., & Rothbart, M. (1982). Perception of out-group homogeneity and levels of social categorization: Memory for the subordinate attributes of in-group and out-group members. *Journal of Personality and Social Psychology, 42,* 1051–1068.

Path–Goal Theory of Leadership

Path–goal theory was initially developed by Robert House to explain workplace leadership. The theory builds heavily on two theories of work motivation: goal setting and expectancy theory. *Goal-setting theory* suggests that an effective way to motivate people is to set challenging but realistic goals and to offer rewards for goal accomplishment. *Expectancy theory* explains why people work hard to attain work goals. People will engage in behaviors that lead to goal attainment if they believe that (a) goal attainment leads to something they value (e.g., increase in pay, status, promotion) and (b) the behaviors they engage in have a high chance (expectancy) of leading to the goal. If people do not value the reward for goal attainment or believe that their behavior is unlikely to lead to goal attainment, then they will not be motivated to work hard.

Path–goal theory builds on these propositions by arguing that effective leaders are those who help their subordinates achieve their goals. According to path–goal theory, leaders have a responsibility to provide their subordinates with the information and support necessary to achieve the work goals. One way to do this is to make salient the effort–reward relationship by linking desirable outcomes to goal attainment (e.g., emphasizing the positive outcomes to the subordinates if they achieve their goals) and/or increasing the belief (expectancy) that their work behaviors can lead to goal attainment

(e.g., by emphasizing that certain behaviors are likely to lead to goal attainment).

The term *path–goal* reflects the belief that effective leaders clarify the paths necessary for their subordinates to achieve the subordinates' goals. Leaders can do this in two main ways. First, leaders can engage in behaviors that help subordinates facilitate goal attainment (e.g., by providing information and other resources necessary to obtain goals). Second, leaders can engage in behaviors that remove obstacles that might hinder subordinates' pursuit of their goals (e.g., by removing workplace factors that reduce the chances of goal attainment).

Leadership Styles

Path–goal theory is a *contingency theory*, proposing that effective leadership is contingent on the leader's adopting a particular style of behavior to match the needs to the subordinate and the situation in which the subordinate is working. The theory identifies four main types of leadership behaviors, each of which can help subordinates attain their goals. *Supportive* leadership involves being considerate of the needs of subordinates and creating a friendly atmosphere to work in. *Directive* leadership involves letting subordinates know what is expected of them, giving clear guidelines, and making sure they know the rules and procedures to get the work done. *Participative* leadership involves consulting with subordinates and taking account of their opinions and suggestions when making decisions. *Achievement-oriented* leadership involves setting challenging work goals, emphasizing the need for excellence in performance, and showing confidence that the subordinates will attain high work standards.

The choice of which style of leadership to use depends on two groups of contingency variables. One group concerns environmental factors that are outside the control of the subordinate (e.g., task structure, authority system, work group), and the other group concerns individual factors that are inherently part of the subordinate (e.g., personality, experience, and abilities).

The theory makes a number of predictions concerning which style of leadership will be most effective in particular situations and with types of subordinates. Because of the large number of contingency factors, there are many potential predictions; some of the main ones are described below.

Supportive leadership should be most effective when the nature of the work is stressful, boring, or dangerous. This is because a supportive style by the leader will increase subordinates' satisfaction and self-confidence and reduce the negative aspects of the situation. This should lead to an increase in the intrinsic valance of the job and the expectation that it will be performed well and lead to the attainment of goals. However, supportive leadership would have little benefit for those subordinates who are satisfied in their work and find it enjoyable (because they already find the work intrinsically motivating).

Directive leadership is most effective when people are unsure what tasks they have to do or when there is a lot of uncertainty within their working environment. This occurs primarily because a directive style clarifies what the subordinates need to do and therefore reduces task ambiguity. In addition, the directive style will make clear the relationship between effort and reward and therefore the expectancy that effort will lead to a valued outcome.

Participative leadership can be effective in unstructured situations because it can increase role clarity, and it can also be effective for people who have a high need to control their environment. Conversely, this style will be less effective for those people who like to be directed at the workplace and do not take on too much responsibility for their outcomes.

Finally, an achievement-oriented style is effective when the work is complex and the environment is uncertain. This is because it can increase subordinates' self-confidence that they are able to attain the goals.

According to path–goal theory, leaders, to be effective, need to do the following: recognize the needs of those they manage and try to satisfy these needs through the workplace, reward people for achieving their goals, help subordinates identify the most effective paths they need to take to reach their goals, and clear those paths so that subordinates can reach their goals. The particular style of leadership that is effective in achieving these outcomes will depend on the contingency factors described above.

The theory has a great deal of intuitive appeal because it can be applied easily to the workplace. It emphasizes understanding the needs of subordinates within the context of their working situation and using the appropriate style of leadership to help subordinates achieve their work goals. One implication of this approach is that leaders need to adopt multiple leadership styles and be able to tailor these styles to the characteristics of the subordinate and the situation. Because of the emphasis on the role of leaders' behaviors rather than their traits, the theory has many applications for leadership training programs.

Robin Martin

See also Charismatic Leadership; Contingency Theories of Leadership; Great Person Theory of Leadership; Group Performance; Interactionist Theories of Leadership; Leader-Member (LMX) Theory; Leadership; Personality Theories of Leadership; Power; Social Identity Theory of Leadership; Transactional Leadership Theories; Transformational Leadership Theories; Vertical Dyad Linkage Model

Further Readings

House, R. J. (1971). A path–goal theory of leadership effectiveness. *Administrative Science Quarterly, 16*, 321–338.

House, R. J. (1996). Path–goal theory of leadership: Lessons, legacy, and a reformulated theory. *Leadership Quarterly, 7*, 323–352.

PERCEIVED GROUP VARIABILITY

Stereotypes are beliefs about the attributes of social categories or groups that potentially affect how the perceiver judges and behaves toward individual group members. They concern the attributes that are typically associated with a social group. But perceivers differ in the degree to which they assume that all group members resemble each other. Accordingly, the *perceived variability* of a group captures the degree to which stereotypes about that group are strong and, accordingly, the degree to which group stereotypes influence judgments of and behavior toward members of that group. If a group is perceived as relatively low in variability, then the social perceiver will expect all members of that group with whom he or she interacts to closely fit the stereotype of the group. In contrast, if a group is perceived as relatively high in variability, then the social perceiver cannot be sure that a specific group member fits the stereotype and will therefore pay more attention to individuating information about the member. Further, when confronted with a low-variability group, people are more confident in the behavioral predictions they make about group members than when confronted with a high-variability group.

Measuring Perceived Group Variability

Different authors have used different methods to measure perceived group variability. Those measures can be grouped into two categories: (1) the *degree of stereotypicality* of the group on a given dimension and (2) the *extent of the dispersion* of the group around the group mean on that dimension. The stereotypicality of a group is measured by questions that ask for the percentage of group members who are consistent with the group stereotype and the percentage who are inconsistent with that stereotype. From these two percentage estimates, a researcher can compute difference scores (percentage consistent minus percentage inconsistent), with lower scores indicating greater perceived group variability (i.e., those who are inconsistent with the group stereotype represent a relatively larger percentage of the group). The dispersion around the mean can be measured in different ways. A researcher can ask about the perceived group range on various stereotypic attributes (where the highest and lowest group members fall) and take the difference between these two. Alternatively, a researcher can ask participants to indicate a perceived distribution of the group on stereotypic

attributes and then compute the standard deviation of that perceived distribution. Research has shown that the two components of perceived group variability (perceived stereotypicality and dispersion) are far from redundant with each other, which suggests that they are two different, relatively independent components of perceived group variability.

Theories of Group Variability Perception

Interest in perceived group variability started with research on the outgroup homogeneity effect. Whether it is measured through group stereotypicality or group dispersion, people consistently perceive outgroups to be less variable than their ingroup. Studies that have demonstrated the outgroup homogeneity effect have used what are called *full ingroup–outgroup designs*, in which members of different groups (e.g., males and females) rate both their own ingroup and the outgroup, using both stereotypicality and group dispersion measures. Outgroup homogeneity has been demonstrated with groups defined by gender, by ethnicity, and by a host of other group categorization variables. It is important to note that this effect is independent of ingroup favoritism, which is the tendency to prefer the ingroup to the outgroup. In other words, although the outgroup homogeneity effect reflects a difference in the way ingroups and outgroups are perceived, it is not the same as dislike of the outgroup relative to the ingroup. Indeed, the outgroup homogeneity effect has been found even when an outgroup is rated on dimensions on which the outgroup stereotype is positive.

A presumed difference in familiarity between ingroups and outgroups has been identified by some as the main factor responsible for the outgroup homogeneity effect. Yet, as previously mentioned, an outgroup homogeneity effect has been demonstrated even with gender groups, which are arguably the two social groups for which there exists extensive familiarity with both the outgroup and the ingroup. It is true that not all research has been able to replicate the outgroup homogeneity effect with gender, and the magnitude of the gender effect may depend on whether perceived stereotypicality or group dispersion is the component of perceived group variability that is assessed.

A persistent question in the perceived variability literature concerns the informational basis of such variability inferences. One model that has been advanced is an *exemplar-based model*, which argues that the different exemplars of a social group that one encounters are stored as separate memory traces and that when one is asked to give an impression about a group, one retrieves stored exemplars of that group and computes an impression based on those retrieved exemplars. Others, however, have argued for an *abstraction-based model*, which posits that one uses each new group member to compute an impression about the group and then stores that impression. The main difference between these two models in explaining perceived group variability is that in the exemplar-based model, the variability depends on which exemplars are used at the retrieval stage, whereas in the abstraction-based model, the variability is an aspect of the group impression that is computed at the encoding stage and revised in the light of subsequent information.

Experiments have been conducted to test the different predictions that are made by the different models. In one study, participants were presented with a group that was either high or low in variability. In addition, the memorability of particular group members was manipulated, with either the more moderate group members being more memorable or the more extreme group members being more memorable. Results were influenced by the variability manipulation but not by the memory manipulation, which lends credence to the abstraction-based model's assumption that variability impressions are constructed online at encoding and not at the retrieval stage, as posited by the exemplar-based model.

Based on the abstraction-based model, an explanation for the outgroup homogeneity effect is that social perceivers have low motivation to update their impressions of groups to which they do not belong. Accordingly, the variability of the outgroup is computed on the basis of the first few encounters with members of that group and is thereafter not likely to be updated. For the ingroup, in contrast, the social perceiver is motivated to construct a more complex and diversified impression. In support of this, researchers have asked participants to think aloud about their ingroup and an outgroup. These think-aloud protocols were then coded. Results showed that for the ingroup, participants made a lot of references to the self and to different subgroups. In contrast, for the outgroup, participants made very few references to the self and to subgroups; instead, the outgroup tended to be discussed as a whole entity.

Perceived group variability is one of the two main factors that underlie the concept of perceived *entitativity*. Entitativity is the degree to which an aggregate of persons is considered to make up a meaningful, or real, group. An important component of entitativity is common fate, or group essence, defined as the degree to which all members of a group share a common core of values and outcomes. More homogeneous groups are perceived as more entitative, and therefore their members are treated more as group members than as individuals.

Effects of Perceived Group Variability

Perceived group variability has been shown to have a variety of effects on social judgment and interaction. As already discussed, members of low-variability groups are judged to more strongly possess the group stereotype and are therefore responded to in a more stereotypic manner. In addition, the ease with which stereotypes are likely to change depends on the perceived variability of the stereotyped group in ways that may not be entirely intuitive. Most models of stereotype change suggest that one is likely to change a group stereotype if one encounters group members who disconfirm that stereotype. But the degree to which such group members actually disconfirm a stereotype is likely to depend in part on the perceived group variability. Someone who is discrepant from the perceived group mean may actually be seen as more discrepant if the group is perceived as very homogeneous than if greater group variability is perceived. As a result, that discrepant group member may actually produce less stereotype change in the case of the homogeneous group because of what has been called *subtyping*: The individual is judged to be such an exception to the rule that he or she is discounted as atypical. In contrast, in the case of a more variable group, that individual may not be discounted, and stereotype change may be more likely to occur.

Charles M. Judd and Nicolas Kervyn

See also Categorization; Entitativity; Outgroup Homogeneity Effect; Stereotyping

Further Readings

Mullen, B., & Hu, L. (1989). Perceptions of in-group and out-group variability: A meta-analytic integration. *Basic and Applied Social Psychology, 10,* 233–252.

Park, B., & Hastie, R. (1987). Perception of variability in category development: Instance- versus abstraction-based stereotypes. *Journal of Personality and Social Psychology, 53,* 621–636.

Park, B., Judd, C. M., & Ryan, C. S. (1991). Social categorization and the representation of variability in formation. In W. Stroebe & M. Hewstone (Eds.), *European Review of Social Psychology* (Vol. 2, pp. 211–245). Chichester, UK: Wiley.

Park, B., Wolsko, C., & Judd, C. M. (2001). Measurement of subtyping in stereotype change. *Journal of Experimental Social Psychology, 37,* 325–332.

Tajfel, H. (1970). Experiments in intergroup discrimination. *Scientific American, 223,* 96–102.

Yzerbyt, V. Y., Judd, C. M., & Corneille, O. (2004). Perceived variability, entitativity, and essentialism: Introduction and overview. In V. Y. Yzerbyt, C. M., Judd, & O. Corneille (Eds.), *The psychology of group perception: Perceived variability, entitativity, and essentialism.* London: Psychology Press.

PERSONALITY THEORIES OF LEADERSHIP

Are you born to be a leader? Are you a "natural"? Or is leadership a set of behaviors and competencies that anyone can develop, given the right experiences, circumstances, and training? The answers to these questions have been debated for centuries. Here, we focus on theories of leadership that would answer with a resounding yes to the first two questions, emphasizing that leadership is deeply embedded within our personalities or in the traits with which we were born. This entry defines and reviews *personality-* and *trait-based theories of leadership* before turning to critiques of these approaches.

Personality- and trait-based approaches to leadership argue that certain individuals have innate characteristics that make them ideally suited for leadership, and these traits or characteristics are what differentiate these leaders from everyone else. Early approaches in this genre included the *great man theories*, which were based on the assumption that the capacity for leadership is inherent—that great leaders are born, not made or developed. These theories often portrayed great leaders as heroic, mythical, and uniquely destined to rise to leadership when their skills were needed. The term *great man* reflects an assumption of these early theories that leadership was a predominantly male quality, especially in the domains of political and military leadership.

One of the first systematic attempts to understand leadership in the 20th century, the great man theory evolved into personality- or trait-based approaches as more modern research revealed that leadership was not inherently male dominated and that leadership could be found and studied in more common settings rather than at the highest levels of organizations or nations. More than a century of research has been conducted on the traits that have been associated to a greater or lesser degree with leadership, and some traits have received consistent support while others have emerged in some studies but not in others. An overview of research on the *Big Five personality factors* and the degree to which each has been linked to leadership is followed by a summary of the five more-specific traits that have been most consistently connected to leadership.

Leadership and the Big Five

Since the 1960s, researchers have examined whether there is a relationship between the basic agreed-on factors that make up personality and leadership. The Big Five personality factors are conscientiousness, agreeableness, neuroticism, openness, and extraversion, which some researchers have labeled the *CANOE* personality model as an easy aid to remembering each factor.

Conscientiousness is defined as an individual's tendency to be organized, thorough, controlled, decisive, and dependable. Of the Big Five factors, it is the personality factor that has been related to leadership second most strongly (after extraversion) in previous research. *Agreeableness*, or an individual's tendency to be trusting, nurturing, conforming, and accepting, has been only weakly associated with leadership. *Neuroticism*, or the tendency to be anxious, hostile, depressed, vulnerable, and insecure, has been moderately and negatively related to leadership, suggesting that most leaders tend to be low in neuroticism. *Openness*, sometimes referred to as openness to experience, refers to an individual's tendency to be curious, creative, insightful, and informed. Openness has been moderately related to leadership, suggesting that leaders tend to be somewhat higher in openness than nonleaders. Finally, *extraversion* is the personality factor that has been most strongly associated with leadership. Defined as the tendency to be sociable (discussed in greater detail below), assertive, and have positive energy, extraversion has been described as the most important personality trait of effective leaders.

Although research on the Big Five personality factors has found some relationships between these overall personality factors and leadership, focusing on more specific traits has led to more consistent findings between effective leadership and the following five traits: intelligence, self-confidence, determination, sociability, and integrity.

Specific Traits Associated With Leadership

Intelligence

A great deal of research suggests that leaders have above-average intelligence. Intellectual ability has been positively associated with cognitive reasoning skills, the capacity to articulate ideas and thoughts to others, and the perceptual ability to recognize important situational factors. Research has focused on the link between intelligence and a leader's development of good problem-solving skills, the ability to adequately assess social situations, and the ability to understand complex organizational issues. Although intelligence has consistently been shown, in a wide variety of studies, to relate positively to leadership, other research has pointed out that it is important that the leader's intellectual ability is not too dissimilar from that of his or her followers. If leaders far surpass their followers in intelligence, they may be unable to express ideas and issues in ways that appeal to or connect with their followers.

Self-Confidence

Additional research has pointed to a consistent relationship between a leader's effectiveness, on one hand, and confidence in his or her skills, technical competencies, and ideas, on the other. Having high self-esteem, a positive regard for one's own ability to lead, and assurance that one's vision or purpose is the right one all help a leader influence others. While some studies have examined self-confidence and others have focused on confidence more generally, it is clear that feeling and communicating certainty about one's own abilities as a leader is a common leadership trait.

Determination or Perseverance

Leadership is often a difficult, thankless, long, and arduous process. Perhaps as a result of this fact, a great deal of research has suggested that leaders must be determined to complete a task or get a job done, even in the face of adversity or when there is less than overwhelming support from others. Leaders show initiative and drive and frequently constitute the motivational energy behind a project or social change movement. Thus, the ability to assert oneself when necessary, be proactive, and continue to push on in the face of obstacles is a key component of leadership. In addition, this determination often involves displaying dominance and a drive to succeed even in the face of initial failures.

Sociability

Sociability is defined as a leader's desire for high-quality social relationships and the ability to maintain and restore positive relationships in difficult times that often involve adversity and crisis. Across studies, leaders often demonstrate the ability to be friendly, extraverted (outgoing), courteous, tactful, and diplomatic. In addition, leaders tend to be sensitive to the needs of others, even at the cost of attending to their own needs. In short, leaders care about the interests of others and put others' interests before their own. Leaders have good interpersonal skills that communicate their concern for others, and they work to smooth out conflicts and disagreements to maintain the group's social harmony.

Integrity

None of the previous traits addresses the fact that smart, confident, determined, and sociable leaders can also be fundamentally immoral and corrupt. The fifth factor, integrity, addresses the finding that leaders tend to be honest and trustworthy, inspiring others to respect them and trust them with important decisions and resources. Leaders are often variously described as loyal, responsible, dependable, and honest. These characteristics inspire the confidence of others and provide evidence that leaders are authentic and have the best interests of the group at heart. This is in stark opposition to individuals who use the efforts and resources of the group for their own prosperity or power and manipulate the group's time and money for their own personal gain (e.g., cult leaders Jim Jones and David Koresh).

Leadership and Emotional Intelligence

In the early 1990s, the concept of emotional intelligence was introduced by Daniel Goleman and others, and it has captured a great deal of attention from practicing leaders and from organizations seeking to enhance the leadership abilities of their employees. Emotional intelligence, abbreviated variously as EQ or EI, is defined as one's ability to perceive and express emotions, understand and reason with emotions, and effectively manage emotions, both in oneself and in others. More recently, a number of assessments have been developed to measure emotional intelligence, and efforts have been made to link emotional intelligence to one's leadership abilities and even one's ultimate successes in life.

There has been considerable debate, however, as to whether emotional intelligence represents a unique construct that is sufficiently different from the five key traits and Big Five personality factors described above. Despite this debate, it seems likely that people who are sensitive to both their own emotions and the emotions of others, and who are adept at managing emotions and accurately discerning their impact, will be more effective leaders.

Critiques of the Trait Approach to Leadership

Similar in many ways to the early great man theories, trait and personality theories assume that people inherit certain qualities and traits that make them suited to be good leaders. By looking at a range of different leaders in a variety of situations over time, trait theorists seek to identify particular personality or behavioral characteristics that leaders share. However, this approach has been criticized for its lack of explanatory power: It is unable to consistently distinguish between leaders and nonleaders. If particular traits are key features of leadership, how do we explain people who possess those qualities but are not leaders? Does an individual need one of these traits, some of them, or all of them to be a good leader? And how do we explain people who have been leaders and exerted widespread influence without possessing some or all of these traits? These questions highlight the difficulties in using trait theories to explain leadership.

Other scholars have pointed out that the recent interest in charismatic leadership essentially represents a neo-personality approach to leadership. Use of the term *charisma* in the popular vernacular focuses primarily on a personalized magnetic appeal that allows leaders to charm and influence others. This approach emphasizes the personal characteristics of the leader to attract and influence others and suggests that charisma is a quality that some leaders can effectively capitalize on to galvanize others into action.

In a similar vein, a prominent critique of the trait or personality approach to leadership is that it discourages individuals from believing they have the "right stuff" to become effective leaders. Approaching leadership as a relationship between leaders and followers or as a set of behaviors and competencies that anyone can develop provides a much more optimistic, democratic, and inclusive picture of leadership. These latter approaches emphasize that given the right experiences, circumstances, and training, each of us has both the capacity and the ability to enact effective leadership, regardless of the specific traits and personality characteristics with which we were born.

Michelle C. Bligh

See also Charismatic Leadership; Contingency Theories of Leadership; Great Person Theory of Leadership; Interactionist Theories of Leadership; Leader-Member (LMX) Theory; Leadership; Path–Goal Theory of Leadership; Power; Social Identity Theory of

Leadership; Transactional Leadership Theories; Transformational Leadership Theories; Vertical Dyad Linkage Model

Further Readings

Goldberg, L. R. (1990). An alternate "description of personality": The Big Five factor structure. *Journal of Personality and Social Psychology, 59,* 1216–1229.

Judge, T. A., Bono, J. E., Ilies, R., & Werner, M. (2002). Personality and leadership: A qualitative and quantitative review. *Journal of Applied Psychology, 87,* 765–780.

Kirkpatrick, S. A., & Locke, E. A. (1991). Leadership: Do traits matter? *Executive, 5,* 48–60.

Lord, R. G., DeVader, C. L., & Alliger, G. M. (1986). A meta-analysis of the relation between personality traits and leadership perceptions: An application of validity generalization procedures. *Journal of Applied Psychology, 71,* 402–410.

Northouse, P. G. (2007). *Leadership theory and practice* (4th ed.). Thousand Oaks, CA: Sage.

PERSONNEL TURNOVER

In today's organizations, in which human capabilities are the key source for competitive advantage, retaining talent has become critical. Turnover, a voluntary or involuntary withdrawal from the organization, exists in all organizations. The cost of turnover in U.S. organizations is estimated in billions of dollars per year. This high cost is primarily due to the need to recruit, select, and train new organizational members as replacements for those who depart. Turnover may interrupt the efficient management of the organization when experienced and knowledgeable employees leave and take with them essential know-how that cannot be easily replaced and can be used by the organization's competitors. Despite its negative consequences, turnover has some positive aspects. It creates an opportunity to replace ineffective employees with more highly skilled ones, opens promotion opportunities, allows newcomers with new ideas and knowledge to join the organization, and fosters innovation. It is not surprising, thus, that the topic of employee turnover in organizations has received substantial attention from both researchers and practitioners.

Voluntary employee turnover has been one of the most studied topics in organizational behavior research, with more than 1,000 studies on the topic in the past century. Research has addressed questions such as why and how people decide to quit their jobs, which factors encourage or disincline them to do so, and what personal and organizational consequences flow from turnover. This entry discusses the turnover decision process, identifies important predictors of turnover in groups and organizations, and describes the consequences of turnover.

The Turnover Decision Process

Voluntarily turnover happens when employees are dissatisfied with their work and experience low commitment to their organization. The relationship between satisfaction and commitment on one hand and turnover on the other has been documented in numerous studies. The relationship between turnover and these predictors, however, is not very strong and is mediated by emotional, cognitive, and behavioral processes. One of the early models that has shaped the course of turnover research was provided by Mobley during the late 1970s. The model describes the experience of dissatisfaction with one's work as arousing thoughts about quitting. These thoughts lead to evaluations of the expected utility of searching for another job and the cost of leaving the current job, to intentions to search, and to evaluations of alternatives. Finding an attractive alternative elicits the intention to quit, which in turn is directly associated with quitting. Research provided empirical support for the model, showed that relationships among the variables in the model can be reciprocal, and identified possible moderators that affect the relationships among the model variables. For example, it was found that in times of high unemployment rates, the relationship between satisfaction and the decision to quit was weaker than during times of low unemployment.

Group Predictors of Member Turnover

Groups may affect members' satisfaction with their work, their commitment to the organization, and, as a result, their decisions to remain in or leave their jobs. The analysis of turnover in groups includes topics such as the influence of group members' characteristics and their relative representation in the group (i.e., diversity) on the tendency to leave the group, the effect of group characteristics such as cohesiveness or culture on members' decisions to leave, the effect of the fit between members' characteristics and characteristics of the group on turnover, and the effect of the group's supervisor on members' decisions to quit.

Group Diversity

Group composition refers to the configuration of members' attributes in the group, including demographic characteristics, education, experience, and attitudes. Group composition affects members' attraction to the group, their satisfaction with other group members, and the social interaction among group members. For example, group composition affects the cohesiveness of the group, as well as the level of task and emotional conflict. Cohesiveness diminishes the tendency to leave the group, whereas conflict increases it.

Several studies have shown that homogeneous groups have lower turnover rates than heterogeneous groups do. The *similarity–attraction* and the *attraction–selection–attrition* theories provide an explanation for this empirical finding. These theories maintain that individuals are attracted to organizations and teams whose members are perceived to be similar to them. Working with similar others contributes to positive self-identity and job satisfaction.

Compared with similar members, dissimilar members are more likely to leave the group. Specifically, members who are dissimilar on such dimensions as age, tenure in the group, date of entry, work experience, or race are more likely to leave their group than similar members are. Individuals who enter the group at the same time or who are the same age are likely to be more tightly bound to one another than are those who are demographically different. Dissimilar members find it more difficult to integrate with other group members and may feel pressure to conform to the group or to leave it.

Group Cohesiveness

Cohesiveness, the degree to which members in a group are attracted to the group or attached to

each other, has also been shown to affect turnover propensities. In most cases, leaving a job also means leaving colleagues. The closer the relationships with colleagues, the more difficult leaving a job is. Indeed, group cohesion is associated with a higher commitment of members to remaining in the group. The attraction to group members hinders member turnover.

Person–Organization Fit

Person–organization fit is the congruence between personal attributes of the individual and attributes of the work context. Personal attributes may include personality traits, attitudes, values, goals, and preferences. Work context includes the culture, norms, and values, as well as goals and other expectations, in the work environment. A better fit between a group member's attributes and the attributes of his or her group increases the likelihood that the member will feel professionally and personally committed to the organization. Poor person–organization fit is associated with higher levels of turnover. For example, it was found that creative members who worked in a relatively structured environment that encouraged habitual and systematic thinking were more likely to leave their jobs than were creative members working in a context that fostered innovation. Similarly, conformists and systematic thinkers showed higher turnover rates when working in an unstructured environment than when working in a structured environment that fit their preferences.

Satisfaction With the Supervisor

Research suggests that the immediate supervisor plays an important rule in the employee turnover decision. Supervisors, perceived as the representatives of the organization, can enhance employees' positive feelings and attitudes toward the organization. Supervisors may also form individual relationships with their employees that shape employees' commitment to the organization and reduce their intention to quit. Perceived supervisor support reduces employee turnover and attenuates the relationship between perceived organizational support and employee turnover. Perceived organizational support becomes more important in the absence of perceived supervisor support.

Consequences of Turnover

Although research on predictors of turnover has accumulated over many years, research on consequences of turnover is more recent. Consequences include *convergent outcomes*, such as the extent to which the group performs its task efficiently and meets quality standards, and *divergent outcomes*, such as whether the group innovates or develops new processes and products. Studies finding that turnover hurts task performance typically focus on convergent outcomes, whereas studies documenting beneficial effects of turnover generally focus on divergent outcomes.

Studies of sports teams, industrial concerns, and service organizations have documented a negative effect of turnover on group and organizational outcomes such as the quality and efficiency of task performance. The departure of members disrupts the smooth functioning of the group and weakens its *transactive memory system*. In groups with well-developed transactive memory systems, members know who knows what and who is good at what and are able to coordinate their activities effectively. When turnover occurs and new members arrive, they must learn not only to perform their individual tasks but also who in the group is good at what and how to coordinate their activities with those of other group members.

The effect of turnover has been found to depend on the extent to which roles in the group are well defined and procedures exist for accomplishing tasks. As examples of contexts that vary along these dimensions, consider two bookstores. One is part of a large chain, in which members have clearly defined roles, and procedures are specified for accomplishing tasks; the other bookstore is an independent establishment owned by an individual who has not developed task performance routines or specified roles for employees. Under the latter condition, much of the bookstore's knowledge is embedded in employees, so their departure would hurt the bookstore's performance. Conversely, in the former case, when jobs are standardized, turnover has been found to have a less negative effect on performance outcomes. When work is standardized, much of the group's knowledge is embedded in its structures and routines, so the loss of an employee has less effect on performance outcomes than in less structured contexts.

Another important contingency in understanding the effect of turnover on groups and organizations is the quality of departing members. Several studies have found that the performance of employees who left an organization was lower than that of those who remained, even when the turnover was voluntary. If it is the poor performers who are leaving an organization, turnover should have a less negative effect on performance. On the other hand, if it is the high performers who are departing, turnover should have a more negative effect on performance. The position of departing members in the unit's social network is another variable likely to affect the relationship between turnover and group performance.

Although studies of convergent outcomes generally find a negative effect of turnover on those outcomes, studies of divergent outcomes, such as innovation, generally find a positive effect of turnover. The departure of organizational members often triggers the arrival of new members who bring new knowledge and approaches to the group. Thus, these newcomers can be a source of innovation—especially when they are high in ability or status, perceived as credible and concerned with the welfare of the group, and share an identity with other group members. Further, the presence of newcomers can stimulate old-timers to develop new ideas and task performance strategies. Thus, teams that experience turnover have been found to be more creative than teams with stable membership.

In short, although turnover can disrupt task performance, it can also stimulate creativity and innovation. More research is needed to understand the conditions under which turnover has negative or positive effects on group outcomes. Research to date has identified important contingencies, including characteristics of departing members and their replacements, features of the group's structures and routines, and whether the desired outcomes are efficiency, quality, or innovation.

Linda Argote and Ella Miron-Spektor

See also Diversity; Group Cohesiveness; Group Learning; Group Performance; Innovation; Minority Influence; Organizations; Transactive Memory Systems

Further Readings

Argote, L. (1999). *Organizational learning: Creating, retaining, and transferring knowledge.* Norwell, MA: Kluwer.

Argote, L., Insko, C. A., Yovetich, N., & Romero, A. A. (1995). Group learning curves: The effects of turnover and task complexity on group performance. *Journal of Applied Social Psychology, 25*(6), 512–529.

Hom, P. W., Caranikas-Walker, F., Prussia, G., & Griffeth, R. W. (1992). A meta-analytical structural equations analysis of a model of employee turnover. *Journal of Applied Psychology, 77*(6), 890–909.

Jackson, S. E., Brett, J. F., Sessa, V. I., Cooper, D. M., Julin, J. A., & Peyronnin, K. (1991). Some differences make a difference: Individual dissimilarity and group heterogeneity as correlates of recruitment, promotions and turnover. *Journal of Applied Psychology, 76*(5), 675–689.

Levine, J. M., Choi, H. S., & Moreland, R. L. (2003). Newcomer innovations in work teams. In P. B. Paulus & B. A. Nijstad (Eds.), *Group creativity: Innovation through collaboration* (pp. 202–224). New York: Oxford University Press.

Mitchell, T. R., Holtom, B. C., Lee, T. W., & Erez, M. (2001). Why people stay: Using job embeddedness to predict voluntary turnover. *Academy of Management Journal, 44*(6), 1102–1121.

Moreland, R. L., Argote, L., & Krishnan, R. (1998). Training people to work in groups. In R. S. Tindale, L. Heath, J. Edwards, E. J. Posvac, F. B. Bryant, Y. Suarez-Balcazar, et al. (Eds.), *Applications of theory and research on groups to social issues* (pp. 37–60). New York: Plenum Press.

O'Reilly, C. A., Caldwell, D. F., & Barnett, W. P. (1989). Work group demography, social integration, and turnover. *Administrative Science Quarterly, 34*(1), 21–37.

Ton, A., & Huckman, R. S. (2008). Managing the impact of employee turnover on performance: The role of process conformance. *Organization Science, 19*(1), 56–68.

PLURALISTIC IGNORANCE

Pluralistic ignorance refers to widespread misperception of the attitudes and behaviors prevalent in one's group due to public misrepresentation of private attitudes. It can lead to conformity to apparent social norms in the absence of actual private support by individuals. In the extreme case, it can lead every individual to believe that he or she is alone in holding an attitude or in practicing a behavior, when in reality every other group member does the same in private. Pluralistic ignorance is typically measured by asking individuals to indicate on a numerical scale how strongly they agree with a statement or how often they engage in a behavior, and then asking them to estimate how much their peers on average espouse the attitude or perform the behavior; the difference between the perceived consensus and the aggregate of individual ratings captures pluralistic ignorance. This entry looks at how pluralistic ignorance is expressed and then discusses its causes and consequences.

A Ubiquitous Social Phenomenon

Many examples of pluralistic ignorance have been documented in small ad hoc groups. When individuals witness an emergency in the presence of others, they are less likely to offer help than when no other bystanders are present (*bystander nonintervention*), in part because when they are trying to understand the situation, they stay impassive, but they mistakenly interpret other people's impassivity as evidence that the situation is not an emergency— a vicious circle leading to less assistance. In a classroom, students confused by a teacher's utterances often mistake their peers' silence for comprehension, and, as a result, a majority of students stay silent and confused, not realizing that no one else understands the material (the *classroom problem*). When discussing an issue about which they initially shared moderate attitudes, group members typically become more extreme (*group polarization*), in part because deviant thoughts are suppressed, and discussants think that everyone else is more extreme than they are. This phenomenon leads groups, in some cases, to a course of action that virtually no member privately supports, again because misgivings are kept under wraps, even if the misgivings are shared by all (one cause of *groupthink*) or because everyone erroneously believes that they are pleasing everyone else (the *Abilene paradox*).

Pluralistic ignorance also explains the persistence of existing social norms in established social groups, which sometimes espouse norms that very few members actually support in private. Thus, members of a campus fraternity were found to resist progressive admission policies that they privately approved because of the false assumption that the rest of the group did not approve of the policies. A majority of incoming college students believe that they are uniquely uncomfortable with heavy drinking, but they keep these misgivings to themselves, sustaining the illusion and leading some to drink excessively in order to match the imaginary heavy-drinking norm. Youth gang members believe that their peers support violence and crime more than they do, which explains the maintenance of deviant gang norms despite individual misgivings. Similarly, both prison guards and inmates believe that their peers hold attitudes much more antagonistic to the other group than those attitudes really are, explaining the maintenance of unnecessarily violent norms.

On a more global scale, pluralistic ignorance explains rapid societal changes, either because a seeming consensus is revealed to have had little real support by individuals (*conservative lag*) or because a minority is able to impose the appearance of consensus on a majority (*liberal leap*). Conservative lags explain why measures no longer supported by a majority live on until they are suddenly revealed to have little foundation. The dramatic fall of European Soviet-inspired regimes at the end of the 20th century illustrates this phenomenon. Private misgivings about these governments were widespread but hidden for many decades, and once expressed, might have led to the governments' quick downfall. In the United States, defunct policies such as Prohibition and racial segregation outlasted their popular support for similar reasons. It has in fact been argued that private opinion polling spelled the end of Prohibition.

Liberal leaps occur when the establishment of pluralistic ignorance allows rapid change. Thus, Tocqueville documented how French revolutionaries managed to strip religion out of daily life with apparent support of the majority—although religious practices were in fact maintained privately and resurfaced quickly once this illusion was dispelled. Revolutionary groups wisely seize first the means of mass communication, which lets the revolutionaries create an illusion of wide support and inhibits reaction by the general population.

Roots of Pluralistic Ignorance

The basic cause of pluralistic ignorance is public misrepresentation of private attitudes. This misrepresentation takes two forms—what gets said, and what does not. On one hand, attitudes believed to be popular are overrepresented. Individuals are more likely to express attitudes believed to be normative, even if it means twisting their real preferences to fit in. Individuals who (earnestly or not) embody this perceived norm receive increased attention and are licensed to advertise their position more freely. Thus, students may boast about their drinking exploits if they believe them to be normative, and the antics of colorful drunkards are discussed with appreciative gusto.

On the other hand, public misrepresentation also involves the silencing of opinions believed to be rare, even if they are really dominant. For example, if some students think binge drinking is stupid, they may not express this opinion at the breakfast table if they think (erroneously) that they are alone in thinking so. One person's silence contributes to the next person's, and a *spiral of silence* ensues.

Pluralistic ignorance rests on a basic social-psychological principle: We believe that the behavior of others reflects who they are and underestimate the role of situations in bringing about their behavior, even when we realize that the same situations affect us. Behavior is seen as a more accurate reflection of character for others than for the self: During a water shortage when showering was forbidden, individuals who bathed thought that other bathers cared less about the community than they did, but nonbathers thought that other nonbathers cared more about the community than they did. This *fundamental attribution error* contributes to pluralistic ignorance because individuals take the behavior of others at face value and disregard the frequent dissembling and complications of social life.

The choices of others are believed to reflect their preferences. In fact, when seeing others choose between two options, individuals see this choice as reflecting liking for the chosen option more than disliking for the rejected option. This again contributes to pluralistic ignorance. Individuals know that they themselves are choosing the lesser of two evils (e.g., in an election between two unpopular candidates) but interpret their peers' choice as reflecting true enthusiasm for the option that receives the most support.

Consequences of Pluralistic Ignorance

The typical consequences of pluralistic ignorance are that unpopular or immoral norms live on, suboptimal decisions are made, and a group's subjective utility is not maximized. Individuals put up with things they should not have to, unnecessarily censor themselves, and conform to norms that very few endorse. One of the deepest theoretical questions raised by pluralistic ignorance is: What should count as the true norm—the perceived consensus that affects public behaviors or the aggregated private attitudes? What counts as the real standards of a community, for example, was questioned in an obscenity trial brought against a Utah video store in 2000, when the defense showed that the number of signatures on a public petition against the store's rental of adult videos was dwarfed by the number of individuals from the same aggrieved community who privately rented or purchased the offensive material.

Pluralistic ignorance can lead to widespread alienation due to individuals' believing they are alone in their views while they are in reality surrounded by a blind crowd of like-minded peers. The U.S. popularity of the Kinsey reports on sex, originally published in 1948 and 1953, can in part be explained by their data-heavy appendixes, revealing as statistically normal some behaviors believed theretofore to be rare and shameful oddities. Ideological isolation can also be felt in polarized debates (e.g., on abortion), in which members of both sides overestimate the extremity of both their opponents' and their peers' opinions (*false polarization*), often feeling like "lone moderates" who are uniquely able to see the complexity and nuances of the issues involved.

On a more positive note, by creating the illusion that new ideas are embraced by all, progressive activists, inspired artists, or visionary leaders can use pluralistic ignorance to bring about much-needed change in a society initially unsure about the proposed path.

Benoît Monin

See also Attribution Biases; Bystander Effect; Conformity; Fads and Fashions; Group Polarization; Groupthink; Informational Influence; Normative Influence; Norms; Reference Groups

Further Readings

Miller, D. T., Monin, B., & Prentice, D. A. (2000). Pluralistic ignorance and inconsistency between private attitudes and public behavior. In D. J. Terry & M. A. Hogg (Eds.), *Attitudes, behavior, and social context: The role of norms and group membership* (pp. 95–113). Mahwah, NJ: Erlbaum.

Monin, B., & Norton, M. I. (2003). Perceptions of a fluid consensus: Uniqueness bias, false consensus, false polarization and pluralistic ignorance in a water conservation crisis. *Personality and Social Psychology Bulletin, 29,* 559–567.

Prentice, D. A., & Miller, D. T. (1993). Pluralistic ignorance and alcohol use on campus: Some consequences of misperceiving the social norm. *Journal of Personality and Social Psychology, 64,* 243–256.

POWER

In social contexts, *power* may be defined as interpersonal or intergroup control over others' resources or outcomes. Occupying positions of power has been shown to affect power holders' cognitive, behavioral, and emotional processes. Findings from research on social power have implications for many psychological outcomes, ranging from close relationships to intergroup relations, as well as outcomes in organizations.

Theoretical Background

Early theorists such as John French and Bertram Raven defined *power* as the ability to influence others, that is, to change others' beliefs, attitudes, or behaviors. Theorists in this tradition have focused on *power bases*—resources that power holders can use to influence others. Power bases include rewards (e.g., offering promotions), coercion (threatened punishment), legitimacy (obeying authority), reference (role-modeling), expertise (knowledge), and information (persuasion). Contemporary theorists such as Susan Fiske, Dacher Keltner, and Deborah

Gruenfeld have drawn from John Thibaut and Harold Kelley's classic *interdependence theory* to offer an alternative definition of power that focuses on the structural properties—that is, the interdependent nature—of relationships between individuals or groups. Specifically, these theorists argue that power is best defined as control over outcomes that are valued by others. Defining power as *outcome control* identifies power as a property of relationships, whereas defining power as influence focuses on the outcomes of power. It is important to note that defining power in terms of outcome control captures the relative nature of power—the amount of control any one individual or group has may vary across situations, over time, and across relationships with different individuals or groups. This definition also distinguishes power from potential correlates, including status and prestige. For example, professors typically have control over their own students' outcomes (e.g., grades) but no control over other students' outcomes. Moreover, their control over student outcomes is independent of status (e.g., whether they have tenure) or prestige (e.g., whether they are recognized internationally by their peers).

Contemporary research on power as outcome control has been driven primarily by two prominent theories: *power-as-control theory* and *power-approach theory*. Power-as-control theory, first proposed by Fiske and colleagues, was developed to explain the role of power in *person perception*, how people process information about others and subsequently form impressions. Predicated on *dual-process* models of impression formation, which distinguish between automatic and controlled cognitive processes, this model argues that social power moderates perceivers' motivation and ability to process information. According to this theory, compared with people who are relatively less powerful, people who are relatively more powerful are less motivated to engage in effortful processing about those in the opposite role because accurate interpersonal judgments are oftentimes not required of them (i.e., their outcomes are not highly dependent on subordinates). Moreover, because powerful people may be subject to greater cognitive demands (e.g., supervising multiple subordinates), they may simply have fewer cognitive resources to attend to subordinates and therefore be less able to engage in effortful cognitive processing. Finally, the power-as-control theory asserts that powerful people can be motivated to attend to subordinates when doing so benefits the power holders' own outcomes (i.e., when subordinates control outcomes of interest to power holders).

Power-approach theory, first articulated by Keltner and colleagues, provides a framework for understanding the consequences of power across a broader range of psychological outcomes, including social cognition. According to this model, having or lacking power has consequences for behavioral regulation—or the tendency to approach or avoid outcomes. Specifically, having power activates approach-related tendencies, whereas lacking power activates inhibition tendencies. These differences in behavioral regulation have important implications for behavior, emotion, and cognition. For example, if increased power is associated with less inhibition, people who hold powerful positions should be more likely to act on their own impulses than should people in less powerful positions.

Methods: How Do People Study Social Power?

Across theoretical perspectives, contemporary researchers have employed two basic approaches to manipulate power differences in laboratory settings. The first approach involves assigning participants to different power roles (e.g., boss vs. employee) that vary in terms of relative outcome control versus dependence. For example, in a high-power role, participants may be told that they are the leader and are responsible for directing a given task, evaluating subordinate workers, allocating chances to win monetary prizes, and so forth. In contrast, participants in a low-power role may be assigned the role of worker and told they must follow the leader's instructions, be evaluated by the leader, and rely on the leader for any chance of winning a prize. In this case, participants are led to believe that the leader has control over the outcomes of workers, whereas workers lack any control over leaders' outcomes. Similar techniques involve role-playing, in which participants are asked to *imagine* themselves in various roles (e.g., art gallery director vs. assistant).

Intergroup power—that is, differences in relative control over group-level outcomes—is typically manipulated through similar techniques.

However, instead of an individual's having control, participants are presented with information that a particular group of individuals has relatively more control over another group's outcomes. Alternatively, researchers may use naturally occurring groups (e.g., men and women) that differ in power. Oftentimes, the use of naturally occurring groups to study intergroup power conflates outcome control with other, related constructs (e.g., status or identity), with implications for interpretation and application of research findings.

Cognitive priming—that is, increasing the cognitive activation of power-relevant constructs—is often used in lieu of manipulating actual outcome control. This technique is often easier to implement (e.g., it does not involve highly deceptive cover stories) and is arguably less susceptible to the potential confounds of naturally occurring power relations (e.g., status). Research has demonstrated that priming people to think about specific concepts or goals can influence emotion, cognition, and behavior outside conscious awareness. With regard to priming power, researchers have relied on a number of techniques. For example, completing word search puzzles that require participants to identify power-relevant words (e.g., authority, boss vs. employee, follower) can increase the accessibility of power-related concepts and subsequently influence behavior. Even subtle cues in the environment can prime power—seating participants in a large, cushioned chair behind a desk versus in a small wooden chair in front of a desk can activate high or low power, respectively. Some researchers have primed power in more overtly conscious ways, such as asking participants to recall a time when they had power over (vs. depended on) another person. Regardless of whether power priming is overt or subtle, the assumption is that the *influence* of the prime occurs outside conscious awareness: Participants are (presumably) not aware that the prime affects their subsequent behavior.

Manipulating power via either priming or role-based techniques typically produces similar results. Moreover, manipulating power in a laboratory setting affords experimental control that cannot be attained in more naturalistic settings where people have power in their daily lives. However, some critics have argued that these manipulations and laboratory settings are too artificial when it comes to assessing the impact of power on some behaviors, such as employee evaluations. Thus, it will be important to replicate laboratory findings in more naturalistic settings.

Interpersonal Power

Interpersonal power refers to power between individuals—when one person controls the outcomes of another (e.g., a boss and employees). Research demonstrates the effects of such power on behavior, emotion, and cognition, including tendencies to stereotype and derogate outgroup members and to sexually harass women.

Behavior

Several empirical studies suggest that having power inclines people to act, consistent with power-approach theory. That is, people in power are more likely to engage in a given action than are people without power. For example, the priming of power has led participants to be more likely to take a hit in blackjack and to stand up to turn off a fan in the room. Parallel effects occur in group settings, where high-power group members tend to speak more often than low-power group members do. This action tendency also affects perceptions of behaviors. Behaviors generally considered risky (e.g., unprotected sex) are perceived as less risky when participants are primed with power.

Alarmingly, having power may also incline people to engage in sexual harassment. Indeed, quid pro quo harassment—when a supervisor withholds or rewards resources in exchange for sexual cooperation—is defined in part by power. Empirical evidence supports a link between power and harassment. For example, researchers have found that men who are predisposed to harass are also likely to cognitively associate the concept of power with sex. In addition, in laboratory studies, men high in the propensity to sexually harass females rate female subordinates as more attractive when the men have been primed to think about having power.

Unfortunately, the effects of power do not apply only to men who are inclined to harass. Additional research has shown that men given control over a hiring decision and asked to interview a female job candidate subsequently sat closer to her during the interview and asked her more sexualized questions. Power may facilitate harassment for both motivational and cognitive reasons. For powerful men, motivated to maintain the status quo, sexual harassment is a way to enforce the existing hierarchy and keep women in low-power roles. Cognitively, power may shift perceptions of sexual harassment. For example, some research suggests that men primed with power rate sexually harassing behaviors (e.g., unwanted touching) as less inappropriate than do men primed with powerlessness.

Emotion

Research examining the link between power and emotion has produced mixed results. Power-approach theory predicts that having power should produce positive emotion, whereas lacking power should produce negative emotion. This prediction is based on research demonstrating a positive correlation between behavioral approach tendencies and positive emotion, as well as between behavioral inhibition and negative emotion. Some empirical research supports the hypothesized power–emotion link. For example, one set of studies tested this prediction in the context of a dyadic interaction. In an initial study, romantic partners rated the extent to which they perceived that they and their partner each had power (defined as amount of influence) in their relationship. These romantic partners then discussed their relationships with one another. As predicted, participants who were perceived to have more power subsequently reported having more positive emotions when discussing their relationships, whereas those perceived to have less power reported more negative emotions. Additional research replicated these findings with strangers who were assigned to power roles and with dyads engaging in negotiations. Although these studies support the predictions of the approach–inhibition model, it is important to note that several other studies have found no effects of power on emotion. These mixed results may simply reflect differences in methods of inducing power. Although priming and role-playing typically yield similar results, parallel effects may not extend to emotion. Studies that employ manipulations of dyadic power roles often produce reliable differences in emotion, whereas those that employ

priming power produce inconsistent results. Further research is needed to resolve these discrepancies.

Cognition

Both power-approach theory and power-as-control theory predict that power promotes relatively less effortful (i.e., more automatic) information processing, whereas powerlessness promotes more deliberative information processing. Recent research, however, suggests that power may have different effects on cognitive processing in different contexts. According to Ana Guinote's *situated focus theory*, powerful people engage in deliberative processing when available information is relevant to their current goals. Several recent studies support this argument. For example, power appears to moderate perceivers' ability to narrow or widen their attentional focus, depending on the demands of the task. In one study, participants primed with high power were able either to selectively attend to background information or to ignore this information as necessary in order to succeed at a cognitive perception task. In contrast, participants primed with low-power concepts were unable to adapt across tasks. More specifically, they performed significantly worse when the task required them to ignore background information, suggesting an inability to narrow attention to fit task demands. This study and others like it point to the need for a better understanding of the complex consequences of power for perception. Moreover, these studies demonstrate a heretofore unidentified cognitive benefit—in the form of cognitive flexibility—for those who have power.

Additional research suggests that power has important consequences for how people think about individuals who belong to different social groups (e.g., racial or ethnic or gender groups). More specifically, occupying positions of power can lead to stereotype-based impression formation processes. Research suggests these processes occur both by *default* (i.e., ignoring stereotype-disconfirming information) and by *design* (i.e., attending more to stereotype-confirming information). In other words, power seems to facilitate reliance on stereotypes for both cognitive and motivational reasons. Cognitively, power holders may have neither the cognitive resources to form accurate impressions nor the motivation to be accurate—using negative stereotypes can legitimate the existing power differences. These attentional differences also translate into evaluations—power holders are more likely to rely on stereotypic information linked to social categories than on individuating traits that distinguish individuals from the social groups to which they belong. The link between power and stereotyping seems to be strongest when people feel less responsible for their judgments (e.g., responsibility norms are weak) and when they feel their powerful positions are less legitimate.

Not only do the powerful tend to rely on stereotypes when evaluating subordinates; they also tend to evaluate subordinates negatively. Meta-analytic studies (which statistically combine findings across a number of studies) confirm the link between power and derogation. In one laboratory study, for example, researchers manipulated whether members of a dyad believed they had power over one another while they engaged in a problem-solving task. When participants were aware that they had power over their partner, they rated their partner more negatively and themselves more positively. Similarly, meta-analyses of data from managers have revealed that as power increases, so do negative evaluations of others and positive evaluations of self.

Intergroup Power

In contrast to interpersonal power, *intergroup power* refers to power *between* groups—when one group has more control over resources than another does (e.g., men typically have more power than women do). Intergroup power can occur between small groups (e.g., work groups or sports teams) as well as broader social groups in society (e.g., groups based on ethnicity or gender). Although power refers to control, it oftentimes is coupled with status at the intergroup level of analysis. This is particularly true when one is studying naturally occurring groups as opposed to those created in the laboratory. A bidirectional relationship between intergroup power and bias seems to exist. Intergroup power can facilitate bias in the form of discrimination. The reverse is also true—bias in the form of stereotypes serves to explain and maintain power differences.

One of the first studies to investigate the effect of intergroup power on intergroup bias used a modified version of the *minimal groups paradigm*. In this paradigm, participants are arbitrarily assigned to one of two groups and are asked to allocate a valued resource (e.g., cash or candies) between the two groups. Consistent with the idea that power can facilitate bias, a positive relationship was found between intergroup power and intergroup discrimination. As people perceived their own group to have more power, they were more likely to distribute resources in a way that disadvantaged the less-powerful outgroup. Additional studies manipulating group status have found similar results, but group power seems to better predict discrimination against outgroups.

Much research has focused on the role stereotypes play in maintaining and justifying existing power imbalances. Many theories have addressed this process, including *system justification theory*, *social dominance theory*, and the *stereotype content model*. Most germane to the discussion of intergroup power is the idea that stereotypes of groups differ in part because of the perceived status of the groups—which often signals differences in resource control. According to the stereotype content model, group status and competition lead to specific stereotypes about and emotions toward different social groups. Specifically, perceptions of different social groups vary along two dimensions: *competence* and *warmth*. For example, in the United States, poor people—who are viewed as low in both status and competition for valued resources—are perceived to be low in both competence and warmth. As a result, poor people are typically viewed with disdain. It is important to note that this theory argues that intergroup power and stereotypes are mutually reinforcing. Thus, controlling resources signals competence, which in turn justifies disparities in resource control.

Current and Future Directions

Because power is a fundamental characteristic of human relationships, and one that varies across relationships, its consequences permeate daily life. Hence, power has far-reaching implications for understanding human behavior across social science disciplines. Currently, psychologists who study social power are moving forward in a number of directions, studying power in a number of different contexts, from the bedroom to the boardroom. Although much research tends to focus on the potential for abuse that comes with having power, there is a renewed interest in recognizing the benefits of having power. Future research within and beyond the field of psychology will benefit from current theories that take a more nuanced approach, recognizing both the pros and the cons of having (or lacking) social power.

Stephanie A. Goodwin and Ann E. Hoover

See also Dominance Hierarchies; Interdependence Theory; Leadership; Need for Power; Power–Dependence Theory; Social Dominance Theory; Status; System Justification Theory

Further Readings

Depret, E., & Fiske, S. T. (1999). Perceiving the powerful: Intriguing individuals versus threatening groups. *Journal of Experimental Social Psychology, 35,* 461–480.

Fiske, S. T., & Berdahl, J. L. (2007). Social power. In A. Kruglanski & E. T. Higgins (Eds.), *Social psychology: A handbook of basic principles* (2nd ed., pp. 678–692). New York: Guilford.

French, J. R. P., & Raven, B. H. (1959). The bases of social power. In D. Cartwright (Ed.), *Studies in social power* (pp. 150–167). Ann Arbor, MI: Institute for Social Research.

Galinsky, A. D., Gruenfeld, D. H., & Magee, J. C. (2003). From power to action. *Journal of Personality and Social Psychology, 85,* 453–466.

Goodwin, S. A., Gubin, A., Fiske, S. T., & Yzerbyt, V. Y. (2000). Power can bias impression processes: Stereotyping subordinates by default and by design. *Group Processes & Intergroup Relations, 3,* 227–256.

Guinote, A. (2007). Behavior variability and the situated focus theory of power. *European Review of Social Psychology, 18,* 256–295.

Keltner, D., Gruenfeld, D. H., & Anderson, C. (2003). Power, approach, and inhibition. *Psychological Review, 110,* 265–284.

Lee-Chai, A. Y., & Bargh, J. A. (Eds.). (2001). *The use and abuse of power.* Philadelphia: Psychology Press.

Simon, B., & Oakes, P. (2006). Beyond dependence: An identity approach to social power and domination. *Human Relations, 59,* 105–139.

POWER–DEPENDENCE THEORY

Power–dependence theory is a structural theory about power in enduring relationships. It describes how individuals' reliance on others for valued resources determines the distribution of power in relationships. Power–dependence theory represents a major shift in the way sociologists think about power. Many earlier theories about power view it as a trait or property of an actor. Power–dependence theory treats power as a characteristic of a relationship and thus focuses on the relationship rather than on the individuals involved in the relationship.

Power–dependence theory was developed by the sociologist Richard Emerson in the 1960s. Power–dependence theory builds on earlier work in sociology by George Homans and Peter Blau and in psychology by John Thibaut and Harold Kelley. Power–dependence theory, together with the earlier work, forms the basis of *social exchange theory*, one of the major sociological social-psychological traditions.

Definitions, Assumptions, and Postulates

Power–dependence theory posits that actors in social relations are dependent on each other to meet certain goals or needs. In an exchange relation, the dependence of one actor on another is determined by the ratio of how much the actor values the resources controlled by the partner to the number of alternative sources the actor has for those resources (resource value vs. resource availability). Power is defined as the potential of one actor to obtain favorable outcomes in an exchange episode at another actor's expense. In an exchange relationship, the first actor has power over the second actor insofar as the first actor controls resources that the second actor values. Power, then, is clearly related to the dependence of the actors on one another. The key postulate of power–dependence theory is that the power of A over B is equal to the dependence of B on A ($Pab = Dba$). Therefore, as A's power over B increases, so does B's dependence on A.

Power–dependence theory has four key assumptions that allow predictions to be made about the behavior of individuals involved in exchange.

First, an individual's behavior is motivated by the desire to increase gain and to avoid loss of valued resources. Second, exchange relations develop in structures of mutual dependence. This means that both parties have some reason to engage in exchange with each other to obtain resources of value; otherwise there would be no need to form an exchange relation. Third, actors engage in recurrent, mutually contingent exchanges with specific partners over time (i.e., they are not engaged in simple one-shot transactions). Last, valued outcomes obey the law of diminishing marginal utility, meaning that after a certain point, each additional resource is of less value.

Expansion Beyond the Dyad

Most interactions between individuals are not isolated. Instead, most social relations are embedded in larger social networks. In his structural theory of power, Richard Emerson expanded his theorizing to larger networks. For Emerson, the structure of the network, or how individuals are connected to each other and the availability of resources across the network, are vital factors necessary to understand power dynamics within a network. In Emerson's terms, networks are composed of relations that are interconnected, so exchange in one relationship affects interaction in other relationships within the network. These connections can be either negative or positive. Connections are termed *negative* if exchange in one relation reduces the frequency of exchange in another relation involving one of the original actors. For example, it is a negative connection if exchange in the focal relationship, A–B, reduces the likelihood of exchange in an alternate relationship between A and C. Conversely, connections are termed *positive* if exchange in one relation increases the frequency of exchange in another relation involving one of the original actors. In the prior example, a connection is positive if exchange in the A–B relationship increases the amount of exchange in the A–C relationship. In addition, networks can include *mixed* connections, which involve both positive and negative connections.

One of the major emphases in the application of power–dependence theory, beginning with the work of Richard Emerson and Karen Cook, was on the structure of connections in exchange networks and the distribution of power. In this early test of power–dependence theory, Emerson and Cook verified that power was an attribute of a structural position in an exchange network rather than an individual trait. Despite the fact that participants were unaware of their position in the exchange network, those participants in high-power positions behaved in a manner consistent with their structural power. That is, those actors in high-power positions acquired more benefits from each exchange than did those actors in low-power positions. Cook and Emerson did find that concerns about equity of resources and commitment between partners reduced the use of power by the high-power actors. These findings shaped much of the subsequent research in the power–dependence paradigm (for more examples, see the entry Social Exchange in Networks and Groups).

Other Key Concepts

In addition to power and dependence, there are four other key concepts that are necessary to understand behaviors in power–dependence relations: reciprocity, cohesion, balance, and power-balancing operations.

Reciprocity, or the cooperative interchange between exchange partners, is often considered to be a vital part of any study of an exchange system. Anthropological studies of exchange networks by scholars such as Claude Lévi-Strauss, Marcel Mauss, and Bronislaw Malinowski placed a strong emphasis on the norm of obligation to reciprocate. In contrast, Richard Emerson viewed the diffuse norm of obligation to reciprocate as something that may emerge over time but not as something intrinsic to social exchange. Emerson argued that the reciprocity observed in ongoing exchange interactions is based on principles of reinforcement, such that in any interaction, if the behavior of A (which is rewarding to B) does not elicit a rewarding behavior from B to A, then there are two options: A will change his or her behavior to elicit a rewarding behavior from B, or the A–B relationship will be terminated.

Cohesion represents the strength of the exchange relation, as well as the likelihood that the relationship will survive a conflict. The relational cohesion of a relationship is the average dependence of the actors in the relation: The higher the mutual dependence, the higher the relational cohesion. This concept has been explored further by Linda Molm and her colleagues, as well as by Edward Lawler and his colleagues. Molm and her colleagues have extensively explored the concept of reciprocity in exchange relations, as well as studying the effect of reciprocity on cohesion and solidarity. Lawler and his colleagues have primarily been concerned with cohesion and solidarity in exchange.

An exchange relationship is *balanced* if the actors are equally dependent on one another (Dab = Dba). Therefore, an imbalanced relationship is one in which there are unequal dependencies, in which one party is more reliant on the other. Balance as described by Emerson is a rare state in exchange relations. The balance in an exchange relation is fragile because actors are motivated to maintain or increase their power in order to increase their benefits and minimize losses. Thus, relationships (even those that begin in a power-balanced state) are likely to ebb and flow between balance and imbalance.

Richard Emerson argued that power-imbalanced exchange relationships are unstable and tend toward balance. He described four balancing mechanisms by which the relationships tend to balance. The mechanisms focus on changes in the value of the resources exchanged or the alternatives for the resources being exchanged. By altering either one of these, the power and dependence of the actors on each other will be changed, but maybe not permanently.

Emerson's four *power-balancing operations* are withdrawal, status giving, network extension, and coalition formation. In a relationship in which A is more powerful than B (i.e., *Pab > Pba* and *Dba > Dab*), the power distribution can move toward balance by B taking one of the following actions. First, B can *withdraw* from the relationship. The second option available to B is called *status giving*. B can balance the relationship by increasing the value to A of the resources B controls. One way B can accomplish this in a relatively low-cost way is by giving status or prestige to A. The next option available to B is *network extension*. By increasing B's number of alternatives, B reduces dependence on A and thus increases B's power in relation to A. Finally, B can attempt to *form a coalition*. B and other alternatives for A join together in a coalition (or some other form of collective action) and reduce the number of alternatives available for A. By decreasing A's alternatives, B and colleagues in the coalition have increased A's dependence on the coalition and thus reduced A's power in relation to the coalition. Of the four power-balancing mechanisms, coalition formation and network extension are the two studied most commonly.

Influence of Power–Dependence Theory

Power–dependence theory has had influence across many domains both inside and outside social psychology. It laid the groundwork for social exchange theory, which is one of the major theoretical programs within sociological social psychology. Social exchange theory builds on the core assumptions and postulates of power–dependence theory to explore micro processes within social networks. Most recently it has been concerned with dynamics of exchange, trust, cohesion, emotion, and solidarity.

Power–dependence theory has also influenced organizational studies, particularly through Jeffrey Pfeffer and Gerald Salancik's *resource dependence perspective*. The key postulate of the resource dependence perspective is identical to power–dependence theory's central argument. Resource dependence theory asserts that organizations have a fundamental need for resources from both outside and within the organization. Those entities that exclusively provide the most needed or valued resources will have the most power in the organization.

Finally, power–dependence theory has influenced the study of social networks within organizations. Illustrative topics of investigation include strategic alliances, collaborative manufacturing enterprises, vertical integration of firms, interlocking directorates, network diffusion of innovative practices, and mergers.

As social scientists turn their focus to the effects of social networks, power–dependence theory provides a way to understand the behaviors of actors within networks and the dynamics of the networks that are likely to emerge over time.

Alexandra Gerbasi

See also Power; Social Exchange in Networks and Groups; Social Networks; Status

Further Readings

Blau, P. M. (1986). *Exchange and power in social life.* New York: Wiley. (Original work published 1964)

Cook, K. S., & Emerson, R. M. (1978). Power, equity and commitment in exchange networks. *American Sociological Review, 43,* 721–739.

Emerson, R. M. (1972). Exchange theory, Part I: A psychological basis for social exchange. In J. Berger, M. Zelditch Jr., & B. Anderson (Eds.), *Sociological theories in progress* (pp. 38–57). Boston: Houghton Mifflin.

Emerson, R. M. (1972). Exchange theory, Part II: Exchange relations and networks. In J. Berger, M. Zelditch Jr., & B. Anderson (Eds.), *Sociological theories in progress* (pp. 58–87). Boston: Houghton Mifflin.

Homans, G. C. (1974). *Social behavior and its elementary forms.* New York: Harcourt, Brace and World. (Original work published 1961)

Pfeffer, J., & Salancik, G. R. (1978). *The external control of organizations: A resource dependence perspective.* New York: Harper & Row.

Thibaut, J. W., & Kelley, H. H. (1959). *The social psychology of groups.* New York: Wiley.

PREJUDICE

Prejudice is one of the defining topics of social psychology and a core theme in the study of intergroup relations. In common parlance and according to the simple definition proposed by Gordon Allport, prejudice can be thought of as "thinking ill of others without sufficient warrant." Influenced strongly by Allport's definition, prejudice has traditionally been conceived of as a negative attitude toward members of a given group, based exclusively on their membership in that group. Literally, the term refers to the process of prejudging people on the basis of their group membership, so in principle, prejudice can be both negative and positive. Thus, more recently, psychologists have expanded the scope of the definition of prejudice in two ways in order to include a broader range of biases that do not necessarily involve antipathy. First, prejudice may reflect more systematically positive responses to members of one's own group (the ingroup) than to other groups (outgroups). Second, prejudice can involve the lowering of the evaluation of a member of a group who deviates from the stereotypic role of that group (e.g., women who succeed in business). This expanded conceptualization serves to align prejudice closely with processes of *stereotyping* and *discrimination*, and, indeed, during the past 50 years, studies of these three processes have been closely intertwined.

Prejudice as a Product of Psychodynamic and Personality Factors

Although topics related to prejudice have been of long-standing interest to psychologists, research in prejudice came to the fore in social psychology in the buildup to and aftermath of World War II. The horrors of the Holocaust fueled a desire to understand the psychological basis of the Nazis' views about, and treatment of, the various social groups that they vilified and persecuted: Jews, homosexuals, gypsies, the disabled.

Much of this early theorizing was heavily influenced by Freudian psychoanalytic theory because of its prominence as a theoretical approach before the war. In the first instance, researchers argued that prejudice was a product of hostility and frustration that was displaced or projected onto members of particular groups that then functioned as scapegoats. According to this model, the behavior of the Nazis was explained by the humiliation that Germany had experienced after World War I and the economic turmoil of the early 1930s.

Among the most influential ideas of this form were those of John Dollard and colleagues, who argued that intergroup hostility and aggression could be understood as an outpouring of the built-up psychic energy produced by frustration. In line with Freudian theory, their model argued that an individual's expression of prejudice had an important cathartic function in releasing pent-up energy and restoring the individual to a state of equilibrium.

Refinements of this idea argued that prejudice reflected the operation of a general process whereby individuals feel frustration toward individuals and groups with power over them and displace those frustrations onto members of other groups that are visible, identifiable, and vulnerable. In this way, groups resolve conflict that they cannot deal with through the creation of conflict with a third party.

Other research in this tradition sought to explain why particular groups are selected as *scapegoats*. Projection theorists suggested that targets are chosen on the basis of characteristics that they are seen to possess and that prejudiced individuals also see in themselves but disapprove of or seek to draw attention away from. In these terms, prejudice is a defense mechanism and a form of denial: People are most prejudiced toward those who are similar to themselves and who remind them of their own limitations and failings.

However, the most influential work within the psychoanalytic tradition was that of Theodor Adorno and other members of the Frankfurt School, as articulated in their classic text *The Authoritarian Personality*. In their exhaustive inquiries into the psychological substrates of anti-Semitism, these researchers interviewed and administered a range of psychometric tests to large numbers of participants. Within these data they identified a number of distinctive patterns of cognition that appeared to differentiate between participants who were prejudiced (authoritarians) and others who were more tolerant or open minded. Specifically, the thought processes of prejudiced individuals were characterized by intolerance of ambiguity, rigidity, concreteness (poor abstract reasoning), and overgeneralization. Such individuals were thus portrayed as being inclined to see the social world in black-and-white terms—evincing strong and disdainful rejection of others who were seen as inferior to themselves and their ingroup. The origins of the authoritarian personality were also traced to individuals' childhood experiences—specifically, to the hierarchical and abusive relationships that authoritarians had with their parents. In contrast, liberals (nonauthoritarians) were believed to be the product of a more equalitarian upbringing and as a result to be more creative and sublimated, more flexible, and less likely to endorse stereotypic representations of others.

Prejudice as a Product of Realistic Group Conflict

The representation of prejudice as a manifestation of a distinct, dysfunctional personality was highly influential, not least because it fit with lay theories that pathologized the prejudiced, representing them as abnormal and the "other." However, this approach was called into question by a number of researchers (notably Roger Brown and, later, Michael Billig) on the basis of a reexamination of relevant data. Their work indicated that the analysis of authoritarianism was oversimplified and that prejudice was not confined to this group. Liberals also demonstrated prejudice in related ways. The principal objection to the psychodynamic approach to prejudice was that it sought to explain widespread phenomena in terms of processes that were mainly abnormal and unique to the individual. The key point about German anti-Semitism—the point that made it so important and so horrific—was that it was an aspect of an ideology common to a large number of people. In short, prejudice seemed to be a *group-level* phenomenon, and its analysis needed to speak to the social reality of *shared* beliefs and practices.

In line with this logic, researchers started to formulate theories of prejudice that focused on the way in which the psychology of prejudice was structured by a person's place within a broader social system. This endeavor was provided with strong empirical foundations by the famous Robbers Cave studies of Muzafer Sherif and colleagues. In this research, conducted in the late 1940s and early 1950s, the researchers assigned boys at a summer camp to different groups and arranged for these groups to compete for goals that only one group could attain. Under these conditions, the groups displayed extreme hostility toward each other. Moreover, this hostility was underpinned by prejudicial attitudes and stereotypes. Significantly, this prejudice was displayed by normal, healthy youngsters in the absence of physical, economic, historical, or personal differences or a history of frustration, exploitation, or repression.

On the basis of these findings, Sherif formulated his *realistic group conflict theory*. This theory asserted that prejudice is an aspect of social conflict and results from social competition for resources. At the same time, as latter phases of the boys' camp studies revealed, prejudice can be ameliorated if group interests are realigned through the introduction of superordinate goals. When the boys had to cooperate and pool resources in order to achieve goals that neither could achieve alone (i.e., if they had superordinate goals), the prejudice that had been displayed when they were in competition gave way to mutual respect and tolerance. Against the view that prejudice is the product of a pathological personality, Sherif had shown that it inhabited the minds of normal human beings and that the same minds that expressed prejudice toward another group could also treat that group with forbearance and understanding.

Recent work has extended the ideas of realistic group conflict theory to systematic differences in social ideology. In particular, work by Jim Sidanius, Felicia Pratto, and colleagues on *social dominance orientation* demonstrates that people differ in the extent to which they believe that the world fundamentally involves competition between groups and that it is appropriate for some groups to dominate other groups. People higher in social dominance orientation exhibit more prejudice toward members of a range of other groups than do people who are lower in social dominance orientation.

Prejudice as a Product of Categorization

A further critical step toward recognition of prejudice as an aspect of a healthy rather than a diseased mind was advanced by Gordon Allport's landmark text *The Nature of Prejudice*, published in 1954. The central theme of this text was that prejudice was not an aberration but an aspect of normal human psychology. Thus Allport's answer to the question "Why do human beings slip so easily into ethnic prejudice?" was "They do so because [its] two essential ingredients—erroneous generalization and hostility—are natural and common capacities of the human mind." Central to the first of these points was Allport's recognition that prejudice relied on the propensity of individuals to engage in social categorization, whereby they reacted to other people in terms as their group membership rather than as individuals. He observed that the "human mind must think with the aid of categories" but also noted that "once formed, categories are the basis for normal prejudgment. We cannot possibly avoid this process. Orderly living depends upon it."

Allport's major contribution was to expand on the nature of the social categorization process as an aspect of individual psychology. In particular, he proposed that prejudice was promoted by the tendency for social categorizations to be associated with differences in value, the primary source of which was a person's group memberships. We tend to like people who are associated with the groups we belong to (ingroups); we are more inclined to dislike, distrust, and reject those who belong to outgroups.

Like Sherif, Allport noted that these things were not set in stone and had the capacity to change. However, like Adorno, Allport (and most other researchers) still clung to the view that categories could be used in a more or less rational manner and that people who are prejudiced are particularly inclined to use dichotomous categories (e.g., believing that ingroups are good and outgroups are bad). Indeed, it was only in 1969, when Henri Tajfel published his influential paper titled "Cognitive Aspects of Prejudice," that the full implications of the cognitive analysis that Allport had pioneered came to fruition.

At the core of Tajfel's treatise was a rejection of prevailing accounts that considered prejudice (and stereotyping) to be irrational and pathological, and an appreciation that prejudice arose from the structure of group memberships and intergroup relations that led to particular cognitions. Prejudice, he argued, is a reflection of people's group memberships and their attempts to understand and explain features of the social world (in particular, the actions of other groups) that impinge on those group memberships.

Tajfel saw three processes as central to this process, categorization, assimilation, and the search for coherence, but it was the first of these that his own empirical work brought to the fore. Coming from a background of research into processes of perceptual judgment, his particular contribution was to show how normal categorization processes could be the basis for biased judgments of individuals on the basis of their group membership. For instance, when participants were shown a series of lines of varying lengths, with the four shortest lines labeled A and the four longest labeled B, and were subsequently asked to recall the length of these lines, the participants tended to accentuate the difference between the two categories of lines by exaggerating the difference between the lengths of the A lines and the B lines and the similarities between lines that were in the same group (A or B). The point that Tajfel abstracted from the study was that the provision of category labels led to systematic distortion in participants' judgment: They saw the two sets of lines as more different than they really were, and they saw lines in the same set as more similar than they really were. Moreover, the critical step that Tajfel took was to recognize the link between these categorization effects and features of prejudicial judgment. These results implied that if judgments of individuals were informed by awareness of their group membership, then those judgments could be systematically distorted such that, on dimensions perceived to be correlated with those group memberships, individuals viewed members of the same groups as more similar to each other and members of different groups as more different from each other than they really were.

This analysis opened the door to a "cognitive revolution" in the study of prejudice and stereotyping that underpinned the greater part of social-psychological research into these topics in the 1970s and 1980s. Indeed, it paved the way for an appreciation of prejudice as an aspect of general *social cognition*. In line with much of Allport's reasoning, this view understood prejudice to arise from cognitive processes (e.g., the accentuation of interclass difference and intraclass similarity) that were normal but nevertheless problematic because they introduced bias into the processing of information about individuals and groups.

A key metaphor here was that of the individual as a *cognitive miser*. Proposed by Shelley Taylor and Susan Fiske, this framework characterized prejudicial (i.e., distorted) stereotypes as a product of the requirement to engage in social categorization in order to preserve limited cognitive resources. Thus prejudice was still seen as erroneous and problematic, but it was now explained as an inevitable, if unfortunate, outcome of the limitations of humans as information processors.

Prejudice as a Product of Social Identity

At the same time that Tajfel's ideas were informing the development of social cognitive approaches to stereotyping and prejudice, his own work was developing in a somewhat different direction. The groundwork for this direction was provided by the *minimal group* studies that he conducted with colleagues in the early 1970s. The purpose of these studies was to identify the minimal conditions that

would lead members of one group to discriminate in favor of the ingroup to which they belonged and against an outgroup. In these studies, participants were assigned to groups that were intended to be as stripped down and meaningless as possible (e.g., based on participants' estimation of the number of dots on a screen or their preference for the abstract painters Klee or Kandinsky). The plan was then to start adding meaning to the situation in order to discover at what point discrimination would show its face.

The key finding of the studies was that even these most minimal of conditions were sufficient to encourage ingroup-favoring responses. That is, when assigning points to anonymous members of the groups, participants tended to deviate from a strategy of fairness by awarding more points to people who were identified as ingroup rather than outgroup members. Significantly, too, this pattern occurred in the absence of a history of conflict, animosity, or interdependence between the groups. There was also no prospect of personal gain. Further research also showed that the minimal group studies have broader relevance to issues of social perception and cognition. For example, participants assigned to minimal groups have been found to describe the outgroup in such studies far less favorably than the ingroup (e.g., as less flexible, less kind, and less fair).

As later argued by John Turner, the most important upshot of the original minimal group studies was that they suggested that the mere act of individuals *categorizing themselves* as group members was sufficient to lead them to display ingroup favoritism. In this, the results challenged established theories of prejudice by demonstrating that discrimination in favor of an ingroup need be underpinned neither by a prejudiced personality nor by realistic conflict or deep-seated (e.g., psychodynamic) motives.

Building on these insights, Tajfel and Turner's *social identity theory* extended this analysis by specifying how social structural factors determined, first, what strategy individuals adopted in their dealings with other groups and, second, whether these strategies were personal or collective. The theory argued that individuals would engage in direct collective competition with an outgroup (e.g., display discrimination of the form shown in the minimal group studies) only when they believed that intergroup relations were insecure in the sense of being perceived to be unstable and illegitimate. In other words, members of low-status groups are predicted to embrace beliefs and act in ways that directly challenge high-status outgroups' status, and those high-status groups are in turn predicted to embrace beliefs and act in ways that defend and justify their position. These dynamics can clearly contribute to prejudice by reinforcing group-based treatment of others that disadvantages them relative to one's ingroup. Critically, though, social identity theorists see such expressions of prejudice as context-specific responses that arise in particular social-psychological conditions and reflect the position of one's group within a particular system of intergroup relations. This analysis was developed though the lens of *self-categorization theory* in Penelope Oakes, Alexander Haslam, and John Turner's 1994 text *Stereotyping and Social Reality*. This theory argued that rather than being irrational, prejudice can be understood to be an aspect of a political process that reflects and advances the perceived interests of those groups with which a person identities in a particular set of social circumstances. In these terms, the problem of prejudice is a problem of politics and ideology (to do with different groups' disagreement about how those interests should be advanced) rather than of group psychology and social perception per se.

Prejudice as a Product of Habit of Mind

Recent research on prejudice proposes that because of the fundamental cognitive and motivational forces that promote prejudice and the reinforcement of particular biases (most notably related to gender, age, race, and ethnicity) through early socialization and cultural experience, people develop prejudices that represent habitual ways of thinking. When individuals are exposed to members or symbols of the outgroup, those individuals' biased thoughts are automatically activated. This spontaneous prejudice, which may not be consciously recognized by people who possess it, is commonly measured with response latency techniques, such as the Implicit Association Test.

The evidence that people may have unconscious (implicit) biases provides support for a number of perspectives on contemporary prejudice (e.g., *aver-sive racism, modern racism, symbolic racism*) that are different from traditional prejudice, which is blatant. In general, many researchers have argued that although the overt expression of many prejudices toward minority groups has declined over time, underlying prejudices remain stubborn and strong but are expressed in covert ways. Researchers have thus argued that while perceivers who belong to dominant groups have learned to control their overt displays of prejudice, they are not able to do so on covert measures. Contemporary prejudice is thus typically expressed indirectly, often couched in support of system-justifying ideologies (such as meritocracy) that benefit the dominant group, and it produces subtle forms of discrimination (e.g., mainly when negative treatment can be justified on the basis of some factor other than group membership). Nevertheless, there is evidence that, even at this unconscious level, processes of stereotyping and prejudice will be sensitive to the identities that are primed in a particular context and to the meaning of those identities in the particular situation at hand. Consistent with this point, there is evidence that social identity and self-categorization processes play a major role in the escalation and reduction of prejudice and in determining people's willingness to express prejudice openly. In particular, a number of studies have shown that people's willingness to express prejudicial attitudes increases markedly if they believe that such an expression is normative for their group and if they identify with that group.

Conclusion

In summary, prejudice comes in several forms. It can reflect either direct negative feelings about members of another group, preference for one's own group or another group, or lowered evaluations of members of another group who violate stereotypic expectations. A number of personality, cognitive, motivational, social, and cultural forces contribute to the development and maintenance of prejudice. In addition, prejudice may be blatant and overt, or it can be harbored unconsciously and covert. In fact, many people who believe they are not prejudiced may be implicitly prejudiced. Under certain circumstances, such as when norms change, implicit biases are expressed more explicitly.

Understanding the causes and nature of prejudice can help guide interventions for reducing prejudice. For example, to the extent that prejudice is based in social categorization and social identity, interventions that alter the way people think about groups and their memberships can ameliorate prejudice. Strategies that encourage people to categorize themselves differently have been shown to lead to change in the treatment and representation of others, even on an implicit level. This is illustrated by a study in which Samuel Gaertner and colleagues defined participants as members of one of two groups, each comprising three members. As in the minimal group studies, this categorization led to intergroup discrimination. After this, however, some participants were induced to *recategorize* the people as either one group of six or as six individuals, and both these recategorization strategies served to reduce intergroup discrimination and prejudice. Specifically, the one-group manipulation increased the perceived attractiveness of former outgroup members, and the separate-individuals redefinition reduced the perceived attractiveness of former ingroup members. Consistent with this point, studies of intergroup contact—which examine the relationship between people's exposure to members of an outgroup and their prejudice toward them—generally find that contact is effective to the extent that it is associated with a softening of the boundaries between ingroup and outgroup and with reduced anxiety about the implications and consequences of future contact.

A key point in the most recent developments in the study of prejudice is that although it is customary for prejudice to be thought of as a process that arises from the processing of information about others ("them"), prejudice is also very much driven by group members' understanding of themselves (as "us"). In this regard, as Stephen Reicher and colleagues have noted, the most pernicious prejudices of the past century have arisen when group members have been encouraged by leaders to develop a theory of their ingroup that first excludes outgroup members, then defines them as a threat to the ingroup, and finally comes to celebrate prejudicial treatment of others as essential for the preservation of that ingroup. Rather than being a matter of cold, detached information processing, such prejudice is fomented in a social cauldron of norms, values, and emotions that group members come to share and that fuel their collective actions in the world. Although much of this "heat" has gone out of social-psychological research in the past 30 years, there is little doubt that it is still keenly felt on the front line of intergroup relations.

S. Alexander Haslam and John F. Dovidio

See also Authoritarian Personality; Categorization; Common Ingroup Identity Model; Discrimination; Hate Crimes; Implicit Association Test (IAT); Implicit Prejudice; Intergroup Contact Theory; Realistic Group Conflict Theory; Social Identity Theory; Stereotyping

Further Readings

Adorno, T. W., Frenkel-Brunswik, E., Levinson, D. J., & Sanford, R. N. (1950). *The authoritarian personality.* New York: Harper.

Allport, G. W. (1954). *The nature of prejudice.* Cambridge, MA: Addison-Wesley.

Gaertner, S. L., Mann, J., Murrell, A., & Dovidio, J. F. (1989). Reducing intergroup bias: The benefits of recategorization. *Journal of Personality and Social Psychology, 57,* 239–249.

Guimond, S. (2000). Group socialization and prejudice: The social transmission of intergroup attitudes and beliefs. *European Journal of Social Psychology, 30,* 335–354.

Haslam, S. A., & Wilson, A. (2000). Is prejudice really personal? The contribution of a group's shared stereotypes to intergroup prejudice. *British Journal of Social Psychology, 39,* 45–63.

Oakes, P. J., Haslam, S. A., & Turner, J. C. (1994). *Stereotyping and social reality.* Oxford, UK: Blackwell.

Reicher, S. D., Haslam, S. A., & Rath, R. (2008). Making a virtue of evil: A five-step social identity model of the development of collective hate. *Social and Personality Psychology Compass, 2,* 1313–1344.

Sherif, M. (1967). *Group conflict and co-operation: Their social psychology.* London: Routledge & Kegan Paul.

Sidanius, J., & Pratto, F. (1999). *Social dominance: An intergroup theory of social hierarchy and oppression.* Cambridge, UK: Cambridge University Press.

Tajfel, H. (1969). Cognitive aspects of prejudice. *Journal of Social Issues, 25,* 79–97.

PRISONER'S DILEMMA

In its simplest form, the *prisoner's dilemma* refers to a *mixed-motive conflict* in which two interdependent decision makers have to decide whether to cooperate with each other or to defect. For each decision maker, the defect choice strictly dominates the cooperative choice (i.e., regardless of what the other person chooses, defection yields a better payoff to the individual than does cooperation). Yet *both* decision makers will be better off if they each choose cooperation rather than if either defects. Hence, there is a choice dilemma.

The prisoner's dilemma derives its name from a prototypic situation in which the police have arrested two people suspected of having committed a bank heist and have placed them in separate, isolated cells so that they cannot communicate. Because the police do not possess adequate material evidence for conviction, they offer each prisoner the option of testifying against the other. If one of the prisoners agrees to confess to the crime (and, in effect, betray the other), that prisoner will be set free, whereas the other prisoner will receive the maximum sentence allowable, 12 years. If both prisoners confess, each receives an intermediate sentence of 6 years. Finally, if neither prisoner confesses, both receive a minimum sentence of only 4 months for the minor offense of loitering near the scene of a crime. Obviously, both prisoners would be best off if both refuse to confess. However, each is tempted to confess. If both do so, however, both are worse off.

When first introduced, the prisoner's dilemma was viewed by social scientists as a simple but powerful analogue of many real-world situations involving interdependent social actors for whom mutual cooperation is attractive but problematic. Such situations include social exchanges, bilateral negotiations, arms races, and the allocation of shared but scarce resources. This entry looks at this line of research as it has developed over time.

Overview and History

The prisoner's dilemma game spawned an enormous amount of empirical research on cooperation and conflict. Part of the appeal of the prisoner's dilemma task as a research tool is that it succinctly captures a fundamental tension between what theories of rational choice predict and what behavioral observations reveal about cooperation and competition in the real world. For example, although *game theory* predicts that both decision makers in a prisoner's dilemma will choose the defecting option, observed rates of cooperation—at least in experimental versions of the dilemma—are often much higher than expected. Moreover, empirical rates of cooperation observed in many natural settings are also greater than predicted by rational choice and game theory models.

Recognizing both its simplicity and its richness, social psychologists have used the prisoner's dilemma paradigm to conduct a very large number of experiments over the past five decades. These experiments have yielded invaluable and reliable insights into the antecedents and consequences of cooperation.

Antecedents of Cooperation

Much of the early psychological research focused on identifying the psychological and social antecedents of cooperation. For example, early studies examined the role of decision makers' expectations about what the other party would do in the situation. These studies showed, for instance, that positive expectations regarding others' cooperativeness enhanced an individual's cooperation rates whereas expectations of competitive behavior predicted defensive competitive behavior in return. Similarly, a number of studies showed that trust in the other person's cooperative motives and intentions made the cooperative choice easier.

Still other studies demonstrated that individual differences in social values (defined in terms of people's distinct preferences for various self–other payoff patterns) influenced cooperation rates. In particular, people with more prosocial and altruistic motives were more likely to cooperate in a prisoner's dilemma situation than were those with more individualistic or competitive social motives. Other studies using the prisoner's dilemma investigated how properties of the choice itself influenced cooperation and noncooperation. For example, studies have shown that the way in which a choice is framed (e.g., whether it is framed in ways highlighting prospective gains or prospective losses to the individual) influences cooperation levels.

Finally, studies explored how the perceived social relationship between the interdependent decision makers influenced their construal of the task and their subsequent choice. For example, studies showed that cooperation rates tended to be higher when individuals believed they were interacting with other members of their own social category or group (ingroup members) than when they thought they were interacting with members of another social group or category (outgroup members).

Another important stream of psychological research on the prisoner's dilemma investigated mechanisms for actually increasing cooperation rates. These studies have generally adopted one of two approaches. The first approach has focused on exploring the efficacy of individual-level behavioral strategies for inducing mutual cooperation. For example, a variety of behavioral strategies employing variations on patterns of reciprocity have been shown to reliably elicit and sustain cooperation. One particularly famous strategy involved the use of gradually increasing cooperative initiatives. The premise behind this approach was that a small initial offer of cooperation would signal to the other party the willingness to be cooperative, without exposing the initiator to excessive amounts of risk. If the small cooperative gesture was reciprocated, then the decision maker could slowly increase his or her cooperation levels. As each level was reciprocated or matched by the other party, participants would move toward higher and higher levels of cooperation. Not surprisingly, studies in this vein also demonstrated that unconditional cooperation was not effective at sustaining cooperation because eventually the other party would be tempted to exploit the unilateral cooperator.

A second approach to eliciting cooperation has focused on the use of structural changes or arrangements that enhance cooperation. Studies in this vein have demonstrated, for instance, that certain forms of communication and discussion before choosing one's response can improve cooperation levels. Furthermore, increasing the salience and certainty of information regarding others' choices can affect cooperation. In particular, unequivocal evidence that others are cooperating has been shown to increase cooperation rates. Increasing the perceived duration of the relationship can enhance cooperation rates as well.

After a period of rather prolific research activity throughout the 1960s and 1970s, enthusiasm for empirical studies using the prisoner's dilemma paradigm waned somewhat. This decline in interest reflected, at least in part, a sense among researchers that the major research questions and most interesting variables influencing cooperation and noncooperation had been investigated in previous research.

A Resurgence of Interest: Iterated Prisoner's Dilemma Game Research

Beginning in the early 1980s, however, innovative research by Robert Axelrod revitalized scientific interest in this line of research. This new work, which focused on cooperation in repeated or *iterated* versions of the prisoner's dilemma, used a clever and, as it turned out, enormously generative computer tournament methodology. Using this computer tournament approach, Axelrod and his associates were able to systematically investigate the comparative efficacy of different choice strategies for inducing and sustaining cooperation over long periods of time.

His results demonstrated, most dramatically, that a very simple strategy known as *tit for tat* was able to outperform even highly complex and cognitively sophisticated decision strategies. In tit for tat, one initially cooperates on the first round of play and thereafter does whatever one's opponent or partner did in the previous round. Axelrod's systematic research further isolated the properties of tit for tat that contributed to its strong performance. In particular, tit for tat is nice (i.e., it always cooperates initially). It is also *provokable* (i.e., it punishes noncooperation immediately). Yet it is also forgiving (i.e., it is willing to return to cooperation after administering a suitable punishment). It also has the advantage, Axelrod suggested, of clarity, thus enabling it to avoid unintentional cycles of mutual defection. In a nutshell, tit for tat is effective at promoting cooperation and deterring exploitation.

Axelrod's computer tournament methodology spawned a large number of studies across multiple disciplines and subfields, including political science, behavioral economics, game theory, sociology, and social psychology. It has led also to the discovery of numerous alternative strategies for eliciting cooperation across a variety of contexts. Thus, although tit for tat proved to be a powerful strategy for eliciting and sustaining cooperation in Axelrod's original tournament, subsequent studies showed that another simple strategy, called *win-stay, lose-switch*, turned out to be quite capable of producing strong and resilient results when paired against a variety of other strategies. As its name suggests, a player using the win-stay, lose-switch strategy continues to use the same strategy so long as that strategy is producing favorable payoffs in its transactions. As soon as it begins to produce inferior payoffs, however, the player switches to another choice.

Another subsequent and promising wave of research has examined the problem of cooperation in what are called "noisy" prisoner's dilemmas. In a noisy prisoner's dilemma situation, players operate under conditions of uncertainty regarding the true level of cooperation of the other player or players. It is interesting to note that when uncertainty of this sort is present, tit for tat performs much more poorly than many other strategies because it tends to set off costly cycles of mutual punishment or retaliation for perceived defections. Stated differently and perhaps somewhat counterintuitively, strict reciprocity does not work so well when information about others' actions is ambiguous. In contrast, strategies that display generosity or leniency by underreacting to others' apparent defections are able to sustain high levels of cooperative exchanges for long periods of time. In a sense, such strategies compensate for the deleterious effects of noise on the interpretation of others' actions.

Simulation work using the Axelrodian paradigm is enjoying considerable vogue and continues to generate new and important insights into the evolution of cooperation and the stability of cooperative regimes.

Current Developments and Future Directions

As a simple but elegant prototype of mixed-motive conflict situations, the prisoner's dilemma game, in all its variations, continues to occupy a special place in the social sciences. Moreover, recent theoretical developments promise to enlarge and enrich early game theoretic perspectives. For example, sociologists and political scientists have become increasingly interested in how group or team identities influence patterns of cooperation and competition. Similarly, there is a great deal of interest in how embedded social structures, such as neighborhoods and network ties, facilitate cooperation and its maintenance.

For example, research in this area has shown that the preservation of social context, even though decision makers within the neighborhood might be changing their individual strategies, can result in high levels of cooperation as well as neighborhoods that are resistant to invasion by predators or cheaters. Other studies have been examining the role of sanctions and norms on the stability of cooperation. The results of these sociological explorations will undoubtedly be more nuanced and refined psychological models of cooperative judgment and choice.

Recently, the prisoner's dilemma has even been viewed as a useful approach for studying cross-cultural or comparative aspects of cooperative choice in dilemma situations. Increasingly sophisticated agent-based modeling techniques suggest the future for prisoner's dilemma research remains bright.

Roderick M. Kramer

See also Cooperation and Competition; Negotiation and Bargaining; Social Dilemmas; Trust

Further Readings

Axelrod, R. (1984). Effective choice in the prisoner's dilemma. *Journal of Conflict Resolution, 24*, 3–25.

Bacharach, M. (2006). *Beyond individual choice: Teams and frames in game theory*. Princeton, NJ: Princeton University Press.

Bendor, J., Kramer, R. M., & Stout, S. (1991). When in doubt: Cooperation in the noisy prisoner's dilemma. *Journal of Conflict Resolution, 35*, 691–719.

Komorita, S. S. (1995). Interpersonal relations: Mixed-motive interaction. *Annual Review of Psychology, 46*, 183–207.

Messick, D. M., & McClintock, C. G. (1968). Motivational bases of choice in experimental games. *Journal of Experimental Social Psychology, 4*, 1–25.

Nowak, M., & Sigmund, K. (1993). A strategy of win-stay, lose-shift that outperforms tit-for-tat in the prisoner's dilemma game. *Nature, 364*, 56–58.

Rapoport, A., & Chammah, A. M. (1965). *Prisoner's dilemma: A study in conflict and cooperation*. Ann Arbor: University of Michigan Press.

Stahl, D. O., & Wilson, P. W. (1994). Experimental evidence on players' models of other players. *Journal of Economic Behavior and Organization, 25,* 309–327.

PROCEDURAL JUSTICE

Procedural justice refers to the fairness of decision-making procedures and of other social and organizational processes. In social psychology, virtually all research on procedural justice refers to *subjective* procedural fairness—the subjective feeling that one has been treated fairly under a given procedure. Early psychological studies of the impact of justice judgments focused on judgments of whether outcome distributions were fair or unfair—a topic called *distributive justice*—without paying much attention to the procedures used to arrive at the outcome allocation. In the early 1970s, however, experimental studies of psychological reactions to various legal procedures showed that procedures have their own impact on feelings of fairness. Psychologist John Thibaut, law professor Laurens Walker, and their colleagues showed that some procedures result in feelings of greater fairness, regardless of whether the outcome of the process was fair or unfair, favorable or unfavorable. The discovery of procedural justice effects was important because it showed that it is possible to increase feelings of fairness by using the right procedure, so that even those who lose or experience negative outcomes can feel fairly treated.

A good example of a procedural justice effect is seen in the first experiment that Thibaut, Walker, and their colleagues conducted on the topic. Participants in that study found themselves involved in a complex dispute resolution process because another member of their team had been accused of cheating. The experiment varied whether the participant knew that his or her teammate had in fact cheated, whether the outcome of the "trial" was favorable or unfavorable (the participant's team was either exonerated or found guilty), and whether the dispute resolution procedure did or did not give the participant a voice in determining what evidence was considered or denied. The results showed a clear effect for the procedure the participant had

experienced. *Voice procedures* were seen as fairer than were procedures that placed all the control and input in the hands of the decision maker. In addition, regardless of whether the participant's team won or lost the trial, and regardless of whether the outcome of the trial conformed to the participant's private knowledge about the teammate's behavior, the voice procedure led to greater satisfaction with the verdict and greater perceived fairness in the trial outcome than did the *mute procedure*. Of course, winning participants were generally more satisfied than losing participants, and correct decisions were generally seen as fairer than incorrect decisions, but in each combination of the other factors, the voice procedure prompted more positive reactions. Subsequent studies have shown that such *voice effects* have a powerful impact on procedural fairness judgments in a variety of organizational and governmental contexts. When people are given an opportunity to control what information is considered by a decision maker, especially when they are given an opportunity to express their views about the situation under consideration, the procedure is seen as fairer.

Subsequent work by Robert Folger and others showed that decisions that come from fair procedures are more readily accepted than those from unfair procedures, a phenomenon Folger dubbed the *fair process effect*. Later research showed that when people believe that the process used to reach a decision is fair, they are more likely to accept the decision. In many of these studies, the way processes were made fair was by including an opportunity for voice on the part of those affected by the decision.

Tom Tyler and his colleagues studied the workings of the fair process effect in political and social contexts and found that judgments of procedural fairness were strongly correlated with the acceptance of authorities' decisions. Tyler also showed that an important factor in people's willingness to obey a law is whether they believe that the process that generated the law was fair. Most of the early studies on acceptance of authority looked at the relationship between procedural fairness judgments and the acceptance of political decisions and laws, but later research showed similar effects for reactions to organizational authorities. In many of these studies, procedural fairness judgments exerted greater influence on the acceptance of authorities' decisions than did distributive justice judgments. While willingness to accept a decision or obey a law can be affected by whether the outcome is favorable to the person in question, believing that the decision or law was generated by fair process has an even greater impact.

Early accounts of the psychology of procedural fairness and the fair process effect relied on assumptions about the role of procedures in ensuring that outcomes would be fair. For example, Thibaut and Walker explained the voice effect they found by suggesting that giving voice to litigants or defendants enhances the perceived likelihood of a fair verdict. Such "instrumental" theories of procedural justice had a difficult time explaining why procedural justice effects were sometimes stronger than effects of distributive fairness, however.

The need for noninstrumental explanations of the psychology of procedural justice is illustrated by an experiment conducted by E. Allan Lind, Ruth Kanfer, and Christopher Earley. Participants were given work goals, which affected their payments for the experiment, using one of three procedures. Some participants had an opportunity to voice their preferences for the goals—this is a typical voice procedure. Others had no opportunity to express their preferences. Instead, they were simply given a goal and put to work—a typical mute procedure. Finally, in a postdecision-voice procedure, the goal was announced, but then participants were given an opportunity to express their preferences. After they had voiced their views, the original goal was repeated and the participants were put to work. Even though the exercise of postdecision voice could not affect the outcome of the goal-setting decision, that procedure was viewed as fairer, resulted in greater acceptance of the goal, and led to better performance than did the mute procedure.

Lind and Tyler have offered a new theory to explain both instrumental and noninstrumental procedural justice effects. Their *group-value model* suggests that there are two ways that people process procedural information to judge its fairness. One way is to evaluate the benefit of the process for their own interests—using an *instrumental fairness processor*, as it were. The other way is to look at the procedure as a manifestation or symbol of how the person in question is valued by the group, organization, or institution that employs

the procedure—using a *group-value fairness processor*. On the one hand, if a procedure seems to recognize the person's standing in the group, organization, or institution, then the procedure is seen as fair. On the other hand, a procedure that seems to deny one's full standing is seen as unfair. From the perspective of group-value theory, voice effects occur because allowing an individual affected by a decision to have a say has positive effects for both the instrumental processor (the voice might convince the authority to make a favorable decision) and the group-value processor (voice indicates that one is a full-fledged member of the group). The fairness effect of the postdecision-voice condition in the Lind, Kanfer, and Earley study can be explained as follows: Even though the postdecision-voice condition had nothing to offer the instrumental fairness processor, it still had a fairness advantage for the group-value processor.

Later work on the psychology of fairness turned to why people should care so much about fairness and why, among fairness judgments, procedural fairness so often carries more weight than distributive fairness. One theoretical approach that addresses these issues is *fairness heuristic theory*, advanced by Lind and Kees van den Bos. Fairness heuristic theory says that people look at the fairness of their treatment as an indicator of whether they can trust a group not to exploit or exclude them. On one hand, when a person receives information or experiences treatment that seems fair, he or she goes into a mode of interaction that is cooperative and supportive of the group in question. On the other hand, when a person experiences unfair treatment, he or she adopts a narrow self-interest approach to the group. Because information is processed early and quickly to serve as the basis of the fairness heuristic, later fairness information is interpreted in light of earlier fairness information. This is where the extra impact of procedural fairness information comes from—we usually know about procedures before we know about outcomes. Van den Bos and others have shown that when outcome information is available before process information, distributive fairness has greater impact.

The psychology of fairness, procedural and distributive, occupies an important place in the psychology of groups and interpersonal relations because it goes to the heart of how people, as individuals, relate to the groups to which they belong. As researchers explore this area, they learn more about the rules, norms, and psychological processes that regulate the person-to-group relationship.

E. Allan Lind

See also Distributive Justice; Justice; Just World Hypothesis; Relational Model of Authority in Groups

Further Readings

Lind, E. A., & Tyler, T. R. (1988). *The social psychology of procedural justice*. New York: Plenum.

Thibaut, J., & Walker, L. (1975). *Procedural justice: A psychological analysis*. Hillsdale, NJ: Erlbaum.

Tyler, T. R. (1990). *Why people obey the law*. New Haven, CT: Yale University Press.

van den Bos, K., Lind, E. A., & Wilke, H. A. M. (2001). The psychology of procedural and distributive justice viewed from the perspective of fairness heuristic theory. In R. Cropanzano (Ed.), *Justice in the workplace: Vol. 2. From theory to practice* (pp. 49–66). Mahwah, NJ: Erlbaum.

PROCESS CONSULTATION

Group interactions involve both content and process. Content is *what* the group is doing. Content includes the group's objective, agenda, discussion topics, and so forth. The content defines the reason the group is getting together. Process is *how* the group conducts its work. Process includes how the group achieves its objective, moves through its agenda, discusses its topics, and so forth. *Process consultation* is an intervention in which an individual, typically from outside the group, helps the group members become more aware of how they do things and then use this awareness to enhance how they operate together.

Process consultation is important to group processes because it can enhance a group's ability to perform its tasks and develop positive relations among its members. This entry describes how process consultation enhances group performance, describes the kinds of behaviors that are observed during process consultation, and discusses how process consultation is conducted.

Enhancement of Group Performance

Process consultation enhances group *functioning* because very few individuals are able to focus on a group's content and process at the same time. Most members have a vested interest in the group's outcome, and all members bring some bias to the group's interactions. Thus, it is difficult for them to be truly objective about how the group is functioning. Moreover, and especially when they have an interest in the outcome of the group's work, most individuals simply cannot attend to the group's process when they are absorbed in the group's content.

Consider the work of a task force that is assembled after a merger of two corporations to make a recommendation regarding which firm's information technology system to use. This is a high-stakes decision: If the two companies have different information technology systems—say that one uses Macintosh computers (Macs) and the other uses PCs—it is likely that employees from the company whose system prevails will get more jobs in the merged organization because they are more familiar with the system that is selected. Members of the task force will be enthusiastic participants in the group's deliberations, pushing for their way of doing things.

Their focus on the *content* of the group's work will detract from their ability to attend to the group's *process*. Deficiencies or dysfunctions in the group's process, in turn, can detract from the group's ability to conduct its work. If members do a poor job of listening to and considering one another's perspectives, then they have defeated the very purpose of using a group to make decisions: to leverage the multiple insights, experiences, and knowledge bases to produce a solution that is superior to what any individual could generate independently.

In cases like this, it is helpful to have a *group facilitator* who can attend to and help enhance the group's process. The facilitator is unbiased—he or she has no vested interest in the group's decision or recommendation. Thus, the facilitator can focus on *how* the group is conducting its work rather than *what* the group is deliberating. Another name for a facilitator is a *process consultant*—someone who is not a full-time member of the group but who attends and participates in group meetings with the express purpose of fostering good group functioning. (Sometimes, a member of the group can act as the process consultant. This typically happens with effectiveness only when the group is relatively mature and has spent time in the past addressing group process issues. For example, an ongoing work team might have each member take a turn being the process consultant at one meeting.)

Key Behaviors

The process consultant is concerned with how the group is functioning—how it achieves its objectives, moves through its agenda, discusses topics, makes decisions, and so on. As Edgar Schein—one of the earliest writers about process consultation—noted, there are two basic kinds of behavior that process consultants look for in examining a group's functioning: task-oriented behavior and maintenance-oriented behavior.

Task-Oriented Behavior

Task-oriented behavior deals with what people say or do to get something done. There are five major elements of task-oriented behavior:

1. *Initiating.* In order for a group to accomplish or make progress on its tasks (the content), there must be some initiating behavior. Examples of initiating behavior include stating the objective or definition of the problem, offering alternatives for working on or solving the problem, setting time limits, building an agenda, and so on.

2. *Information and opinion seeking and giving.* Communication is the essential process by which the group accomplishes its tasks. Information seeking and giving, and opinion seeking and giving, are vital task-oriented behaviors. Examples include questions and statements such as these: What more do we know about this problem? I've got more data that may help. What do people think about these alternatives? Here's my opinion on that issue.

3. *Clarifying and elaborating.* The reason for calling the group together in the first place rests on the assumption that no individual has the

answer. Clarification helps sharpen members' understanding of the specifics involved. Elaborating on someone else's inputs is the essence of collaboration. By asking for clarification and by building on the ideas of others, a group moves toward creative solutions to complex problems that are beyond any single individual's capability.

4. *Summarizing.* To further help a group operate with full information, effective summarization is an important function. Reviewing the points that have been covered, the ideas under consideration, the decisions made and pending, and so on can help a group determine where it has been, where it is, and where it needs to go.

5. *Consensus testing.* Consensus testing is checking to see whether the group is close to a decision. Even if the group is not ready for a decision, testing can still serve the important function of reminding the group that it is there to achieve some objective and within some time constraint. This is a productive form of time keeping.

Maintenance-Oriented Behavior

Maintenance-oriented behavior deals with how people behave toward one another in performing the task and, ultimately, with how cohesive the group members feel. There are four main elements of maintenance-oriented behavior:

1. *Gatekeeping.* Group members often behave in ways that make it difficult for others to make their own contributions. For example, repeatedly interrupting a person and dominating the conversation can create a situation in which the interrupted person stops contributing. Gatekeeping—that is, regulating the communication gates—ensures that everyone has at least the opportunity to contribute. For example, a member may state, "We haven't heard everyone's opinion on this, so let's go around the table and see what people think."

2. *Encouraging.* Encouraging can serve a function similar to that of gatekeeping. For various reasons, some individuals do not jump in as quickly or consistently as others do as the group conducts its work. These individuals may need some encouragement if they are to be willing

and able to make a contribution or to continue making contributions if their first attempts fall flat, sound disorganized, or are immediately discounted by others.

3. *Harmonizing and compromising.* Harmonizing and compromising are efforts to bring the group together in a shared perspective. However, their use and value must be carefully examined in each particular situation. When used too hastily, they can detract from the group's effectiveness. In some situations, it may be very important first to confront the fact that a serious disagreement exists and then to strive to find a creative, integrative solution before resorting to a compromise or next-best solution. When used as a mechanism to avoid real differences of opinion, harmonizing and compromising result in a state of false security.

4. *Standard setting and testing.* These are efforts to test whether the group is satisfied with its procedures or to suggest procedures and standards. Standard setting and testing can involve pointing out explicit or implicit norms that have been set in the group.

How Process Consultation Is Conducted

Process consultation also involves observing patterns of interaction among group members. One of the easiest aspects of group process to observe is the pattern of communication. Who talks in the group, for how long, and how often? Who do people look at when they talk—single others (possibly potential supporters of their point of view), the full group, or no one? Who talks after whom or who interrupts whom? What style of communication is being used (assertions, questions, tone of voice, gestures, etc.)?

Process consultation is done most often through direct observation of the group and, at appropriate times, through raising questions or making observations about what has been happening in the group. The group could be ongoing, such as a regular work team, or it could be temporary, such as the task force described earlier, charged to recommend whether the merged company should go with Macs or PCs.

In some cases, process consultation is used to identify and address deficiencies in group effectiveness

or dysfunctions in group interactions. For example, a group that repeatedly falters at implementing decisions made by its members may suffer from problems associated with clarifying support during the decision-making process. In other cases, process consultation can be used to make a relatively effective group even better. In these cases, the process consultant observes the group in action, provides the group members feedback on the observations, and then engages the members is discussing and applying the observations to their situation.

Although process consultation has been practiced for 40 years, only a modest amount of research has been conducted to assess its effectiveness in improving the ability of groups to accomplish work. Findings of research on process consultation are unclear, especially when the findings relate to task performance. A number of difficulties arise in trying to measure performance improvement as a result of process consultation. One problem is that most process consultation is conducted with groups performing mental tasks, such as decision making; the outcomes of such tasks are difficult to evaluate. A second issue is that process consultation typically is combined with other interventions; isolating the impact of process consultations from those of the other interventions is difficult.

Literature reviews on the effectiveness of process consultation have concluded that it has positive effects on participants, according to self-reports, in areas including greater personal involvement, higher mutual influence, and enhanced group effectiveness. One recent study noted that process consultation tends to be most effective when managers have the personal resources to engage in self-evaluation and personal development and thus to participate in such a process.

Mitchell Lee Marks

See also Group Development; Group Performance; Group Problem Solving and Decision Making; Team Building; Teams; Work Teams

Further Readings

Schein, E. (1969). *Process consultation: Its role in organization development.* Reading, MA: Addison-Wesley.

PROCESS GAIN AND LOSS

Process gain and *loss* are labels covering a long research tradition in social psychology that examines how and to what degree group processes affect group performance, with the earliest work occurring over 100 years ago. Sometimes, group processes can lead to performance that exceeds expectation, referred to as *process gains*. More often, group processes lead to performance that falls below expectations, referred to as *process losses*. Work on process gains and losses has focused on both performance by the group as a whole and the effects on the performance of an individual who is working as a member of the group.

This entry looks at research about process gains and losses in two principal categories, coordination and motivation. Coordination gains and losses result from how well the group coordinates its efforts or resources while performing the task. Motivation gains and losses stem from the effects that group membership has on the amount of effort each individual member contributes to the task.

Coordination Gains and Losses

Group Problem Solving

Early work on group problem solving seemed to show that group interaction led to process gains, in that groups were two to three times as likely as individuals to be able to solve basic logic and word problems. However, both gains and losses are relative and must be defined in terms of some baseline, or expectation. This early work used the "average" individual as the baseline to which group performance was compared. Research has shown that many basic group processes can lead groups to perform better than their average member. For example, simple majority or plurality processes (i.e., the alternative that has the most support in the group gets chosen by the group) often lead to superior performance by groups compared with the performance of the average individual. Such processes are quite commonplace in group decision-making situations because of their high level of accuracy relative to the amount of information gathering and cognitive effort that they require from the group.

Most social-psychological research on groups has used *potential* group performance as the baseline against which process gains and losses are measured. In problem-solving situations in which a particular choice alternative can be considered correct or best, a common baseline used is *truth wins*; that is, if any member of the group initially favors the correct or best answer (i.e., has truth), then the group will choose that alternative. Based on this baseline criterion, most groups show process losses in problem-solving situations.

Although groups typically perform better than their average member, they often do not perform as well as their best member. Research has shown that groups rarely perform as well as a truth-wins model predicts they should. On problem-solving tasks, groups often perform near the predictions of a *truth supported wins* model (i.e., a group will be able to solve the problem only if at least two of the members can solve the problem). This level of performance is still better than the average individual but is below the group's potential performance.

Brainstorming

A second area in which results were interpreted initially as process gains but were later seen as process losses involved *brainstorming* in groups. Early research showed that groups asked to generate ideas or solutions generated far more items than did single individuals working alone. However, many later studies have shown that sets of noninteracting individuals, or nominal groups, often perform better than interacting groups of the same size. In regard to brainstorming, two of the major reasons for these performance losses are *production blocking* and *cognitive interference*. Production blocking occurs because group members try to produce responses at the same time, so someone must wait to contribute. This creates a coordination loss. In addition, ideas presented by other members tend to interfere with individual cognitive processes used to generate ideas.

Information Sharing

A third area in which coordination problems lead to performance decrements involves information sharing in groups. A number of group tasks require members to share information in order to reach an optimal solution or decision. However, research has shown that members tend to discuss and place more weight on information that they all share than on information that is uniquely held by each individual member. Shared information is often relevant and valid, but if group members do not share task-relevant information that only they know, then their group is less likely to perform up to its potential. A number of studies have shown that groups will choose inferior options supported by shared information even though they have enough information to demonstrate that a different alternative is superior.

If group members each have unique task-relevant information and subsequently share that information during group discussion, then their groups can perform at levels above what is possible for any individual members. Recent research has argued that the unique information brought by members of multidisciplinary scientific research teams affords such teams better odds of making significant scientific contributions compared with teams whose members are drawn from a single scientific discipline. Recent empirical and simulation findings also show that members who bring complementary strategies to a decision problem can produce decision outcomes that are superior to those possible by groups sharing a single strategy. Unfortunately, if most of the members share a particular strategy or orientation toward a problem, then that particular strategy or orientation will dominate other strategies that may be available to the group, even if the shared strategy is suboptimal or invalid.

Implicit and Explicit Coordination

A final area in which coordination losses have been demonstrated involves *implicit* and *explicit coordination*. Most groups rely on implicit coordination, which simply evolves (without discussion) as the group works on the task. Although groups learn to coordinate their actions, the process can be slow, and coordination rarely becomes optimal. Explicit coordination or planning is often viewed as a positive way for groups to begin a task. However, left to their own devices, groups rarely spend much time planning and often spend no time at all at it. Forcing groups to plan in advance of attempting to perform a task can thus improve performance.

Motivation Losses

Much of the early research on process losses assumed they were due to coordination problems. However, research designs using tasks that allowed for estimates of performance decrements due to lack of coordination showed that actual group performance was often below estimates based on coordination problems alone. Thus, researchers began to focus on motivation losses as well and coined the term *social loafing* to describe them.

Social loafing occurs when group members are working on a common task in which individual contributions are difficult to assess and the odds of the group's achieving its goal are high or the goal is of little value to group members. Under these circumstances, members put less effort into the task than they do when working on the task as an individual. The actual presence of other group members is not necessary. Simply knowing that other people are working on the task and that there are no specific or assessable individual member goals can lead members to loaf. Loafing has been observed on physical and cognitive tasks, by both males and females, and in many different cultures.

Social loafing can also stem from more strategic aspects of behavior in groups. *Free riding* occurs when members can reap the benefits of the groups' behavior regardless of the amount of effort they extend. For example, if others refrain from dumping their garbage into a common lake, then the lake will remain usable, even if one member continues to dump garbage in it. Many group settings allow for free riding, so some groups create negative incentives (penalties or expulsion from the group) to reduce its prevalence. Free riding can also lead to further motivation losses by others who feel they are being played for suckers. If typically conscientious members think others are free riding, then the conscientious members will exert less effort themselves to avoid being taken advantage of.

Although social loafing is probably the most widely studied form of motivation loss in groups, other processes can also lead to effort reductions. For example, *social anxiety* created by evaluation apprehension can lead group members to limit their participation. In situations in which members are not confident of their abilities or ideas, they may hold back to avoid the appearance of incompetence. Fear of evaluation can stem from characteristics of the specific group (e.g., other members are of higher status) or a general anxiety that some people have about working in groups. Groups composed of members who enjoy working in groups tend to perform better than groups of comparable ability whose members feel uncomfortable in group environments.

Motivation losses can also occur because of social comparison among group members. Often, group members do not know exactly how much time and effort they should devote to a task. In such situations, they will look to the other members of the group for cues. On idea generation tasks, for example, if one member of the group appears to have given up, then other members of the group will soon cease their performance as well. In highly cohesive groups, members may actually ostracize a member for expending more effort than others in the group are. And when groups set goals for themselves and for individual members, people often set lower goals for others than they do for themselves, maybe to ensure that all members can reach their goals. Thus, groups can generate norms for effort expenditure that are well below potential effort levels.

Motivation Gains

Although much of the research on motivation in groups has focused on losses, recent evidence points to circumstances that produce motivation gains. These situations tend to be the opposites of those that lead to losses. When group goals are highly valued and some members feel that they have more resources than other members have, they will put in extra effort to compensate for the potential limitations of those other members. Such compensation effects occur when a group member fears that others will loaf or free ride, especially if the group goal is important for that member.

Another situation in which motivation gains have been observed involves tasks in which the least competent member determines the group's performance (conjunctive tasks). When members do not differ greatly in ability, lower-ability members will work harder so as not to keep the group from reaching its full potential. This has been referred to as the *Köhler effect*, after the German scientist who first discovered the phenomenon. For such effects to occur, lower-ability members must be able to compare their performance to that of higher-ability members, and they must believe that their extra effort will lead to performance comparable to the performance of more capable members.

R. Scott Tindale and Rebecca Starkel

See also Brainstorming; Common Knowledge Effect; Group Memory; Group Motivation; Köhler Effect; Ringelmann Effect; Social Compensation; Social Facilitation; Social Loafing

Further Readings

Karau, S. J., & Williams, K. D. (1993). Social loafing: A meta-analytic review and theoretical integration. *Journal of Personality and Social Psychology, 65,* 681–706.

Larson, J. R., Jr. (2007). Deep diversity and strong synergy: Modeling the impact of variability in members' problem-solving strategies on group problem-solving performance. *Small Group Research, 38,* 413–436.

Laughlin, P. R., Bonner, B. L., & Miner, A. G. (2002). Groups perform better than their best member on letters-to-numbers problems. *Organizational Behavior and Human Decision Processes, 88,* 605–620.

Nijstad, B. A., & Streobe, W. (2006). How the group affects the mind: A cognitive model of idea generation in groups. *Personality and Social Psychology Review, 10,* 186–213.

Stasser, G., & Stewart, D. D. (1992). The discovery of hidden profiles by decision making groups: Solving a problem vs. making a decision. *Journal of Personality and Social Psychology, 63,* 426–434.

Steiner, I. (1972). *Group process and productivity.* New York: Academic Press.

Weber, B., & Hertel, G. (2007). Motivation gains of inferior group members: A meta-analytical review. *Journal of Personality and Social Psychology, 93*(6), 973–993.

PROTESTANT WORK ETHIC

The *Protestant work ethic* (PWE) is an ideology or worldview that emphasizes self-discipline and commitment to work. Its main tenet is that hard work leads to success. A core value in the United States and many Western countries, this view is embodied in sayings such as "the early bird gets the worm" and stories such as *The Little Engine That Could*, a classic children's book. Shared endorsement of the PWE helps create a common belief system that can explain both individuals' status within a group and different groups' relative status positions within society (i.e., higher-status individuals and groups must have acquired their status through hard work). Consequently, belief in the PWE is related to attitudes toward both advantaged and disadvantaged individuals and groups and has different meanings as a function of an individual's own status and the status of a social group.

History and Background

The term *Protestant ethic* was coined by Max Weber in his book *The Protestant Ethic and the Spirit of Capitalism* (first published in 1904 in German). Weber argued that Reformed Protestantism, through the teachings of Martin Luther and John Calvin, redefined the value and meaning of work in humans' lives and created a new work ethic, the PWE. In this belief system, work and the prosperity resulting from it were accorded a high value because they were taken to be evidence that an individual or group had been given the grace of God and was among "God's elect." In turn, PWE helped bring about and support economic growth through capitalism.

Contemporary social-psychological definitions and uses of the term commonly strip it of its religious foundations. Instead, it is conceptualized as an ideology or worldview whose main tenet is that hard work leads to success. It is often studied in conjunction with other core U.S. values and beliefs (e.g., meritocracy, individual economic mobility) that justify the status quo. The PWE provides a meaningful way in which individuals can perceive and interpret their social world, furnishing them with a sense of order and predictability.

As many ideologies do, the PWE contains both descriptive and prescriptive elements. Endorsers of the PWE think that it both describes the true nature of the world (i.e., that individuals and

groups who are committed to and disciplined in their work will achieve success) and prescribes how they should behave (i.e., that hard work should lead to success and that idleness should lead to failure).

A variety of self-report scales have been used to measure the PWE. Most measures primarily focus on the value of hard work, which is the fundamental dimension of the PWE. However, other scales also measure the related concepts of leisure, religion and morality, and independence from others. One of the first and best-known scales was created by Herbert Mirels and James Garrett. Recent assessments divide the PWE into two component meanings. The opportunity-focused component is thought to be primary and stresses the equal opportunity individuals and groups have to succeed through hard work. The status-focused component uses the PWE to explain existing status differences between individuals and groups.

Endorsement of the PWE is related to a variety of psychological and demographic variables. Specifically, individuals who endorse the PWE tend also to score higher on measures of self-discipline and willpower, perseverance and endurance, and autonomy. High-PWE people are also more likely to endorse other status-justifying beliefs, such as meritocracy and belief in a just world. Strength of endorsement of the PWE also differs among different groups in society (e.g., among racial or ethnic groups or between political liberals and conservatives). Therefore, although the PWE is a pervasive belief system in many Western societies, meaning that the majority of individuals endorse it to some extent, there is also considerable variability in level of endorsement among individuals and groups. In particular, low-status individuals and members of low-status groups are somewhat less likely to believe in the PWE (or to believe in it to a lesser degree).

Consequences for Group Processes

Within groups, a shared belief in the PWE serves several important functions. First, it contributes to a common meaning system for understanding the world and provides an explanatory mechanism for individuals' status within a group. For group members to communicate effectively, they must have a shared system of meaning for interpreting and acting in the world. The PWE provides this system of meaning. Through a mutual endorsement of the PWE, group members share an implicit value of hard work and diligence. This common understanding helps foster a shared set of priorities and behavior patterns. For example, members of a group are able to take for granted that people will strive for success through hard work, and they will agree that such behavior should be rewarded. In addition, group members can rest assured that if they themselves work hard, they will be rewarded.

Second, belief in the PWE justifies the status hierarchy of the individual members within the group. Given a shared endorsement of the PWE, group members will be in agreement concerning each individual's position within the group. High status will be conferred only on those who work hard, and any individual who works hard will be assigned such status. Conversely, low status will be accorded to those who do not work hard. A common belief in the PWE will lead group members to share the belief that status positions are just and accurate reflections of each individual's hard work and merit, which will help maintain order and harmony within the group and legitimize the status quo. Thus, although low-status individuals will be seen as unable or unwilling to succeed, belief in the PWE means that all group members, low and high status, will agree with these attributions.

Finally, belief in the PWE can impact self-esteem. This can happen through an increase (or decrease) in individuals' personal self-esteem after their own successes (or failures), for which they are given "credit" because of their individual efforts and perseverance (or idleness and apathy). The PWE can also affect group members' collective self-esteem through attributions made by self or others for group-level success or failure. Endorsement of the PWE can heighten a successful group's level of collective self-esteem by crediting the group for the group's superior performance. However, for poor-performing groups, endorsement of the PWE can have the opposite effect. It can lead groups to be blamed for their failure, consequently lowering group members' collective self-esteem.

Consequences for Intergroup Relations

Belief in the PWE also influences several intergroup processes. First, endorsement of the PWE influences perceptions of outgroups and their members. If the cause of differential group status in a society is generally thought to be the efforts of groups and their members, then belief in the PWE is often accompanied by the belief that a group's high or low status is deserved or legitimate. Through such a belief, the approbation of high-status groups and their members, as well as the derogation of low-status groups and their members, becomes justified. The more that individuals endorse the PWE, the more negative their attitudes tend to be toward groups that hold lower status in society, such as Blacks and people who are overweight, poor, homeless, or living with AIDS.

Individuals who strongly endorse the PWE are also more likely to exhibit negative behavior toward low-status individuals and groups. For example, the more individuals who are not themselves homeless endorse the PWE, the less charitable behavior they display toward homeless people. The PWE also is associated with greater ingroup blame among members of low-status groups. Blaming their own group's low status or disadvantage on their group's lack of hard work or discipline may lead individuals to lessen their identification with or commitment to their group.

Despite the negative effects that the PWE may have for attitudes toward and treatment of lower-status groups and their members, low-status individuals may continue to endorse the PWE given its explanatory power, its prevalence in the broader society (see above), and the sense of personal control over outcomes it may provide.

It is important to note that the relation between endorsement of the PWE and derogation of low-status groups and their members may depend on the particular aspect of the PWE that individuals endorse (e.g., opportunity focused or status focused). Whereas the opportunity-focused form of the PWE is egalitarian and does not address status differences between groups, the status-focused form explains existing status differences between groups and individuals as resulting from differing levels of ability and/or effort. This latter form thus justifies high-status groups' advantages and low-status groups' disadvantages. It is only this latter dimension of the PWE that, when endorsed, leads to derogation of low-status groups and individuals. Endorsement of the former, the egalitarian and opportunity-focused dimension, leads to a belief that all groups and individuals are equal in their ability and chance to succeed.

Brenda Major and
Sarah Sachiko Martin Townsend

See also Ideology; Just World Hypothesis; Status; System Justification Theory

Further Readings

Furnham, A. (1990). *The Protestant work ethic: The psychology of work-related beliefs* and *behaviours.* New York: Routledge.

Katz, I., & Hass, R. G. (1988). Racial ambivalence and American value conflict: Correlational and priming studies of dual cognitive structures. *Journal of Personality and Social Psychology, 55,* 893–905.

Levy, S. R., West, T. L., Ramirez, L., & Karafantis, D. M. (2006). The Protestant work ethic: A lay theory with dual intergroup implications. *Group Processes and Intergroup Relations, 9,* 95–115.

RACIAL AMBIVALENCE THEORY

Racial ambivalence theory is an explanation of White people's attitudes and behavior toward Black people. The theory holds that many Whites are fundamentally ambivalent about Blacks. That is, their attitudes toward Blacks are a potent mixture of extreme positive and negative evaluations. Also, compared with their behavior toward other Whites, about whom they are not ambivalent, Whites' behavior toward Blacks is extremely positive or negative. Hence, there is an ambivalence amplification effect. Although racial ambivalence theory is grounded in race relations in the United States, it may, to some extent, be applicable in other contexts. This entry describes the theory and its application.

Background and History

Irwin Katz, his colleagues, and other social scientists noted that White people's attitudes toward Blacks in the United States are not evaluatively straightforward. The researchers reasoned that Whites' complex attitudes toward Blacks are best understood as ambivalent. Katz and others found evidence that this ambivalence is based on conflicting values. Whites' negative attitude toward Blacks is the result of the former's endorsement of the Protestant work ethic, whereas their positive attitudes toward Blacks are the result of their support for humanitarian–egalitarian values. These values come into conflict because Blacks are viewed as deviant—due to apparent lack of effort on their own behalf—*and* disadvantaged.

Ambivalence Amplification

Katz and colleagues demonstrated that people's ambivalent attitudes toward Blacks can result in amplification of positive or negative evaluations, as manifested in actions directed at members of that minority. In a series of studies, Katz and colleagues demonstrated that Whites—especially if they were high in racial ambivalence—behaved in either extremely negative or extremely positive ways toward Blacks. Dependent measures included Whites' tendency to (a) help a Black phone surveyor, (b) do a favor for a Black person whom they unintentionally harmed, and (c) denigrate a Black person whom they harmed.

Mechanisms of Ambivalence Amplification

Katz and colleagues' explanation for ambivalence amplification is largely psychodynamic: Whites experience psychological discomfort caused by their ambivalence, akin to the psychological discomfort caused by cognitive dissonance. This psychological discomfort can be resolved by eliminating the cognitive inconsistency that caused it—that is, by strengthening one side of the conflict. Thus, Whites act in accord with either their extreme positive or extreme negative evaluation. This behavior strengthens one side of the conflict, thereby reducing dissonance and the experience of discomfort.

Other researchers have proposed alternative explanations for the amplification effect. Walter Stephan and Cookie Stephan argued that intergroup contact (e.g., between Whites and Blacks) results in heightened anxiety. An increase in anxiety leads, in turn, to a host of consequences, including norm-based behavior (either good or bad) and biased information processing (due to a narrowing of attentional focus). Patricia Linville and Ned Jones, in contrast, highlighted the role of schema complexity in amplification effects. They argued that Whites' schemata for Blacks are less complex, resulting in a greater impact of positive or negative evaluative information about the minority. In support, the researchers demonstrated that White people have simpler cognitive schemata for Blacks than they do for Whites. Linville and Jones also established that possession of a simple schema for a group results in comparatively extreme evaluations of that group.

Applications and Extensions

The ambivalence amplification hypothesis has been applied to other domains, including research on White Canadians' ambivalence about native Canadians, people's ambivalence about feminists, and behavior toward people with disabilities. Racial ambivalence theory is arguably the progenitor of subsequent theories of racism, including symbolic racism (Don Kinder and David Sears), aversive racism (Sam Gaertner and Jack Dovidio), and (in)congruencies in implicit and explicit racial attitudes (L. S. Son Hing).

As with racial ambivalence theory, those accounts hold that Whites' attitudes toward Blacks are a volatile mixture of contradictory cognitions and behavioral inclinations. Gaertner and Dovidio, for example, have argued that Whites' attitudes toward Blacks are positive and based on egalitarian values and sympathies for past injustices. Also, however, Whites have negative attitudes toward Blacks—of which they are unaware.

Similarly, Son Hing and colleagues have identified people who have positive explicit attitudes toward Asians but negative implicit attitudes. Compared with people who are truly low in prejudice, these aversive racists show prejudiced behavior and exhibit less prejudice when they are made mindful of their hypocritical stance.

Racial ambivalence theory and its findings demonstrate that Whites' attitudes toward Blacks cannot be understood simply as more or less negative. Rather, Whites' attitudes are a mixture of both positive and negative evaluations. This contention introduces a significant but essential complexity to any understanding of relations between the two races.

Moreover, the existence of these ambivalent attitudes does not mean that Whites' behavior toward Blacks will simply be some sort of average of Whites' positive and negative attitudes. To the contrary, this ambivalence means that Whites' behaviors toward Blacks will often be extreme and seemingly arbitrary. Katz and his colleagues' analysis is trenchant and compelling and has informed subsequent thinking and research on attitudes and behaviors involving minorities, racial or otherwise.

Ian Newby-Clark

See also Ambivalent Sexism; Aversive Racism; Implicit Prejudice; Intergroup Anxiety; Modern Forms of Prejudice; Modern Racism

Further Readings

Bell, D. W., & Esses, V. M. (2002). Ambivalence and response amplification: A motivational perspective. *Personality and Social Psychology Bulletin, 28,* 1143–1152.

Gaertner, S. L., & Dovidio, J. F. (1986). The aversive form of racism. In J. F. Dovidio & S. L. Gaertner (Eds.), *Prejudice, discrimination, and racism* (pp. 61–89). Toronto, ON, Canada: Academic Press.

Katz, I., & Hass, R. G. (1988). Racial ambivalence and American value conflict: Correlational and priming studies of dual cognitive structures. *Journal of Personality and Social Psychology, 55,* 893–905.

Katz, I., Hass, R. G., & Wackenhut, J. (1986). Racial ambivalence, value duality, and behavior. In J. F. Dovidio & S. L. Gaertner (Eds.), *Prejudice, discrimination, and racism* (pp. 35–59). Toronto, ON, Canada: Academic Press.

Linville, P. W., & Jones, E. E. (1980). Polarized appraisals of out-group members. *Journal of Personality and Social Psychology, 38,* 689–703.

Stephan, W. G., & Stephan, C. W. (1985). Intergroup anxiety. *Journal of Social Issues, 41,* 157–175.

RACISM

Racism represents an organized system of privilege and bias that disadvantages a set of people on the basis of their group membership. Racism is enforced by the intentional or unintentional actions of individuals and the operation of institutional or societal standards that, in concert, produce disparities, by race or by social categories such as national origin, ethnicity, religion, and cultural beliefs or ideologies, that are *racialized* and assumed to reflect biological differences. There are two defining elements of racism. The first element is the culturally shared belief that groups have distinguishing race-based characteristics that are common to their members. The second factor is that the perceived inherent racial characteristics of another group are held to be inferior or that those of one's own group are superior to those of other groups. In its very essence, racism involves not only negative attitudes and beliefs but also the social power that enables these attitudes and beliefs to translate into disparate outcomes that disadvantage other races or offer unique advantages to one's own race at the expense of others. The term *racism* was popularized by its use in the 1968 *Report of the National Advisory Commission on Civil Disorders*.

Racism is related to concepts such as discrimination (unjustified negative behavior), prejudice (an unfair attitude associated with group membership), and stereotypes (generalized beliefs about a group and its members), but it is a more encompassing term than any of these. Because racism is a culturally shared system of beliefs, it may be supported by "scientific evidence" of group difference and inferiority and may be sanctioned by social norms, policies, and laws. Although racism typically involves negative attitudes, it may instead reflect a paternalistic orientation, which fosters the dependency of a group or a set of beliefs that may ostensibly be favorable in some ways but that systematically limits the opportunities for group members and undermines their dignity.

Whereas psychologists have typically studied stereotypes, prejudice, and discrimination in terms of intrapsychic (e.g., cognitive, motivational, or psychodynamic) processes and interactions between individuals, racism operates significantly at broader social levels, as well. James Jones has identified three applications of the term *racism*. The first is *individual racism*, which relates to the joint operation of personal stereotypes, prejudice, and discrimination to create and support disparities between members of different groups. The second is *institutional racism*, which refers to the intentional or unintentional manipulation or toleration of institutional policies (e.g., poll taxes, admissions criteria) that unfairly restrict the opportunities of particular groups of people. The third is *cultural racism*. Cultural racism involves beliefs about the superiority of one's racial cultural heritage over that of other races and the expression of this belief in individual actions or institutional policies. Thus, cultural racism includes elements of individual and institutional racism. Because of its broad scope and emphasis on institutions as well as individuals, racism is a common focus of research in political science and sociology, as well as in psychology. These three applications of racism—individual, institutional, and cultural—are considered in separate sections of this entry.

Individual Racism

Individual racism is closely affiliated with racial prejudice. Although prejudice has generally been conceptualized as an attitude, prejudice scales often include items concerning the defining elements of racism—specifically, endorsement of statements about innate group differences, the relative inferiority of the other group, and policies that reinforce or exacerbate group differences in fundamental resources (e.g., employment opportunity, health). Approaches to individual racism have emphasized both blatant and subtle influences.

Some of these approaches focus on functional aspects of individual racism that fulfill personal needs and desires. Much of the traditional work on personality and prejudice was based on a Freudian psychoanalytic model that assumes that prejudice is an indicator of an underlying intrapsychic conflict. The consequences of this conflict are projection, displacement, and the development of an authoritarian personality—and ultimately the expression of individual racism. Alternatively, nonpsychodynamic models have proposed that prejudice and racism are the result of motivations to restore feelings of self-esteem, achieve a sense of superior status, or support a social hierarchy that favors one's group. Social dominance orientation represents an individual difference in support for group-based systems of social stratification that typically benefit one's own group. Other approaches, which have focused on commonalities across people rather than on individual differences, have viewed prejudice and individual racism as attitudes, which, like other attitudes, are acquired through socialization and are functional.

Many contemporary approaches to individual racism acknowledge the persistence of blatant, intentional forms of racism but also consider the role of automatic or unconscious processes and indirect expressions of bias. For example, because of common socialization experiences that involve repeated exposure to racial stereotypes, Whites automatically activate stereotypes of Blacks on the actual or symbolic presence of Blacks. Although both high- and low-prejudiced people, distinguished by their scores on self-report measures of prejudice, are equally aware of cultural stereotypes and show similar levels of automatic activation, only low-prejudiced people make a conscious attempt to prevent those negative stereotypes from influencing their behavior. Moreover, low-prejudiced people are more likely to have personal standards prescribing that they behave in a nonprejudiced way toward Blacks, internalize these standards more strongly, and experience more compunction and guilt when they deviate from these standards—which in turn motivates efforts to behave in a less biased way in the future.

Regardless of conscious motivations, implicit stereotypes and prejudice form a foundation for pervasive bias associated with racism. In fact, implicit (automatic or unconscious) and explicit (deliberative or conscious) prejudice and stereotypes are largely unrelated. Implicit attitudes are typically assessed through techniques that tap stereotypic associations and require split-second responding that is usually beyond an individual's control; explicit prejudice is commonly measured through self-reports. Whereas the vast majority of White people in the United States, for instance, report explicitly that they are not racially prejudiced, the majority of Whites show implicit racial biases. However, there is some debate as to whether these implicit measures reflect merely knowledge of culturally shared stereotypes or the personal endorsement of these beliefs.

A dissociation between automatic responses and self-reported prejudice is also consistent with other conceptions of the contemporary nature of individual racism among Whites. In contrast to "old-fashioned" racism, which is blatant, *aversive racism* represents a subtle, often unintentional form of bias that characterizes many White people in the United States who possess strong egalitarian values, endorse a politically liberal ideology, and believe that they are nonprejudiced. Aversive racists also possess negative racial feelings and beliefs (which develop through normal cognitive biases and socialization) of which they are unaware or that they try to dissociate from their nonprejudiced self-images. Because aversive racists consciously endorse egalitarian values, they will not discriminate directly and openly in ways that can be attributed to racism; however, because of their negative feelings, they will discriminate, often unintentionally, when their behavior can be justified on the basis of some factor other than race (e.g., questionable qualifications for a position). Thus, aversive racists may regularly engage in discrimination while they maintain a nonprejudiced self-image.

Whereas aversive racism represents subtle bias among generally liberal Whites who endorse nonprejudiced values and beliefs, *symbolic racism* reflects subtle prejudice associated with traditionally conservative values. Specifically, symbolic racism reflects the unique assimilation of politically conservative, individualistic values and negative racial affect. It involves the denial of contemporary discrimination and negative beliefs about Blacks' work ethic, which produces resentment of Blacks' demands and special benefits given to Blacks because of their race. Like aversive racism, the negative effects of symbolic racism are observed primarily when discrimination can be justified on the basis of factors other than race. Thus, even though aversive racism and symbolic racism perspectives often predict similar behaviors, such as resistance to policies designed to benefit Blacks, they hypothesize different underlying processes.

Both traditional overt forms of individual racism and contemporary subtle forms can contribute to social policies that form the basis of institutional racism. In particular, blatant racial prejudice relates to support for policies that unconditionally restrict the rights and opportunities of minority groups, whereas subtle racism is associated with support for the status quo or for restrictions when other justifications (e.g., lack of credentials) are available.

Institutional Racism

Institutional racism involves the differential impact of policies, practices, and laws on members of racial groups and on the groups as a whole. Institutional racism can develop from intentional racism (e.g., limiting immigration on the basis of assumptions about the inferiority of other groups), motivations to provide resources to one's own group (e.g., attempts to limit another group's voting power), or as a by-product of policies with one explicit goal but with unintended systematic race-based effects (e.g., differential mandatory penalties for trafficking crack and powder cocaine).

Explicitly race-based policies are typically associated with the development of ideologies that justify them. Historically, for example, White people in the United States developed racial ideologies that helped justify the laws that enabled them to achieve two important types of economic exploitation: slavery and the seizure of lands from native tribes. Thus, although the belief that race is a biological construct is fundamental to racism, race is also regarded as a social construction that permits and ideologically justifies the exploitation of one group by another. The particular group that becomes racialized (e.g., Blacks, Italians, Jews) depends on the function it serves for the dominant group. For instance, during the period of significant immigration from southern Europe to the United States during the early 1900s, which generated social and economic threats to many people in the United States, Italians were characterized as racially intellectually inferior. In Nazi Germany, Jews were racialized and dehumanized for economic and political gain.

Moreover, although individual racism may produce actions such as political support for laws and policies that lead to institutional racism, institutional racism operates at a level independent of individual racism. Institutional racism does not require the active support of individuals, intention to discriminate, or even the awareness of discrimination. Racism becomes *ritualized* in ways that minimize the effort and energy individuals and groups must expend to support it.

Institutional racism is typically not widely recognized as being racist or unfair because it is embedded in laws (which are normally assumed to be right and moral), is ritualized, and is accompanied by racial ideologies that justify it. The media and public discourse often direct attention away from potential institutional biases and instead focus on common connections or shared identities that can promote more harmonious group relations while preserving group-based disparities, privilege, and disadvantage in the status quo. Once social norms, laws, and policies are established, awareness of unfair treatment and consequences is needed to stimulate individual or collective action for social change toward equality.

Because institutional racism is not necessarily intentional or explicitly race based, its operation often must be inferred from the presence of systematically different outcomes for different racial groups—outcomes that can logically be traced to the differential and unfair impact of policies, even those that might appear not to be race related. These effects may appear economically (e.g., in loan policies), educationally (e.g., in admission and financial aid policies), in the media (e.g., over-representation of groups associated with violence or poverty), in the criminal justice system (e.g., racial differences in receipt of the death penalty), and in mental and physical health (e.g., social stress). Racial ideologies and values often also become deeply embedded in the fiber of one's culture and thus define what is normal and appropriate for the society in general.

Cultural Racism

Cultural racism occurs when one group exerts the power to define cultural values for the society. It involves not only preference for the culture, heritage, and values (ethnocentrism) of one's own group but also the imposition of this culture on other groups. As a consequence, the essence of racism is communicated to and by members of all racial groups in everyday activities and is passed on across generations.

James Jones, for example, has identified five fundamental domains of human experience on which cultures differ: time, rhythm, improvisation, oral expression, and spirituality (the TRIOS model). Dominant U.S. culture has valued a future time orientation, stable and predictable rhythms of activity, planning ahead rather than improvising, written over oral expression, and a belief in personal control instead of an emphasis on spirituality. Beyond this model, cultures differ systematically in their emphasis on individual outcomes or collective outcomes. The United States reflects an individualistic culture. To the extent that adherence to these cultural standards is valued, rewarded, and defined as normal at the expense of racial groups who express other cultural values, cultural racism may be operating.

Racism that is institutionalized and becomes embedded in the culture can also affect the personal identities and ideologies of minority group members in fundamental ways. In particular, racial identities develop as a function of one's experiences as a group member and how one interprets, internalizes, and adjusts to those experiences. The racial identity and the culture of Blacks in the United States, for example, have been hypothesized to reflect an evolutionary component, which developed from the cultural foundation of an African past, and a reactionary component, which is an adaptation to the historical and contemporary challenges of minority status in the United States. Because of the pervasiveness of racism, Blacks in the United States may internalize racial stereotypes, which when activated, even without endorsement, can adversely influence their performance in significant ways (e.g., through the adverse impact of *stereotype threat* on achievement test performance).

Under some circumstances, members of the target racial group may adopt system-justifying ideologies of the dominant cultural group that distract attention from group-based disparities and inequity. Thus, members of a disadvantaged group may develop a "false consciousness," in which they fail to recognize and not only comply with but also endorse cultural values that systematically disadvantage them. For example, an exclusive emphasis on individually oriented meritocracy may obscure cultural and institutional forces in racism and lead to an overreliance on individual rather than collective action needed to address racism. Thus, the unique power of racism resides in how it can persuade members of different groups to think, interpret, behave, and react in ways that contribute to the perpetuation of racial disparities and reinforce racism, without necessarily involving their intention, awareness, or active support.

Conclusion

In summary, racism represents a particular constellation of racial stereotypes, prejudice, and discrimination. Stereotypic differences are assumed to reflect racial differences; prejudicial attitudes may be in the form of negative attitudes toward other racial groups or reflect positive beliefs in the racial superiority of one's own group; discrimination may occur intentionally or unintentionally and personally or impersonally. Whereas individual racism is closely affiliated with prejudice, institutional racism involves the operation of social and institutional policies that unfairly benefit the dominant group and/or unfairly affect other racial groups adversely. Cultural racism, which includes elements of both individual and institutional racism, represents the imposition of the dominant group's cultural standards on other racial groups in the society.

Although racism may involve overt antipathy and bigoted intent, it also can operate unconsciously but pervasively at the individual, institutional, or cultural level. Because it can become ritualized in custom and policy and rationalized by racial ideologies, racism can often go unrecognized or unacknowledged. Also, because these ideologies are so embedded within the fabric of society, once their consequences are recognized, there may be resistance to the changes that may be necessary to ameliorate the problem.

John F. Dovidio and Samuel L. Gaertner

See also Authoritarian Personality; Aversive Racism; Civil Rights Legislation; Discrimination; Modern Racism; Prejudice; Slavery; Social Dominance Theory; Symbolic Racism

Further Readings

Adorno, T. W., Frenkel-Brunswik, E., Levinson, D. J., & Sanford, R. N. (1950). *The authoritarian personality.* New York: Harper.

Allport, G. W. (1954). *The nature of prejudice.* Reading, MA: Addison-Wesley.

Bonilla-Silva, E. (2006). *Racism without racists: Color-blind racism and the persistence of racial inequality in the United States.* Lanham, MD: Rowman & Littlefield.

Dovidio, J. F., & Gaertner, S. L. (2004). Aversive racism. In M. P. Zanna (Ed.), *Advances in experimental social psychology* (Vol. 36, pp. 1–51). San Diego, CA: Academic Press.

Dovidio, J. F., Glick, P., & Rudman, L. A. (Eds.). (2005). *On the nature of prejudice: Fifty years after Allport*. Malden, MA: Blackwell.

Feagin, J. R. (2006). *Systemic racism: A theory of oppression*. New York: Routledge.

Frederickson, G. M. (2002). *Racism: A short history*. Princeton, NJ: Princeton University Press.

Gaertner, S. L., & Dovidio, J. F. (1986). The aversive form of racism. In J. F. Dovidio & S. L. Gaertner (Eds.), *Prejudice, discrimination, and racism* (pp. 61–89). Orlando, FL: Academic Press.

Jones, J. M. (1997). *Prejudice and racism* (2nd ed.). New York: McGraw-Hill.

Jost, J. T., & Major, B. (Eds.). (2001). *The psychology of legitimacy: Emerging perspectives on ideology, justice, and intergroup relations*. New York: Cambridge University Press.

National Advisory Commission on Civil Disorders. (1968). *Report of the National Advisory Commission on Civil Disorders*. New York: Bantam Books.

Sears, D. O., & Henry, P. J. (2005). Over thirty years later: A contemporary look at symbolic racism. In M. P. Zanna (Ed.), *Advances in experimental social psychology* (Vol. 37, pp. 95–150). San Diego, CA: Academic Press.

Sidanius, J., & Pratto, F. (1999). *Social dominance: An intergroup theory of social hierarchy and oppression*. New York: Cambridge University Press.

REALISTIC GROUP CONFLICT THEORY

Realistic group conflict theory (RGCT) states that competition between groups for finite resources leads to intergroup stereotypes, antagonism, and conflict. Such competition creates incompatible goals for members of different groups because one group's success in obtaining those resources prevents the other group from obtaining them. Such conflicts of interest lead to the development of ingroup norms that foster negative reactions to the outgroup, backed by punishment and rejection of those ingroup members who deviate from those norms.

Just as RGCT argues that *competition* for desired but limited resources creates intergroup conflict, it also argues that *cooperation* in pursuit of superordinate goals, mutually desired outcomes that are unobtainable without such cooperation, has the potential over time to reduce intergroup conflict and to create positive relations among members of cooperating groups. This entry describes the background of RGCT, examines major research findings, and discusses the theory's importance.

Background, History, and Major Research Findings

RGCT was given its name by anthropologist Robert LeVine and psychologist Donald Campbell, who formulated and cross-culturally tested propositions based on existing psychological, sociological, and anthropological research on ethnocentrism and group conflict. In the course of this work, they grouped theories explaining ethnocentrism into several categories (reference group theory, frustration–aggression–displacement theory, etc.), including one they dubbed *realistic group conflict theory*. They used this term to refer to "the set of all theories that generate the ethnocentrism syndrome from the competitive struggle of groups with incompatible interests" (LeVine & Campbell, 1972, p. 72).

As indicated above, the core idea in RGCT is that intergroup stereotyping, prejudice, and hostility emerge when groups have conflicting interests, and specifically when one group's success blocks the other's goal attainment. RGCT includes a large number of specific predictions about the way in which clashing interests between groups influence both ingroup functioning and intergroup relations. For example, RGCT predicts that conflict with outgroups enhances ingroup solidarity. It also predicts that the more another group stands in the way of one's own group's attainment of desired goals, the greater the hostility created toward that other group. Some of these propositions have stimulated much more research than others.

Robbers Cave

The research most commonly cited in discussions of RGCT is a series of three studies by Muzafer Sherif and colleagues conducted between 1949 and 1954, in which boys of 11 to 12 years of age attended summer camps that were set up to study intergroup behavior, although the boys were not aware of this fact. The third and most famous of these studies was the Robbers Cave experiment. The goal of the first phase of this study was to have two sets of previously unacquainted boys each coalesce into a group, with differentiated status positions, group norms, and the like. To achieve this end, campers were divided into two groups, each of which engaged with ingroup members in a series of enjoyable activities (preparing food at a "hideout," deciding how to spend money the group had won, etc.).

During the next week, in the experiment's second phase, when the campers in the different groups interacted for the first time, the situation was structured so that the two groups had incompatible interests. Specifically, the groups were brought into initial contact in a series of competitive activities (baseball games, a treasure hunt, etc.), during which each accumulated points toward valued prizes to be given to the group with the highest cumulative score.

In the final stage of the study, during its 3rd week, the functional relationship between the groups was drastically changed by the introduction of superordinate goals. Specifically, a series of situations was engineered that required the cooperation of members of both groups to meet highly valued goals that neither group alone could achieve (the camp's water tank needed to be repaired to restore water service, etc.).

The development of norms and relationships within and between the groups at the camp under competitive and cooperative conditions was studied extensively by means of a wide variety of methods. Consistent with the main tenet of RGCT, when members of the two groups began to interact competitively in the study's second phase, negative relations developed between them. Specifically, as the boys began to interact under competitive conditions, outgroup members were derogatively stereotyped and became the targets of aggressive behavior, including name calling, stealing and burning the other group's flag, raiding the other group's cabin, and preparing weapons such as socks filled with rocks. In addition, members of both groups overrated the performance of members of their ingroup relative to that of members of the outgroup.

During the first day or two of the study's third phase, when the tournament sparking the competition between the groups was over, members of the two groups were brought into contact in situations such as waiting for a movie to start and shooting off fire crackers, which involved neither competitive nor superordinate goals. Heckling and avoidance of outgroup members were evident. However, with the subsequent introduction of superordinate goals fostering cooperation, relations between the two groups gradually improved to the point that by the end of the study, the campers cheered the idea of returning home on one bus, and members of one group used prize money to buy all campers a treat.

Later Studies

Subsequent research conducted by anthropologists, sociologists, and psychologists has provided considerable support for the basic tenets of RGCT. For example, one study found that group threat (measured by group size and economic conditions) explains most of the variation in average prejudice scores in 12 European countries, and another replicated the finding that individuals overestimate the performance of ingroup members compared with outgroup members. A study conducted in Lebanon with Christian and Muslim 11-year-olds who were randomly assigned to one of two groups at a summer camp lent further support to the idea that realistic group conflict promotes aggression, although this study did not support all Sherif's conclusions.

In addition, some work has focused on extending RGCT's basic ideas. For example, Lawrence Bobo has argued that *perceived* threat to group interests can cause negative relations, regardless of whether the perception is accurate. This line of argument is supported by more recent findings suggesting that the perception of a realistic threat animates negative attitudes toward immigrants in the United States and toward ultraorthodox Jews on the part of Israeli adults who are not ultraorthodox themselves. It is interesting that the study conducted in Israel also suggested that ingroup identification moderates the link between perceived threat and aggression. However, generally speaking, RGCT has inspired relatively little research in the past two or three decades, possibly because its basic tenets are so widely accepted.

Critiques and Challenges

No theory is without its critics, and RGCT is no exception. For example, one study concluded, on the basis of a failure to replicate many of Sherif's findings in research on established patrols in a Boy Scout troop during a camp experience, that when individuals are initially well acquainted with each other, intergroup competition does not yield either the strong outgroup hostility and denigration or the increase in ingroup solidarity that RGCT predicts. However, this study ignored the fact that the patrols were also part of a larger scout troop, creating a shared superordinate identity that may well have influenced the way in which relations between patrols developed.

A stronger challenge to RGCT comes from *social identity theory*, where substantial research has demonstrated clearly that groups need not be in actual competition for ingroup bias to arise. However, RGCT makes no claim that it fully explains intergroup relations. Furthermore, there is no doubt that the kinds of negative attitudes and behaviors evidenced in Sherif's research were much more extreme than those typically studied by social identity theorists. So it is possible that mere shared group membership may foster ingroup favoritism but that conflicting interests are necessary to call forth the very strong negative attitudes and behaviors evident in Sherif's studies. Further, it may well be that the degree to which individuals identify with their groups influences the extent to which a conflict of interest between their group and another evokes negative attitudes and behaviors toward the outgroup.

Another challenge to RGCT comes from the observation that intergroup conflict often involves those with different amounts of initial power and status, which was not the case in the classic RGCT studies. In situations involving groups that differ in initial power and status, it may be difficult to establish superordinate goals, and even if that is possible, the result of working to achieve those goals might well be different from when the groups start out roughly equal to each other. It is also important to recognize that third parties often play an important role in creating or resolving intergroup conflicts and that their role is ignored by RGCT.

Assessing Its Importance

In contrast to many theories that were prevalent when RGCT emerged in the 1950s and 1960s,

including work on the *authoritarian personality* and the frustration–aggression–displacement hypothesis, RGCT does not posit individual psychological processes as the underlying origin of intergroup tensions and conflict. Indeed, in order to provide a test of the basic idea that the functional relationship between groups causes intergroup conflict and stereotyping rather than preexisting tensions between members of different social categories or deviant personal proclivities, the boys selected to participate in classic summer camp experiments were all middle class, from the same racial group (White), and "normal" with regard to school performance, social relationships, and personal adjustment.

Instead of focusing on individual psychological processes, RGCT emphasizes the role that group processes play in creating and ameliorating intergroup tensions. It does this by highlighting the role of conflicting interests in creating intergroup tensions and emphasizing the ways in which ingroup processes can promote and support intergroup conflict. It also de-emphasizes individual psychological explanations for negative intergroup relations by stressing how a change from competitive to cooperative functional relations between groups can profoundly change the nature of relations between members of those groups.

RGCT is similar to *contact theory*, another very influential theory regarding intergroup relations, which had its origins at about the same time. Both stress the importance of the structural aspects of the contact situation in influencing the development of relationships between members of different groups. However, RGCT was a more radical departure from prevailing thought at the time because it focused attention on the way in which group processes rather than individual psychological processes lead to intergroup tensions. Although there is currently relatively little active theoretical or empirical work stemming directly from RGCT, it is widely acknowledged as having fundamentally enriched our understanding of intergroup relations.

Janet Ward Schofield

See also Cooperation and Competition; Intergroup Contact Theory; Intergroup Violence; Sherif, Muzafer; Social Identity Theory

Further Readings

Campbell, D. T. (1965). Ethnocentric and other altruistic motives. In D. Levine (Ed.), *Nebraska Symposium on Motivation* (Vol. 13, pp. 283–311). Lincoln: University of Nebraska Press.

Diab, L. N. (1970). A study of intragroup and intergroup relations among experimentally produced small groups. *Genetic Psychology Monographs, 82,* 49–82.

Jackson, J. W. (1993). Realistic group conflict theory: A review and evaluation of the theoretical and empirical literature. *Psychological Record, 43*(3), 395–404.

Kahn, A., & Ryen, A. H. (1972). Factors influencing the bias towards one's own group. *International Journal of Group Tensions, 2,* 33–50.

LeVine, R. A., & Campbell, D. T. (1972). *Ethnocentrism: Theories of conflict, ethnic attitudes, and group behavior.* New York: Wiley.

Quillian, L. (1995). Prejudice as a response to perceived group threat: Population composition and anti-immigrant and racial prejudice in Europe. *American Sociological Review, 60*(4), 586–611.

Sherif, M., & Sherif, C. W. (1966). *Groups in harmony and tension: An integration of studies on intergroup relations.* New York: Octagon Books.

Struch, N., & Schwartz, S. H. (1989). Intergroup aggression: Its predictors and distinctiveness from in-group bias. *Journal of Personality and Social Psychology, 56*(3), 364–373.

Tyerman, A., & Spencer, C. (1983). A critical test of the Sherifs' Robber's Cave experiments: Intergroup competition and cooperation between groups of well-acquainted individuals. *Small Group Behavior, 14*(4), 515–531.

REFERENCE GROUPS

A *reference group* is a group or collectivity that is used as a standard or frame of reference by an individual in evaluating his or her own abilities, attitudes, or beliefs or in choosing a behavior. Reference groups help orient people and may comprise noninteracting individuals, status categories, or members of social groups. Reference groups may be groups to which an individual currently belongs, groups to which an individual once belonged, or groups to which an individual aspires to belong. They may be real, tangible groups, present or not present, or even imaginary.

Psychological groups may be defined as reference groups when (a) the individual is aware of those composing the group; (b) the individual identifies himself or herself as a member, former member, or potential member; and (c) the group is seen as emotionally or cognitively significant for the individual. Most people have multiple reference groups, and the groups may be conflicting or mutually sustaining. Those groups may be positive (used to provide standards of comparison or as sources for values, norms, and attitudes) or negative (used to provide standards of comparison in direct opposition with those of the group or as sources of values, norms, and attitudes formed in direct opposition to the group).

Early History

Herbert Hyman is credited with first using the term *reference group* in 1942 (although others at that time also conceived of the use of groups for relative evaluation) in an examination of the distinction between objective and subjective status. He was concerned with the factors that influence people's evaluations of their social standing or status. For Hyman, an individual's subjective status is relative; it is a person's conception of his or her own position in comparisons with others. He asked the participants in his investigations whether they ever thought about their social standing in relationship to others and found that not only did most of them think about their relative superiority in relation to others, but they sometimes did not use actual groups for comparison. Instead, they used general social categories such as occupation, race, or class.

Subjects rarely used the total population as a reference group but rather used smaller, more intimate groups. One person, for example, used authors who wrote the books he read rather than all authors as a reference group. Subjects were also more likely to use different reference groups for different domains, such as social standing, looks (physical attractiveness), and economic status.

About the same time as Hyman's research was being conducted, Theodore Newcomb was investigating the process of political attitude shifts among Bennington College students during their college careers. Although he did not use the term *reference groups* to characterize the source of influence, his study did provide a systematic investigation of reference groups and their influence on attitudes. He focused on how students changed their beliefs from the standards of their families in the students' first college years to the standards of the more liberal college community in the students' junior and senior years. He found that the students beginning their college careers tended to use the seniors as their frame of reference instead of their own classmates, although the younger students tended to assume that their attitudes matched those of the majority of their classmates.

In a 1950 reexamination of *The American Soldier* studies conducted by Samuel Stouffer and associates, Robert K. Merton and Alice Kitt used the concept of *comparative reference groups* to explain relative deprivation. Men in the military used different reference groups as a source of comparison and, depending on which group they used, reported feelings of satisfaction and deprivation, feelings that were often inconsistent with their actual levels of suffering. Only when they thought that their suffering was relatively greater than others' did they express dissatisfaction. The men used reference groups to which they did not belong to define the relative quality of their circumstances. Merton and Kitt called these *nonmembership reference groups*. Also in 1950, Merton and Alice Rossi synthesized previous research in their work titled "Contributions to the Theory of Reference Group Behavior," creating visibility and prominence for the concept.

Another major refinement of the concept was presented in 1952 in Harold H. Kelley's paper on the two functions of reference groups. Kelley distinguished between the normative function and the comparative function of reference groups. First, individuals may be motivated to gain or maintain acceptance in groups, perhaps to find friendship, a mate, or simply a companion. This type of group has a normative function in that it encourages and enforces acceptable behavior, attitudes, and values through awarding or withholding recognition to the individual.

The college community in Newcomb's study at Bennington illustrates the normative function of a reference group. Not only did these college students develop a set of political attitudes that were largely accepted by the students as they progressed through their college careers, but students were motivated to assimilate these values in order to be accepted by the group. In comparing the liberal students who shifted in their values with the conservative students who did not, Newcomb also distinguished between *positive reference groups*, in which attitudes are formed in accordance with the norms of the group, and *negative reference groups*, in which attitudes are formed in opposition to the norms of the group.

Reference groups may also provide standards of comparison for evaluations of oneself, others, and the world. Kelley called this the comparative function. Illustrated in Hyman's research, groups were used as standards or comparison points against which people evaluate their own prosperity.

It should be noted that although the features of the different types of reference groups led to their conceptualization as separate and distinct, different features may occur together within the same group. A group of classmates, for example, may have both a normative function (encouraging conformity to academic norms) and a comparison function (as a source of academic standards for evaluation) in its group influence.

Morton Deutsch and Harold Gerard conducted a study in 1955 to confirm and extend Kelley's distinction by examining how reference groups could provide both normative social influence and informative social influence simultaneously. They used Solomon Asch's experimental paradigm to test hypotheses predicting greater normative social influence when members are more involved in a group and when a member perceives that his or her actions can be identified. In the first condition, the participants in the experiment made judgments about the lengths of lines while in face-to-face interaction with three confederates. In the second condition, the participants were separated by partitions and pressed a button to indicate their judgments anonymously. In the third condition, Deutsch and Gerard forced involvement of the participants in the group by instructing the participants that the most successful group would receive tickets to a Broadway play.

Confederates of the researchers in all three groups gave mostly inaccurate judgments about the lines on the cards, and normative social influence was measured by the degree of a participant's conformity with the confederates' judgments. Greater conformity was found when participants were working for a prize and when participants' actions could be identified. The researchers reasoned that the groups of confederates served as normative reference groups because it was unlikely that subjects were using the groups to gain information. The correct judgments were somewhat obvious, and it is more likely that participants wanted to be accepted by the group, especially if they were working together to win tickets to a play. Participants likely did not want to be responsible for the group's losing the prize because then they would be rejected by the group, particularly if they could be identified.

In another condition with face-to-face interaction, in which participants were asked to judge the lines from memory, informational influence also was high. A group influenced its members by providing information about which line was correct, and participants thought that they were wrong in their own judgments and believed that the group was correct.

Expansions and Criticisms

Although this distinction between normative and informational influence from reference groups has been the basis for much subsequent research, many researchers suggest that it is too simple a distinction. Jonathan Turner, in a discussion of role-taking and reference group behavior, suggested four kinds of reference groups: the *identification group* (a source of values when individuals take the role of another), the *interaction group* (members are conditions for an individual's action), the *evaluation group* (its influence is determined by how much an individual values the group), and the *audience group* (a normative group that attends to and evaluates an individual's behavior).

Eleanor Singer, who with Hyman edited a volume on reference group theory and research in 1968, made the point that the two types of reference groups differentiated by Kelley may not always be empirically distinct. In a later article, John Turner compared informational influence with normative influence, pointing out that informational influence can be socially mediated and is, therefore, normative. Norms also may be informative about the appropriateness or correctness of preferences and values. He suggested that the distinction more correctly refers to the source of change when reference groups exert influence. When the influence is normative, the source of change comes from others; when the influence is informational, the source of change comes from the self.

Probably the most frequent criticisms have more to do with the largely circular explanation found in reference group theory rather than with the term itself. The theory specifies that reference groups determine behavior while groups that are found to influence behavior are reference groups. Theorists fight against this deterministic reasoning, however, and emphasize the process whereby individuals define the situation and how actors may accept or reject influence.

Importance

For more than 65 years, the concept of reference groups has stimulated sociological and social-psychological research. The concept underscores the idea that reference groups are not simply one's membership groups. Groups that are not one's own or that one is not a member of also may be used as frames of reference.

The concept has been widely used in research, particularly through the 1950s and 1960s, when it reached its height in popularity. Since then, its theoretical prominence has diminished. As others have pointed out, because membership and non-membership groups are such an important part of life in complex societies, the value of the concept of reference groups is in assisting in the understanding of the relationship between the individual and the larger society. By far the largest number of empirical studies focuses on normative reference groups, beginning with Newcomb's early work on the normative influence of the college community on college students at Bennington. Subsequent normative studies measure reference group influence on such features as prosocial behavior, student alcohol consumption, and sorority binge eating. Lesser empirical attention has been given to the comparative effects of reference groups; comparative effects are found in studies of variables such as job satisfaction, class inequality perceptions, self-evaluations for the blind and for those who are mentally ill, and self-appraisals of academic performance.

Kathy J. Kuipers

See also Asch, Solomon; Common Ingroup Identity Model; Group Socialization; Informational Influence; Normative Influence; Norms; Support Groups

Further Readings

Felson, R. B., & Reed, M. D. (1986). Reference groups and self-appraisals of academic ability and performance. *Social Psychology Quarterly, 49,* 103–109.

Hyman, H. H., & Singer, E. (1968). *Readings in reference group theory and research*. New York: Free Press.

REFERENT INFORMATIONAL INFLUENCE THEORY

Referent informational influence theory is the social identity theory of social influence in groups. It considers normative influence and informational influence—separate concepts in the thinking of other social scientists—as part of a single influence process linked to group membership and social identity. This entry describes the background and content of the theory and then summarizes relevant research and implications.

Traditionally, social influence has been accounted for in terms of individual needs such as the need for approval and liking or the need for rational assessment of the social world. These two types of needs have been translated into two qualitatively different forms of influence: *normative influence,* which reflects public compliance as a result of social pressure, and *informational influence,* which reflects private acceptance of the nature of reality. However, according to *social identity theory,* this distinction is problematic because it artifactually separates aspects of social influence that need to be considered together as part of a single process. Within social identity theory, informational and normative influence emanate from a single process called *referent informational influence.*

History and Background

Referent informational influence theory arises from social identity theory and, more specifically, *self-categorization theory.* It was developed by John Turner and his colleagues as the conceptual component dealing with social influence. According to Turner and colleagues, *social influence* results from the process of self-categorization, whereby individuals come to see themselves as group members and thus in possession of the same group-defining attributes as other members of their group. Through the processes of self-categorization and referent informational influence, individuals come to learn about the appropriate ways of thinking and behaving as a group member and assign these characteristics to themselves.

In referent informational influence theory, the traditional distinction between informational and normative influence is replaced by a single process. For group members, what is normative is highly informative about appropriate and correct beliefs and behaviors in particular contexts. Moreover, the subjective validity of information is established by ingroup norms; information from members of our groups is seen as more valid than information from members of other groups.

In referent informational influence theory, conformity to the group norm is the result of a three-stage process. First, people must categorize themselves and identify as group members. Then, as a consequence of self-categorization, a context-specific group norm is constructed from available, and usually shared, social comparative information. Because the identity-consistent behavior of prototypical group members is a direct source of such information, these people often occupy an effective leadership role in the group—an idea that underpins Michael Hogg's *social identity theory of leadership.* The newly formed norm is represented as a group prototype that serves to describe and prescribe the beliefs, attitudes, feelings, and behaviors that maximize the differences between groups and minimize the differences within groups (the *metacontrast principle*).

Finally, group members internalize these norms through assimilation of the self to the prototype (a process called *depersonalization*) and use them as guides to their own behavior. Moreover, because the norm is internalized as part of the individual's self-concept and is linked to his or her membership in that group, the norm exerts influence over behavior even in the absence of surveillance by other group members. Identification-based conformity is a process not of surface behavioral compliance but of genuine cognitive internalization of group attitudes as one's own.

Referent informational influence theory has little to say about the role of outgroups—groups to which the individual does not belong—and outgroup norms in group-mediated behavior. Although it is acknowledged that non-ingroup members can be informative about group norms—by informing the individual what not to do—the most immediate and direct source of information about group norms is seen to be other group members, particularly prototypical group members (i.e., individuals who seem to embody what it means to be a group member). Moreover, if outgroups do influence the behavior of ingroup members, this influence is seen to be the result of compliance, whereby individuals go along with social norms because of the power of the other group rather than because of its true persuasive influence.

Evidence

Referent informational influence theory unifies our understanding of social influence in several respects. Processes such as normalization, conformity, and innovation are all seen as processes of influence related to the establishment, maintenance, or change of group norms. Research by Dominic Abrams and his colleagues demonstrated the role of referent informational influence in social influence phenomena previously considered or explained in terms of normative or informational influence, including norm formation, conformity, and group polarization. This research has supported the argument advanced in referent informational influence theory that informational and normative influence are inextricably linked to group membership.

Studies of norm formation, such as those conducted by Muzafer Sherif using the autokinetic paradigm, have found that under ambiguous conditions, people converge quickly on an agreed frame of reference—or norm. Such results are taken as clear evidence of informational influence: Under uncertainty, individuals accept the information provided by others as evidence about reality. However, social identity researchers have found that the group membership of the other people in the situation has a profound effect on norm formation. Individuals converge only with people categorized as similar to the self (i.e., other ingroup members) and actually diverge from people categorized as dissimilar to the self (i.e., outgroup members).

Studies of conformity using Solomon Asch's paradigm, in which people are confronted with a majority that makes incorrect judgments about unambiguous stimuli, have found that people go along with an incorrect majority in public but do not accept their judgments in private. This study is seen to be a classic example of normative influence. However, social identity researchers have found that levels of conformity in the Asch paradigm are a function of group membership. People do not necessarily conform blindly in public conditions; rather, individuals conform to the behavior of ingroup members and resist influence from outgroup members. In other words, normative pressure to comply is dependent on the self-definition of the target of influence. It is only when the individual and the majority share group membership that influence is likely to occur.

Group polarization is the tendency for group discussion to produce a group decision or position that is more extreme than the average of the individuals' prediscussion attitudes and opinions and is in the direction already favored by the group. This phenomenon has been explained in terms of either normative or informational influence: Opinions become polarized because of the perceived value of other opinions or because people are exposed to new information that produces an information shift. However, research within the social identity approach has demonstrated that group polarization is a function of the self-categorization of the individuals involved in the group discussion. Group polarization occurs only when people expect to agree with their fellow discussants—that is, when people are engaged in discussion with ingroup members and not outgroup members. Thus, group polarization reflects conformity to what people perceive to be the ingroup norm.

Debate

One of the key concepts in referent informational influence is the idea of depersonalization. Through depersonalization, people come to see themselves and other category members less as individuals and more as interchangeable exemplars of the group prototype. Moreover, as a function of depersonalization and assimilation to the group prototype or norm, group members are seen to follow automatically the behavior prescribed by the group norm. In other words, an automatic link is posited between thinking of oneself as a group member and group normative attitudes and behavior. However, it has been argued that this notion fails to account for individual variation in the way that people can express their group membership. Although the processes that make a social identity salient are often relatively automatic, responses to a salient identity, such as group behavior, are likely to be under some degree of conscious control and can be influenced by contextual factors, such as the presence or absence of an audience or power relations between the groups.

A description of the ways in which the behavior of group members can be strategic can be found in the *social identity model of deindividuation effects* (SIDE). The SIDE model, developed by Stephen Reicher and his colleagues, combines social identity with notions of self-presentation and strategic behavior to provide a fuller account of group behavior in social contexts and to account for individual variability in the relationship between the individual and the group.

Joanne R. Smith

See also Conformity; Depersonalization; Group Polarization; Informational Influence; Normative Influence; Self-Categorization Theory; Social Identity Model of Deindividuation Effects; Social Identity Theory; Social Identity Theory of Leadership

Further Readings

Abrams, D., Wetherell, M., Cochrane, S., Hogg, M. A., & Turner, J. C. (1990). Knowing what to think by knowing who you are: Self-categorization and the nature of norm formation, conformity, and group polarization. *British Journal of Social Psychology, 29*, 97–119.

Hogg, M. A., & Turner, J. C. (1987). Social identity and conformity: A theory of referent informational influence. In W. Doise & S. Moscovici (Eds.), *Current issues in European social psychology* (Vol. 2, pp. 139–182). Cambridge, UK: Cambridge University Press.

Reicher, S. D., Spears, R., & Postmes, T. (1995). A social identity model of deindividuation phenomena. *European Review of Social Psychology, 6*, 161–198.

Turner, J. C. (1991). *Social influence.* Milton Keynes, UK: Open University Press.

RELATIONAL COHESION THEORY

Relational cohesion theory explains how and when people who are exchanging things of value develop stable, cohesive relations. It starts from the idea that people tend to interact or do things with others because they get something they value or want from those others. They give something to the other and receive something in return. This is termed a *social exchange.* The valued "goods" that are exchanged may be tangible or intangible. Employees exchange their labor for pay, clients exchange money for services, neighbors exchange assistance with each other's yards, coworkers exchange advice and information, roommates exchange respect for each other's belongings, and friends exchange emotional support for each other.

Overview

Social exchanges are instrumental in the sense that people engage in exchange to get something for themselves, and they may not care what the other gets. Unless people have some sort of commitment to each other, you would expect them to always be searching or "on the lookout" for better exchange partners and to readily leave one relationship for another. Social ties or relations would be like economic markets in this sense, governed and shaped purely by self-interest. Relational cohesion theory asks, Under what conditions will people in social exchange develop a commitment to their relationship?

Commitment is defined as the tendency for people to keep exchanging with the same person or to stay in a relationship despite good or better alternatives. If people have a commitment, they will not be as inclined to search for better alternatives or to choose an alternative over their current relationship if one becomes available. Relational cohesion theory, as the name implies, argues that social cohesion produces a strong form of commitment that involves not just staying in the relationship but also giving gifts without strings attached (unilaterally) and partaking in new joint activities or ventures that require or imply trust in the other's goodwill. The theory contends that such commitments form because social exchanges produce emotions (or feelings), and under certain conditions, people associate their individual feelings with their relationship or shared group affiliation. When this occurs, people come to value not only the things they personally get from the exchange but also the relationship or group affiliation in itself.

According to the theory, social cohesion has a structural and a perceptual dimension. *Structural cohesion* is based on the degree of interdependence, that is, how dependent the people are on each other. Structural cohesion is strong if both people in an exchange are highly dependent on each other for valued rewards (high mutual dependence, or interdependence) and if they are equally rather than unequally dependent on each other. Structural cohesion, however, is an unrealized potential. It makes salient to people that they are involved in a joint task or activity with another and that they cannot accomplish the task alone or without the other.

The fact that they "need" each other for this purpose is important, but it does not necessarily lead to actualized or realized cohesion. Actual or realized cohesion has to be produced and perceived by the people themselves in their interactions with each other. Once cohesion is realized, people tend to become committed and thus are inclined to stay in their relationship, give each other gifts, and trust each other enough to partake in new cooperative ventures that expand or grow their relationship.

Central Assumptions

Relational cohesion theory indicates that structural cohesion is realized through the emotions and feelings that emerge from repeated social exchanges among the same persons. An emotion is an evaluation state of the human organism that has cognitive, physiological, and neurological elements. When you feel an emotion, you "feel it all over," so emotions refer to generalized states of the human organism. In relational cohesion theory, the emotions of concern are mild states that people often experience in their daily lives, such as feeling good, up, satisfied, bad, down, or dissatisfied. The theory identifies conditions under which such everyday feelings are attributed to relations or groups within which social exchanges occur. This is what causes relational or group commitments to become emotionally based. There are four main points in the theory.

First, social structures bring people together by making them dependent on each other and giving them incentives to interact and exchange. Who exchanges with whom and how often are determined by these interdependencies and associated incentives. People choose to exchange with those from whom they receive the greatest reward or payoff, and at this point, they are oriented only to their own rewards. However, relationships form and evolve when the exchange occurs frequently and repeatedly among the same people. The reasons for this are the next points.

Second, successfully arriving at exchanges with another is an accomplishment that gives people an "emotional buzz." They feel good about accomplishing the exchange task, whereas unsuccessful efforts to exchange make them feel bad. Repeated exchanges or failures at exchange create patterns of feeling good or bad with another person. Moreover, because social exchange is inherently a joint task, people are likely to believe that their relationship is one reason they are able to repeatedly solve the task (or fail at it). People infer that their emotions, felt individually, are jointly produced by what they share, such as their relationship or group affiliation.

Third, the theory argues further that positive feelings make more salient the relationship people have to each other and lead them to perceive their relationship as a unifying force in the situation. Thus, repeated exchange produces positive feelings, and these feelings, in turn, foster perceptions of a cohesive relationship, that is, one coming together rather than coming apart. People orient their behavior more to the other and to this relationship than before because the relationship is now a distinct object or force in the situation. They are prepared to do more things on behalf of their relationship with the other, even if it involves costs or sacrifice on their part. Thus, the instrumental, self-interest foundation of their original exchanges evolves into an expressive, symbolic relation with intrinsic value. People continue exchanging with the same others in part to affirm and maintain a valued social relationship.

Fourth, combining the above three points, there is a three-part sequence or process through which a social structure (dependencies) produces commitment: exchange to emotion to cohesion. The effects of social structures are indirect and occur only when this process is produced, that is, when exchange produces positive emotions and these emotions generate perceived cohesion. Commitments to relations will not occur if structures do not generate repeated patterns of exchange among the same people, if those exchanges do not give people an "emotional buzz," or if the resulting emotions do not lead the people to perceive a cohesive relationship with each other.

Related Research

Many laboratory experiments have been conducted to test the predictions of relational cohesion theory. These experiments bring two or more people together to negotiate agreements across a series of episodes of negotiations and vary people's mutual dependence on each other (high vs. low) and also their relative dependence (equal vs. unequal). The evidence strongly supports the idea that equal dependence and more mutual dependence promote commitment behaviors, but only indirectly, through the exchange-to-emotion-to-cohesion process.

Second, the exchange-to-emotion-to-cohesion process has been supported under a variety of different conditions, such as in groups of three working on a joint venture, in networks with four people, and with different types or forms of social exchange. Thus, the idea that frequent exchange produces more positive feelings and more positive feelings produce more perceived cohesion is well founded at this point.

Finally, the theory suggests, more generally, that the effects of group processes on group commitments are strongest when the tasks generate a strong sense of shared responsibility among the people involved in social exchange. Highly joint tasks create a sense of shared responsibility among people doing the task together, and social exchange is one example of a joint task. If people give credit to themselves and not the others for success at a joint task (low sense of shared responsibility), then repeated success at the task should have no effects on cohesion and commitment.

On the other hand, if people give all those involved credit for success (high sense of shared responsibility), the effects of emotions felt on cohesion and commitment should be strong. In this way, the theory of relational cohesion helps explain how and when group processes are likely to produce group cohesion and affective group commitments. Group cohesion and commitment should be especially strong when the structure of the task and the behaviors of people in accomplishing it generate a strong sense of shared responsibility for the results.

Edward J. Lawler

See also Group Cohesiveness; Group Emotions; Group Structure; Social Exchange in Networks and Groups

Further Readings

Lawler, E. J., & Thye, S. R. (2006). Social exchange theory of emotions. In J. E. Stets & J. H. Turner (Eds.), *Handbook of the sociology of emotions* (pp. 295–320). New York: Springer.

Lawler, E. J., Thye, S. R., & Yoon, J. (2000). Emotion and group cohesion in productive exchange. *American Journal of Sociology, 106,* 616–657.

Lawler, E. J., Thye, S. R., & Yoon, J. (2006). Commitment in structurally-enabled and induced exchange relations. *Social Psychology Quarterly, 69,* 183–200.

Lawler, E. J., & Yoon, J. (1996). Commitment in exchange relations: Test of a theory of relational cohesion. *American Sociological Review, 63,* 89–108.

RELATIONAL MODEL OF AUTHORITY IN GROUPS

One of the primary challenges faced by leaders of all types of groups—work groups, organizations, student groups, athletic teams, and religious sects, for example—is how to get group members to follow the rules they establish and the directives they issue. More generally, authority figures face the challenge of getting group members to act in ways that advance group goals, such as getting them to work hard, organize their efforts with other group members, and do things that may be in the group's interest even if they do not benefit the individual. Groups that cannot successfully master this challenge are not likely to be viable for very long. For this reason, it is essential that leaders focus on overcoming this challenge.

Indeed, it is this challenge that, in many ways, makes leadership necessary in the first place.

Many theories attempt to specify how group authorities can best master the challenge of shaping group members' behavior. The traditional perspective adopted by many of these theories is that leaders can best accomplish this by issuing directives and making strict rules that establish how group members should behave. Of course, leaders must also take steps to ensure that those directives and rules are followed, which requires close monitoring of group members' behavior, as well as the provision of rewards to group members who comply and punishment to those who do not. The principle that underlies these approaches is that group members cannot be relied on to follow the rules established by authorities, and thus, systems that entice them to do so must be put in place.

The *relational model of authority* (the *relational model*), however, takes a somewhat different approach. This model argues that when group members consider group authorities as legitimate—that is, as deserving of the power they wield and as using that power appropriately—members will take it on themselves to follow group rules and to act in ways that benefit the group. Furthermore, the model argues, group members will do this without close supervision and without the provision of rewards and punishments. This enables groups to devote their energy and resources to other functions and thus enables them to function more effectively. In this entry, both traditional and relational approaches are explored in more detail.

Traditional Approaches

Many traditional theories about leadership and authority relations are based on the assumption that group members must be compelled and coerced into following the directives of group leaders and into submitting to rules set by the group. According to such theories, leaders must implement systems that directly control group members' behavior. This can be done by instituting reward and incentive systems for good behavior and/or punishment systems for poor behavior, both of which require leaders to closely monitor group members' behavior. This establishes a system that encourages group members to engage in desired behaviors and to refrain from undesired behaviors.

The underlying premise of this approach is that group members are fundamentally self-interested actors who engage in behaviors that benefit them and avoid behaviors that do not. Such a notion implies that group members will not follow the rules put forth by group authorities unless those rules have tangible benefits for them. Rewarding compliance and punishing noncompliance address this condition by aligning each group member's behavior with his or her self-interest. The ability of group authorities to lead, therefore, rests on their ability and power to monitor group members, as well as on the power they wield to provide rewards and dispense punishments.

To appreciate relational models, it is important to note some of the implications of these more traditional approaches. One such implication is that group members will follow group authorities only when they believe their behavior will be observed by those authorities. When their behavior is not observed, group authorities cannot determine whether to provide incentives for compliance or punishments for noncompliance. Given this, the group member's primary reason for engaging in the behavior has essentially been removed.

Another implication is that group members will follow group authorities only when the members believe those authorities can actually dispense the incentives and punishments associated with particular behaviors. Scarce resources, weak leadership, and inadequate support systems can all hinder the ability of group authorities to do this. As such, group authorities' ability to shape group members' behavior is highly contingent on whether group authorities have sufficient resources to closely monitor group members and follow through with the incentives and punishments they specify.

This approach is problematic because it requires that a considerable portion of group resources—which could be put to other uses—be devoted to ensuring group members' compliance with group authorities' directives. What's more, when groups experience periods of resource scarcity, they are unable to devote the resources needed to shape group members' behavior at precisely the time when it is most important to do so. It is also important to note that even when group authorities do have the resources to successfully monitor and reward or punish behavior, actually doing so comes at a significant cost. They risk communicating to group members that the group does not trust them, which can in turn hurt members' commitment to the group. Similarly, this can damage the dynamic between group authorities and individuals because the relationship between the two comes to be dominated by these command-and-control processes. Finally, this approach sends a message to group members that following group rules may not be in their self-interest because they need to be coerced into compliance via extrinsic rewards and punishments.

The Relational Model

The relational model of authority, which suggests a very different approach to getting group members to follow directives and rules, stands in contrast to these traditional leadership approaches. In particular, the relational model argues that group members will be intrinsically motivated to follow group authorities when the members see those authorities as legitimate. Legitimacy refers to group members' perceptions that authorities deserve the power they hold (i.e., that they have achieved their power through appropriate means and continue to exercise that power appropriately). When authorities are seen as legitimate, the decisions they make and the rules they establish are imbued with a sense of legitimacy and correctness, and group members feel that they *should* follow those decisions and rules. In contrast, when authorities are regarded as illegitimate, their decisions and rules may seem to have little merit, and group members are unlikely to feel any obligation to follow them. Perceptions of legitimacy, therefore, determine the extent to which group members feel that they should or should not comply with authorities. This, in turn, shapes group members' actual behavior.

In suggesting that members will follow their group's authorities even in the absence of monitoring, rewards, and/or punishments, the relational model's framework is a more viable model of how authorities can lead groups. According to the model, group members can be counted on to follow group authorities out of their own intrinsic desires, and thus, their compliance with rules and directives set forth by authorities is not contingent on outside rewards or other factors. The benefits of this perspective are readily apparent when contrasted with the downsides of other approaches.

First, the relational model does not require the expenditure of resources to gain group members' compliance, because members follow authorities of their own volition. This frees these resources for other, more productive uses. Moreover, members can be relied on to follow group authorities even when group resources are scarce. In addition, dynamics among members and between members and their authorities are not damaged, as this framework does not communicate the authorities' distrust of the group's members. Finally, this approach does not imply that following group authorities is not in the individual's self-interest.

There is a critical question that follows from the relational model: What are the factors that cause group members to regard authorities as legitimate? Legitimacy is a powerful tool that enables leaders to gain effective compliance from followers. The relational model argues that the roots of legitimacy lie in group members' judgments of the underlying fairness of group authorities' decision making and their treatment of the group's members.

Such fairness judgments, known as *procedural justice judgments*, have been shown to have a significant impact on judgments of the legitimacy of group authorities. Group authorities who make fair decisions (i.e., those who are consistent, unbiased, and accurate in their decision making) are more likely to be considered legitimate. In addition, group authorities that treat members fairly by showing appropriate respect for them, listening to them, and showing concern for them are also more likely to be viewed as legitimate. It is important to note that these procedural fairness judgments are different from the fairness judgments group members make about the outcomes received from group authorities—known as *distributive fairness judgments*.

The distinction between procedural and distributive fairness is comparable to the distinction between means (procedural justice) and ends (distributive justice). Although people care about both procedural and distributive fairness (i.e., they care about the fairness of both the processes they experience and the outcomes they receive), their judgments of procedural justice have the most significant impact on whether they view group authorities as legitimate. In short, legitimacy comes more from a sense that authorities engage in fair processes and less from the outcomes people receive from them.

Why is procedural justice so important to members' perceptions of their authorities as legitimate? The relational model argues that procedural justice is important because it is a cue that group members can use to evaluate their relationship with the group's authority figures. Judgments that a group authority is procedurally fair lead group members to view their relationship with that authority positively. This, in turn, makes group members feel that the authority recognizes their status within the group and that they can trust the authority. When their relationship with the authority is validated in this way, members are more likely to regard the authority's power as legitimate. As noted, this in turn makes them more likely to take it on themselves to follow policies established by those authorities.

The relational model's key tenet is that group authorities can best overcome the challenge of shaping group members' behavior by making decisions and treating members with fairness. In doing so, authorities communicate a positive message to group members about their membership in the group and their relationship to the authorities, which, in turn, leads group members to conclude that the authorities deserve the power they wield. This approach to shaping group members' behavior has many upsides—especially when compared with approaches that attempt to shape behavior via extrinsic means—because these strategies are far less taxing on group resources, less damaging to group dynamics, and more likely to yield desired behaviors across a wider range of circumstances and for longer times. Therefore, the relational model of authority represents an important framework for effective leadership.

Steven L. Blader

See also Leadership; Power; Procedural Justice

Further Readings

Lind, E. A., & Tyler, T. R. (1988). *The social psychology of procedural justice*. New York: Plenum.

Tyler, T. R., & Blader, S. L. (2005). Can businesses effectively regulate employee conduct? The antecedents of rule following in work settings. *Academy of Management Journal, 48*, 1143–1158.

Tyler, T. R., Boeckmann, R. J., Smith, H. J., & Huo, Y. J. (1997). *Social justice in a diverse society*. Boulder, CO: Westview.

Tyler, T. R., & Lind, E. A. (1992). A relational model of authority in groups. In M. Zanna (Ed.), *Advances in experimental social psychology, 25*, 115–191. New York: Academic Press.

RELATIVE DEPRIVATION

Relative deprivation is the sense of being deprived of something to which one believes one is entitled and the subsequent emotions, such as anger, frustration, and resentment. Feeling deprived is determined not by objective conditions of deprivation but rather by subjective comparison with others who are apparently better off.

The construct of relative deprivation has been around for a long time, more than six decades, and is employed in many social sciences, including social psychology, sociology, economics, and political science. It has been used to predict a wide variety of behaviors, ranging from the individual experience of stress and depression to civil insurrection and participation in political upheaval and other forms of collective action. Although researchers have theorized and operationalized relative deprivation differently, and sometimes inconsistently, its core is defined by the grievance of injustice.

Relative deprivation captures this sense of injustice, specifies the conditions under which it is expected to arise, and predicts its consequences. There are significant theoretical linkages with *social identity theory*, and there are significant and persistent conceptual and methodological problems in relative deprivation research. However, the relative deprivation construct continues to be of value in describing and understanding social behavior. This entry traces the theory over time, places it in a context of other ideas, and summarizes its primary challenges.

Historical Background

The term *relative deprivation* was coined by the U.S. sociologist Samuel Stouffer in the classic *American Soldier* volumes (1949). Stouffer and his colleagues conducted extensive studies of morale among U.S. troops fighting in Europe in World War II. Their research program was vast, but of primary interest here is a seeming paradox they observed in how satisfied different service units were with their promotion opportunities. Military police faced few prospects of promotion yet were more satisfied with those prospects than were air corpsmen, who had objectively much better prospects of more rapid promotion.

Stouffer and his colleagues suggested that these different levels of satisfaction could be understood as the disappointment of failed high expectations that had been formed though comparisons with others. Servicemen working in units with low rates of promotion were led to have low expectations of success when they themselves applied for promotion, and hence they were not terribly dissatisfied if they missed out on promotion. On the other hand, servicemen working in units with high rates of promotion were led to expect promotion when they applied, and hence they were dissatisfied if they missed out. Ostensibly the same objective outcome—failing to get promoted—led to significantly different experiences depending on one's prior expectations, which had been formed by the surrounding social context. Dissatisfaction stemmed from feeling deprived relative to others.

The idea of relative deprivation was similar to several other constructs and minitheories being developed in the social sciences in the postwar years, most notably Robert Merton's concept of reference groups, Harold Kelley's theorizing about comparison level of alternatives, and Leon Festinger's social comparison theory. Theories (or minitheories) about relative deprivation were also being developed, more or less independently, by researchers in social psychology, sociology, and political science.

All these different developments were brought together in 1967 in a significant theoretical synthesis by Thomas Pettigrew into what he termed *social evaluation theory*. Although that term has never gained currency, Pettigrew's specification of relative deprivation as a mesolevel process tying micro psychological processes to macro sociological processes has had wide and long-lasting influence. So too has his concern with the policy and political implications of social-psychological theories such as relative deprivation. Unfortunately, this policy dimension has been more in token observance than in material engagement.

Early formulations of a theory of relative deprivation treated it as the result of an intergroup

comparison and used it to explain various social phenomena. In the 1960s, relative deprivation was commonly employed to help explain participation in widespread civil unrest in the United States. These explanations focused on Blacks' dissatisfaction with access to jobs, education, fair pay, and so on, relative to Whites, as the primary grievance fueling participation in civil unrest.

Similarly, but in a converse manner, in his 1966 classic *Relative Deprivation and Social Justice*, the English sociologist Walter Runciman used the intergroup comparative nature of relative deprivation to help explain why members of the English working class did not participate in collective action to change the social order in which objectively they do not fare as well as other classes. Tackling the classic Marxist conundrum of why the working classes do not revolt in the face of objective evidence of their exploitation, Runciman proposed that members of the English working class do not evaluate the fairness of their conditions relative to members of other, more privileged classes. Instead, they make such evaluations relative to other members of the working class, often to people in their immediate social networks of friends and family. In other words, it is the failure to engage in intergroup comparisons that explains the absence of grievance in the face of intergroup inequality and exploitation.

Runciman introduced the distinction between egoistic and fraternalistic relative deprivation. These two kinds of relative deprivation have since come to be known as *personal* and *group relative deprivation*, respectively, at least in part because the term *fraternalistic* was awkward in later research examining relative deprivation in working women. The newer labels also provide a clearer link to social identity theory, discussed in more detail below. Egoistic or personal relative deprivation refers to feelings of grievance arising from comparisons between self and other individuals. In Runciman's research, those other individuals were usually friends and family members. The social comparisons involved are individualistic; group memberships are not involved, except to quietly circumscribe the range of other individuals with whom one might compare.

In contrast, fraternalistic, or group, relative deprivation arises from invidious comparisons between one's ingroup and some outgroup. It is these social comparisons between groups that provide the fuel for intergroup conflict and social change. Research has consistently shown that the experience of individual relative deprivation predicts individual-level outcomes such as stress and depression, which are not predicted by the experience of group relative deprivation. Conversely, the experience of group relative deprivation predicts social or group-level responses such as engaging in social protest and attempting to change the status quo, which are not predicted by individual relative deprivation.

The theory of relative deprivation was, in its early years, clearly a theory focused on intergroup relations and social change. Despite this focus, the theory still remained concerned with relative deprivation as an experience of individuals situated in a social context. This theoretical complexion started to change in the 1970s. The U.S. political scientist T. R. Gurr formulated relative deprivation as a perceived discrepancy between an individual's value expectations and value capabilities and argued that fraternalistic forms of relative deprivation are best conceptualized as special cases of egoistic relative deprivation. This individualistic formulation reduced the construct of relative deprivation by removing it from the intergroup, social comparative context of earlier work. In contrast to this individualistic, reductionistic approach to the construct of relative deprivation, Gurr's empirical research inferred relative deprivation from aggregate measures of objective conditions of deprivation at a national level.

Other research on relative deprivation at this time was also becoming more individualistic, or at least more focused on personal forms of relative deprivation. Notable among this research was a significant and influential model of personal relative deprivation proposed by Faye Crosby in 1976. Crosby proposed a set of five necessary and sufficient conditions to define those in a state of relative deprivation: People must see others possessing something they lack, must want it, must feel entitled to it, must think it feasible to attain it, and must not blame themselves for not having it.

Crosby further specified three variables that mediate the effects of relative deprivation: whether one blames oneself or society for not having the desired object, one's perceived level of personal control (the extent to which one believes one's actions can influence or affect society), and the actual opportunities for effecting change. Depending on the pattern of these mediating variables, the experience of relative deprivation will lead to stress symptoms, attempts at self-improvement, attempts at constructive social change, or violence against society.

Crosby's model significantly influenced relative deprivation research for many years. It provided a powerful attempt at a theoretical integration of the extant literature and a rare attempt at a formal specification of the construct of relative deprivation, its preconditions, behavioral outcomes, and variables mediating those outcomes. She was also the first to posit that relative deprivation is not a construct that can be measured directly but rather is a theoretical variable to be inferred from a set of preconditions.

Subsequent research came to be directed at assessing each of the model's preconditions to determine whether each is either necessary or sufficient as a precondition of relative deprivation and also at assessing the role of the proposed mediators. The model was limiting in several ways, however. Arguably, proposing that relative deprivation should be assumed from the satisfaction of a set of preconditions rather than measured directly became a diversion in the further development of the theory. Certainly, most recent research has returned to the direct assessment of relative deprivation, at least partly because attempts to empirically resolve issues about the preconditions never reached resolution. The model was naïve in its formulation of the behavioral outcomes of relative deprivation. And the model was too mechanistic and not sensitive enough to context-specific influences on the experience of injustice to accommodate the closer integration with social identity theory that was to come in the 1980s and later.

Theoretical Linkages

One of the most notable, important, and influential theoretical developments in social psychology generally in the past two decades has been the development of social identity theory. Flowing from early work by the European social psychologist Henri Tajfel and first fully specified by Tajfel and John Turner, social identity theory articulates the linkages between social categorization processes, social comparison processes, and social identity.

Social identity is closely tied to social category memberships, the value of which to an individual can be assessed only through social comparison processes involving self, the ingroup, and relevant outgroups. Negative social comparisons threaten social identity, motivating various intergroup strategies to enhance the sense of positive intergroup differentiation. These strategies can include direct challenges to the intergroup status quo. Social identity theory has clear similarities to relative deprivation theory, a point recognized by Tajfel in his early, nascent formulations of social identity theory. The past two decades have seen significant work elaborating the relationships between relative deprivation and social identity theories.

The two theories primarily complement each other, synthesizing different historical and methodological traditions. Relative deprivation research has strong lineage from sociology and political science and has often relied on survey methods, whereas social identity research comes predominantly from experimental social psychology. Relative deprivation research has typically focused more on the consequences of relative deprivation, whereas social identity research has focused more on the cognitive processes linking categorization to social comparison outcomes. Relative deprivation research has focused exclusively on judgments of justice and injustice, whereas social identity research has had a broader approach to the dimensions of social comparison, out of which judgments of justice often naturally emerge as important points of comparison. Relative deprivation research has tended to assume which social category memberships (social identities) are important to people, whereas social identity research has focused intensely on this issue. These points of difference are not fundamental incompatibilities between the two approaches but rather points of differential emphasis.

Conceptual and Empirical Challenges

The two approaches share some common theoretical problems too. These problems afflict all the family of Pettigrew's social evaluation theories and persist despite consistent research attention. Prime among these are problems in the social comparison process—namely, specifying which groups will be chosen as a comparison referent and along which

dimensions comparisons will be made. Festinger's original formulation of social comparison theory in 1954 set out careful predictions that, all other things being equal, people will seek similar, rather than dissimilar, others for comparison, that comparisons will be about particular opinions or abilities, and that in the case of abilities, the comparison other will be slightly better than the comparer.

Festinger's theory, however, was concerned only with individual comparisons that people make to evaluate their opinions and abilities. The comparisons at the core of both relative deprivation and social identity theories often involve inter- or even intragroup processes and are made by people concerned with evaluating procedural or distributive justice. Under such situations, people tend not to make comparisons with similar others but instead often compare with dissimilar others. And the dimensions of comparison are more varied than just opinions and abilities. However, all social evaluation theories suffer from an inability to predict which others (individuals or groups) will be selected as the comparison other, as well as an inability to predict what the dimensions of comparison will be. These problems continue to be the major theoretical hurdle facing relative deprivation and social identity theories.

Another major issue for relative deprivation research, and to a lesser degree for social identity research, concerns a distinction between cognitive and affective components of the construct. At its core, the construct of relative deprivation is a hot, affective, motivational response to a grievance. However, many operationalizations of relative deprivation are cold and cognitive. This disjunction helps explain why many studies find only modest relationships between relative deprivation and outcome measures; generally, stronger relationships are found when measures of relative deprivation include the affective component. This makes sense intuitively. Recognizing a discrepancy (the cognitive component of relative deprivation) translates into action only if one cares strongly about the discrepancy and the discrepancy violates one's sense of fairness and justice.

Recognizing the role of the affective component of relative deprivation has led researchers recently to expand the analysis of group-based emotions. Emotions are usually thought of as individual, psychological, private experiences.

However, emotions arise through social interaction, often involving groups, and are shared and regulated socially. Whether talking of personal or group relative deprivation, recognizing a discrepancy between what is and what one believes ought to be results in attempts to change the status quo only when that recognition makes one angry. Anger is the fuel of discontent. But it is not the only emotion that may be produced by the recognition of deprivation. Sadness, fear, shame, envy, and anxiety are all possible emotional responses, and each leads to a different sort of behavioral response.

Just as there are many possible emotional responses to the recognition of deprivation, so too are there different emotional responses to the recognition of advantage and privilege. The flip side of relative deprivation (sometimes referred to as *relative gratification*) has come to researchers' attention in recent years as an important component of political change. Some earlier analyses of personal and group relative deprivation suggested that those who are doubly deprived (i.e., suffering both personal and group relative deprivation) are the most likely to engage in collective action. Others suggested that the vanguard of collective action is composed of people who are group deprived and personally advantaged, because it is they who have the greatest resources available to tackle the group deprivation.

More recently, though, it has come to be recognized that the privileged have an important political role to play in addressing social inequalities. Many members of privileged groups do not recognize their group's superior position, or they explain it away as a legitimate reflection of deservingness. However, some accept that their group is unfairly privileged and that others suffer deprivation as a result. Common emotional responses to this view can be indignation and shame. These typically do not lead to political action, though. That comes from feeling outrage and anger.

Thus, it can be seen that emotions play a critical role in determining responses to perceptions of deprivation, whether one is deprived or privileged. The waxing of research attention to the emotional side of judgments of unfairness and inequality returns relative deprivation to its origins. Cognitive processes are essential in appraising the fairness of personal and group outcomes, to be sure, but

emotional processes provide the pathway to different kinds of behaviors.

Iain Walker

See also Justice; Social Comparison Theory; Social Identity Theory

Further Readings

Crosby, F. J. (1982). *Relative deprivation and working women*. New York: Oxford University Press.

Pettigrew, T. F. (1967). Social evaluation theory: Convergences and applications. In D. Levine (Ed.), *Nebraska Symposium on Motivation* (Vol. 15, pp. 241–311). Lincoln: University of Nebraska Press.

Smith, H. J., & Kessler, T. (2004). Group-based emotions and intergroup behavior: The case of relative deprivation. In L. Z. Tiedens & C. W Leach (Eds.), *The social life of emotions* (pp. 292–313). Cambridge, UK: Cambridge University Press.

Tajfel, H., & Turner, J. C. (1979). An integrative theory of intergroup conflict. In W. G. Austin & S. Worchel (Eds.), *The social psychology of intergroup relations* (pp. 33–48). Monterey, CA: Brooks/Cole.

Tyler, T. R., Boeckmann, R. J., Smith, H. J., & Huo, Y. (1997). *Social justice in a diverse society*. Boulder CO: Westview.

Walker, I., & Smith, H. J. (Eds.). (2002). *Relative deprivation: Specification, development, and integration*. New York: Cambridge University Press.

RESEARCH METHODS AND ISSUES

Group processes can be conceptualized as the mechanisms or intervening factors that connect properties of groups (e.g., group size, average skill level, diversity, or identity) to outcomes. Examples include the actions or communication that groups engage in while making decisions, negotiating, or coordinating their activities. These behaviors are driven by the group's task and associated performance goals, creating interdependencies among group members that lead to coordinated and actively integrated behavior. It is this set of behaviors that researchers investigating group processes attempt to capture and analyze.

Scholars have suggested that to fully understand how people organize, we must consider an individual's behavior and how others react to that behavior before we can predict how that person will behave at a later time. Mapping this process of interaction can provide insight as to what triggers certain behavior, what patterns of behavior are likely to occur, and what patterns are likely to facilitate high-quality outcomes. Studying group processes thus enables the researcher to address "how" questions, such as how new ideas are introduced within groups or how the process of planning influences which ideas are finally adopted.

The measurement of group processes poses challenges to the researcher that are distinct from those posed by the measurement of group properties. This entry is thus an overview of the primary issues faced by researchers in measuring group processes. First, it presents an overview of group process research methods and their implications for theory and analysis. Second, it addresses specific methodological issues faced by group process researchers that pertain to capturing and analyzing data.

Overview of Group Process Research Methods

This section provides an overview of the methods for capturing and analyzing group processes, focusing on the differences between capturing group processes via self-reports versus third-party observations and static versus dynamic approaches to data analysis. Because the survey methods that underlie self-report measures of group process are well known, this section pays more attention to methods of direct observation and associated data-analytic approaches.

Capturing Group Process: Self-Reports Versus Direct Observation

To capture group process data, the researcher typically has a choice of obtaining the data either from members' self-reports or from third parties directly observing the group. Self-reports measure group members' subjective perception of the group's actual processes, usually via survey responses after the group has completed the task. Direct observation methods, in contrast, rely on the (relatively) objective assessment of group processes by trained observers, either in real time or from recordings (typically audio or video). If the

researcher is interested in a global measure of group processes (e.g., cooperation), then Likert-type scales (e.g., scoring 1 for *never* through 5 for *always*) can be used by observers to assess the interaction. However, if the researcher is interested in dynamic processes, or if more detailed differentiation of behavior is required, then the raw data from these recordings need to be coded and analyzed.

The first step involves transforming the recording into meaningful units of analysis. This transformation typically occurs through a process of *unitizing* (i.e., identifying units of behavior) and then classifying behaviors according to a *coding scheme*. The coding scheme is a set of rules or guidelines for coders to identify the unit to be coded (e.g., thought, sentence, speaking turn, paragraph), category labels, definitions, and rules of thumb for distinguishing between categories and using context (i.e., statements surrounding the unit of interest) to interpret meaning. Regardless of whether a coding scheme is adapted from previous research or designed from scratch, its development is a pivotal step in the research process because the classification scheme has a profound influence on the researcher's ability to test and support hypotheses.

Analyzing Group Process: Static Versus Dynamic Approaches

There are two alternative approaches to analyzing group process data obtained from direct observation methods: static and dynamic. A *static* approach considers the total (or relative) amount of a given behavior collapsed over time. For example, cooperation might be measured by counting the instances of cooperative behaviors that occur during a team meeting. Using a static approach by aggregating group process data over time is appropriate when a researcher is interested in capturing the general approach used by a group or the relative usage of different task strategies (e.g., independent vs. interdependent work or cooperation vs. competition). Frequencies (or relative frequencies) are typically used to explain how inputs affect outcomes (e.g., group composition → *information exchange* → innovativeness).

The decision whether to analyze absolute or relative frequencies will be guided by one's theory of group behavior. If the given behavior is theorized to influence a group outcome regardless of the amount of other behaviors present, then *absolute frequencies* are more appropriate. But if one is interested in the relative impact of a behavior within the overall interaction, then *relative frequencies* are more appropriate. Relative frequencies are typically calculated by dividing the absolute frequency of a given behavior by the total behavior exhibited by the group. Frequencies of behavior are subsequently related to the phenomenon of interest by means of regression techniques. The use of frequencies, however, assumes no temporal relationships among behaviors, no unique person-to-person interactions, and it does not allow for the possibility that low-frequency events can have a profound influence on the group.

Alternatively, group process can be measured using a *dynamic* approach, looking at group behavior over time. Using this approach, researchers can measure sequences of behavior at a very fine-grained level, or they can measure broader phases of behavior over longer periods of time.

Sequences capture the direct communication exchange between group members and can be used to predict group outcomes. For example, a group discussion in which members reciprocate information sharing so that there is a back-and-forth exchange throughout the meeting will have outcomes that differ from those of a group discussion in which information is shared sequentially by each member, followed by a vote. Outcomes in the former group can be expected to be more positive than outcomes in the latter group because members are building on one another's ideas. These differences in outcomes would best be explained by comparing the sequences of information exchange within the group. In contrast, reporting total frequencies of information exchange might result in the false conclusion that information exchange does not influence the quality of group decisions.

Phases of group process are also dynamic in that they capture the broader group processes that unfold over time. Phases can be predetermined via theory (e.g., phases of group development), time divisions (e.g., meetings divided into quarters), or observation (emergent phases based on patterns within the data). Researchers who study phases are often interested in understanding the process itself rather than using it to predict specific group outcomes. However, it is not uncommon for prescriptive models to be developed on the basis of observations of phase patterns in successful groups.

Sequential analysis techniques identify patterns of recurring behavior over time. Such techniques typically look at transitions from one type of behavior to another. Recurring patterns are then identified and tested for significance. Popular analytic techniques include lag sequential, Markov chain, log linear, and phase analyses. *Lag sequential analysis* captures the effect of a given behavior on other behaviors that occur in lags (e.g., units) later. Thus, lag sequential analysis can capture immediate or later (lagged) responses. *Markov chain* and *log linear* analyses examine the likelihood that specific chains of behavior will occur. *Phase analysis* captures emergent phases in groups. The researcher first defines what constitutes a phase (e.g., clusters of similar behaviors or important events that serve as a transition in the process), and then the analysis is used to identify when phases actually begin and end within a given group.

Researchers interested in adopting direct observation methods to measure group process face a distinct set of practical and theoretical issues. These issues can be categorized according to whether they pertain to capturing or analyzing group process data.

Methodological Issues: Capturing Group Process

Group processes are typically observed either in laboratory experiments or in in-depth, small-sample case studies in the field. Although experiments can be conducted in the field, they are rare because of the difficulties in both manipulating variables and recording group process for large numbers of groups.

Research Design

Group process research that uses traditional experimental design aggregates data across groups to look for similar patterns within conditions and differences in patterns across conditions. The research goals are typically to link group process to inputs or outcomes or to test for mediation. A prototypical study might manipulate the complexity of a group's task, examine how groups plan and perform in each condition, and then use mediation analysis to examine how the task's complexity influenced planning and subsequent performance.

In contrast, when the process itself is of interest to the researcher, then it may be more appropriate to examine group functioning in real-world contexts through in-depth examination of specific situations. These studies typically focus on a single group or small set of groups and systematically examine behavior over time. This approach is sometimes used out of necessity, because of the difficulty in obtaining access to large numbers of naturalistic groups in organizational settings. Although the generalizability across contexts may be limited, the depth of understanding is often greater, and one can avoid potential biases associated with averaging data across groups to reach conclusions about the processes of any one group.

The decision about which research design to adopt eventually depends on the research goals and the feasibility of implementing a particular design.

Direct Observation Versus Self-Reports

Capturing group process from self-reports is appropriate insofar as members' perceptions guide their reactions and behaviors. However, relying on perceptual data to identify and measure group process introduces two sources of bias that can lead to measurement problems. The first source of bias, inaccurate recall, is introduced as a result of the situation, intervening events, or members' inattention to the group process. Furthermore, the relevant group process might not be identifiable by group members during the interaction. Important group processes could occur at an aggregate level that is not immediately discernible. Even the most helpful participants cannot describe broad patterns of the group interaction. Alternatively, group processes could also occur subconsciously when people react to one another's behavior. In both cases, self-reports of group process would not be able to capture the phenomena of interest.

The second source of bias involves subjectivity of assessment. A group member's perception of the group process might be influenced by a number of factors, such as past experiences, individual differences, status within the group, and knowledge of performance. If the researcher's goal is to understand reactions to group interactions, then capturing these perceptions via self-reports is necessary. But if the goal is to capture the fundamental nature of interaction in the group, then these biases will create measurement problems and interfere with the research objective.

Data Collection

Collecting data on group processes can pose a unique challenge to researchers. Several decisions need to be made regarding the medium of data collection: Should the data be recorded or collected in real time? If recorded, are audio or video recordings necessary? Should the verbal portion of the recordings be transcribed, or can coding be done directly from the tapes?

Recording Versus Real-Time

Obtaining a recording of the group's process is always preferable to collecting all the data in real time. Recording allows one to code the data at the coder's rather than the group's pace. Ideally a researcher would also observe the group interaction while recording because observation provides an opportunity to detect nuances that may be lost in recording. However, it is not always possible to record group interactions, especially when studying groups in field settings, due to concerns of confidentiality. In many of these situations, coding in real time is the only option. Using a simple coding scheme and having multiple, highly trained coders will increase the likelihood of reliable data collection. More detailed coding schemes make real-time coding difficult because they require coders to make complex coding decisions quickly. This difficulty, combined with the inability to review a past code assignment, increases the risk of unreliable coding. Use of multiple coders can reduce this concern by providing multiple assessments of the interaction.

Regardless of whether interactions are captured in real time or via recordings, researchers must consider whether group members' awareness of being observed is affecting the group processes. Although basic research ethics demand that participants consent to being observed or recorded, the effect of this knowledge on group processes can be minimized in a number of ways. Recording devices should be as inconspicuous as possible, such as behind one-way mirrors in the lab or strategically placed. When this is not possible, group members can be given more time to interact so that they can adapt to the presence of the observer or recording device.

Audio Versus Video Recording

Interest in nonverbal behavior and/or in identifying speakers will drive the choice of video or audio recordings. Whereas audio recordings are less expensive and easier to obtain, they preclude the collection of nonverbal behavior and make it difficult to identify speakers. However, the latter problem can be overcome by using a multitrack audio-recording device and recording each speaker on a separate track. Video recordings allow speakers to be identified, but camera placement is important to ensure a clear view of all group members. This might require the use of several cameras, depending on the configuration and size of the group and room. If multiple cameras are used, it is useful to link them to a common time code or use a video mixer to facilitate integration among the separate recordings.

Advances in software packages have improved the interface between video recordings and coding equipment, making the use of video recordings more attractive. The use of audio versus video recording is also influenced by the research setting. It is often difficult to obtain permission to videotape group processes in organizational settings where concerns about anonymity and confidentiality are strong. However, several organizations use videotapes of group decision making as sources of feedback for managers. Tapping into ongoing efforts might increase the odds of gaining video access.

Alternative recording media are also available. For example, computer-mediated communication involving e-mail and Internet chat systems is easily recorded with software programs that have been developed for such purposes. More recently, online communities have been used as an archival source of group interactions. Group Decision Support Systems software also provides the opportunity to record written interaction while employing the system. Handwriting recognition systems are also available for saving handwritten coding and field notes.

Transcriptions

Before coding recorded data on verbal interactions, the researcher must decide whether to transcribe the verbal interaction. With transcripts, one can code from the transcripts alone or in combination with the recording. Without transcripts, one must code from the recordings alone. Transcription, especially of videotapes, is time-consuming and potentially expensive if one must use professional transcription services. Although direct coding of recordings is tempting for this reason, it is more difficult to reliably identify the units to be coded (i.e., obtain unitizing reliability) without transcripts.

If one chooses not to transcribe verbal interaction but rather to work directly from the recordings, the recordings need to be indexed by means of time codes. The use of digital technology facilitates this process because each frame is indexed when it is saved. These time codes can be used by the coders to identify the beginning and ending of each unit to be coded. Behavioral coding assessments can then be linked to the location on the video through the use of the time codes.

Methodological Issues in Analyzing Group Process

Unit of Analysis

An issue raised by adopting direct observation approaches to studying group process concerns the appropriate unit of analysis. When sequences are to be analyzed, the unit of analysis can vary from a single utterance that contains meaning to a speaking turn or to a back-and-forth exchange. When phases are to be analyzed, the units of analysis are the phases themselves.

At the lowest level of aggregation, an *act* refers to a single expressed idea or activity that is displayed by a group member. At the next level of aggregation, *speaking turns* are defined as beginning when an individual takes the floor and ending when that person stops talking or another group member begins. Hence, speaking turns can involve single or multiple acts. When the unit of analysis is at the level of acts or speaking turns, sequential behavior can easily be examined. When acts are the unit of analysis, the focus is on the flow of messages, regardless of who is speaking.

When speaking turns are the unit of analysis, the focus is often the interactive nature of the group process.

At the opposite end of the aggregation spectrum is a conceptualization of group process as a series of fixed *phases* or *stages*, the study of which can provide insight into such phenomena as group socialization and group development. In the literature on these topics, phases of group membership and stages of group development are assumed to affect the interactions among members. Phases can also be conceptualized as flexible. *Flexible models* account for the fact that group processes do not progress in an orderly fashion but rather advance in fits and starts, with regression to prior stages being a common event. Flexible models thus allow for more complex modeling of the group's process.

Decisions regarding choice of unit type must be linked to the research question being asked, with special sensitivity to the appropriate level of analysis and to where, in action and speech, relevant meaning resides. If too small a unit is selected, then meaning can be lost because the individual statements convey a different meaning from that conveyed by a speaking turn. Redundancy may also be added as a result of separating immediate restatements that simply repeat previous messages rather than add new information. In contrast, information can be lost if too large a unit is selected. If multiple categories of statements are made during a speaking turn, then the researcher must decide which code best represents the behavior within a given unit. To aid such decisions, *dominance schemes*, which identify the kinds of behavior that are expected to have the greatest impact on the interaction, can be developed. Alternatively, the first or the last code within the unit might be retained. Regardless of the approach that is used, the risk of losing valuable information remains.

An issue related to choosing an appropriate unit of analysis is whether to capture group processes at predetermined intervals rather than throughout a group interaction. This method, known as *time sampling*, provides a glimpse of group activities at a particular point in time. For example, one might be interested in the exertion of effort at the beginning, middle, and ending of a work session. The researcher needs to determine the window of time

to sample and an appropriate sampling interval. These issues will depend on the theory about what phases of work are meaningful and on how long it takes to get a representative view of the processes of interest. Time sampling can also be an expedient approach to data collection, transcription, and coding because it does not require attention to the entire interaction.

Coding Scheme Design

General Versus Task Specific

In designing a coding scheme, one of the first issues the researcher has to consider is whether a general or a task-specific scheme is more appropriate. General schemes are exhaustive, logically complete classification systems that can be applied across task types, whereas task-specific schemes index behaviors associated with performing the specific task at hand.

Task-specific schemes complement the use of domain-specific theories of group behavior but lack the generalizability of general schemes. However, several researchers have noted that because of the large number of factors that can influence the interdependencies among group members, it may not be possible to generalize group process across tasks. The task-specific approach supports the call by these researchers for midrange theories relevant to performance effectiveness under specified circumstances.

Theory Derived Versus Data Derived

What is the basis for determining how a behavior should be classified? Should the classification system be derived theoretically or from the data? In practice, the distinction between the two is blurred because human behavior is too complex to anticipate all relevant behaviors without some direct experience with the group and its task(s). Thus, a hybrid approach is typically adopted, in which the coding scheme is continually refined by iterating between theory and data. An appropriate first step in this strategy is to develop categories based on theoretical predictions about the types of behavior that are expected to be important. This brings us to issues about how exhaustive and detailed a coding scheme should be.

Exhaustiveness

Both theoretical and analytical concerns are relevant to this issue. If one is interested in detailed interaction patterns, then coding all verbal behaviors may be important. However, if some behaviors are not theoretically interesting, but all behavior must be classified (such as when conducting a sequential analysis), a "miscellaneous" or "other" category can be used. If the miscellaneous category turns out to contain substantial information, then the researcher can always create new codes to reclassify these behaviors.

Depth of Coding Scheme

The more detailed the scheme, the more fine-grained the discrimination will be among behaviors. As the number of categories increases, the risk of combining two behaviors that potentially serve different purposes is thus reduced. However, the downside of the proliferation of categories is twofold. First, coding becomes more difficult as categories become less distinct. Coding errors are more likely, lowering reliability and potentially necessitating the combination of categories. Second, as the number of categories increases, the frequency of behavior in each category necessarily decreases. Low-frequency categories are problematic for most statistical methods, especially sequential data analysis techniques. The issue of how detailed the scheme should be ultimately depends on the goal of the analysis, that is, whether global or detailed interaction patterns are of interest.

Code Application

The reliability and validity of a measure are issues that should concern all researchers. For group process research, the two kinds of reliability of concern are unitizing reliability and interpretive reliability. *Unitizing reliability* refers to the degree of agreement regarding identification of the units to be categorized, whereas *interpretive reliability* refers to consistency in applying labels to the units. High reliability of both types suggests that raters are coding from the same set of units and applying labels consistently to these units.

To ensure high interpretive reliability, it is best to unitize and code the data in separate passes because errors in unitizing will have a strong impact on interpretive reliability. When units do not align, codes will be applied differently and cannot be compared. This is especially important when one is coding from recordings, in which it is more difficult to identify the specific unit to which a code was assigned.

Low reliability suggests that the interpretation and application of labels between coders is inconsistent. This could be due to an overexhaustive coding scheme that makes it more difficult for coders to distinguish among behaviors. Inconsistencies between raters could also be attributed to the imprecise definitions of labels. In the former case, reliability can be increased by collapsing categories. In the latter case, more precise definitions and additional practice will enable coders to better discriminate.

Interpretive validity refers to the degree to which a coding scheme produces the information it was designed to obtain. How accurately do the applied labels represent what group members actually mean? Coding schemes can be validated through the use of theoretically derived coding schemes, participants' reflections and interpretations, or some combination of the two.

Conclusion

Group processes are inherently complex, and that complexity is reflected in the methods that have been developed to study them. This has often discouraged researchers who are interested in group processes but are unfamiliar with the necessary measurement methods or daunted by their difficulty. Although time-consuming, these methods are tractable and worthwhile in that the direct examination of group process can provide insights that no other method can. Findings from research on group processes can illuminate critical interactions within groups, deepening our understanding of the relationship between group attributes and outcomes.

Laurie R. Weingart and Kenneth Goh

See also Group Development; Interaction Process Analysis; SYMLOG

Further Readings

Bales, R. F., & Cohen, S. P. (1979). *SYMLOG: A system for the multiple level observation of groups.* New York: Free Press.

Boyatzis, R. E. (1998). *Transforming qualitative information: Thematic analysis and code development.* Thousand Oaks, CA: Sage

Edmondson, A. C., & McManus, S. E. (2007). Methodological fit in management field research. *Academy of Management Review, 32,* 1155–1179.

Fleiss, J. L. (1971). Measuring nominal scale agreement among many raters. *Psychological Bulletin, 76,* 378–382.

Futoran, G. C., Kelly, J. R., & McGrath, J. E. (1989). TEMPO: A time-based system for analysis of group interaction process. *Basic and Applied Social Psychology, 10,* 211–232.

Gottman, J. M., & Roy, A. K. (1990). *Sequential analysis: A guide for behavioral researchers.* New York: Cambridge University Press.

Guetzkow, H. (1950). Unitizing and categorizing problems in coding qualitative data. *Journal of Clinical Psychology, 6,* 47–58.

Hewes, D. E. (1979). The sequential analysis of social interaction. *Quarterly Journal of Speech, 65,* 56–73.

Holmes, M. E., & Poole, M. S. (1991). Longitudinal analysis. In B. Montgomery & S. Duck (Eds.), *Studying interpersonal interaction* (pp. 286–302). New York: Guilford.

Kelly, J. R. (2000). Interaction process analysis in task performing groups. In A. P. Beck & C. M. Lewis (Eds.), *The process of group psychotherapy: Systems for analyzing change* (pp. 49–65). Washington, DC: American Psychological Association.

Morley, D. D. (1987). Revised lag sequential analysis. In M. L. McLaughlin (Ed.), *Communication yearbook 10* (pp. 172–182). Newbury Park, CA: Sage.

Poole, M. S., Folger, J. P., & Hewes, D. E. (1987). Analyzing interpersonal interaction. In M. E. Roloff & G. R. Miller (Eds.), *Interpersonal processes: New directions in communication research* (pp. 220–256). Newbury Park, CA: Sage.

Poole, M. S., & McPhee, R. D. (1994). Methodology in interpersonal communication. In M. Knapp & G. R. Miller (Eds.), *Handbook of interpersonal communication* (pp. 42–100). Thousand Oaks, CA: Sage.

Trujillo, N. (1986). Toward a taxonomy of small group interaction coding systems. *Small Group Behavior, 17,* 371–394.

Tuckman, B. W. (1965). Developmental sequence in small groups. *Psychological Bulletin, 63,* 384–399.

Weingart, L. R. (1997). How did they do that? The ways and means of studying group processes. In L. L. Cummings & B. M. Staw (Eds.), *Research in organizational behavior* (Vol. 19, pp. 189–239). Greenwich, CT: JAI Press.

Weingart, L. R., Olekalns, M., & Smith, P. L. (2004). Quantitative coding of negotiation behavior. *International Negotiation, 9,* 441–455.

RIGHT WING AUTHORITARIANISM

Right wing authoritarianism (RWA) describes a relatively stable dimension of individual differences in social attitudes and beliefs. At the low extreme of this dimension are beliefs and attitudes favoring individual freedom, personal autonomy, social diversity, social novelty, change, and innovation, while the high authoritarian extreme is characterized by beliefs and attitudes that favor maintaining traditional socially conservative values, lifestyles, morality, and religious beliefs; respect and obedience for established laws, norms, and social authorities; and strict, tough, punitive social control.

This dimension also has broader attitudinal implications. Persons low in RWA tend to be ideologically liberal and left wing, favoring the political Left and "progressive" social change; are more open and sympathetic to minorities, immigrants, and foreigners; and oppose nationalism, ethnocentrism, and militarism. Persons high in RWA tend to be more politically conservative and ideologically right wing, oppose social change, and tend to be more nationalistic and ethnocentric, being in particular less favorable to minorities, immigrants, and foreigners in general. This entry looks at the theory of the authoritarian personality and how it is linked to political and ideological conservatism, then examines current trends in this research.

Theory of the Authoritarian Personality

This individual-difference dimension of RWA attitudes was originally identified in the 1930s by social scientists such as Erich Fromm and Wilhelm Reich. They suggested that these attitudes have their psychological basis in a particular kind of personality characterized by underlying needs for strong national authority and hostility to outgroups or minorities. This, they suggested, helped explain the rise of right wing fascist movements and virulent anti-Semitism in Europe at the time. The theory was developed and furnished with some empirical support in 1950 in a classic volume, *The Authoritarian Personality*, by Theodor Adorno, Else Frenkel-Brunswick, Daniel Levinson, and Nevitt Sanford.

Their research showed that prejudiced attitudes, such as anti-Semitism, were not held in isolation but were part of a broader ethnocentric pattern involving a generalized dislike of outgroups and minorities. Together, these attitudes formed part of the broader right wing authoritarian social attitude dimension. The authors classified these authoritarian social attitudes into nine categories or hypothesized traits that they assumed together constituted the authoritarian personality dimension. These nine traits were conventionalism (rigid adherence to conventional middle-class values), authoritarian submission (submissive, uncritical attitudes toward authorities), authoritarian aggression (tendency to condemn, reject, and punish people who violate conventional values), anti-introspection (opposition to the subjective, imaginative, and tender-minded), superstition and stereotypy (belief in mystical determinants of the individual's fate, disposition to think in rigid categories), power and toughness (preoccupation with the dominance–submission, strong–weak, leader–follower dimension; identification with power, strength, toughness), destructiveness and cynicism (generalized hostility, vilification of the human), projectivity (disposition to believe that wild and dangerous things go on in the world; the projection outward of unconscious emotional impulses), and finally an exaggerated concern with sexual goings-on.

Adorno and colleagues' theory of the authoritarian personality suggested that these traits arose from underlying psychodynamic conflicts originating from harsh, punitive parental socialization in early childhood. This was presumed to create underlying feelings of resentment and anger toward parental authority, later generalized to all authority, and feelings that were repressed and replaced by deference and idealization of authority, while the underlying repressed anger and aggression were displaced as hostility toward deviant persons, outgroups, and minorities.

Adorno and his colleagues also developed a psychometric scale to measure this authoritarian personality, which they named the *F scale* (believing the items expressed implicitly profascist sentiments). Research did indeed show that persons scoring high on the F scale were characterized by higher levels of generalized prejudice toward outgroups and minorities and were more ethnocentric, socially conservative, and politically right wing.

This theory attracted enormous attention initially, and the F scale became widely used. Critics, however, noted methodological flaws in the research and pointed out that the theory ignored authoritarianism of the left. The F scale was found to have serious psychometric flaws, most notably the all-positive formulation of its items, so that scores were heavily contaminated by the response style of acquiescence (the general tendency of people to agree rather than disagree). When this was corrected, the items of "balanced" versions of the F scale lacked internal consistency and so could not be measuring a single unitary syndrome or dimension. As a result of this and other nonsupportive findings, interest in the F scale and the theory of the authoritarian personality largely dissipated during the 1960s.

Contemporary Developments: RWA and Social Dominance Orientation

In 1981, an important book by Robert Altemeyer reported the development of a new and psychometrically robust measure of right wing authoritarianism, the RWA scale. Altemeyer succeeded in this by narrowing and refining the concept to just three of the original categories or traits identified by Adorno and colleagues—that is, conventionalism, authoritarian submission, and authoritarian aggression—which correlated together strongly enough to define a single unitary attitudinal dimension.

During the past three decades, the RWA scale has been widely used to measure right wing authoritarianism and has been largely responsible for reviving social scientific interest in the concept and establishing its importance as an individual-difference construct relevant to social behavior. Research by Altemeyer and others has confirmed that the social attitudinal dimension measured by the RWA scale was highly stable in individuals during periods of as long as 20 years and was powerfully associated with right wing political orientation, religious fundamentalism, social traditionalism, resistance to change, preferences for structure and order, and general prejudice against outgroups and minorities. Some research suggests that persons high in RWA are behaviorally less flexible and process social information in a more biased fashion, although other research suggests that this may be so only under stressful or threatening conditions.

Research on RWA has also not supported Adorno and colleagues' earlier hypothesis that these attitudes were formed in early childhood. Instead, Altemeyer's and others' findings suggested that RWA attitudes were largely formed through social learning and personal experiences and crystallized during late adolescence. Despite this, and the finding that these attitudes are generally stable over time, research has also shown that they can be substantially changed by experiences throughout the life cycle. Thus, RWA scale scores decrease substantially with liberal higher education and increase as a result of becoming a parent and being exposed to threats to societal security and stability.

A new development in research on authoritarianism came in the 1990s when Jim Sidanius and Felicia Pratto proposed the concept of social dominance orientation (SDO), which described a second relatively stable dimension of social attitudes in individuals, distinct from RWA. The items of their SDO scale, which measured this dimension, express a general attitudinal preference for intergroup relations to be hierarchical rather than equal, with more powerful groups having the right to dominate weaker ones.

Research has shown that the SDO scale powerfully predicts sociopolitical and intergroup phenomena similar to those predicted by the RWA scale, such as generalized prejudice, intolerance, right wing political party preference, nationalism, punitiveness, and militarism, but it is uncorrelated or only weakly correlated with RWA, indicating that they comprise relatively independent dimensions.

Conclusion

In contrast to the early research of Adorno and colleagues, new findings have shown not just one but two distinct dimensions of authoritarian social attitudes. The original idea that these attitudes are expressions of basic personality has, however, survived. Many contemporary researchers, including Altemeyer himself, have argued that RWA and SDO directly represent two different authoritarian personality dimensions, with RWA a submissive authoritarian personality and SDO a dominant authoritarian personality.

During the past decade, however, this "personality assumption" has been questioned. Critics have pointed out that the RWA and SDO scales consist of items solely assessing social attitudes and that there is no evidence that they measure personality in the sense of behavioral dispositions. Instead it has been argued that RWA and SDO seem to be attitudinal expressions of basic social values, with RWA expressing collective security or conservation values (valuing social stability, tradition, security, cohesion, and order) and SDO expressing enhancement values (valuing power, dominance, achievement, and superiority). This approach helps explain the kinds of social attitudes that constitute each of these dimensions, the relative stability of the beliefs constituting these dimensions in individuals, and their capacity to be changed by exposure to particular social experiences and events (such as social threat in the case of RWA).

John Duckitt

See also Anti-Semitism; Authoritarian Personality; Prejudice; Social Dominance Theory

Further Readings

Adorno, T., Frenkel-Brunswick, E., Levinson, D., & Sanford, N. (1950). *The authoritarian personality.* New York: Harper.

Altemeyer, B. (1981). *Right-wing authoritarianism.* Winnipeg, MB, Canada: University of Manitoba Press.

Altemeyer, B. (1996). *The authoritarian specter.* Cambridge, MA: Harvard University Press.

Altemeyer, B. (1998). The other "authoritarian personality." In M. Zanna (Ed.), *Advances in experimental social psychology* (Vol. 30, pp. 47–92). San Diego, CA: Academic Press.

Duckitt, J. (2001). A dual process cognitive–motivational theory of ideology and prejudice. In M. P. Zanna (Ed.), *Advances in experimental social psychology* (Vol. 33, pp. 41–113). San Diego, CA: Academic Press.

Duckitt, J. (2009). Authoritarianism and dogmatism. In M. Leary & R. Hoyle (Eds.), *Handbook of individual differences in social behavior* (pp. 298–317). New York: Guilford.

Sidanius, J., & Pratto, F. (1999). *Social dominance: An intergroup theory of social hierarchy and oppression.* Cambridge, UK: Cambridge University Press.

RINGELMANN EFFECT

The *Ringelmann effect* is a systematic reduction of individual effort on a task as the number of people performing the task increases. The effect, named after Maximilien Ringelmann, who first reported it in 1913, was described in 1927 by Walther Moede in a German journal on industrial psychology. According to Moede, Ringelmann found that when groups of coworkers pulled on a rope, their collective group performance was inferior to the sum of their abilities to pull it individually. Furthermore, as a group increased in size from one to eight members, the discrepancy between the group's potential and its actual performance increased progressively. Assuming that men pulling a rope individually perform at 100% of their ability, Moede wrote that two-man groups perform at 93% of the average member's pull, three-man groups at 85%, and so on, with eight-man groups pulling with only 49% of the average individual member's ability. In other words, although a group's absolute pull increased with its size, its per-person performance declined.

Ringelmann's original 1913 article, on which Moede's report was based, was not rediscovered until 1986, by David Kravitz and Barbara Martin. They also learned that Ringelmann was a French agricultural engineer (not a German, as was assumed earlier), whose experiments were conducted in the 1880s. Thus, Ringelmann's studies are arguably the earliest truly social-psychological experiments ever performed, although their results were not published until much later (and after Norman Triplett's better known early experiments on social facilitation had been published). Moreover, Ringelmann did not specifically refer to rope pulling when he reported progressive performance declines with increases in group size. He had, however, interpreted his findings as attributable to poor social coordination, whereby the more people (or animals!) one adds to a group, the more likely it is that they will fail to coordinate their efforts effectively, that is, by not pulling at the same time or at the same angle.

The Ingham Project

Although Moede's report was widely cited in the subsequent literature on group performance, no replication of Ringelmann's research was published until 1974, when Alan Ingham, George Levinger, James Graves, and Vaughn Peckham reported a partial confirmation of Ringelmann's effect in two tightly controlled laboratory experiments. Their initial aim was to ascertain the generality of the effect. Having found some confirmation in their Study 1, their Study 2 investigated the relative importance of coordination versus motivation losses. Ingham and colleagues' work was inspired by Ivan Steiner's theorizing about a group's actual productivity, which he postulated is determined by potential productivity minus losses due to faulty process. Steiner identified two types of *process losses*: *coordination loss* and *motivation loss*.

Ingham built a 27-foot-long apparatus that could contain groups of up to six people pulling on a taut rope 1 meter above the ground, from which the force of their pulls was electronically recorded. (Six was the maximum number of pullers whose joint efforts could practically be studied in his laboratory.) Study 1 replicated Ringelmann's decrements for the pulls of two and three coworkers—finding decrements of 9% in two- and 18% in three-person groups—but it found almost no further losses after the addition of a fourth, fifth, or sixth coworker.

Study 2 was therefore designed to eliminate the possibility of coordination losses and thus to estimate the contribution of motivation losses to decrements in individuals' rope pulls. To ascertain this, individual participants (situated in the Number 1 spot in the apparatus) pulled in the presence of five experimenter confederates. The participants pulled in ostensible groups of 1 (alone), 2, 3, 4, 5, or 6 (in random order across subjects) but actually pulled all alone in every instance. Without exception, all participants assumed (as they reported in postsession interviews) they had indeed pulled in groups of six different sizes. Once again, performance declined significantly with the addition of the first and second perceived coworker, but then it leveled off for perceived group sizes of four to six.

This second study, then, found strong evidence for a motivation loss, thus undercutting the sufficiency of the earlier coordination loss explanation. Note, however, that Ingham and colleagues' apparatus required all subjects to pull at the same angle, and their verbal prompts encouraged all subjects to pull at the same time; this may have minimized possible coordination losses. In their conclusions, therefore, Ingham and his coauthors were careful to delimit the context in which their results were obtained and suggested ways in which groups might experience gains rather than losses in their performance.

Later Research

Two contrasting lines of research have followed from the 1974 attempt to replicate Ringelmann. One line of work relabeled the term *motivation loss* as *social loafing* and extended it to other kinds of tasks. For instance, in an early and influential study, Bibb Latané, Kipling Williams, and Stephen Harkins found evidence of social loafing in their carefully designed studies of noise levels when subjects shouted or clapped either singly, in pairs, or in four- or six-member groups. Their per-member performance in Experiment 1 dropped from 100% singly to 71% in pairs, 51% in fours, and 40% in sixes. In their more tightly controlled Experiment 2, it dropped to 66% in pairs and to 33% in six-person groups. Parallel social loafing effects have been found in other laboratory research as well as in real-life social group contexts—such as in Soviet collective farms.

The second line of research has pursued the opposite tack, confirming the possibility of significant increases in group performance under specified conditions. One such motivation gain is the Köhler effect—based on O. Köhler's early research on motivation gains in coworking groups. Essentially, individuals working in a group context may under certain conditions boost their efforts and consequent output either when they feel they are competing with others in a comparative context or when they believe their own effort is indispensable to the group's success.

George Levinger

See also Group Motivation; Group Performance; Köhler Effect; Social Loafing

Further Readings

Ingham, A. G., Levinger, G., Graves, J., & Peckham, V. (1974). The Ringelmann effect: Studies of group size and group performance. *Journal of Experimental Social Psychology, 10,* 371–384.

Kerr, N. L., Seok, D., Sambolec, E. J., Lount, R. B., Jr., & Park, E. S. (2007). Psychological mechanisms underlying the Köhler motivation gain. *Personality and Social Psychology Bulletin, 33,* 828–841.

Kravitz, D. A., & Martin, B. (1986). Ringelmann rediscovered: The original article. *Journal of Personality and Social Psychology, 50,* 936–941.

Latané, B., Williams, K., & Harkins, S. (1979). Many hands make light the work: The causes and consequences of social loafing. *Journal of Personality and Social Psychology, 37,* 822–832.

Moede, W. (1927). Die Richtlinien der Leistungs-Psychologie [Guidelines of performance psychology]. *Industrielle Psychotechnik, 4,* 193–209.

Ringelmann, M. (1913). Recherches sur les moteurs animes: Travail de l'homme [Research on animate sources of power: The work of man]. *Annales de l'Institut National Agronomique, 2e serie-tome XII,* 1–40.

ROLES

In society, people spend much of their lives in groups. In groups, people hold various positions. Tied to these positions are *roles*, which refer to the expectations that guide people's attitudes and behavior. For example, on a college campus, there is the position of student. Tied to the student position are roles or sets of expectations, including learning new knowledge and skills, establishing an area of study, passing courses, acquiring a degree, and so forth, that define what it means to be a student. We learn expectations tied to different positions in society from others, such as our parents, peers, educators, and the media. In general, if we have information about the roles people occupy in a situation, we are in a good position to predict their behavior.

This entry reviews several aspects related to roles. First, some general concepts found in the literature on roles are presented. Then four role theories are identified, along with what is central in each theory. Finally, four role processes that have received attention in the literature are discussed: role-playing, role-taking, role identity, and role differentiation.

General Role Concepts

A social position is a category in society that an individual occupies. These categories are varied.

They can include one's occupation, such as nurse, pastor, or mother. They can refer to the kinds of people it is possible to be in society, such as rebel or intellectual. They also can refer to one's biological attributes, such as being female or young. When a person assumes a position in a situation, certain expectations are attached to the position, and others behave toward the person based on these expectations. It is these expectations that the term *role* designates. For example, the position of friend may include the expectation of being supportive, trustworthy, and loyal. The position of worker may include the expectation of being hardworking, efficient, and responsible.

More than one expectation may be tied to a social position. Furthermore, expectations can be specific or general in the behavior to which they refer. They can require specific performances, or they can simply suggest a script within which much flexibility is possible. For instance, a general expectation of a mother is that she be nurturing. Some women may fulfill this expectation by being physically affectionate while others may fulfill it through encouraging and supportive talk with their child. Expectations also can refer to a minimal part or a large part of one's range of interactions. For example, the role of male carries with it many expectations, such as being dominant and assertive and taking the lead. These expectations will be applicable to a wide range of interactions at home, at school, at work, and with friends. In contrast, the role of fraternity member carries with it expectations that typically are relevant with friends or at school; thus they are applicable to a smaller range of interactions.

Members of a society share the expectations associated with positions. It is through the socialization process that the members learn these expectations. The members of a society cannot be taught the expectations unless there is societal agreement or consensus as to what those expectations are. With consensus, individuals are expected to conform to or abide by those expectations. One way to ensure conformity is for people to verbalize the expectations and pressure others to follow them.

Role Theories

Four major theories on roles have developed: functional role theory, structural role theory, symbolic interactionist role theory, and cognitive role theory. *Functional role theory* developed in the work of the sociologist Talcott Parsons. For functionalists, roles are consensual expectations that guide behavior. In turn, behavior is functional for the maintenance of society. Roles are the shared normative expectations that prescribe and explain people's behavior as they occupy social positions. Individuals learn these normative expectations from others in society and are expected to conform. Conformity to roles helps explain how society remains stable and orderly.

Structural role theory, like functional role theory, considers society as a functional unit. As in functional role theory, roles are defined as patterned behaviors attached to social positions in society. Structural role theory emphasizes the idea that because society is composed of multiple and reciprocal social positions, such as parent–child, employer–employee, teacher–student, and so forth, there are corresponding multiple and reciprocal roles. The structural perspective was influenced by the work of anthropologist Ralph Linton, who made a distinction between *status* (position) and role. Status is a set of rights and duties, and a role represents the implementation of those rights and duties in interaction. For Linton, status and role are inseparable. One cannot exist without the other.

Symbolic interactionist role theory examines roles not from the point of view of society, as functional or structural role theory do, but from the point of view of the individual. Roles are expectations, but they may be heavily laden with norms, demands as to how to behave in a specific situation, and the evolving definition of the situation as understood by the actor. This perspective was influenced by the work of Erving Goffman and his concept of dramaturgy.

Goffman viewed social interaction as analogous to a theater in which actors have a script that they play out in front of an audience. Individuals take on roles in an interaction in the same way that actors take on their parts in a play. For Goffman, roles are the activities individuals would enact if they abided by the normative demands of a position. This is different from role performance, which is the actual conduct of an individual based on the person's interpretation of the role.

Cognitive role theory, like symbolic interactionist theory, addresses roles from the point of view of the individual. The emphasis is on the expectations associated with roles. Theorists examine the social factors that give rise to the expectations, how these expectations are perceived by individuals, how these expectations can be measured, and the relationship between expectations and behavior. Bruce Biddle, one cognitive role theorist, has maintained that role expectations can appear in societal norms, preferences, and beliefs. In this way, role expectations are much more pervasive in society than simply being associated with societal positions.

The macro orientation to roles in functional and structural role theory and the micro orientation to roles in symbolic interactionist and cognitive role theory can be integrated into a general theory of roles. At one level, we can see how the patterns of behavior across individuals create general patterns that constitute the social structure and social order. At another level, we can see how roles guide behavior in interaction for any one individual. Both levels of analysis are important in understanding roles.

Role Processes

Four important role processes have captured the attention of many researchers: role-playing, role-taking, role identity, and role differentiation. Role-playing emerged out of cognitive role theory, role-taking and role identity developed out of symbolic interactionist role theory, and role differentiation developed out of functional role theory.

Role-Playing

Role-playing, a term coined by psychologist Jacob Moreno, involves imitating behaviors that are associated with a social position. Role-playing is a basic strategy for learning roles. It appears spontaneously in the behaviors of children and grows in complexity as the child matures. When children role-play, they gain important information about how to perform a role. For instance, children may learn to play the role of mother by first observing their mother feeding, cleaning, and clothing her children. By imitating these observed behaviors while playing "house" with their friends, the children obtain a better understanding as to what is involved in the role of mother.

Role-playing has been used as a technique in laboratory studies to simulate difficult group situations to which researchers would not otherwise have access. For example, in the well-known Stanford Prison Experiment, Philip Zimbardo and his colleagues had Stanford University undergraduates play the roles of prisoners and guards to simulate the prison environment and study the interaction among guards and inmates. Within a short time, participants in the simulation found themselves deeply involved in their roles. Guards became hostile, and the prisoners became psychologically fragile. The researchers had to end the experiment before the scheduled deadline because of the emerging psychological harm to the participants. This study demonstrated that when individuals identify with their roles and play them out, they can closely approximate what happens in groups.

Role-Taking

The social philosopher George Herbert Mead made an important contribution to the study of roles by highlighting the process of role-taking, or taking the perspective of others into account in interaction. Individuals put themselves in the place of others and see the world as the others see it. Mead maintained that role-taking was crucial in the development of the self. Specifically, as we take the view of others into account and see things from others' vantage point, we come to see how others view us and to view ourselves in a similar manner. When individuals evaluate themselves in the same way as others evaluate them, a *self* has emerged. Role-taking facilitates not only self-development but also coordinated interaction. In seeing things through others' eyes, individuals are able to anticipate responses of others and adjust their own behavior accordingly.

Role-taking has cognitive and affective aspects. In *cognitive role-taking*, the individual infers another's thoughts, motives, or intentions. In *affective role-taking*, a person infers the emotional state of another. Some have defined affective role-taking to involve empathy, which is feeling what another is feeling. In general, it is better to infer what others are thinking *and* feeling than to infer what they are thinking *or* feeling. In taking into account the cognitive and emotional dimensions of others, observers have more information by which to gauge their own response in the situation.

Role-taking also varies along the dimensions of accuracy, range, and depth. In the first instance, one may take the role of others but not correctly discern others' thoughts or feelings. One may simply "project" onto others what one is thinking rather than accurately identifying the thoughts and motives of others. Role-taking range has to do with people's ability to infer the thoughts and feelings of a wide variety of people. Such individuals may be able to identify the views and emotions of both men and women, for instance. Finally, role-taking depth is the ability of individuals to infer what others are thinking and feeling across a range of areas in their lives. More generally, it is grasping another's total worldview. It is understanding others in depth and in detail.

Within groups, role-taking facilitates communication, a shared understanding within the group, and coordinated activity. If problems emerge in the group, acknowledging others' perspectives can ease conflict and tension. Role-taking is also an important mechanism for social control in a group. If a group member decides to engage in counternormative behavior, taking the role of other group members and inferring that their reaction will be negative may lead the group member to avoid enacting the counternormative behavior. Thus, persons inhibit behaviors they think the group will disapprove of and choose behaviors that support and maintain the group's goals.

Role Identity

Most interaction in groups is not between whole people but between the different aspects of people having to do with their roles. For each role a person holds, there is a corresponding identity associated with it. Thus, people have role identities. A role identity consists of the meanings and expectations individuals claim for themselves while in a role. In other words, what does it mean to a person to be a student, a friend, or a worker? These meanings and expectations individuals attribute to themselves while in a role become their role identity standards. These role identity standards guide their behavior while playing out their roles in situations.

As there are roles and counterroles in situations, there are also identities and counteridentities.

When one claims a role identity in a situation, there is an alternative role identity claimed by another to which it is related. For example, in the role of student, the student identity is enacted as it relates to the corresponding counterrole of teacher. Similarly, the husband identity is played out in a situation as it relates to the wife identity, and so forth. Sometimes, one's expectations associated with a role identity may differ from the expectations others associate with that role identity in the situation. When this happens, individuals may discuss these differences and compromise on a set of expectations so that interaction can proceed.

Because individuals hold multiple roles in society, they have multiple role identities. The many role identities individuals claim are organized in a hierarchy. The role identities highest in the hierarchy of role identities are those that individuals are most likely to play out across situations. Individuals are more committed to these identities in the sense that the number of people they are connected to through having the particular identity is large, and the connection to these others is strong. For example, those who are more committed to the student identity should be tied to many others based on this identity, and the ties with those others should be deep.

The successful enactment of role identities in groups activates a sense of self-efficacy. Individuals see that they are effective in living out the expectations set by their role identity standards. They gain a sense of control over their environment and confidence in their own abilities. For this reason, claiming and playing out role identities in groups is an important source of feeling good about the self.

Role Differentiation

Leadership role differentiation, an idea developed by Robert F. Bales and Philip E. Slater, refers to the emergence in groups of two specialized leadership roles: a *task leader* and a *socioemotional leader*. The task leader is often the person who provides the best guidance and ideas toward the attainment of the group's goals. In an effort to get things done, however, the task leader may be pushy and openly antagonistic. Although this person makes an impact on the group's opinion, his or her assertive behavior may create tension in the group. Thus, a socioemotional leader emerges to ease the tension and soothe hurt feelings in the group. This person might tell a joke at the right moment or provide emotional support to someone whose feelings were hurt. The person helps release tension and maintain good spirits within the group. This is often the best-liked member of the group. Thus, we have the development of leadership into two distinct roles played by different individuals.

Later research on task and socioemotional role differentiation revealed that role differentiation does not always occur in groups. It tends not to occur when the leader is given the authority to lead in the group and when the task activity is seen as legitimate. When an experimenter appoints a person to be the leader in a group, thus giving the person the authority to lead, role differentiation is less likely to occur than when the leader is not authorized by the experimenter. Role differentiation also is less likely to occur when the task activity of the group is accepted, such that group members interact as if there is a "task ethic" (performing the task that is asked of them, arriving at conclusions, obtaining a consensus, etc.). Under leadership legitimacy and task legitimacy, fewer group members challenge the leader's role or the task activity. This leads to fewer problems in the group, and thus there is less need for a socioemotional leader.

Early research on the family applied the concept of role differentiation to men's and women's specialized roles in the home. Men took on the task or instrumental role by financially providing for the family through work in the labor force, and women assumed the socioemotional, or expressive, role by being the primary caretaker. This division of labor was functional for the maintenance and continuation of the family.

Alice Eagly has argued that given the specific roles that women and men occupy in the family and in society more generally, we come to have different expectations for them. This is her *social role theory* for understanding *gender roles* in society. She argued that the content of gender roles involves attributing communal characteristics to women and agentic characteristics to men. *Communal characteristics* reflect a concern with the welfare of others. They involve affection, interpersonal sensitivity, and nurturance. *Agentic characteristics* involve assertion, control, and confidence. These characteristics are consistent with the greater investment of women in the domestic role and the greater investment of men in the worker role.

Jan E. Stets and Yvonne Thai

See also Gender Roles; Group Structure; Leadership; Norms; Role Transitions; Symbolic Interactionism

Further Readings

Biddle, B. J. (1986). Recent developments in role theory. *Annual Review of Sociology, 12,* 67–92.

Biddle, B. J., & Thomas, E. J. (1966). *Role theory: Concepts and research.* New York: Wiley.

Eagly, A. H. (1987). *Sex differences in social behavior: A social-role interpretation.* Hillsdale, NJ: Erlbaum.

Stryker, S., & Statham, A. (1985). Symbolic interaction and role theory. In G. Lindzey & E. Aronson (Eds.), *Handbook of social psychology* (pp. 311–378). New York: Random House.

ROLE TRANSITIONS

A role refers to the normative expectations associated with a position in a social system. *Role transitions* refer to the psychological and, if relevant, physical movements between positions within or between social systems, including disengagement from one role (*role exit*) and engagement in another role (*role entry*). This process includes *macro role transitions* between sequential roles, such as a high school student's becoming a university student, and *micro role transitions* between simultaneous roles, such as a woman's shifting subtly between her roles of wife and mother at the dinner table.

Although most research focuses on either role exit or role entry, the nature of each can strongly influence the other. For example, an involuntary layoff can impair one's acceptance of the role of retiree, and a transfer to a better school can ease the pain of leaving school friends behind. Also, role transitions involve what Victor Turner refers to as *liminality*, wherein a person is temporarily between roles, and the psychological grip of each is reduced. Liminality allows time and psychological space to make sense of the old before having to fully embrace the new, and it allows new ways of thinking, feeling, and acting to percolate.

This entry discusses role entry and role exit in the context of macro transitions, in which an individual goes from outsider to insider and vice versa, and then considers micro transitions.

Macro Role Transitions

According to the work of Blake Ashforth, role transitions are particularly difficult if they are of high magnitude (the new role differs greatly from the old, such as a shift from a nonsupervisory to a supervisory role), socially undesirable (e.g., imprisonment), involuntary (e.g., job demotion), unpredictable (the nature of the transition is hard to anticipate, such as a minor league athlete awaiting a call-up to the majors), individual rather than collective (the person goes through the process without the benefit of peers), or irreversible (e.g., becoming a parent) and if the transition period is short (leaving little time to prepare for exit and entry, such as suddenly being widowed). The more difficult the transition, the less likely the newcomer will be effective and satisfied in the new role and its associated group.

Role Entry

Regardless of how difficult the transition may be, role entry typically involves a period of mutual adjustment between the individual and the group. As Richard Moreland and John Levine have put it, newcomers tend to enter as *quasi-members* and become *full members*—with "all of the privileges and responsibilities associated with group membership"—only when they are socialized and accepted by the group. Accordingly, the group tends to exert a large impact on the individual. Because it is hard for the individual to anticipate the demands and nuances of the new role and the group(s) within which it is embedded, entry often fosters surprise and uncertainty, which motivate the new member to learn about the situation.

Elizabeth Morrison has stated that learning focuses on technical information about how to perform tasks, referent information about role expectations, social information about other people and one's relationships with them, appraisal information about how one is evaluated, normative information about the group's nature, and political information about the distribution and use of power and status. Because newcomers are naïve and lack credibility, they are predisposed to adapt to the situation in order to fit in. Thus, individuals tend to be most amenable to personal change when they first enter a new situation. To that end, groups may actively socialize newcomers through some mix of mentors, initiation rites, training, "on the job" trial and error, and observation of senior members.

As for the flipside of the mutual adjustment—the individual's impact on the group—individuals often take the initiative to learn about the situation and to shape it more to their own wants and needs. The more experience, knowledge, and skill they bring to the new role, the more leeway they are usually allowed to modify the role. Through seeking information about the status quo, seeking feedback about their behavior and performance, building relationships, negotiating with group members about their mutual expectations, and modifying the role directly, newcomers can influence the role and the group.

The result of this mutual adjustment between newcomer and group is that role entry is typically a combination of personal change in the newcomer, role modification, and group change. Although some theoretical models view personal change and role change as opposite poles on a continuum (either the newcomer changes or the role does), research suggests that they are relatively independent: Adjustment may reflect little personal and role change, much change in both, or change in one but not the other. Nigel Nicholson has argued that the more discretion a newcomer has and the more novel the role is to him or her, the more likely that adjustment will entail both personal change and role modification (and presumably group change).

Research on the *ABCs of role entry*, summarized by Ashforth, indicates that newcomers can feel (*A* for affect), act (*B* for behavior), or think (*C* for cognition) their way into becoming comfortable with their new role. For example, newcomers can identify with a role or group long before becoming able to act as competent members, and this identification may motivate role-consistent behavior; conversely, as newcomers begin enacting their new role, they may come to feel more at home in it and see themselves as bona fide members (what Robert Granfield termed "making it by faking it"). The ABCs are mutually reinforcing such that positive adjustment is a meld of thinking of oneself as a member, feeling comfortable in the role, and performing it effectively. An important element in this process is *social validation*, in which one's peers and other relevant individuals (e.g., group leader, external audiences) respond positively to how one enacts the role, to the *role markers* (e.g., attire, grooming) one displays, and to one's performance outcomes. Validation, in short, involves recognizing and treating newcomers as legitimate members.

Finally, role transitions *within* a group should be mentioned briefly. Movement between positions within a group is less common than movement between groups. Examples of the former include a group member's assuming the role of group leader, treasurer, or social events organizer. Because the group member in question is already known to the other members, the period of mutual adjustment is usually short. However, because the initial intragroup relationships were predicated on the member's original role, the transition to the new role typically requires some recalibration of the relationships. For example, it may prove somewhat awkward if one's peer suddenly becomes one's supervisor.

Role Exit

A role exit can be voluntary or involuntary. Involuntary exit occurs when a group decides to remove a member from a role, typically because of task or social problems. In Harold Garfinkel's words, a *degradation ceremony*, such as being fired from a job, may be used to formally strip the role from the person, thereby communicating the separation to the individual and the group and reaffirming the values and standards of the role for remaining members. However, members often do not have the power to terminate peers in groups that lack a formal structure. Instead, more subtle actions on behalf of the group can coerce a member to leave, such as ostracizing the individual or revoking benefits that make the role desirable.

Voluntary role exits are more complex because of the role of choice in the process. This discussion of voluntary exits is adapted from Helen Rose Fuchs Ebaugh's landmark work. Voluntary role exits often begin when certain events—disappointments, external changes (e.g., relocating for a spouse's job, seizing a sudden opportunity), milestones, and internal events (e.g., growing job burnout)—prompt doubts about the role or group. If the doubts persist, the individual may search for information to confirm or disconfirm them. However, the stronger the doubts, the more likely that he or she will seek—and therefore find—confirmation. Incidents that may have aroused little notice earlier may become imbued with meaning, and the doubts may spread from specific concerns to general ones. The individual may turn to trusted others both inside and outside the group for impartial advice, and depending on their responses, the doubts may be weakened or strengthened. However, if the doubts are strong, the individual is likely to seek others who will simply reinforce them. The individual may even act provocatively (e.g., complaining, breaking rules) to precipitate a reaction from the group, thereby bringing the issue to a head.

As doubts crystallize, the individual may seek and weigh alternatives. Often, the alternatives must outweigh the strong pull of inertia, personal ties, sunk costs (e.g., time invested), and so on. Where the transition is counternormative (e.g., dropping out of school), knowledge of others who have traveled the same road may normalize the transition. The more attractive the feasible alternatives, the more likely the role exit. If the individual is leaning toward exit, his or her psychological focus may shift from the current role to the anticipated one. Indeed, psychological exit almost always precedes physical exit in the case of voluntary role transitions (although psychological exit may well continue into the new role as one strives to make sense of the experience). Even with a concrete alternative in hand, a turning point—typically a further event such as a new disappointment—is often required to precipitate a break with the role and to justify that break to others. Indeed, a seemingly insignificant event can serve as a last straw. For example, Ebaugh reported that a convent's decision to forbid smoking triggered the exit of a nun, even though she was not a smoker: The rule symbolized the disconnect between her values and those of the convent.

A farewell party or other rite of separation may be used to mark the transition and help the individual and group reach closure. By a celebration of individual discontinuity, social continuity is preserved. Finally, the individual needs to come to terms with the role experience and fold it into his or her ongoing life narrative. Ebaugh referred to this process as constructing an *ex role* (e.g., alumnus).

Although voluntary role exit has been described here in fairly linear and rational terms, it should be noted that the process is fraught with emotion, bias, and contradiction and may involve iterations of the various steps. Role exits are typically associated with ambivalence because the individual may experience relief at resolving his or her doubts, excitement and apprehension at the prospect of beginning anew, guilt at abandoning role obligations, and grief at leaving peers. Thomas Schmid and Richard Jones found that even prison inmates felt somewhat ambivalent about their impending release from prison.

Micro Role Transitions

Unlike macro role transitions, micro transitions tend to be temporary and recurrent, involving the juggling of simultaneous roles, such as mother, stockbroker, gym member, and so on. According to Christena Nippert-Eng and Ashforth, a given pair of roles can be arrayed on a continuum ranging from highly segmented to highly integrated. Highly segmented roles tend to have little similarity in their goals, values, beliefs, norms, interaction styles, and time horizons, and there tends to be little overlap in the physical location or the membership of the respective groups.

Accordingly, highly segmented roles, such as mother and stockbroker, have boundaries that are relatively inflexible (i.e., tied to specific settings and times) and impermeable (i.e., permit few cross-role interruptions). Segmentation decreases the blurring between role identities and reinforces the role boundaries. The mother does not cease being a mother while at work; however, the role of mother is not usually salient. Generally, the greater the segmentation between two roles, the greater the contrast in their identities. Indeed, the stockbroker role may occasionally induce the woman to act in quite unmotherlike ways. Because of the relatively inflexible and impermeable role boundaries, high segmentation increases the magnitude of the role transition. The person must exit the stockbroker

role and enter the mother role, crossing the boundaries. Boundary crossing is facilitated by personal and collective rites of passage that signal a change in roles (e.g., turning off the office equipment and driving home). As with macro transitions, boundary crossing entails liminality while the woman suspends her role as a stockbroker, unwinds from her workday, and prepares to reengage with her family in the role of mother. Micro role transitions tend to become easier over time as individuals develop routines for transitioning between roles.

Conversely, highly integrated roles, such as a son's working in the family business, tend to have similar identities, be embedded in similar contexts, and overlap in the physical location and the membership of the respective groups. Accordingly, highly integrated roles have relatively flexible and permeable boundaries, and each role may interrupt the other unpredictably. The son may interact with his mother in terms of both their family relationship (son–mother) and their work relationship (employee–manager), with the focus oscillating between the two. As this example suggests, high integration decreases the magnitude of the role transition; indeed, the transitions tend to be frequent, perhaps irregular and unpredictable, and involve little conscious awareness. However, integration increases role blurring and thus confusion as to which role is operating. The challenge that individuals face in integrated roles, then, is to create and maintain artificial boundaries to reduce the role blurring to tolerable levels. Thus, the son may insist that the family not talk business when at home.

Blake E. Ashforth and Kristie M. Rogers

See also Group Socialization; Inclusion/Exclusion; Initiation Rites; Multiple Identities; Organizations; Personnel Turnover; Roles

Further Readings

Ashforth, B. E. (2001). *Role transitions in organizational life: An identity-based perspective*. Mahwah, NJ: Erlbaum.

Ebaugh, H. R. F. (1988). *Becoming an ex: The process of role exit*. Chicago: University of Chicago Press.

Garfinkel, H. (1956). Conditions of successful degradation ceremonies. *American Journal of Sociology, 61*, 420–424.

Granfield, R. (1991). Making it by faking it: Working-class students in an elite academic environment. *Journal of Contemporary Ethnography, 20,* 331–351.

Moreland, R. L., & Levine, J. M. (1984). Role transitions in small groups. In V. L. Allen & E. van de Vliert (Eds.), *Role transitions: Explorations and explanations* (pp. 181–195). New York: Plenum.

Morrison, E. W. (1995). Information usefulness and acquisition during organizational encounter. *Management Communication Quarterly, 9,* 131–155.

Nicholson, N. (1984). A theory of work role transitions. *Administrative Science Quarterly, 29,* 172–191.

Nippert-Eng, C. E. (1996). *Home and work: Negotiating boundaries through everyday life.* Chicago: University of Chicago Press.

Schmid, T. J., & Jones, R. S. (1993). Ambivalent actions: Prison adaptation strategies of first-time, short-term inmates. *Journal of Contemporary Ethnography, 21,* 439–463.

Turner, V. W. (1969). *The ritual process: Structure and anti-structure.* Chicago: Aldine.

ROMANCE OF LEADERSHIP

Leadership is one of the most discussed, studied, and written about topics in our society. Should it be? The *romance of leadership* (ROL) is an attributional approach to leadership that attempts to understand when and why we recognize and give credit to leaders for influencing and changing our institutions and societies. First introduced by leadership scholar James R. Meindl and colleagues, this approach highlights the fact that leaders and leadership issues often become the favored explanations for both positive and negative outcomes in organizations. In addition, subsequent research has demonstrated that people value performance results more highly when those results are attributed to leadership and that a halo effect exists for leadership: If an individual is perceived to be an effective leader, his or her personal shortcomings and poor organizational performance may be overlooked. This entry defines the ROL perspective and then turns to implications and critiques of this approach.

The Theory

Based on a series of studies, the ROL suggests that we overwhelmingly tend to favor leaders and leadership as the causal force behind the activities and outcomes of organizations. In part, a critical response to a prevailing emphasis on the importance of *leaders* in the leadership process (as opposed to an emphasis on followers or the situation), the ROL theory was developed to call attention to the fact that whatever the "true" impact of leaders and leadership in organizations and societies, leadership as a concept has attained an immense—and perhaps often unwarranted—popularity in our understanding of the world. Simply stated, despite centuries of study and decades of formal research, the concept of leadership remains largely elusive and resistant to attempts to unravel its mystique. Yet we continue to believe in its import and efficacy, even in situations in which we have no direct evidence to support this belief.

The ROL was introduced as one of the first explicitly *follower*-centric approaches in an effort to balance the many leader-centric approaches that dominated leadership research and practice. Meindl pointed out that leadership had attained a seemingly heroic, larger-than-life status and urged us to consider the implications of relaxing the often taken-for-granted assumption that leadership is important in its own right. Particularly in light of the growing appreciation of external factors and the surrounding environment in which organizations operate, he suggested that we need to question and systematically explore the value and significance of leadership in modern organizations.

The ROL approach helps highlight and question the esteem, prestige, charisma, and heroism attached to various forms of leadership. In addition, the vast majority of research and popular business attention has focused on leadership as a positive force on followers and society. As a result, the ROL perspective questions our collective fascination with leadership and our emphasis on heroism, charisma, and the glorification of leadership in the face of any real evidence that a given leader is really worthy of such praise.

Implications of the ROL Approach

Leadership Portrayals in the Media

The ROL is often reflected in the images of leaders that are produced in the mass media. More often than not, leaders are presented in the form of portraits of successful individuals or images of great leadership figures, and popular leadership books are touted as never-before-revealed secrets of leadership effectiveness. These images reflect our appetite as a society for leadership products and behaviors that promise to enrich and improve our lives. In addition, such compelling images of leadership appeal to our cultural fascination with the power of leadership and serve to fixate us on the personas and characteristics of leaders themselves (especially high-profile leaders). However, this one-sided emphasis on the positive forms of leadership can be dangerous, for it suggests that leaders are inherently positive forces for individuals, organizations, and humanity as a whole.

Exploring previous writing and scholarship on leadership provides an important window into our beliefs, both as individuals and as a society, about the topic: what constitutes leadership, why it is important, what makes it successful, and what decisions or assumptions we make about the effects of leadership. Our basic assumptions about leadership are influenced by how it is defined and discussed in popular books and media and by the types of leadership that are both publicly idealized and sometimes demonized as well. An analysis of popular leadership books, for example, reveals that leaders are seen as effecting change, possessing great experience and knowledge, and providing their followers with opportunities to reach their unique potential. These conceptualizations all fit our cultural stereotypes of "great" leadership. The ROL perspective encourages us to question and debate the functions that leadership serves within society, as well as the broader trends that inform our discussion about what leadership is, what good leadership looks like, and how we decide whether a leader has truly made an impact.

Followers and Followership

The ROL also draws attention to followers' perceptions of leadership as worthy of study in their own right, in parallel to or independent of how the leader actually behaves. As a result, the theory has fostered research into the needs of followers and situational factors that may create greater or lesser susceptibilities to leadership. In addition, the theory emphasizes that followers socially construct images of leadership, meaning that the interactions among followers about a leader may be just as important as the actual behaviors of the leader in understanding the leadership process. As a result, researchers have examined issues such as how leadership influence spreads among followers, even in cases in which followers have had no direct contact with or exposure to a leader. Specifically, understanding followers' emotional reactions to a leader plays an important role in followers' conclusions about whether their leader is an effective or "good" leader, worthy of extravagant stock options or a vote to remain in political power.

Another important implication of the ROL approach is that sense-making processes are integral to understanding leadership and may help us understand why leadership is so enigmatic. Stated more simply, individuals learn what leadership is and what to make of leadership behaviors through their interactions with one another. Followers' decisions to attribute leadership to an individual are to a large extent the result of their interactions and communications with each other, in which they share information about the leader and compare one another's views about what his or her behavior means. Followers are thus viewed as active, powerful players in the leadership process and not passive, compliant, obedient "sheep" at the mercy of their leaders. In addition, followers' psychological needs, ideas about what leadership should look like, and decisions about what leaders are responsible for all play crucial yet underexamined roles in the leadership process.

The ROL perspective also provides another view on charismatic leadership, suggesting that *charisma* is itself a socially constructed phenomenon that says as much about followers and the situation as it does about leaders. For example, Meindl found that individuals in leadership roles are perceived to be more charismatic to the extent that the organization they lead undergoes a crisis turnaround (e.g., moving from loss to profit) rather than a crisis decline (e.g., moving from profit to loss). In addition, attributions of charisma to a leader are not solely grounded in the direct interactions between leaders and followers but rather are strongly impacted by followers' interactions with their peers as well.

Through this approach, we can more readily understand why there are so many discrepancies in perceptions of charisma and a given leader's charismatic appeal. We can also examine how followers vary in their susceptibility both to the belief in the efficacy of leadership and to the charisma of a leader. For example, research suggests that the first followers to succumb to the charismatic "virus" are likely to be high in agreeableness and emotional intensity. In addition, this approach highlights the importance of one's social network in understanding perceptions of leadership and suggests that those who are more central and connected to others are more likely to spread charismatic appeal to others.

Critiques of the ROL Theory

Despite efforts to characterize it as such, Meindl continually pointed out that the ROL perspective was not antileadership but simply an alternative to most existing theories and perspectives that place great weight on the leaders themselves and assume that leaders' actions all have equal importance and significance. Thus, the ROL perspective does not reject or minimize the importance of leaders in leadership but simply argues that it is easier to believe in leadership than it is to prove it. In addition, Meindl pointed out that we need to continually question the prevailing emphasis on leaders to the detriment of followers. Overall, the ROL suggests that we need to complement existing leader-centered approaches with more follower-centered approaches and take into account the social-psychological processes among followers in understanding the leadership phenomenon.

Michelle C. Bligh and Jeffrey C. Kohles

See also Charismatic Leadership; Great Person Theory of Leadership; Leadership; Personality Theories of Leadership; Transactional Leadership Theories

Further Readings

Bligh, M. C., & Meindl, J. R. (2004). The cultural ecology of leadership: An analysis of popular leadership books. In D. M. Messick & R. M. Kramer (Eds.), *The psychology of leadership: New perspectives and research* (pp. 11–52). Mahwah, NJ: Erlbaum.

Shamir, B., Pillai, R., Bligh, M. C., & Uhl-Bien, M. (Eds.). (2007). *Follower-centered perspectives on leadership: A tribute to the memory of James R. Meindl.* Greenwich, CT: Information Age.

Meindl, J. R. (1990). On leadership: An alternative to the conventional wisdom. In B. M. Staw & L. L. Cummings (Eds.), *Research in organizational behavior* (Vol. 12, pp. 159–203). Greenwich, CT: JAI Press.

Meindl, J. R. (1995). The romance of leadership as a follower-centric theory: A social constructionist approach. *Leadership Quarterly, 6*(3), 329–341.

Meindl, J. R. (1998). Thanks—And let me try again. In F. Dansereau & F. J. Yammarino (Eds.), *Leadership: The multiple-level approaches, Part B. Contemporary and alternative* (pp. 321–326). Stamford, CT: JAI Press.

Meindl, J. R., Ehrlich, S. B., & Dukerich, J. M. (1985). The romance of leadership. *Administrative Science Quarterly, 30*, 78–102.

RUMOR

A *rumor* is an unverified account or explanation of an event that is transmitted from person to person. Rumors may be transmitted for specific reasons, such as to blame a person or group member for a particular action or to harm a reputation. However, rumors can also provide useful information in ambiguous situations.

At a group level, sharing information in the form of rumors can enhance group cohesion and strengthen emotional ties within the group. At an individual level, sharing rumors can help reduce stress due to uncertainty. Although rumors can be transmitted without distortion of the original account, they often become distorted as they are passed on from person to person. In the case of rumors about groups, the information that survives in distorted rumor transmission is most likely to be information that is consistent with preexisting group stereotypes.

History and Background

One of the first psychological examinations of rumor was a study conducted by Gordon Allport and Joseph Leo Postman in 1945. In this study, participants were asked to describe an illustration to another person who had not seen the illustration. Then the recipient of the description was asked to reproduce it for another person and so on for several retellings of the description. Each participant's account was recorded. Allport and Postman found that many of the features of the original message disappeared as the message was passed along the chain of recipients. In particular, approximately 70% of the details of the message were lost in the first five or six transmissions. Similar findings occurred across many different types of pictures with different settings and contents.

Allport and Postman described three processes that occur in rumor transmission. The first—*leveling*—refers to the process whereby the rumor becomes shorter and less complex, a process that happens quickly. The second—*sharpening*—refers to the process whereby certain features of the rumor are selected for transmission and are often exaggerated. Finally, *assimilation* refers to the distortion of the information as a result of subconscious motivations, attitudes, and prejudices. There is some empirical support for this three-part process. For example, in 1951 T. M. Higham found evidence for distortion of messages transmitted from person to person in a laboratory setting. However, it was found that this was the case only for messages that did not affect participants' interests. For *ego-involved* messages that did affect participants' interests, the transmissions were less distorted.

More recent research also suggests that a rumor will not always be a distorted account of the original information and depends on other factors. In particular, the results of studies not based in laboratories show much less distortion of rumors than in Allport and Postman's study. Further, the amount of rumor distortion appears to be dependent on the recipients' anxiety and whether recipients take a critical or uncritical approach to the content of the message. Information contained in rumors can reduce anxiety in the face of uncertainty. People therefore transmit rumors in part to reduce stress in ambiguous situations. However, people can also take a critical or uncritical approach to the information contained in the message. If recipients take a critical approach, the rumor will not be distorted and may even be refined. On the other hand, when recipients take an uncritical approach, it is more likely that the rumor will become distorted. This is particularly likely in crisis situations, in which people are unable to attend to the information as closely as they normally might.

The Social Functions of Rumor

Rumor and Motives

Rumors are often initiated and elaborated for a reason. That is, the source of the rumor typically has an ulterior motive in passing it on to others. One reason is to harm the reputation of an individual or group. For example, a group member can propagate a rumor about another group so that the other group appears in a negative light to others; this increases the likelihood that the group will be disliked. In this respect, spreading a negative rumor about one group can enhance the position of the group responsible for the rumor. A group can also spread a rumor that blames another group for a significant event or wrongdoing. In this case, blame may be deflected from the ingroup, and the reputation of the target outgroup can be significantly tarnished.

In more extreme cases, spreading rumors about groups and group members can notably affect intergroup relations, provoke conflict, or reinforce group status hierarchies. A good example of this was the prevalence in the late 1800s and early 1900s of race-related rumors in which Blacks were frequently accused of crimes and put to death by illegal lynch mobs. These atrocities were based largely on hearsay and rumor for which no evidence was offered. Of course, the spreading of rumors also occurs at a more innocuous level and is commonly known as *gossip*, *idle talk*, or rumor about the private affairs of others. However, although the information transmitted in this manner is typically trivial, it can also be the result of a malicious attempt to undermine another person (or group member), harm the person's reputation, or worse.

Rumor and Information Sharing

People devote a great deal of attention to gathering and sharing information about themselves and others. This information is very important. By understanding the self and others, people are more able to function in the social world. Rumor is a vital part of this information-gathering and information-sharing process. It can also help forge social cohesion and emotional bonds within a group. The evolutionary psychologist Robin Dunbar suggests that people spend about 60% of their conversations gossiping about their own lives and those of others. Dunbar also argues that rumor and gossip are the human equivalent of social grooming among primates, which actually reduces stress and stimulates the immune system. Another, related function of gossip and rumor is that people use them to cope with and explain situations beyond their control. Some research carried out in organizational settings demonstrates that rumors thrive in contexts in which there is an absence of trust. For example, in unstable organizational settings containing distinct groups (e.g., manager, worker) with different agendas, rumor transmission can help people come to terms with their own position within the group.

Receiving rumors also gives people information about what is happening within the group. This information helps them keep in touch with their groups, which facilitates their survival within the group. Being out of touch means that people do not have the fundamental social knowledge they may need in order to understand and function within their group. Also, propagating rumors performs important social functions for the sender. In particular, being the source of a rumor within a group places the sender in a position of being a source of useful information that the group can use to answer questions and solve problems. This therefore identifies the person as a valuable member of the group.

Because social knowledge is so fundamental to social relationships, rumor can be characterized as a collective explanation process. In 2004, Prashant Bordia and Nicholas DiFonzo carried out a study that supports this idea. They analyzed a set of archived Internet message board discussions containing rumors. It was found that the plurality of the statements (nearly 30%) could be coded as sense-making statements, which in particular involved attempts to understand a social process or solve a problem. Bordia and DiFonzo also found that each rumor went through a specific pattern of development in which a rumor was introduced for discussion, then information about the rumor was volunteered and discussed, and finally a resolution was arrived at or interest in the rumor was lost. Rumors therefore performed the important social functions of information sharing and sense-making, and once those functions were achieved, the rumors were no longer interesting.

Rumor and Stereotype Communication

When passing information about group members on to others, people can choose to transmit stereotype-consistent or stereotype-inconsistent information. What types of information people choose to transmit about groups has implications for how rumors about groups are spread. Yoshihisa Kashima and colleagues have carried out a program of research using the *serial reproduction* paradigm, in which participants are asked to tell a story about a person to another participant, who then tells the story to another participant, and so on for a small number of retellings of the story. Results demonstrate that communicators generally pass on more stereotype-consistent information than stereotype-inconsistent information. For example, in one study, in which participants were asked to retell a story containing gender-stereotypical and counterstereotypical information, more gender-stereotypical details than counterstereotypical details were transmitted. Researchers argue that this is one way in which stereotypes and prejudice are perpetuated. In terms of rumors, this finding can therefore potentially have negative consequences. One example is how rumors of violence, rape, and looting spread after the 2005 tragedy of Hurricane Katrina in New Orleans, Louisiana. Details of these stereotypical behaviors of people in disaster situations were transmitted widely across the media although later evidence suggested that most of these reports were based on unfounded rumors. The spread of these wild rumors did very little good for race relations in the city.

Further research shows that transmission of information about groups is also dependent on the extent to which people feel as though they share beliefs in common with the people they are communicating to. If people perceive that they share common beliefs with others, then they are more likely to pass information on. Rumors about groups therefore may be transmitted to the extent to which people think that others will endorse the rumor.

Widespread Rumors: Conspiracy Theories

A good example of widespread rumor transmission is the phenomenon of conspiracy theories. Scholars characterize *conspiracy theories* as attempts to explain the ultimate cause of an event (usually a political or social event) as a secret plot by a covert alliance of powerful individuals or organizations rather than as an overt activity or natural occurrence. Attempts to explain why people believe conspiracy theories have focused on people's need to explain events that are beyond their control. In particular, some researchers view conspiracy theories as a response to powerlessness; in the face of increasingly vast and anonymous bureaucratic forces, conspiracy theories allow people to come to terms with the possibility that these underlying forces shape their future. Similarly, others view conspiracy theories as a means for less powerful individuals to imagine themselves in posession of powerful, or secret, information.

Conspiracy theories are therefore a powerful and attractive form of rumor. They are powerful because they can reach many people, especially in the age of the Internet, where information can be spread rapidly. Further, conspiracy theories are often the result of a hidden agenda by a smaller group of people and can facilitate their objectives. For example, one well-known conspiracy theory is that homosexuals are intentionally spreading HIV, which can have an adverse impact on how this group is perceived and treated in society. Spreading such a conspiracy theory is one way to propagate antigay attitudes and realize an antigay agenda. Conspiracy theories are also powerful because they are difficult to disconfirm. As a result, they can be very persuasive.

Finally, conspiracy theories are an attractive form of rumor because they help people deal with the uncertainty and anxiety caused by significant world events. Like rumors in general, conspiracy theories address ambigious events with a definitive and persuasive explanation, which can minimize stress and anxiety.

Karen M. Douglas

See also Conspiracy Theories; Evolutionary Psychology; Informational Influence; Normative Influence; Prejudice; Social Representations; Status; Stereotyping; Trust

Further Readings

Allport, G. W., & Postman, L. J. (1947). *The psychology of rumor*. New York: Holt.

DiFonzo, N., & Bordia, P. (2007). *Rumor psychology: Social & organizational approaches*. Washington, DC: American Psychological Association.

Dunbar, R. (1996). *Grooming, gossip and the evolution of language*. Cambridge, MA: Harvard University Press.

Knopf, T. A. (2006). *Rumors, race and riots*. London: Transaction Books.

McCauley, C., & Jacques, S. (1979). The popularity of conspiracy theories of presidential assassination: A Bayesian analysis. *Journal of Personality and Social Psychology, 37*, 637–644.

S

SCAPEGOATING

Scapegoating is an extreme form of prejudice in which people blame an outgroup as intentionally having caused their own group's misfortunes, motivating harsh actions against the scapegoated group. Scapegoating explanations have been offered for events ranging from the execution of "witches" in early modern Europe to 20th-century genocides such as the Holocaust. Initial theories of scapegoating relied on Freudian psychodynamics and, later, the frustration–aggression hypothesis. Both view scapegoating as a spontaneous venting of frustrations displaced onto an innocent group, chosen merely because it is weak and vulnerable, making it a convenient target. These theories, however, have difficulty explaining which minorities will be scapegoated and how scapegoating becomes a coordinated social movement that organizes violent actions (rather than a series of unconnected, individual hate crimes).

A newer model of scapegoating suggests instead that, during difficult times, socioeconomically successful (not "weak") minority groups face particular risk for scapegoating. Only successful minorities are popularly viewed as having the ability (e.g., social position, influence, and power) as well as the intent to cause widespread harm. This entry describes classical scapegoating theory and discusses how it has been modified to explain contemporary instances.

Classic Scapegoating Theory

Freud hypothesized that unconscious motives, especially basic drives for sex and aggression (which constitute the *id*), often lead people to behave in irrational ways. The id inevitably comes into conflict with social norms that seek to shape, control, and limit how its drives are expressed. Individuals internalize these norms, creating the *superego* (or conscience), which represses socially unacceptable drives (e.g., to aggress). Repression, however, is insufficient because the id's drives continually create mental energy that seeks behavioral release. Thus, unless individuals can channel their impulses constructively (e.g., express aggression through sports participation), they may displace aggression onto others while avoiding the superego's censure by constructing socially acceptable justifications or rationalizations to legitimize their hostility.

Displaced aggression is rationalized through psychologically projecting one's own faults and conflicts onto others. For example, "I want to harm others" is mentally transformed to "They want to harm me and therefore deserve my hostility." Minority groups that society already derogates present convenient, socially acceptable targets for projection and displaced aggression, making it easier for people to scapegoat them. Freud believed that after people vent their frustrations through aggression, they experience catharsis (a sense of relief and temporary diminishment of the aggressive drive). This model is notoriously

723

difficult to test, and although there is some empirical support for projection, the notion that expressing aggression diminishes subsequent violence has been disproved: Acting violently (even by punching a pillow) makes subsequent violence more (not less) likely.

Frustration–aggression theorists preserved Freud's displaced aggression assumption but argued that aggressive impulses are typically caused by obstacles to goal-directed behavior (not intrapsychic conflict). For instance, failing to land a coveted job might elicit frustration and, in turn, the impulse to aggress. When individuals cannot retaliate against the true source of frustration, perhaps because the other is powerful and might retaliate, they may displace aggression onto weak and vulnerable victims (e.g., a child who is mad at a parent might lash out instead against a younger sibling). In this view, minority groups become targets of displaced aggression because they happen to be in a weak position, unable to retaliate.

While the frustration–aggression approach emphasizes external obstacles and the Freudian view focuses on internal psychological conflict as initial sources of frustration, they have much in common. Both suggest that individual frustrations lead people to vent (much like a boiling kettle must release steam or explode), both characterize scapegoating as irrationally displaced aggression, and both suggest that the rationalizations people use to justify their hostility have nothing to do with the true reasons for their aggression.

Critics have long expressed objections to both the Freudian and the frustration–aggression approaches to scapegoating. Given that many minorities may occupy weak social positions, which one will be chosen? In instances of genocidal attack, why do so many people happen to choose the same group to scapegoat? Is it mere coincidence that a host of people simultaneously resolve their individual frustrations by venting on the same target group in a coordinated manner (as happens in genocides)? Because classic scapegoating theories remain rooted in psychological approaches focused on individualized frustrations rather than the social psychology of group identification, they are ill equipped to explain mass scapegoating as a collective event.

Newer Approaches to Scapegoating

Subsequent approaches have focused on shared or collective (not individual) frustrations as the distal source of scapegoating. Ervin Staub noted that difficult life conditions frustrate basic human needs (e.g., for security, optimism, group esteem). Shared frustrations (e.g., an economic depression) motivate people to construct explanations that diagnose the source of acute societal problems and suggest possible solutions. This process has been labeled social or collective attribution. In this view, people are not necessarily irrational or driven by unconscious impulses. Rather, they attempt to use an adaptive problem-solving strategy to deal with pressing problems that have frustrated their basic needs.

Massive social problems, however, may defy easy explanation or solution. Peter Glick's ideological model of scapegoating posits that only explanations that fit long-standing cultural biases and belief systems, such as group stereotypes, will appeal to large segments of a society. For example, imagine living in 17th-century Europe. You would probably accept the commonly held belief that some people (namely witches) are malevolent and possess supernatural powers.

Now imagine a plague that kills off one third of your village. In the absence of knowledge about how diseases are transmitted, how would you explain this horrible event? You might assume that somebody or some group must have caused the plague, and, in an early modern European cultural context, witches made likely candidates. After all, witches were "known" to have special powers that might produce diseases, as well as to have evil intentions. (By contrast, imagine how you might ridicule and reject a well-informed time traveler who tried to convince you that an invisible "virus" was the true cause.) Thus, a normally adaptive and rational motive to explain negative events can nevertheless yield wholly incorrect beliefs that lead people to scapegoat innocents (such as the tens of thousands burned as "witches").

What leads people collectively to decide that a specific group caused their misfortunes? Logically, for a group to have produced collective ills such as a plague, an economic depression, or political chaos, they must be powerful (i.e., capable of shaping widespread social outcomes) and also ill-intentioned (i.e., have the desire to harm others). Glick argued that socioeconomically successful or powerful minority groups are at particular risk of being the objects of scapegoating in times of shared, difficult social conditions. Such groups may be tolerated when social conditions are favorable but immediately suspected of malfeasance when things go bad.

Conspiracy theories, the hallmark of scapegoating, exaggerate the power wielded by the scapegoated group, which "explains" how it could have caused such widespread harm. However, many people may view a conspiracy theory as plausible when it is built on a kernel of truth—the relative success and influence of the minority group within the society. In addition, scapegoat ideologies fan the resentment that people often feel toward successful minorities (especially when most of society is suffering).

The Nazis, for example, complained bitterly of the prominence of Jews in business, science, government, and art. Indeed, as a group, the Jews were relatively successful in Germany before the Nazi era. Unfortunately, their very success fed into the Nazis' belief that only an international Jewish conspiracy (which allegedly allowed Jewish industrialists to profit from German misery) could have caused Germany to lose World War I and suffer a subsequent depression. Similarly, in Rwanda, the Tutsi—who were subjected to a genocidal attack during the 1990s by elements of the Hutu majority—were traditionally a high status, powerful minority. Thus, they could plausibly be blamed for Rwanda's economic depression and other social problems.

In addition to fixing blame, scapegoat ideologies offer a "solution" to society's problems—typically the elimination of the group that allegedly caused the misfortunes (e.g., the Nazis' "final solution" to the "Jewish problem"). From the perspective of people who adhere to such an ideology, aggression against the scapegoated group is psychologically justified as a necessary form of self-defense against a diabolically clever enemy. Genocides are organized affairs, initiated by a core of true believers convinced of the need to murder the group that allegedly caused their miseries. Thus, it remains vitally important to understand the psychology of scapegoating to prevent future genocidal attacks.

Peter Glick

See also Anti-Semitism; Authoritarian Personality; Frustration-Aggression Hypothesis; Genocide; Hate Crimes; Holocaust; Right Wing Authoritarianism

Further Readings

Allport, G. W. (1979). *The nature of prejudice.* Cambridge, MA: Perseus Books. (Original work published 1954)

Glick, P. (2005). Choice of scapegoats. In J. F. Dovidio, P. Glick, & L. A. Rudman (Eds.), *On the nature of prejudice: 50 years after Allport* (pp. 244–261). Malden, MA: Blackwell.

Staub, E. (1989). *The roots of evil: The psychological and cultural origins of genocide.* Cambridge, UK: Cambridge University Press.

SCHISMS

A *schism* refers to the secession of at least one *faction* (i.e., an ideologically distinct subgroup) from a social group. The breakaway faction(s) may either join a different group or create a new group. Schisms are common. They can occur in every type of group, including small aggregates (scientific expeditions, sports teams), middle-range groups (political parties, religious institutions, industrial organizations), and large communities (nations, ethnic groups). Whenever they occur, schisms have significant repercussions. They can quite dramatically affect beliefs, values, and behaviors *within* groups and transform relationships and equilibrium *between* groups. In sum, schisms constitute one of the most basic and consequential phenomena in the life of groups and in their interrelationships. This entry provides an overview of related research, presents a social-psychological model of schisms, discusses the model's limitations, and briefly describes related constructs.

Empirical Research on Schisms

Social scientists have long been interested in conflict and discord within groups. However, the dynamics of schisms remain relatively underresearched. Existing research can be classified into three distinct strands.

First, several researchers have conducted in-depth studies of specific schisms. In particular, sociologists have investigated religious and organizational schisms, political scientists have studied schisms within political parties and institutions, and anthropologists have focused on schisms in small non-Western villages (note that anthropologists often use the term *fission* instead of *schism*). Although these researchers have proposed explanations for each schismatic event that they have studied, they have rarely attempted to create a general theoretical model.

One notable exception is the Scottish anthropologist Victor Turner. In the 1950s, he studied schisms in Ndembu villages located in the North-Western province of Zambia. He was interested in the process leading a subgroup within a village to detach itself and build a separate settlement. Turner contended that a schism takes the form of a *social drama*. This is a sequence of ritual actions that can be grouped into four distinct phases: (1) breach of regular social relations; (2) widening of the breach until it becomes coextensive with important subgroups; (3) implementation of adjustive mechanisms, such as legal procedures or public rituals; and (4) reintegration of the disturbed subgroup or recognition of irreparable breach between the conflicting aggregates. Turner's work has been very influential among social anthropologists. However, while it points to general patterns of behavioral manifestations that may punctuate all schisms, it does not describe underlying mechanisms that supposedly produce a schism, and therefore it does not offer a truly explanatory model.

Second, some sociologists have reviewed several schisms and offered a list of group structural characteristics that make a schism more or less likely to happen. For instance, John Wilson noted that schisms are more frequent (a) in either very dogmatic groups or groups in which there is a totally open truth, (b) in groups in which clique formation is easy, (c) in groups lacking institutionalized methods for resolving conflicts, and (d) in groups in which decision-making processes are either highly centralized or highly decentralized.

Third, a group of social psychologists led by Fabio Sani has worked toward the construction of a general model aimed at explaining the social-psychological mechanisms that produce a schism. Their model is based on extensive empirical research on various schisms. For instance, one piece of research was a retrospective investigation of the split that took place in the Italian Communist Party in 1991 as a consequence of a change of name, symbol, and program. Another piece of research assessed the antecedents and consequences of the schism that occurred within the Church of England in the mid-1990s over the ordination of women to the priesthood. The model and its limitations are discussed below.

The Social Psychology of Schism

Group Norms and Identity

Some years ago, British social psychologists Henri Tajfel and John Turner argued that members of a group share a powerful sense of "we" and "us," in that they feel part of something that transcends their individuality. To survive as a meaningful entity, a group needs some degree of unity. Therefore, the group's members assume that they should broadly agree on the norms (beliefs, values, attitudes, and behaviors) that characterize the group's identity and thus its members' social identity. But far from being set in stone, the group's norms are subjected to an incessant process of debate and negotiation. In the course of such a process, norms may be adjusted, modified, or even rejected and replaced with new norms.

From Perceived Identity Subversion to Schism

Although normative change is an inherent aspect of all groups, group members tend to distinguish between changes that improve and strengthen group identity, which are welcome, and changes that deny and subvert group identity, which constitute a threat and therefore are feared. Because the nature of the relationship between a new norm and the group identity is arguable, there may be situations in which factions form around different understandings of such a relationship. Basically, while the members of a faction may see a new norm as fully consistent with the group's identity, or even as reinforcing it, the members of another faction may consider the new norm to be profoundly inconsistent with and even negating the group's identity and denying its "true" essence. This disagreement will often trigger a schism.

This is what happened in the schisms mentioned above. For instance, in the Italian Communist Party schism, the trigger was the fact that while the majority saw the newly adopted symbolism and program of the party as a necessary development in line with the party identity, a substantial subgroup of party members saw the change as a profound rupture with the history and identity of the party. As a consequence, the subgroup that opposed the change left the party to create a new one, which in their opinion retained the identity of the Italian Communist Party.

The same mechanisms applied to the schism in the Church of England. That is, the majority group, which had voted in favor of the ordination of women to the priesthood, saw this change as fully consistent with scriptures and tradition and as a necessary development that strengthened the group's identity. On the other hand, a minority of members perceived the ordination of women as inconsistent with scriptures, tradition, and the will of God and therefore as transforming the Church of England into a completely different group and irreconcilably subverting its identity. Many of these members eventually left the Church of England to create a new, small, breakaway church or to join either the Roman Catholic Church or the Orthodox Church.

Why should the perception that the group's identity has been negated lead to a schism? The model points to three reasons.

First, witnessing a profound denial of the group's identity makes members acutely aware of the existence of two ideologically incompatible factions within the group and raises the all too real probability that the group will be deeply fractured and divided and will not really be able to function as a single entity any longer.

Second, recognizing their group as having a different and undesired identity lowers members' sense of group identification and collective self-esteem. Members feel estranged from the group and no longer feel a sense of pride in belonging to or being part of it.

Third, the fact that the changed group identity is radically different from one's ideal group identity, and from what one thinks the group's identity ought to be, generates negative emotions. In particular, this generates dejection-related emotions (disappointment, sadness), agitation-related emotions (apprehension, uneasiness), and, in some cases, even strong anger and resentment toward those members who are seen as responsible for the change.

These three reactions lead people to consider a schism to be a viable option. A schism would allow them to escape from a group that is divided, with which they do not identify any longer, and that causes them painful emotions.

The model described here also specifies that those group members who are dissatisfied with the change, and therefore experience the reactions described above, will be more or less likely to join a schism depending on how much voice they perceive they have within the group. If they believe that, because of their position, they will be marginalized and isolated within the group, then their likelihood of joining a schism will be relatively high. On the contrary, if they sense that they will be respected and valued, then their likelihood of leaving the group will be lower.

Limitations of the Model

This model has two main limitations. First, it is derived from analyses of schisms in groups in which identity was of primary importance and, therefore, threats to identity caused turmoil and preoccupation that eventually led to schism. However, some smaller, face-to-face groups, such as a research team or a music band, might not place such importance on identity. This implies that the model might be more applicable to some types of groups than to others.

The second, related, limitation stems from the fact that the model is derived from situations in which a conservative faction secedes from a group because of an unacceptable change endorsed by a more progressive, reformist majority. However, there are situations in which a reformist faction secedes from the group because it advocates change that is staunchly opposed by a conservative majority. Whether the model can be adapted to this circumstance is yet to be established.

Related Phenomena and Constructs

Some other phenomena studied by social scientists are strongly related to or partially overlap the notion of schism. One of these is *factionalism*, which refers to the existence of competing and conflicting factions within a group. This phenomenon is generally seen as a logical precondition of schism but not as a schism itself. For instance, in his 1931 entry for the *Encyclopedia of Social Sciences*, Harold Lasswell stated that when factions turn into groups of higher order, the term *factionalism* is no longer appropriate. Consistent with this, the majority of research on factionalism focuses on descriptions and explanations of faction formation and development, rather than on schism as a consequence of these processes.

It should be noted, however, that some scholars, such as the psychoanalyst Wilfred Bion and his followers, use the term *schism* to refer to divisions and conflict between small subgroups within psychotherapy groups, for which the concept of factionalism would be probably more appropriate. In contrast, other scholars use the term *factionalism* very broadly to apply to disputes between different political parties.

Another phenomenon related to schism is *defection*. Like the term *schism*, *defection* is used to indicate the departure of members from a group. Defectors are said to experience a sense of ideological detachment from a group and a loss of faith in the group's beliefs and values. However, in this case, the emphasis is on the action of one or more individuals rather than on collective action undertaken by members of a more or less organized faction. This notion is very similar to the notion of *exit*, which is used by Albert Hirschman to signify one of the possible options that members of firms, organizations, and states may choose in times of organizational decline. Finally, some sociologists, such as Lewis Coser and Stuart Wright, point out that some defectors make special efforts to attack their former group and to negate its worldview, and they use the term *apostasy* to indicate this specific phenomenon.

Fabio Sani

See also Collective Movements and Protest; Collective Self; Conformity; Group Development; Group Dissolution; Norms; Social Identity Theory

Further Readings

Sani, F. (2005). When subgroups secede: Extending and refining the social psychological model of schisms in groups. *Personality and Social Psychology Bulletin, 31,* 1074–1086.

Sani, F. (in press). When subgroups secede: A social psychological model of factionalism and schism in groups. In F. Butera & J. Levine (Eds.), *Hoping and coping: How minorities manage their social environments.* Cambridge, UK: Cambridge University Press.

Sani, F., & Reicher, S. (1998). When consensus fails: An analysis of the schism within the Italian Communist Party (1991). *European Journal of Social Psychology, 28,* 623–645.

Turner, V. W. (1957). *Schism and continuity in an African society: A study of Ndembu village life.* Manchester, UK: Manchester University Press.

Wilson, J. (1971). The sociology of schism. In M. Hill (Ed.), *A sociological yearbook of religion in Britain* (Vol. 4, pp. 1–20). London: SCM.

SELF-CATEGORIZATION THEORY

Self-categorization theory describes how the cognitive process of categorization, when applied to oneself, creates a sense of identification with the social category or group and produces the array of behaviors that we associate with group membership: conformity, stereotyping, ethnocentrism, and so forth. Self-categorization theory was developed by John Turner and his colleagues at the University of Bristol and described in a classic 1987 book. It is an integral part of *social identity theory*, often referred to as the *social identity theory of the group*, to differentiate its cognitive and general group emphasis from Henri Tajfel and John Turner's 1979 social identity theory of intergroup relations, which places more emphasis on motivational and intergroup dimensions.

In describing self-categorization theory, this entry gives some historical background and then discusses key features and elaborations of the theory. These include the structuring of social categories around prototypes, the processes of categorization and depersonalization, attraction among group members and the bases of group solidarity and cohesion, intergroup behavior, motivations associated with social and self-categorization, the process of psychological salience of self-categories or social identities, how groups influence their members, and processes that make some individuals influential while others are marginalized.

Historical Background

During the late 1960s and early 1970s, Henri Tajfel championed a cognitive perspective on intergroup relations. He believed that basic cognitive processes associated with how we categorize people as members of groups lie at the psychological core of an array of intergroup behaviors, in particular prejudice, discrimination, and stereotyping. This perspective gathered momentum through collaboration with John Turner and a focus on the comparisons people make between groups, particularly between a group they belong to (ingroup) and groups they do not belong to (outgroups), and on the role of self-definition and self-evaluation as a group member (*social identity*) in intergroup behavior.

This led to Tajfel and Turner's classic 1979 statement of the social identity theory of intergroup relations, which focused on how the interplay between social identification, the pursuit of positive intergroup distinctiveness, and beliefs about the nature of intergroup relations impacted cooperation and competition between groups. During the early 1980s, Turner and his colleagues turned their attention (back) to the mechanics of group identification, asking what exactly, psychologically speaking, a group is and what basic social-cognitive processes generate group identification and associated group processes and behaviors. In so doing, Turner and his colleagues revisited and greatly elaborated the role of social categorization in order to produce the social identity theory of the group—self-categorization theory.

The original 1987 statement of self-categorization theory was very specific in its focus on levels of inclusiveness (how categorical distinctions are made within high order similarities; e.g., people are categorized as Scottish or English within the context of all being British, and as British or French within the context of all being European) and on depersonalized self-perception (how categorizing oneself depersonalizes self-perception and behavior to conform to the defining attributes of the category to which one belongs). Very quickly, however, many, if not most, social identity and self-categorization researchers relaxed the focus on levels of inclusiveness and broadened the depersonalization concept to apply to the perception of other people as well. It is this broader perspective that is described here.

Categories and Prototypes

Human groups are social categories that people mentally represent as *prototypes,* that is, complex (fuzzy) sets of interrelated attributes that capture similarities within groups and differences between groups. Prototypes maximize *entitativity* (the extent to which a group is a distinct and clearly defined entity) and optimize metacontrast (the extent to which maximal similarity among members of the group is balanced with maximal difference between the group as a whole and a relevant outgroup). If I say to you "French," what comes immediately to mind is your prototype of that national group—possibly something to do with berets, baguettes, and bicycles. However, if in thinking about the French, you are contrasting them to the Dutch, then bicycles may not be part of the prototype because it is not an attribute that differentiates the categories very sharply—the Dutch also do a lot of cycling.

Overwhelmingly, we make binary categorizations in which one of the categories is the group that we are in, the ingroup. Thus, prototypes not only capture similarities within the ingroup but also accentuate differences between our group and a specific outgroup. Ingroup prototypes can therefore change as a function of the specific outgroup to which we are comparing our group. In this way, prototypes are context dependent.

Categorization and Depersonalization

The process of categorizing people has predictable consequences. Rather than seeing them as idiosyncratic individuals, we see them through the lens of the prototype: They become depersonalized. Prototype-based perception of outgroup members is more commonly called *stereotyping*: We view "them" as being similar to one another and all having outgroup attributes. We can also depersonalize ingroup members and ourselves in the same way. When we categorize ourselves, we view ourselves in terms of the defining attributes of the ingroup (*self-stereotyping*), and because prototypes also describe and prescribe group-appropriate ways to think, feel, and behave, we think, feel, and behave group prototypically. In this way, self-categorization, which generates a sense of belonging, attachment, and identification with the group, not only transforms the way we view ourselves but also transforms our behavior to comply with ingroup norms, producing normative behavior among members of a group.

Feelings for Group Members: Social Attraction

Social categorization affects how we feel toward other people. Feelings are governed by how prototypical of the group we think other people are, rather than by personal preferences, friendships, and enmities. In this way, liking becomes depersonalized social attraction. Furthermore, because within one's group there is usually agreement over prototypicality, prototypical members are liked by all—they are "popular." Likewise, less-prototypical members are unpopular and can be marginalized as undesirable deviants.

Another aspect of social attraction is that outgroup members are liked less than ingroup members. Outgroupers are very unprototypical of the ingroup. Social attraction also occurs because our ingroup prototypes are generally more favorable than our outgroup prototypes (we do all we can to secure an evaluative advantage of our own group over relevant comparison outgroups). Thus, liking reflects not only prototypicality but the valence of the prototype.

Intergroup Behavior

This tendency for ingroup prototypes to be more favorable than outgroup prototypes represents *ethnocentrism*—the belief that all things ingroup are superior to all things outgroup. Ethnocentrism exists because of the correspondence, through social identification and self-categorization, between how the group is evaluated and how we are evaluated. Thus, intergroup behavior is a struggle over the relative status or prestige of one's ingroup—a struggle for positive ingroup distinctiveness and social identity. Groups with higher status fight to protect their evaluative superiority; groups of lower status struggle to shrug off their social stigma and promote their positivity. It is this aspect of social identity theory that is fully theorized by Tajfel and Turner's 1979 social identity theory of intergroup relations.

Motivational Processes

For the social identity theory of intergroup relations, the key motivational process is self-enhancement in group terms and the management of collective self-esteem. At the group level, this motivation is manifested as an intergroup struggle for positive distinctiveness. Self-categorization theory originally had little to say about motivation. Instead, it focused on process. However, it contained the implicit assumption that categorization might satisfy a basic human need to structure one's perceptions, attitudes, and behaviors and locate oneself in the social world.

Building on this idea, Michael Hogg developed *uncertainty-identity theory*, first published in 2000 and then more fully in 2007, presenting it as a motivational explanation of social identity processes and self-categorization effects to complement the motivational role of self and group enhancement. According to uncertainty-identity theory, people strive to reduce feelings of uncertainty about their social world and their place within it. In other words, they like to know who they are and how to behave and who others are and how they might behave. Social identity, through the processes of self-categorization and depersonalization, ties self-definition and behavior to prescriptive and descriptive prototypes. Social identity reduces uncertainty about who we are and about how we and others will behave and is particularly effective if the social identity is clearly defined by membership in a distinctive, high-entitativity group. Research confirms that uncertainty, especially about or related to self, motivates identification, particularly with high-entitativity groups.

Another motivational perspective on social identity processes based on self-categorization is offered by Marilynn Brewer's 1991 *optimal distinctiveness theory*. According to this theory, people are simultaneously motivated to stand out and be separate from other people, on one hand, and to fit in and be included by others, on the other hand. As a resolution of these competing motives, they seek a state of optimal distinctiveness. Large groups satisfy the inclusiveness motive but not the distinctiveness motive, and small groups do the opposite. Thus, people prefer to identify with midsized groups, or they seek a degree of intragroup differentiation (based on roles or subgroups) against the background of identification with a larger collective.

Psychological Salience

A social identity or self-category comes into play psychologically to govern perceptions, attitudes, feelings, and behavior when it is psychologically salient. People draw on readily accessible social identities or categorizations (e.g., gender, profession)—ones that are valued, important, and frequently employed aspects of the self-concept (chronically accessible in memory) or self-evident and perceptually obvious in the immediate situation (situationally accessible). People use accessible identities to make sense of what is going on around them, checking how well the categorization accounts for similarities and differences among people (structural or comparative fit) and how well the stereotypical properties of the categorization account for people's behavior (normative fit). People try out different categorizations, and the categorization with optimal fit becomes psychologically salient. Although largely an automatic process, salience is influenced by motivations to employ categorizations that favor the ingroup and do not raise self-uncertainty.

Influence in Groups

People in groups adhere to similar standards, have similar attitudes, and behave in similar ways. They conform to group norms and behave group prototypically. Self-categorization is the cognitive process responsible for depersonalization and thus for causing individual group members to behave prototypically or normatively—transforming their self-concept and behavior to be identity consistent. The social identity theory of influence, *referent informational influence theory*, builds on self-categorization theory but also discusses processes responsible for identifying and configuring the ingroup prototype or norm.

Clearly, members will be highly vigilant for and attentive to information that accurately conveys what the prototype or norm is. In gauging what the appropriate group norm is, people pay attention to the behavior of people who are most informative about the norm. Typically, these are people who are generally considered to be prototypical and who are behaving in ways that are not inconsistent with the wider parameters of the group's identity. In many contexts, these people are the group's leaders. Indeed, this idea is the foundation of the *social identity theory of leadership*. However, outgroup members and marginal ingroup members can also be informative in a more indirect way: What they are is what the ingroup is not.

Relative Prototypicality and the Psychology of Marginalization

Flowing from this discussion of how group members determine the appropriate group prototype is the observation that in groups, not every member is equally prototypical. Instead, some members are considered more prototypical than others, and there can be more or less intragroup consensus on this. A member who is consensually perceived to be highly prototypical will be extremely influential within the group, functioning as an effective leader who can influence the group's identity and destiny. A member who is consensually perceived to be nonprototypical will find it very difficult to exert influence and will often be vilified and marginalized by the rest of the group and possibly ejected from the group. Where consensus on prototypicality is low, members are effectively disagreeing about what the group is or should stand for—conditions that produce conflict that may lead to schisms and possible group disintegration.

Michael A. Hogg

See also Depersonalization; Optimal Distinctiveness; Referent Informational Influence Theory; Schisms; Social Identity Theory; Uncertainty-Identity Theory

Further Readings

Hogg, M. A. (2006). Social identity theory. In P. J. Burke (Ed.), *Contemporary social psychological theories* (pp. 111–136). Palo Alto, CA: Stanford University Press.

Hogg, M. A. (2007). Uncertainty-identity theory. In M. P. Zanna (Ed.), *Advances in experimental social psychology* (Vol. 39, pp. 69–126). San Diego, CA: Academic Press.

Oakes, P. J., Haslam, S. A., & Turner, J. C. (1994). *Stereotyping and social reality.* Oxford, UK: Blackwell.

Turner, J. C. (1982). Towards a cognitive redefinition of the social group. In H. Tajfel (Ed.), *Social identity and intergroup relations* (pp. 15–40). Cambridge, UK: Cambridge University Press.

Turner, J. C., Hogg, M. A., Oakes, P. J., Reicher, S. D., & Wetherell, M. S. (1987). *Rediscovering the social group: A self-categorization theory.* Oxford, UK: Blackwell.

SELF-ESTEEM

The term *self-esteem* is attributed to William James, who defined it as feelings about the self resulting from comparisons of the *actual self* to the *ideal self*. More recently, self-esteem has come to reflect an individual's evaluation of his or her *self-worth*. With regard to intergroup relations and group processes, the following issues are of primary importance: (a) types of self-esteem, (b) self-esteem as an outcome or a predictor of intergroup discrimination, (c) the impact of experiencing discrimination on self-esteem, (d) implicit self-esteem, (e) the role of self-esteem in terror management, (f) the differentiation of self-esteem from group identification and group status, and (g) contingencies of self-worth. The relationship of self-esteem to intergroup phenomena is the primary focus of this entry. However, a discussion of dimensions and types of self-esteem is necessary before discussing how self-esteem relates to group processes and intergroup relations.

Types of Self-Esteem

Initially, researchers defined self-esteem as a stable personality trait relative to how individuals felt about themselves. More recently, however, the term *self-esteem* has broadened to encompass different dimensions. One way to classify dimensions of self-esteem is as global, trait based, or domain specific.

Global self-esteem refers to stable aspects of the self-concept (e.g., "I feel I have a number of good qualities"). Common global measures of self-esteem include the Rosenberg Self-Esteem Scale and the Collective Self-Esteem Scale. Global measures of self-esteem are best conceptualized as predictor variables because their stability makes them difficult to change after experimental manipulation.

Trait-based measures of self-esteem address feelings that may fluctuate (e.g., "I feel inferior to others at this moment"). A common measure of trait self-esteem is the State Self-Esteem Scale. Trait self-esteem, because it can fluctuate, is appropriate for use as both a predictor (i.e., it can be manipulated) and a dependent measure (i.e., it may change after experimental manipulations).

Domain-specific self-esteem comprises specific aspects of the self-concept and may fluctuate (e.g., "I have good reading comprehension"). Domain-specific self-esteem measurement generally focuses on specific areas of mastery, such as academic or physical self-concept. Like trait self-esteem, domain-specific self-esteem can be conceptualized as a predictor or a dependent measure.

For intergroup purposes, self-esteem may be further distinguished as measuring personal or collective (social) aspects of the self. *Personal self-esteem* reflects how much individuals value themselves. For example, a personal self-esteem scale might include items such as "I wish I could have more respect for myself." *Collective self-esteem* addresses how much individuals value the groups or collectives of which they are members. Typical collective self-esteem measurement items might include, "In general, I'm glad to be a member of the social groups I belong to."

Still another way to categorize self-esteem is as an explicit or an implicit measure. *Explicit* measures of self-esteem involve traditional paper-and-pencil tasks wherein individuals answer direct questions. Most self-esteem scales involve explicit measurement. In contrast, *implicit* measures involve computer-based reaction time tests. For example, a common implicit measure requires the individual to pair words relevant to the self, such as *I* or *me*, with positive or negative words, such as *worthy* or *useless*. Those who associate "self" words with positive traits more quickly than with negative traits attain higher implicit self-esteem scores. This approach is often termed *indirect* or *nonconscious measurement*. Implicit self-esteem deserves special mention because implicit or nonconscious measures are commonly defined as outside conscious control. This definition seems to conflict with the characterizations of self-esteem as self-evaluative. However, some researchers argue that, regardless of the nonconscious aspect of the measure, the feelings measured are in fact elicited by the self and do guide reactions to stimulus.

Self-Esteem in Intergroup Discrimination

The role of self-esteem in group processes and intergroup relations is rooted in self-enhancement motivations. Individuals strive to focus on positive information about the self and to make evaluations and attributions that support positive self-evaluations. At an intergroup level, there also exists a group enhancement motivation. *Social identity theory* states that individuals define themselves in terms of their group memberships and seek to maintain a positive identity through association with positively valued groups and through comparisons with other groups.

Social identity theory posits a central role for self-esteem relevant to intergroup relations. However, interpretations of the theory suggest competing perspectives on the role of self-esteem. One perspective states that intergroup discrimination, or ingroup-favoring evaluations, enhance self-esteem. Intergroup discrimination involves either evaluations that derogate members of other groups or evaluations wherein both groups are evaluated positively but the ingroup receives a more positive evaluation. In either case, discrimination involves enhancing the relative value of the ingroup. Because positive identities are a product of membership in positively valued groups, people show bias as a means of enhancing their self-esteem. A competing perspective proposes that depressed self-esteem promotes ingroup bias. That is, individuals with low self-esteem are motivated to enhance their group as a means of increasing deficient self-esteem.

Both perspectives suggest a central role for self-esteem in intergroup processes, but the two perspectives do not seem logically consistent. In particular, if ingroup bias improves self-esteem and people with low self-esteem are more likely to show bias, how is it that some individuals are chronically low in self-esteem? The different dimensions of self-esteem detailed below help resolve this inconsistency.

Self-Esteem as an Outcome of Intergroup Discrimination

There is some support for the proposition that discrimination against outgroups enhances self-esteem for those who discriminate. However, it appears that only trait, domain-specific, and social aspects of self-esteem increase after the opportunity to discriminate. This suggests that discrimination improves aspects of self-esteem that are not static (i.e., trait and domain-specific) and those that are relevant to feelings derived from group memberships (i.e., collective or social aspects).

Self-Esteem as a Predictor of Intergroup Discrimination

The question most commonly asked by researchers interested in self-esteem as a predictor of intergroup discrimination is, Who shows more bias,

individuals with high self-esteem or individuals with low self-esteem? Empirical evidence suggests that individuals with high personal self-esteem demonstrate more bias. However, under conditions in which self-consistency needs are met (e.g., people with low self-esteem can discriminate without making claims of superiority), individuals with high and individuals with low self-esteem show similar levels of bias on both personal and collective measures. Broadly, data suggest that individuals higher in global personal self-esteem show more ingroup bias, indicating that social identity theory predictions regarding the motivational role of self-esteem are not supported.

Research examining self-esteem as a predictor and as an outcome of discrimination behaviors highlights important issues about different domains of self-esteem. In the case of the link between self-esteem and intergroup discrimination, competing predictions were resolved through consideration of the different forms of self-esteem.

Self-Esteem of Those Who Experience Discrimination

Another issue of interest is how being the target of group-based discrimination impacts self-esteem. Black people in the United States, a long-standing target of discrimination, generally report higher self-esteem than do groups with fewer discrimination experiences. However, some other groups that have suffered discrimination, such as women and the overweight, show deflated self-esteem. Research examining effects of discrimination on self-esteem suggests that appraisals of the discrimination and how the individual perceives the outcomes of the discrimination mediate its impact on self-esteem.

The Emerging Role of Implicit Self-Esteem

Implicit self-esteem measures are relatively new. Although the source of some controversy, many perspectives suggest that consideration of both implicit and explicit measures is important because they predict different behavioral outcomes. In addition, implicit and explicit measures are often unrelated, suggesting that they are independent constructs.

Work on the impact of implicit self-esteem on intergroup attitudes suggests that increases in implicit self-esteem motivate ingroup-favoring responses. However, other research indicates that individuals who possess low implicit self-esteem and high explicit self-esteem are more likely to demonstrate ingroup bias. Still other work finds that high implicit self-esteem is associated with ingroup favoritism only when the ingroup is high status. The relationship between implicit self-esteem and intergroup bias appears ripe for continuing investigation.

Terror Management and Self-Esteem

Terror management theory posits that self-esteem serves a fundamental role in buffering anxiety derived from reminders of mortality. In this view, mortality reminders motivate a striving for self-esteem to offset anxiety. The primary mechanism for bolstering self-esteem is adhering more strongly to one's cultural worldview. Many outcomes corresponding to bolstering the cultural worldview are relevant to intergroup relations.

For example, one strategy for bolstering the worldview (and thus bolstering self-esteem) is evaluating the ingroup favorably and outgroups unfavorably, provided that the ingroup is viewed positively and outgroups are viewed negatively. However, when outgroups are viewed favorably, mortality reminders promote more positive outgroup evaluations. In short, mortality reminders make responses extreme. Individuals evaluate positively valued groups more positively and negatively valued groups more negatively.

Self-Esteem Versus Status and Group Identification

Other useful distinctions are between self-esteem and group status and between self-esteem and group identification. There is a long tradition of investigation of the effects of status on ingroup bias. Often group status, defined as the relative standing of the group in relation to other groups, is equated with self-esteem. However, individuals who are members of low-status or stigmatized groups are no more or less likely to have low self-esteem than are members of high-status or nonstigmatized groups. Thus, it seems that negative aspects of social identity, such as low status, can become disassociated from self-esteem.

It is also useful to distinguish *group identification* from self-esteem. Although measures used to assess group identification often include items that tap aspects similar to those defined as collective self-esteem, group identification focuses on how strongly people are committed to their groups. In contrast, collective self-esteem addresses the feelings derived from group memberships. Collective self-esteem and group identification are sometimes viewed interchangeably. However, empirical evidence suggests that stronger group identification, but not greater collective self-esteem, predicts increased ingroup bias.

Contingencies of Self-Worth

Recent work on contingencies of self-worth focuses on characteristics that constitute global self-esteem. That is, these contingencies are the domains that contribute to an individual's global self-esteem. Some individuals may base their self-esteem on physical appearance, others on academic performance, and still others on religious faith or some other domain. Contingencies of self-worth explain a number of paradoxical influences of self-esteem. For example, empirical data demonstrate that Black people in the United States are less likely to place value on approval from others and so are less likely to have their self-esteem impacted by discrimination (i.e., disapproval from others). Although there is presently little work examining the relationship between contingencies of self-worth and prejudice, this area represents an interesting avenue for future investigation.

Christopher L. Aberson

See also Collective Self; Identification and Commitment; Ingroup Allocation Bias; Racism; Social Identity Theory; Status; Stigma; Terror Management Theory

Further Readings

Aberson, C. L., Healy, M. R., & Romero, V. L. (2000). Ingroup bias and self-esteem: A meta-analysis. *Personality and Social Psychology Review, 4,* 157–173.

Bosson, J. K., Swann, W. B., Jr., & Pennebaker, J. (2000). Stalking the perfect measure of implicit self-esteem: The blind men and the elephant revisited? *Journal of Personality and Social Psychology, 79,* 631–643.

Crocker, J., & Wolfe, C. T. (2001). Contingencies of self-worth. *Psychological Review, 108,* 593–623.

Hogg, M. A., & Abrams, D. (1990). Social motivation, self-esteem, and social identity. In D. Abrams & M. A. Hogg (Eds.), *Social identity theory: Constructive and critical advances* (pp. 28–47). New York: Springer-Verlag.

Kernis, M. H. (Ed.). (2006). *Self-esteem issues and answers: A sourcebook of current perspectives.* New York: Psychology Press.

Luhtanen, R., & Crocker, J. (1992). A collective self-esteem scale: Self-evaluation of one's social identity. *Personality and Social Psychology Bulletin, 18,* 302–318.

Major, B., & O'Brien, L. T. (2005). The social psychology of stigma. *Annual Review of Psychology, 56,* 393–421.

Rubin, M., & Hewstone, M. (1998). Social identity theory's self-esteem hypothesis: A review and some suggestions for clarification. *Personality and Social Psychology Review, 2,* 40–62.

Solomon, S., Greenberg, J., & Pyszczynski, T. (2000). Pride and prejudice: Fear of death and social behavior. *Current Directions in Psychological Science, 9,* 200–204.

SELF-FULFILLING PROPHECY

A *self-fulfilling prophecy* occurs when an originally false expectation leads to its own confirmation. One classic example of a self-fulfilling prophecy was bank failures during the Great Depression. Even banks with strong financials sometimes were driven to insolvency by bank runs. Banks make money by taking in deposits and then lending that money to others. If (as happened during the Great Depression) a false rumor starts that the bank is insolvent (incapable of covering its deposits), a panic ensues, and depositors want to withdraw their money all at once before the bank's cash runs out. When the bank cannot cover all the withdrawals, it actually becomes insolvent. Thus, an originally false belief has led to its own fulfillment.

Self-fulfilling prophecies are important to the understanding of intergroup relations. Under just the right (or wrong) conditions, inaccurate social stereotypes may lead to their own fulfillment. For example, members of groups stereotyped as more intelligent, competent, or likable can, through the operation of self-fulfilling prophecies, actually become more intelligent, competent, or likable

than members of groups stereotyped as less intelligent, competent, or likable. Thus, self-fulfilling prophecies may contribute to the maintenance, not only of stereotypes themselves, but of the group differences and inequalities that give rise to those stereotypes.

Such processes, however, are limited, and the extent to which they contribute to group differences and inequalities is the subject of considerable controversy in the research literature. This entry discusses what that literature does and does not tell us (including some common misconceptions) about self-fulfilling prophecies.

Early Research

The earliest empirical research on self-fulfilling prophecies examined whether teachers' false expectations for their students caused students to achieve at levels consistent with those teachers' expectations. Repeatedly, although not always, research demonstrated that teacher expectations are indeed self-fulfilling—students (sometimes) come to perform at levels consistent with their teachers' originally false expectations.

This research has been interpreted by many scholars as providing a powerful insight into social, educational, and economic inequality. Teacher expectations seem to systematically advantage students from already advantaged backgrounds (e.g., Whites, middle-class students) and disadvantage students from already disadvantaged backgrounds (e.g., ethnic minorities, lower-class students). To the extent that education is a major stepping-stone toward occupational and economic advancement, self-fulfilling prophecies, it would seem, constitute a major social force operating to keep the disadvantaged in "their place."

Further support for self-fulfilling prophecies was provided by additional early research showing that social stereotypes can indeed be self-fulfilling. Classic studies showed that both physical attractiveness and racial stereotypes could be self-fulfilling. When men interviewed a woman who they falsely believed was physically attractive (accomplished through the use of false photographs in non–face-to-face interviews), not only were the men warmer and friendlier to her, but she became warmer and friendlier in response. Moreover, when White interviewers treated White interviewees in the same cold and distant manner they used with Black interviewees, the performance of the White interviewees suffered.

Self-fulfilling prophecies have been demonstrated in a wide variety of educational, occupational, professional, and informal contexts. They have been demonstrated in experimental laboratory studies, experimental field studies, to naturalistic studies. Indeed, it is fairly easy to string together a few of the classic studies to tell a compelling story about how teachers' expectations, employers' expectations, and expectations in everyday interactions victimize people from stigmatized social groups. And, indeed, that is exactly what some observers have done. The logic here is quite simple. Stereotypes are widely shared and inaccurate. Stereotypes lead to inaccurate expectations. These expectations, in turn, are self-fulfilling. According to this perspective, self-fulfilling prophecies constitute a major source of social inequalities and social problems.

The Limits of Self-Fulfilling Prophecies

For several reasons, however, evidence for the power of self-fulfilling prophecies is far from conclusive. First, some of the classic studies had major methodological problems. Second, many have proven difficult to replicate. Third, the overall power of self-fulfilling prophecies, especially as obtained in naturalistic studies that do not involve experimenters intentionally creating false expectations in participants, is not large at all. Fourth, there currently is about as much evidence that positive self-fulfilling prophecies improve the performance of low-achieving students as there is that negative self-fulfilling prophecies harm their performance. Fifth, considerable evidence indicates that people are not rudderless ships, relentlessly tossed around on the seas of other people's expectations. Instead, people have their own motivations and goals that enable them to successfully combat others' false expectations.

Overall, therefore, the evidence does not justify a simple picture of self-fulfilling prophecies as powerful and pervasive sources of social problems. But the picture gets even fuzzier when other research is added to the mix. Although not all stereotypes are 100% accurate, most of the empirical studies that have assessed people's beliefs about groups and then compared those beliefs to criteria regarding what those groups are actually like (Census reports, results from hundreds of empirical studies, self-reports) find that people's beliefs correspond with groups' characteristics quite well. Indeed, the accuracy of people's stereotypes (the extent to which people's beliefs about groups correspond with what those groups are actually like) is one of the largest relationships in all of social psychology.

In addition, the shared component of stereotypes is typically even more accurate than is the individual or idiosyncratic component. People do not rigidly and powerfully apply their stereotypes when judging individuals. They readily jettison their stereotypes when clear and relevant personal information is available about the person being judged, and overall, the effect of stereotypes on judging individuals is generally quite small. Thus, some of the key assumptions underlying the "self-fulfilling stereotypes are a powerful and pervasive source of social problems" story—that stereotypes are widely shared and inaccurate and that they powerfully distort expectations for individuals— seem to be largely invalid.

A second important assumption underlying the argument for the power of self-fulfilling prophecies is that even if these prophecies are small in any given study, those small effects, because they likely accumulate over time, can become quite large and hence at least partially account for major social inequalities. For example, let's say that teacher expectations increase the IQ of high-expectancy students only 3 points per year and decrease the IQ of low-expectancy students only 3 points per year. If these effects accumulate, then at the end of 6 years, there would be a 36-IQ-point difference between two students who started out with identical IQ test scores but different expectancies.

However, empirical research on self-fulfilling prophecies in education has not provided any evidence of accumulation. Every study that has tested the accumulation hypothesis has not only failed to confirm it but has found the opposite. Rather than accumulating to become larger and larger over time, the effects of self-fulfilling prophecies in the classroom dissipate over time—they become smaller and smaller. Why this happens is not currently well understood. Given the evidence for generally high accuracy in teacher expectations, strongly erroneous teacher expectations may be the exception rather than the rule. Thus, students may be highly unlikely to be the target of the same type of erroneous expectation year after year, thereby limiting the likelihood that they will be subjected to the same erroneous expectation (and its self-fulfilling effects) year after year.

Nonetheless, the story about the role of self-fulfilling prophecies in social problems should not be completely discarded. Self-fulfilling prophecies probably do play some modest role in social inequalities. First, some of the largest self-fulfilling prophecy effects ever obtained have been found among students from stigmatized social and demographic groups (Blacks, lower social class students, and students with histories of low achievement). Second, even though educational self-fulfilling prophecies do not accumulate, they can be very long lasting. Some evidence shows that sixth-grade teacher expectations have self-fulfilling effects as far out as 12th grade. Third, the types of diagnostic labels often used in educational contexts—learning disabled, emotionally disturbed, neurologically impaired—are inaccurately applied sufficiently often that they may frequently create inaccurately low expectations that are indeed self-fulfilling. Because these labels have a veneer of scientific credibility, it may be much harder for students so labeled to shake the inaccurate expectations produced by them.

Conclusion

Given the highly mixed nature of the evidence, what conclusions about self-fulfilling prophecies are currently justified?

- Self-fulfilling prophecies are a real phenomenon and occur in many settings, including laboratories, classrooms, courtrooms, and jobs.
- In general, self-fulfilling prophecies do not greatly influence people. Occasionally, however, they can be quite powerful.
- Self-fulfilling prophecies in the classroom dissipate over time. There is insufficient research to reach any conclusion about whether they accumulate or dissipate in other contexts, such as the workplace or family.
- In general, self-fulfilling prophecies probably play a real yet relatively modest role in creating or maintaining social inequalities based on

characteristics such as race, ethnicity, social class, gender, and attractiveness. Nonetheless, there may be some contexts in which this role is quite large.

Lee Jussim

See also Children: Stereotypes and Prejudice; Discrimination; Minority Groups in Society; Stereotyping

Further Readings

Jussim, L., Eccles, J., & Madon, S. J. (1996). Social perception, social stereotypes, and teacher expectations: Accuracy and the quest for the powerful self-fulfilling prophecy. In M. P. Zanna (Ed.), *Advances in experimental social psychology* (Vol. 29, pp. 281–388). San Diego, CA: Academic Press.

Jussim, L., & Harber, K. (2005). Teacher expectations and self-fulfilling prophecies: Knowns and unknowns, resolved and unresolved controversies. *Personality and Social Psychology Review, 9,* 131–155.

Rosenthal, R., & Jacobson, L. (1968). *Pygmalion in the classroom: Teacher expectations and student intellectual development.* New York: Holt, Rinehart & Winston.

Snyder, M. (1984). When belief creates reality. In L. Berkowitz (Ed.), *Advances in experimental social psychology* (Vol. 18, pp. 247–305). New York: Academic Press.

SELF-MANAGING TEAMS

Teams are a fundamental part of most manufacturing, service, and high technology companies and most nonprofit organizations. Some teams operate in a face-to-face setting, whereas others are geographically distributed. Some occur within a single organization, whereas others contain members from multiple organizations. *Self-managing teams* (SMTs) share some features common to traditional work groups, including group goals, a set of interdependent tasks, and the challenge of coordinating tasks and member skills to create a group product or service. What distinguishes SMTs is their control over the decision-making process. In traditional work groups, managers decide who is in the group and how and when members interact with one another. In an SMT, many of these decisions are made by the group. This entry examines the ways in which SMTs differ from traditional work groups, the outcomes of SMTs, challenges for future research on SMTs, and limitations of SMTs.

To understand the difference between traditional work teams and SMTs, consider the example of a manufacturing facility that produced blades for jet engines. The plant was organized into SMTs. Each SMT decided who could join the group, what jobs people would work on, and how the jobs were to be done. In addition, each SMT disciplined members of the group and evaluated members' competencies in order to determine compensation. In an SMT operation, activities such as maintenance and quality control are part of the group's responsibilities rather than independent support operations. The fundamental idea is that the responsibility and authority for all the major work decisions are held by the team rather than by some organizational hierarchy. However, all SMTs are not the same. The major differences among SMTs concern the scope and number of decisions the group controls. The critical criterion of an SMT is that the majority of work decisions are made by the group.

Impact on Outcomes

How do these structural features of SMTs affect group and organizational effectiveness, and what is the rationale for designing groups this way? Some key mediating mechanisms have been proposed to account for the presumed effectiveness of SMTs. First, compared with traditional work groups, SMTs provide workers with greater levels of autonomy, responsibility, freedom, and variety—factors documented in the literature to create high levels of motivation. Second, SMTs demand greater levels of coordination than do traditional work groups. The group members, rather than a supervisor, are responsible for making coordination effective, and they have control over their environment. In well-designed SMTs there are high levels of cohesiveness and strong norms supporting cooperation. Third, given the group's responsibility for managing the major production decisions, most SMTs exhibit high levels of problem solving. Instead of relying on a supervisor or others in the

organization to solve a problem, the group takes responsibility. A fourth mediating mechanism, related to the three listed above, is a focus on learning. In SMTs, the group strives to continuously develop new repertoires to enhance performance.

The potential consequences of these higher levels of motivation, coordination, problem solving, and learning are that SMTs should achieve high performance goals. Also, group members should express high levels of satisfaction and commitment over time. Furthermore, SMTs should be characterized by lower absenteeism, turnover, and accident rates than are traditional work groups.

What are the empirical findings regarding SMTs? Evidence suggests that SMTs can improve performance, but only when they are effectively implemented and institutionalized in organizations. Performance is measured both objectively (in terms of productivity and quality) and subjectively. High customer satisfaction is another outcome sometimes associated with SMTs. Finally, there is some evidence that withdrawal behavior (e.g., turnover, absenteeism) is lower in SMTs. In regard to mediators of SMT effectivness, research suggests that SMTs produce greater effort and problem solving, which in turn lead to higher performance. To date, little effort has been made to investigate how SMTs influence other important group processes, such as leadership, conflict management, role ambiguity, and emergent control systems.

Challenges for Future Research

One challenge for future research is clarifying how SMTs differ from tradititional work groups. Asserting that a group is an SMT is common in the literature. But the definition of an SMT is based on the group's control over a variety of decisions. In many studies, the specific decisions the group does or does not make are not well specified, and hence ambiguity exists about whether the group is indeed an SMT. A second challenge is understanding the evolution of SMTs over time. When a group is initially given control over a new set of decisions, it is not surprising that there are positive performance changes. Longitudinal designs are needed to assess how SMTs evolve over time and whether the changes associated with new groups persist. A third challenge involves increasing the use of control groups, which are absent in most of the studies on SMTs. A fourth challenge is being clear about the level of analysis for measuring the consequences of SMTs. Because SMTs are group-level phenomena, measurement needs to be at that level. A final challenge involves carefully specifying how the organizational contexts in which SMTs are embedded affect their performance.

Limitations of SMTs

Several constraints on the diffusion and long-term effectiveness of SMTs deserve mention. First, because SMTs represent a fundamental change in the way organizations are structured, they are often resisted. Second, if SMTs are introduced into organizations in which traditional work teams also remain in place, conflicts between the two kinds of groups may reduce the long-run viability of the SMTs. A third limiting factor involves the group's task structure. Because SMTs are designed for groups in which members have high task interdependence, they are unlikely to be effective in situations in which members primarily work alone (e.g., service technicians).

SMTs are likely to remain part of the organizational landscape. At the same time, the nature of work is changing—it is becoming more distributed and global and placing a higher premium on knowledge work. It will be interesting to see how SMTs adapt to this changing environment.

Paul S. Goodman and Uriel J. Haran

See also Group Cohesiveness; Group Learning; Group Problem Solving and Decision Making; Job Design; Team Performance Assessment; Teams; Work Teams

Further Readings

Bishop, J. W., & Scott, K. D. (2000). An examination of organizational and team commitment in a self-directed team environment. *Journal of Applied Psychology, 85*(3), 439–450.

Goodman, P. S., Devadas, R., & Hughson, T. L. G. (1988). Groups and productivity: Analyzing the effectiveness of self-managing teams. In J. P. Campbell & R. J. Campbell (Eds.), *Productivity in organizations* (pp. 295–327). San Francisco: Jossey-Bass.

Kirkman, B. L., & Rosen, B. (1999). Beyond self-management: Antecedents and consequences of team empowerment. *Academy of Management Journal, 42*(1), 58–74.

Morgeson, M. D., Johnson, M. A., Campion, G. J., & Medsker, T. (2006). Understanding reactions to job redesign: A quasi-experimental investigation. *Personnel Psychology, 59*(2), 333–363.

Wageman, R. (2001). How leaders foster self-managing team effectiveness: Design choices versus hands-on coaching. *Organization Science, 12*(5), 559–577.

SELF-STEREOTYPING

Self-stereotyping occurs when individuals' perceptions of their own characteristics correspond to the characteristics attributed to a social group to which they belong (i.e., stereotypes of their group). Researchers commonly measure self-stereotyping in one of two ways. The first way involves measuring the extent to which individuals attribute to themselves those characteristics commonly thought to describe their group. For example, it is a common belief that women in general are poor at math. Assessing whether individual women feel as if they are poor at math would be consistent with this way of measuring self-stereotyping. The second way researchers assess self-stereotyping is by measuring how similar individual group members think they are to their group or to a typical group member. For example, a researcher may ask individual members of an ethnic group how similar they are to a typical member of their ethnic group.

Some researchers use the term *self-stereotyping* more broadly to describe circumstances in which individual members of a group embrace stereotypic beliefs about their group, when group members behave in line with prevailing stereotypes of their group, and when members of a group have low self-esteem because their group as a whole is devalued within society. However, these uses of the term are less common and do not conform to the definition provided above.

History and Importance

Historically, self-stereotyping was assumed to be an unavoidable negative consequence of membership in a socially devalued group. Conceptualizing self-stereotyping more broadly than is done today, classic theories of the self and intergroup relations argued that the way society views a group undoubtedly shapes how individual group members see themselves. It was believed that members of socially devalued groups must see themselves negatively because they internalize society's negative image of their group. Thus, the importance of self-stereotyping was derived from the assumption that it represented a pervasive harmful consequence of being socially devalued.

In more recent thinking, the importance of self-stereotyping is thought to rest on the functions that it serves. According to some researchers, most notably system-justification theorists, self-stereotyping serves to justify inequitable social systems. That is, self-stereotyping among members of disadvantaged groups is thought to translate into beliefs and behaviors that excuse and perpetuate their disadvantaged status, lending credence to existing group inequalities. Other notable perspectives contend that self-stereotyping is a means by which individuals can feel close to or distinct from others.

At the intergroup level, self-stereotyping can increase a sense of connection to members of one's own group, thereby creating a sense of group cohesion and solidarity, or decrease the degree to which one's group seems similar to other groups. At the interpersonal level, self-stereotyping can facilitate positive interactions with people who believe group stereotypes to be true. Research delineating other functions needs to be done.

Theory and Evidence

Several perspectives describe the circumstances in which self-stereotyping is more or less likely to occur. One important perspective, *self-categorization theory*, contends that the likelihood of self-stereotyping depends on whether people are categorizing themselves in terms of either a personal or a group identity at a given moment in time. As individuals shift from a personal identity to a group identity, the likelihood of self-stereotyping increases. This is because individuals who are thinking about themselves in terms of their personal identity define themselves using characteristics that differentiate them from other members of their group. In contrast, individuals who are thinking about themselves in terms of a group identity compare themselves with members of other groups, defining themselves using shared ingroup characteristics that differentiate their group from other groups.

Two forms of evidence support this perspective. First, factors thought to increase the degree to which people think of themselves in terms of group identities have been shown to increase self-stereotyping. For example, situational cues that increase the degree to which a group membership comes to mind, such as completing a demographics sheet containing items inquiring about one's group membership, increase self-stereotyping. Self-stereotyping also increases as the distinctiveness of a given group membership within a particular situation increases. For example, being the only Black person at a board meeting should increase the likelihood that one thinks of the self in terms of this group membership, and therefore this situation should increase self-stereotyping. Second, self-stereotyping has been shown to depend on those to whom people compare themselves. Men and women in social or cultural contexts that foster cross-gender comparisons have been shown to exhibit greater self-stereotyping than those in contexts that foster within-gender comparisons.

The motivation to feel close to one's own group or differentiate one's group from other groups also determines self-stereotyping. Investigating the role of the former motivation, researchers found that individuals whose desire to feel included in important ingroups is threatened engage in greater self-stereotyping to fulfill this need. For example, if a sorority member momentarily feels that she is very different from the other members of her sorority, an important group identity, she may attempt to quell this feeling by engaging in self-stereotyping.

Exemplifying the role of the latter motivation, individuals who feel their group is threatened because of low status or insufficient distinctiveness from other groups will engage in self-stereotyping as a means to enhance the sense that their group is unique. An honors student who learns that honors students and other students on campus are fairly similar, for example, may engage in self-stereotyping by seeing himself or herself as highly academically motivated in order to restore a feeling of being distinct from other students. People who are highly identified with their group are particularly likely to respond to such temporary and chronic threats to the group with increased self-stereotyping, even when the relevant group traits are negative.

Finally, stereotypes have been shown to influence how people see themselves via shared understandings about the self developed in long-term relationships and in the course of daily social interaction with others. Self-stereotyping is more likely if one thinks that a close other holds stereotypic beliefs about one's group than if the other person is thought to hold counterstereotypic beliefs. For example, self-stereotyping is more likely if a woman thinks that her mother believes that women are poor at math than if she thinks her mother believes women are good at math. Also, people who think a new person with whom they want to get along holds stereotypic beliefs, as opposed to counterstereotypic beliefs, about their group are more likely to see themselves in a stereotypic manner.

Future Directions

The understanding of self-stereotyping has advanced over time. The nature of self-stereotyping as well as those conditions that give rise to it are better understood. However, many fertile avenues for research remain. One important task is further distinguishing the circumstances under which self-stereotyping occurs with respect to positive group characteristics only, negative group characteristics only, or both. In some research, self-stereotyping is selective and occurs only for positive traits. In other research, self-stereotyping occurs for both positive and negative traits. Another important question is whether and when self-stereotyping translates into corresponding behavior. For example, for members of groups commonly associated with poor academic abilities, does self-stereotyping translate into poor academic performance?

Jeffrey R. Huntsinger and Stacey Sinclair

See also Categorization; Self-Categorization Theory; Self-Esteem; Social Identity Theory; Stereotyping

Further Readings

Guimond, S., Branscombe, N. R., Brunot, S., Buunk, A. P., Chatard, A., Désert, M., et al. (2007). Culture, gender and the self: Variations and impact of social comparison processes. *Journal of Personality and Social Psychology, 92,* 1118–1134.

Onorato, R. S., & Turner, J. C. (2001). The "I," the "me," and the "us": The psychological group and self-concept maintenance and change. In C. Sedikides & M. Brewer (Eds.), *Individual self, relational self and collective self* (pp. 147–170). New York: Psychology Press.

Pickett, C. L., Bonner, B. L., & Coleman, J. M. (2002). Motivated self-stereotyping: Heightened assimilation and differentiation needs result in increased levels of positive and negative self-stereotyping. *Journal of Personality and Social Psychology, 82,* 543–562.

Sinclair, S., Huntsinger, J., Skorinko, J., & Hardin, C. D. (2005). Social tuning of the self: Consequences for the self-evaluations of stereotype targets. *Journal of Personality and Social Psychology, 89,* 160–175.

SENSITIVITY TRAINING GROUPS

Sensitivity training groups provide training in a small-group setting for people who want to gain greater awareness and understanding of themselves and of their relationships with others. In contrast to psychotherapy groups, in which people seek relief through therapeutic intervention from an emotional disturbance (such as depression), sensitivity training groups generally involve people who are healthy yet have a desire for personal growth. Examples of problem areas in which growth is often sought include shyness, talkativeness, inability to express anger, and discomfort with emotional closeness.

Understanding sensitivity training groups is important because their focus on healthy individuals has widespread societal applicability. These groups are offered by organizations and agencies to help members of a community learn how to better understand and appreciate differences in other people. They often address societal concerns such as gender sensitivity; multicultural sensitivity, including gay, lesbian, bisexual, and transgendered cultures; and sensitivity toward those who are disabled in some way. This entry examines how such groups developed and how they work; it also reviews points of debate and current use of such programs.

History

In the early 1900s, scholars began to take an interest in crowd psychology, which translated by the 1920s into an interest in studying normal social groupings and interactions to find solutions to social problems. In the 1930s, Kurt Lewin developed his field theory to understand the nature of individuals in the context of their experience of their social environment. Lewin also began research aimed at promoting social change.

The development of what was called the *training laboratory* was a collaborative effort of Leland Bradford, Ronald Lippitt, and Kenneth Benne, all of whom joined with Lewin in the summer of 1946 to run a workshop at Connecticut's State Teachers College. According to Lippitt, one evening, as they met to discuss the day's training, three of the training participants came in and indicated they wanted to listen to the discussion. Lewin agreed, and he and his colleagues tried to proceed as if the participants were not present.

When the discussion's focus turned to the behavior of one of these participants, that participant became agitated and declared that the scientists' view of her group's interactions was not correct, and she commenced to offer her own perceptions. Later in the discussion, the same happened with one of the other participants—she, too, had a different perception of what had occurred within the group that day. At the end of the discussion, the three trainees asked if they could come back the next night for the discussion of that day's training events. The next night all 50 of the trainees came, and they all continued to come back every night of the training. According to Lippitt, this feedback and process review session became the most significant training event of the workshop.

This account of the emergence of the sensitivity training group is compatible with Lewin's three-stage model of group decision making: (1) *Unfreezing* occurs when the participant has a basic attitude, belief, or behavior disconfirmed or called into question; (2) *moving* occurs when the participant feels safe and secure and uses information obtained from the group's feedback to arrive at new attitudes, beliefs, or behaviors; and (3) *freezing* reflects the extent to which the new changes are internalized. According to Kurt Back, the training group (T-group) provided a new method for unfreezing a group, and the strong interactions and emotions that came with feedback were a sign of accomplishing this change.

At the time of their inception in the 1940s, T-groups focused on teaching U.S. communities techniques for participatory democracy. In the 1950s, the groups shifted to a focus on individual growth, self-knowledge, and maturation. In the mid-1960s, the original aims of the laboratory method were renewed with the launch of the *Journal of Applied Behavioral Science* as a forum to critically reevaluate this field.

Thirty years after the birth of T-groups, there were three main types of these unstructured learning groups. The traditional T-group, also called *laboratory training*, emphasized interpersonal relationships and the development of interpersonal skills by allowing group members to interact in an unstructured environment and then analyze the dynamics of what had occurred. *Organizational development groups*, also called *human relations training*, used T-groups to address interpersonal problems at work and to change the culture of their organizations. Because group members were also coworkers, dynamics of the interactions would often have long-term positive and/or negative effects in the work environment. Finally, *personal expression groups* focused on personal growth and development, including the examination of personal beliefs, biases, and prejudices. With the shift away from a focus on dynamic group learning, personal expression groups came to be known as sensitivity training groups. *Encounter groups*, a type of sensitivity training group that gained popularity in the late 1960s, are sensitivity training groups that allow group members opportunities to have interpersonally intimate experiences with other group members. These latter two terms are often used synonymously in the literature.

Goals and Format

The goals of sensitivity training groups are to help participants develop sensitivity to and awareness of their own feelings and reactions, to increase their understanding of group interactions, and to help them learn to modify their behavior. These goals include specifics such as increasing one's awareness of one's own feelings in the here and now, increasing one's ability to give and receive feedback, increasing one's ability to learn from experiences, increasing one's understanding of the impact of one's behavior on other people, and increasing one's ability to manage and use conflict.

To accomplish these goals, sensitivity training groups do not focus on discussion of a particular topic, the presentation of information, or problem solving but rather on the process of the group's interactions, such as the feelings of group participants and the communication of those feelings. Participants' concerns about issues such as intimacy, authority, and inclusion or exclusion in the group come to the surface and become the content and work of the group.

The format most commonly used for sensitivity training is a group consisting of 7 to 12 people who meet together with a group leader on an outpatient basis once a week for a specified time. However, *marathon groups* meet continuously for lengthy periods, such as 12 to 24 hours, providing a highly intense experience without interruptions. The leader of the group is referred to as the *trainer* but is more of a facilitator than an expert or teacher, helping the group make its own decisions and maximize its resources.

In general, these groups are highly experiential, including activities such as discussions, games, and exercises that produce high levels of involvement by participants, thereby producing increased learning. Although experiential, groups are relatively unstructured; indeed, the group itself is accountable for developing the structure, and in this process, interpersonal styles and habits of the participants become evident. Participants who are self-centered, manipulative, rebellious, or pacifying, or who continue to remain disengaged, reveal themselves, and the group gives them feedback on their behavior.

This process takes on predictable developmental stages. These stages are given various names throughout the literature, but their descriptions are the same: (a) *initial encounter* describes the beginning of the group, when participants are cautious about exchanging personal material; (b) *interpersonal confrontation* describes the work stage, in which the focus of the group is directed to individual members and there is substantial negative feedback and/or invalidation of participants' personal beliefs, which provides participants with an opportunity to reconstruct their beliefs and/or expectations of others; and (c) *mutual acceptance* refers to the concluding phase, when the work has lessened, participant relationships become more relaxed and positive, and participants make efforts to patch up sources of conflict and tension from earlier training sessions.

Some researchers believe that the disconfirmation of a participant's beliefs creates a motivation or "felt need" to learn, that the acceptance or support offered by the group creates the climate in which the participant can change, and that these paradoxical stances are essential for effective learning in sensitivity training groups. The groups thus provide a testing ground for group members to "try on" new behaviors, attitudes, and beliefs.

Points of Debate

Sensitivity training has been controversial because of suggestions that participants could suffer emotional harm that would render the training method unethical. For example, the group may promote exposure, frankness, or even attacks within the group that participants would not normally engage in or be exposed to in their lives outside the group. Such experiences might have undesirable enduring consequences for participants.

Furthermore, despite some researchers' firm beliefs that confrontation or disconfirmation of a participant's basic feelings, attitudes, or behavior is necessary for change to occur, research does not support this belief. Favorable outcomes have also been reported by participants who received only support from the group, allowing them to feel safe or accepted. These findings provide an invitation to current sensitivity training group leaders to eliminate controversial confrontational methods and replace them with those that would provide more support of group members. Doing so would allow leaders to facilitate personal growth in group members without the risk of harming them emotionally.

There are two other main points of debate in the literature. First, there is concern about the moral implications that this type of encounter may have for an individual and for the community at large. Within sensitivity training groups, standards and norms are relative: They are determined in situ by the group and hinge on a basic assumption that the group should be trusted. Organizations that believe in universal moral standards or absolutes, such as some churches, do not support the use of sensitivity training groups.

Second, findings from research examining the effectiveness of sensitivity training are mixed. In some studies, participation in sensitivity training groups has been shown to change behavior. However, there is a question about the persistence of these changes over time. Also, some research suggests possible negative outcomes for some participants. Furthermore, in hospital settings, research found that social skills groups that focused on learning appropriate behaviors and eliminating inappropriate behaviors through the use of behavioral techniques such as rehearsal, feedback, and modeling fared significantly better than sensitivity training groups did in producing changes in their participants.

Research on sensitivity training groups has largely faded. One reason is that although such groups were originally associated with basic laboratory-based psychology, these groups now have a very successful life of their own outside scientific psychology. Sensitivity training is now largely a clinical and applied discipline. With no identifiable basic social science discipline to call their own, sensitivity training groups have few norms for performance or evaluation.

Current Status

Concerns and research issues led to a virtual extinction of sensitivity training groups as they had existed in the 1960s and early 1970s. For example, in the early years, sensitivity training groups and human relations training were the focus of many books and were included in psychotherapy literature reviews, yet in current publications it is difficult to find mention of either of these topics in other than a historical sense. However, as reported by John Beck, many sensitivity training group participants reported highly fulfilling experiences, in addition to expressing positive sentiments of excitement, involvement, enjoyment, and fun.

In the 1970s, efforts were made to develop training programs to address the continued interest of participants through widely marketed for-profit companies. For example, the company LifeSpring, founded in 1974 by John Hanley, used Large Group Awareness Training to present training in a seminar format but split participants up into dyads to accomplish the small-group training experiences and goals of the earlier groups. By 1989, more than 300,000 participants had enrolled in these seminars. Although the company no longer exists, the *personal growth movement* continues with widespread fervor in other formats, and many companies, such as Momentus and the Great Life Foundation, offer intrapersonal training based on LifeSpring. There are also groups that have a greater focus on interpersonal training, such as Conscious Loving and Living, developed by Gay and Kathlyn Hendricks. The ongoing popularity of these programs provides contemporary evidence of the personal value participants place on this type of training.

Gary M. Burlingame and
Debra Theobald McClendon

See also Cooperation and Competition; Group Learning; Lewin, Kurt

Further Readings

Back, K. W. (1972). *Beyond words: The story of sensitivity training and the encounter movement*. New York: Russell Sage.

Back, K. W. (1978). *The search for community: Encounter groups and social change*. Boulder, CO: Westview.

Golembiewski, R. T., & Blumberg, A. (Eds.). (1977). *Sensitivity training and the laboratory approach: Readings about concepts and applications* (3rd ed). Istasca, IL: F. E. Peacock.

Lewin, K. (1948). *Resolving social conflicts*. New York: Harper & Row.

Lewin, K. (1951). *Field theory in social science*. New York: Harper & Brothers.

Miner, J. B. (2005). *Organizational behavior: Essential theories of motivation and leadership*. Armonk, NY: M. E. Sharp.

SEXISM

Sexism refers to attitudes and behaviors based on sex stereotypes, or cultural assumptions attached to being male or being female that disadvantage and discriminate against individuals on the basis of sex. Central to sexism are beliefs that men and women have inherently and essentially different traits. Manifested in socialization, interactions, and institutions, these beliefs maintain differences between men and women, affecting individuals in many different ways. This entry begins by reviewing common stereotypes based on gender, then examines the consequences for women, and briefly summarizes discrimination against men.

Sex Stereotypes

Studies find that widely held gender beliefs exist in the United States. In general, these beliefs hold that women are more *communal* and men are more *agentic*. Accordingly, women are often believed to be more competent at tasks that are characterized as more expressive and socioemotional in nature (e.g., nurturing and caring for others), while men are believed to be more competent at tasks that are more instrumental in nature (e.g., starting a business). In addition to these specific assumptions, men are considered to be generally more status worthy and more competent at tasks that "count." Because communal tasks are often devalued, women are usually seen as less competent than men, although they are generally considered the "nicer" sex.

Sex stereotypes are pervasive in that they are learned during childhood and maintained throughout the life course. From an early age, children learn that sex is a significant attribute of self and that being female is supposedly different from being male. To make sense of this difference, children often imitate behaviors of their same-sex parent, and parents may in turn encourage gender-appropriate behaviors through endorsing gender-specific hobbies (e.g., cooking for girls and sports for boys), rewarding gender-typical acts (e.g., girls behaving well and boys being assertive), and punishing or discouraging gender-atypical acts (e.g., girls acting aggressively and boys playing with dolls).

In addition, in childhood and adolescence, teachers and peers may help reinforce not only the notion that women and men are different but also the belief that men are more status worthy than women. Within the classroom, teachers may subconsciously pay more attention to boys, thereby creating a heightened sense of superiority and importance among the male students. Outside the classroom, peers may ostracize both girls who are tomboys and boys who "act like girls," but such stigmatization is often harsher on boys than on girls. The differential sanctioning of gender-deviant behavior is hence suggestive of men's higher status because it implies that it is more acceptable for women to partake in male-typed activities but less acceptable for men to exhibit feminine behaviors.

The early socialization of gender beliefs can significantly constrain perceptions of self-competence. For instance, research finds that given the cultural belief that boys are better at mathematics than girls are, parents often attribute boys' successes in mathematics to talent but girls' successes in mathematics to effort. Such attribution bias can lead to feelings of competence among boys and feelings of incompetence among girls, even if the two groups do not objectively differ in their actual performance in mathematics. Thus, sex stereotypes can prevent and discourage girls from pursuing a male-dominated field even if they are as competent as the male sex in that field. Indeed, a number of studies find that, when exposed to the belief that men are more competent than women at a task, men develop not only higher ratings of self-competence in that task but also higher aspirations to work in a field related to that task, even if there is no actual gender difference in competence. One implication, then, is that sex stereotypes can help explain the persistent segregation of men and women in different fields of study, occupations, and jobs.

Aside from early socialization, sex stereotypes are maintained in interactions throughout the life course. In this light, two theories in social psychology, *status characteristics theory* and *expectation states theory*, provide useful frameworks for understanding the mechanisms by which gender beliefs are created and upheld.

According to status characteristics theory, an attribute is a status characteristic when cultural beliefs attach a greater value and competence to one category of the attribute than another. Gender is therefore a status characteristic in that cultural beliefs denote not only sex differences in general levels of competence (thus making gender a *diffuse* status characteristic) but also sex differences in specific types of competence (thus making gender a *specific* status characteristic). The beliefs attached to the different categories of gender, in turn, have implications for how individuals see and act toward one another in social relations.

According to expectation states theory, cultural beliefs attached to a status characteristic translate into performance expectations and ultimately behaviors when the status characteristic is salient in the particular social relational context. Specifically, in collective, task-oriented situations, to the extent that a status characteristic is related to the task outcome, the stereotypes associated with that status characteristic shape expectations that actors form for themselves and others. What this theory predicts, then, is that in situations in which gender is salient, sex stereotypes will influence what individuals expect from one another. Congruent with this prediction, experimental research in mixed-sex settings finds that men have an advantage over women in task behaviors (e.g., visual dominance, assertive gestures) when given a masculine task or a gender-neutral task, whereas women have an advantage over men when given a feminine task.

The resulting implication is that in interactions in which gender is salient, individuals expect others to treat them in ways that are consistent with widely held gender belief. That is, men and women are better at different tasks, but men are generally more competent than women. Behaviors then follow expectations in self-fulfilling ways: Men are given more opportunities to act and more positive feedback when they are presumed to be more competent at the task, whereas women take the dominant role when the task is considered a feminine one.

The maintenance of sex stereotypes in interactions thus reinforces and legitimates the belief that men and women are different. This belief can serve as a basis of discrimination, especially in situations in which individuals enter a group or position that is dominated by the other sex. In particular, research finds that women in traditionally male-dominated work settings (e.g., engineering) or positions (e.g., CEOs) often face a double bind: Whereas their work requires them to be agentic and aggressive, they are also expected to be communal and warm. As the requisite behavior contradicts gendered expectations, women in these situations often experience a *backlash*, as they are seen as too aggressive, unfriendly, and therefore deviant from the way others believe they should be. As a result, women looking to work in customarily male occupations or jobs may be less favorably considered or evaluated, and their legitimacy may be questioned. This, in turn, can disadvantage women in their career choices, advancement, and mobility.

Consequences of Sexism

Sex stereotypes thus affect not only individual behaviors and social relations but also larger social structures. In particular, research suggests that gender inequality in the labor market can be at least partly explained by discrimination based on sex stereotypes. It is important to note, however, that sex stereotypes often emerge in subtle and nonconscious ways. Gender beliefs emerge in social relations through the process of sex categorization, that is, the labeling of self and others as either male or female. Studies in cognitive psychology suggest that sex categorization often occurs automatically and unconsciously; that is, sex is one of the first categories with which individuals sort and make sense of self and others. As categorization inherently exaggerates differences between groups and minimizes differences within groups, sex categorization activates ingroup preferences as well as sex stereotypes, thereby distorting and biasing perceptions and evaluations of others.

Workplace Discrimination

Men tend to be predominant in the workplace, and this can be disadvantageous to women. As individuals in powerful positions are often male, ingroup preferences can result in the favoring of men over women in hiring and promotion practices. Furthermore, widespread beliefs about gender and competence can lead not only to the placement of men and women into different jobs but also to the placement of men in higher positions and women in lower positions. Given the assumption that men are generally more competent than women, employers may also credit men more often for their successes, leaving women with less recognition for their achievements.

Although they are subtle, acts of nonconscious discrimination can over time accumulate into real advantages and disadvantages. Discrimination based on sex, however, can also occur in other ways. Related to gendered assumptions about competence are gendered assumptions about men's and women's roles in the family. Though women's participation in the labor force has increased, women are still seen as wives and mothers before they are workers and providers, whereas men are seen as workers and providers before they are husbands and fathers. The persistent assignment of the nurturing role to women and the provider role to men can lead not only to increased work–family conflicts for women but also to discrimination against mothers in the workplace. Like gender, motherhood can be seen as a status characteristic with its own set of stereotypes. In particular, it is often assumed that mothers are less competent and less committed to work, given their primary childbearing and childrearing responsibilities. Given this belief, employers may see mothers as less hirable and less promotable, in turn disadvantaging mothers in their workplace pursuits. This belief can also affect women who are not mothers, because employers often assume that most women will become mothers.

Discrimination based on motherhood therefore constitutes another barrier for women in the labor market. Indeed, recent research indicates a wage penalty for motherhood, suggesting that employer discrimination against mothers can be one reason for the depression of women's earnings. Furthermore, studies suggest that employers could also "statistically" discriminate. According to this perspective, employers are seen as profit-maximizing actors who use sex stereotypes as a means to screen applicants with respect to work productivity and commitment to work. As mentioned earlier, given the cultural assignment of domestic responsibilities to women, employers often assume that women are less productive, less committed to work, and more likely to quit than men are. As such, hiring or promoting female workers poses significant risks and high costs, and employers may accordingly not hire women or not promote women, or they may allocate women to lower positions with lower turnover costs. In this sense, although employers may believe that they are making rational decisions, their actions may nonetheless constitute discrimination based on inaccurate beliefs.

Other Outcomes

In general, employer discrimination based on sex stereotypes occurs in fairly subtle and covert ways. However, sex stereotypes can emerge in a more overt manner through sexual harassment. Broadly, sexual harassment refers to unwelcome verbal or physical behavior of a sexual nature directed at a person or group in institutional settings such as education or the workplace. Such behavior can come from authority figures (e.g., teachers or employers) as well as peers (e.g., classmates or coworkers) and often involves disparagement or disapproval of a certain sex based on beliefs about that sex. For instance, research finds that women studying or working in customarily male fields often encounter sexist remarks that question women's abilities (e.g., women's management skills), imply their inappropriateness for studying or working in those fields (e.g., calling law "a man's game"), and maintain their difference from their male counterparts (e.g., the doctor vs. the "lady doctor"). Such experiences with sexual harassment can lower women's satisfaction with their work, elevate their levels of stress, and increase their likelihood of changing their academic or career plans.

In addition to discriminatory behaviors, sexist beliefs may be embedded within institutions in more direct ways. One example is the devaluation of women's work. It is widely documented that there is a wage penalty for working in occupations that are female dominated. That is, controlling for occupational characteristics and occupational demands, female-dominated occupations tend to pay less than male-dominated occupations. Research further finds that there is a wage penalty associated with nurturance. That is, jobs that require nurturing skills pay less. Given that nurturance is a trait usually linked to women, these findings imply that occupations are valued in ways that are consistent with the stereotype that men's abilities, and hence tasks associated with men are worth more than women's abilities and feminine-typed tasks. Thus, as much as the gender gap in pay may be due to discrimination against women, it may also be due to systematic gender bias in the compensation structures in the labor market.

Knowledge-producing institutions are also not impervious to gender beliefs. Up until the mid-20th century, most academic research focused largely on men in both methodology (e.g., studying only men) and scope (e.g., studying only men's issues). Interpretations of research findings also favored men and reinforced sex stereotypes. As an example, the finding that men and women have different brain sizes was interpreted as evidence for actual gender differences in competence. Since then, women have increased their participation in research, and studies including women have likewise expanded. However, it remains true that women's issues are often marginalized or neglected. Men continue to be seen as the standard for the typical human subject in research, and findings continue to compare women against an implicit male norm rather than assess gender differences on equal grounds. Further, though most studies now incorporate both men and women in their research methods, findings regarding gender differences are not always discussed or applied in the real world. Gender bias hence exists even in institutions where objectivity is the ideal, and given that these institutions are linked to the production of knowledge, such bias may result in the further reproduction of sex stereotypes.

It has also been argued that there is a general lack of gender sensitivity in social institutions. Research on professional education (e.g., medical school and law school), for one, finds little inclusion and little discussion of gender issues in the classroom and in educational texts. The marginalization of gender not only can result in a lack of gender awareness but also can leave individuals unprepared for gendered experiences in later career practices. Likewise, at the workplace, gender insensitivity can go beyond sexual harassment in that characteristics that are considered inherent in jobs may be laden with gendered connotations. In some cases, gender-specific job titles (e.g., stewardess) may be used to imply the gender-appropriateness of different types of work, and specific job requirements (e.g., heavy lifting) may be used to favor a particular gender in hiring and promotions. Moreover, despite legal sanctions against blatant discrimination based on sex, the underreporting of sexual harassment and the lack of intervention and resolution for cases that are reported indicate a need for effective policies and stronger enforcement of policies. Similarly, despite the prevalence of work–family conflicts, there remains a dearth of family-friendly policies at the workplace. The lack of discussion and action regarding the work–family balance can be particularly disadvantageous to women because most women shoulder the bulk of domestic responsibilities.

Sexism Against Men

Although the term *sexism* is generally applied to the treatment of women, there is recent discourse regarding sexism against men, or *reverse sexism*. In this perspective, widely held gender beliefs are seen as disadvantageous not only to women but also to men. A recent example is a court suit filed by a male high school student against his school, claiming that schools are designed to disadvantage boys in that they reward behaviors more often expected from girls (e.g., compliance) while punishing behaviors more often expected from boys (e.g., rebelliousness).

Discrimination against men, however, has been documented in more than the educational setting. In the criminal justice system, the gender gap in conviction and imprisonment rates may partly reflect the stereotype that men are more aggressive and therefore more capable of violent crimes. Specifically, some research finds that although men and women are equally likely to initiate violence, women are less often charged with domestic abuse than men are because of the belief that women are less aggressive and therefore less capable of abusive acts. Bias against men has also been documented in the legal system. In family court, fathers are much less likely than mothers to obtain child custody in divorce cases. Possibly this reflects the stereotype that women are more nurturing and therefore better parents than men are.

Discrimination in the labor market can also be directed at men. Just as women in male-dominated occupations face significant gender bias at the workplace, men who wish to pursue female-dominated occupations (e.g., nursing, elementary school teaching) find themselves discriminated against by others, who label these men as effeminate, weak, and passive. The overarching sentiment is that these men are not only acting inappropriately against norms of masculinity but are also stepping down in status by pursuing female-typed work. As sanctions for gender-deviant behaviors are usually harsher on men than on women, such discrimination can strongly discourage men from pursuing female occupations, thereby contributing to men's dramatic underrepresentation in female-dominant fields.

Even men who choose to pursue and work in female-dominant occupations face discrimination from those within. The nature and consequences of such discrimination, however, could be seen in a positive light. In particular, because of the assumption that men are generally more competent than women are, specifically at instrumental tasks, men in female occupations are often encouraged to "move up" into higher-paying administrative positions (e.g., head nurse, school principal). This is a sharp contrast to women's experiences in male-dominated occupations, in which they face backlash and hence difficulty in moving up the ladder. Thus, whereas women in male occupations face a *glass ceiling*, men in female occupations face a *glass escalator* that ultimately leads to better career outcomes. However, while these are considered positive outcomes, men may not necessarily intend or desire them, even though they may nonetheless take positions in higher ranks.

Manwai C. Ku

See also Ambivalent Sexism; Discrimination; Feminism; Gender and Behavior; Gender Roles; Modern Sexism; Prejudice; Sexual Harassment; Stereotyping

Further Readings

Correll, S. J. (2004). Constraints into preferences: Gender, status, and emerging career aspirations. *American Sociological Review, 69*, 93–113.

Reskin, B. F. (2002). Rethinking employment discrimination. In M. F. Guillen, R. Collins, P. England, & M. Meyers (Eds.), *The new economic sociology: Developments in an emerging field* (pp. 218–244). New York: Russell Sage.

Ridgeway, C. L., & Correll, S. J. (2004). Unpacking the gender system: A theoretical perspective on cultural beliefs and social relations. *Gender & Society, 18*, 510–531.

Williams, C. L. (1992). The glass escalator: Hidden advantages for men in the female professions. *Social Problems, 39*, 253–267.

Sexual Harassment

Most legal and scholarly definitions of *sexual harassment* refer to any form of unwanted sexual attention that occurs at work or in school. Sexual harassment may include, among other behaviors, unwanted touching, exposure to offensive materials, offensive joking, or demands for sexual favors. In the view of many scholars and activists, sexual harassment is best conceived of as a form of sexual violence.

The term *sexual harassment* entered public consciousness during the second wave of the feminist movement, in the 1960s and 1970s, and attention to the problem of sexual harassment was raised further after the 1979 publication of Catherine MacKinnon's groundbreaking book, *Sexual Harassment of Working Women*. Since that time, social psychologists, sociologists, and other scholars have developed a large literature on the topic, and legal protections against sexual harassment have been enacted and increasingly expanded. Sexual harassment shapes intergroup relations at school and work and highlights how various dimensions of power such as gender and age shape experiences within these important social institutions.

This entry reports sexual harassment prevalence rates, outlines the two major types of sexual harassment covered under U.S. law, and then describes social scientific explanations for sexual harassment.

Prevalence and Reporting

The experience of sexual harassment is not limited to one age or gender. Studies show that women and men of all ages may be subjected to sexual harassment. As many as 70% of women and 45% of men have experienced sexual harassment in the workplace, while up to 80% of students in Grades 8 through 11 and 65% percent of college students say they have been sexually harassed. Even so, many experts believe that sexual harassment remains underreported. Those who experience harassment may be reluctant to report it because of concerns about possible retaliation such as demotion, job loss, or stigmatization.

Indeed, research has shown that targets of sexual harassment may face such consequences as a result of reporting harassment. Oftentimes harassers hold some power over their targets, making reporting potentially even more difficult. Although sexual harassment is sometimes popularly represented as the result of some misunderstanding or overreaction, research shows that it is in fact a powerful tactic used by some individuals to exert power over others through sexual intimidation tactics.

Types of Sexual Harassment

In the United States, two forms of sexual harassment are recognized under the law. The first, *quid pro quo* or "something for something," refers to instances when sexual demands are made, or threatened to become, a condition of or basis for employment or school-related decisions such as grades or access to school activities. This type of harassment is usually directed at a subordinate by a person of power within an organization.

The second type of sexual harassment, *hostile environment*, can occur among individuals who have the same amount of power within an organization or among those of different statuses. Hostile environment harassment refers to the existence of sexual conduct or materials in the workplace that unreasonably interfere with a person's ability to perform her or his job or school tasks or when such conduct creates a hostile, intimidating, or offensive working or learning environment. In most cases, a pattern of unwelcome sexual conduct must typically be shown in order to qualify as hostile work environment harassment. On very rare occasions, a single incident may qualify as hostile work environment harassment if the event is particularly severe.

Since the U.S. Supreme Court decision in *Meritor Savings Bank v. Vinson* in 1986, employees have been protected from sexual harassment under Title VII of the 1964 Civil Rights Act. Students in educational programs and activities that receive federal funding are protected under Title IX of the Education Amendments of 1972. Most sexual harassment complaints fall under the category of hostile environment harassment.

A recent legal trend in the United States is that courts have begun to recognize and apply sexual harassment protections in same-sex cases in addition to more typical male-on-female harassment cases. For example, in the 1997 case of *Doe v. Belleville*, a federal appellate court considered the case of a young man who was physically harassed and threatened with sexual assault by his male coworkers, and in 1998 the U.S. Supreme Court considered a case (*Oncale v. Sundowner Offshore Services*) in which a man was subjected to numerous sexual humiliations, attacks, and threats of rape by male coworkers.

Explanations for Sexual Harassment

At its core, sexual harassment is about power. More specifically, research shows that sexual harassment is a gendered expression of power used to regulate and modify gendered behavior within the social institutions of school and work. In particular, because it exists within the present cultural context in which masculinity is valued over femininity, sexual harassment may be used to assert men's dominance over women, as in the case of male-on-female harassment. Social scientists have found that organizational settings where women work in occupations traditionally thought to be men's domain may be especially likely locations where sexual harassment occurs. Public awareness of such organizational cultures has increased in part because of recently popular films such as *North Country*.

Sexual harassment may also be used to force individuals to adhere to mainstream gender norms. For example, men who do not adhere to masculinity norms associated with power, dominance, and heterosexuality may be subject to sexual harassment. Men with egalitarian gender views and those who do not adhere to masculine norms for self-presentation, perhaps by wearing earrings or dressing in other ways considered feminine, have also been found to be more likely than other men to experience harassment.

In addition to gender, dimensions of power such as age, social class, and sexuality have been linked to instances of and explanations for sexual harassment. Young people tend to be in positions at school and work in which older individuals wield power over them. Research has shown that young workers specifically may be more vulnerable to sexual harassment than their older counterparts because their lack of experience in the workplace tends to coincide with a general lack of knowledge about workplace rights and appropriate workplace interactions. Workers and students from disadvantaged social class positions may also be more vulnerable to sexual harassment. In the workplace particularly, those from lower social classes may be less willing or able to leave harassing job situations. Finally, research shows that lesbian, gay, bisexual, and transgendered individuals are more likely to experience sexual harassment than are others. Thus, sexual identity is yet another dimension of power that shapes sexual harassment experiences.

It is important to note that gender, age, sexuality, and social class are not simply individual characteristics. Instead, these dimensions of power are imbued throughout organizations and social institutions and therefore shape experiences of and responses to sexual harassment in schools and workplaces. In sum, multiple dimensions of power operate together to form the context of group processes and intergroup relations. Sexual harassment is an expression of power to which a range of individuals may be subject and that occurs within a variety of social contexts and institutions.

Amy Blackstone

See also Affirmative Action; Discrimination; Feminism; Gender and Behavior; Gender Roles; Power; Prejudice; Sexism; Stereotyping

Further Readings

Gruber, J. E., & Morgan, P. (Eds.). (2005). *In the company of men: Male dominance and sexual harassment.* Boston: Northeastern University Press.

Hill, C., & Silva, E. (2005). *Drawing the line: Sexual harassment on campus.* Washington, DC: American Association of University Women Educational Foundation.

MacKinnon, C. (1979). *Sexual harassment of working women: A case of sex discrimination.* New Haven, CT: Yale University Press.

Welsh, S. (1999). Gender and sexual harassment. *Annual Review of Sociology, 25,* 169–190.

Zippel, K. S. (2006). *The politics of sexual harassment: A comparative study of the United States, the European Union, and Germany.* Cambridge, UK: Cambridge University Press.

SHARED MENTAL MODELS

When it comes to the interaction between humans and machines, it is clear that people develop an understanding of how machinery works. This understanding, or *mental model*, guides how the individual interacts with machines. Cognitive psychologist Philip Johnson-Laird used this term to describe a reasoning process that could be applied to practical problems. He argued that mental models help people draw conclusions about how things work, deduce the relationship between units, and predict outcomes. The notion of mental models has since been widely used to describe internal cognitive representations of complex systems.

During the late 1980s, interest in team performance increased dramatically, due in part to several well-publicized incidents that were attributed to faulty teamwork (e.g., the downing of a commercial airliner by the Navy's USS *Vincennes*, the close call at the Three Mile Island nuclear energy plant, and an Air Florida crash in Washington, D.C.). Given the urgent need to understand and improve the performance of such critical teams, researchers extended the construct of mental models to teams. Most notably, Jan Cannon-Bowers and her colleagues began to analyze *shared mental model*—knowledge that is common or shared among team members. Shared mental models allow team members not only to understand their own work requirements but also to predict the needs and actions of their teammates. When accurate, these predictions should lead to better coordination and thus better teamwork.

Good examples of shared metal models are often seen in sports teams. Take basketball, for example. One player passing the ball to a second player without looking is called a *blind* or *no-look pass*. In analyzing this skill, we have to assume that the player who passes the ball is predicting that his or her teammate will be in a position to catch it (or else the pass would not be made). By the same token, the player receiving the pass is likely to have put himself or herself in a position to catch the ball. At a minimum, he or she is probably not caught completely off guard by the pass. This case illustrates how two team members are coordinating *implicitly* (without communicating) and demonstrates the use of shared mental models.

Researchers have described four types of mental models that might be shared among group members and thereby improve the group's performance. Each model contains different types of information about the task and the team.

1. A *task model* includes the overall goals and requirements of the task, task strategies, and parameters that circumscribe and limit the task.

2. A *team interaction model* includes the roles and responsibilities of individual members and the group's understanding of interaction requirements.

3. A *team model* includes team members' understanding of one another's knowledge,

skills, abilities, preferences, strengths, weaknesses, personal styles, and so on.

4. An *equipment model* includes a shared understanding of the use of available equipment in accomplishing the task and of how the performance of various team members needs to be coordinated to be successful.

So, for example, if team members have different task models, then they may approach the task differently and have trouble coordinating their actions. By the same token, if team members have different ideas about how they are supposed to interact (team interaction models), they will probably run into difficulties. When team models are not shared, team members will not have a good sense of one another and can make bad assumptions about what teammates need or are likely to do. Taking the basketball example, even highly skilled players can fail when they are not familiar with each other. Several Olympic "dream teams" have suffered this fate. Finally, in situations in which the team interacts with complex equipment, different equipment models can hinder coordination (a cockpit crew is a good example).

Although there is much agreement among analysts about the existence of shared mental models, there is still much debate about exactly how to define them. For example, some have interpreted the term *shared* to mean knowledge, implying that team members need to hold identical models. However, this interpretation is not completely accurate. For example, it is clear that surgical teams must coordinate their actions, but individual team members certainly do not have identical knowledge. Instead, each team member brings his or her own unique set of knowledge and skills to bear. So it is more reasonable to conclude that some *portion* of the individual members' mental models must be shared to ensure coordinated performance.

Measuring Shared Mental Models

Empirical research on shared mental models has lagged far behind theoretical analyses of them. This gap may be attributed, in part, to the difficulty in measuring this rather elusive construct. Obviously, there are no direct measures of mental models or shared mental models, because both are cognitive processes that occur in the minds of team members. Hence, researchers are forced to infer the existence of shared mental models from team members' questionnaire responses or from observations of a team's performance. Both techniques are imprecise and have been the subject of some criticism. For this reason, efforts to improve them continue.

In one popular method to assess shared mental models, task experts are first asked to generate a list of important concepts related to performance of the task at hand, including the steps that must be taken to complete the task. This list of concepts is then given to another set of experts, who are asked to rate how similar each concept is to each of the others. Sometimes this is done by printing each concept on an index card and asking experts to sort them into related piles (*card sorting*). The goal is to figure out the relatedness among concepts. These data are fed into statistical packages (e.g., *Pathfinder*) that produce an overall "map" of the experts' mental models. To assess the sharedness of mental models among team members, each team member is asked to do the same concept-sorting task, and the software calculates how similar the representations (maps) are among team members.

Although methods such as this are widely used, focusing only on the similarity of knowledge among team members may be misguided. Some suggest that it is important to assess the *accuracy* of these models as well. For example, if team members have a highly shared mental model of a situation, but that mental model is incorrect, then they will all be wrong (and likely fail). Obviously, both sharedness and accuracy are likely to be factors in performance.

Empirical Research on Shared Mental Models

As noted, research on shared mental models has progressed rather slowly. Most research has focused on establishing the relationship between shared mental models and team performance. For the most part, a small to moderate positive relationship has been found. Moreover, the accuracy of team mental models explains a significant amount of variance in performance when added to the similarity of models as a predictor.

Other researchers have investigated training approaches that might help create shared mental models within teams. At least three approaches have been proposed. The first of these is *cross training*, in which team members are allowed to experience the roles of their teammates. The rationale here is that if team members play one another's roles, then they will have a much better appreciation of how to support one another later on. Researchers have demonstrated that this is indeed a promising approach. However, there have also been some negative results, so more work is needed. A second approach is *interpositional knowledge training*. This entails training team members directly in the roles and responsibilities of their teammates. This approach has undergone little research (although what exists is encouraging) and thus requires further attention. The third approach is *team self-correction training*. This approach emphasizes intrateam feedback skills that help team members refine their mental models following performance. For example, this kind of intrateam debriefing often occurs in softball teams (frequently in a bar after the game): Team members recall individual plays from the game and discuss ways they could have handled things better. These exchanges are natural mechanisms that teams use to try to improve their performance. To date, however, few studies have been done to assess the utility of such exchanges.

Future Directions in Shared Mental Models Research

Several challenges exist in fully understanding the nature and development of shared mental models. Recent critiques have suggested that the concept of shared mental models is too limited to clarify the role of cognition in team performance and that issues such as the accuracy of shared mental models need further exploration. From the empirical perspective, there is a need for more research on shared mental models. Relatively little is known about how these models evolve, what they should contain, or how to improve them. For example, a recent statistical review of team training found only seven empirical studies that evaluated the effectiveness of training approaches thought to improve shared mental models.

Jan Cannon-Bowers and Clint Bowers

See also Group Mind; Group Performance; Socially Shared Cognition; Team Performance Assessment; Teams; Transactive Memory Systems

Further Readings

Cannon-Bowers, J., Salas, E., & Converse, S. (1993). Shared mental models in expert team decision making. In N. J. J. Castellan (Ed.), *Individual and group decision making: Current issues* (pp. 221–246). Hillsdale, NJ: Erlbaum.

Johnson-Laird, P. (1983). *Mental models: Towards a cognitive science of language, inference, and consciousness*. Cambridge, MA: Harvard University Press.

Mohammed, S., Klimoski, R., & Rentsch, J. (2000). The measurement of team mental models: We have no shared schema. *Organizational Research Methods, 3*(2), 123–165.

Thorsden, M. L., & Klein, G. A. (1989). Cognitive processes of the team mind. *Proceedings of the IEEE Conference on Systems, Man, and Cybernetics*, 46–49.

Yoo, Y., & Kanawattanachai, P. (2001). Development of transactive memory systems and collective mind in virtual teams. *International Journal of Organizational Analysis, 9*(2), 187–208.

SHERIF, MUZAFER (1906–1988)

Few can match the impact that Muzafer Sherif had on social psychology in the mid-20th century. His interests were wide ranging, including the self, social judgment, communication, reference groups, and attitude formation and change. But his most influential work was his early research on social norms and perception in the mid-1930s and his intergroup relations experiments carried out some 20 years later. The latter experiments provided the basis for his *realistic conflict theory*. It is his work on these two topics, based on an innovative use of the experimental method, that had major impact on both theory and research in social psychology. The common threads in his work were the ways that attitudes, internalized norms, and aspects of the self provide people with a frame of reference and anchor the way that they perceive, judge, and think.

Sherif's Personal and Intellectual History

According to the historian Gardner Murphy, who also supervised Sherif's PhD dissertation, social psychology in the 1930s saw the disparate contributions of F. C. Bartlett's studies of (socially transmitted) remembering, the German school of Gestalt psychology, and Kurt Lewin's field theory to North American social psychology. What Sherif supplied was the alignment of an experimental commitment with real-life observations that together defined how people respond socially. This holistic approach was new in its time and was the substance of two major publications, *Some Social Factors in Perception* (1935), based on Sherif's dissertation, and its expansion in his *Psychology of Social Norms* (1936).

Sherif was born in 1906 in Turkey, completed a master's degree there, and then earned a second master's degree at Harvard in 1932. He returned to a post as instructor at the Gazi Institute, in Ankara, Turkey, where he commenced an investigation of norm formation. He then reentered the United States to continue his work at Harvard and completed his PhD dissertation on this topic at Columbia University in 1935 under Murphy's supervision. He returned to Turkey again in 1937, taking the first of several academic posts there and doing both basic and applied research in social psychology. He was ultimately appointed to a professorship at Ankara University. He left his homeland for the last time in 1945, extremely concerned by Turkish support for Nazism. In particular, he rejected the acceptance of genetic racial theory by the Turkish government and by officials and colleagues at his university. His protests led to his temporary arrest. His eventual release and return to the United States was sponsored by the U.S. State Department and aided by several American academics, including influential figures such as Hadley Cantril, Leonard Doob, and Murphy.

In 1945, Sherif married Carolyn Wood, who became an eminent social psychologist in her own right. Together, they coauthored several publications, including key works reporting experimental studies of intergroup relations. He held posts at several institutions, spending the longest time at the University of Oklahoma, and finally moved to his last position, at Pennsylvania State University, where he worked until his retirement in 1972. He received a number of prestigious awards and honors throughout his distinguished career.

Sherif's Major Contributions

Social Norms

In the mid-1930s, Sherif commenced his seminal work on social norms. He argued that, to establish a range of possible behavior, individuals use the behavior of others to provide a frame of reference. By default, people accept the average or middle views of others as likely to be more correct than their own. Further, he believed that this process underlies the origins of social norms. Sherif put this theory to the test in a series of classic studies designed to induce a group norm. The task was based on the autokinetic effect, an illusion in which a fixed pinpoint of light in a completely dark room appears to move. In fact, the apparent movement is caused by eye movement in the absence of a physical frame of reference. In the experiment, people in small groups were asked in turn to estimate how far they thought the light had moved. Making a response in this task is difficult, so people are highly uncertain. To counter this uncertainty, individuals used what others in their group had to say as a frame of reference, and over time group members converged in their estimates. This convergence was evidence that a norm had emerged. For example, one group might judge that the light had moved 2 inches, and another group might judge that it had moved 6 inches. In contrast, people tested alone were much more variable in their estimates over the same number of trials. The group norm persisted when members were later tested individually, indicating that the norm had been internalized.

Sherif's autokinetic experiment signaled his strong commitment at the outset of his career to the experimental method and was hailed as a pioneering study. Together with Solomon Asch's experiments on conformity to group pressure and Stanley Milgram's studies of obedience to authority, Sherif's experiment is one of the most often cited studies in social psychology dealing with social influence. It was his demonstration of the experimental formation of a social norm that prompted Asch, as he himself acknowledged, to study conformity to group pressure.

Realistic Conflict Theory

Sherif believed that an explanation of group behavior could not result from the analysis of individual behavior and that the origins of *ethnocentrism* lay in the nature of intergroup relations. He argued that ethnocentrism is based on intergroup conflict and that this conflict arises when groups compete for scarce resources.

Sherif based his theoretical ideas on three field experiments conducted in boys' summer camps between 1949 and 1954, the most famous of which was the Robbers Cave experiment. These experiments were organized as follows:

1. The boys arrived at the camp, where they engaged initially in various campwide activities through which they formed friendships.

2. The boys were then divided into two separate groups, such that some of their friends were in the ingroup and others were in the outgroup. The groups were isolated from each other by living in separate bunkhouses and playing and working separately. In a short time, the two groups developed different norms. Even without intergroup contact, some outgroup stereotyping occurred.

3. Next, the two groups were brought together to engage in organized intergroup competitions in sports and other activities. This led to fierce competition and intergroup hostility, which was manifested in various ways. Ethnocentrism and intergroup aggression increased, often leading to an even higher level of ingroup solidarity. Even harmless encounters became hostile: If the groups shared the camp dining room, a meal was a chance for the groups to throw food at each other. Intergroup relations deteriorated so dramatically that two of the experiments were terminated at this point.

4. In one experiment, it was possible to proceed to a fourth stage. The two groups were provided with *superordinate goals*—ones that they both desired but were unable to achieve alone. In one instance, during a day's outing, the boys discovered that their truck was stalled, a real setback because it was their only means of driving for food. It took the combined effort of both groups pulling on a rope to get it started.

In other words, the groups needed to share their efforts and to work for a common cause. Sherif found evidence for a gradual improvement in intergroup relations following a series of cooperative intergroup interactions that allowed superordinate goals to be achieved.

These classic experiments demonstrated a number of things:

- Stereotyping occurred before actual competition between the groups.
- Prejudice and discrimination arose as a consequence of real intergroup conflict.
- Personality factors, such as authoritarianism and dogmatism, did not play an important role in the intergroup hostility.
- Ingroups formed despite the fact that some initial friends were outgroup members.
- Simple contact between members of groups in conflict was not enough to improve intergroup relations.

Realistic conflict theory was the most widely accepted theory of intergroup conflict prior to the development of Henri Tajfel and John Turner's *social identity theory*. According to realistic conflict theory, incompatible goals lead to tension and hostility between groups, and intergroup harmony depends on the shared perception and realization of goals that require intergroup cooperation for their achievement.

Realistic conflict theory has been further supported by other naturalistic experiments. Competition for scarce resources appears to be a sufficient condition for conflict to occur. *Social identity theory* argues that the mere awareness that two separate groups exist may also be sufficient to prompt intergroup discrimination. The two theories do not contradict each other. Rather, they highlight complementary factors that account for prejudice, discrimination, and intergroup conflict.

Graham M. Vaughan

See also Asch, Solomon; Conformity; Cooperation and Competition; Ethnocentrism; Ingroup Allocation Bias; Minimal Group Effect; Norms; Obedience to Authority; Realistic Group Conflict Theory; Reference Groups; Social Identity Theory

Further Readings

Sherif, M. (1935). A study of some social factors in perception. *Archives of Psychology, 27,* 1–60.

Sherif, M. (1936). *The psychology of social norms.* New York: Harper.

Sherif, M., Harvey, O. J., White, B. J., Hood, W., & Sherif, C. (1961). *Intergroup conflict and cooperation: The Robbers Cave experiment.* Norman: University of Oklahoma, Institute of Intergroup Relations.

Sherif, M., & Sherif, C. W. (1953). *Groups in harmony and tension: An integration of studies in intergroup relations.* New York: Harper & Row.

Sherif, M., & Sherif, C. W. (1964). *Reference groups.* New York: Harper & Row.

Sherif, M., & Sherif, C. W. (1969). *Social psychology.* New York: Harper & Row.

SLAVERY

Slavery is an ancient and complex social system that permits the control of and often the actual ownership of an individual and his or her labor by another. This institution often blends into other forms of forced labor, which include a vast array of relationships that extend from formal systems, such as serfdom, indentured servitude, and conscription, to informal systems of family labor and to even illegal control of labor and other services. This complex and constantly changing system of servitude has played a central role in many societies since before the agricultural revolution and still exists in informal and illegal manifestations today. This entry focuses on the history of slavery within North America and the United States and its relationship to the development of intergroup relationships among races, classes, and sections within the United States.

Early Development of Slavery

Racial slavery helped fuel a virulent racism that became and has remained a central theme in the history of the United States until this day. The institution also led to class tensions within the South between slave owners and poorer Whites and created sectional tensions that led to the U.S. Civil War (1861–1865). This system began with the Portuguese voyages down the African coast during the later 15th century. These early adventurers purchased slaves from Africans located along the coast and transported the slaves back to Portugal or began to use them to produce sugar on their Atlantic islands or a little later in Brazil. By 1600 a new form of racial, plantation-based slavery had taken root in the Americas.

Slavery quickly spread throughout the Americas. During the early and mid-17th century, the British and other European powers moved into the West Indies and began producing sugar. In North America, Dutch and British colonists began to import slaves, and by the early 18th century, plantation-based racial slavery had become well established in Maryland, Virginia, and Carolina.

The British and their colonists established a system of slavery that differed considerably from the ancient system and less decidedly from the Portuguese and Spanish models. Unlike those in most of the ancient institutions, slaves in the Americas faced perpetual servitude not only for themselves but also for their descendants. Slavery also became associated with color or African background. Slavery, as a legal institution, had died out in northern and western Europe during the Middle Ages, and although individuals from this region could be forced to labor as indentured servants, criminals, or prisoners of war, they could not be perpetually enslaved. Africans, on the other hand, even if baptized as Christians, could be kept in perpetual bondage. The British system treated individual slaves as real or personal property. Owners could buy or sell them as individuals, could use them as collateral for loans, could rent or hire them out to others, and could will them to their descendants. Unlike other systems in which slaves performed a variety of roles as soldiers and bureaucrats owned by the state or became incorporated into families, British North American slavery became based on large-scale commercial agriculture. Slaves also worked as artisans, domestics, urban and rural laborers, and sailors and at a wide variety of occupations, of course, but the plantation remained the economic foundation of the American institution.

Race, unlike the situation in earlier and other forms of slavery, played a central role. Slavery became limited to Africans, and race became a symbol of freedom and slavery. The British also imported large numbers of indentured servants and convicts, but these individuals became free after their term of servitude. Unlike the situation in the Iberian colonies, the difficulties of manumission in the British system led to a much smaller proportion of free Africans and thus intensified the linkage of race to slavery.

By 1776 the conditions of servitude had become well established in all the British North American colonies. Every one of the colonies had legislated a slave code that gave owners control over their property and awarded only extremely limited rights to slaves. The codes differed from colony to colony, but all accepted the ideal of perpetual servitude and the protection of the property rights of owners. The colonists through their legislatures passed these slave codes, which were unknown in northern and western Europe.

The American Revolution brought independence to the United States but only limited changes for slaves. Between 1776 and 1804, several of the newly created states began the process of ending slavery. Vermont led off by ending slavery in its 1777 constitution, and New York and New Jersey ended this process in 1799 and 1804, respectively. New Jersey would be the last state until the Civil War to move toward eventual abolition. Because none of the southern states followed this lead, the United States, after 1804, became sectionally divided by slavery between the northern, so-called free, states (the North) and the states to the south (the South), which continued the institution.

U.S. Slavery, 1790–1860

During the 1790s, the industrial revolution, spearheaded by the rapid development of the British textile industry, fueled the demand for cotton, which quickly became the leading cash crop of the Carolinas and Georgia. When the United States purchased Louisiana in 1803, sugar and cotton production based on slavery spread into these new territories. Meanwhile, the action of Congress to outlaw the importation of slaves in 1807 led to the rapid development of an interstate slave trade as owners in the Chesapeake and other areas of the upper South began to sell or transport slaves to the cotton and sugar lands in the central states of the South.

Between 1810 and the Civil War, slavery played a central role in the economic, social, cultural, and eventually the political history of the United States.

From the 1820s to the Civil War, slave-produced cotton alone accounted for around half of the value of all exports from the United States, and tobacco and other slave-produced commodities added another tenth. U.S. commercial and financial institutions became heavily involved in supporting the shipment of these products to Europe, and a rapidly developing textile industry in the northeast became dependent on Southern cotton. The U.S. merchant marine, the second largest in the world, transported most of the cotton to Liverpool and other ports in Britain and Europe. By the eve of the Civil War, slaves accounted for around $4 billion worth of property, which accounted for at least 20% of the total wealth of the United States and which compares to a gross domestic product of $4 billion for the nation in 1860. Slavery had become big business.

Slavery created a powerful, wealthy elite that played an important role in Southern and national history. This small group dominated the economic activity in the Southern states and played a vital role in their social composition. Slavery intensified class divisions within the South as the minority of households that owned slaves looked down on the majority of poorer Whites. A virulent racism also became associated with the system. Many Southerners saw it as a system of racial control while Northerners associated Africans with slavery. Thus the endemic racism prevalent in the nation during these decades continued after the Civil War and continued to play a powerful role in U.S. history well after the destruction of slavery.

Life for slaves within this powerful institution remained controlled yet complex. In theory, slaves possessed very limited rights, but in practice, the amount of control slaves actually possessed depended on the constant interactions among themselves, their masters, and other Whites. Even under slavery, many found space to create and protect families, to develop cultural and religious practices, and to sell products in local, often illegal markets. Different situations also produced diversity. Life on a large sugar plantation in Louisiana differed from the life of a single slave on a small western Virginia farm. The status of a field hand in Mississippi differed from that of a skilled iron worker in the Shenandoah Valley. The situation of slaves hired out to a railroad company differed from that of slaves working as domestics in Baltimore, Richmond, or New Orleans. There was a variety of environments for slavery, but the power to buy and sell, to hire out, or to punish meant that the owner retained an enormous amount of control.

Abolition and Civil War

This institution, which had become central to the nation, created both attackers and defenders. Some people in the United States, influenced by Enlightenment and/or evangelical ideals, began to criticize the institution, and by the 1830s a small but active group of abolitionists had sprung up in several Northern, or free, states. Africans, both freed and enslaved, also attacked the institution. Many freed Africans joined the abolitionists or aided fugitive slaves to escape into enclaves for free Blacks in the North or in Canada. Slaves ran away, sometimes rebelled, and committed other actions against the institution. Slavery always had its defenders, and these attacks brought forth a full-fledged defense based on the deep cultural and historical roots of the institution, its acceptance in the Bible and among early Christians, and the virulent racism common to all regions of the nation. The North never became dominated by the abolitionists, but many people in the United States began to question the morality of the institution. On the other side, Southerners, now influenced by a powerful proslavery rhetoric, began to demand Northern acceptance of the institution.

Slavery had long been a sporadic political issue. Debates at the Constitutional Convention, in the early 1790s, and over Missouri between 1819 and 1821 had riled politicians, but the Mexican War, in the 1840s, placed the slavery issue in the midst of national politics. When the United States seized Mexican territory, the debate flared over whether slavery should be permitted in these newly acquired possessions. The Free-Soilers, not abolitionists, wanted to contain the extension of slavery, but many Southerners, now convinced by a proslavery argument, believed it to be in the best interest of the nation for slavery to expand. After serious sectional confrontations, Congress cobbled together the compromise of 1850, which failed because Free-Soilers, in the North, attacked the Fugitive Slave Law and many extreme Southerners believed their section had gained little. The passage of the Kansas–Nebraska Act in 1854 led to the battles over "bleeding Kansas" and the formation of a new Free Soil Republican party. The efforts of President James Buchanan and his administration to admit Kansas as a slave state inflamed politics so much that when abolitionist John Brown attacked Harper's Ferry in 1859, leading Southern politicians demanded that Congress pass legislation that would protect slavery in the national territories. This demand led to the division of the Democratic Party in early 1860, the election of Lincoln in late 1860, and the secession of slave states. By the spring of 1861, the Civil War had begun.

At first the Lincoln administration merely wished to reverse secession, but in early 1862, Congress passed legislation ending slavery in the territories and providing for compensated emancipation in the District of Columbia. The war continued, and Lincoln moved forward with his famous Proclamation, which freed slaves only in areas under Confederate control as of January 1, 1863. Congress, realizing that such a proclamation might be eventually ruled unconstitutional, passed after serious division the Thirteenth Amendment to the U.S. Constitution, ending slavery as a legal institution, in early 1865.

The courts later decided that the Thirteenth Amendment, which abolished slavery, also prohibited peonage and other forms of forced labor. This ended the ancient institution of slavery within the United States. Abolishing the institution of slavery did not end its impact on intergroup relations, however. Racism remained a central feature in U.S. politics and society. While class conflict based on slavery died away in the South, the results of slavery, the Civil War, and abolition helped create a strong Southern sectional identification that persists to this day. The ancient institution ended in the United States in 1865, but its impact remains with us today.

Van Beck Hall

See also Apartheid; Dehumanization/Infrahumanization; Discrimination; Minority Groups in Society; Prejudice; Racism

Further Readings

Fogel, R. (1989). *Without consent or contract: The rise and fall of American slavery*. New York: Norton.

Kolchin, P. (1993). *American slavery, 1619–1877*. New York: Hill and Wang.

Morgan, P. D. (1998). *Slave counterpoint: Black culture in the eighteenth century Chesapeake and Lowcountry*. Chapel Hill: University of North Carolina Press.

Ransom, R. L. (1989). *Conflict and compromise: The political economy of slavery, emancipation, and the American Civil War*. Cambridge, UK: Cambridge University Press.

SOCIAL CLASS

The *social class* of individuals or groups refers to their hierarchical position in society. The bases of class are complex and sometimes ambiguous and vary among societies and historical periods. In contemporary industrialized societies, social class is generally determined by a small set of socioeconomic factors including educational attainment, occupation, income, and ownership of assets. In such societies, we may refer to an individual's membership in *a* social class, being a group of people who typically have a designated name or label (such as *working class* or *upper middle class*). However, this categorical judgment is not as simple as it seems. For example, people with low-prestige occupations may nonetheless be very wealthy. Relatively uneducated people may rise to very prestigious occupations in corporate life or the arts. The appropriate weighting of each of the socioeconomic factors we have mentioned in determining class is implicit, ambiguous, and often controversial. People may see themselves as working class whereas others may see them as middle class. The bases of class are contested by sociologists as well as by lay people. The primary focus of this entry is the social psychology of class.

Defining Social Class

For the most part, social class is not inherited in the sense that a person is guaranteed to retain the class status that he or she was born with. However, some societies retain aspects of ancient hereditary class systems, such as the caste system of India and the aristocracy of Britain. Further, even when there is no formal inheritance of class, one's family background remains an important factor in determining one's social class in adulthood. For example, an upper-class heritage is often signaled by an individual's manners, accent, and taste. These help the individual win the esteem required to maintain that class position through life. These and other forms of *cultural capital* are also used in fine-grained class distinctions such as that between *old money*, or people who have been upper class for some generations, and the *nouveaux riches*, who have risen in class ranks via the recent attainment of wealth.

It also helps upper-class individuals that they tend to have access to social connections, education, and other factors that open up opportunities for them to acquire resources and prestige. Further, class systems tend to be upheld by differences in the expectations of higher- and lower-class individuals. Those born into highly disadvantaged backgrounds may not expect to occupy esteemed positions in society as adults. This diminished expectation, relative to those from higher-class backgrounds, may lead to diminished motivation.

The number and type of social classes in a society appear to depend largely on the dominant mode of economic production. Anthropologists have observed that some tribal hunter–gatherer societies are non-stratified. In these societies there are no nominal social classes, leadership is not inherited, and indeed in some cases it is not even assigned permanently to individuals. On the other hand, as agriculture begins to dominate an economy, a class distinction often arises between those who own productive land and those who work it for them. This specific class distinction is a manifestation of the most fundamental class distinction possible—that between the *powerful* and the *powerless*. Even so, small and isolated agricultural communities such as the crofters of the Scottish Highlands are sometimes characterized by a relatively classless *smallholder* mode of organization, in which each family owns and works a small plot of land.

With the rise of industrialization and the associated expansion of trade, the class system typically begins to get more complex, in particular with the appearance of new middle classes, comprising merchants, professionals, highly skilled workers, and bureaucrats. Although the middle classes typically do not have power over others (unlike the upper classes), they have a greater degree of autonomy than working classes do by virtue of their possession of assets such as land, housing, stocks, and economically valuable skills. Although most contemporary social scientific models make finer class distinctions (such as upper middle class vs. lower middle class), most reflect the essentially tripartite structure of upper, middle, and working classes.

Theories

Different theories within the social sciences take different views, sometimes radically different, of the origins and nature of social class. For the sociobiologist E. O. Wilson, class inequality may be a consequence of the evolution of people who are genetically suited to occupy high- or low-status positions. However, this position is difficult to reconcile with the variety and fluidity of class structures in human societies. Furthermore, genetic evidence for the hypothesis is lacking.

In contrast, for Karl Marx, class ultimately stems not from human nature but from excess production. When agriculture and industry are efficient enough to produce more than is required, a ruling class that owns the means of production emerges, as does a working class that supplies the labor required to produce things. In capitalist systems, these classes are the *bourgeoisie*, or *capitalist*, class and the wage-earning *proletariat*, respectively. Relationships between these two groups of people are characterized by a particular kind of antagonism termed *class conflict*. Class conflict stems from the fact that the bourgeoisie is motivated to perpetuate its exploitation of the proletariat, whose members for their part are motivated to overthrow it.

The Marxist analysis of class has, of course, been hugely influential both in social science and in many of the important political events of the previous two centuries. The political impact of Marxism is perhaps the most striking demonstration yet of the reactivity of social science: The study of social processes has the potential to change those processes, in ways both intended and unintended. However, Marxist social theory has attracted a fair amount of criticism. One criticism is that its essentially bipartite model of class, which distinguishes the bourgeois from the proletariat, glosses over class distinctions of much economic and cultural significance, such as that between the middle and working classes. Another is that it tends to overemphasize the conflictual aspects of class relationships and to underemphasize the cooperative dimension. In the corporate environment, wage earners, executives, and shareholders have common as well as divergent interests and may express a high degree of identification with the corporation regardless of their role within it. Even a class system as stark as feudalism was characterized by reciprocity, whereby the lower classes pledged their homage, loyalty, labor, and/or military service in exchange for the right to use land. Another criticism is that Marxism gives priority to class compared with the other social categorizations—such as gender, race, and religion—which also organize human experience and society and provide fertile ground for conflict. The notion of a society divided and in conflict along unidimensional class lines seems to be almost an ideal in Marxist theory—at least as a necessary stage in the realization of a classless utopia.

Despite the controversy that has surrounded it, some of the key insights of Marxist theory have been enormously influential in social psychology. Three of its most prominent theories, *social identity theory*, *social dominance theory*, and *system justification theory*, are heavily indebted to Marx. For example, each theory is concerned with the distinction between what Marx called *false consciousness* and *class consciousness*, which refer to ignorance and awareness, respectively, of one's position in the class system, the inequalities and injustices of the class system, the common interests of individuals within class groupings, and the competing interests of those in different social classes.

Key Research Findings

Each of these theories is also concerned, in part, with one of the key findings to emerge from empirical investigations of class. Namely, individuals from lower social classes are more likely than upper-class individuals to engage in self-defeating behaviors. These findings are consistent with Marx's claim that individuals from lower classes are prone to participate in their own oppression. Jim Sidanius and his colleagues have labeled this phenomenon *behavioral asymmetry*. For example, lower social class is one of the strongest psychosocial predictors of poor health indicators such as obesity and Type II diabetes, as well as adverse health behaviors such as smoking and consumption of refined sugars. It also predicts low motivation and disengagement in educational settings, contributing to educational underachievement. Class is a major risk factor for many forms of criminality. Furthermore, individuals from lower-class backgrounds are more likely than those from upper-class backgrounds to vote for political parties whose policies are contrary to their economic self-interest. Social psychologists have helped make explicit, refined, and complemented Marx's analysis of the psychological mechanisms that work to perpetuate systems of social class.

For example, according to the *relative deprivation hypothesis*, aggressive behavior is potentiated by a sense of frustration at being denied opportunities that are afforded to others. According to both *system justification theory* and *social dominance theory*, individuals from lower classes are motivated, as are people from higher classes, to perceive the economic system in which they are embedded as just. As a result, individuals from lower classes are prone to see their relatively lowly position as deserved and to internalize negative stereotypes of their social class, with adverse impacts on self-esteem and motivation. According to social identity theory, individuals from lower social classes may be diverted from collective action by the perception that class boundaries are permeable. Under these conditions, pursuing social mobility as an individual may seem more attractive and fruitful than doing so on behalf of one's class group. Further, working-class people may seek to preserve some of the very characteristics that tend to perpetuate economic disadvantage, such as a lack of participation in university education and a high degree of manual skill, as cherished tokens of a distinctive and subjectively positive social identity.

Researchers have recently shown that a phenomenon known as *stereotype threat* can also adversely affect persons of low socioeconomic status. Stereotype threat is the tendency for people from stigmatized groups to perform poorly because they fear confirming a negative stereotype. The performance of people from lower social classes on a test of scholastic aptitude declined when they were merely asked questions about their socioeconomic status shortly before the test, compared with members of a control group, who were not given those questions. Answering the questions appeared to make their social class salient to the members of the experimental group, together with the associated stigmatizing stereotypes about low academic ability.

One of the most intensive lines of social-psychological investigation into social class has been literature on the consequences of accent. Spoken accents in many countries convey information about social class. In the United Kingdom, speakers with strong regional accents (e.g., a Birmingham accent) are perceived to hail from a lower-class background. Much the same thing is true in the United States, where certain accents, such as those hailing from parts of the South, are sometimes accorded lower class status. In Australia and New Zealand, accents vary much less according to region than they do according to class. Observers ascribe less prestige and aesthetic value to lower-class accents and rate the quality of an argument lower when it is expressed in a lower-class than in a middle- or upper-class accent. These findings are consistent with the notion that accents are a form of cultural capital used to denote and thus to regulate and perpetuate class distinctions.

Additional Considerations

Despite the valuable insights that have been provided by social psychologists, it is clear that overall they have paid much less attention to social class than to other systems of inequality, such as race and gender. Although there is a popular conception—shared by some scholars—that the relevance of social class is declining, it is clear that people are still aware of class and discriminate on the basis of class and that the disadvantages confronting those from the working or lower classes are many. According to national health statistics in the United Kingdom, the life expectancy of those in the lower socioeconomic brackets is some 8 years less than that of the middle classes. Similar to other stigmatized minorities, *ethnophaulisms*, or derogatory labels, such as *chav, oaf, oik, bogan,* and *working stiff*, are reserved for members of the working classes. There are also Internet hate sites devoted to them, and these sites use language that would be unthinkable and indeed illegal if applied to racial or gender groups. It appears therefore that there is scope for further social-psychological contributions to the study of class.

Robbie M. Sutton

See also Discrimination; Power; Prejudice; Social Dominance Theory; Social Identity Theory; Status; Stigma; System Justification Theory

Further Readings

Giddens, A. (1981). *The class structure of the advanced societies.* London: Hutchinson.

Giles, H., & Powesland, P. F. (1975). *Speech style and social evaluation.* London: Academic Press.

Jost, J., Banaji, M. R., & Nosek, B. (2004). A decade of system justification theory: Accumulated evidence of conscious and unconscious bolstering of the status quo. *Political Psychology, 25,* 881–919.

Sidanius, J., & Pratto, F. (1999). *Social dominance orientation: An intergroup theory of social hierarchy and oppression.* New York: Cambridge University Press.

Spencer, B., & Castano, E. (2008). Social class is dead, long live social class! Stereotype threat among low socioeconomic status individuals. *Social Justice Research, 20,* 418–432.

Wilson, E. O. (1975). *Sociobiology: The new synthesis.* Cambridge, MA: Harvard University Press.

SOCIAL COMPARISON THEORY

A good many things that people need to know about themselves, they learn by observing the actions of other people and reasoning from what they observe to implications for themselves. They interpret the meanings of those observed actions and decode the implications of those actions for their own opinions and abilities. Sometimes this is a simple process. At a faculty–student picnic, I foolishly join in the 100-yard dash and learn that all the students finish considerably ahead of me. I thus infer that my previous belief that I am a really fast runner needs to be corrected. Or I hold the opinion that a new television show is clever and cool and make the mistake of saying so, only to discover that my ingroup of friends unanimously thinks it is stupid and boring.

Social Comparison of Abilities and Opinions

Many social scientists had recognized aspects of these phenomena, but Leon Festinger was the first to systematize them in his 1954 theory of social comparison processes. Festinger initially cast the theory as a theory about how an individual could self-assess. In the first example above, what I'd learn about is my own abilities; in the second example, it is the validity of my opinions. And learning from the actions of others about one's abilities and opinions was the process that Festinger sought to analyze.

Festinger's theory assumed that the goal of individuals was to form accurate perceptions of their abilities, and that is certainly a reasonable goal to hold. Knowing my abilities will enable me to make sensible decisions about what I should attempt and not attempt. If I can jump about 12 feet, then I'd better not try to clear a 15-foot creek! If I am a really good mathematician, I have some ideas about careers at which I could succeed.

However, other motives are also involved when one compares one's ability to that of others. Having a high and having a low level of ability are equally informative about what we should attempt but are quite different in their impact on us. Having a high level of ability generally heightens one's self-esteem, while discovering one has a low level of ability is harmful to self-esteem. *Abilities* are qualities that it is good to be good at, and self-esteem is bolstered and enhanced by possessing those qualities. Similarly, doing poorly at something that matters is a blow to one's self-esteem.

Having accurate assessments of one's own abilities and having high self-esteem can be thought of as motives of the individual, the sorts of motives that Festinger suggested social comparison facilitated. However, more interpersonal motives are in play in social comparison situations as well. How well I perform when I am performing in public influences people's perceptions and opinions about me. Because I am often surrounded by groups whose opinions matter to me, I am often concerned with managing the impressions that people form of me. The *impression management* problem arises most acutely when I give a poor performance—that is, a performance that normally would be interpreted as signaling a low ability. Social comparison therefore is as much about dynamics within and between groups as it is about motives within an individual.

But a performance is not always a perfect guide to the underlying ability of the performing individual. More specifically, a flawed performance does not always indicate an inadequate person. I can run slowly because I am out of practice or have leg cramps or am distracted by problems at work or have any number of other momentary or long-term "handicaps." Call this the *performance-ability gap*. If we broaden our discussion here, we can access what psychologists call the *psychology of excuses*. Although I can act in ways that seem to signal a poor moral character or a crude set of standards about how to behave, I often try to convince others that I am not personally flawed.

Skilled excuse makers are able to convince others that the performance they have just given, which ordinarily would signal something discrediting about them, should instead be attributed to some external cause—the hidden difficulty of the task, the fact that they have been misinformed, and so on. The task here is to manage the attributions that others would otherwise make about us. More specifically, we seek to make sure that performances that typically would be interpreted as revealing something unfavorable about us are instead attributed to other causes. The ability to carry this off requires great tacit knowledge and subtle signaling skills, things that many of us possess.

The process of comparing our opinions with those of others requires a separate analysis. First it is important to distinguish between opinions that have a factual content and those that are based on taste, preference, or social convention. If I am comparing my opinion about a factual matter with that of a person who is an expert on the topic and discover we disagree, I do not need to take his or her opinion as certainly true, but I had better check further to see if he or she may be right. If my opinion is about a matter of taste, preference, or social convention, then I need to understand what it is that I would be signaling if I were to express that opinion. One way of understanding this is by learning the opinions of others on the topic and doing some social calibration regarding the social standing of those others and the consequences of agreeing or disagreeing with them. This is difficult to describe in the abstract but easy in a specific

case. Imagine that I secretly prefer paintings of an idealized version of the late Elvis Presley on black velvet backgrounds to paintings by Mondrian. I discover that a group of bikers at the local bar also prefers the Elvis paintings, while my superiors in the law firm where I work prefer Mondrian. I then have some idea of what it would cost me to express my preference for Elvis while at work. I might also try to discover the reasons behind the Mondrian preference of my superiors. As a result, I might decide that my reasons for preferring Elvis are good ones, and so I would silently maintain that preference, or I might decide that their reasons are more compelling than mine, and so I would move toward their preference.

Reference Groups

The central message of social comparison theory is that people are greatly affected by the information they get from the persons around them. Yet we know that there are people who are able to maintain an opinion about how to dress or whom to vote for that is at odds with the opinions of others. How do they sustain their views? One answer is given by *reference group theory*, which is a version of a social comparison theory. Reference group theory presumes that the persons whose opinions sustain and validate our opinions are not necessarily those who are physically near us but rather those to whom we "refer our behavior." An example would be a high school football player who learns what "cool" behavior is by comparing his behavior with that of the clique of "jocks" in his high school. He pays no attention to the behavior of those ordinary students who physically surround him in the classroom—their views on how to behave mean nothing to him because he does not care about their opinions of him.

This analysis suggests an interesting interpretation of how it is that people who are deviant according to the standards of the group in which they are physically embedded sustain their deviance. They do so by referring their behavior to the standards of some other group that is psychologically present in their remembered experience and agrees with their own standards, in contrast to the "uncivilized" group in which they currently find themselves. One way of describing what is going on here is that people who are apparently deviants in the group that physically surrounds them do not feel anxious and fear rejection, as most deviants do, but instead are serene in their conviction of the superiority of the standards of some other group. In some cases we genuinely admire people who show such convictions. An example might be missionaries who go into other cultures and attempt to model a life based on the Golden Rule. In other cases, such as crusaders who violently tried to convert others to their religion, we see evil or perhaps mental illness. Being sustained in our beliefs and behaviors by reference to the opinions and standards of a group of absent others is an intrinsically complicated endeavor but a very human one.

Social Comparison, Happiness, and Well-Being

Another aspect of social comparison deals with the consequences of comparing aspects of our lives with the lives of those around us or those in the public media. The general suggestion arising from the social comparison perspective is that our level of happiness with our lives, or more generally our sense of well-being, depends on these comparisons. In materialist societies, such as contemporary Western, capitalist countries, these comparisons are often assumed to generate largely negative consequences for large groups of citizens who are below other groups on one or more of the standard dimensions of comparison. Because the communications media—now largely television and magazines—tend to feature the lifestyles of the "rich and famous" disproportionately, these negative consequences may be quite common.

To equip ourselves to examine this topic, we need to distinguish between two kinds of deprivation. On one hand, *objective* or *physical deprivation* occurs when an individual falls short of the conditions and resources necessary to sustain life. Lack of nourishing food, clean water, and adequate shelter are prototypical examples of physical deprivations, but today we would perhaps extend the list to include medical care for illnesses and wounds, education sufficient to succeed in modern societies, chances to engage in remunerated labor, and many similar services and commodities. In our society, the earnings from remunerated labor are generally what we exchange for these commodities and services. And we have a term to describe the situation of those

who fall below adequate sustenance—they fall below the *poverty line*, that is, below the level necessary to purchase the necessities of life.

On the other hand, *relative deprivation* occurs when an individual believes that he or she lacks conditions or resources that others possess, coupled with the feeling that he or she is either *entitled* to possess them or can at least *aspire* to possess them. Relative deprivation can be sufficiently powerful to trigger *revolutions of rising expectations*. The notion here is that when a country that has had a constant low supply of services and commodities available to citizens suddenly experiences a rise in the supply of these services and commodities, but they are available only to the more powerful segments of society, then those who do not have access to these services and commodities feel relatively deprived. This in turn motivates these "deprived" people to overthrow the power structure to gain access to services and commodities that they did not previously aspire to possess.

Services and commodities that one aspires to possess may also have powerful effects on individuals. Kurt Lewin made the point that affluent people in the United States need only a few of the things they want. We need nourishing food, but we go out for sushi; we need water, but we pay extra to drink designer water. Moreover, things like sushi and designer water motivate us to work. Lewin called them *quasi-needs*. John Kenneth Galbraith commented that our current affluent Western societies count on our desires to acquire these goods to keep the demand for them high enough to keep the economy moving forward.

The psychological mechanisms of social comparison that create a desire to possess goods that others possess are useful to think through. The usual answer is that envy is the mechanism that creates a strong desire on the part of "deprived" individuals to possess those goods that more privileged individuals possess. However, this may be too simple an analysis, as well as one that allows those of us who can afford luxury goods to be comfortable owning them while those of us who are less well-to-do must go without.

Another explanation suggests that possession of certain goods conveys status to the possessor. Call these *positional goods*. In order to function as a positional good, a good must be public in nature. That is, people must see the possession and know who the possessor is. Large, elegant houses fit the definition, as do expensive cars, fine jewelry, and fashionable clothes. In every behavior setting, certain goods signal that the possessor has high status.

Thus, more than envy drives the desire to possess whatever the trappings of high status are in any particular setting. Having high status is an advantage. For example, it can signal respectability and reliability. Advice columns for job seekers consistently stress the importance of "dressing professionally," which often means looking just a bit better than the other candidates. In housing markets, real estate agents know that a house in a "good neighborhood" is worth much more than the same house in a less desirable neighborhood. In addition to conveying status, owning the house in the good neighborhood may have other advantages. "Good neighborhoods" tend to have good schools, to some extent because in the United States, for example, property taxes support schools. What is a good school? Among other things, a good school is one with a good record of getting its graduates admitted to good colleges. Living in good neighborhoods with good schools thus confers real advantages on children. More generally, cues of high status convey real advantages on the people who possess them.

Consider next a different kind of status, namely, one's "standing" to participate in group functions. Norman Rockwell nicely illustrated this kind of status in his painting titled *Town Meeting*. In the center of the painting is a workman addressing the yearly meeting that small New England towns hold to decide issues that are important to their citizens. Around the workman are seated other, better-dressed people, often in coats and ties, while the workman is wearing a flannel shirt and a worn leather work jacket. But the better-dressed citizens are listening attentively to the workman, presumably because his residence in the community gives him the standing to command other townspeople's attention to the ideas he is expressing. Having the standing to participate in group functions not only allows a person to influence group actions but is also a major determinant of a person's sense of self-worth.

Conclusion

Two related themes are included under the heading of social comparison. The first emphasizes learning about one's own qualities, generally abilities and opinions, by comparing manifestations of these qualities with those of other people. The second theme involves justice and personal aspirations. Given the possessions that others around us have, to what are we entitled? Stated differently, how does observing the possessions of others affect what we aspire to possess? This second theme is sometimes thought of as an envy-driven process, but it can also be based on the desire for status.

Social comparison began as a relatively narrow theory about how people assess their abilities and opinions but has been transformed into a more general framework for explaining many of the phenomena that are central to social psychology. As Serge Guimond has recently reminded us, social comparison processes drive a variety of assessment processes among individuals, among groups, and across cultures.

John Darley

See also Collective Movements and Protest; Distributive Justice; Festinger, Leon; Justice; Procedural Justice; Reference Groups; Relative Deprivation

Further Readings

Crosby, F. (1976). A model of egotistical relative deprivation. *Psychological Review, 83*, 85–113.

Festinger, L. (1954). A theory of social comparison processes. *Human Relations, 7*, 117–140.

Franks, R. (2007). *Falling behind: How rising inequality harms the middle class*. Berkeley: University of California Press.

Galbraith, J. K. (1958). *The affluent society*. Boston: Houghton Mifflin.

Goethals, G., & Darley, J. M. (1977). Social comparison theory: An attributional approach. In J. M. Suls & R. L. Miller (Eds.), *Social comparison processes: Theoretical and empirical perspectives* (pp. 259–278). Washington, DC: Hemisphere.

Guimond, S. (2006). *Social comparison and social psychology: Understanding cognition, intergroup relations, and culture*. Cambridge, UK: Cambridge University Press.

Snyder, C., Higgins, R., & Stucky, R. (1983). *Excuses: Masquerades in search of grace*. New York: Wiley.

SOCIAL COMPENSATION

Social compensation is superior effort exerted when an individual works on a collective task as compared with working individually or coactively. Collective tasks involve combining all group members' contributions, which means that members are evaluated together. Coactive tasks involve individuals working in the presence of others but not combining their contributions, which means that evaluations can be made individually. Social compensation involves working hard to make up for other group members whose performances are expected to be inferior.

For example, a group of product executives might be asked to generate as many uses as they can for a new product. If someone believes that other group members are not capable of or willing to perform well at this task, and the outcome of this collective task is important, then that person will work especially hard to generate more uses for the product in order to make up for the possibility that other group members will not generate many uses. If someone is working alone, then he or she will not be concerned with a group's overall outcome and will not try to make up for others' lack of effort. If someone believes that others can or will work hard, then the typical response is *social loafing* (putting less effort into a collective task than if one were working alone or coactively). This entry looks at the phenomenon of social compensation, related research, and practical implications.

Background

Tasks are often completed in groups, such as committees, sports teams, juries, marching bands, and quality control teams. Numerous tasks are completed collectively, in that an individual's contributions are pooled with the contributions of coworkers to form a single outcome, such as a decision, a score (in a sports game), a musical performance, or an inspected product. Some of the earliest social-psychological research investigated how groups work together to complete a task. Social psychologists were particularly interested in how working in groups affects the motivation, effort, and productivity of individuals.

In early research on this topic, Max Ringelmann wanted to understand why, when he added a second ox to a team pulling a plow, the plowing did not get done twice as fast. Ringelmann explored this issue by studying the performance of men pulling on a rope. He found there was a loss of motivation when the men collectively pulled on the rope, compared with when they pulled as hard as they could individually. He speculated that this reduction of individual effort on a collective task was merely an artifact of coordination problems and was not psychological in nature.

However, researchers in the 1970s found that when lack of coordination was ruled out, *social loafing* remained a robust psychological phenomenon. Social loafing occurs when individuals expend less effort collectively, when the outcome is dependent on how everyone performs, than they do coactively, when individuals work by themselves but in the presence of others. Social loafing can be reduced or eliminated through several means, such as increasing the identifiability or evaluability of the individual members' contributions, enhancing personal involvement with the task, elevating the uniqueness of individual contributions, or strengthening group cohesiveness.

When social loafing cannot be reduced through these tactics, however, an individual may feel he or she has to compensate for the loafing of other group members. Take a classroom project, for example. Teachers often divide a class into small groups, and each group member will receive the same grade for whatever project the group is instructed to complete. From the beginning, one individual in the group may recognize that the other group members are less motivated to earn a high grade than he or she is. The highly motivated individual may then try to make up for the other students' lack of motivation by working especially hard on the project.

When Social Compensation Occurs

Two conditions must be present for social compensation to occur. Otherwise, social loafing is the more likely outcome. The first condition is the expectation that other group members will contribute insufficiently to the group effort. The expectation that group members will perform insufficiently may result from a general predisposition to have little trust in others' ability or reliability or from particular information that other group members are unable or unwilling to perform on the specific task.

Ironically, high-trusting individuals are more likely to take advantage of others during a collective task by letting them do most of the work (socially loafing). Individuals high in interpersonal trust expect the other group members to carry their weight, whereas those low in interpersonal trust expect others to loaf. Similarly, particular information implying greater effort or ability by coworkers is more likely to lead to social loafing.

The second condition that is necessary for social compensation to occur is that the outcome be important or meaningful to the individual. If the outcome of a task is not important to an individual, then there is no need to compensate for poorly performing coworkers. However, if the outcome of a task is meaningful, then an individual will be motivated to avoid group failure by compensating for poorly performing coworkers. This is consistent with *expectancy-value models* of effort and with *self-validation theories*, which argue that people will exert effort on a task only to the degree they believe their effort will produce a valued result. Individuals may not necessarily demonstrate a complete lack of motivation, but their motivation will be based on how directly related they think their efforts are to producing a favorable outcome.

Even if the two qualifying conditions are satisfied, social compensation may not occur for other reasons. For instance, when it is possible to leave a group, individuals may just abandon the collective task to avoid a negative evaluation caused by the poor performance of other, loafing group members. Only when there is no other option are people "forced" to socially compensate. And after compensating repeatedly for other group members, a person may come to feel "used" and thus stop compensating. Continuing to socially compensate may lead to the *sucker effect*, whereby a person realizes that he or she is being exploited and thus chooses to stop compensating and join the other group members in their loafing. Finally, as group size increases, so too does the difficultly associated with compensating for the increasing number of group members who are loafing. Social compensation is thus less common when people are working together in large groups.

Conclusion

By understanding what causes some group members to loaf and others to compensate, researchers can understand how to optimize group performance by reducing motivation losses. Researchers can investigate conditions that promote social compensation so that it occurs more often. Increasing social compensation might be especially helpful during emergency situations, where detrimental bystander effects can occur. The *bystander effect* occurs when an individual is less likely to aid in an emergency situation when others are present compared with being the only one available to help.

Social compensation has implications for working groups and organizations. Persistent experiences of social compensation may cause employees to avoid jobs or settings that involve group work. Being forced into situations in which social compensation might be needed could cause distress to potential compensators. A student, learning that her grade would depend on a collective group assignment, once lamented to one of us, "I know that I will have to work harder than everyone else in my group." She knew from past experiences that she would likely have to compensate for other group members because they were unlikely to help her get the high grade that she desired.

More often than not, people who are concerned to ensure that their group succeeds are people who are valuable to an organization. Understanding how to prevent such persons from always being forced to socially compensate (which could cause them to burn out) might help organizations retain these workers. Finally, it is interesting that social compensation has primarily negative origins: distrust or knowledge of inferior effort or motivation on the part of one's coworkers. A more positive wellspring of social compensation, *esprit de corps* (group spirit), has yet to be demonstrated.

Kipling D. Williams and James H. Wirth

See also Group Performance; Köhler Effect; Social Loafing; Sucker Effect

Further Readings

Kerr, N. L. (2001). Motivational gains in performance groups: Aspects and prospects. In J. Forgas, K.

Williams, & L. Wheeler (Eds.), *The social mind: Cognitive and motivational aspects of interpersonal behavior* (pp. 350–370). New York: Cambridge University Press.

Shepperd, J. A. (1993). Productivity loss in performance groups: A motivation analysis. *Psychological Bulletin, 113*, 67–81.

Williams, K. D., Harkins, S. G., & Karau, S. J. (2003). Social performance. In M. A. Hogg & J. Cooper (Eds.), *Handbook of social psychology* (pp. 328–346). London: Sage.

Williams, K. D., & Karau, S. J. (1991). Social loafing and social compensation: The effects of expectations of coworker performance. *Journal of Personality and Social Psychology, 61*, 570–581.

SOCIAL DARWINISM

Social Darwinism is the belief that the fittest or strongest among individuals, groups, or nations should survive and flourish, while the weak or unfit should be allowed to perish. This view was advocated by Herbert Spencer, a British sociologist who attempted to apply Charles Darwin's theory of biological evolution to the development of human societies. Social Darwinism became popular in the late Victorian era in England, the United States, and elsewhere. Another social interpretation of Darwin's biological views was promoted by Francis Galton. His view and its theoretical offshoot, later known as eugenics, have also been associated with social Darwinism. This entry first reviews Spencer's and Galton's views on developments of human faculties and human societies and then describes the trajectory that social Darwinism took in societies and social sciences in the late 20th century. It then explains how advocates of social Darwinism commit a common but fatal logical fallacy (the *naturalistic fallacy*) and confuse Darwinian science with a particular ethical position, a position that is incompatible with contemporary moral values.

Spencer's Evolutionary Progressivism

In 1857 Spencer, under the influence of Thomas Malthus's 1798 work (*An Essay on the Principle of Population*), published his major work, *Progress: Its Law and Causes*. It was 2 years before Charles Darwin published his seminal, 1859 work, *On the Origin of Species*. Spencer's later theorizing (e.g., see *First Principles*, published in 1860) was strongly influenced by Darwin's ideas.

Spencer applied Darwin's ideas to interpret social phenomena. He coined the term *survival of the fittest*, maintaining that through competition and natural selection, social evolution would lead to prosperity and personal liberty unparalleled in human history. Spencer argued that the individual (rather than the collective) evolves, and thus government intervention should be minimal in social and political domains. This view fit well with the dominant ideologies of the capitalist economics in the late 19th century, especially those of laissez-faire economics, and it was strongly supported by both intellectuals and businessmen, including Andrew Carnegie, who hosted Spencer's visit to the United States in 1883.

Spencer's theory was essentially a prescriptive, ethical theory. He did not simply argue that natural selection descriptively works with humans much as Darwin theorized it worked with animals and plants, but that the survival of the fittest in human society is morally correct and should be promoted. As a result, social Darwinism was used to justify various political and economic exploitations that are generally inconsistent with modern moral values, including colonialism, imperialism, neglect of poor living and working conditions, oppression of labor unions and similar organizations, and so on.

Among others, a major problem with social Darwinism as an ethical theory is that the theory commits what is called the naturalistic fallacy in philosophy, whereby an *ought* statement is derived rather directly from an *is* statement. That is, it is a logical error to assume that what is natural is equivalent to what is morally correct. Social Darwinism made this fatal error in using the principle of survival of the fittest not only to explain how human society might actually operate (a statement that could, in principle, be verified empirically) but also to prescribe morally how social institutions (and human society in general) ought to be designed. Although social Darwinism arguably had some beneficial effects (e.g., providing the poor with resources for production and education rather than simply with handouts), its moral basis is now widely rejected.

Galton's Eugenics

Intrigued by Darwin's 1859 work, Galton, a British scientist and Darwin's cousin, became interested in heritability of many aspects of human variation, ranging from physical characteristics to mental characteristics and from facial appearance to fingerprint patterns. Using various biographical records, Galton developed statistical techniques to quantify the heritability of human abilities. In *Hereditary Genius*, published in 1869, he summarized these findings and argued that biological inheritance is much more critical in determining human character and intelligence than are environmental influences. Besides reporting his scientific findings, Galton went on to argue that the notion of heredity should occupy a central place when one considered social morals. According to his view, certain social welfare policies (e.g., asylums for the insane) allowed "less fit" members of society to survive and reproduce faster than "more fit" ones, and this trend eventually would lead to degradation of the society by "inferiors." Galton thus maintained that social morals should be changed so that people would become more conscious of heredity in their decisions about reproduction.

In his 1883 book, *Inquiries Into Human Faculty and Its Development*, Galton coined the term *eugenics* from the Greek word *eu* (well) and the suffix *-genes* (born). Although Galton did not personally advocate eugenic social policies that promoted governmental coercion of so-called inferiors, such mandatory eugenics began to be practiced in the early 20th century. The most infamous example was provided by Nazi Germany's eugenics programs, which led to the sterilizations of thousands of individuals whom the Nazis viewed as mentally and physically "unfit" and to mass killings of "undesirable" people, including Jews, Roma, and homosexuals during the Holocaust.

Social Darwinism in the Late 20th Century

Social Darwinism gradually lost its popularity and support after World War I. Ironically, the term *social Darwinism* was later popularized by a U.S. historian, Richard Hofstadter, in his 1944 work, *Social Darwinism in American Thought*, which discredited Nazi Germany's ideologies along with its eugenic policies.

Around the same time, anthropologists Franz Boas, Margaret Mead, Ruth Benedict, and others also severely criticized social Darwinism. They emphasized the role of culture in differentiating humans from other animals and rejected social Darwinism's biological foundations. It is important to note that the criticisms from these anthropologists (Boas in particular) were originally directed only against the notion of "evolutionary progressivism" advocated by Spencer—the notion that assumes that all societies progress through the same stages in the same sequence and that societies can thus be ordered, from less well-developed, inferior ones to more highly developed, superior ones. Obviously, Spencer's is a notion with little scientific basis. However, later generations of anthropologists also broadly rejected Darwinian, biological approaches to the development of human societies in favor of a sociocultural approach. Such resistance to applying Darwinian concepts and analyses to the study of human society rapidly became dominant in the social sciences.

During the 1960s, biological approaches to study human social behavior and human society resurfaced, after the "modern evolutionary synthesis" was completed in biology. Biologists such as William Hamilton, Robert Trivers, and others extended their theories to explain origins of human cooperation, mate selection, and human sociality in general. In 1988, the Human Behavior and Evolution Society was founded by investigators who unapologetically used evolutionary theory to analyze human nature. Since then, the Society has expanded substantively to overlap with many social science disciplines, including psychology, anthropology, psychiatry, economics, law, political science, and sociology. Sharing a common metatheoretical perspective, the biological and evolutionary approaches have yielded highly successful cross-disciplinary collaborations, including modern behavioral genetics, analysis of human sociality, and research on neural underpinnings of social cognition. In social psychology, these approaches have also spurred reexaminations of traditional questions, including research on adaptive efficiencies of group behavior, biological roots of intergroup behavior, and so on.

However, despite its broader scientific acceptance, biological and evolutionary approaches to studying human behavior and society have also met with substantial opposition. For example, in 1975, when biologist Edward Wilson argued in *Sociobiology: The New Synthesis* that genetics exerts a greater influence on human behavior than scientists had previously thought, he was labeled as a racist by both liberals and conservatives who favored the idea that human behavior was determined by enculturation. But in fact what Wilson claimed in his book was not particularly extreme: He maintained that human behavior cannot be understood without taking *both* biology and culture into account.

Confusion of Social Darwinism With Darwinism

As exemplified above, many negative reactions to Darwinism arise from the confusion of Darwinism with social Darwinism. Darwinism is a scientific theory whose ultimate value can be judged only empirically. On the other hand, social Darwinism is an ethical theory purporting that the fittest should flourish while the unfit should be allowed to die. Aside from their names and a couple of basic Darwinian notions that social Darwinism misused (e.g., directional evolution that underlies survival of the fittest), these two theories share very little. Nevertheless, many of the negative reactions to a Darwinian approach to understanding human behavior and human society continue to stem from antipathy for social Darwinism, its unconventional moral values, and its illogical foundation (viz the naturalistic fallacy).

Tatsuya Kameda

See also Eugenics; Evolutionary Psychology; Holocaust; Racism; System Justification Theory

Further Readings

Barkow, J. H., Cosmides, L., & Tooby, J. (Eds.). (1992). *The adapted mind: Evolutionary psychology and the generation of culture.* Oxford, UK: Oxford University Press.

Hawkins, M. (1997). *Social Darwinism in European and American thought, 1860–1945: Nature as model and nature as threat.* Cambridge, UK: Cambridge University Press.

Hofstadter, R. (1992). *Social Darwinism in American thought.* Boston: Beacon. (Original work published 1944)

Pinker, S. (2003). *The blank slate: The modern denial of human nature.* New York: Penguin.

Schaller, M., Simpson, J., & Kenrick, D. (Eds.). (2006). *Evolution and social psychology.* New York: Psychology Press.

Wilson, E. O. (2000). *Sociobiology: The new synthesis.* Cambridge, MA: Belknap. (Original work published 1975)

SOCIAL DECISION SCHEMES

Social decision scheme (SDS) *theory* provides a mathematical framework for predicting group choices from group member preferences. A *social decision scheme* is a representation of a decision process that yields predicted group decisions given the initial preferences of members. As an example, consider a committee of employees who must choose among three health insurance plans being considered by their employer. The committee is composed of four employees, and each has a preferred plan. The four members may agree or disagree, but the goal is to endorse collectively one plan. Combining such individual preferences to obtain a collective decision encompasses both voting rules and a social influence process. Voting or decision rules are explicit or implicit rules for determining the group choice based on members' final votes. Common rules are majority (the alternative with 50% + 1 votes wins), unanimity (the alternative with all votes wins), and plurality (the alternative with more votes than any other wins). In addition to using voting rules, small groups also typically discuss the decision options, and preferences change as a result of information exchange, persuasion, and social pressure. In the aforementioned example, assume that the committee adheres to a majority decision rule: Three of the four members must ultimately agree to adopt a particular health plan. Unless they begin with such a majority, they will likely discuss the health care plans, and the preferences that individuals bring to the group may change during this discussion. SDS theory captures how different alignments of initial preferences are channeled through voting and social influence processes to yield a collective choice.

The fundamental question in the SDS approach is, What is the committee likely to decide, given the initial preferences of its members or, more generally, given the preferences of the people who are potential members of the committee? The four elements of SDS are (1) individual preferences, (2) group preference composition, (3) social decision schemes, and (4) group choices. This entry considers each of these.

Individual Preferences

Choices are defined on a finite set of mutually exclusive and discrete alternatives. In the previous example, these alternatives are the three health insurance plans: Plan A, Plan B, and Plan C. More generally, the decision set is denoted as $a = \{a_1, a_2, a_3, \ldots, a_n\}$, where n is the number of alternatives. Individual preferences are often summarized as the probabilities that a randomly chosen group member will prefer each alternative. These probabilities are summarized in a vector, $p = \{p_1, p_2, p_3, \ldots, p_n\}$, where p_i is the probability than an individual will prefer alternative a_i.

Group Composition: Distinguishable Distributions

Information about each group's preference composition is summarized in a *distinguishable distribution*, $r = \{r_1, r_2, r_3, \ldots, r_n\}$, where r_i is the number of group members who prefer alternative a_i. In the aforementioned example, the preferences of the four members of the group can be distributed over the three choices in 15 different ways, yielding 15 possible distinguishable distributions. One of these is {2, 1, 1}, in which two prefer Plan A, one prefers Plan B, and one prefers Plan C. Other possibilities include {4, 0, 0}, {3, 1, 0}, {3, 0, 1}, {2, 2, 0}, and so forth. Each of these possibilities represents a unique alignment of support among the possible choices. A core idea in SDS theory is that this initial alignment of support foretells what choices the group is likely ultimately to make. To illustrate, contrast a group with a {3, 1, 0} distinguishable distribution with one having a {1, 2, 1} distribution. There are numerous reasons (adoption of majority rules, consensus pressures, etc.) to expect that the {3, 1, 0} group is more likely to adopt Plan A than is the {1, 2, 1} group.

In short, it matters how groups are composed. In SDS applications, group composition can be directly observed or can be estimated. In direct observation, the preferences of group members are solicited before or at the onset of group interaction and thereby the distinguishable distribution of each group identified. In estimation, the probabilities of obtaining each of the possible distinguishable distributions are estimated from information about the distribution of opinions in the population of potential group members. A common assumption is that groups are composed by random selection. Under random selection, the probability of obtaining each of the distinguishable distributions can be estimated if the probability distribution of individual preferences in the population of potential group members, p, is known. In the previous example, suppose that an independent survey revealed that 40% of employees favored Plan A, 30% favored Plan B, and 30% favored Plan C. That is, $p = \{.4, .3, .3\}$. Using the multinomial probability function, the probability of selecting randomly four members who all favor Plan A ($r = \{4, 0, 0\}$) is .026, $r = \{2, 1, 1\}$ will occur with a probability of .173, and so on. In this manner, the probability of obtaining each of the 15 possible distinguishable distributions can be computed. The complete set of observed or estimated relative frequencies of the possible distinguishable distribution is contained in a vector, $\pi = \{\pi_1, \pi_2, \pi_3, \ldots, \pi_m\}$, where m is the number of possible distinguishable distributions.

Social Decision Schemes: The Relationships Among Distinguishable Distributions and Group Choices

The *social decision scheme matrix* (*D* matrix) is the mechanism for summarizing propositions about the relationships between group preference compositions and group choices. The rows of the *D* matrix are defined by the possible distinguishable distributions, and the columns are defined by the possible group choices. To conserve space, consider a simpler example of the four-person committee deciding between two, rather than three, health care plans. In this case, there are five distinguishable distributions, and the *D* matrix would have the form given in Table 1.

The entries in the *D* matrix within the rectangle are the probabilities, d_{ij}, of the group's choosing the *j*th option given that opinions are distributed as in the *i*th distinguishable distribution. Specifying

Table 1   The General Form of the D Matrix for Two Alternatives and Four Members

r	Group Choice	
(r_A, r_B)	Plan A	Plan B
(4, 0)	d_{11}	d_{12}
(3, 1)	d_{21}	d_{22}
(2, 2)	d_{31}	d_{32}
(1, 3)	d_{41}	d_{42}
(0, 4)	d_{51}	d_{52}

the values of these entries gives expression to theoretical ideas about group process. For example, the idea that majorities win because they can outvote, persuade, and pressure minorities suggests a *majority-wins* scheme, given in Table 2.

Table 2   A Majority-Wins Decision Scheme

r	Group Choice	
(r_A, r_B)	Plan A	Plan B
(4, 0)	1.0	0.0
(3, 1)	1.0	0.0
(2, 2)	0.5	0.5
(1, 3)	0.0	1.0
(0, 4)	0.0	1.0

Notice that in this simple example of majority wins, an anomaly arises in the {2, 2} case, which has no majority. Decision schemes often require that theorists address such anomalies by providing a *subscheme* for distinguishable distributions that are not resolved by the major scheme. In this case, we might propose that the faction will win that has the most convincing arguments for its plan. However, having no way of determining a priori which faction this will be, one may simply predict that the {2, 2} case has a 50% chance of going either way.

Consider another conception of a group's decision-making process: *truth wins*. Suppose that the group engages in an exhaustive exchange of what members know about the two plans, and the group selects the plan that is supported by the preponderance of information aired in discussion.

Further imagine that the prominent features of Plan A are superior to those of Plan B but that the fine print of Plan A negates its apparent superiority. If an individual reads and understands this fine print, the individual favors Plan B, but otherwise, the individual favors Plan A. Further assume that the group will select Plan A unless one or more members have detected this critical fine print that damns Plan A. This process is dubbed *truth wins* because only one member needs to support the correct or best choice for the group to adopt it. Such a truth-wins process generates a distinctly different D matrix from the one generated by the majority-wins idea.

Table 3   A Truth-Wins Decision Scheme

r	Group Choice	
(r_A, r_B)	Plan A	Plan B
(4, 0)	1.0	0.0
(3, 1)	0.0	1.0
(2, 2)	0.0	1.0
(1, 3)	0.0	1.0
(0, 4)	0.0	1.0

The Fundamental Equation of SDS Theory: Predicting Group Choices From Individual Preferences

The ultimate goal is to transform ideas about the decision process into predictions of group choices. Given the estimated or observed relative frequencies of distinguishable distributions summarized in $\pi = \{\pi_1, \pi_2, \pi_3, \ldots, \pi_m\}$ and a defined D matrix, the distribution of group choices can be predicted. Let $P = \{P_1, P_2, P_3, \ldots, P_n\}$, where n P_i is the probability that a group will choose the ith alternative. Then P is given by

$$P = \pi D.$$

To continue the foregoing example, suppose that a poll of employees revealed that 60% favored Plan A and 40%, Plan B. Then, randomly selecting members for the four-person committee would result in the estimate of π being {.13, .35, .35, .15, .03}.

Using the majority-wins D matrix from above, Equation 1 expands to

$$P = \{ .13, .35, .35, .15, .03 \}$$

$$\begin{vmatrix} 1.0 & 0.0 \\ 1.0 & 0.0 \\ 0.5 & 0.5 \\ 0.0 & 1.0 \\ 0.0 & 1.0 \end{vmatrix} = \{ .65, .35 \}.$$

That is, operating under a majority-wins decision scheme, about two thirds of four-person groups would select Plan A. By way of comparison, the same computation using the truth-wins D matrix from above yields a prediction that only 13% of these groups would select Plan A.

A model-testing approach permits one to evaluate comparatively the validity of competing ideas about decision-making processes by (a) converting competing ideas about process into D matrices, (b) generating the predicted distributions of group choices, and (c) comparing these predictions to observed outcomes.

Capturing Decision Processes

SDS theory can be used to explore the effects of various features of the decision environment on group process. For example, one prominent line of research by Patrick Laughlin and his colleagues considers the effect of task character and member capabilities on decision processes. They contend that an important feature of the task environment is the *demonstrability* of the correct or best decision. A task is said to be highly demonstrable if the following conditions are met: (a) the correct choice is identified by a mutually shared system of inference, (b) there is sufficient information to identify the correct choice, (c) members preferring inferior options are able to understand the reasoning that leads to the correct choice, and (d) members preferring the correct choice are able and sufficiently motivated to present the information and arguments that demonstrate the superiority of the best choice. Logic and math problems are prime examples of tasks that are potentially high in demonstrability, whereas judgments of aesthetics are not. However, demonstrability also depends on characteristics of the group members. A math problem

that is highly demonstrable for a group of advanced math majors may be low in demonstrability for remedial math students. In the latter case, a member with the right answer may not be able to articulate the reasoning that produces the correct answer, and the others may not understand the rationale if it is presented. Laughlin showed that the number of supporters needed for a decision alternative to be adopted by the group increases as the demonstrability of the decision decreases. That is, a choice involving a task with low demonstrability (e.g., an aesthetic judgment) may require a majority (majority wins) or a supramajority (two-thirds–majority wins) to determine the group choice, whereas the solution to a demonstrable logic problem may require only a minority of one (truth wins) or two (*truth-supported wins*) to be chosen by the group.

Prospecting: Going Beyond Existing Data

A useful feature of SDS is that it permits one to explore the effects of group size and changes in individual preferences on group decisions. For example, suppose that majority wins adequately describes the decision process of the four-person committee deciding among health care plans. Then, SDS theory can predict the effects of changing committee size or changing the individual preferences in the population of potential group members.

Garold Stasser

See also Collective Induction; Conformity; Dynamical Systems Approach; Group Problem Solving and Decision Making; Group Task; Minority Influence

Further Readings

Davis, J. H. (1973). Group decision and social interaction: A theory of social decision schemes. *Psychological Review, 80,* 97–125.

Davis, J. H., & Kerr, N. L. (1986). Thought experiments and the problem of sparse data in small-group research. In P. Goodman (Ed.), *Designing effective work groups* (pp. 305–349). San Francisco: Jossey-Bass.

Laughlin, P. R. (1999). Collective induction: Twelve postulates. *Organization Behavior and Human Decision Processes, 80,* 50–69.

Stasser, G. (1999). A primer of social decision scheme theory: Models of group influence, competitive model testing and prospective modeling. *Organization Behavior and Human Decision Processes, 80,* 3–20.

SOCIAL DEVIANCE

Social deviance, broadly defined, applies to any behavior, belief, or appearance that violates prevailing social norms. Norms are social standards concerning what members of a group expect and believe is acceptable conduct in a given situation. The power of norms to govern individual behavior derives from the perception that others endorse and will enforce the normative standards. When an individual's or a minority group's behavior, belief, or appearance deviates from normative standards, the individual or the group members risk becoming the targets of social disapproval and other forms of punishment. Examples of social deviance range from minor breaches of social etiquette to major violations of the law. This entry examines the development of thinking about social deviance, describes current perspectives on crime and punishment, and then examines the group dynamics of social deviance and its impact on social change.

Historical Background and Perception of Deviant Behavior

Before the Enlightenment, it was widely accepted that social deviance was compelled or facilitated by demonic or otherwise nefarious supernatural forces. Social Darwinism in the late 19th and early 20th centuries recast this basic idea using a new, "scientific" vocabulary. Instead of supernatural forces, it was thought that inherited biological traits compelled individuals to engage in deviant behavior. Cesare Lombroso (1836–1909) argued that the physical appearance, cultural practices, and criminal behavior of marginal or lower status social groups reflected such "degenerative" biological traits.

Beginning with classical criminologists such as Cesare Beccaria (1738–1794) and Jeremy Bentham (1748–1832), explanations of deviant behavior have shifted away from such essentialist beliefs. The preponderance of findings from contemporary research on deviant behavior suggests that it is overwhelmingly, and with rare exception, rooted in social processes rather than an individual's fundamental traits. However, the belief that deviant behavior reflects innate deficiencies in the character of individuals or social groups continues to circulate as conventional wisdom. Near the end of the 20th century, the essentialist argument that inherited genetic differences could account for racial disparities in criminal behavior (and other social inequalities) reemerged despite its dismissal by professional academics and criminologists.

If essentialist arguments are fundamentally flawed, then what explains their public popularity? It is likely that essentialist explanations for deviant behavior remain alluring because they seemingly conform to everyday observation. Social-psychological research has demonstrated that individuals are inclined to attribute the cause of another person's behavior to that person's personal character traits, even when relevant situational or environmental factors clearly account for the behavior. This bias is particularly strong when the behavior is perceived as unexpected, extraordinary, or threatening or has seemingly negative consequences—all common features of social deviance.

Contemporary Understandings of Social Deviance

Many normative standards are codified into laws, and violations of the law are classified as crimes. Criminologists investigate the causes and consequences of this particular type of social deviance. Criminal deviance differs from other types in that it exposes the deviant to state-mandated punishments. While legal standards may define legally appropriate conduct at any given time, laws change over time and differ from one jurisdiction to the next.

The rise of the labeling perspective in the 1960s challenged the assumption that certain behaviors were invariably deviant. The majority of researchers now recognize that the labeling of particular individuals or social groups as deviant often says as much about the power of the labeler as it does about the behavior of those who are labeled.

The normative standards adopted by an observer will determine whether the observer defines another person as deviant. Because individuals belong to multiple social groups, a given behavior may be subject to evaluation according to different and at times contradictory standards. For example, parents who choose to work long hours instead of seeing their children may be evaluated as deviant when the standard of familial norms is applied, but they may be evaluated as conforming when the standard of workplace norms is applied. Likewise, premeditated killing can evoke widespread disapproval and a long prison sentence, but it may bring popular acclaim and honors when authorized during times of war. Therefore, what constitutes social deviance is in the eye of the observer rather than a necessary feature of the observed person or the person's behavior. While there may be widespread consensus over definitions of deviance, such definitions are never exempt from challenge or change.

The stigma of deviance can impact members of many social categories (e.g., race, gender, sexual orientation). Stigmatization can create social barriers for individuals because others categorize them as belonging to a particular group. For example, recent research has demonstrated that even when actual amounts of deviant behavior and social neglect are taken into account, neighborhoods with a higher concentration of Black residents are perceived as more deviant and disorderly than are comparable White neighborhoods. In addition, research on employment opportunities in New York City found that Black male applicants with no criminal history had the same chance of receiving a job interview as equally qualified White male felons.

Punishment

Social deviance is closely associated with the punishments it often elicits from observers. Punishing a deviant symbolically reinforces a group's normative standard and sense of collective identity. Although the specific type of punishments available to any given group may vary from mundane (e.g., stern looks, disregard) to dramatic (e.g., public humiliation, physical abuse, death), all groups wield both active and passive forms of punishment. Active punishments directly penalize a deviant (e.g., reprimands, monetary fines, physical pain), whereas passive punishments either curtail or suspend a deviant's access to social interaction and valued resources. Although active punishments are more recognizable, passive punishments can be equally distressful, particularly if the deviant closely identifies with the group or is otherwise highly dependent on the group for important resources.

The standard punishment for serious criminal deviance in most modern societies is imprisonment. For most of human history, imprisonment was not considered *the* punishment, but rather a means to hold criminals awaiting trial or punishment. Modern imprisonment encapsulates both active and passive forms of punishment in that it imposes deprivations on inmates while also curtailing their access to civil society.

The Group Dynamics of Social Deviance

Social groups distinguish themselves from one another according to the normative standards of behavior and appearance each attempts to embody. The very existence of a group is premised on its ability to distinguish itself from other, perhaps very similar, social groups. Examples include the characteristic behaviors and appearances associated with various high school cliques or that distinguish college sororities from one another. Social identity theory argues that members of a given group possess a mental image of the qualities that define an ideal group member. These group *prototypes* are mental representations of the values, traits, and behaviors that exemplify the group and distinguish ingroup from outgroup members. Individuals who conform to the group prototype receive evaluations that are more positive and are granted higher status by fellow group members. Those who deviate from the group prototype are viewed negatively and risk marginalization within the group or exclusion from the group altogether.

In groups that are motivated to achieve a goal, such as winning a competition, solving a problem, or accomplishing some other activity, group members often consider deviance a threat to the group's overall performance. In such goal-motivated groups, members typically expect some measure of personal gain if the group achieves its goals. Therefore, members have a stake in maximizing the group's effectiveness by personally conforming to group norms and supporting the punishment of deviant behavior. For example, if a lower ranking member fails to display proper deference to higher ranking members—perhaps by refusing to follow directions or assuming the right to oversee and direct the activity of others—that member risks social disapproval and punishment. Because assertive behavior is normatively inconsistent with lower ranking positions, other members typically view such behavior as an illegitimate use of power that undermines group efforts. However, group members will treat the same behavior performed by those with higher rank as legitimate and welcome contributions to the group's efforts.

Because their behavior diverges from group norms, deviant individuals or minority groups are vulnerable to social exclusion. However, the negative impact of a deviant label can sometimes be reduced or avoided altogether by demonstrating a general commitment to the group or by explicitly framing one's behavior or ideas as motivated by a desire to promote group success.

Deviance as Dissent and Impetus for Social Change

By posing a challenge to conventional norms, social deviance can also be a powerful means of affecting social change. Although deviants run the risk of marginalization by undermining either the group's identity or its productive efficacy, every normative standard was at some time a new—perhaps deviant—behavior or idea. Rather than merely serving as a target for group disapproval, social deviance can, by posing a challenge to the status quo, also redefine a group prototype or promote innovative strategies for group achievement.

One consequence of social norms is that they can perpetuate public compliance even when private support for the behavior or ideas they secure is weak or waning. Public compliance has a self-fulfilling effect of maintaining the perceived consensus and strength of normative standards. In situations such as these, acts of social deviance have the potential to unmask the façade of group consensus and stimulate a change in normative expectations. When taken as a potential alternative to normative social practices or beliefs, social deviance is akin to the concept of *social dissent*.

Individuals or minority groups that acquire the deviant label can expect challenges by those vested in the normative status quo and those with competing visions of acceptable behavior or ideas. Initially, fellow group members will attempt to "correct" the deviant's errant behavior or beliefs through gentle persuasion or subtle verbal and nonverbal cues. If the deviant behavior persists, the individual may become the target of more forceful punishments. These punishments are often a very effective means of correcting, or at least

suppressing, social deviance. However, the behavior and ideas of a deviant often become more alluring to others when the deviating individual does not succumb to social pressure but instead endures in the face of it.

Again, social controls on deviance typically prevail in countering immediate challenges to the status quo. However, like the proverbial squeaky wheel getting the oil, because social deviance is unexpected or unfamiliar, it attracts the attention of others. By attracting attention, deviants receive an opportunity to influence other group members in ways that their conforming brethren do not. Although the deviants' influence may not be immediately apparent, research demonstrates that counternormative ideas sometimes alter the subsequent decision-making behavior of people who are exposed to them. Therefore, while social deviance may often fail to influence a group at any given time, it can indirectly alter a group's future trajectory by drawing attention to, and raising questions about, taken-for-granted normative expectations.

Brian Colwell

See also Anticonformity; Conformity; Deviance; Essentialism; Legitimation; Normative Influence; Social Identity Theory; Status Characteristics/ Expectation States Theory; Stigma; Subjective Group Dynamics

Further Readings

Becker, H. S. (1963). *Outsiders: Studies in the sociology of deviance.* New York: Free Press.

Cullen, F. T., Gendreau, P., Jarjoura, G. R., & Wright, J. P. (1997). Crime and the bell curve: Lessons from intelligent criminology. *Crime & Delinquency, 46*(6), 387–411.

Marques, J. M., Abrams, D., Páez, D., & Hogg, M. A. (2003). Social categorization, social identification, and rejection of deviant group members. In M. A. Hogg & S. Tindale (Eds.), *Group processes* (pp. 400–424). Malden, MA: Blackwell.

Nemeth, C., & Nemeth-Brown, B. (2003). Better than individuals? The potential benefits of dissent and diversity for group creativity. In P. B. Paulus & B. A. Nijstad (Eds.), *Group creativity: Innovation through collaboration* (pp. 63–84). New York: Oxford University Press.

Ridgeway, C. (1993). Legitimacy, status, and dominance behavior in groups. In S. Worchel & J. A. Simpson (Eds.), *Conflict between people and groups* (pp. 110–127). Chicago: Nelson-Hall.

Sampson, R. J., & Raudenbush, S. W. (2004). Seeing disorder: Neighborhood stigma and the social construction of "Broken windows." *Social Psychology Quarterly, 67*(4), 319–342.

SOCIAL DILEMMAS

Social dilemmas are situations in which private interests are at odds with collective interests. Such situations arise because people frequently attach more weight to their short-term selfish interests than to the long-term interests of the group, organization, or society to which they belong. Many of the most challenging issues people face, from the interpersonal to the intergroup, are at their core social dilemmas.

Consider these examples. As individuals, we are each better off when we make use of public services such as schools, hospitals, and recreational grounds without contributing to their maintenance. However, if we each acted according to our narrow self-interest, then these resources would not be provided, and everyone would be worse off. Similarly, in the long run, everyone would benefit from a cleaner environment, yet how many people are prepared to voluntarily reduce their carbon footprint by saving more energy or driving or flying less frequently?

Definitions and Metaphors

Social dilemmas are formally defined by two properties: (1) each person has an individual rational strategy that yields the best outcome in all circumstances (the noncooperative choice); (2) if all individuals pursue this strategy, it results in a deficient collective outcome—everyone would be better off by cooperating. Researchers frequently use experimental games to study social dilemmas in the laboratory. An experimental game is a situation in which participants choose between cooperative and noncooperative alternatives, yielding consequences for themselves and others in terms of their monetary outcomes.

The literature on social dilemmas has historically revolved around three metaphorical stories, the prisoner's dilemma, the public good dilemma, and the commons dilemma, and each of these stories has been modeled as an experimental game. The *prisoner's dilemma game* was developed by scientists in the 1950s. The cover story for the game involved two prisoners who are separately given the choice between testifying against the other (noncooperation) or keeping silent (cooperation). The outcomes are such that each of them is better off testifying against the other, but if they both pursue this strategy, they are both worse off than if they remain silent.

Table 1   Payoff Matrix for Prisoner's Dilemma

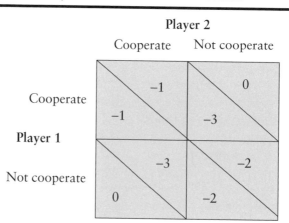

Notes: Payoffs represent number of years in prison associated with a cooperative choice (remaining silent) or a noncooperative choice (testifying against the other); lower diagonals reflect payoffs for Player 1, and upper diagonals reflect payoffs for Player 2. As can be seen, each player is better off testifying against the other, provided that the other remains silent (the first player goes free, whereas the second players goes to prison for 3 years). Yet if both players testify against each other, then both players are worse off (they each serve a prison sentence of 2 years) than if both remained silent (they each serve for only 1 year).

The *public good dilemma* has the same properties as the prisoner's dilemma game but involves more than two individuals. A public good is a resource from which all may benefit regardless of whether they contributed to the good. For instance, people can enjoy the city parks regardless of whether they contributed to their upkeep through local taxes. Public goods are nonexcludable: Once these goods are provided, nobody can be excluded from using them. As a result, there is a temptation to enjoy the good without making a contribution. Those who do so are called *free riders*, and although it is rational to free ride, if all do so, then the public good is not provided, and all are worse off. Researchers study primarily two public good dilemma games in the laboratory. Participants get a monetary endowment to play these games and decide how much to invest in a private fund versus a group fund. It is individually rational to invest in the private fund, yet all would be better off investing in the group fund because this yields a bonus. In the continuous game, the more that people invest in the group fund, the larger their share of the bonus. In the step-level game, people get a share of the bonus if the total group investments exceed a critical (step) level.

Finally, the *commons dilemma* was inspired by the metaphor of the Tragedy of the Commons, a story about a group of herders having open access to a common parcel of land on which their cows graze. It is in each herder's interest to put as many cows as possible onto the land, even if the commons is damaged as a result. The herder receives all the benefits from the additional cows, and the damage to the commons is shared by the entire group. Yet if all herders make this individually rational decision, the commons will be destroyed, and all will suffer. Compare this with the use of nonrenewable resources such as water or fish: When water is used at a higher rate than the reservoirs are replenished or when fish consumption exceeds the reproductive capacity of the fish, then we face a tragedy of the commons. The experimental commons game involves a common resource pool (filled with money or points) from which individuals harvest without depleting it. It is individually rational to harvest as much as possible, but the resource collapses if people harvest more than the replenishment rate of the pool.

Theories of Social Dilemmas

Social dilemmas have attracted a great deal of interest in the social and behavioral sciences. Economists, biologists, psychologists, sociologists, and political scientists alike study when people are selfish or cooperative in a social dilemma. The most influential theoretical approach is *economic game theory* (i.e., *rational choice theory* or *expected utility theory*). Game theory assumes that individuals are rational actors motivated to maximize their utilities. *Utility* is often narrowly defined in terms of people's economic self-interest. Game theory thus predicts a noncooperative outcome in a social dilemma. Although this is a useful starting premise, there are many circumstances in which people may deviate from individual rationality, demonstrating the limitations of economic game theory.

Biological and evolutionary approaches provide useful complementary insights into decision making in social dilemmas. According to *selfish gene theory*, humans (like any other organism) have evolved to maximize their inclusive fitness, the number of copies of their genes passed on to the next generation. Under certain conditions, selfish genes can produce cooperative individuals. For instance, it could be profitable for family members, who share a portion of the same genes, to help each other because doing so facilitates the survival of their genes. *Reciprocity theories* provide a different account of the evolution of cooperation. In repeated social dilemma games between the same individuals, cooperation might emerge because people can punish a partner for failing to cooperate. This encourages reciprocal cooperation. Reciprocity can explain why people cooperate in dyads, but what about larger groups? Evolutionary theories of *indirect reciprocity* and *costly signaling*, which assume that there are indirect benefits derived from a cooperative act, may be useful in explaining large-scale cooperation. When people can selectively choose partners to play games with, it pays to invest in getting a cooperative reputation. Through being cooperative, individuals can signal to others that they are kind and generous people, which might make them attractive partners or group members.

Psychological models offer additional insights into social dilemmas by questioning the game theory assumption that individuals pursue their narrow self-interest. *Interdependence theory* suggests that people transform a given social situation into one that is consistent with their motivational and strategic preferences. Playing a prisoner's dilemma with close family or friends, for example, will change the outcomes so that it becomes rational to cooperate. Whether individuals approach a social dilemma selfishly or cooperatively might also depend on what attributions they make about other players, such as whether they believe others are greedy or cooperative. Similarly, *goal–expectation theory* assumes that people might cooperate under two conditions: They must (1) have a cooperative goal and (2) expect others to cooperate. Another psychological model, the *appropriateness model*, questions the game theory assumption that individuals rationally calculate their outcomes. Instead, many people base their decisions on what people around them do and use simple heuristics, like an equality rule, to decide whether to cooperate.

Solutions to Social Dilemmas

Studying the conditions under which people cooperate might lead to recommendations for solving social dilemmas in society. The literature distinguishes between three broad classes of solutions—motivational, strategic, and structural—that vary in whether they assume actors are motivated purely by self-interest and in whether they change the rules of the social dilemma game or leave them intact.

Motivational Solutions

Motivational solutions assume that people have other-regarding preferences. Considerable literature on social values shows that people have stable preferences for how much they value outcomes for self versus others. Research has concentrated on three social motives: (1) individualism, or maximizing one's own outcomes regardless of others; (2) competition, or maximizing one's own outcomes relative to others; and (3) cooperation, or maximizing joint outcomes. The first two orientations are referred to as *proself orientations* and the third as a *prosocial orientation*. There is much support for the idea that prosocial and proself individuals behave differently when confronted with a social dilemma in the laboratory or the field. People with prosocial orientations weigh the moral implications of their decisions more and see cooperation as the most intelligent choice in a social dilemma. When there are conditions of scarcity, such as a water shortage, prosocials harvest less from a common resource. Similarly, prosocials are more concerned about the environmental consequences of, for example, taking the car or public transport.

Research on the development of social value orientations suggests an influence of factors such as family history (prosocials have more sibling sisters), age (older people are more prosocial), culture (Western cultures have more individualists), sex (more women are prosocial), and even university course (economics students are less prosocial). However, until we know more about the psychological mechanisms underlying these social value orientations, we lack a good basis for interventions.

Many people also have *group-regarding preferences*. People's group association is a powerful predictor of their social dilemma behavior. When people identify highly with a group, they contribute more to public goods and harvest less from common resources. Group identifications have even more striking effects when there is intergroup competition. When social dilemmas involve two or more groups of players, there is much less cooperation than when individuals play. Yet intergroup competition also facilitates intragroup cooperation, especially among men. When a resource is depleting rapidly, people are more willing to compensate for selfish decisions by ingroup members than outgroup members. Furthermore, the free-rider problem is much less pronounced when there is intergroup competition. However, intergroup competition can be a double-edged sword. Encouraging competition between groups might serve the temporary needs of ingroup members, but the social costs of intergroup conflicts can be severe for either group. It is not entirely clear why people cooperate more as part of a group. One possibility is that people become genuinely more altruistic. Other possibilities are that people are more concerned about their ingroup reputation or are more likely to expect returns from ingroup than outgroup members. This question needs further investigation.

Another factor that might affect the weight individuals assign to group outcomes is the possibility of communication. A robust finding in the social dilemma literature is that cooperation increases when people are given a chance to talk to each other. It has been quite a challenge to explain this effect. One motivational reason is that communication reinforces a sense of group identity. Another reason is that communication offers an opportunity for moral suasion so that people are exposed to arguments to do what is morally right. But there may be strategic considerations as well. First, communication gives group members a chance to make promises and explicit commitments about what they will do. Yet it is not clear whether many people stick to their promises to cooperate. Similarly, through communication people are able to gather information about what others do. However, in social dilemmas, this information might produce ambiguous results: If I know that most people cooperate, might I be tempted to act selfishly?

Strategic Solutions

A second category of solutions is strategic. In repeated interactions, cooperation might emerge when people adopt a tit-for tat (TFT) strategy. TFT is characterized by making a first cooperative move and then mimicking your partner's subsequent moves. Thus, if the partner does not cooperate, you mimic this move until he or she starts to cooperate. Computer tournaments in which different strategies were pitted against each other have shown TFT to be the most successful strategy in social dilemmas. TFT is a common strategy in real-world social dilemmas because it is nice but firm. Think, for instance, about marriage contracts, rental agreements, and international trade policies that all use TFT tactics. However, TFT is quite an unforgiving strategy, and in noisy real-world dilemmas, a more forgiving strategy might be better.

Even when partners might not meet again, it could be strategically wise to cooperate. When people can selectively choose whom to interact with, it might pay to be seen as a cooperator. Research shows that cooperators create better opportunities for themselves than do noncooperators: Cooperators are selectively preferred as collaborative partners, romantic partners, and group leaders. This occurs, however, only when people's social dilemma choices are monitored by others. Public acts of altruism and cooperation, such as charity giving, philanthropy, and bystander intervention, are probably manifestations of reputation-based cooperation.

Structural Solutions

Structural solutions change the rules of the game by either modifying the social dilemma or removing the dilemma altogether. Not surprisingly, many studies have shown that cooperation rates go up as the benefits of cooperation increase. Field research on conservation behavior has shown that selective incentives in the form of monetary rewards are effective in decreasing domestic water and electricity use. Furthermore, experimental studies show that cooperation is more likely if individuals have the ability to punish defectors. Yet implementation of reward and punishment systems can be problematic for various reasons. First, there are significant costs associated with creating and administering sanction systems. Providing selective rewards and punishments requires support institutions to monitor the activities of both cooperators and noncooperators, and these institutions can be quite expensive to maintain. Second, these systems are themselves public goods because one can enjoy the benefits of a sanctioning system without contributing to its existence. The police, army, and judicial systems will fail to operate unless people are willing to pay taxes to support them. This raises the question whether many people want to contribute to these institutions. Experimental research suggests that particularly low trust individuals are willing to invest money in punishment systems, and a considerable portion of people are willing to punish noncooperators even if they personally do not profit. Some researchers even suggest that altruistic punishment is an evolved mechanism for human cooperation. A third limitation is that punishment and reward systems might undermine people's voluntary cooperative intention. Some people get a "warm glow" from cooperation, and the provision of selective incentives might crowd out their cooperative intention. Similarly, the presence of a negative sanctioning system might undermine voluntary cooperation. Research has found that punishment systems decrease the trust that people have in others. Thus, sanctioning is a delicate strategy.

Boundary structural solutions modify the social dilemma structure, and such strategies are often very effective. An often studied solution is the establishment of a leader or authority to manage a social dilemma. Experimental studies on commons dilemmas show that overharvesting groups are more willing to appoint a leader to look after the common resource. There is a preference for a democratically elected prototypical leader with limited power, especially when people's group ties are strong. When ties are weak, groups prefer a stronger leader with a coercive power base. The question remains whether authorities can be trusted in governing social dilemmas, and field research shows that legitimacy and fair procedures are extremely important in citizens' willingness to accept authorities.

Another structural solution is reducing group size. Cooperation generally declines as group size increases. In larger groups, people often feel less responsible for the common good and believe, rightly or wrongly, that their contribution does not matter. Reducing the scale—for example through dividing a large-scale dilemma into smaller, more manageable parts—might be an effective tool in raising cooperation.

Another proposed boundary solution is to remove the social from the dilemma by means of *privatization*. People are often better in managing a private resource than a resource shared with many others. However, it is not easy to privatize movable resources such as fish, water, and clean air. Privatization also raises concerns about social justice because not everyone may be able to get an equal share. Finally, privatization might erode people's intrinsic motivation to cooperate.

Conclusion

As social dilemmas in society become more pressing, there is an increasing need for policies. It is encouraging that much social dilemma research is applied to areas such as organizational welfare, public health, and local and global environmental change. The emphasis is shifting from purely laboratory research to research testing combinations of motivational, strategic, and structural solutions. It is also noteworthy that social dilemmas are an interdisciplinary research field with participation from researchers from various behavioral sciences who are developing unifying theoretical frameworks (such as evolutionary theory) to study social dilemmas. For instance, there is a burgeoning neuroeconomics literature that uses neuroscience methods to study brain correlates of decision making in social dilemmas. Finally, social dilemma researchers are increasingly using more dynamic experimental designs to see, for instance, what happens if people can voluntarily or involuntarily enter or exit a social dilemma or play different social dilemmas at the same time within different groups.

Mark van Vugt

See also Commons Dilemma; Cooperation and Competition; Evolutionary Psychology; Free Riding; Group Problem Solving and Decision Making; Leadership; Negotiation and Bargaining; Prisoner's Dilemma; Social Identity Theory

Further Readings

Axelrod, R. A. (1984). *The evolution of cooperation.* New York: Basic Books.

De Cremer, D., & van Vugt, M. (1999). Social identification effects in social dilemmas: A transformation of motives. *European Journal of Social Psychology, 29,* 871–893.

Kollock, P. (1998). Social dilemmas: Anatomy of cooperation. *Annual Review of Sociology, 24,* 183–214.

Messick, D. M., & Brewer, M. B. (1983). Solving social dilemmas: A review. In L. Wheeler & P. Shaver (Eds.), *Review of personality and social psychology* (Vol. 4, pp. 11–44). Beverly Hills, CA: Sage.

Ridley, M. (1997). *Origins of virtue.* London: Penguin Classics.

van Lange, P. A. M., Otten, W., De Bruin, E. M. N., & Joireman, J. A. (1997). Development of prosocial, individualistic, and competitive orientations: Theory and preliminary evidence. *Journal of Personality and Social Psychology, 73,* 733–746.

van Vugt, M., & De Cremer, D. (1999). Leadership in social dilemmas: The effects of group identification on collective actions to provide public goods. *Journal of Personality and Social Psychology, 76,* 587–599.

Weber, M., Kopelman, S., & Messick, D. M. (2004). A conceptual review of social dilemmas: Applying a logic of appropriateness. *Personality and Social Psychology Review, 8,* 281–307.

Yamagishi, T. (1986). The structural goal/expectation theory of cooperation in social dilemmas. In E. Lawler (Ed.), *Advances in group processes* (Vol. 3, pp. 51–87). Greenwich, CT: JAI Press.

SOCIAL DOMINANCE THEORY

Social dominance theory addresses the question of why all large human societies with economic surplus are structured as group-based hierarchies. Social dominance theory integrates ideas from a broad variety of social science theories, including *authoritarian personality theory, social identity theory, realistic group conflict theory, Marxism, feminism, evolutionary psychology, elite theory, social representations, symbolic racism theory,* and others. Social dominance theory is a multilevel theory, explaining how processes within individuals, such as prejudice and stereotyping, interface with practices of groups and institutions. Further, social dominance theory considers how cultural ideologies organize patterns of behavior to structure group-based power in societies. This entry provides an overview.

Structure of Group-Dominance Societies

Whether their government is theocratic, democratic, monarchical, or communist, societies have a three-part, group-based structure, with adults dominating children, men exercising more power than women, and at least one socially defined group that includes men, women, and children (e.g., a race, religion, class, caste, or sect) exercising more power than at least one other group. Social dominance theory emphasizes how these three kinds of group-based hierarchy—age, gender, and arbitrary set—intersect. Therefore, social dominance theory does not view each kind of hierarchy as a subset of something else.

Across societies, economic systems, and historical time, the definition of the arbitrary groups and their predominance has varied substantially. For example, Muslims no longer dominate around the Mediterranean. There has been less societal variability in gender and age dominance, likely because of the universal presence of families. Thus, although some societies revere older people and some do not, and although some societies have gender parity in their national legislatures and many do not, gender inequality and age inequality are more constant and less lethal than arbitrary-set inequality.

For a society to sustain group-based inequality, it must systematically distribute whatever people value (e.g., wealth, prestige, health care, pleasant living places) and whatever they devalue (e.g., danger, difficult jobs) more in favor of the dominant arbitrary group than subordinate groups. A major vehicle for such unequal distribution is discrimination by institutions. As documented in their 1999 book, Jim Sidanius and Felicia Pratto found that, the world over, corporate employers, financial institutions, schools, and health facilities provide better opportunities, resources, and services to members of dominant groups than to members of subordinate groups. Discrimination by individuals also systematically sustains inequality because people tend to discriminate in like fashion.

Legitimizing Myths

The coordination among different actors in both individual discrimination and institutional discrimination such that certain groups are favored and others disfavored is largely accomplished through shared legitimizing myths. Legitimizing myths are cultural ideologies that prescribe how people with certain social identities should act and be treated by others, what social priorities are important, or who deserves what. The contents of these myths can be quite varied within and between cultures and across historical time.

For example, propositions (and attitudes) that justify Christian discrimination against Muslims have ranged from the theological conception that Muslims were unholy (disgust) to the view that Muslims immigrate to the West to take jobs (resentment) and to the assumption that most Muslims are terrorists (fear). In social discourse and persuasive processes, legitimizing myths make practices or outcomes that sustain inequality seem justified, natural, and necessary, or they may obscure the fact that practices produce inequality by framing it as something else (e.g., equal opportunity, for the greater good, modern, traditional, efficient).

The "truth value" of these myths cannot be determined, but they have the property of making themselves come true by coordinating discrimination. For example, a stereotype that a subordinate group is criminal can contribute to more extensive policing of that group, higher conviction rates, and thus to a disproportionate number of convicted criminals among that group.

Myths that serve to sustain inequality are hierarchy enhancing. Myths that promote greater equality are hierarchy attenuating. Legitimizing myths can change their hierarchical function when people replace the meanings with social practices that have opposite implications for hierarchy. For example, the Protestant work ethic developed as a hierarchy-attenuating myth because it privileged the mercantile class over the nobility that ruled western Europe. At present in the United States, the type of meritocracy derived from the Protestant work ethic privileges people who already have wealth, education, and the customs that are considered high status, namely, Whites.

Social Dominance Orientation

When people have freedom of choice over their actions, social dominance theory assumes that whether they discriminate in hierarchy-enhancing or hierarchy-attenuating ways, and whether they choose hierarchy-attenuating or hierarchy-enhancing roles, is influenced by a general value they have for group inequality versus equality. This psychological orientation is called social dominance orientation. People who are relatively high in social dominance orientation (unegalitarian) have been found to endorse sexist beliefs, to support more conservative than liberal political parties, and to endorse prejudice against the local subordinate group more than do people lower in social dominance orientation.

This finding has emerged in the United States, Sweden, Israel, New Zealand, South Africa, Canada, Spain, France, Belgium, Mexico, Australia, Lebanon, China, Taiwan, Italy, and elsewhere, even though the contents of sexism, the particular political system and political parties, and the subordinate arbitrary group and measures of prejudice differ from society to society. Social dominance orientation also correlates with prejudice based on nationalism and sexual orientation. Social dominance orientation is a robust individual difference measure of group prejudice, and it accounts for variability in prejudice independent of right wing authoritarianism and political–economic conservatism. Social dominance orientation reliably predicts a variety of discriminatory behaviors in experiments and is relatively stable over time, although it can change with educational socialization.

It is not known what causes a person to become relatively high or low in social dominance orientation, but there are consistent correlations between social dominance orientation and other variables across nations. Men are consistently higher in social dominance orientation than women are, and, in most studies, people in the dominant ethnic or sexual-orientation groups are also higher in social dominance orientation than people in the

subordinate ethnic or sexual-orientation groups. People lower in social dominance orientation tend to be higher in empathy, benevolence, openness, agreeableness, and universal values than are people higher in social dominance orientation. People higher in social dominance orientation assume that the world is a zero-sum competition, and their motivation not to lose this competition can lead them to be callous and hostile. However, social dominance orientation is unrelated to being task focused or efficacious. Some have argued that there are developmental antecedents to social dominance orientation. For example, John Duckitt has hypothesized that people who are raised with little affection develop a dog-eat-dog worldview and become higher in social dominance orientation.

Behavioral Asymmetry

Because social dominance theory is fundamentally about group differences in power, it has explicitly theorized about the social and psychological situations of dominance and subordination. One important principle it has explicated is that of behavioral asymmetry, which states that behaviors that are generally self- or group beneficial will be more likely to be performed by members of dominant than members of subordinate groups. Sidanius and Pratto have reviewed an array of such behaviors. For example, Blacks are less likely to spend time studying and are less likely to follow their doctor's orders than Whites are. The fact that people in subordinate groups do not act in ways that favor themselves as much as do people in dominant groups is, then, another bias that contributes to group inequality.

A special case of behavioral asymmetry is ideological asymmetry. The principle of ideological asymmetry holds that psychological factors that are expected to be associated with social dominance orientation, such as ingroup identification and endorsement of hierarchy-enhancing ideologies, will be more strongly associated among dominant group members than among subordinate group members. For example, ethnic identification is more strongly associated with social dominance orientation among Whites than among Blacks and Latinos in the United States. In fact, even people in nonhegemonic societies, such as Lebanon, have been shown to favor the global hegemony of the United States if they are high in social dominance orientation. Related predictions concerning group differences in the relations among identity, ingroup bias, and system justification have been derived from social identity theory and system justification theory, but often relying on the concept of social dominance orientation.

Gender and Group Dominance

Social dominance theory recognizes that men play a special role in maintaining group dominance in that men monopolize the forceful institutional roles that sustain not just order but group dominance, including judiciary, lawyers, militaries, and police. The primary targets of forceful control by such institutions are men in subordinate groups. Moreover, men are overrepresented (compared with women) in unofficial coalitions that use force to exert power, including criminal gangs, substate terrorist groups, and revolutionary and liberation movements that use violence. In some sense, then, considerable intergroup violence is actually conflict between coalitions of men, although of course women and children can also participate in and suffer from such conflicts. This is one fact that shows that gender inequality and arbitrary-set inequality interlock and are not just special cases of each other.

Women are more likely than men to do hierarchy-attenuating work, or work that disproportionately benefits members of low-power groups, such as social work and volunteer work that aid the poor, the sick, and immigrants. Gender differences in obtaining roles that attenuate or enhance hierarchy are not due only to gender differences in social dominance orientation but also to sex discrimination in hiring.

Power Dynamics

The apparatus of social dominance theory outlines how social inequality could be made more or less severe and also more or less stable. Societies should be relatively more egalitarian to the extent that they are not wealthy, have hierarchy-attenuating ideologies strongly linked to their cultural values and social identities, have more women with political power, have more gender equality in caregiving roles, and have less privileging of punitive and military institutions. Societies that have widely shared legitimizing myths will tend to be more stable in inequality, both because of social consensus and because hierarchy-attenuating myths and actors will tend to curb the excesses of hierarchy-enhancing myths and actors. Elite groups that rely more on violence than on legitimizing myths to maintain dominance are likely to be unstable, because they produce resentment. Moreover, once these groups have been removed from power, a power vacuum occurs that invites multiple parties to engage in conflict until a new dominating order is established.

Felicia Pratto

See also Authoritarian Personality; Discrimination; Dominance Hierarchies; Ideology; Power; Prejudice; Racism; Social Identity Theory; System Justification Theory

Further Readings

Altemeyer, B. (1998). The other "authoritarian personality." In M. P. Zanna (Ed.), *Advances in experimental social psychology* (Vol. 30, pp. 48–92). San Diego, CA: Academic Press.

Duckitt, J. (2001). A dual-process cognitive-motivational theory of ideology and prejudice. In M. P. Zanna (Ed.), *Advances in experimental social psychology* (Vol. 33, pp. 41–113). San Diego, CA: Academic Press.

Guimond, S., Dambrun, M., Michinov, N., & Duarte, S. (2003). Does social dominance generate prejudice? Integrating individual and contextual determinants of intergroup cognitions. *Journal of Personality & Social Psychology, 84,* 697–721.

Pratto, F., Liu, J., Levin, S., Sidanius, J., Shih, M., Bachrach, H., et al. (2000). Social dominance orientation and the legitimization of inequality across cultures. *Journal of Cross-Cultural Psychology, 31,* 369–409.

Pratto, F., Sidanius, J., & Levin, S. (2006). Social dominance theory and the dynamics of group power: Taking stock and looking forward. *European Review of Social Psychology, 17,* 271–320.

Pratto, F., Sidanius, J., Stallworth, L. M., & Malle, B. F. (1994). Social dominance orientation: A personality variable predicting social and political attitudes. *Journal of Personality and Social Psychology, 67,* 741–763.

Sidanius, J. (1993). The psychology of group conflict and the dynamics of oppression: A social dominance perspective. In S. Iyengar & W. McGuire (Eds.),

Explorations in political psychology (pp. 183–219). Durham, NC: Duke University Press.

Sidanius, J., & Pratto, F. (1999). *Social dominance: An intergroup theory of social hierarchy and oppression.* New York: Cambridge University Press.

SOCIAL ENTRAINMENT

The *social entrainment model* was introduced by Joseph McGrath and Janice Kelly to provide a general framework for understanding some aspects of social behavior over time. The term *entrainment* is borrowed from the biological sciences, in which an internal rhythmic process is "captured" and modified by another cycle. For instance, we know that there are a number of cyclic processes within the body, such as body temperature, urinary output, and various hormonal cycles, that have become entrained to one another so that they operate in synchrony with respect to their regularly spaced recurrence.

These cycles can also be affected by various outside forces that might affect their onset, offset, or synchronization. For instance, the day–night cycle acts as a powerful entraining signal for synchronizing many of the body's cyclic processes. In "free-running" conditions, or in conditions in which the outside pacing influence of the day–night cycle is removed, these cycles continue to approximate a 24-hour periodicity. Thus, the circadian fluctuations will persist for a time, even after the pacing event has been removed, until disentrainment from the 24-hour periodicity occurs or until a new entraining signal is imposed. When the outside pacing event is again imposed on these processes, such as when the day–night cycle is reintroduced, the 24-hour periodicity again becomes strongly entrained.

By analogy, the term *social entrainment* describes the many human social rhythms that are influenced by other social rhythms or by external pacing events. Social entrainment can also occur between individuals. For instance, some researchers have found that individuals in conversation will modify their conversation patterns toward that of their partner. At an even more macro level, there is an entrainment of life activity patterns that can become disrupted when a worker changes to an off-time shift. Social entrainment refers to all those cycles of behavior, at the individual, group, or organizational level, that are captured and modified by one another or by an external pacer that may serve to regulate those behaviors. This entry summarizes the original model and related empirical research.

Components of the Model

McGrath and Kelly assumed that these notions of rhythm, entrainment, and external pacing events might be useful for thinking about human behavior over time. Their ideas were formalized in 1986 as the *social entrainment model*. The model consists of four components that refer to entrained and unentrained rhythms of behavior and to possible external pacing conditions.

The first component of the model, *rhythm*, refers to the various endogenous rhythmic processes that may be inherent in the organism under study. Many aspects of human behavior seem to have cyclic or rhythmic qualities. For instance, individuals have fairly predictable activity cycles, perhaps influenced by various biological cycles. Individuals also seem to have various base-rate preferences for the amount of talking or for appropriate turn-taking that they might prefer in a group interaction. Rebecca Warner and others have found that patterns of sound and silence in interacting dyads seem to operate in recurring patterns or rhythms. Organizations also often have predictable, seasonal fluctuations. Thus, rhythmic aspects of behavior can occur on individual to organizational levels and can range in periodicities from fractions of seconds to lifetimes.

The second component, *mesh*, refers to some process through which various rhythms become synchronized. In biology, it is sometimes possible to specify the organ or area responsible for the entrainment. In human social behavior, on the other hand, such a mechanism must often be inferred. For example, individuals entering an interaction with various personal tempos for conversational behavior must negotiate or somehow adopt a scheme for synchronizing individual preferences. Others have suggested a similar mechanism at the level of social systems, such that organizations must somehow develop a *negotiated temporal order* in order to achieve smooth organizational coordination.

The third component, *tempo*, refers to the patterns of behavior that result as a consequence of this synchronization. For example, after individual conversational preferences are synchronized, there is a resulting pattern of sound and silence, or other behaviors, within the interaction. Other examples might include a pattern of individual task performance, daily recurrent patterns of activity and rest, or yearly productivity patterns in an organization.

The final component, *pace*, refers to potential outside pacing events that might influence the onset, offset, or periodicity of the specified rhythms. The biological example is the day–night cycle that synchronizes circadian cycles to a 24-hour periodicity. Examples of pacing events for human behavior include changes in work schedule and abrupt changes in time zones. Each of these examples has implications for onset and offset of activity cycles. For example, time limits often act as powerful pacing events that obviously affect the onset and offset of activities but that also affect the periodicities of behavior within those time limits.

The social entrainment model therefore suggests that when looking at human behavior, we might want to examine a number of features. In particular, we might want to examine (a) rhythms of behavior, (b) synchronization between rhythms of behavior, (c) how various external pacing events might affect these rhythms, and (d) how these altered rhythms might persist over time.

Related Research

Most of the empirical work on social entrainment has focused on the third and fourth of these issues, namely, how external pacing events might alter rhythms and how these altered rhythms might persist over time. For example, Kelly and her colleagues have found that *time limits* can serve as powerful potential pacing events, and these researchers have gathered a body of evidence concerning the initial altering (entraining) effects of time limits and how these entrained patterns persist over time. More specifically, they find that short initial time limits (or time pressure) cause individuals and groups to work at a faster rate of performance, but with lower quality, and that these initial effects persist over multiple trials.

Conversely, long initial time limits cause individuals and groups to work at slower rates of performance, but with higher quality, and these initial effects also persist over multiple trials. Their work also shows similar entrainment effects for interpersonal communication patterns. Short time limits cause groups to focus more specifically on task-oriented communications, as opposed to nontask and personal communications, and these effects also persist over multiple trials.

Deborah Ancona and her colleagues have similarly documented powerful external pacing events in organizations. Organizations can have periods of speeded-up activity and periods of sloweddown activity that can define a rhythm of activity. These rhythms can be influenced by eternal events, such as seasonal demand or quarterly accounting cycles. Behavior in teams operating within organizations also responds to internal pacing events, such as those that are defined by phases of task completion or by deadlines. Ancona thus has stated that teams must engage in a *dance of entrainment* as they choreograph their activities to mesh with internal and external pacing events over time.

Janice R. Kelly

See also Group Development; Group Performance; Group Task; Norms; Teams

Further Readings

Ancona, D. G., & Chong, C. L. (1996). Entrainment: Pace, cycle, and rhythm in organizational behavior. *Research in Organizational Behavior, 18,* 251–284.

Ancona, D. G., & Waller, M. J. (2007). The dance of entrainment: Temporally navigating across multiple pacers. *Research in the Sociology of Work, 17,* 115–146.

Farmer, S., & Seers, A. (2004). Time enough to work: Employee motivation and entrainment in the workplace. *Time and Society, 13,* 265–284.

Kelly, J. R. (1988). Entrainment in individual and group behavior. In J. E. McGrath (Ed.), *The social psychology of time: New perspectives.* Newbury Park, CA: Sage.

McGrath, J. E., & Kelly, J. R. (1986). *Time and human interaction: Toward a social psychology of time.* New York: Guilford.

Social Exchange in Networks and Groups

Research on social exchange in networks and groups is primarily concerned with the more or less enduring relationships that develop over time. The research has been concerned with interactions, both within and between groups and networks, in which individuals attempt to obtain the resources or benefits they desire. One of the major concerns has been how the connections between individuals influence their likelihood of obtaining the resources they desire, and as a result, how interactions can then reshape the connections between individuals in networks and groups.

History and Background

The exchange perspective on networks and groups has origins in several disciplines, including psychology, sociology, anthropology, and economics. There were two major influences from the field of psychology. First is the work by John Thibaut and Harold Kelley, *The Social Psychology of Groups*, which was extremely influential in the early works on exchange in sociology. In addition, the work of B. F. Skinner had a strong influence on the work of George Homans and subsequently of Linda Molm. In cultural anthropology, the works of Claude Lévi-Strauss, Bronislaw Malinowski, and Marcel Mauss were especially influential.

Three of the earliest theorists writing about social exchange in networks and groups were George Homans, Peter Blau, and Richard M. Emerson. They set the groundwork for most of the subsequent research on exchange in networks and groups. Each of these theorists had significant influence on the development of this field of study.

Homans's primary focus was the social behavior that emerged as a result of mutual reinforcement of two parties involved in a dyadic exchange. He was greatly influenced by the work of Skinner and borrowed Skinner's ideas on reinforcement as a mechanism for change within networks. Homans's theoretical consideration of distributive justice, power, status, authority, leadership, and solidarity is based on an analysis of direct exchange between individuals in groups.

Blau focused on the links between microsocial behavior and the groups, organizations, and institutions in which individual relations are embedded. Blau was interested primarily in the reciprocal exchange of benefits and the types of relationships and social structures that emerge from this kind of social interaction.

For Emerson, the relationship between power and social structure was the central theoretical problem in social exchange in groups and networks. Two of Emerson's distinct contributions are his fundamental insight into the relational nature of power and his extension of power–dependence theory to analyze the social networks created by exchange relations. Subsequent work by Karen Cook, Barry Markovsky, David Willer, John Skvoretz, Edward Lawler, Linda Molm, Phillip Bonacich, Noah Friedkin, and others built on these developments.

Types of Exchange

The principles of social exchange in groups and networks can be applied to most human interactions, but individuals do not interact with all other individuals the same ways, nor is it acceptable to engage in certain types of interaction to procure certain resources (i.e., one is unlikely to negotiate birthday gifts). Several possible types of interaction within groups and networks have been specified. The broadest distinction between types of exchange is between direct and indirect exchanges. *Direct exchange* is a relationship in which each actor's outcome is directly dependent on another actor's behavior. *Indirect exchange* is an exchange relationship in which each actor's outcome is dependent, not on the person he or she gave to, but rather on either a collective entity or another member of the network.

There are three major types of direct exchange: negotiated, reciprocal, and productive exchange. In *negotiated exchange*, actors engage in a joint decision process, such as explicit bargaining, in which they seek agreement on the terms of the transaction. It is easy to identify the benefits received by individuals in any given transaction. All sides of the transaction must agree to the terms of the transaction for it to occur. Most economic exchanges take this form, as do many social exchanges (negotiating over chores or social activities).

In contrast, in *reciprocal exchange*, actors' contributions to the exchange are separately performed and not explicitly negotiated. In reciprocal exchange, an actor initiates exchanges individually, by performing a beneficial act for another actor or a group, without knowing whether, when, or to what extent the other actor will reciprocate this beneficial act. If a relationship forms, it often takes the shape of sequential actions characterized by mutual obligations. Reciprocal exchange often occurs within intimate social relations in which explicit negotiation over resources or benefits would violate norms. But reciprocal exchange also occurs in situations such as the workplace, where individuals may help one another on projects, with implicit expectations for reciprocity in the future.

Studies of negotiated and reciprocal exchange generally focus on the interaction within a network of exchange. Early work on social exchange within groups and networks typically examined dyadic exchange relationships. Now, most research focuses on exchange relations embedded within larger exchange networks or groups. Emerson defined an *exchange network* as a set of two or more connected exchange relations. Two exchange relationships are connected if the frequency or value of exchange in one relationship affects the frequency or value of exchange in another.

The third major form of direct exchange is *productive exchange*. In this form of interaction, all the parties of the exchange contribute and benefit from a single transaction. Groups engage in productive exchange when they act collectively, each member contributing to produce a socially valued outcome that benefits all group members. Productive exchange is similar to what other social psychologists have called cooperation or coordination. Research on productive exchange generally focuses on the group, in which individuals work together to achieve some valued outcome. The structure of the group (i.e., the way each group's members are connected) has not typically been studied. Instead, research on productive exchange, such as that by Lawler and his colleagues, has focused on issues of coordination, solidarity, cohesion, and affect.

In *indirect* or *generalized exchange*, one actor gives resources to another, but resources are reciprocated not by the recipient but rather by a third party. Thus, generalized-exchange systems involve a minimum of three actors. From the perspective of the recipient, the obligation to reciprocate is not necessarily directed to the benefactor but instead to one or more actors who are implicated in a social exchange situation with the benefactor.

There are two main types of generalized exchange: network-generalized exchange and group-generalized exchange. In *network-generalized exchange*, each individual gives goods or services directly to one other individual and receives goods or services from a different individual in the same network. The *Kula ring* trade in the Trobriand Islands studied by Malinowski is the most famous example. The Kula ring involved the exchange of necklaces of red shells in a clockwise fashion between islands, while bracelets of white shells were exchanged in a counterclockwise direction. In *group-generalized exchange*, individuals contribute to a public or collective good and receive benefits from the same public or collective good. Barn raising, in which a community comes together to build a barn for one of its members, is an example of group-generalized exchange.

The majority of the theorizing on social exchange in groups and networks emphasizes direct exchange. The following sections describe the major trends and findings.

Power

By embedding the exchange relation within a network of connections, Emerson fostered a new era of exchange studies. The inclusion of networks allowed theorists to consider the effects of having alternatives for valued resources, that is, structural power. Emerson, and later his colleague Cook, developed power–dependence theory, which describes how variation in the number of alternatives for valued resources and the value of the resources one controls determine one's relative power in an exchange network. One of the major findings in this tradition is that an actor's relative position in a network produces differences in the use of power. Unequal power then manifests itself in the unequal distribution of rewards across positions in a social network.

David Willer and Barry Markovsky have also studied power within networks and groups. They assume that power is determined by the number of alternative connections available to an actor within a network. They distinguish between two types of networks, *strong* and *weak power networks*. The difference between the two types of networks stems from the likelihood of actors being excluded from exchange. In strong power networks, some actors in the network (low-power actors) must be excluded from the exchange, and some actors (high-power actors) must be included in the exchange. High-power actors in strong power networks are likely to obtain almost all, if not all, the resources available in the network. On the other hand, in weak power networks, it is possible to exclude any actor in the network in an exchange. The likelihood of being excluded from the exchange depends on an actor's position in the network. In weak power networks, high-power actors benefit proportionally more than do lower power actors.

Commitment

In addition to the study of power, the phenomenon of commitment became a central focus of those interested in exchange dynamics within groups and networks. Commitment has generally been conceived of as repeated interaction with one partner to the exclusion of other potential partners in the group or network. Commitment became central to the work on exchange in networks and groups because it presented a serious theoretical problem. Scholars who study exchange in groups and networks generally assume that actors try to maximize outcomes they desire. However, committing to a partner when an individual has alternatives is not a rational decision.

Seminal work by Cook and Emerson and their students has established that, in general, individuals value low uncertainty and often act to minimize uncertainty in interactions. Cook and Emerson found that greater uncertainty led to higher levels of commitment with particular partners. Commitment between partners reduces the uncertainty of finding a partner for trade and ensures a higher frequency of exchange. Peter Kollock examined behavioral commitments in environments that allow actors to cheat one another in their exchanges. In situations in which opportunism is possible, a commitment to a specific trustworthy partner is often the easiest solution to the problem of uncertainty. He found that actors were willing to forgo potentially more profitable exchanges with untested partners in favor of continuing to transact

with known partners who had demonstrated their trustworthiness in previous transactions (i.e., they did not misrepresent the value of their goods).

Toshio Yamagishi and Karen Cook have found that, in conditions of low uncertainty, actors are much more likely to avoid forming commitments to specific partners in order to maximize their access to valued resources. And Yamagishi and Cook have found that, under conditions of high uncertainty, actors form exclusive commitments to a specific partner in the network in an attempt to avoid the possibility of exploitation by unknown actors who enter the exchange network.

Affect and Affective Commitment

More recently, the concept of commitment has expanded beyond the traditional behavioral measures of repeated exchange to include measures of affective commitment. This effort has been led by Lawler and his colleagues, as well as by Molm and her colleagues. This shift to understand the role of emotions in exchange represents an important return to fundamental issues of social solidarity and cohesion in networks and groups.

Among the more recent efforts to examine the nonstructural elements of social exchange in networks and groups is the work of Lawler on relational cohesion, as well as Molm's research on variations in affective responses to different types of exchange. Lawler and his colleagues developed the *affect theory of social exchange* to explain the effects of emotional responses to exchanges on relationships within networks and groups and exchange outcomes, including the degree of commitment and solidarity within the network or group. The goal of this work has been to develop a more comprehensive theory of exchange in networks and groups that includes emotions as a key element in the formation and continuation of relationships within networks and groups.

Molm and her colleagues have examined the effects of *type* of exchange (reciprocal or negotiated) on affective commitment within networks and groups. Molm and her collaborators have argued that reciprocal exchange is inherently more risky than negotiated exchange. Because exploitation is always possible, actors in reciprocal exchange risk giving benefits unilaterally while receiving little or nothing in return. Moreover, these researchers have argued that affective commitment is more likely to form in reciprocal exchange than in negotiated exchange. Because of the inherent risk, actors are likely to attribute a partner's positive behaviors to personal traits and intentions, which results in the emergence of stronger positive feelings in reciprocal exchange than in negotiated exchange.

Trust

In addition to work on affect and affective commitment, understanding the formation of trust relationships has become an important area of research on exchange in networks and groups. The earliest work on trust formation stressed the importance of positive exchange behavior in the network or group. Blau argued that by cooperating with a partner, one indicates that one is less likely to take advantage of one's partner. It is these actions that can help build relationships within and between networks and groups. Blau argued that actors in reciprocal exchange start with small gifts. If those are returned, the actor is perceived as trustworthy, and subsequently, larger gifts may be given. In addition, Kollock has shown how the risk of exploitation can have extreme effects on perceptions of trustworthiness. In his study, when sellers were able to mislead the buyers about the quality of the goods to be purchased (i.e., a potential for opportunism existed), truthful information was associated with high levels of perceived trustworthiness, but dishonest information was associated with high levels of distrust.

Molm and her colleagues have also studied how different types of exchange (which vary in risk) affect perceptions of trust. They have argued that trust should be higher in reciprocal exchange than in negotiated exchange, precisely because the fear of exploitation should be stronger in reciprocal exchange. This effect is magnified by the attribution of behaviors to a partner's personal traits, which allows trust to be attributed to that partner within a network or group.

While the majority of social-psychological studies on exchange have focused on direct exchange, interest in generalized exchange has increased recently. Yamagishi and Cook compared the two types of generalized exchange and found that network-generalized exchange systems promote higher levels of participation than do group-generalized exchange systems (controlling for the size of the

network or group). They also found that mutual trust between members of these groups leads to higher levels of participation in the exchange. This effect is especially pronounced in network-generalized exchange.

In addition, Molm and her colleagues have begun including generalized exchange in their comparisons between types of exchange. They have found that network-generalized exchange produces higher levels of solidarity, perceived trust, and positive affect within groups and networks than do either reciprocal or negotiated exchange. They have argued that indirect reciprocity, typified by network-generalized exchange, produces stronger feelings of group attachment and solidarity. The work by Molm and her colleagues typifies one of the major trends in exchange studies, namely, to compare how different network structures and exchange types impact different social-psychological outcomes.

Future Directions

The work discussed here focuses on interaction within one type of exchange, but real-world studies of exchange relationships show that exchange relations are multiplex and can evolve through time. One of the challenges of the study of social exchange in networks and groups is to understand the causes and consequences of changes in the type of exchange. Another area for future work on social exchange in networks and groups is to use the theoretical tools developed in the laboratory to explore real-world social networks. The work on social exchange in networks and groups has primarily been limited to highly controlled experimental studies, but the theoretical framework has the potential to help us better understand interaction in naturally forming groups and networks.

Alexandra Gerbasi

See also Cooperation and Competition; Negotiation and Bargaining; Power; Power–Dependence Theory; Social Networks

Further Readings

Blau, P. M. (1986). *Exchange and power in social life.* New York: Wiley. (Original work published 1964)

Cook, K. S., & Emerson, R. M. (1984). Exchange networks and the analysis of complex organization. In

S. B. Bacharach & E. J. Lawler (Eds.), *Research in the sociology of organizations* (pp. 1–30). Greenwich, CT: JAI Press.

Emerson, R. M. (1972). Exchange theory, part I: A psychological basis for social exchange. In J. Berger, M. Zelditch Jr., & B. Anderson (Eds.), *Sociological theories in progress* (pp. 38–57). Boston: Houghton Mifflin.

Emerson, R. M. (1972). Exchange theory, part II: Exchange relations and networks. In J. Berger, M. Zelditch Jr., & B. Anderson (Eds.), *Sociological theories in progress* (pp. 58–87). Boston: Houghton Mifflin.

Homans, G. C. (1974). *Social behavior: Its elementary forms.* New York: Harcourt, Brace, Jovanovich. (Original work published 1961)

Kollock, P. (1994). The emergence of exchange structures: An experimental study of uncertainty, commitment, and trust. *American Journal of Sociology, 100,* 313–345.

Lawler, E. J., Yoon, J., & Thye, S. R. (2000). Emotion and group cohesion in productive exchange. *American Journal of Sociology, 106,* 616–657.

Markovsky, B., Willer, D., & Patton, T. (1988). Power relations in exchange networks. *American Sociological Review, 53,* 101–117.

Molm, L., & Cook, K. S. (1995). Social exchange and exchange networks. In K. S. Cook, G. A. Fine, & J. S. House (Eds.), *Sociological perspectives on social psychology* (pp. 209–235). Boston: Allyn & Bacon.

Yamagishi, T., & Cook, K. S. (1993). Generalized exchange and social dilemmas. *Social Psychology Quarterly, 56,* 235–248.

SOCIAL FACILITATION

In 1956, Roger Bannister used an inventive strategy to achieve the world's first 4-minute mile. He had two friends pace him, each for one lap, just under the needed pace. Bannister's strategy illustrates *social facilitation.* This term refers to cases in which individuals improve their performance when they are in the presence of conspecifics (i.e., members of the same species). These conspecifics can be observers, others performing the same activity, or others who just happen to be present. This facilitation, however, occurs only on simple tasks in which the correct response is well learned. In contrast, on complex tasks in which the correct response is not well learned, the presence of conspecifics usually detracts from performance, a phenomenon known as *social impairment.* The fact that the presence of others intensifies reactions (either correct or incorrect) has implications for a wide array of behaviors in human groups, including mobs, teams, and work groups. For example, recent research indicates that the presence of others can facilitate intergroup stereotyping. This entry describes research regarding social facilitation, one of the oldest research topics in social psychology.

History

In 1897 Norman Triplett observed that bicycle racers rode faster against competitors than against a clock. He then conducted experiments verifying that children wound a fishing reel faster when they had competitors. Other researchers found that, when conspecifics were present, ants moved more sand, chicks ate more feed, and dogs ran faster. Knut Larsson reported that rat pairs copulated more if they were in the presence of other copulating rat pairs. In one intriguing study, Robert Zajonc and his associates found that cockroaches ran faster down a straight runway to escape a light if the runway was lined with acrylic cubicles containing other cockroaches. Similarly, humans eat more, purchase more, and jog faster when they are in the presence of other people. In short, responses are intensified in terms of speed, vigor, or probability of occurrence when humans, insects, and animals are observed by an audience or are performing with coactors. Because so many of the early studies reported improvements in performance in others' presence, the term *social facilitation* came to be synonymous with the impact of such social presence and to some degree remains so today.

However, by the 1930s it had become apparent that, occasionally, having people work together on a task could also impair performance. Thus, if people collaborate on a single group task such that their individual contributions are masked, *social loafing* rather than social facilitation occurs. In addition, even on noncollaborative tasks (in which one's individual output is easily assessed), working alongside coactors (or before an audience) impairs performance in some cases. For example, such social conditions impair performance when people work on Greek epigrams or complex computer problems. Such results initially provoked some confusion. However, in a classic 1965 paper, Zajonc offered an integrative explanation for these outcomes that reinvigorated research on this topic.

Theoretical Views

Zajonc's Drive View

Zajonc suggested that both social facilitation and social impairment occur because the presence of others elevates *drive*, also called *arousal* or *excitement*. Drive level is important because it is known to intensify performance on easy tasks, in which correct performance is pretty much automatic. This occurs because drive (e.g., hunger) is known to intensify *dominant responses*—responses that are highly likely as a result of training or inborn tendencies. On easy tasks, the correct response is dominant, and therefore drive should serve to facilitate correct performance. On difficult tasks, however, incorrect responses tend to be dominant, and therefore drive should intensify these responses, thereby impairing correct performance. Thus, according to Zajonc, increased drive can lead to *either* performance facilitation or impairment. Zajonc's cockroach study illustrates his theory. The same cockroach "rooting section" that facilitated performance in a straight runway (where the dominant response of running forward is "correct") inhibited performance on a task that required the insects to emit a nondominant response (slowing down and turning right).

After 20 years, it became clear that there was strong support for Dr. Zajonc's basic predictions. A 1984 meta-analysis "averaged" the findings of 241 studies. As predicted, social conditions did indeed facilitate performance on simple tasks and impair performance on complex tasks. What remained unclear, however, was why.

Evaluation Theory

Zajonc argued in 1965 that such facilitation or impairment should occur whenever others are *merely present*. Other researchers, however, have maintained that facilitation or impairment—at least among humans—is due to participants' worrying about looking bad to others. Consistent with this viewpoint, there is evidence that nonevaluative audiences do not provoke social facilitation or impairment. For example, several studies indicate that joggers do not jog faster when potential observers are inattentive. However, in support of the "mere-presence" view, other research indicates that even when people should not feel anxious about evaluation (e.g., during a pretask warm-up period), they show evidence of social facilitation while typing their names in front of a blindfolded observer. In another study, A. W. Rajecki reported that the simple presence of a blindfolded display manikin triggered social facilitation. In short, the question regarding the impact of mere presence remains unsettled.

Distraction–Conflict Theory

According to distraction–conflict theory, social facilitation or impairment occurs because we have a strong tendency to pay attention to conspecifics. In experiments, this tendency conflicts with our need to pay close attention to the experimental task. The tendency to pay attention to conspecifics should be particularly strong if these others are competing against us or evaluating us or are unusual in some fashion. This tendency produces *attentional conflict*, that is, indecision regarding where and when to direct our attention. Such *approach–approach conflict*, in turn, is known to produce the type of drive or arousal to which Zajonc alluded.

This view explains the effects of evaluation anxiety by assuming that worrying creates *internal* distraction (Will I perform well enough? Do I look silly?). Similarly, the inconsistent effects of mere presence discussed above can be explained by assuming that when the presence of others is unusual, it provokes attentional conflict. However, when it is not unusual, it does not. Thus, the presence of a blindfolded manikin (which few people have encountered before) might well lure participants' attention from an experimental task, thereby provoking attentional conflict.

Supporting this model, mechanical distractions have been found to provoke the same social facilitation effects and physiological reactions as an audience, and social facilitation occurs only when coactors work on comparable tasks (where the urge to socially compare is strong). In one ingenious study, Brad Groff required participants to examine the face of an evaluating observer. Given that this particular task *required* participants to monitor the observer, there was no attentional conflict between performing the task (watching the observer) and attending to the audience (i.e., the single observer). As predicted, in this condition no social facilitation occurred.

Critique

One serious problem with these versions of drive theory is that evidence for elevated arousal (e.g., blood pressure) in social conditions is mixed. Thus, the meta-analysis described above revealed that arousal was elevated on complex tasks but not on simple ones. In addition, John Cacioppo in 1990 carefully assessed arousal measures and found no evidence of heightened arousal when people were observed.

Research by James Blascovich and his associates suggests that physiological reactions in social conditions may be more specific than Zajonc assumed. This work indicates that when individuals in social conditions feel that they can meet the demands posed by a task, they show increased cardiac output, dilation of their arteries, and improved blood flow to the muscles (i.e., a *challenge reaction*). This reaction is associated with improved task performance. However, when people feel that they probably cannot meet the task demands, they exhibit a *threat reaction*, which is known to impair performance. This reaction is marked by increased vascular constriction and increased blood pressure. These findings suggest that social facilitation or impairment is not due to a simple increase in arousal, as Zajonc suggested, but rather to a more complex set of bodily reactions.

Attention Theory

In contrast to drive theory, some have suggested that attentional processes may explain social facilitation effects. A revision of distraction–conflict theory points out that when people are overloaded with more stimuli than they have time to process, they narrow the range of cues to which they attend. If they are working on a well-learned task, this narrow focus allows them to better "home in" on the few key cues demanding attention. If, however, a complex task requires people to process a wide array of cues, such a narrow focus will hurt performance. This explains how the model accounts for both facilitation and impairment effects.

Several recent studies support this perspective. Dominique Muller and Fabrizio Butera reported in 2007 that coaction increased participants' ability to focus on two key stimuli—a slash and a tilted S—while it decreased their tendency to falsely report seeing these items as a dollar sign (a dominant–familiar response). Similarly, Pascal Huguet reported that coaction increased individuals' ability to focus on the color of letters making up a word and decreased their tendency to read the word (a dominant response). In short, 99 years after Triplett's original report, researchers still continue to explore the causes and dimensions of social facilitation, one of the fundamental findings in group psychology.

Robert S. Baron

See also Group Motivation; Group Performance; Social Compensation; Social Loafing; Sports Teams; Teams

Further Readings

Aiello, J. R., & Douthitt, E. A. (2001). Social facilitation from Triplett to electronic performance monitoring. *Group Dynamics: Theory, Research, & Practice, 5,* 163–180.

Baron, R. S. (1986). Distraction-conflict theory: Progress and problems. In L. Berkowitz (Ed.), *Advances in experimental social psychology* (pp. 1–40). New York: Academic Press.

Lambert, A. J., Payne, B. K., Jacoby, L. L., Shaffer, L. M., Chasteen, A., & Khan, S. (2003). Stereotypes as dominant responses. *Journal of Personality and Social Psychology, 84,* 277–295.

Muller, D., & Butera, F. (2007). The focusing effect of self-evaluation threat in coaction and social comparison. *Journal of Personality and Social Psychology, 93,* 194–211.

Zajonc, R. B. (1965). Social facilitation. *Science, 149,* 269–274.

Social Identity Model of Deindividuation Effects

The *social identity model of deindividuation effects* (SIDE model) explains how group behavior is affected by *anonymity* and *identifiability*. There are many social situations in which people interact in relatively anonymous ways. In social interactions on the Internet, for example, people often use pseudonyms or avatars (pictures) to identify themselves, and even e-mail addresses do not typically provide much information about senders. Another example is the anonymity people experience when they are in a crowd. An important question, therefore, is how anonymity affects people's behavior.

SIDE was developed as an alternative to *deindividuation theory*. Deindividuation theory suggests that anonymity leads to a loss of self-awareness, and this loss leads to a rise in antinormative behavior. But deindividuation research shows contradictory results: Anonymity in groups often leads to more normative behavior. SIDE suggests this is because anonymity makes people self-define themselves less as persons but *more* as members of the social group to which they belong. This increased salience of social group membership (or social identity) leads to increased adherence to the norms of the group.

Today, SIDE is used to explain the effects of anonymity and social isolation in various settings, and an extensive body of research has examined its propositions. Taken as a whole, this research demonstrates that anonymity and identifiability have profound consequences for intergroup relations, group processes, and individual self-definition. Research on SIDE has particularly focused on crowds and collective action, online teams, electronic relationships and virtual communities, and, recently, on social effects of surveillance (e.g., by means of cameras or electronic tagging). This entry first reviews the historical and scientific background of the SIDE model and then explains the model in some detail.

Background

Deindividuation theory was developed to explain the phenomenon that in crowds, people become capable of acts that rational individuals would not normally endorse. In a crowd, people may become disinhibited and behave antinormatively. Soccer hooliganism is one example. Deindividuation theory argues that this behavior occurs because of the anonymity of the crowd. If you are anonymous, you are not paid attention to as an individual, and

this makes you less able and less motivated to regulate your actions. If you do not or cannot regulate your actions, you can no longer adhere to existing social norms, and your behavior may be disinhibited. The psychological state of deindividuation therefore involves a severely reduced ability to exercise self-control.

Research has shown that deindividuation does not tell the whole story, however. For example, questions have been raised about the existence of the psychological state of deindividuation. Even more problematic is that the outcomes predicted by deindividuation theory are actually quite rare. Historical evidence shows that most crowds are peaceful and orderly. And even when they are violent, crowds are typically disciplined and capable of sophisticated patterns of behavior. These characteristics are inconsistent with the deindividuation theory prediction of disinhibition.

SIDE has taken these inconsistencies as the basis for a new model. Its prediction is different from that of deindividuation theory. SIDE predicts that in the crowd (as well as in other "deindividuating" situations), group members are highly sensitive to situational norms that are specific to their psychological ingroup. What happens in the crowd is *not* that individuals become less self-aware. Rather, according to SIDE, the crowd leads individuals to pay attention to a different aspect of the self.

SIDE builds on social identity and self-categorization theory, which propose that one's sense of self is made up of personal identity and multiple social identities, all of which combine to shape one's personality. Social identities are likely to become the basis for self-definition when that social identity is *salient*, such as when making comparisons between "them" and "us." One consequence of salience is *depersonalization*. Depersonalization is not the same as deindividuation or a loss of self. Rather, depersonalization refers to a switch to a group level of self-categorization in which self and others are seen in terms of their group identities.

As a consequence of depersonalization, perceptions of the outgroup become more stereotypical. Self-perceptions also shift: Self and other ingroup members become interchangeable, and the individual self-stereotypes in terms of group attributes. Depersonalization thus transforms individuals into group members who regulate their behavior according to ingroup norms. It is important to note that, in contrast to deindividuation, the psychological state of depersonalization does not imply a loss of rationality or behavioral disinhibition. Rather, the individual behaves rationally and regulates behavior according to ingroup standards. These ideas from social identity theory and self-categorization theory are the foundations of SIDE.

Development of the SIDE Model

The SIDE model was named in 1991 by Martin Lea and Russell Spears. The most comprehensive statement of the model was provided in 1995 by Stephen Reicher, Russell Spears, and Tom Postmes. According to SIDE, a social identity approach can account for many of the effects observed in deindividuation research and in the crowd. But in order to understand the effects of anonymity and identifiability on group behavior, one also has to take the social and intergroup context into account. SIDE proposes that these two elements, anonymity and social context, when combined have both cognitive and strategic effects.

Cognitive Effects of the SIDE Model

As described above, to be immersed in a group to the point that one feels anonymous may make social identity quite salient. Research demonstrates that if people feel anonymous in a group, their group identities become more salient and lead to depersonalized social perceptions of others and the self. According to SIDE, this occurs principally because (visual) anonymity obscures individual features and interpersonal differences. As a result of the decreased visibility of the individual within anonymous groups, the process of depersonalization is accentuated, and group members are more likely to perceive the group as an entity. The net result is that people perceive self and others in terms of stereotypical group features and are influenced accordingly.

Many online groups, for example, are bounded by strong feelings of community and shared social identity. This occurs even when the members of these online communities do not know each other individually or have never met in person. SIDE research shows that the anonymity of individuals within such groups obscures the differences between "me" and "you," actually helping these group members to maintain their sense of unity. Differences within the group may otherwise distract attention from the collective ("us" as a *group*).

It is important to note that there are situations in which social identities become salient also when, or precisely because, individuals are identifiable. This is particularly the case when individual features provide information about a person's group memberships. People's faces may sometimes reveal things about them as individuals, but faces may also reveal that people are members of particular social groups, which may then become salient (this is likely to be the case for important social identities such as gender and race, to which most people are very sensitive).

SIDE thus describes the cognitive process by which the salience of social identity is affected by the absence or presence of individuating information. It is important to note that this process can operate only to the extent that some sense of groupness exists from the outset. Research shows that if individuals interact anonymously with others with whom they believe they have very little or nothing in common, anonymity can then become a cover for them to do whatever they wish. Thus, anonymity also provides the freedom for individual group members to do whatever they would like to do, independently of the group, because it prevents the group from carefully monitoring them. Juxtaposing the two possibilities, either anonymity in the group has the effect of amplifying a shared social identity that, however rudimentary, is already in place, or anonymity can amplify the individual independence that exists in contexts in which no shared identity is available. The latter process, whereby anonymity provides the opportunities for people to express and develop identities independent of the social influence of the group, is further elaborated in the strategic SIDE.

Strategic Effects of the SIDE Model

Anonymity also has strategic consequences: It affects the ability to express personal and social identities. Strategic concerns come into play when an outgroup has more power than the ingroup and when the norms of both groups are at odds with each other. This is often the case in organizations, for example, in which managers have more power than workers and, sometimes, different ideas about what the workers should be doing. In such cases, the identifiability of ingroup members to the outgroup will shift the power balance between groups. Identifiability to a more powerful outgroup limits the degree to which the ingroup's identity can be expressed freely and without sanction on those dimensions on which ingroup norms conflict with outgroup standards and values and that are punishable or otherwise sanctionable. Conversely, anonymity to a more powerful outgroup may be a convenient instrument for the ingroup to express itself on those same dimensions. For example, workers may use the cloak of anonymity to thwart the wishes of management.

The strategic SIDE thus proposes that anonymity may be "used" by less powerful groups to express aspects of their identity. This may appear to be similar to the effects that anonymity has for accountability in classic deindividuation theory. However, unlike deindividuation theory, SIDE takes account of the intergroup context within which identifiability and anonymity occur. Thus, a loss of accountability does not result in the disinhibited or *random* antinormative behavior *of individuals* that deindividuation theory is concerned with. Rather, according to SIDE, anonymity affects the ability of a *group* to express its identity and thus to engage in targeted and ingroup normative behavior, thereby changing power relations between groups.

This idea of strategic SIDE effects is illustrated by the patterned and targeted behavior that can be observed in the crowd. During the Los Angeles riots of 1994, for example, Black rioters and looters were very particular about the shops they targeted, nearly all of which were Asian businesses. This is not an isolated example—historical research shows that crowd violence often has a highly symbolic function.

In addition to anonymity between groups, SIDE considers strategic effects of anonymity within groups. Here, SIDE has particularly explored the consequences of anonymity (as well as isolation) from other ingroup members. On one hand, this anonymity deprives individual group members of social support from their fellows, and this lack of social support may hinder their ability to express their ingroup identity in the face of a powerful and unsympathetic outgroup. Thus, making workers anonymous to each other may discourage them from resisting management's wishes. On the other hand, the knowledge that other ingroup members are unable to identify the self may allow group members (in particular low identifiers) to feel less committed to ingroup norms.

Contributions of SIDE

SIDE's main contributions have been with respect to real crowds and virtual groups. SIDE's explanation of crowd behavior provides a new perspective on why crowds become a threat to public order. This perspective has informed practical interventions to change and improve police tactics for crowd control, such as during major European soccer tournaments. With respect to online behavior, SIDE has contributed the understanding that anonymity is not a barrier to the formation of productive and pleasing online relations. This has informed the design of systems for computer-supported collaborative learning and knowledge-sharing technologies. As a result, SIDE has been one of the key perspectives to predict and explain the enormous success of the Internet for communication and the maintenance of social relations.

Tom Postmes

See also Deindividuation; Depersonalization; Norms; Self-Categorization Theory; Social Identity Theory

Further Readings

Lea, M., & Spears, R. (1991). Computer-mediated communication, de-individuation and group decision-making. *International Journal of Man-Machine Studies, 34,* 283–301.

Postmes, T., & Spears, R. (1998). Deindividuation and anti-normative behavior: A meta-analysis. *Psychological Bulletin, 123,* 238–259.

Postmes, T., Spears, R., & Lea, M. (1998). Breaching or building social boundaries? SIDE-effects of computer-mediated communication. *Communication Research, 25,* 689–715.

Reicher, S., Spears, R., & Postmes, T. (1995). A social identity model of deindividuation phenomena. *European Review of Social Psychology, 6,* 161–198.

Spears, R., & Lea, M. (1994). Panacea or panopticon? The hidden power in computer-mediated communication. *Communication Research, 21,* 427–459.

Spears, R., Postmes, T., Lea, M., & Wolbert, A. (2002). The power of influence and the influence of power in virtual groups: A SIDE look at CMC and the Internet. *Journal of Social Issues, 58,* 91–108.

SOCIAL IDENTITY THEORY

When people interact in groups or think of the way their group relates to other groups, they do not always think of themselves as separate individuals (I am John). Instead, they may think of themselves and act as group members (I am an environmentalist). In psychology, a distinction is therefore made between people's personal identities (referring to their individual self) and their social identities (indicating the group self). *Social identity theory,* which was originally developed by Henri Tajfel and John Turner in the 1970s, focuses on the interplay between personal and social identities. Its aim is to specify and predict the circumstances under which individuals tend to think of themselves either as individuals or as group members. The theory also considers the consequences of personal and social identities for individual perceptions and group behavior.

Over the years, many researchers and theorists have found this a useful analytical framework. A large body of research has accumulated to specify the basic processes involved, which has led to several refinements and extensions of social identity theory over the years. The theory has also been applied to analyze and understand a range of societal problems (most notably in the area of stereotyping and intergroup conflict) and a variety of topics in organizational behavior (such as leadership, team motivation, and organizational commitment). This entry looks at the background of this concept and then discusses several key elements of the theory and some common misunderstandings about what it says.

Background and History

Social identity theory developed out of a series of studies conducted by Tajfel and his colleagues in the early 1970s, which are commonly referred to as the *minimal group studies.* These were designed to identify the minimal conditions that would lead individuals to discriminate in favor of the *ingroup,* to which they belonged, and against an *outgroup.* For this purpose, participants were assigned to groups that were intended to be as empty and meaningless as possible. Nevertheless, when people were asked to assign points to other research participants, they systematically awarded more points to ingroup members than to outgroup members. In doing this, they maximized the relative gain for ingroup compared with outgroup members, even when this implied awarding a lower number of points to the ingroup. The results of these minimal group studies were interpreted by arguing that the mere act of categorizing individuals into groups can be sufficient to make them think of themselves and others in terms of group memberships instead of as separate individuals. This deviated from common views at the time, namely, that an objective conflict of interest is a central factor in the emergence of intergroup conflict.

Thus, social identity theory originated from the conviction that group memberships can help people instill meaning in social situations. Group memberships help people define who they are and how they relate to others. Social identity theory was developed as an *integrative* theory, as it aimed to connect cognitive (thought) processes and (behavioral) motivation. Initially, its main focus was on intergroup conflict and intergroup relations more broadly. For this reason, the original form has been referred to as the *social identity theory of intergroup relations.*

Later elaborations by John Turner and his colleagues on the cognitive aspects relevant to social identification further specified how people interpret their own position in different social contexts and how this affects their perceptions of others (e.g., stereotyping), as well as their own behavior in groups (e.g., social influence). These elaborations represent *self-categorization theory,* or the *social identity theory of the group.* Together, self-categorization theory and social identity theory can be referred to as the *social identity approach.*

Cognitive Processes

Social identity theory was developed to explain how individuals create and define their place in society. According to the theory, three psychological processes are central in this regard: social categorization, social comparison, and social identification. *Social categorization* refers to the tendency for people to perceive themselves and others in terms of particular social categories. That is, as relatively interchangeable group members instead of as separate and unique individuals. For example, we can think of someone as Jane, a feminist, instead of as Jane, an ambitious woman.

Social comparison indicates the process by which people determine the relative value or social standing of a particular group and its members. For instance, school teachers may be seen as having higher social standing than garbage collectors. Compared with university professors, however, school teachers can be seen as having lower social standing.

Social identification reflects the notion that people generally do not perceive social situations as detached observers. Instead, their own sense of who they are and how they relate to others is typically implicated in the way they view other individuals and groups around them. For university professors, the conclusion that school teachers have lower social standing than they do affects how they think of themselves and how they relate to other university professors and to school teachers.

Someone's social identity is then seen as the outcome of these three processes (social categorization, social comparison, and social identification). *Social identity* can be defined as the individual's knowledge of belonging to certain social groups, together with some emotional and value significance of this group membership. Thus, while one's *personal identity* refers to self-knowledge associated with unique individual attributes, people's social identity indicates who they are in terms of the groups to which they belong.

Motivation

Social identity theory considers motivated behavior as a direct consequence of the cognitive processes that define people's social identities. According to the theory, social behavior can be represented in terms of a bipolar continuum. At one pole of this continuum, behavior is determined solely by the character and motivations of the person as an individual (interpersonal behavior). This is the case, for instance, when you do not want to talk to someone because he or she does not smile at you. At the other pole, behavior derives solely from the person's group membership (i.e., intergroup behavior). This happens when you do not want to talk to someone because he or she was raised in a different religion from you. The significance of this distinction is the implication that intergroup and interpersonal behavior are qualitatively distinct from each other: Groups are not just collections of individuals, and group behavior cannot be explained in terms of interpersonal principles.

As a result, much of what we know about psychological processes underlying individual thoughts and behaviors may not apply in group situations. For instance, a robust phenomenon in social psychology is that people are motivated to think positively of themselves. If necessary, they do this by blaming others for their individual failures. In some cases, however, people may care so much about the groups to which they belong that they sacrifice their individual interests or positive self-views to help or benefit the group. This is the case when an individual soccer player takes the blame for a team loss: Upholding the image of the team is more important than maintaining a positive view of his or her own abilities as a soccer player. Social identity theory helps us understand these types of responses, which cannot be explained from standard theories about the cognitions and motivated behaviors of separate individuals.

Social identity theory assumes that a basic motivation guiding people's responses as group members is the desire to establish a positively distinct social identity. That is, people seek to establish a meaningful social identity by specifying how the group they belong to differs from relevant other groups, for instance in terms of characteristic traits (Dutch people are stingy), attitudes (university students care for the environment), or behaviors (workers at this company provide a high service level to customers).

People generally prefer to maintain a positive image of the groups to which they belong. As a result of social identity processes, people are inclined to seek out and emphasize positively valued traits, attitudes, and behaviors that can be seen as characteristic for the ingroups they belong to. This may also cause them to focus on less favorable characteristics of outgroups or to downplay the importance of positive outgroup characteristics. The tendency to favor one's ingroups over relevant outgroups can emerge in a variety of responses, including the distribution of material resources or outcomes between ingroup and outgroup members, the evaluation of ingroup versus outgroup products, attributions for ingroup versus outgroup performance and achievement, and communications about the behavior of ingroup versus outgroup members.

Strategies for Status Improvement

When it was first developed, the central goal of social identity theory was to explain the origins of conflictual relations between different social groups, even in the absence of a conflict over scarce resources. The motivation to establish a positive social identity is considered to lie at the root of such intergroup conflict, as members of disadvantaged groups strive for the improvement of their group's position and social standing, whereas members of advantaged groups are motivated to protect and maintain their privileged position. This is why the theory specifies in considerable detail the different ways in which group members may try to cope with group-based disadvantage or with the threat of position loss.

Parallel to the behavioral continuum distinguishing between interpersonal and intergroup behavior, the theory specifies a continuum of different social belief systems. One pole of this continuum locates situations in which individuals hold the conviction that they can move as free agents from one group to another (*individual mobility belief system*). The defining feature of this individual mobility belief system is the notion that group boundaries are permeable. Permeable group boundaries indicate that individuals are not bound or restricted by their group memberships in pursuing position improvement. Permeable group boundaries imply that people's opportunities and outcomes depend on their individual talents, life choices, and achievements rather than on their ethnic origin or the social groups to which they belong.

The other pole is defined by the belief that changes in social relations depend on groups' modifying their positions relative to each other (*social change belief system*). Beliefs about the likelihood that the position of one's group relative to other groups can change indicate status security. This depends on the perceived stability and legitimacy of existing status differences between groups. According to the theory, status stability and legitimacy tend to mutually influence each other: When positions are subject to change, existing intergroup differences in status appear less legitimate. Conversely, when the legitimacy of existing status differences between groups is questioned, this is likely to undermine the perceived stability of such relations. These different belief systems, in turn, determine what people are most likely to do when they pursue a (more) positive social identity. The theory distinguishes between three types of strategies: individual mobility, social competition, and social creativity.

Individual mobility can help individual group members improve their own situation by dissociating the self from a devalued group and seeking association with (or inclusion in) another group that has higher social standing. This is the case when a member of an ethnic minority group pursues a university education to be able to secure a job and advance in a professional career. When group boundaries are seen as permeable, people are more likely to engage in individual mobility attempts. Pursuit of individual position improvement can lead people to denounce or deny their membership of the devalued group, as individual success often requires that they adopt a lifestyle or display behaviors that are characteristic for groups with higher standing.

Female managers who display masculine behavior, immigrants who avoid talking about their family background, or gays or lesbians who bring an opposite-gender friend to an office party all can be seen as displaying this type of response. An important consequence of individual mobility attempts is that it remains an individual-level solution for social devaluation. Because these individuals are unlikely to be seen as representative members of the devalued group, their individual success does not necessarily help improve the image of their group as a whole.

Social competition indicates the tendency to confront existing status differences at the group level by collectively outperforming other groups or acquiring more resources or better outcomes. This is what firms do when they compete for a position on the *Fortune* 500 list. People are most likely to engage in social competition when intergroup status differences seem insecure (i.e., illegitimate and/or unstable). Social competition is a group-level strategy in that it requires group members to draw together and combine forces to help each other improve their joint performance or outcomes.

Social creativity is a strategy that can be used when actual improvement of individual or group positions is not feasible or is undesirable (e.g., because group boundaries are impermeable and group status differences are stable and legitimate). Social creativity implies that people adapt their perceptions of the ingroup's standing. This can be achieved in different ways. One possibility is to introduce alternative dimensions of comparison in order to emphasize ways in which the ingroup is positively distinct from relevant outgroups. An example of this strategy would be female workers' focusing on their greater sensitivity to interpersonal relations rather than addressing the notion that they are less competitive or ambitious than male workers. A second possibility is to reevaluate existing group characteristics to enhance ingroup perceptions. For instance, to make people more appreciative of the potential contribution of their group, ethnic minority group members can point at the importance of cultural diversity in organizations. A final possibility is to compare one's group with another reference group in order to make the current standing of the ingroup appear more positive. Migrant workers, for instance, can cope with their less favorable position in the labor market by thinking of the ways they are still better off than workers in their country of origin.

Social creativity strategies are generally characterized as cognitive strategies because they alter people's perceptions of their group's current standing instead of altering objective outcomes. Nevertheless, it has been demonstrated that these strategies can constitute a first step toward the achievement of social change. Because social creativity strategies help preserve identification with and positive regard for the ingroup, even when it has low status, over time these strategies can empower group members to seek actual position improvement for their group.

Forms of Identity Threat

Even though original statements of social identity theory focused on low group status as a source of identity threat and a cause for motivated behavior, later additions to the theory have suggested different forms of identity threat. In addition to *group status threat*, implying that the perceived competence of the group is devalued, group members can experience *social identity threat* when the moral behavior of their group is called into question. This form of threat is sometimes experienced even by group members who can in no way be held personally accountable for their group's behavior, such as people who experience collective guilt and shame about the role their country played in slavery, which happened long before they were born.

Group members can also experience social identity threat when they think their group is not sufficiently acknowledged as a separate entity with unique characteristics. This form of threat is referred to as *group distinctiveness threat*. It is experienced when different groups of people are included in larger, more inclusive groups, nations, or organizations, such as members of linguistic minorities who strive for political autonomy, or workers of a small company that is taken over in an organizational merger. *Categorization threat* occurs when individuals are treated as group members at times they would prefer not to be, as when a woman who is a lawyer is addressed in court on the basis of her gender instead of her profession. *Acceptance threat* occurs when individuals fail to gain acceptance and inclusion in the groups of which they consider themselves a member, such as when a manager of Asian descent is not invited to join the local business club.

To cope with these forms of social identity threat, group members will show different responses depending on the degree to which they identify with the group. Whereas low identifiers will focus on addressing and improving their personal situation, high identifiers tend to respond in ways that relieve the threat for the group as a whole. The degree to which individuals identify with a particular group thus not only is an outcome of social identity threat (when individuals are reluctant to identify with a group that is devalued) but also determines the ways in which they are likely to respond to such threat. In addition to the perceived characteristics of the social structure (and the opportunities and restrictions implied), the psychological significance of a group membership and the loyalty and commitment to the group and its members also determine how people cope with identity threat.

Common Misunderstandings

Because of the elaborations and specifications that were added over the years, it is not always clear what social identity theory predicts and what it does not. Some misunderstandings have emerged as a result. First, it is important to note that low group status does not always induce ingroup favoritism. Other forms of threat can be more important, such as when the necessity to establish a distinct group identity overrules the desire to achieve a positive social identity. Furthermore, different group-level or individual-level strategies may be used to cope with low group status.

Second, the desire to achieve a positive identity does not imply that people identify with groups only to the extent that doing so serves their personal self-interests or because they are interdependent on other group members. In fact, to the extent that people derive a personal sense of value and meaning from the group, they may sacrifice their personal self-interest to serve the group, sometimes even to an extreme degree (e.g., suicide terrorists).

Third, the awareness that people belong to a group does not imply that they identify with, support, or defend the group. The different aspects and processes involved in social identification do not necessarily go together. The fact that people categorize themselves as members of a particular group does not imply that they value or care for the group. Conversely, people can subjectively identify with a group while acknowledging that they do not fulfill the criteria for membership or while conceding that this subjective identification does not yield them a positive social identity.

Naomi Ellemers

See also Collective Self; Ingroup Allocation Bias; Minimal Group Effect; Multiple Identities; Realistic Group Conflict Theory; Referent Informational Influence Theory; Relative Deprivation; Self-Categorization Theory; Self-Stereotyping; Social Identity Model of Deindividuation Effects; Social Identity Theory of Leadership; Tajfel, Henri; Uncertainty-Identity Theory

Further Readings

Ellemers, N. (1993). The influence of socio-structural variables on identity management strategies. *European Review of Social Psychology, 4,* 27–57.

Ellemers, N., Spears, R., & Doosje, B. (1999). *Social identity: Context, commitment, content.* Oxford, UK: Basil Blackwell.

Haslam, S. A. (2004). *Psychology in organizations: The social identity approach.* London: Sage.

Hogg, M. A., & Abrams, D. (1988). *Social identifications: A social psychology of intergroup relations and group processes.* London: Routledge.

Postmes, T., & Branscombe N. R. (in press). *Rediscovering social identity: Core sources.* London: Sage.

Tajfel, H., & Turner, J. C. (1979). An integrative theory of intergroup conflict. In W. G. Austin & S. Worchel (Eds.), *The social psychology of intergroup relations* (pp. 94–109). Monterey, CA: Brooks-Cole.

Turner, J. C., Hogg, M. A., Oakes, P. J., Reicher, S. D., & Wetherell, M. S. (1987). *Rediscovering the social group: A self-categorization theory.* Oxford, UK: Blackwell.

SOCIAL IDENTITY THEORY OF LEADERSHIP

Leadership is a core feature of groups and ranges from leaders of small teams through corporate chief executive officers (CEOs) to national and global leaders who stride the world stage. It is difficult to imagine groups that do not have some form of leadership. Leaders coordinate and motivate the actions of group members to achieve group goals, but they also set the goals and provide an overall vision for the group.

Most leadership research is conducted outside social psychology, in the organizational sciences, and focuses principally on organizational leadership and the psychology of the CEO. One feature of leadership that has been underemphasized by this literature is its identity function: Leaders define what a group stands for and thus the identity of the group's members. We look to our leaders to define who we are and thus what we should think, how we should behave, how we should view the world, and how others are likely to view us. The *social identity theory of leadership*, originally published by Michael Hogg in 2001 and further developed by Michael Hogg and Daan van Knippenberg in 2003, draws on social identity theory to provide an identity-focused analysis of leadership.

This entry describes the components of the social identity theory of leadership in the context of its grounding in aspects of *social identity theory* and *self-categorization theory*. When people identify relatively strongly with a group, social identity processes come into play to make leaders more effective if they are perceived by the group to be a good fit with the group's norms and identity. Such leaders are influential and "popular"; are perceived to have relatively high status; are imbued with legitimacy, trust, and charisma; are allowed to be innovative and transformative; are effective entrepreneurs of identity; and are effective at integrating different subgroups and identities.

Group Membership, Social Identity, and Leadership

Groups vary in their *psychological salience*, that is, how important and central members feel the group is to their sense of who they are and thus how strongly they identify with the group. Psychological salience can be a relatively enduring property of a particular social identity and group membership, but it can also vary from context to context. For example, your national identity might be an important orienting principle for your behaviors, perceptions, and interactions in almost all contexts, or it might come to the fore only when you are visiting a foreign country where you stand out.

For the social identity theory of leadership, the key premise is that where the psychological salience of group membership is elevated, effective leadership rests firmly on the extent to which followers consider the leader to possess *prototypical* properties of the group—those attributes that followers believe define the group and distinguish it from other groups. In this analysis, group members as followers play a significant role in configuring the characteristics of the group's leadership or even creating the leadership to begin with. Members are more likely to follow a leader whom they consider most able to construct a group identity that is acceptable to them.

As people identify more strongly with a group, they pay more attention to the group prototype and to what and who is more prototypical (research shows that under these circumstances, members have good knowledge about the relative prototypicality of group members). This is because the prototype defines the group's membership attributes and thus members' own self-concept and identity. In these contexts where group membership is psychologically salient, being perceived to be a highly prototypical leader makes one more influential. There are a number of basic social identity and social-psychological reasons for this.

Appearing to Have Influence

First, when people identify strongly with a group, the cognitive process of categorizing themselves as group members transforms their attitudes and behaviors to conform to the prototype of the group, a process described by self-categorization theory as *depersonalization*. Because people in a group generally tend to share the same prototype of their group (i.e., it is a group norm), this self-categorization–based process of depersonalization generates *conformity*.

Group members behave in similar ways that conform to the group norm. Thus members appear to be influenced by the prototype and therefore by those members who are actually more group prototypical. Prototypical members are perceived to have disproportionate influence over the rest of the members of the group. Prototypical leaders appear to be more effective sources of influence than are less prototypical members.

Being "Popular" and Having Status

Second, when members identify strongly with a group, they significantly base their liking for other members on how prototypical they feel those others are, rather than on personal preferences or idiosyncratic attributes. Thus, they like more-prototypical members more than they like less-prototypical members. Because there is usually significant agreement on the prototype, the group as a whole likes prototypical members; they are consensually popular in group terms.

Research shows that identification and group salience produce relatively consensual liking for more-prototypical group members over less-prototypical members. Being liked makes it easier to be influential—research shows we are significantly more likely to comply with requests from and to agree with people we like. Thus, prototypical leaders are popular in the eyes of their followers and are readily able to gain compliance with their ideas. In other words, they can exercise effective leadership. Furthermore, this popularity creates a status difference between consensually popular leaders and their followers. When, as is often the case, there is a leadership clique rather than a solo leader, this status difference may become a genuine intergroup status difference within the group, in which case the seeds of destructive leader–follower conflict may be sown.

Legitimacy, Trust, and Innovation

Third, prototypical members typically find the group more central and important to self-definition and therefore identify more strongly with it. They have a greater investment in the group and thus are more likely to behave in group-serving ways. They embody group norms more exactly, and they are more likely to favor their group (the ingroup) over other groups (outgroups), to treat ingroup members fairly, and to act in ways that promote their group. Research confirms that enhanced identification is associated with greater conformity to norms and stronger ingroup favoritism and with fairer treatment of fellow ingroup members and more pronounced promotion of the group's goals and welfare.

These behaviors confirm a person's group prototypicality and membership credentials and encourage other members of the group to trust that the person is acting in the best interest of the group even when it may not appear to be so. In other words, prototypical leaders are furnished with legitimacy and group membership–based trustworthiness. Followers invest their trust in prototypical leaders, which paradoxically allows such leaders to diverge from group norms and be less conformist and more innovative and transformational than nonprototypical or less prototypical leaders. Innovation and transformation are key components of effective leadership. Leaders are expected to provide an identity focus and a transformative vision for the group, not merely to manage the day-to-day life of the group.

Charisma and Leadership

Finally, because the prototype is so central to group life, information related to the prototype stands out in people's minds against the background of other information about the group. Because prototypical leaders are the most direct source of information about the group prototype, they stand out as figural against the background of the group. Members pay close attention to their leaders and, as in other areas of social perception and inference, attribute their leaders' behavior to invariant underlying personality attributes or *essences*. In the context of leadership, this process causes followers to construct a charismatic leadership personality for their leader. After all, the general class of behaviors that is being attributed to personality includes being the source of influence, being able to gain compliance from others, being popular, having higher status, being innovative, and being trusted.

In this way, *charisma*, which plays an important role in transformational leadership, is an emergent property of social identity–based group processes rather than a static personality attribute that is brought by individuals to the group. The perception of charisma further facilitates effective and innovative leadership on the part of a prototypical leader. For example, a new departmental head promoted from the ranks might initially seem just like the rest of us, but if members identified strongly with the department and the new head was highly prototypical, then we might gradually attribute his or her influence over us to charismatic personality rather than prototypicality.

Leaders as Entrepreneurs of Identity

These social identity leadership processes extend leaders' considerable power to maintain their leadership position. Because they are trusted, given latitude to be innovative, and invested with status and charisma, prototypical leaders are very effective prototype managers, or entrepreneurs of identity. By consolidating an existing prototype, modifying it, or entirely reconstructing it, they can define what the group stands for and what the social identity of its members is.

One of the key attributes of effective leadership is precisely this visionary and transformational activity in which leaders are able to change what the group sees itself as being. For example, during the 1980s, the British prime minister, Margaret Thatcher, constructed an imperially assertive and proud British identity around an iconic image of herself as Boadicea, a first-century British queen who led a British uprising against the occupying forces of the Roman Empire.

There are many strategies that prototypical leaders can employ to manage their prototypicality and shape their group's identity. There is evidence that they can talk up their own prototypicality and/or talk down aspects of their own behavior that are nonprototypical, identify deviants or marginal members to highlight their own prototypicality or to construct a particular prototype for the group that enhances their own prototypicality, secure their own leadership position by vilifying contenders for leadership and casting the latter as nonprototypical, and identify as relevant comparison outgroups those that are most favorable to their own ingroup prototypicality.

Leaders can also engage in a discourse that elevates or lowers the salience of the group to its members. If you are a highly prototypical leader, elevating the group's salience and strengthening members' identification with the group will provide you with the leadership benefits of high prototypicality, and if you are not very prototypical, then lowering the group's salience and weakening members' identification will protect you from the leadership pitfalls of not being very prototypical. Generally, leaders who feel they are not, or are no longer, prototypical strategically engage in a range of group-oriented behaviors to strengthen their membership credentials.

Intergroup Leadership

A feature of leadership situations that is underemphasized is that leaders more often than not have to provide integrative leadership to quite distinct subgroups that can sometimes have hostile relations with one another—for example, providing unifying national leadership for Sunnis, Shi'ites, and Kurds in Iraq. In these cases, the identity function of leadership is particularly prominent. The challenge for leaders is to provide an overarching identity that does not subtract from or threaten people's cherished subgroup identities and then to configure themselves, as leaders, as prototypical of this acceptable overarching identity.

Identity entrepreneurship plays a particularly important role here, as does the psychology of transforming intergroup conflict into intergroup harmony. Research in this area suggests that one set of strategies involves recognizing and respecting the distinctiveness and value of subgroup identities but configuring subgroup relations within the overarching identity as different groups with important shared goals working together on the same team. It is important to prevent one group from feeling that its attributes are relatively underrepresented in the superordinate identity.

A Concluding Caveat

With respect to this description of the social identity theory of leadership, there is one important caveat to bear in mind. Social identity leadership processes occur, or occur more strongly, only in groups with which members identify strongly. As the group's salience or members' strength of identification with it weakens, social identity leadership processes also weaken. Leadership becomes less strongly based on how prototypical the leader is of the group and more strongly based on other factors, such as how charismatic the leader is or how well the leader matches people's general or more specific schemas of the properties a leader should possess to fulfill a particular group function.

Michael A. Hogg

See also Charismatic Leadership; Contingency Theories of Leadership; Great Person Theory of Leadership; Group Composition; Interactionist Theories of Leadership; Leader-Member Exchange (LMX) Theory; Leadership; Path–Goal Theory of Leadership; Personality Theories of Leadership; Self-Categorization Theory; Social Identity Theory; Social Identity Theory of Leadership; Transactional Leadership Theories; Transformational Leadership Theories; Vertical Dyad Linkage Model

Further Readings

Ellemers, N., de Gilder, D., & Haslam, S. A. (2004). Motivating individuals and groups at work: A social identity perspective on leadership and group performance. *Academy of Management Review, 29,* 459–478.

Hogg, M. A. (2001). A social identity theory of leadership. *Personality and Social Psychology Review, 5,* 184–200.

Hogg, M. A. (2007). Social psychology of leadership. In A. W. Kruglanski & E. T. Higgins (Eds.), *Social psychology: Handbook of basic principles* (2nd ed., pp. 716–733). New York: Guilford.

Hogg, M. A. (2008). Social identity theory of leadership. In C. L. Hoyt, G. R. Goethals, & D. R. Forsyth (Eds.), *Leadership at the crossroads: Leadership and psychology* (Vol. 1, pp. 62–77). Westport, CT: Praeger.

Hogg, M. A., & van Knippenberg, D. (2003). Social identity and leadership processes in groups. In M. P. Zanna (Ed.), *Advances in experimental social psychology* (Vol. 35, pp. 1–52). San Diego, CA: Academic Press.

van Knippenberg, D., van Knippenberg, B., De Cremer, D., & Hogg, M. A. (2004). Leadership, self, and identity: A review and research agenda. *Leadership Quarterly, 15,* 825–856.

Social Impact Theory

Social impact theory was proposed by Bibb Latané in 1981 to predict how and when sources of social influence will affect a target of influence. It is a very broad theory, seeking to encompass a variety of thoughts, feelings, behaviors, and physiological states. When other people are sources of social influence on a target person, impact is predicted to be a multiplicative function of the strength, immediacy, and number of sources. When other people are cotargets of social influence, social impact is predicted to be divided as an inverse power function of the strength, immediacy, and number of the targets. The theory was proposed as a descriptive model, or metatheory, as opposed to an explanatory one. It was influenced by ideas in sociology, astronomy, geography, and psychophysics. Social impact theory accounts for a wide range of research results in social influence domains such as conformity, compliance, and obedience. More recently, a dynamic version of the theory has been used to generate predictions about the emergence of cultural phenomena. This entry describes the principles of the theory, assesses its strengths and limitations, and examines the evolution of dynamic social impact theory.

Principles of Social Impact Theory

The first principle of the theory, the *principle of social forces*, is expressed mathematically as follows: $\hat{i} = f(SIN)$, where $\hat{i}$ stands for the magnitude of social impact, f is a function, S is strength of the sources, I is immediacy (e.g., closeness in space or time), and N is number of sources. Strength includes such things as the salience or importance of a source and may be operationally defined by manipulating such source variables as authority, socioeconomic status, or expertise. Immediacy can be thought of as the ease with which a message may be communicated, and it is often operationally defined as physical proximity. Number is simply how many sources of social influence there are. As strength, immediacy, and number of sources of social influence increase, the magnitude of social impact on a target is expected to increase. The proposed multiplicative relationship implies that if any one of the three parameters (strength, immediacy, or number) is zero, no social impact will occur.

The second principle of the theory, the *psychosocial law*, is expressed as follows: $\hat{i} = sN^t$, $t < 1$, where $\hat{i}$ = the magnitude of social impact, s is a scaling constant, N is the number of sources, and t is an exponent with a value less than 1. Conceptually, the psychosocial law was modeled after S. S. Stevens's psychophysical law, which proposed that the subjective psychological intensity of a stimulus increases as the objective intensity increases, but it follows a law of diminishing returns. That is, each new source adds additional pressure to change a target's thoughts, feelings, or behavior, but the social impact of each new source adds less and less pressure to change. For example, the first source (increasing from 0 to 1) has more impact than the sixth (increasing from 5 to 6).

Research on *conformity* provides mixed support for the psychosocial law. In Solomon Asch's classic studies, the first source of influence resulted in very little conformity. Instead, the largest increase in conformity occurred when the number of sources was increased from two to three. Later conformity research, including Stanley Milgram's research in which confederates stood on a street corner in Manhattan and looked up at the sixth floor of a building, provides support for the psychosocial law, which predicts diminishing returns as the number of sources increases. Other research, including work on stage fright and the perceived importance of news events, also supports the predictions of the psychosocial law. In studies of stage fright, for example, as perceived audience size increased from 1 through 16, participants rated their subjective tension to increase as a predicted power function of the size of the audience. Increasing the strength of the audience (age given as either early teens or late 30s) similarly increased the subjective tension experienced by participants.

The third principle of the theory relates to *multiplication versus division of social impact*. When there are multiple targets of social impact, the following formula applies: $\hat{i} = s/N^t$, $t < 1$, where $\hat{i}$ is the magnitude of social impact, s is a scaling constant, N is the number of targets, and t is an exponent with a value less than 1. That is, social impact gets divided among multiple targets as a function of their strength, immediacy, and number. The larger a given audience, the smaller the amount of expected social impact a source will have on each audience member.

Support for the third principle is provided by the large body of research on the *bystander effect*, which shows that as the size of a group of observers of an emergency increases, the likelihood that any of them will provide help decreases. Another phenomenon supporting the principle of division of impact is *social loafing*, or the tendency for people to put forth less effort on a task as group size increases.

Strengths of the Theory

Social impact theory has been quite influential, appearing in most social psychology textbooks' accounts of social influence. One reason for its popularity is that Bibb Latané (like Kurt Lewin in his field theory) drew a powerful analogy between physical forces and social forces. Latané termed it a "lightbulb" theory: Just as the amount of light that shines on a target may be affected by the strength (wattage), immediacy (closeness), and number of lightbulbs, sources of social impact may vary along similar dimensions. The lightbulb analogy provides a vivid image that makes the theory easy to understand.

Social impact theory is also very general. It ties together research results from different domains of social influence, including conformity, compliance, obedience, and persuasion. For example, Milgram conducted experiments in which study participants were asked to play the part of "teachers" and were told by an "experimenter" to administer electric shocks to "students" who gave wrong answers to questions. In fact, actors played the experimenter and the students, and no shocks were actually administered. In variations of the experiment, the participants' obedience to the experimenter's instruction to administer shocks increased or decreased as a function of the situation. For example, in one variation, obedience dropped off sharply as the victim was moved closer to the teacher—from being in the next room without voice feedback to giving voice feedback, then to being in the same room, and then to the teacher's having to physically force the victim to place a hand on the shock plate. These results illustrate the effects of immediacy of the victim. Immediacy of the experimenter in the Milgram obedience studies had the opposite effect: As the experimenter moved physically farther away from the teacher, obedience dropped dramatically. Levels of obedience in other variations of the experiment can be interpreted in terms of strength and number.

Another strength of the theory is that it ties together seemingly disparate phenomena. For example, models of *persuasion* have posited different processes to explain the effects of influence by majority versus minority influence. Social impact theory has been used to explain how both majority and minority sources are influential as a function of their strength, immediacy, and influence. For example, a small yet high-strength minority source may overcome the numerical advantage of a majority faction.

The theory is also quite useful. Because strength, immediacy, and number can be easily conceptualized and operationally defined, social impact theory can make practical suggestions to those wishing to increase their influence over others or to resist influence attempts. For example, when people are soliciting donations for charity, increasing strength (by dressing more formally), immediacy (by standing closer), and number of the people asking for donations has been shown to increase the amount of money raised.

Limitations of the Theory

The original version of social impact theory was a static one, in that it assumed that targets of social influence were passive recipients of social impact.

The theory did not take into account the dynamic nature of social influence—that is, the idea that people are by turns both sources and targets of social influence in their everyday interactions. A later version of the theory, described below, incorporated this dynamic aspect of social impact.

One criticism of social impact theory is that there has been much more empirical support for the effects of number of sources and targets than for the effects of strength and immediacy. Operational definitions of strength are also difficult to specify in a quantifiable manner. For example, a physician may be a higher-strength source of influence in medical matters than a physician's assistant might be, but how much higher is difficult to determine a priori. Indeed, definitions of strength often seem to be circular: Higher-strength sources are those that exert more influence on an audience. Strength may also be an idiosyncratic function of pairwise relationships between sources and targets—a source of influence may be very high in strength to one person and very low to another. Support for predictions regarding the effects of immediacy has also been mixed. A meta-analysis showed that immediacy had stronger effects on self-reported measures of social impact than on behavioral measures.

Social impact theory is more of a descriptive than an explanatory theory. It specifies the level of social impact likely to occur as a function of strength, immediacy, and number of sources and targets of social influence, but it does not specify why the impact will occur. However, ideas derived from theories in evolutionary psychology may help transform social impact theory into a more explanatory model. For example, Robert Boyd and Peter Richerson have postulated that it may be adaptive for humans to adopt the thoughts, feelings, and behaviors of prestigious (i.e., high-strength) group members as well as the majority of group members (explaining the effects of number). Tatsuya Kameda and Reid Hastie have made a similar evolutionary argument for the validity of majority opinion.

Dynamic Social Impact Theory

In 1990, Latané published a dynamic version of social impact theory in collaboration with Andrzej Nowak and Jacek Szamrej. In this line of research, inspired by the dynamical systems approach to

science, computer simulation was used to determine what the theory would predict for a population of agents obeying the laws of social impact theory. Results of thousands of computer simulations of social impact, in which a variety of parameters, such as group size and communication networks, were varied, showed that four group-level phenomena consistently emerged over time:

1. *Consolidation*, or a reduction in diversity at the group level, occurs as the majority faction typically gains new members at the expense of the minority.

2. *Clustering*, or the tendency for agents to become more similar to nearby neighbors over time, occurs because of the principle of immediacy.

3. *Correlation* across initially unrelated issues emerges as clusters of different issues overlap.

4. *Continuing diversity* also occurs as the group maintains different factions instead of converging on the majority opinion or an average group-level opinion.

These four phenomena have been observed to emerge in spatially distributed groups of people discussing issues with each other through both computer-mediated and face-to-face communication. They have also been shown to occur in existing groups of spatially distributed people. For example, attitudes toward alcohol use clustered by dormitory floor within a building and within buildings on a college campus.

The dynamic version of social impact theory has been quite useful in explaining cross-cultural differences in thoughts, feelings, and behaviors. It provides a psychological mechanism for the formation, emergence, and change of norms within and between groups over time and explains how these cross-cultural differences may derive from day-to-day social influence. For example, the often-demonstrated individualism–collectivism distinction between European and Asian cultures provides an example of clustering.

Social impact theory has thrived as an explanation for social and cultural phenomena because it fulfills the criteria of a good theory: It is parsimonious, logically coherent, general, and testable.

Since its inception, it has guided research using a variety of methods, including descriptive field studies, experimental laboratory studies, and computer simulation. As it becomes a more explanatory theory, it will continue to guide future research aimed at understanding and explaining the social world.

Martin J. Bourgeois

See also Bystander Effect; Communication Networks; Conformity; Culture; Dynamical Systems Approach; Obedience to Authority; Social Loafing; Social Networks

Further Readings

Harton, H. C., & Bourgeois, M. J. (2005). Cultural elements emerge from dynamic social impact. In M. Schaller & C. S. Crandall (Eds.), *The psychological foundations of culture* (pp. 42–76). Mahwah, NJ: Erlbaum.

Latané, B. (1981). The psychology of social impact. *American Psychologist, 36,* 343–365.

Latané, B., & Bourgeois, M. J. (2001). Dynamic social impact and the consolidation, clustering, correlation, and continuing diversity of culture. In M. A. Hogg & R. S. Tindale (Eds.), *Blackwell handbook of social psychology: Group processes* (pp. 235–258). Oxford, UK: Blackwell.

Mullen, B. (1985). Strength and immediacy of sources: A meta-analytic evaluation of the forgotten elements of social impact theory. *Journal of Personality and Social Psychology, 48,* 1458–1466.

Nowak, A., Szamrej, J., & Latané, B. (1990). From private attitude to public opinion: A dynamic theory of social impact. *Psychological Review, 9,* 362–376.

Social Loafing

Social loafing is the tendency for people to reduce their efforts and work less hard on a task when working in a group than when working individually. It represents a potential productivity barrier to any group or team in which individual efforts are combined into a group product. Thus, it is important to design groups carefully to avoid the potential for reduced individual motivation. This entry describes the background of work on social loafing, its key principles, several theories that attempt to explain it, and some related issues.

History and Background

The motivational effects of groups on individuals have long been of interest to social and organizational psychologists. In perhaps the earliest social-psychological studies, conducted in the 1880s, Max Ringelmann designed a rope-pulling apparatus that allowed him to measure the strain exerted both by individuals and by groups of varying sizes. When he asked male volunteers to pull on a rope, either alone or in groups ranging in size from two to six people, he found that as group size got larger, the total force exerted was progressively lower than would be predicted from the simple addition of individual efforts. This raised the possibility that collective tasks could reduce the motivation of individuals, though the performance reduction in these studies could also have been due to process loss, or poor coordination of the efforts of individual group members.

Nearly a century later, in 1974, Alan Ingham and colleagues designed a paradigm that sought to separate motivation loss from process loss. Individuals were asked to pull on a rope either alone or in groups of varying sizes across a number of trials. However, on some of these trials, when individuals believed they were pulling with others, they were actually pulling alone. The deception was masked with the use of confederates and by having participants wear blindfolds. Ingham and colleagues replicated the performance reductions with increasing group size found by Ringelmann and also showed that reductions occurred both on actual trials (in which participants really pulled with others) and on pseudogroup trials (in which they pulled alone but believed they were pulling with others). The latter finding suggested that working in groups can reduce individual motivation.

To control for mere presence, distraction, and evaluation concerns that can vary with changes in group size, social loafing researchers usually compare individual performance on a collective task (in which members' inputs are combined into a group total) with individual performance on a coactive task (in which individuals work in the presence of others but their inputs are counted individually), while keeping group size the same across these two conditions. As in the research by Ingham and colleagues, pseudogroups are often employed to allow researchers to study individual performance on tasks in which the individuals simply believe their outputs are being combined into a group product.

A seminal study by Bibb Latané and colleagues in 1979 nicely illustrates these features. Participants were asked to shout as loudly as possible, both alone and with others. Participants were asked to wear blindfolds and headphones that played masking noise that prevented individuals from hearing whether others were shouting. Participants shouted in both actual groups and pseudogroups, in which they were told they were shouting with others but actually shouted alone. Individual efforts were still reduced on these pseudogroup trials, showing that a significant percentage of the reduced performance on group tasks was due to reduced motivation, as distinct from coordination loss. Latané and colleagues were also the first to use the term *social loafing* to describe the tendency of individuals to reduce their efforts on group tasks.

Key Findings

Thus far, more than 100 studies have been conducted on social loafing. These studies have examined individual motivation within groups in both laboratory and field settings, in a variety of countries, and across a wide array of tasks. The results converge to show that social loafing is a fairly robust phenomenon that generalizes across settings, tasks, and subject populations. A 1993 meta-analysis by Steven Karau and Kipling Williams showed that, across 78 studies run before that date, social loafing was moderate in magnitude, consistently found across studies, and comparable in magnitude to a variety of other social-psychological effects.

Social loafing has been observed across a wide range of tasks that require different types of effort. These tasks have included physical tasks such as swimming or pulling on a rope, work-related tasks such as typing or managing an in-box of information, creative tasks such as listing thoughts or writing songs, cognitive tasks such as identifying signals on a computer screen or navigating mazes, and evaluative tasks such as rating the quality of poems and editorials. Although the average magnitude of social loafing appears to be lower in Eastern cultures (which are more collectivistic in orientation) than in Western cultures (which are more individualistic), significant social loafing effects have been documented in a number of different countries, including the United States, Canada, Germany, France, Norway, Japan, China, Taiwan, and Jordan. Similarly, although the magnitude of social loafing is often lower among women than among men, significant effort reductions are typically found for both sexes. Finally, although laboratory studies have predominated, social loafing effects have also been documented in groups in a variety of field settings, including sports teams, organizational work groups, sales teams, songwriting teams, and classroom project teams.

Although social loafing appears to be a fairly robust phenomenon, it does not occur in all groups, and a number of moderating variables have been identified that can reduce or eliminate it. Specifically, a number of studies have shown that social loafing can be reduced or eliminated by making individuals more identifiable or accountable for their contributions, making tasks more meaningful or personally relevant to individuals, strengthening group cohesiveness, providing comparison standards for performance, providing performance incentives, punishing poor performance, making individual contributions more unique and less redundant with those of other members, closely matching the personality of individual members to the demands of the group task, and increasing feelings of task efficacy.

Finally, in addition to research that has established moderators of social loafing, there is also a relatively small but growing body of research that has documented specific conditions under which working in groups can actually enhance individual motivation. Examples are research on the *Köhler effect* and *social compensation*.

Theories of Social Loafing

A number of theories of social loafing have been advanced. Among these, three perspectives have been especially prominent in the literature. First, the *evaluation potential perspective* posits that social loafing occurs because individual inputs can typically be clearly identified on individual or coactive tasks but are often much harder or even impossible to evaluate on group or collective tasks.

A programmatic series of studies by Stephen Harkins, Kate Szymanski, and their colleagues provides support for this viewpoint. Those researchers have shown that social loafing can often be eliminated by making individual inputs on a collective task identifiable to individuals, their teammates, or an outside party, while also providing an objective or social comparison standard with which those inputs can be evaluated.

Second, Bibb Latané's *social impact theory* posits that individuals can be either sources or targets of social influence and that the influence experienced in a social situation depends on the strength (status or legitimacy), immediacy (proximity in a physical or psychological sense), and number of sources and targets present. When working individually, people experience the full influence of the demand from an outside source of influence (such as a boss or an experimenter) to work hard. But when working in a group, that influence is diffused across all the members of the group. This viewpoint is consistent with a number of studies showing that social loafing effects often become larger as group size increases.

Third, several researchers have used *expectancy-value models* to explain social loafing. Those models posit that social loafing occurs because people's perceptions that their efforts will be instrumental in producing valued outcomes are weaker in group than in individual performance contexts. Because efforts are combined into a group total on collective tasks, and because rewards are often distributed across members, there may be less of a link, or contingency, between one's efforts and desired outcomes when one is working with others in a group. This perspective appears to be broadly consistent with many of the established moderators of social loafing.

All three theories contribute to a greater understanding of social loafing, with the expectancy-value approach appearing to offer integrative potential and with the evaluation potential and social impact perspectives providing strong insights into more specific social loafing contexts.

Relationships With Other Phenomena

Because the impact of groups on individuals is a fundamental problem in social and organizational psychology, it is not surprising that social loafing is relevant to many other phenomena that have been studied using somewhat different paradigms. One related phenomenon, *social facilitation*, occurs when the presence of other people affects an individual's task-related motivation, leading to better performance on simple or well-learned tasks and worse performance on complex or novel tasks.

At first glance, this would appear inconsistent with social loafing research, in which working with others reduces individual motivation. However, the two phenomena are fully compatible when the nature of the presence of others is considered. In social loafing research, the others present are coworkers with whom one combines efforts into a group product, whereas in social facilitation research, the others present are either coactors or observers who might potentially evaluate one's efforts but who are not contributing to one's work as teammates. Thus, social facilitation research shows that the presence of others as observers or coactors tends to increase motivation (perhaps because of arousal, distraction, or evaluative concerns), whereas social loafing research shows that the presence of others as teammates or coworkers tends to reduce motivation (at least under many conditions of group work).

Related issues arise in *social dilemmas*, situations in which actions that are beneficial to the individual in the short term tend to be detrimental to the group in the long term. Social dilemma research, which often focuses on resources that are shared by groups, communities, or societies, has found that individuals often contribute less than their fair share to public goods such as recycling centers and public television stations and take more than their fair share from pooled resources such as energy grids or agricultural commons. Social loafing can be seen as a type of "defection" within social dilemmas, such that individuals engage in uncooperative behavior by contributing less than their fair share to a group product or outcome. Although social loafing and social dilemmas often have been seen as separate bodies of research, there is the potential for insightful dialogue between them, a potential that has been partially realized by a number of scholars within the past 30 years.

Steven J. Karau

See also Free Riding; Group Motivation; Köhler Effect; Ringelmann Effect; Social Compensation; Social Dilemmas; Social Facilitation; Social Impact Theory; Sucker Effect

Further Readings

Ingham, A. G., Levinger, G., Graves, J., & Peckham, V. (1974). The Ringelmann effect: Studies of group size and group performance. *Journal of Personality and Social Psychology, 10,* 371–384.

Karau, S. J., & Williams, K. D. (1993). Social loafing: A meta-analytic review and theoretical integration. *Journal of Personality and Social Psychology, 65,* 681–706.

Kravitz, D. A., & Martin, B. (1986). Ringelmann rediscovered: The original article. *Journal of Personality and Social Psychology, 50,* 936–941.

Latané, B., Williams, K., & Harkins, S. (1979). Many hands make light the work: The causes and consequences of social loafing. *Journal of Personality and Social Psychology, 37,* 822–832.

Liden, R. C., Wayne, S. J., Jaworski, R. A., & Bennett, N. (2004). Social loafing: A field investigation. *Journal of Management, 30,* 285–304.

SOCIALLY SHARED COGNITION

The *cognitive revolution* in psychology moved the field from simply observing the relationship between environmental stimuli and behavior to attempting to understand how people mentally represent both the environment and their behavior within it. At first, these representations were seen as located within individual brains. Consequently, cognition was seen as an individual phenomenon. The cognitive revolution was seen as one reason for the decline of research on group-level phenomena during the 1960s and 1970s. However, more recent conceptualizations of the role of cognitive processes in social behavior have led to a resurgence in group research. One of the most influential concepts underlying this resurgence is the notion of socially shared cognitions.

The idea that cognition is a social phenomenon is not new. Early theorists such as George Herbert Mead and Lev Vygotsky argued that the way people view and interpret the world is influenced by their social environment. Unfortunately, this idea was slow to be integrated into mainstream cognitive and social psychology. Early cognitive theories of language and person perception focused on how information (e.g., words, perceptions of others) was represented in an individual's mental structure. However, research began to show that the same word or stimulus was represented very differently when presented in different contexts. In addition, research found that the meaning attributed to particular messages differed when they came from different social groups. Finally, research on how speakers interpreted messages they gave (or were about to give) showed that interpretations changed as a function of the group to which the message was given and even just as a function of presenting the message. Thus, both what we think and how we think change as a function of the social and cultural context within which such thinking occurs. In general, the social context leads people within that context to believe similar things and think about the world in similar ways, which is the basic definition of *socially shared cognition*.

How Shared Cognitions Develop

There are a number of different ways in which cognitions become shared among a particular social or cultural group. First, evolution has played a major role in shaping how cognitions are shared and in what ways. For example, evolved tendencies toward affiliation (e.g., need to belong) ensure healthy amounts of social contact, which is necessary for shared cognitions to develop. The brain structures designed for language interpretation and production are also central to the processes involved in shared cognitions. Common experience is also important for shared cognitions. People who share a particular location experience the same environment and learn to adapt to that environment in similar ways. Recent dynamic models of social influence have shown that simply living in the same geographic location leads to belief convergence among people.

However, most shared cognitions are probably developed through social perception and interaction. Virtually all cultures and societies have in place mechanisms for teaching their young the shared "truths" as defined by the culture or society. Schools, churches, libraries, museums, and so forth all serve as vehicles for socialization, helping ensure that knowledge and values considered valid or appropriate are shared among the members of a society or culture. In addition to these formal mechanisms, simply observing the behavior of others and interacting with them will lead to shared cognitions. Social comparison is another major influence on people's behavior, particularly in new or uncertain situations. People use social comparison both to detect appropriate behavior and opinions and to validate the correctness of their own behavior and opinions. Norms for appropriate behavior in a particular situation are learned quickly, even if those norms conflict with more accepted or prescribed rules for behavior. For example, even though littering is considered inappropriate behavior (a prescriptive norm), research has shown that people are much more likely to litter after being reminded of the prescriptive norm (do not litter) in settings where others have obviously littered (a descriptive norm).

Beliefs about the world are also shared through social interaction. Many stereotypes that people hold come not from direct experience with the stereotyped group but rather from social interactions in which the stereotypes are mentioned or used without refutation. Such general societal or cultural beliefs have been referred to as *social representations*—common ways in which a group of people represents its world. Social representations are both learned and strengthened through social interaction. When people make statements consistent with social representations, both the speaker's and the recipients' belief in the representation are strengthened. Research has shown that speakers who expect a group of people to believe certain things tend to "tune" their message or statements to fit those beliefs. In addition, after the speaker has tuned the message, his or her own beliefs become more consistent with those of the audience—the "saying-is-believing" effect. Research has shown that social comparison and interaction influence cognitions of all types, even those that are formed through objective experience.

Selection and socialization processes in groups also lead to socially shared cognitions. People often join (or leave) groups because they believe the other members of the group have beliefs and values that are similar (or dissimilar) to their own. Research has shown that people like others who are similar to themselves and seek out similar others for social interaction. Thus, groups often form because of the cognitions that members share, and groups may dissolve when such sharing declines. And when groups admit new members, they tend to recruit people who will think and act in appropriate (i.e., similar) ways and to exclude or expel people with dissimilar beliefs or behaviors. Thus, groups often start out with shared cognitions and then regulate entry and exit to ensure that sharedness is maintained.

Another main contributor to socially shared cognitions is social identity. People tend, in part, to define themselves by the groups in which they are members. When those group memberships are made salient, people look to the group to organize their beliefs and to guide their behavior. Thus, people who define themselves as members of a group tend to share many beliefs and ideas with other members of that group. Research has demonstrated that when social identities are strong, group members' thoughts and behaviors tend to move toward their idea of a *prototypic* group member, a person who embodies the qualities that make the group distinctive (usually in positive ways). The conceptualization of this prototypic member is shared among the members of the group, and their thoughts and behaviors converge accordingly. Recent research has shown that social identity can be both a cause and an effect of shared cognitions. Members who think similarly tend to see themselves as a group, and this increases their identity with that group. Moreover, members who identify strongly with a group change their beliefs and ideas to match more closely with those of other group members.

Implications of Shared Cognitions in Groups

One of the main findings in the literature on small groups is that ideas that are shared among group members tend to influence the group consensus process. The most important of these may be shared decision preferences, as exemplified by majority decision processes. Many societies, institutions, and smaller collectives, either explicitly or implicitly, follow some form of majority or plurality rule. A vast number of studies on small-group decision making have found that a simple *majority-wins* or *plurality-wins* model does a very good job of describing the group decision outcome. Such processes tend to exacerbate individual preference trends at the group level, leading groups to be more polarized, or extreme, in their positions relative to individuals. Moreover, majority and plurality processes also tend to be perceived as fairer than most other decision processes, and, in most cases, majority and plurality processes are quite accurate. Recent computer simulations have shown that majority decision processes maximize relative accuracy for very little cognitive or computational effort. If a group simply chooses to do what most of its members want to do in the first place, then on average that group will do quite well, and the members will be satisfied with its choices.

Another topic that has received major research attention concerns the degree to which information is initially shared among group members. Early research on groups tended to assume that unshared information (information known by only one group member) would be brought up and shared during group discussion, allowing groups to outperform individuals in most information-processing tasks because each member would bring unique information to the discussion. However, research has shown that groups tend mainly to focus on information that is initially shared by most or all group members. The *hidden profile paradigm* was instrumental in demonstrating this effect. In this paradigm, information is distributed among group members in such a way that the information they share favors one decision alternative, but if all information were pooled during discussion (shared as well as unshared information), then a different decision alternative is obviously superior. Under these circumstances, groups often reach consensus on the alternative that is supported by the shared information rather than discovering the best alternative available. The dominance of shared information tends to be strongest when individual members commit to their preferred alternatives before group discussion, the information load on the group is high, and reaching consensus is more important than making an accurate or optimal decision.

The degree to which information is shared among group members also has other consequences for group process and performance. A group member's mention of a piece of information that others also know tends to confirm the validity of the information, making it more important for defining the group's eventual choice. The person who mentions the information is also perceived as more competent and is liked better by other group members. In addition, members of the group who share a greater amount of information with other members (i.e., are more *cognitively central*) are often seen as group leaders and have a disproportionate influence on the group decision. Thus, there appears to be an individual member benefit for mentioning information that others know. However, even in situations in which a member may not know what information he or she shares with others, shared information has a greater probability of being mentioned simply because a greater number of people know and therefore can mention it.

There is also a growing body of evidence that shared strategies or ways of representing a task can also affect both group process and performance. For example, research on juries has found that the shared instructions associated with the *reasonable doubt criterion* increase the likelihood of acquittals, relative to other jury instructions. Looking at the influence processes, the reasonable doubt criterion gives factions that favor acquittal a greater chance of winning, even if they do not represent a majority. Although groups usually outperform individuals, they tend to perform worse than the average member would have performed alone in situations in which the group members share an inappropriate task strategy. Again, a shared strategy can allow minorities with incorrect responses that are aligned with that strategy to win out over majorities with correct responses. This trend is reversed when group members share an appropriate task strategy. For example, using the hidden profile paradigm, groups are much better at discovering the optimal alternative when they share a task strategy of information sharing. If the members know that they share this strategy, they do even better. Recent research on negotiation shows a similar pattern of results. Parties in a negotiation who frame the negotiation in similar terms and understand how their opponents are thinking tend to have better overall outcomes. Thus, it seems that both sharing cognitions and knowing that the cognitions are shared can influence group performance and process.

Knowing what information is shared or not shared (i.e., shared metacognition) is a crucial component of *transactive memory*. Transactive memory systems involve distributing responsibility for remembering different types of information across members of the group. By purposely assigning different information to different members, the group's overall memory capacity is increased. However, this is effective for group performance only if all members share the metaknowledge of who knows what. The group can use the information effectively only if each member knows who to go to for the information that is needed. In this case, the cognitions themselves are not shared, but the knowledge of where the cognitions are located is shared.

Transactive memory systems are seen as one key component of *shared mental models* in teams. Two types of shared mental models are important for team performance: (1) mental models of the team and how the members are related to one another and (2) mental models of the task on which the team is working. Research has shown that both types of shared mental models are important and that the metaknowledge associated with knowing that information is shared among team members is also important. Transactive memory systems are part of the *team mental model*. They allow group members to realize who knows what in the group and who needs certain types of information when it becomes available. Other aspects of the team mental model involve the roles and leadership responsibilities of group members and the most important goals for performance.

The *task mental model* depends on the specific demands required by the task on which the team is working. Although individual members must know their roles and the behaviors for successful performance of those roles, it is also important for them to have a clear representation of the overall task, as well as an understanding of the interdependencies among various members. Research has shown that teams whose members share both team and task mental models perform better than teams whose members do not share such mental models. A recent program of team training for airline crews, called cockpit resource management, has been very effective in reducing errors and improving safety. The system is based on clearly defined task mental models, with an emphasis on a particular shared team mental model involving clear channels of communication and information

exchange unhampered by status differences. Recent expansions of the program to other teams (e.g., hospital surgical teams) have produced similar positive results.

Shared social identities have also been found to affect group processes and outcomes. Groups whose members strongly identify with the group show greater levels of cohesiveness and tend to polarize more in group-normative directions relative to groups with less strongly identified members. Stronger shared identities also lead to greater adherence to group norms and greater cooperation within the group. Groups with strong shared identities show greater commitment to group goals and are less tolerant of ingroup members who show antinormative behavior. Unfortunately, a strong shared social identity can also have negative consequences. Strongly identifying group members are more likely to engage in ethically questionable behavior that favors the group, unless part of the group identity involves adherence to high ethical standards. Groups with strong social identities are also more competitive and aggressive relative to groups with less strongly identifying members, particularly in intergroup settings. Much research has recently focused on how to harness the positive aspects of shared social identity while inhibiting the more negative aspects.

Socially shared cognition is still a relatively new area of research. Research on the best way to measure socially shared cognitions of different types is ongoing, and no general consensus has yet been reached. In addition, the interplay among socially shared cognitions, metacognitions, identities, and so forth has only recently begun to be explored. Although young, the area has already produced a number of classic insights and will probably remain vibrant for years to come.

R. Scott Tindale and Sarah Stawiski

See also Common Knowledge Effect; Group Memory; Group Mind; Group Polarization; Hidden Profile Task; Minority Influence; Social Identity Theory; Social Representations

Further Readings

Cannon-Bowers, J. A., Salas, E., & Converse, S. (1993). Shared mental models in expert team decision making.

In N. J. Castellan Jr. (Ed.), *Individual and group decision making: Current issues* (pp. 221–246). Hillsdale, NJ: Erlbaum.

Resnick, L. B., Levine, J. M., & Teasley, S. D. (1991). *Perspectives on socially shared cognition*. Washington, DC: American Psychological Association.

Stasser, G., & Titus, W. (1985). Pooling of unshared information in group decision making: Biased information sampling during discussion. *Journal of Personality and Social Psychology, 48,* 1467–1478.

Swaab, R., Postmes, T., van Beest, I., & Spears, R. (2007). Shared cognition as a product of, and precursor to, shared identity in negotiations. *Personality and Social Psychology Bulletin, 33,* 187–199.

Thompson, L., & Fine, G. A. (1999). Socially shared cognition, affect, and behavior: A review and integration. *Personality and Social Psychology Review, 3,* 278–302.

Thompson, L., Levine, J. M., & Messick, D. M. (Eds.). (1999). *Shared cognitions in organizations*. Mahwah, NJ: Erlbaum.

Tindale, R. S., & Kameda, T. (2000). Social sharedness as a unifying theme for information processing in groups. *Group Processes and Intergroup Relations, 3,* 123–140.

Tindale, R. S., Meisenhelder, H. M., Dykema-Engblade, A. A., & Hogg, M. A. (2001). Shared cognitions in small groups. In M. A. Hogg & R. S. Tindale (Eds.), *Blackwell handbook in social psychology: Group processes* (pp. 1–30). Oxford, UK: Blackwell.

Wiener, E. L., Kanki, B. G., & Helmreich, R. L. (Eds.). (1993). *Cockpit resource management*. San Diego, CA: Academic Press.

SOCIAL MOBILITY

Understanding the psychological processes associated with unequal collective power and status is critical to understanding intergroup relations. *Social mobility* is a central construct in the context of group inequality. Defined as the extent to which an individual can, and does, move from one group to another, social mobility focuses attention on members of low-status groups and their potential to move to a group of higher status. For example, within nations, individual members of a low-status group might engage in upward social mobility by directing their efforts toward joining the middle class. Similarly, individuals from a poor or troubled nation might emigrate to a country that promises economic advancement. This entry summarizes research on how social mobility works, examines what happens when social mobility is perceived as possible or impossible, and reviews some of the challenges for those making such changes.

Social Mobility and Social Identity

For members of a group to engage in *social mobility*, the hierarchically arranged system of groups must be open. That is, the intergroup configuration must have a clearly defined set of characteristics that permits members of one group to gain entrance into another group. In an open system, then, an equity principle of justice prevails—an individual's inputs, as deemed important by society, govern how far up the intergroup hierarchy that person may climb.

By contrast, in a closed system of hierarchically arranged groups, social mobility is impossible. Formal caste structures and slavery are examples of closed systems in which there are no opportunities for upward social mobility. When confronted with a closed system, the only option available for an individual to improve her or his status is *social change*. That is, only an improvement in the status of the entire group will cause the individual's personal status to change for the better. Social change involves collective action designed to improve the group's status, and this improvement will be at the expense of the high-status group. Clearly, social change strategies in the face of a closed system involve some level of intergroup conflict. Because the conflict involves groups of unequal power and status, the usual diplomatic and military strategies associated with conflict between equal-status groups will not likely yield the desired results for the low-status group. Thus, collective actions such as terrorism and rioting often emerge as groups lacking power and status search for strategies to successfully confront high-status groups.

Social identity theorists have been influential in drawing the conceptual distinction between *social mobility* and *social change*. They articulated these two social strategies for upward mobility by pointing to the importance of group identity for understanding the self. Their proposition is that people strive to attain a group identity that is distinct and positive. Well-being is reinforced when individuals identify with a group that has high status and is regarded positively.

Presumably, members of a low-status group will be motivated to improve their group-based identity by engaging in upward social mobility. But in real-world intergroup situations, it has proven difficult to predict when, and indeed whether, members of a disadvantaged group will take individual or collective action to improve their group-based identity. Social identity theorists have proposed that if members of a disadvantaged group perceive that mobility is possible and that their disadvantaged status is unfair, then they will engage in behavior designed to improve their status and, by extension, their group identity.

Perceiving Social Mobility as Possible

It is no easy matter for members of a low-status group to confidently perceive that mobility is possible. They may well be motivated to improve their social identity by perceiving that they are participating in a group hierarchy that is open to mobility. But members of high-status groups have a vested interest in a more closed hierarchical group structure. They are motivated to protect their own positive group identity, and if the system were completely open, they might risk demotion to a low-status group.

Even using objective statistical analyses, it is often difficult for members of a low-status group to decide whether mobility is possible. Consider analyses regarding upward mobility in contemporary society. On one hand, there are statistics that indicate that certain visible minority groups and women are overrepresented in low-status groups. On the other hand, there are indications of increased participation of visible minority groups and women in high-status positions. But there are also statistics pointing to a widening gap between elite members of minority groups and the vast majority of other group members. Statistics about educational achievement are also confusing. There are statistics that describe a narrowing of the educational achievement gap between groups that have historically underperformed and more privileged groups. However, equally compelling analyses indicate that the narrowing is related to lowered educational standards for those who have historically

underperformed and their participation in less demanding programs.

Given these ambiguities, an understanding of the extent to which social mobility is possible falls squarely into the lap of social psychologists. It is people's perceptions, not objective reality, that govern their behavior, and social psychologists focus much of their attention on these perceptions.

When Social Mobility Is Impossible

The real-world observation that few low-status groups actually engage in collective action despite their disadvantaged position is theoretically interesting. Although attention naturally turns to dramatic instances of rebellion, coups, and terrorism, social psychologists have focused most of their efforts on understanding the less dramatic but more pervasive tendency of members of low-status groups to accept their disadvantaged position.

This acceptance of a disadvantaged position seems to be rooted in a psychological need to believe that one's personal relations and intergroup relations are just and fair. This belief is a profound one because it offers people a framework within which to think, feel, and behave with others. It also provides a measure of predictability and certainty and thereby allows for meaning in life. Hence people are reluctant to believe that the hierarchical arrangement of groups in society is unfair. It is precisely this desire to perceive the world as fair that leads members of low-status groups to believe that they must deserve their disadvantaged status.

Research in social psychology has shown that, indeed, members of low-status groups do endorse the status quo hierarchy of groups as much as members of high-status groups do. Research has also shown that members of low-status groups cling to the belief that they deserve their disadvantaged position even when they are exposed to relatively blatant examples of group-based discrimination.

To reinforce the belief that the intergroup hierarchy is fair, high-status groups may foster group stereotypes. For example, stereotyping a low-status group as lacking in intelligence or lazy allows members of a low-status group to understand why they are not upwardly mobile and why high-status group members deserve their advantaged position.

Conclusion

Social mobility, or movement between groups of differing status, can have profound effects on people's well-being. Moreover, it is very much a social-psychological issue in that it raises fundamental questions about when and how members of a low-status group engage in upward mobility and, alternatively, when and how they come to accept their disadvantage. These questions are likely to elicit theoretical and empirical attention for many years to come.

Donald M. Taylor

See also Collective Movements and Protest; Social Dominance Theory; Social Identity Theory; System Justification Theory

Further Readings

Hogg, M. A. (2007). Uncertainty-identity theory. In M. P. Zanna (Ed.), *Advances in experimental social psychology* (Vol. 39, pp. 69–126). San Diego, CA: Academic Press.

Jost, J. T., & Banaji, M. R. (1994). The role of stereotyping in system-justification and the production of false consciousness. *British Journal of Social Psychology, 33*, 1–27.

Sidanius, J., & Pratto, F. (1999). *Social dominance: An intergroup theory of social dominance and oppression.* Cambridge, UK: Cambridge University Press.

Tajfel, H., & Turner, J. C. (1979). An integrative theory of intergroup conflict. In W. G. Austin & S. Worchel (Eds.), *The social psychology of intergroup relations* (pp. 33–47). Monterey, CA: Brooks/Cole.

Taylor, D. M., & Moghaddam, F. M. (1994). *Theories of intergroup relations: International social psychological perspectives.* Westport, CT: Praeger.

SOCIAL NETWORKS

Social networks is a field of study that focuses on the pattern, or structure, of relations among a set of actors. For example, while traditional explanations of career success often focus on a person's training or education, a social network perspective would emphasize his or her connections to others within an organization. Similarly, while leadership is often thought of as a set of personal abilities and skills, a social network analysis would focus on the leader's relations with others—for example, the relations between the leader and his or her followers or the bridging role the leader provides to outside groups—both of which might enhance or inhibit the leader's effectiveness.

To understand how social network analysis is different from other perspectives on social phenomena, it is useful to understand the distinction between *units* of analysis and *levels* of analysis. The unit of analysis refers to the aggregation of people into units of interest as primary actors in a system. For example, the field of social networks is sufficiently interdisciplinary that one can find studies of networks of all kinds of units, including people, organizations, industries, and even nations. For present purposes, however, this entry focuses on social networks in which people are the unit of analysis.

The *level* of analysis, in contrast, is more complex because it refers to different aggregations of the structural or relational features of interest, and it may be best described by example. Consider a network made up of N friends. We can identify the levels of analysis of this network on a log scale from 0 to 3 as follows: Level 0 refers to the network structure as a whole, Level 1 refers to properties of the N actors in the network, Level 2 refers to properties of the individual dyadic relations between all pairs of actors in the network, and Level 3 refers to the perceptions that each of the N actors has of the dyadic relationships in the network. Each level of analysis sheds light on a different aspect of the social relations that characterize the network. The different insights that can be gained from the levels of analysis are illustrated in Figures 1 and 2 (both adapted from real examples of work teams).

Level 0: Structure as a Whole

The first level of analysis, Level 0, yields one observation of interest in a given network of N actors. It addresses several questions: What is the overall shape of the network, how is this shape characterized, and what effect does this shape have on the performance and behavior of the group as a whole? Different shapes have different implications for

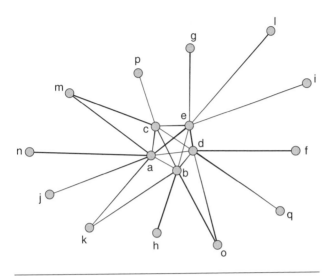

Figure 1   Core–Periphery Structure

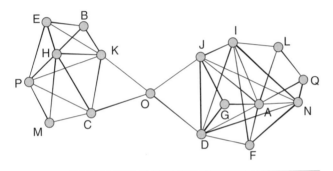

Figure 2   Bow Tie Structure

what people see, how they think, and how the group or system behaves. In Figures 1 and 2, both networks are about the same size, and they have approximately the same number of overall ties, but their shapes are quite different. Figure 1 is a classic *core–periphery* structure, made up of a small group of people (the *core*) who are well connected to each other and who have ties to those on the periphery. (If there is just one person in the core, the structure is called a *star*.) Those on the periphery have ties to the core but relatively few ties to each other. This structure represents highly centralized work groups, which often have efficient group processes when the task they face is relatively simple and routine. But this structure can also evolve toward a hierarchical power distribution, in which the core coordinates to reinforce its power advantages and the periphery becomes disenchanted with this inequity. This leads to negative group dynamics that can undercut the efficiency of this structure.

The structure in Figure 2 has a very different shape, a classic bow tie, showing two relatively densely connected subgroups connected by one (or sometimes a few) bridging individuals. The integrity of the overall structure is quite fragile because keeping it connected is heavily dependent on one person (O), without whom the subgroups would be totally separated. Not only is this structure fragile, but the coherence within the subgroups and the relative lack of connection between the subgroups tends to devolve into two local subgroup identities (we–they attitudes). If the group's purpose is to perform an overall integrated task, then this structure can interfere with necessary subgroup cooperation and coordination.

These two examples only scratch the surface of the range of structural wholes that can be described in a Level-0 analysis. Most groups are not as classic, or prototypical, in their structure as those in Figures 1 and 2. Usually, structures are complex and messy, and the question is not what type of structure they are but rather how close, or similar, they are to particular ideal types. Measures of such closeness abound and carry with them different implications for group processes and outcomes. For example, the *E–I index* measures the extent to which a structure is characterized by a preponderance of external ties (that bridge across group boundaries) versus internal ties (that connect people within the group). Having a high E–I index score, indicating predominantly bridging ties, has been found to facilitate a group's ability to deal with or survive crises.

A secondary question is, What leads to different structural shapes? Since most network structures are emergent (i.e., not preplanned but rather evolving through a set of recurring, sometimes random, interactions), the question becomes, What governs which shape will predominate? Although there is much work to be done to answer this question, it has been argued that the structures illustrated in Figures 1 and 2 occur frequently. For example, Michels's *iron law of oligarchy* argues for the inevitable evolution of social systems toward a core–periphery structure (Figure 1), with a small group of leaders coordinating to dominate the whole structure. On the other hand, Watts's work on "small worlds" suggests that, in large-scale networks, clustering such as that in Figure 2 is rather common.

Level 1: The Individual Actor

Individuals bring with them to the social situation a set of attributes (e.g., age, education, experience, attitudes, beliefs). The network analyst adds to this list an assessment of the advantages a person has because of his or her position within the network. A Level-1 analysis addresses the following question: What is the consequence to the individual who occupies a certain position in the network?

The most prominent concept used in asking Level-1 questions is *centrality*. There are three basic types of centrality: degree, closeness, and betweenness (although extensions and varieties of each exist). *Degree centrality* is simply the count of the number of ties a person has in the network. In Figure 2, Person A has the highest degree centrality (8 ties), whereas person B has the lowest (3 ties). People with high degree centrality are often identified as the informal leaders of the group.

Efficient communication and information transfer within a group are critical to its proper functioning. The social network provides a road map of how this communication flows within and between groups. The more steps it takes (equivalent to the number of intermediaries who must be traversed) to reach someone in another part of the network, the more remote that target is. A critical issue, then, is how quickly one can reach others through the network. This ability is often assessed by *closeness centrality*, which measures the average number of steps it takes for an individual to reach everyone else in the network. A person with high closeness centrality can reach others in relatively few steps; a person with low closeness centrality has to go through many intermediaries in order to reach everyone in the network. Those high in closeness centrality, therefore, are more likely to be able to disseminate information quickly through the network. Another advantage is that they are more likely to pick up rumors or other bits of information that percolate through the network. When such information transfer is critical to the group, closeness centrality becomes a valuable asset to the individual who holds it.

While both degree and closeness centrality are useful guides to understanding an individual's advantages and contributions to the group processes, it is *betweenness centrality* and related measures that are most important to success in a social network. Betweenness centrality captures the extent to which an individual is on critical paths between others in the network. Returning to Figure 2 (the bow tie), we see that Person A has the most ties (highest degree centrality). But we also see that most of the people A is tied to are also tied to each other. Thus, none of the people A is tied to are dependent on A to get a message to any of the others; they can easily go around A to reach their targets. Despite A's popularity, he or she has low betweenness centrality in this network.

In contrast, whereas Person O has only 4 ties, these ties are critically situated so that individuals in the left side of the graph are highly dependent on O to reach those on the right side (and vice versa). O is critically located between many other pairs of individuals in the network and thus has high betweenness centrality. Because of the dependency that others have on those with high betweenness centrality, this index is often predictive of the power and influence an individual has in the group or organization.

A close relative of betweenness centrality is Ronald Burt's concept of *structural holes*. Recall that A had low betweenness because most of the people A is tied to are already tied to each other and thus they can easily go around A. The people O is tied to, in contrast, have far fewer options. It is this lack of ties, called *holes*, that gives rise to O's betweenness and power advantages. Measures of structural holes and betweenness are conceptually linked and empirically correlated, but the research on structural holes has focused more on the performance consequences of the group's members. Those individuals surrounded by structural holes have been shown to be more productive, to develop more creative ideas, and to get promoted more quickly in organizations. There are costs, though, in that being the bridge between different groups (as O is in Figure 2) can lead to role conflict and stress.

Level 2: The Dyad

Since position within the network has such a powerful effect on participants' opportunities and constraints, researchers have explored a deeper question, namely, how do these (almost $N \times N$) dyadic network ties form? Why do we choose particular others to be our friends? Several factors can help us answer these questions.

First, there is the general principle of *homophily*. People prefer to interact with others who are similar to themselves. People of similar demographic characteristics (e.g., race, sex, age, education) tend to associate with each other. People will also tend to associate with others who share similar beliefs and attitudes.

Another prominent factor that influences the formation and retention of network ties is *propinquity*. Whether two people communicate or form a relationship is heavily influenced by the physical distance between them. For example, two people with offices beside each other will tend to communicate more often than will two people with offices on separate floors.

A third factor is *affect*. People have a tendency to interact with others whom they like. This may seem obvious, but the extent to which affect dominates people's choices is sometimes surprising. For example, suppose you need technical help on a task. Suppose further that you have a choice to seek help from either a *competent jerk* (someone you view as technically able to address your question but whom you do not care for personally) or a *lovable fool* (someone you like but who is relatively incompetent). It turns out that most people will choose the lovable fool over the competent jerk in work settings.

Level 3: Cognitive Social Structures

Beyond actual dyadic interactions, there are also people's perceptions of networks. That is, while the network can have structural effects on individuals, if a participant in the network believes the network is different from what it really is, that perception may influence his or her perceived options and subsequent behavior. For example, the person who is the manager of the workgroup in Figure 2 might want to introduce changes in the role assignments of his or her work crew. A cursory examination of this network is likely to lead the manager to see that he or she should take into consideration the fact that these two distinct subgroups might view any changes with suspicion if the changes favor members of one subgroup over the other. Moreover, in seeking to implement the new assignments, the manager could take advantage of O's unique role as a bridge between the two subgroups. In contrast, if the manager believes

that the network is one large, undifferentiated group with network ties densely distributed across the board, then he or she may not take these group dynamics into account in trying to implement the new role assignments.

Each of the N participants in the network has his or her own perception of what the network is like. Taken together, these N perceptions are called the *cognitive social structure* of the network. Since each participant has a view of who is tied to whom, this amounts to approximately N^3 assessments of the structure (N perceptions of almost $N \times N$ dyads).

Research in this area has produced several interesting findings. First, participants' perceptions of the network have direct consequences for their behavior, as illustrated by the above example about the group in Figure 2. Moreover, *accuracy* of network perception facilitates a participant's ability to accomplish his or her goals in the group. In particular, an individual's accuracy leads to power, over and above the power emanating from his or her formal position or the power attributable to his or her centrality in the network.

Research has explored predictors of network perceptions and their associated biases. These perceptions are influenced by many factors, some of which lead to substantial misperceptions and inaccuracy. For example, there is a tendency to see more solid groupings and clusters of ties than actually exist. This bias is strongest for those people who are closest to the perceiver (we prefer that our friends be friends with each other). We also have relatively little insight about those parts of the network that are distant from us as perceivers. This results in an accelerated rate of inaccurate perceptions as a function of distance, simply because of lack of information. In combination, these two sources of bias result in the most accurate assessments of dyadic ties for those who are at an intermediate distance from perceivers.

Conclusion

The field of social networks provides a perspective on social phenomena that focuses on relationships among individual actors as the core building block of group and individual behavior. Different levels of analysis emerge from this perspective, ranging from the micro (Level 3) to the macro (Level 0). Each of these provides insights into how individuals operate in groups and how groups interact. Moreover, levels of analysis can inform each other: Perceptions can lead to ties, strategic ties can lead to central network positions, and stratification of these positions can lead to systemic behavior. By examining these network relationships, we gain a unique understanding of complex social situations.

David Krackhardt

See also Cliques; Communication Networks; Dyads; Group Composition; Homophily; Levels of Analysis; Social Relations Model; Status

Further Readings

Burt, R. S. (2005). *Brokerage and closure: An introduction to social capital.* Oxford, UK: Oxford University Press.

Casciaro, T., & Sousa Lobo, M. (2008). When competence is irrelevant: The role of interpersonal affect in task-related ties. *Administrative Science Quarterly, 53*(4), 655–684.

Cross, R., Parker, A., & Sasson, L. (2003). *Networks in the knowledge economy.* New York: Oxford University Press.

Kilduff, M., & Krackhardt, D. (2008). *Interpersonal networks in organizations: Cognition, personality, dynamics, and culture.* Cambridge, UK: Cambridge University Press.

Kilduff, M., & Tsai, W. (2003). *Social networks and organizations.* Thousand Oaks, CA: Sage.

Wasserman, S., & Faust, K. (1994). *Social network analysis: Methods and applications.* Cambridge, UK: Cambridge University Press.

Social Relations Model

The *social relations model* (SRM), developed by David Kenny and Lawrence LaVoie, offers both a conceptualization scheme and a set of analytical tools for studying interdependent perceptions and behaviors related to group processes and outcomes at multiple levels of analysis. The model assesses the degree of similarity of perceptions or behaviors within groups (e.g., whether everyone in the group thinks that a given member is credible or whether members direct their comments to a particular person) and whether that similarity holds at the individual, dyadic, and group levels of analysis. The SRM decomposes ratings members make about or behaviors directed to other members into three basic components, each of which is used to answer a set of specific questions regarding group and interpersonal processes.

A typical SRM study of small groups employs a round-robin design, in which each member rates every other member on some measure (although some studies use a block design, in which a subset of members rates another subset), so round-robin designs are assumed in the remainder of this entry. Self-ratings are possible, although not necessary. Excluding them, however, precludes several interesting analyses. Depending on the research questions and purposes of the study, ratings can be obtained before, during, or after interaction, and, in some cases, ratings are obtained at *zero-acquaintance*, before members get to know one another. The result is that in a group of size N, each member rates and is rated by the $N - 1$ other members on the variable or measure of interest.

According to the SRM, three main components of perception (as derived from the ratings) are the perceiver, target, and relationship effects. The *perceiver effect* describes the tendency to view or rate a set of targets similarly. For example, a given member might be predisposed to rate all his or her colleagues high on credibility. The perceiver effect indexes *assimilation*, which is the extent to which a person provides similar ratings of the other group members. The *target effect* describes the set of judgments a set of perceivers makes about a target. For example, some members may be perceived uniformly as having high credibility, perhaps because of their behavior or institutional position. The term *consensus* is attached to the target effect. Finally, the *relationship effect* is the unique perceptions a perceiver has of a target relative to other targets. *Uniqueness* is the extent to which one's perception of the target cannot be explained by consensus and assimilation. From these three components, one is able to ask several questions, including those related to *assumed similarity*, which is the correspondence between self-perceptions and one's perceptions of others, and *self–other agreement* (i.e., the correlation of self-perceptions and others' perceptions).

The variation of judgments at different levels of analysis is at the heart of the SRM. The perceiver and target variances are at the individual level. If members of four-person groups rate each other on credibility, there are four mean perceiver scores (each person rates the other three members) and four mean target scores (each person is rated by the three other members). Those means will likely differ or vary from one another. The term *target variance* refers to the variability of the four means for each of the four targets in the group, whereas *perceiver variance* indexes variation in the mean perceiver scores. (The actual computation of the variances is complex and is averaged across groups.) If there is little or no variance in the target effect, for example, then the rating one receives is not different from that received by others. If there is sufficient perceiver or target variance, then one can examine the extent to which the ratings vary with other variables of interest. For example, a researcher might hypothesize that the number of contributions to discussion correlates with credibility ratings received.

The relationship component is a dyad-level effect. It is likely that the ratings made by a given perceiver vary. For example, Person A's ratings of Persons B, C, and D are 3, 4, 5, respectively, on a 7-point credibility scale, with higher numbers indicating greater credibility. The ratings for a given target provided by the other three members of the group also likely vary. If ratings vary within perceivers and targets, then there is some degree of covariance. For example, Person A's rating of B's credibility might mirror B's rating of A on that measure, but those ratings likely differ from the ones A and C give each other, and so on. This indexes the degree to which members perceive or act toward one another above and beyond effects attributed to particular characteristics of perceivers and targets. Finally, there is the group-level effect; group means might differ. For example, some groups might have higher mean credibility scores than do others.

Another important aspect of the SRM is *reciprocity*: Perceptions and behaviors are often correlated within groups. Reciprocity often has ramifications for group processes because one's perceptions and behaviors are related to those of one's colleagues. As with the three main components of the SRM, reciprocity occurs at both the individual and the dyad levels of analysis. *Generalized reciprocity* is at the individual level

because it is the correlation of one's actor and target effects, and it addresses whether the ratings one receives correspond with those one provides. For example, if other group members rate a particular member as credible, does that member rate his or her colleagues as credible? *Dyadic reciprocity* refers to the similarity of ratings of pairs of members—if Person A thinks B is credible, does B think A is credible? Most conceptualizations of reciprocity are implicitly at the dyadic level, but in practice the two levels are confounded. The SRM offers a way to partial one effect from the other.

Kenny, among others, has reviewed the SRM literature and noted some trends in SRM components. Most notably, consensus is small compared with assimilation and uniqueness, but is often evident, at least for some types of measures, at zero-acquaintance (at which some obvious features of the target are linked to the measure in question). Surprisingly, consensus does not increase with acquaintance. Instead, it takes a relatively short time, or just a small number of actions performed by the target, for consensus to stabilize. Assimilation tends to decrease with increased acquaintance because individuation-based processes supplant generalized processing. Uniqueness, as noted, is a fairly stable feature of interpersonal interaction.

The SRM is an important lens for viewing group processes. It is clear that process depends on individual, dyadic, and group-level characteristics, and the SRM is designed to capture them with just one set of ratings. It is also evident that a large part of the process is interdependent such that what one says, thinks, and decides is related to what other members do, say, and decide. The SRM captures interdependence at three distinct levels of analysis. It is important to note that, assuming sufficient variation in the judgments or behaviors of interest, group scholars can examine the correlates or causes of the effects or use them to predict other features of group processes and outcomes. For example, the quality of arguments made during discussion likely is associated with perceptions of credibility, or the distribution of perceptions depends on the type of task (e.g., whether it has a correct answer). The SRM allows researchers to ask a new set of questions regarding a variety of phenomena related to group processes and outcomes.

Joseph A. Bonito

See also Interdependence Theory; Levels of Analysis; Research Methods and Issues

Further Readings

Bonito, J. A. (2003). A social relations analysis of participation in small groups. *Communication Monographs, 70,* 83–97.

Kenny, D. A. (1994). *Interpersonal perception: A social relations analysis.* New York: Guilford.

Kenny, D. A. (2004). PERSON: A general model of interpersonal perception. *Personality & Social Psychology Review, 8,* 265–280.

Marcus, D. K. (1998). Studying group dynamics with the social relations model. *Group Dynamics, 2,* 230–240.

Swann, W. B. J., Kwan, V. S. Y., Polzer, J. T., & Milton, L. P. (2003). Fostering group identification and creativity in diverse groups: The role of individuation and self-verification. *Personality & Social Psychology Bulletin, 29,* 1396–1406.

SOCIAL REPRESENTATIONS

Social representations are lay conceptions of complex phenomena that are important, relevant, and attention grabbing for society as a whole or for specific groups or communities within society. Examples of these phenomena include addiction, AIDS, climate change, intelligence, gender differences, and role of genes in people's character. Because these are important phenomena, they have sophisticated, technical, scientific explanations. However, we are not all trained biochemists, psychologists, sociologists, climatologists, and so forth, and yet we still have a desperate need to understand and communicate about these phenomena. Social representations fill this need. The study of social representations is the study of how everyday explanations arise and are sustained in society.

Background

According to the social psychologist Willem Doise, the theory of social representations is a general approach to understanding how collective processes affect the way that people think. The theory has its roots in a distinction made by the sociologist Émile Durkheim, who defined *individual* representations, in contrast to *collective* representations, as internal states that cannot be shared with others. In order to be communicated, such internal states are transformed into words, images, and symbols that can be collectively shared. Lucien Lévy-Bruhl, an anthropologist, further distinguished between two modes of collective thinking: a rational mode, which he considered typical of "civilized" cultures, and a mystic mode, typical of "primitive" cultures. Jean Piaget used this same distinction, arguing that rational thinking gradually replaces mystic thinking as a person develops through childhood into adulthood. However, from a social-psychological perspective, Serge Moscovici demonstrated that the two modes of thinking actually coexist in adult thought. People reason differently in different situations. Notably, mystic thinking is well suited to many situations in social life, such as when people are engaged in convincing or charming others, interpreting new events, or predicting the future.

From Mental Representations to Social Representations

A nice example of how mental representations are socially structured comes from the way people conceive of groups. The psychological literature contains various conceptions of groups. Groups are sometimes conceived of as resulting from a partitioning of the social world into mutually exclusive categories of people. In each category, all the group members share the same basic characteristics, which become the "essence" of the group. Other conceptions stress a limited number of attributes that carry weight in the definition of a prototype of the group. Group membership is based on whether an individual possesses enough of these attributes. Because each group member's characteristics match to a differing degree the group's prototype, heterogeneity arises from comparisons among group members. Still other conceptions posit that a group consists of the accumulation of concrete memories about individuals who have been previously encountered during personal contacts, learned from the media, and so on. Such groups promote even more heterogeneity among the group members.

From the standpoint of social representations theory, these conceptions are not mutually exclusive. Fabio Lorenzi-Cioldi has provided evidence that the way we conceive of groups is influenced by where we are positioned in a social hierarchy. Those with power and status emphasize beliefs in a society of loosely related individuals who are striving for mobility based on individual merit. They thus come to define themselves mainly as individual persons whose group membership does not make a relevant or important contribution to their self-definition. People positioned lower in the social hierarchy tend to describe themselves in terms of attributes that are associated with their group membership, making the self coextensive with all the other members of the group.

This example suggests that conceptions of groups cannot be understood without taking into consideration the broader social context in which conceptions operate. Seemingly universal and antagonistic conceptions of groups are in fact concurrent and compatible, and their form reflects the social position of the conceiver. The social representations perspective shifts the theoretical focus from the formal properties of conceptions of a group to the properties of the perceivers' social context. The study of social representations thus answers the question, Which social regulations engage which reasoning in which contexts? The answer to this question points to two sociocognitive dynamics, called objectification and anchoring.

Objectification and Anchoring

In his seminal work on the presentation and communication of psychoanalysis in the French press, Moscovici introduced *objectification* and *anchoring* as the two thought processes that provide the impetus for the emergence of social representations.

Objectification

To objectify means to turn abstract, unfamiliar ideas into concrete, familiar ideas. Thus, objectification "domesticates" reality by fitting reality into preexisting interpretative categories and standards that are provided by our shared culture. People understand abstract information with the help of knowledge (analogies, metaphors, images) that they already possess. Hence, to objectify means to superimpose a concrete image on something abstract, making the latter *recognizable* and ready for communication.

In his study of the social representation of the theory of psychoanalysis, Moscovici showed that the partitioning of the psyche into "organs"—for instance, the conscious and the unconscious as two aspects located in the outer and the inner parts of the brain—made the theory more familiar.

Illustration: The Social Representation of the Androgynous Person in Psychology

The transformation of the concept of androgyny in psychology illustrates how scientists promote and legitimize a socially desirable construct out of the prevalent social representations of sexual ambiguity (androgyny) as deviance. The social climate that gave rise to the concept of androgyny was characterized by theories and lay conceptions of sex differences that associated the simultaneous display of masculine and feminine properties with concrete images of psychological maladjustment, such as sexual ambivalence and homosexuality. The concept of psychological androgyny as co-presence of masculine and feminine attributes has been developed to repudiate this concrete imagery of the sexually unhealthy character (the familiar). However, although the *co-presence* concept was a novel idea, it did not break clearly with more traditional prescriptions of appropriate sex-typed behavior. The notion of a person embodying characteristics of both sexes was poorly equipped to bypass the stigma of sexual maladaptation—such a person was socially represented as determined by, yet contrary to, nature.

To circumvent this interpretation, theorists proposed a new perspective that supplanted the problematic masculine-versus-feminine contrast. From the idea of simple co-presence of masculine and feminine attributes, the definition of androgyny mutated toward the idea of a fusion of these attributes. Researchers advocated a hybrid being, an individual who blended the sex-typed characteristics into new ways of being.

The final conception of transcendence aimed at rectifying further deficiencies with the blending notion. Androgyny now referred to a person in whom the masculine and the feminine had disappeared, making obsolete a cognitive schema based on masculine versus feminine. The popular objectification of the androgyne was circumvented for good with a scientific conception that conceptualized the androgyne in terms of what "s/he" was not or did not do. The androgynous person became colorless, incorporeal, and indemonstrable by commonsense standards, and thus no longer reducible to lay conceptions of homosexuality and hermaphroditism.

Anchoring

Anchoring refers to the act of naming and categorizing. *To anchor* means to reduce new, unfamiliar, and strange ideas to ordinary words and images, that is, to set them in a familiar universe that makes them readily intelligible and interpretable. In his analysis of the images of psychoanalysis in the Catholic, communist, and popular press, Moscovici showed that psychoanalysis was transformed into an interpersonal relationship between psychoanalyst and patient. Thus it was assimilated either to the practice of confession or to a relationship tainted with sexuality.

Illustration: The Faithfulness Gene

Serge Moscovici and Miles Hewstone distinguish scientific thought from representational common sense in terms of their differing form and content. However, common sense is increasingly based on scientific discoveries relayed through the mainstream media. Information is incorporated into preexisting knowledge and beliefs, thus facilitating its assimilation and transformation.

Consider, for instance, how people interpreted the report in *Nature* of a laboratory experiment concerning the affiliative tendencies of a species of rodent. When this complex information was diffused by newspapers, the discovery of the impact of vasopressin on the sociability of voles was translated into the discovery of a faithfulness gene that explained fidelity in human romantic relations. The transformed information was understood by laypeople in line with their particular belief about the role of genes in human social behaviors. For those rejecting genetic explanations, the discovery contradicted their belief. Hence, it was associated with a potential genetic manipulation of human beings. These people organized their representation of the discovery around the dangerous consequences of the faithfulness gene for the future of romantic relations. For people believing in the genetic explanation of social behavior, the scientific information did not threaten preexisting beliefs. Consequently, their representation was related to descriptive accounts of the experiment. They restricted the discovery to the genetics of animals and did not evoke their implications for humans. Thus, the same initial message produced very different stories at the end of the communication chain.

Objectification of the scientific message was initially driven by communication concerns. In order to understand the discovery and communicate an understandable version of it, individuals focused on intriguing aspects of the message and associated those aspects to lay vocabulary. Attitudinal concerns, in the anchoring phase, modulate the story in order to assimilate the message into preexisting knowledge and beliefs.

Communication Processes

The transformation of information follows different routes depending on the group within which information is disseminated. Because social representations are elaborated through daily exchanges, conversations, and discussion, a focus on communication processes is central to the study of social representations.

Diffusion, Propagation, Propaganda

Moscovici distinguished between three modalities of communication, depending on the nature of interindividual and intergroup relations. When a new idea is emerging, the first communication phase is *diffusion* of information. The new information is spread evenly across a group so that a common reference point and body of knowledge are created that facilitate circulation and communication of information within the group. The second phase begins when specific groups intervene to organize the communication network according to knowledge and beliefs. The message is targeted to members of various groups, who in turn develop perspectives on what to think about the developing debate. Some experts within the group may *propagate* a principle for weighting the different elements of the network in order to consolidate the group's particular perspective. Other individuals, most often minorities, develop a strong perspective through the use of *propaganda* hinging on recognition of conflicting social relations within the group. This form of communication is aimed at selecting true and false knowledge and opinions from common knowledge. Positions resulting in propagation are expressed as flexible attitudes, whereas those stemming from propaganda are inflexible and stereotypical.

Illustration: Changing Conceptions of Drug Abuse

The debate over drug abuse shows an interesting evolution. In the 1960s, the consumption of illicit products was linked to antiestablishment rebellion. Drug abuse was emphatically condemned and rejected as an illegal and dangerous contamination of youth. However, difficulties in treating this "social problem" led some experts and practitioners to argue that the classification of drugs in terms of legal language should be replaced with a public health viewpoint. The distinction between legal and illicit drugs was replaced by an addiction measure, based on the deleterious health effect of the product. Thus a legal product such as alcohol became as harmful as an illicit one such as marijuana.

Through its entry into common parlance, this technical debate transformed the social representation of drugs to one in which legal and health perspectives converged. The consequence has been a more flexible and global approach to drugs by the legal system—such as promotion of increasingly strict tobacco smoking bans in many countries around the world. However, the emphasis on addiction has played up the negative aspects of legal drugs such as tobacco and alcohol and engaged a polarized public discourse resembling propaganda—which has led in the case of tobacco to potential criminalization of smokers.

The social representations perspective, with its emphasis on multiple levels of analysis—individual, group, and society—is a truly social-psychological approach to the generation of hypotheses about how people explain the world they live in and the ways they cope with social problems. As it stands now, a few process principles (objectification and anchoring, diffusion, propagation, and propaganda) have shown their capacity to help elucidate the form and content of social representation.

Fabio Lorenzi-Cioldi and Alain Clémence

See also Conspiracy Theories; Ideology; Levels of Analysis; Moscovici, Serge; Rumor; Socially Shared Cognition

Further Readings

Deaux, K., & Philogène, G. (Eds.). (2001). *Representations of the social.* Oxford, UK: Blackwell.

Doise, W., Clémence, A., & Lorenzi-Cioldi, F. (1993). *The quantitative analysis of social representations.* London: Harvester-Wheatsheaf.

Moscovici, S. (2008). *Psychoanalysis: Its image and its public.* Cambridge, UK: Polity Press. (Original work published 1961)

Moscovici, S., & Hewstone, M. (1983). Social representations and social explanations: From the "naïve" to the "amateur" scientist. In M. Hewstone (Ed.), *Attribution theory: Social and functional extensions* (pp. 98–125). Oxford, UK: Blackwell.

Mugny, G., & Carugati, F. (1989). *Social representations of intelligence.* Paris: Maison des Sciences de l'Homme.

SOCIOEMOTIONAL AND TASK BEHAVIOR

In problem-solving groups, individual members engage in different types of behavior, including *task behavior*, which focuses on the external problem to be addressed, and *socioemotional behavior*, which addresses the feelings that arise as a result of group interaction. This entry describes these two types of behavior and examines the leadership styles of group leaders who focus on each one.

Starting in 1947, social psychologist Robert F. Bales, at Harvard University, began studying roles in problem-solving groups. For the time, his methods were quite innovative. Small groups were observed through one-way mirrors, and all behavior was recorded. The observed groups were composed of five male Harvard undergraduates. They were given a human relations case and were told to discuss it for about 40 minutes and then dictate a recommended solution into a tape recording at the end of their session. After some refinement, Bales devised a set of 12 behavior categories that trained judges could code while observing ongoing interaction. Generally, 15 to 20 acts were coded every minute.

The 12 categories of behavior included some that were directly relevant to solving the problem the group was asked to address. Three of these are *gives suggestion*, *gives information*, and *asks for opinion*. Other categories refer to emotional expression related to interpersonal interaction—for example, *shows tension release*, *shows antagonism*, and *shows solidarity*. Overall, 56% of the coded behaviors were considered problem-solving attempts, and 44% included reactions to those attempts. In general, a task-related initiative would produce both a task-related response and some emotional response. For example, one person might offer a suggestion, a second might give an opinion about that suggestion, and a third might express annoyance, causing the first person to look embarrassed.

One overall conclusion from these and related studies is that when groups work on problems, two kinds of issues come into focus—those related to the challenge of solving the problem confronting the group and those that involve addressing and managing the feelings that the interaction produces. Such emotions are almost always apt to be a feature of group interaction directed toward solving a problem, especially if the problem is ambiguous or difficult. Thus some behavior has to be directed toward the task, and some toward relationships and emotions.

A second conclusion from such studies is that while each person engages in behavior related to both challenges, some people focus more on the task, others focus more on feelings, and some are quite balanced. Whether any individual at any instant, or over time, focuses more on the external task or more on emotions within the group will depend on two things. First, what are the individual's own inclinations? What role or roles is he or she most comfortable performing? Second, how do others in the group behave? That is, any individual's behavior is shaped by his or her own personality and by the behavior of others. As pioneering psychologist Kurt Lewin observed many years ago, behavior is a function of the person and the environment.

Regardless of the cause, some individuals in groups become *task specialists* and others become what Bales called *socioemotional specialists*. This development has implications for leadership. Is the leader likely to be one of these specialists or instead a person who can deal effectively with both the challenges of the group's task and the dynamics arising from the group's feelings? An initial hypothesis was that there would be a status order in which the person who contributed most to problem solving would also be the best liked. This hypothesis was not supported. Neither the person who was most active nor the person who was rated as having the best ideas was typically the best liked. Instead, it was found that there seemed to be two leaders in many groups, one who was regarded as the *task leader* and one who seemed to be the *socioemotional leader*. This finding suggested the hypothesis of two complementary leaders, one focusing on the task and the other on emotions and relationships. This hypothesis included the idea that the two leaders might get along quite well, their complementary skills combining to promote both group success and group happiness. The idea that leadership involves these two roles is supported by research published by Ralph Stogdill in 1948. Stogdill found that two categories of leader behavior are *initiating structure* and *showing consideration*.

The phenomenon of two complementary leaders, or a bifurcated leadership structure, might emerge for two reasons. First, an individual leader may only rarely be skilled enough to effectively lead toward both task accomplishment and toward group cohesiveness. Second, it may be that there are inherent incompatibilities between task roles and socioemotional roles. On one hand, the task-oriented leader needs to move people and direct and organize them. Behaviors directed toward that end disturb and perhaps antagonize people. On the other hand, the relationship-oriented leader cannot both soothe ruffled feathers and issue orders, so that leader will stay away from directing tasks. Thus, the inherent conflict between moving people and soothing them is a challenge for leadership and opens the door to bifurcated leadership.

Task-Oriented Versus Relationship-Oriented Leadership Styles

In many organized groups, just one person has the formal authority to lead. Unless that individual is the rare person who can successfully choreograph both task leadership and socioemotional leadership, he or she is likely to prefer one style to the other. This possibility was the starting point for Fred Fiedler's highly influential *contingency theory of leadership*. According to the social psychologist Martin Chemers, Fiedler's emphasis on task-focused versus socioemotionally focused leadership grew out of his research on psychotherapists who were more distant versus more accepting. This work led Fiedler to ask questions about the relative effectiveness of leaders who were more or less interpersonally oriented. Fiedler's important work on leadership led to a number of conclusions. First, leaders could be reliably distinguished as primarily valuing either interpersonal relations or goal accomplishment. Second, these two different kinds of leaders are effective in different kinds of situations. Third, the differential effectiveness of such leaders depends largely on whether their values and competencies match the demands of the situation. When there is a good match between the leader's personal qualities and the demands of the situation, the leader is more likely to feel confident and become active and directive and therefore effective. In these *in-match* situations, the leader is likely to experience *flow*, which Mihaly Csikszentmihalyi has described as a *dynamic state of consciousness* marked by feelings of engagement, confidence, and control.

After years of research, Fiedler devised a simple measure that has proven remarkably effective in identifying relationship versus task-oriented leaders—the Least Preferred Coworker (LPC) Scale. Individual leaders are asked to consider the one coworker "with whom you have had the most difficulty in getting the job done." The leaders rate the coworkers on dimensions such as pleasant–unpleasant, accepting–rejecting, and trustworthy–untrustworthy. Essentially, they indicate whether they think those difficult coworkers are good people or not. The high-LPC leader is one who values interpersonal relations and grants that the difficult coworker is a decent human being, even though he or she is a detriment to accomplishing goals. The low-LPC leader has no patience for the troublesome colleague and roundly condemns him or her.

Fiedler also identified three variables that determine how much control the leader has or, in somewhat different terms, how favorable the situation is for leadership. These variables are the quality of the leader–follower relationships in the group, the

clarity and difficulty of the task facing the group, and the degree of power or authority the leader has by virtue of his or her formal position or role in the group. A highly favorable situation, in which the leader has lots of control, is one in which there are good relationships between the leader and the followers, the task is easy and clear, and the leader's position provides a good deal of formal authority. An unfavorable situation is one in which the opposites hold: The leader and the followers relate to each other poorly, the group faces a difficult and ambiguous task, and the leader does not have much formal power. Of course, most situations are neither that good nor that bad. Quite often the situation is moderately favorable, giving the leader a moderate degree of control.

Fiedler's major contribution was to show that low-LPC leaders, who value task accomplishment over good interpersonal relations, are more effective than high-LPC leaders when the situation is either very good or very bad. In very good situations, the leader can provide structure and direction without worrying about ruffling any feathers. In very bad situations, the leader does not have time to address hurt feelings or interpersonal conflict and instead must take charge and tell people exactly what to do. Both these situations call for the strengths of the low-LPC leader. In contrast, in moderately favorable situations, followers need some direction, but they also need to be treated with dignity, and their feelings warrant attention. These are the conditions that play to the values and competencies of the relationship-oriented, high-LPC leader.

A great deal of research has focused on Fiedler's contingency theory of leadership. On the whole, the research has supported it. Task-oriented and socioemotionally oriented leaders indeed thrive in different contexts. In those situations that play to their strengths, they are active and confident, and the groups they are leading do well. If there is a mismatch between the particulars of the situation and a leader's values and behavior, the leader's effectiveness is significantly diminished.

George R. Goethals

See also Charismatic Leadership; Contingency Theories of Leadership; Great Person Theory of Leadership; Interactionist Theories of Leadership; Leader-Member Exchange (LMX) Theory; Leadership; Path–Goal

Theory of Leadership; Personality Theories of Leadership; Social Identity Theory of Leadership; Transactional Leadership Theories; Trasformational Leadership Theories; Vertical Dyad Linkage Model

Further Readings

Bales, R. F. (1958). Task roles and social roles in problem-solving groups. In E. Maccoby, T. M. Newcomb, & E. L. Hartley (Eds.), *Readings in social psychology* (pp. 437–447). New York: Holt, Rinehart & Winston.

Bales, R. F. (1970). *Personality and interpersonal behavior*. New York: Holt, Rinehart & Winston.

Chemers, M. M. (1997). *An integrative theory of leadership*. Mahwah, NJ: Erlbaum.

Chemers, M. M., & Ayman, R. (1993). *Leadership theory and research*. San Diego, CA: Academic Press.

Csikszentmihalyi, M. (1982). Toward a psychology of optimal experience. In L. Wheeler (Ed.), *Review of personality and social psychology* (pp. 13–36). Beverly Hills, CA: Sage.

Fiedler, F. E. (1993). The leadership situation and the Black Box in contingency theories. In M. Chemers, M., & R. Ayman (Eds.), *Leadership theory and research* (pp. 1–28). San Diego, CA: Academic Press.

Stogdill, R. M. (1948). Personal factors associated with leadership: A survey of the literature. *Journal of Psychology, 25*, 35–71.

SOCIOMETER MODEL

Despite widespread public interest in the topic, many people do not realize that there are numerous definitions of self-esteem. Some psychologists conceptualize self-esteem as a fundamental human need to feel good about oneself, some conceptualize self-esteem as a reasoned tally of one's positive attributes, and still others conceptualize self-esteem as an emotional state. The *sociometer model of self-esteem* proposes that self-esteem is an interpersonal monitor—a *sociometer*—that provides real-time feedback about the quality of one's social bonds and provokes behaviors aimed at maintaining positive social relationships with one's ingroup members. Hence, this theory, proposed by Mark Leary and his colleagues, is a distinctly social-psychological theory of self-esteem because it proposes that the self-esteem system plays an important role in helping people navigate their social worlds.

How exactly does self-esteem perform this important interpersonal function? Leary suggests that to answer this question, one must first understand the general nature of *regulatory systems*. According to evolutionary psychologists, the human mind is composed of a number of distinct regulatory modules that evolved to solve unique psychological, physical, or social problems that influenced survival or reproduction in the prehistoric past. For example, the pain regulatory system evolved to help people avoid hurt and injury. Like all regulatory modules, the pain system comprises monitoring, signaling, and behavioral components: The pain system monitors the body for signs of injury, then signals a potential injury with feelings of pain; these feelings of pain motivate behaviors aimed at avoiding further physical damage.

Just as avoiding injury was essential for survival and reproduction in humans' evolutionary past, so too was maintaining acceptance by one's group. People depended on their group for protection from predators, for help gathering food and caring for young, and for care and protection during bouts of illness or physical incapacitation. Without such support, an individual would have been at a severe disadvantage in the biological race to produce healthy offspring and raise them to adulthood. Because of the importance of social bonds for survival and reproduction, sociometer theory proposes that people possess a regulatory module that evolved to ensure that people are at least minimally accepted by their group while also avoiding outright rejection. Specifically, the self-esteem system is proposed to be an interpersonal monitor—a sociometer—that performs exactly this function.

First, one's sociometer regularly, effortlessly, and often automatically monitors the environment for cues regarding one's *relational value*, which is the degree to which one is valued by others. Such cues may come from the external environment in the form of social feedback or from interpersonal experiences, but people may also glean information about their relational value from their memories of past social experiences or from their anticipation of future social events. In response to such social cues concerning one's relational value, the sociometer produces a signal that indicates whether acceptance or rejection is imminent. If social feedback suggests that a person's relational value is high, the person experiences increases in *state self-esteem* (i.e., transitory increases in feelings of self-worth). In contrast, if feedback suggests that a person's relational value is low, then the person experiences decreases in state self-esteem (i.e., transitory decreases in feelings of self-worth).

In turn, such changes in state self-esteem are thought to motivate social behaviors. If relational value is high, the positive affective signal motivates people to approach a desired social situation or target, whereas if relational value is low, the aversive affective signal motivates people either to work to repair the damaged relationship or, if repair is not possible or is too risky, to avoid the relationship and thus avoid the hurt feelings that it prompts. In this latter instance, people would then be motivated to find substitute sources of acceptance through building new relationships in the group, thereby replenishing their depleted sociometer.

The preceding discussion has focused on the role played by state self-esteem in regulating social relationships. However, *global self-esteem* (a person's overall sense of self-worth) plays an equally important regulatory role. Research suggests that people rely on their global self-esteem to predict future interpersonal outcomes: Individuals with higher self-esteem (HSEs) anticipate acceptance from future relational partners, whereas individuals with lower self-esteem (LSEs) anticipate a more chilly interpersonal reception. These differing social expectations seem to have a marked influence on people's behavioral response to social cues concerning their relational value.

For example, HSEs eagerly seek new social opportunities whereas LSEs remain hesitant to enter novel social situations unless acceptance is virtually guaranteed. In addition, LSEs tend to respond to hurt feelings by avoiding the person who caused them pain, whereas HSEs respond with efforts to repair the relationship. For example, in romantic relationships, on the day after a conflict, HSEs attempt to repair their relationship by seeking closeness with their romantic partner, whereas LSEs attempt to limit their risk of rejection by emotionally distancing from their partner.

In summary, sociometer theory proposes that both state and global self-esteem play important roles in helping people regulate their interpersonal relationships. Transitory increases or decreases in state self-esteem provide real-time feedback about the quality of people's social bonds, whereas people rely on their global self-esteem to predict future social outcomes and choose interpersonal behaviors that will minimize the risk of rejection and optimize the probability of acceptance.

Implications for Group Processes and Intergroup Relations

An important implication of the sociometer model of self-esteem is that one's feelings of self-worth are ultimately determined by the group to which one belongs. If the group is generally accepting, then an individual will have higher self-esteem; if the group is ambivalent about one's value or is outright rejecting, then an individual will have lower self-esteem. But what factors determine an individual's value as a relational partner?

An individual's social value will be determined in large part by the individual's *social role*. Social roles are positions that one can hold either within a larger social structure or within a particular relationship. Other people will expect and desire occupants of a given social role to possess the traits that allow occupants of that role to successfully fulfill role requirements. Typically, such role requirements constitute behaviors that will benefit the other members of one's ingroup. For example, the female gender role fundamentally involves the adoption of a relational self-construal, wherein one's primary motivation is to maintain harmonious relationships. In reflection of this, girls are encouraged to develop other-oriented, communal traits, and grown women who possess traits such as warmth, kindness, and responsiveness are highly valued as relationship partners.

Because an individual's social value is ultimately determined by the social roles he or she occupies, research suggests that the monitoring component of the self-esteem system is also affected by one's social role. For example, consider the role of an opera singer. The best opera singers possess musicality, emotional expressiveness, and perfect pitch. More important, opera singers who possess those qualities are generally admired by their peer group. This association with actual acceptance leads opera singers' self-esteem system to become particularly sensitive to feedback about such traits, such that positive feedback leads to increases in state self-esteem, and negative feedback leads to decreases in state self-esteem. In contrast, mathematical abilities are not predictive of acceptance for opera singers, presumably because mathematical abilities will not benefit an opera singer's ingroup, so opera singers' state self-esteem is not sensitive to feedback about mathematical abilities. Conversely, in the social role of a physicist, mathematical skills *do* predict one's relational value and offer potential benefits to ingroup members, whereas singing abilities fade in importance. Hence, a physicist's state self-esteem is sensitive to feedback about his or her math skills but not about his or her singing abilities. It is important to remember that the opera singer and the physicist did not choose to have sociometers that monitor social feedback about singing abilities or mathematical skills. Their ingroup members made this choice for them by accepting or rejecting occupants of those social roles who possessed, or lacked, singing ability and mathematical abilities, respectively.

This suggests that the sociometer is able to attend selectively to certain types of social feedback. This may explain why members of stigmatized social groups do not necessarily have lower self-esteem. Research suggests that members of stigmatized groups have a number of protective strategies that allow them to maintain relatively high self-esteem in the face of negative social feedback. They may attribute negative social feedback to prejudice; they may compare their social outcomes to those of other ingroup members rather than to those of outgroup members; and they may devalue traits or attributes on which their group fares poorly. By using these techniques, members of stigmatized groups may be directing their sociometers to focus on feedback from the people whose opinions matter most for survival and reproduction: one's ingroup members.

Danu Anthony Stinson and John G. Holmes

See also Attachment Theory; Evolutionary Psychology; Looking-Glass Self; Roles; Self-Esteem

Further Readings

Anthony, D. B., Holmes, J. G., & Wood, J. V. (2007). Social acceptance and self-esteem: Tuning the sociometer to interpersonal value. *Journal of Personality and Social Psychology, 92,* 1024–1039.

Crocker, J., & Major, B. (1989). Social stigma and self-esteem: The self-protective properties of stigma. *Psychological Review, 96,* 608–630.

Leary, M. R. (2004). The sociometer, self-esteem, and the regulation of interpersonal behavior. In R. F. Baumeister & K. D. Vohs (Eds.), *Handbook of self-regulation: Research, theory, and applications* (pp. 373–391). New York: Guilford.

Murray, S. L., Holmes, J. G., & Collins, N. L. (2006). Optimizing assurance: The risk regulation system in relationships. *Psychological Bulletin, 132,* 641–666.

SOCIOMETRIC CHOICE

Sociometric choice is a method of measuring group members' relationships by asking them to identify others with whom they are or wish to be connected in a specific situation. These choices identify relations of attraction and repulsion, or liking and disliking, in the group. Jacob L. Moreno proposed the *sociometric choice test* in 1934 as a key element of sociometry—the study of the pattern of interrelations between members of a group. The sociometric method dominated the field of sociology from the 1930s through the 1950s and has been used in group therapy and developmental work on children's peer groups. Patterns of sociometric choice can predict important outcomes, such as group performance and member influence. For this reason, sociometry promised early on to aid the optimal configuration of groups, such as families, schools, and factories. This entry examines the elements of the theory, its early applications, and future directions for this line of research.

Measurement

Sociometry introduced rigorous measurement techniques for studying the microrelations within groups and communities. At the heart of sociometry was the sociometric choice test, which asked group members to report the most, and sometimes the least, preferred members for a specific purpose or circumstance. For example, school children would name three classmates with whom they would most like to play, workers would identify the people with whom they would most want to work on a committee, and military personnel would list the two people in their company whom they would most like to take home on a leave.

Different forms of the choice test vary in how many others the respondent may list as preferred or not preferred in a given circumstance. What is common, however, is that these self-reports are neither explicit evaluations of other group members nor overall liking or disliking reports about others irrespective of a specific context. Some scholars have suggested that other measurement techniques, such as the method of *rank order* (ranking in order of preference all group members) and *paired comparisons* (indicating the preferred person in each possible pairing of group members), are suitable substitutes for the traditional sociometric choice test.

Sociometrists aggregate their choice data in a variety of ways to indicate member roles in the group and features of the group. Members who are highly chosen by others are *popular,* those who are infrequently chosen are *isolates,* those who select many others as friends are *positives,* and those who select few others are *negatives. Pairs* are two members with mutually reciprocal bonds, and *cliques* are subgroups of three or more members with reciprocal bonds.

Sociometric choices also can be used to identify group *cohesiveness* (overall level of attraction in the group) and *density* (degree of mutual preference in the group). Member choices may be organized in a *sociogram,* which is a figure in two-dimensional space that maps member interrelations. Each group member is represented as a lettered or numbered circle. Lines between the circles indicate connections between members, and arrows indicate the direction of attraction. Today, computer software aids the creation of sociograms.

Causes and Consequences

Some have criticized sociometric research for measuring member choices but not the reasons behind them. However, research has identified several situational and personal factors that can influence sociometric choices. For example, physical proximity influences friendship choices such that people prefer those who are close by. When classroom seats or dormitory rooms are assigned randomly, students choose as friends those who were seating

companions or dormitory roommates. People also choose as friends others whom they perceive as similar to themselves in values, beliefs, and interests, although contact with dissimilar people may mitigate this tendency. Members who hold a different opinion from the rest of a group are less preferred as future group mates than are those who conform to the group norm. And status influences sociometric choices in military units—service personnel report liking and choosing high-status members to take home on a leave.

Ultimately, the value of sociometric choice comes from its ability to predict important individual and group outcomes. Research has shown that individuals who are highly chosen in sociometric tests perform better and make fewer errors on certain tasks in organizations. Military groups that have greater sociometric density are characterized by more member satisfaction and better performance. Group members who are highly chosen for leadership positions are more likely to engage in leadership behaviors during group discussion (e.g., high participation and influence). Children who are identified as popular in camp situations are more influential and imitated by others. In school settings, children who are chosen as friends by others engage in more cooperative and obedient classroom behavior. Given the importance of predicting individual and group performance for organizational researchers and managers, the ability of the sociometric choice test to predict performance is a notable benefit.

Sociometric Choice in Use

Although much sociometric research has focused on the causes and consequences of sociometric choice, this was not the purpose of sociometry as laid out by its founder. Moreno argued that understanding the reasons behind sociometric choices was unnecessary. He believed, instead, that knowing the choices and putting them into action were critical. His point was that sociometric choices should be used. Two examples of such usage are group therapy and social engineering.

One way to put sociometric choice into action is through *group therapy,* a term first used by Moreno. In one form of such therapy, group members discuss their sociometric choices and the reasons behind them (rather than reporting their choices privately). Members reveal to fellow group members whom they most and least prefer as friends or coworkers and the reasons for their choices. These discussions, as one can imagine, can be threatening and uncomfortable. Therefore, using appropriate discussion procedures and promoting effective communication are of utmost importance. One way to make members more comfortable is to allow them to express their reservations about the interaction or halt it at any time. Moreno believed that such honest discussion of members' liking preferences would promote personal growth and interpersonal insight.

In the late 1920s and early 1930s, when Moreno was formulating sociometry, social engineering was a popular idea (e.g., some psychologists were interested in eugenics, controlled breeding to promote the ideal population). Moreno's hope was that sociometry would be used to create utopian groups, communities, and societies. He envisioned that sociometric choice would be used to achieve ideal group compositions, better performance, and improved member relations. For example, urban planners might foster social integration by providing a framework for mapping an entire community. Moreno hoped that, by understanding social interrelations in small groups, sociologists would be able to extrapolate such knowledge to the larger society.

History and Future Direction

Moreno had grandiose dreams for sociometry, some of which (e.g., social engineering) were not realized. In 1937, Moreno started the journal *Sociometry*, which highlighted sociometric theory and research. This journal had great influence in shaping the field of microsociology. After two decades of managing the journal on his own, Moreno handed it over to the American Sociological Society (now the American Sociological Association). By 1979, sociometric methods had become less focal in the field of sociology, and, for this reason, the journal was renamed *Social Psychology Quarterly*—its name to this day.

Very little sociometric testing is used today relative to its heyday, but its impact in shaping sociology and other fields (e.g., developmental psychology and psychotherapy) is notable. Many ideas originally laid out in sociometry have

contributed to the understanding of *social networks* and the development of network analysis. It is in this direction that the study of group member interrelations is likely to continue in the future.

Gwen M. Wittenbaum

See also Group Cohesiveness; Inclusion/Exclusion; Opinion Deviance; Social Networks; Therapy Groups

Further Readings

Cadwallader, T. W. (2001). Sociometry reconsidered: The social context of peer rejection in childhood. *International Journal of Action Methods: Psychodrama, Skill Training, and Role Playing, 53*, 99–118.

Katz, N., Lazer, D. Arrow, H., & Contractor, N. (2005). The network perspective on small groups: Theory and research. In M. S. Poole & A. B. Hollingshead (Eds.), *Theories of small group research: Interdisciplinary perspectives* (pp. 277–312). Thousand Oaks, CA: Sage.

Lucius, R. H., & Kuhnert, K. W. (1997). Using sociometry to predict team performance in the work place. *Journal of Psychology: Interdisciplinary and Applied, 13*, 21–32.

Moreno, J. L. (1956). The sociometric school and the science of man. *Sociometry, 18*, 271–291.

Remer, R. (1995). Strong sociometry: A definition. *Journal of Group Psychotherapy, Psychodrama, & Sociometry, 48*, 69–74.

SPORTS TEAMS

Sports teams share the properties of many other groups, in that they are composed of two or more individuals who possess a common identity, have common goals and objectives, share a common fate, exhibit structured patterns of interaction and modes of communication, hold common perceptions about group structural elements such as norms and roles, are personally and instrumentally interdependent, reciprocate interpersonal attraction, and consider themselves to be a group.

An intercollegiate tennis doubles team provides a useful example of this definition. The team contains, of course, two athletes, both of whom would describe themselves as partners on a team (common identity). Also, the two athletes would share numerous goals for both practices and competitions and experience success and failure as a collective (common fate). The brief, often single-word communications they exchange during a rally, their dynamic adjustments in rushing toward and retreating from the net, and their pre-serve signals to convey intended postserve court positions all reflect structured patterns of interaction and communication. To play doubles tennis clearly requires task interdependence. Also, the considerable time spent traveling to and from competitions and waiting for a match to begin inevitably lead to social interdependence and interpersonal attraction. Finally, and not surprisingly given all the above, the two athletes would consider themselves to be a team.

In considering themselves to be a team, the athletes exhibit one of the fundamental tenets of social identity theory, namely, social *categorization*. Considerable indirect evidence also highlights the presence of two fundamental consequences of this categorization—*identification* with the ingroup and *comparison with/bias against* outgroups. The purpose of this entry is to outline what we know about the role that sports plays in the dynamics of ingroups (teams) and their relationships with outgroups (including opponents, fans, and the media).

The Sports Team as an Ingroup

In 1995, Roy Baumeister and Mark Leary presented an elegant case for the proposition that we have an innate need to belong to groups. In our evolutionary past, creating bonds with others increased our chances of survival. Thus, the desire for interpersonal attachments is thought to be a fundamental human motivation. Membership in sports teams, just like membership in other social groups, satisfies this need to belong. In fact, consistent with *social identity theory*, being a member of a team forms an important part of an individual's self-concept. When we belong to a group, our identity is derived, at least in part, from that group.

In examining the sports team as an ingroup, two important aspects to consider are the team's structure (e.g., norms and roles) and its processes (e.g., decision making). The discussion in this section focuses on how these factors influence team members' thoughts, emotions, and behaviors, as well as the team as a whole.

Group Norms

Team norms represent an unwritten code of conduct for group member behavior. They provide members with guidelines as to what behaviors are expected. In addition to being informational, norms serve an integrative function. Athletes who understand and adhere to team norms are integrated into the group, whereas athletes who consistently violate team norms are sanctioned and may eventually (if the behavior persists) be rejected from the team. Perhaps the most important function of group norms is to ensure that a team performs as a unit as opposed to a collection of individuals.

Research in sports has found that teams develop norms for a variety of contexts, including competition, practice, the off-season, and social events. Regardless of the context, the most dominant norm in sports teams involves work output. A team puts pressure on its members to give maximal effort in competition, work hard in practice, and train hard in the off-season. Research also has found that these performance norms influence both the individual and the team. At the individual level, stronger performance norms exert greater social influence. At the group level, teams with higher performance norms are more successful.

It is also important to note the negative side of group norms. Not all norms enhance team performance. An example of a negative norm that inhibits performance is the expectation that one should be abusive to other team members (e.g., rookies, training personnel). Perhaps the most troubling aspect of negative norms is that they can persist over several seasons—long after the athletes who were instrumental in their development have departed.

Group Roles

While norms represent general expectations for the behavior of all team members, roles reflect specific expectations concerning how members who occupy a certain position on the team should behave. Every member of a sports team has a role. For example, hockey teams have enforcers—members who are expected to serve (as a National Hockey League coach suggested) as a "nuclear deterrent." Each role is unique and contributes to a team's success. In fact, a team's effectiveness relies on each person's carrying out his or her designated role effectively.

Role clarity is a cornerstone of effective team performance. Research has shown that *role ambiguity* (the flip side of role clarity) can arise among athletes regarding the *scope* of their responsibilities (is being an enforcer sufficient, or am I also expected to be a productive member of the offense?), the *behaviors* necessary to carry out role responsibilities (in my role as an enforcer, am I expected to fight or simply serve as a deterrent by my presence?), the *consequences* of failing to carry out role responsibilities (if I don't fight, will I be benched, reprimanded, cut from the team?), and how role performance will be *evaluated* (is it sufficient to simply fight, or do I have to win the majority of the encounters?). Role ambiguity has been shown to be moderately (and negatively) related to athlete performance. Other aspects of the roles associated with athlete performance include *role satisfaction*, *role acceptance*, *role efficacy*, and *role conflict*.

Shared Beliefs

Shared beliefs are a pervasive cognitive attribute of groups. Despite individual differences in personalities and histories, members of sports teams develop similar beliefs. Team members are exposed to the same experiences, and each member's interpretation of an event is influenced by how his or her teammates interpret that event. The interdependence and interaction among teammates result in shared beliefs. Research with sports teams has provided empirical support for the presence of strong shared beliefs about *collective efficacy* (i.e., confidence in the team as a collective), *cohesion*, *group norms*, and *performance attributions* (explanations advanced for factors in team success and failure).

Attributional Style

Performance attributions made by team members can evolve into a team attributional style. Individuals are often characterized as having either an *adaptive* (*optimistic*) or *maladaptive* (*pessimistic*) style. Attributional style has been linked to an individual's emotions, expectancies, and future behavior. In studies investigating attributional style at the group level, researchers have examined newspaper quotations from professional athletes. It has been found that team members explain team losses in a similar manner, in that teams tend to be either collectively optimistic (e.g., "we lost only because our opponent outworked us tonight") or collectively pessimistic (e.g., "we lost because we have no talent"). Furthermore, the team's attribution style has been found to correlate with its future performance, such that optimistic teams tend to perform better than pessimistic teams during the next season.

The Sports Team and Its Relationship With the Outgroup

Trash Talking

Traditionally, sports psychology research has focused on the ingroup—the thoughts, feelings, and behaviors characteristic of the members of a team. Little research attention has been directed toward relationships between teams. Nonetheless, there is substantial anecdotal evidence that the bias, prejudice, and stereotyping displayed by ingroups toward outgroup members in other contexts also are present within sports. Take trash talking, for example, one of the most reviled phenomena in sports. Trash talking involves verbal barbs or abuse directed at opponents, both on and away from a court or field. Trash talking is widespread—almost universal—despite rules in many sports that seek to eliminate it.

Race is the only topic considered off limits for trash talking. Thus, an opponent's family (including "yo mamma"), physical imperfections or unusual characteristics, and mental limitations are all potential targets. Taunts that might produce physical retaliation in any other context are considered "part of the game" in sports. In fact, the target of trash talking often takes pains to show that he or she is not negatively affected by it.

Violence

In sports, especially in football, rugby, water polo, wrestling, and hockey, describing behavior directed at opponents (the outgroup) as violent poses some difficulties. Body contact is an integral part of competition, and athletes enter competition expecting aggressive tactics from opponents. However, all sports have sanctions against what are considered excessively dangerous acts. It is not physical contact per se that is problematic—it is contact exerted to violate, damage, or abuse an opponent. Although sports such as hockey, basketball, and baseball have a long tradition of inter-team violence, there has been a noticeable increase over the past 15 years in both the frequency and severity of violence in sports—an epidemic of violence, according to some scholars. No one is sure why this increase has occurred.

In sports, a number of constituencies consider themselves part of the ingroup. They include athletes, coaches, parents, fans, and support personnel, such as trainers. Constituents forming the outgroup are numerous as well. They include the other team, its supporters, and often officials and the media. Violence has been perpetrated by virtually every constituent of the ingroup against virtually every constituent of the outgroup. Many examples can be cited. A Massachusetts father of a 10-year-old hockey player beat a coach to death over what was perceived to be intolerably rough play against his child on the ice. Manchester United's Eric Cantona assaulted a fan who allegedly had subjected him to racial slurs. The Miami Hurricanes and Florida International University's Golden Panthers engaged in a bench-clearing brawl sparked by a point-after-touchdown incident. Ten players from the New York Knicks and Denver Nuggets were ejected from a game after a brawl instigated by Carmelo Anthony. After an attack from behind by Todd Bertuzzi of the Vancouver Canucks, Colorado Avalanche's Steve Moore was hospitalized with three broken vertebrae. Ron Artest and Jermaine O'Neal of the Indiana Pacers exchanged punches with Detroit Pistons fans. And the list goes on. Violence is prevalent in sports, despite many efforts to eliminate it.

The Home Advantage

A significant factor in an ingroup's relationship with an outgroup is territoriality. This should not come as a surprise, given the number of popular expressions that highlight the special nature of the home, such as "home sweet home," "home is where the heart is," and "there's no place like home." Countries in international competitions and teams in professional sports profit from competing in a place they call home.

For example, countries win more medals when they host the Olympic Games than they do in immediately preceding or subsequent games. Another interesting example is provided by results from Fédération Internationale de Football Association World Cup competitions. They have been held 18 times. In that period, host nations have placed first, second, or third a total of 10 times—an overall 55% success rate. Given that in two of the competitions—1994 in the United States and 2002 in Korea and Japan—the host nations were improbable possibilities for a top-three finish, the host nations' record is impressive.

At the team level, the home advantage has been well documented in professional sports. A home advantage has been found in every sport, although the magnitude varies. For example, in baseball, football, ice hockey, basketball, and soccer the home advantage is 53%, 57%, 58%, 61%, and 62%, respectively.

The above notwithstanding, not every team in every league enjoys a home advantage. For example, when Steven Bray analyzed National Hockey League results from 1974 to 1993, he found that slightly more than one third of the teams won fewer than 50% of their home games. Generally, however, if inept teams are going to win, there is a greater probability that they will do so at home than on the road.

The reasons underlying the home advantage have been examined extensively. No single factor has been identified, and the factors that appear important in some contexts are not always so in others. With this caveat, it seems that the major causes are the crowd, the officiating (because of the crowd influence), the visiting team's travel, and familiarity with the home facility.

Conclusion

The term *competition* comes from the Latin word *competere*, which means to seek together, to coincide, and to agree. This utopian notion that members of opposing sports teams are working toward a common goal, when in fact they are participating in a zero-sum contest in which a plus (win) for one team necessarily means a minus (loss) for the other team, is not supported by research or by popular (media) reports. Outgroup members in sports are subjected to the same bias, prejudice, and stereotyping present in other group situations.

Albert Carron and Kim Shapcott

See also Cooperation and Competition; Group Cohesiveness; Group Structure; Intergroup Violence; Norms; Prejudice; Roles; Social Identity Theory; Socially Shared Cognition; Stereotyping

Further Readings

Beauchamp, M., & Eys, M. A. (2007). *Group dynamics advances in sport and exercise psychology: Contemporary themes.* London: Routledge.

Buford, B. (1992). *Among the thugs: The experience and seduction of crowd violence.* New York: Norton.

Carron, A. V., Hausenblas, H. A., & Eys, M. A. (2005). *Group dynamics in sport* (3rd ed.). Morgantown, WA: Fitness Information Technology.

STANFORD PRISON EXPERIMENT

The Stanford prison experiment (SPE) was an experiment designed to examine the power of an institutional environment—prison, in particular—to shape and control the behavior of persons placed inside it. Using college student participants who were selected for their normality and randomly assigned to be prisoners or guards, the study ended unexpectedly early because of the dramatic and extreme results. It has assumed a prominent place in debates over the causes of extreme behavior in powerful situations or settings, especially in the criminal justice system.

Study Design and Findings

The SPE was conducted in 1971 by a group of Stanford research psychologists, led by Philip Zimbardo, and his two graduate students, Craig Haney and Curtis Banks. The experiment was designed to control for the individual personality variables (e.g., narcissism, authoritarianism) that are sometimes used to attempt to explain behavior in prison and other institutional settings. That is, the researchers in the SPE neutralized the explanatory argument that pathological traits alone accounted for extreme and abusive behavior in severe institutional setting such as prisons. They did this by (a) selecting a group of participants who were psychologically healthy and had scored in the normal range of numerous personality variables and (b) assigning participants to the role of either prisoner or guard on a completely random basis. The behavior that resulted when these otherwise healthy, normal participants were placed in the extreme environment of a simulated prison would therefore have to be explained largely if not entirely on the basis of the characteristics of the social setting in which they had been placed.

The setting itself was designed to be as similar as possible to an actual prison, given a number of obvious practical and ethical constraints. Constructed in the basement of the Psychology Department at Stanford University, the "Stanford County Prison" had barred doors on the small rooms that served as cells, cots on which the prisoners slept, a hallway area that was converted to a prison "yard" where group activities were conducted, and a small closet that served as a short-term "solitary confinement" cell for disciplining unruly prisoners. The prisoners wore uniforms that were designed to de-emphasize their individuality and underscore their powerlessness. In contrast, guards donned military-like garb, complete with reflecting sun glasses and nightsticks. Guards generated a set of rules and regulations that in many ways resembled those in operation in actual prisons, and prisoners were expected to comply with the guards' orders. However, guards were instructed not to resort to physical force to gain prisoner compliance.

Despite the lack of any legal mandate for the "incarceration" of the prisoners, and despite the fact that both groups were told that they had been randomly assigned to their roles (so that, for example, guards knew that prisoners had done nothing to "deserve" their degraded prisoner status, and similarly, prisoners knew that the guards had no special training or actual legal authority over them), the behavior that ensued was remarkably similar to behavior that takes place inside actual prisons. It also was surprisingly extreme in intensity and effect. Thus, initial prisoner resistance and rebellion were met forcibly by guards, who quickly struggled to regain their power and then proceeded to escalate their mistreatment of prisoners throughout the study, at the slightest sign of affront or disobedience.

As the guards' control over the prisoners increased, the tensions between the two groups intensified, and the harassment of the prisoners worsened. For example, the guards conducted a series of "counts"—times when prisoners were removed from their cells in order to be counted but which quickly deteriorated into occasions for verbal and other forms of abuse and humiliation that the guards directed at them. In some instances, the guards conspired to physically mistreat prisoners outside the presence of the experimenters and to leave prisoners in the solitary confinement cell beyond the 1-hour limit that the researchers had set.

Conversely, prisoners resisted the guards' orders at first but then succumbed to their superior power and control. Some prisoners had serious emotional breakdowns in the course of the study and had to be released from participation. Other prisoners became compliant and conforming, rarely if ever challenging the "authority" of the guards. Despite the fact that the researchers could not keep the prisoners in the study against their will (and they had been informed at the outset of the study of their legal right to leave), as the study proceeded prisoners "petitioned" the prison "administrators" for permission to be "paroled" and returned passively to their cells when their requests were denied. By the end of the study, they had disintegrated as a group. The guards, in contrast, solidified and intensified their control as time passed. Although some of the guards were more extreme and inventive in the degradation they inflicted on the prisoners and some were more passive and less involved, none of the guards intervened to restrain the behavior of their more abusive colleagues. Although the study was designed to last for 2 full weeks, the extreme nature of the behavior that occurred led the researchers to terminate it after only 6 days.

A post hoc analysis of the SPE data showed that the careful screening of the participants and their random assignment to the roles of prisoners and guards had effectively controlled for any significant personality-based, or dispositional, explanation of the results. That is, there were no significant personality differences between the SPE participants and the normal population (i.e., the group means for guards and prisoners did not fall outside the 40 to 60 percentile range of the normative male population on any of the dimensions of the personality inventory that was used), no personality

differences between the guards and prisoners could explain their very different behavior in the study, and no personality differences within either group reliably predicted variations in their in-prison behavior.

The SPE's Larger Implications

Controversial from the outset and widely discussed since it was conducted, the study has come to stand in psychology and related disciplines as a demonstration of the power of situations—especially extreme institutional settings such as prisons—to shape and control the behavior of the persons in them. The results of the study undermine the notion that extreme social behavior can only—or even mostly—be explained in terms of the extreme characteristics of the persons who engage in it. Instead, the SPE warns us to look more carefully at the characteristics of the settings in which extreme behavior occurs.

The SPE also stands as a challenge to what might be termed the *presumption of institutional rationality*—that is, the tendency to assume that institutions operate on the basis of an inherent rationality that should be accepted rather than questioned. Instead, the SPE (itself the most "irrational" of prisons, in the sense that the guards had no legal authority over the prisoners, who had committed no crimes that warranted their punishment) suggests that a kind of "psycho-logic" may operate in these settings that controls role-bound behavior, whether or not that behavior furthers legitimate goals. That is, despite the fact that the guards had no genuine authority over the prisoners and the prisoners had done nothing illegal to legitimize their mistreatment, the guards reacted to violations of rules that they arbitrarily constructed as if they were mandated to do so (and often did so forcefully, in ways that caused apparent pain and distress for the prisoners).

The SPE was conducted in the early 1970s, and its results and implications were widely disseminated in the years that immediately followed. The study was often cited as a prominent example of research that contributed directly to the "situational revolution" in psychology—the insight that context plays a powerful role in shaping people's thoughts and actions, especially in extreme settings (such as ones where social pressures are brought acutely to bear, where marked imbalances of power exist, and where all aspects of patient, inmate, or prisoner behavior are subject to control). It helped lead to the now more widely accepted proposition that no account of behavior can avoid a careful assessment of the situational influences on what people do, the things they believe, and even how they think.

The study also promised to have an impact on prison policy, at least in the years that immediately followed. This was a time in the history of the criminal justice system in the United States when the nation appeared open to fundamental reform of its crime control policies and penal practices. The message of the SPE—that context very much mattered in general and that, specifically, prison and prison-like environments had the inherent capacity to set powerful social-psychological forces in motion that could negatively affect the behavior of staff members and have adverse consequences for inmates—resonated perfectly with the spirit of these times.

However, for reasons that appeared more political than scientific, the nation's prison and crime control policies soon began to move in a fundamentally different direction. In the waning years of the 1970s and in the several decades that followed, the situational message of the SPE had little impact in correctional circles. Although evidence continued to mount in psychology and related disciplines that past and present circumstances and situations played a powerful role in influencing behavior, not only in penal institutions but in the origins of the criminal behavior those institutions were intended to address, sentencing laws and prison policies were implemented that seemed to ignore the most important lessons of the *situational revolution*. That is, crime control practices during these years focused even more narrowly on individual-level wrongdoing to the exclusion of situational models of crime prevention, and the potential role of context and circumstance in crime causation was increasingly discounted, even in sentencing guidelines (where "social factors" were explicitly deemed irrelevant).

In more recent years, however, the implications of the SPE became part of the national dialogue that occurred in response to the widely publicized abuse of prisoners at Abu Ghraib, Iraq, by members of the U.S. military. There appeared to be direct parallels between some of the mistreatment perpetrated by the guards in the SPE and the abuse that was inflicted on the prisoners at Abu Ghraib. Here, too, the explanation that situational forces had overcome the dispositions of the otherwise normal, healthy soldiers who perpetrated the abuse seemed cogent. The analysis of the behavior of the guards in the SPE *and* at Abu Ghraib pointed away from a "few bad apples" assessment of blame and focused instead on the abuse-engendering circumstances in which the guards functioned—a "faulty barrel" assessment, if you will—as well as the responsibility of the persons who created and maintained such a flawed environment for monitoring prisoners and guards alike.

Craig Haney and Philip G. Zimbardo

See also Intergroup Violence; Obedience to Authority; Power

Further Readings

Haney, C. (2006). *Reforming punishment: Psychological limits to the pains of imprisonment*. Washington, DC: American Psychological Association.

Haney, C., Banks, C., & Zimbardo, P. (1973). Interpersonal dynamics in a simulated prison. *International Journal of Criminology and Penology, 1,* 69–97.

Haney, C., & Zimbardo, P. (1977). The socialization into criminality: On becoming a prisoner and a guard. In J. Tapp & F. Levine (Eds.), *Law, justice, and the individual in society: Psychological and legal issues* (pp. 198–223). New York: Holt, Rinehart & Winston.

Haney, C., & Zimbardo, P. (1998). The past and future of U.S. prison policy: Twenty-five years after the Stanford prison experiment. *American Psychologist, 53,* 709–727.

Zimbardo, P. (2007). *The Lucifer effect: Understanding how good people turn evil*. New York: Random House.

Zimbardo, P., Maslach, C., & Haney, C. (1999). Reflections on the Stanford prison experiment: Genesis, transformations, consequences. In T. Blass (Ed.), *Obedience to authority: Current perspectives on the Milgram paradigm* (pp. 193–237). Hillsdale, NJ: Erlbaum.

STATUS

The *status* of individuals and groups refers to their social rank defined in terms of prestige or esteem.

Because status brings respect and deference, it is also closely associated with power. It is surely one of the most fundamental parameters governing the lives of humans and other social animals. It is also something that can be negotiated, constructed, challenged, and perpetuated in the process of social interaction. It is therefore of interest to social psychologists as both an independent variable (i.e., a cause) and a dependent variable (i.e., an effect). Indeed many research studies have examined status from both these perspectives, revealing much about the sources, the consequences, and the unfolding dynamics of status within and between groups.

The Intragroup Dynamics of Status

One of the early findings to emerge from the empirical scrutiny of group processes is that groups tend to form unequal status hierarchies. Seldom are groups arranged along entirely egalitarian lines. The Harvard sociologist Robert F. Bales convened small decision-making groups of undergraduate students and found that typically within the first hour-long meeting, a hierarchy of status had developed. Bales documented four specific, interdependent dimensions of status. High-status members (1) initiated and (2) were granted more opportunities to participate in decision making. Further, their ideas were (3) rated more favorably by and (4) had more influence over their peers. Usually, these status hierarchies formed quickly and smoothly. Where power struggles did occur, they postponed but did not cancel the development of a stable, unequal status hierarchy.

Status within these hierarchies can be earned or *achieved* on the basis of one's actions, or it can be assigned or *ascribed* on the basis of inherited characteristics, such as the status of one's family, race, or gender. This distinction is reflected in *expectation states theory*, by Joseph Berger. According to this theory, the status that group members grant to an individual depends on how much they expect he or she will help to contribute to realizing the group's goals. Individuals with characteristics that are *task relevant*, such as expertise and talent, will tend to be granted high status. But also, *diffuse* status characteristics, such as family, race, and gender, influence group members' perception that an individual may assist the group. Therefore, they influence the status

awarded to an individual. Indeed these traits are often more apparent than task-relevant characteristics in the early stages of group formation. They may therefore have an unduly powerful influence on the initial assignment of status.

This process, sometimes referred to as *status generalization,* illustrates how individuals' status outside the group affects their status within the group. It means that similar people tend to occupy high- and low-status positions within groups, even when the formation of each group is entirely independent. For example, when groups are composed of both men and women, men tend to occupy the high-status positions, be those groups political, cultural, religious, or economic. Thus, status hierarchies within local groups tend to enact and replicate global status hierarchies.

Once status hierarchies are formed, they tend to be reinforced and legitimized by group processes. A person's status characteristics influence the size of the contribution to the group's goals that the person will make. When a large contribution is expected of an individual, he or she tends to be given every opportunity to make one. Such individuals are given opportunities to contribute earlier than other members. Identical contributions are evaluated more favorably if made by a high- rather than a low-status individual. They are also rewarded more richly: Rewards within groups are assigned as a legitimizing marker of status independent of the value of a person's contribution to a group. Nowhere does this point seem to be illustrated more clearly than cases in which large salaries, bonuses, and pensions are paid to high-status executives even after the spectacular failure of the companies for which they are responsible.

The importance of family, race, and gender to status can be attributed to longstanding discriminatory systems of class, racism, and sexism, by which members of some social categories are advantaged relative to others. This is not the case, however, for the effect of height on status. The power of height to confer status seems to be reliable in both experiments and field studies, which show, for example, that CEOs are taller than average and that tall job applicants are more likely than others to be successful. The link between status and height is implicit in the etiquette of many cultures, in which low-status individuals bow, curtsey, or even sit or kneel to confirm the higher status of high-status individuals. It is also implicit in the pervasive cultural metaphors identified by the psycholinguist George Lakoff and the philosopher Mark Johnson in their book *Metaphors We Live By*. According to their analysis, metaphors such as "social climber," "upper class," and "ideas above one's station" reflect an underlying cultural equation of social status with physical height.

The role that status plays in regulating social interaction affects much more than the tendency to engage in "bowing and scraping." The social psychologist Roger Brown has suggested that across all known human cultures, status plays a key role in a universal norm that governs communication and intimacy. In societies that are stratified according to status, people reserve a respectful mode of communication for those who are either higher in status than themselves or socially distant. For example, in Medieval English, *thou* was used to address inferiors and familiar people, while *you* was reserved for superiors and strangers. This is an example of the so-called *T–V distinction* present in many languages (named after the French language, in which *tu* is familiar and *vous*, respectful). Similarly, the use of titles and surnames in address is associated with communication directed to someone who is either unfamiliar or who is higher in status, whereas use of first names signifies communication that is directed to an equal, an inferior, or someone with whom the speaker is close. Furthermore, any relaxation in formality is usually suggested by the communicator with higher status. Thus it is more typical for professors to suggest that a student address them by their first names than vice versa. Being high in status confers the privilege of control over intimacy.

Status has other powerful effects on the way that social interactions unfold from moment to moment. Studies of nonverbal language have shown that compared with persons of lower status, those high in status gaze more into the eyes of their conversation partners while talking, touch others more, stand in a more erect posture, and criticize more frequently. Conversation analyses have shown that people of higher status interrupt others more and are more likely to direct who takes turns in the conversation. Conversely, judicious use of these high-status types of body language and conversational style can sometimes be an effective way to win status.

In addition to affecting the body language of communicators and how they take turns in communication, status has effects on how communicators express themselves verbally. For example, in some settings, low-status speakers tend to use more polite and tentative language. Consistent with expectation states theory, this phenomenon is most likely to manifest itself when people of lower status talk to those higher in status and when the basis of status (e.g., gender, race, occupation, or class) is perceived to be relevant to the goals of the conversation.

Consequences of Intragroup Status

Once achieved, it is clear that social status has many social-psychological effects. High-status people are also likely to receive more flattery and more measured and mitigated forms of critical feedback, and they are likely to benefit from others' attempts to ingratiate themselves. However, discrepancies in status can raise suspicion about the motives of those who engage in ingratiation, as has been shown in research by the social psychologist Roos Vonk. Vonk found that attempts by low-status individuals to win the hearts and minds of high-status individuals with flattery and similar tactics of ingratiation may be seen for what they are and may subsequently backfire, producing less, rather than more, liking. Pithily, Vonk labeled this finding the *slime effect*. It is perhaps not surprising that independent observers, more than those who are personally being flattered and ingratiated, are more prone to the slime effect. Independent observers are less likely to suspect that the flattery may be strategic rather than heartfelt.

Status can also be seen as a form of social capital, allowing individuals to achieve their goals by exerting power or influence over others. A number of studies show that compliance is more likely to requests made by individuals with higher status and by representatives of organizations with higher status. One of the most famous demonstrations of the effect of status on compliance was provided by Stanley Milgram's studies of obedience. In these studies, participants complied with requests from an experimenter to deliver ostensibly strong doses of electricity to an innocent stranger. The effect generalizes to much more mundane and arguably less distressing requests, such as the calls for small donations made by charity workers. A parallel literature on so-called *source credibility* shows that a similar effect applies to persuasion. Attitudes are more likely to shift toward persuasive messages from high-status sources than from low-status sources. For example, identical editorials are more persuasive when attributed to prestigious newspapers than to less-prestigious tabloids.

Furthermore, a person's status may make him or her attractive to both individuals and groups. For example, high social status tends to confer sexual attractiveness on men, in particular. Evolutionary psychologists explain this effect in terms of the biological and social imperative for women to invest in their children and therefore to select mates who are likely to be willing and able to support them materially and socially. Alternatively, it is possible to explain this effect in terms of economic necessity and culturally determined sex roles.

In addition, groups are often keen to recruit individuals with high social status because the groups perceive these individuals to be able to assist in the realization of group aims. For example, the recruitment of high-status individuals allows groups to bathe in the associative glow of their prestige. High-status individuals may be able to employ their enhanced capacity for social influence to enhance ingroup cohesion and to successfully negotiate with external parties in the interests of the group.

Given all the social benefits that status confers, it is not surprising that it is also beneficial to physical well-being. A number of studies link status to health and longevity, even when related factors such as wealth are controlled for. One of the most striking and well-publicized examples was uncovered by University of Warwick economists Andrew Oswald and Matthew Rablen in 2005. They analyzed the life span data available for a sample of 524 nominees for the Nobel Prizes in physics and chemistry in the first half of the 20th century. The average life span of these nominees was 76 years, but the 135 winners among this group were found to have lived approximately 2 years longer when other factors, such as country of origin, were controlled for. The number of nominations received by scientists was not predictive of their life span, and neither was the size of the monetary award given to each laureate. As Oswald noted in an interview subsequent to the publication of this research, winning the Nobel Prize per se seemed to confer "a kind of health-giving magic."

Further research is required to establish precisely how social status translates to physical health and longevity. The prestige, power, and other forms of social capital conferred by status may play a role. But also, the health benefits of status may operate rather more directly. Researchers have observed immediate physiological responses to social status in human and nonhuman animals alike. For example, animals who are experimentally locked into a low-status or *subdominant* position display endocrinological changes involving elevated levels of harmful, stress-related chemicals in the blood. These changes are associated with heightened vigilance, agitation, and motivational disorientation. Low status therefore appears to be an aversive and unhealthy state for many social animals. In some animals, however, these effects disappear once status hierarchies have been established and each animal settles into its place in the regime. In these cases, animal behavior is reminiscent of some of the patterns predicted by Theodor Adorno's *authoritarian theory of personality* and its descendants, such as Robert Altemeyer's theory of *right wing authoritarianism*.

Social-Psychological Theories of Responses to Intra- and Intergroup Status

Social-psychological theories offer differing perspectives on how people respond to their position within their group and to their group's status within an intergroup hierarchy. According to both *social dominance theory* and authoritarian theories, many people prefer contexts in which there is a clear status hierarchy of groups to situations in which groups have equal status. Social dominance theory also suggests that people actively seek a dominant position for their group and support measures that might further this aim. In contrast, right wing authoritarianism is thought to lead to acquiescent or "yielding" responses to high status. Each theory derives support from a range of sources, including studies in which individual differences in social dominance orientation and right wing authoritarianism are measured. Individuals who are high in right wing authoritarianism and, depending on the social context, social dominance orientation prefer marked status hierarchies at both the interpersonal and the intergroup levels of society.

In contrast, *just world* and *system justification* theories are premised on the idea that people generally prefer to see the intra- and intergroup hierarchies that they occupy as fair. This means that if individuals occupy low-status positions within their group, they are apt to perceive themselves as deserving of that status. Reductions in self-esteem and especially perceptions that one is lacking in status-relevant attributes such as competence tend to follow. Similarly, members of low-status groups may be prone to *outgroup favoritism* in an unconscious attempt to justify their collective position, endorsing negative stereotypes of their own group and seeing higher-status groups as superior to their own on key traits such as competence.

According to these theories, how people feel about their personal status is more or less the same as how they feel about their group status. In contrast, *social identity theory* postulates a subtle interplay between people's perception of the status of themselves and their group. For example, members of low-status groups are less likely to take action to improve their collective lot if they perceive that group boundaries are permeable and that their personal status may therefore improve. They are also less likely to take action if they perceive the low status of their group to be legitimate and if they are unaware of alternative social contexts in which their group may have higher status. If status relations between groups are seen as illegitimate and alterable, then social identity is said to be insecure. When social identity is insecure, individuals are likely to take action to address the low status of their group.

The specific strategy that group members may use to enhance their status depends on contextual factors such as what is practical in the circumstances and how other groups react. For example, group members may, when possible, engage in social competition, in which they strive to better rival groups on the dimensions on which they are currently perceived as inferior. Or they may engage in strategies classed as *social creativity*. These strategies include attaching positive value to attributes that were hitherto seen as negative, choosing other attributes as the basis of compari-son with the outgroup, and choosing to compare themselves against other outgroups.

Of course, the status of one's own group in relation to others is not merely of symbolic importance, relevant only to collective self-esteem. Often, as recognized by social identity theory, it determines the resources that groups can gain for themselves. It also determines what groups can do to each other. According to Susan Fiske's *stereotype content model*, group members are motivated to know what other groups can do and want to do to their group. This means that they are particularly interested in two types of traits, namely, *competence* (is the group capable or not?) and *warmth* (does it mean well or ill?). High-status groups tend to be seen as competent but cold, whereas low-status groups are often seen as warm but incompetent. These stereotypes are likely to help observers justify inequality and to cope with conflicting information (e.g., prevailing negative representations of an outgroup on one hand, but a normative ban on prejudice on the other). Also, the stereotypes tend to offer an explanation for how the high- and low-status groups got where they are.

In general, it is probably fair to say that research and theorizing thus far permits more definite conclusions about the status of individuals than about the status of groups. For example, there is much research on how individuals come to achieve a certain level of social status but rather less on how groups do this. Typically, research and theory focus on how groups respond to a given level of status, a question that is hotly contested by a number of theories. Consensus has yet to be reached on key problems such as whether, and in what circumstances, high-status groups exhibit more prejudice and ingroup favoritism than low-status groups do. Nonetheless, it is clear that status is a crucial variable at the intra- and intergroup levels of human behavior.

Robbie M. Sutton

See also Authoritarian Personality; Discrimination; Dominance Hierarchies; Group Structure; Power; Right Wing Authoritarianism; Social Class; Social Dominance Theory; Social Identity Theory; Status Characteristics/Expectation States Theory; Status Construction Theory; Stereotypes; System Justification Theory

Further Readings

Hogg, M. A. (2001). A social identity theory of leadership. *Personality and Social Psychology Review*, 5, 184–200.

Kroger, R. O., & Wood, L. A. (1992). Are the rules of address universal? IV: Comparison of Chinese, Korean, Greek, and German usage. *Journal of Cross-Cultural Psychology*, 57, 416–425.

Levine, J. M., Moreland, R. L., & Choi, H. (2001). Group socialization and newcomer innovation. In M. A. Hogg & S. Tindale (Eds.), *Blackwell handbook of social psychology: Group processes* (pp. 86–106). Oxford, UK: Blackwell.

Marmot, M. (2004). *Status syndrome: How your social standing directly affects your health and life expectancy*. London: Bloomsbury.

Ridgeway, C. L. (2001). Social status and group structure. In M. A. Hogg & S. Tindale (Eds.), *Blackwell handbook of social psychology: Group processes* (pp. 353–375). Oxford, UK: Blackwell.

Ridgeway, C. L., & Smith-Lovin, L. (1999). The gender system and interaction. *Annual Review of Sociology*, 25, 191–216.

Turner, J. C., & Brown, R. (1978). Social status, cognitive alternatives and intergroup relations. In H. Tajfel (Ed.), *Differentiation between social groups* (pp. 201–234). London: Academic Press.

STATUS CHARACTERISTICS/ EXPECTATION STATES THEORY

When members of juries, project teams, or study groups differ by gender, race or ethnicity, or even physical attractiveness, how do these differences affect members' conduct? More generally, how does social status, the prestige one possesses based on one's differentially valued social distinctions, affect people's behavior during group encounters? *Status characteristics theory* (SCT), which is a part of the theoretical research program called *expectation states theory*, explains this group-level phenomenon. SCT describes the social-psychological process that produces a *status hierarchy*—a rank order of people that is based on social prestige— within certain kinds of groups. Knowing the particulars of SCT has allowed researchers to craft powerful intervention strategies designed to inhibit the deleterious effects of status inequalities. This entry describes how this line of research developed, what SCT says about group relations, and how the ideas have been applied in interventions.

What Is Expectation States Theory?

During the 1960s, three researchers at Stanford University developed expectation states theory: Joseph Berger, Bernard Cohen, and Morris Zelditch Jr. The type of formal theory they used, along with the subject matter they studied, became known as the *Stanford tradition* of sociological social psychology.

Expectation states theory is not a unitary theory but rather a theoretical research program comprising a set of interrelated, middle-range theories. SCT is one of this set of middle-range theories, as is *reward expectation states theory*, *status legitimation theory*, *source theory*, *status construction theory*, and many others. Several similarities exist among these theories, but the two most central and important concepts that unite them are expectation state and status situation.

Expectation State

An expectation state is an out-of-awareness anticipation or hunch about one's capacity to engender the behaviors, attitudes, and competence necessary to elicit more (or less) deference from other group members. Expectation states have four important properties.

1. They are activated nonconsciously. People are not aware of the instantaneous mental process that occurs when expectation states begin to affect their actions. Psychological social psychologists refer to this kind of mental activity as implicit processing, as opposed to explicit processing, which entails conscious thinking.

2. An expectation state is a relative notion: People cannot have a higher level of expectation for their actions if they do not compare their capacities with those of others within a group.

3. An expectation state is distinctive to the specific social situation. Just because an expectation state is triggered in one situation does not mean that it will be triggered in other situations.

4. An expectation state is unobservable, in that we cannot directly measure when an expectation state is activated. However, we can presume that an expectation state has been activated by observing the behavioral inequalities displayed by group members. These differences in behavior are indicators of the presence of an activated expectation state.

The type of expectation state central to SCT is the performance expectation: an out-of-awareness anticipation of one's capacity and abilities relative to those of other group members to complete a group task successfully.

Status Situation

The other important concept central to expectation states theory is the status situation. This is a micro-encounter in which two or more people work on a task given to a group to complete successfully. Roles for each group member are not formally assigned before the beginning of the group's work. Rather, group members organize their roles and behaviors informally, on their own, as they carry out the task.

In formal theoretical terms, a group's circumstance is considered to be a status situation if the group meets two criteria, or scope conditions: The group must be both task oriented and collectively oriented. Scope conditions are situations in which researchers are able to guarantee that the propositions of expectation states theory will apply. If a group is both task oriented and collectively oriented, then the group falls within the boundaries specified by theories involving expectation states. If a group does not meet these scope conditions, theorists are not assured that the propositions for the theory being applied will be confirmed, nor are they certain that an expectation state will be activated.

Task-oriented groups are those whose members are committed to completing a task that they perceive as having either a successful or unsuccessful outcome. Collectively oriented groups are those whose members believe that it is necessary, and in fact right and proper, for them to take each other's behaviors and opinions into account when completing the task. Examples of task-oriented and collectively oriented groups include juries during deliberations, special project teams assembled

within businesses, and study groups of students who are assigned a project for which they will all receive the same grade.

With the notions of expectation states and status situations, researchers have proposed several theories to describe how status hierarchies affect groups. This entry focuses on SCT. To introduce this theory, some important concepts must first be defined.

What Is a Status Characteristic?

A status characteristic is any recognized social distinction that has attached to it widely shared beliefs about at least two categories, or states, of the distinction. Those possessing one category, the positive state, are more valued socially than those possessing the complementary category, the negative state. Different states of a status characteristic confer social advantages and disadvantages on actors who have the traits and attributes associated with the respective state.

Status characteristics convey assessments of individuals' capacities to other actors. SCT posits that the different states of the status characteristic will be attached to differential evaluations of ability. For example, gender is a status characteristic with the positive state typically being male and the negative state being female. In general, there are widely held cultural beliefs suggesting that men possess higher ability than do women on a large range of tasks.

Two types of status characteristics exist. A *specific status characteristic* is one that is applicable to one type of task and is associated with a distinct performance expectation. For instance, ability to do calculus is a specific status characteristic: Those who possess the positive state are expected to be able to solve calculus problems; those who possess the negative state are considered much less likely to have the ability to solve this type of math problem. A *diffuse status characteristic* is one that is both applicable to more than one type of task and is associated with a general performance expectation. Gender is a diffuse status characteristic: Males are believed to have more ability on many tasks, such as solving math problems and mechanical difficulties in cars, than do females. And males are often viewed as more competent in general than are females.

It is essential to note that ability evaluations surrounding the different states of diffuse status characteristics are based on perceptions and cultural belief systems, and not necessarily on reality. For example, the gender gap in the math SAT scores has narrowed to the point that it is no longer statistically significant. However, the perception that males are better in math than females are still persists in our society.

It is also crucial to note that, not always but often, diffuse status characteristics mirror the macrolevel social inequalities of a society. For example, in the United States, experimental tests have demonstrated that race, ethnicity, physical attractiveness, military rank, sexual orientation, and occupational ranks and positions are diffuse status characteristics. One could demonstrate that these status characteristics are also the general axes of inequality in the United States, representing systems of unequal income distributions, educational attainment, and the like.

Finally, the nature of the task may determine which state of a diffuse status characteristic is positive and which is negative. For instance, in 1988 John Dovidio and his colleagues demonstrated that male was the negative state and female was the positive state on a sewing task, even though many tailors are male. Because sewing is widely believed to be a female-centric task, the states of the status characteristic gender were reversed, compared with general attitudes about the relationship between competence and gender.

The Status-Organizing Process

How do status characteristics organize behavior in groups? Which ones matter? What if I possess a positive state on one status characteristic but a negative state on another—do they somehow cancel each other out? These questions are answered by SCT. Its assumptions explicate a status-organizing process, often referred to as *status generalization*. The status-organizing process described by SCT is one in which status characteristics and their concomitant ability evaluations, based on widely shared beliefs and perceptions, result in observable behavioral inequalities during microencounters.

At this point, it is important to note that expectation states theorists do not believe that the status generalization process describes how group members *should* behave. These researchers do not support the notion that women should be evaluated lower than men, for example. In fact, the primary motivation for most expectation states theorists is first to recognize that social inequalities exist and affect behavior and then to study how these adverse circumstances can be changed. Without understanding the processes that create inequalities, even the best-intentioned programs designed to eradicate them may not make a difference. Understanding the deleterious consequences of status generalization is the first step in eliminating those consequences.

Status generalization occurs within groups that fit within the scope conditions of expectation states theory. In lay terms, that means the group members are working together to achieve a shared goal. Five assumptions depict status generalization.

The first is called the *salience assumption*. It describes the conditions under which status characteristics activate status generalization. We possess states of myriad status characteristics, so which ones matter for the process? The salience assumption states that those status characteristics that discriminate between actors, the ones in which at least one group member possesses one state and another member the complementary state, will activate status generalization. Also, if a status characteristic is perceived as culturally linked to the task at the start of a group encounter, even if it does not differentiate members, then it will still be salient. An example of this situation would be a group of three men working on a sewing task. Gender does not distinguish group members but is salient because it is related to the task.

The second assumption is called the *burden of proof assumption*. It refers to whether a status characteristic that becomes salient remains salient. For a status characteristic to stay germane to the situation, group members need do nothing. Unless group members know that the status characteristic has nothing to do with the task, they perceive it as if it is pertinent to the situation. However, to "deactivate" the salient characteristic, group members must actively dissociate the status advantages and disadvantages conferred on group members by that salient status characteristic. In other words, the burden of proof for whether a status characteristic is relevant to a task at hand lies with someone who might persuasively demonstrate its irrelevance. For example, suppose a group of individuals is gathered to fix a broken-down car. Unless these people know for sure that gender is not relevant to fixing a car, then gender will remain salient during the period that the group works together. If, however, a mechanic joins the group and firmly states that neither men nor women are better at fixing cars, then the status characteristic may no longer be salient.

The third assumption is called *sequencing*. If new information about status characteristics is made known to a group, or if new people join the group, then the new information is added to the original group members' status ordering. However, a trace of the initial ordering would remain and affect group behavior as long as the original members stay within the group. The restructuring done with the new information would follow the rules proposed by the salience and burden of proof assumptions.

The fourth assumption states that group members combine all the information conveyed by salient status characteristics. All status information from positive states is combined into one grouping and assigned a positive score; all negative information is combined into another grouping and assigned a negative score. This *combining process* includes a weighting scheme such that for each grouping, any additional, similarly signed information has less incremental effect on the overall positive or negative grouping score (this is known as the *attenuation effect*). Combining also includes a second weighting scheme such that those status elements more relevant to the task have a higher impact on the positive or negative grouping scores. Finally, after taking the weighting schemes into consideration, the positive and negative grouping scores are added together. This computation, known as the *principle of organized subsets*, creates a performance expectation profile that is compared with others' profiles. A group member's expectation advantage or disadvantage can be calculated by subtracting another member's performance expectation profile from his or her own. A group's rank order of these expectation profiles represents the *theoretical power and prestige order* of the group—the status hierarchy. It is important to remember that this mathematical procedure is a heuristic for how people process status information,

not necessarily an actual cognitive model. A complete graph-theoretic rendering of this model is presented in the book titled *Status Characteristics and Social Interaction: An Expectation States Approach*, published in 1977 by Joseph Berger and his colleagues.

The fifth and final assumption, the *basic expectation assumption*, posits that the theoretical power and prestige order will translate into the behavior of the group members who will display behavioral inequalities. The unequal distribution of behaviors is referred to as the *observable power and prestige order*. If person A has a higher performance expectation profile than person B (i.e., person A has more status than person B), then A will receive more action opportunities to participate in the task, make more performance outputs to solve problems related to the task, obtain higher performance evaluations, and exert more influence than B will. Other behaviors that would likely indicate A's performance expectation advantage over B are differential rates of gesturing, disparate rates of maintaining eye gaze, and unequal ratios of fluent to nonfluent speech.

Two final comments are warranted. First, the processes associated with the five assumptions occur among group members simultaneously. Because of widely shared cultural understandings about the information provided by status characteristics, the processes will be the same and will happen concurrently for all group members. Second, cultural understandings about status characteristics, and not necessarily individual meanings, are what trigger status generalization. So, for example, a woman may personally believe that she is as competent as, or even more competent than, any man working on a task with her. However, she may also believe that men get paid more than women and are generally perceived as being more competent than women. She will expect that the other group members will respond to male workmates in a fashion consistent with these shared beliefs. These beliefs will activate status generalization (if gender is a salient status characteristic) despite her personal beliefs about her own abilities.

Interventions

Researchers have created intervention strategies to prevent status-organizing processes from happening or to impede these processes once they have occurred. A good example is the work of Elizabeth Cohen, a former professor at Stanford University. Cohen recognized that student groups assigned to work on classroom projects often experience status generalization. She devised two interventions to reduce this tendency—the *multiple abilities* and the *assigned competence* treatments. In the former intervention, teachers develop group tasks that require many roles with associated abilities for completion. Teachers then tell students that their task requires the contributions of all group members, because people are not good at every role. In the latter intervention, teachers observe students' behaviors in groups to determine students' typical status positions. During subsequent group tasks, teachers tell students to pay attention to the abilities of low-status group members, because these students can make useful contributions to task completion. There is some evidence that these interventions can reduce status generalization in classrooms.

Alison J. Bianchi

See also Dominance Hierarchies; Group Structure; Implicit Prejudice; Power; Self-Fulfilling Prophecy; Status; Status Construction Theory

Further Readings

Berger, J., Fişek, M. H., Norman, R. Z., & Zelditch, M., Jr. (1977). *Status characteristics and social interaction: An expectation states approach.* New York: Elsevier.

Berger, J., Rosenholtz, S., & Zelditch, M., Jr. (1980). Status organizing processes. *Annual Review of Sociology, 6,* 479–508.

Berger, J., & Webster, M., Jr. (2006). Expectations, status, and behavior. In P. J. Burke (Ed.), *Contemporary social psychological theories* (pp. 268–300). Stanford, CA: Stanford University Press.

Cohen, E. G. (1982). Expectation states and interracial interaction in school settings. *Annual Review of Sociology, 8,* 209–235.

Dovidio, J. F., Brown, C. E., Heltmann, K., Ellyson, S. L., & Keating, C. F. (1988). Power displays between women and men in discussions of gender-linked tasks: A multichannel study. *Journal of Personality and Social Psychology, 55,* 580–587.

Ridgeway, C. L., & Walker, H. A. (1995). Status structures. In K. S. Cook, G. A. Fine, & J. S. House (Eds.), *Sociological perspectives on social psychology* (pp. 281–310). Boston: Allyn & Bacon.

Wagner, D. G., & Berger, J. (2002). Expectation states theory: An evolving research program. In J. Berger & M. Zelditch Jr. (Eds.), *New directions in contemporary sociological theory* (pp. 41–76). Lanham, MD: Rowman & Littlefield.

Webster, M., Jr., & Foschi, M. (1988). Overview of status generalization. In M. Webster Jr. & M. Foschi (Eds.), *Status generalization: New theory and research* (pp. 1–20). Stanford, CA: Stanford University Press.

STATUS CONSTRUCTION THEORY

Status construction theory describes social processes that transform nominal differences among people—such as ethnicity, sex, occupation, or religion—into status distinctions in a society or population. A social difference becomes a status distinction when people develop beliefs that those in one category of the social difference (e.g., Whites, men) are more socially respected and are presumed to be more competent at socially valued tasks than are those in another category of that difference (e.g., people of color, women). These status beliefs, when widely shared in the population, have consequences for inequality among both individuals and social groups. Thus, to explain how a social difference becomes a status distinction, status construction theory describes (a) how status beliefs can be created and spread in interpersonal encounters among socially different actors and (b) the social conditions under which these beliefs are likely to become widespread in the population.

A distinctive aspect of status beliefs is that both those in the social category favored by a belief and those in the category less favored by the belief hold similar beliefs that "most people" view the favored group as better than the other group. As beliefs about what "most people" think, status beliefs are a type of social reputation. Status construction theory proposes one set of processes by which such status beliefs could form, although there are likely to be other ways as well. This entry examines how the theory developed, summarizes its contents, and briefly reviews supporting evidence.

Historical Overview

Status construction theory developed in the context of a well-established body of theory and research on status hierarchies among individuals in groups. Beginning in the 1950s, a long tradition of empirical research, particularly that associated with status characteristics and expectation states theories, showed that the influence and deference individuals attain in groups is powerfully shaped by differences among them in social characteristics that carry status value in the larger society. Differences in occupation and sex, for instance, affect people's influence on juries.

It was unknown, however, how status beliefs developed about such social differences. Drawing on this body of research, status construction theory argues that if existing status beliefs are powerfully at play in encounters among people who differ in socially recognized ways, then such encounters are also likely to be arenas in which new status beliefs are created, spread, and maintained.

The theory takes as a starting point the existence of a social difference that is widely recognized in a population but about which no shared evaluation has yet developed. It also assumes that people from different categories of this social difference are interdependent in that they must regularly cooperate in order to achieve what they want or need. Under these conditions, the theory argues, the local contexts in which people from different social categories encounter one another have the potential to induce the participants to form shared status beliefs about their difference.

Basics of Status Construction Theory

The theory's arguments about how local encounters create status beliefs can be summarized as follows. In cooperative, goal-oriented encounters between categorically different people, interpersonal hierarchies of influence and status are likely to develop among the participants just as they do in virtually all goal-oriented encounters. Such interpersonal influence hierarchies develop implicitly, through multiple small behaviors. One person speaks up, for instance, while another holds back or responds hesitantly. Because participants rarely notice these behaviors, the actual origins of their influence hierarchy are usually obscure to them at the same time that the categorical difference between them is salient. As a consequence, there is a probability that the participants will associate their apparent difference in esteem and competence in the situation with their corresponding categorical difference.

To the extent that this association between the categorical difference and influence appears to be consensually accepted in the situation, rather than resisted or challenged, it seems socially valid to the participants. The backing of legitimate authority will also make the correspondence between difference and influence seem socially valid to participants. If the same association with influence is repeated for these participants in subsequent encounters with people from the other category, its apparent validity will be further strengthened.

Eventually, the apparent validity of the association between the categorical distinction and influence in encounters induces actors to believe that, whether they like it or not, "most people" outside the encounters also would accept that people who differ on the categorical distinction also differ in esteem and competence. In this way, actors form generalized status beliefs about the categorical distinction even when these beliefs disadvantage their own categorical group.

Once people form status beliefs about the distinction, they carry these beliefs to their next encounters with those from the other group who may not be aware of the belief. Yet, by treating categorically different others according to the new status belief, belief holders induce at least some of the others to take on the belief as well. In effect, they "teach" the others the belief by acting on it. This in turn creates a diffusion process that spreads the new status belief in the population.

The theory's second set of arguments focuses on the structural conditions under which beliefs formed in encounters can disseminate widely. The most important condition is whether there is an unequal distribution between the groups of some factor, such as material resources or technology, that is helpful in gaining influence in intercategory encounters. If so, it becomes likely that people from the categorical group with more of the factor (e.g., the richer group) will more often than not emerge as the most influential actors in encounters with people from the group with less of the factor (the poorer group). This causes the intercategory encounters taking place all across the population to continually foster more status beliefs favoring the structurally advantaged group than favoring the other categorical group. As these beliefs spread through future encounters, beliefs favoring the structurally advantaged group will eventually overwhelm counterbeliefs and become nearly consensual in the population. Thus, the theory argues that if a factor that creates an influence advantage in encounters is unequally distributed between categorical groups, status beliefs favoring the structurally advantaged group will develop and spread to become widely shared in the population.

Although the theory frames its arguments in terms of the creation of new status beliefs, it also explains the maintenance of existing beliefs. If structural conditions described by the theory are currently present, such as an inequality in resources between categorical groups, then status construction processes will act to maintain status beliefs about the categorical difference, whether or not these processes played a role in the actual historical origins of these status beliefs. Thus, status construction processes can cause status beliefs based on race, gender, or other social differences to persist in contemporary societies even after the original historical causes of those status beliefs have disappeared.

Supportive Evidence

Two types of evidence support these theoretical arguments. Computer simulations have shown that if encounters between socially different actors actually do create and spread status beliefs as the theory argues, then the development of nearly consensual status beliefs about the difference would indeed be a logical result of the structural conditions the theory posits. In addition to this logical support, experiments have examined whether people do form and spread status beliefs in encounters with different others.

These experiments have shown that people form clearly defined status beliefs about a previously unevaluated categorical difference from only two repeated encounters with members of the other category in which influence hierarchies developed that corresponded to actors' categorical difference. Participants formed beliefs favoring the categorical group that was consistently more influential in the encounters even when these beliefs cast the participant's own group as lower status. Research has also demonstrated that the formation of status beliefs in these encounters turns on social validity, as the theory argues. When the apparent consensual acceptance of the influence hierarchies in these encounters was challenged by a participant, status beliefs did not form.

Additional experiments have shown that when the influence hierarchies in these intercategory encounters are biased by a structural factor, such as material resources, the beliefs that people form favor the resource-advantaged category, as predicted. Moreover, once people form status beliefs in encounters, they spontaneously treat the next person they encounter from the other category according to their new belief (although men do this more quickly than women do). Finally, there is evidence that, by treating someone in the situation according to the belief, people can spread their beliefs to others, creating a diffusion process that allows beliefs to spread widely.

Cecilia L. Ridgeway

See also Dominance Hierarchies; Group Structure; Power; Status; Status Characteristics/Expectation States Theory

Further Readings

Ridgeway, C. L. (1991). The social construction of status value: Gender and other nominal characteristics. *Social Forces, 70,* 367–386.

Ridgeway, C. L. (2006). Status construction theory. In P. Burke (Ed.), *Contemporary social psychological theories* (pp. 301–323). Stanford, CA: Stanford University Press.

Webster, M., & Hysom, S. J. (1998). Creating status characteristics. *American Sociological Review, 63,* 351–379.

STEPLADDER TECHNIQUE

The *stepladder technique* is a structured procedure designed to facilitate effective group decision making. The goal is to ensure that the thoughts and ideas of all members are made available to the group so that they can be considered while the group is reaching a decision. The importance of this goal is underscored by research by Gary

Stasser, James Larson, and others indicating that groups frequently fail to consider relevant information and that this can seriously impair the quality of group decisions. This entry describes the technique and looks at research outcomes.

The stepladder technique was developed by Steven Rogelberg, Janet Barnes-Farrell, and Charles Lowe. It involves the sequential entry of members into a discussion group. The order in which members enter the group is randomly determined. At the first step, two of the group members (the core group) discuss the issue and reach a tentative understanding. Next, a third person joins the group and shares his or her thoughts with the members of the core group. This is followed by a discussion among the three members. Next, a fourth person joins the group, shares his or her thoughts, and additional group discussion ensues. This procedure continues until all group members have presented and discussed their ideas. At that point, the group reaches a final decision.

In addition to the sequential entry of members into the discussion, the technique involves other procedures. Group members are provided with the decision task and given time to think about it before group discussion. The discussion is structured so that each person added to the core group is required to state his or her thoughts before learning the ideas and preferences of the other members. As each member is added, the group is given adequate time for discussion. The final decision is not made until all members have provided their thoughts and the entire group has discussed the problem and potential solutions.

The stepladder technique was designed to overcome some of the more common sources of process losses in groups. Process losses are ineffective group processes that limit the effectiveness of groups. Process losses frequently occur in group discussions and often keep groups from performing as effectively as they potentially could. In decision-making groups, a few members may dominate the discussion while other members participate little or not at all. As demonstrated by Michael Diehl, Wolfgang Stroebe, and others, members may fail to participate because they can easily slack off on group projects, they feel their contributions are not needed, or they are shy or inhibited by other members. Often only a very few suggestions are considered before a group reaches

a decision. Once one suggestion begins to get support, this tends to inhibit other members from adding new suggestions. Group members may be reluctant to openly disagree with positions of high-status members. Thus, members may remain silent rather than offer alternative perspectives. Members frequently conform to the ideas of other members because they do not want to disagree openly or because they devalue their own ideas when they find that these ideas differ from the group consensus. The stepladder technique is an attempt to limit these problems.

The initial two-person discussion and the sequential addition of members who must share their thoughts and potential solutions with the other group members serve to ensure that all members participate in the group discussion. Members' expressing their ideas before hearing the opinions of others should lessen conformity pressures and result in a wider range of ideas and potential solutions. This feature not only increases the chances that a high-quality solution is proposed, but it also exposes any conflicting views that may exist. The consideration of opposing viewpoints within a cooperative framework can lead to more careful deliberation and a more refined solution. Thus, the stepladder technique offers an approach that can lead to a more complete use of member expertise and promises to improve the quality of group decision making.

Research Evidence

Only a limited number of empirical studies have been conducted to evaluate the stepladder technique, but they indicate that the technique can lead to meaningful improvements in group decision performance. Groups using the stepladder technique reach decisions of higher quality than do groups using unstructured methods (in which all members work collectively to reach a decision). Moreover, the decision made by a stepladder group is likely to exceed the quality of the individual decision made by the best member of the group.

Some potential reasons the stepladder technique facilitates effective group decisions have been investigated. Compared with group members using unstructured methods, members of groups using the stepladder technique report positive climate effects (e.g., less pressure to conform, better teamwork) and greater levels of effort. Although these factors may lead to decisions of higher quality, their impact on performance of stepladder groups has not been assessed. Evidence also suggests that the stepladder technique leads to more effective use of group members' expertise. In stepladder groups, but not in conventional groups, the most expert member is more likely than other members to report having ample opportunity to express his or her ideas. There is also evidence that the most expert member exerts the most influence on the group decision in stepladder groups, but not in conventional groups. Finally, in stepladder groups, but not in conventional groups, the performance of the best member is highly related to group decision quality. Although these factors may account for some of the improvements in decision effectiveness in stepladder groups, additional work is needed to understand when and why such groups are effective.

Despite the fact that, in stepladder groups, members of the core group participate in all discussions and other members enter later, these latter people do not experience the group less favorably or have less impact on group decisions. That is, members added later do not differ from those in the initial core in terms of influence, feelings of involvement, or cohesion. Finally, it is worth noting that, while the stepladder technique leads to more effective group decisions, there is some cost in terms of time. This time cost may be inconsequential in some cases, but the technique may not be appropriate when time demands are extreme.

Some efforts have been made to study the boundary conditions of the effectiveness of stepladder groups. For example, when the technique was first developed, the timing of entry of members into the group was controlled by the researcher. Later studies have indicated that the technique is also effective when group members themselves determine the timing of entry of new members. In addition, although the stepladder technique was initially used with face-to-face groups, recent studies have examined its utility with virtual groups (in which members are not located together but instead interact via electronic communication). Results indicate that the technique leads to more effective decisions for groups that communicate via a telephone conference call, but not for those in which members interact by sending computer-based text messages.

The reasons for this discrepancy are not clear, but they may be related to factors such as the quantity or distribution of communication, availability of paralinguistic cues, or members' feelings about the group—factors that may differ across the two types of virtual groups.

Directions for Future Research

Additional research is needed on the boundary conditions for the effectiveness of stepladder groups. For example, all the studies to date have used a single type of task, the survival exercise. In this task, participants rank order items in terms of their utility for survival in an inhospitable environment, such as a remote area during severe winter conditions. Studies that examine the effectiveness of the technique across a variety of other tasks would therefore be useful. Another area in which additional work is needed involves group size. At present, all studies have used four-person groups. It is possible that the technique may prove too cumbersome and time-consuming for use with larger groups.

Studies to date have used laboratory groups in which members typically are unacquainted and there is no existing group structure. Because such groups are in some ways similar to project teams and virtual teams used in organizations, findings from laboratory studies may well generalize to these types of groups. It is less clear, however, how well the technique will work in intact teams in which members work together for long periods of time. One question concerns the willingness of members of intact teams to continue using the technique. Because of the persistence of norms and resistance to change in such groups, their members may revert to more traditional modes of group discussion once the intervention is over. An evaluation of the long-term use of the stepladder technique in intact work groups would therefore be worthwhile.

In summary, the stepladder technique is a very promising approach to group decision making. It seems to minimize a number of process problems that limit the effectiveness of conventional decision-making groups. However, additional work is needed to specify the conditions under which the technique is effective.

Glenn E. Littlepage

See also Conformity; Delphi Technique; Group Problem Solving and Decision Making; Hidden Profile Task; Social Loafing

Further Readings

Rogelberg, S. G., Barnes-Farrell, J. L., & Lowe, C. A. (1992). The stepladder technique: An alternative group structure facilitating effective group decision making. *Journal of Applied Psychology, 77,* 730–737.

Rogelberg, S. G., & O'Connor, M. S. (1998). Extending the stepladder technique: An examination of self-paced stepladder groups. *Group Dynamics: Theory, Research, and Practice, 2,* 82–91.

Rogelberg, S. G., O'Connor, M. S., & Sederburg, M. (2002). Using the stepladder technique to facilitate the performance of audioconferencing groups. *Journal of Applied Psychology, 87,* 994–1000.

Thompson, L. F., & Coovert, M. D. (2002). Stepping up to the challenge: A critical examination of face-to-face and computer-mediated team decision making. *Group Dynamics: Theory, Research, and Practice, 6,* 52–64.

West, M. A. (2004). *Effective teamwork: Practical lessons from organizational research* (2nd ed.). Malden, MA: BPS Blackwell.

Stereotype Threat

Stereotype threat occurs when people confront the possibility that their own behavior could confirm a negative stereotype about a group to which they belong. The fear associated with confirming an unwanted stereotype can prevent a person from performing up to his or her true potential, and when this occurs for many members of a stigmatized group, the average performance of the group is decreased, creating the appearance that the group lacks ability in that domain.

Stereotype threat research helps to explain long-observed gender and racial differences in performance, particularly in standardized testing. These persistent gaps in performance have fueled an ongoing controversy over whether race differences in IQ scores or sex differences in math performance are due to environmental factors, such as socioeconomic disadvantages or a history of biased socialization, or to biological factors, such as genetic, hormonal, or neurological differences that correlate with race or sex.

Stereotype threat enters this debate as a theory that takes a different approach. It argues that even if one could perfectly match students for their biological or environmental history, the mere knowledge of gender or racial stereotypes would create group differences in performance that give the appearance of group differences in ability. By pointing to situational factors that help produce these performance differences, stereotype threat offers a more optimistic account that lends itself to solutions. This entry will summarize when stereotype threat occurs, who is most susceptible, the psychological mechanisms by which performance is impaired, and how stereotype threat can be reduced.

How and When Is Stereotype Threat Elicited?

Stereotype threat was first documented empirically by Claude Steele and Joshua Aronson in 1995. In one seminal study, Black college students performed worse than their White peers on a task that was described to them as a diagnostic measure of verbal ability, an effect that paralleled the race gap typically found on standardized tests. However, when the same task was described to a second half of the sample as a simple laboratory exercise and unrelated to intelligence, Black students performed significantly better on the task, and their performance was not significantly different from that of their White counterparts after their prior SAT scores were taken into account. This effect demonstrates that subtle situational cues can impair performance and exacerbate the appearance of group differences in ability.

Since the phenomenon was first identified, stereotype threat has been firmly established as an effect that can be created for any group in the right situation. Stereotype threat has been examined as a cause of women's underperformance in math, Latinos' underperformance on intellectual tests, and older adults' poorer memory performance. White men, a group that is not typically stigmatized, show lower performance on a math test when told that their ability will be compared with that of Asian men, a group stereotyped to be mathematically superior. Studies also show that Asian American women perform better on a math test when reminded of their Asian background but perform worse when reminded of their gender. Again, this result shows that simple features of the situation, such as reminders of one's race or gender, can affect how one performs.

Stereotype threat has also been shown outside the classroom, in athletic performance. For example, White athletes do worse at a golf putting task when told that the task measures natural athletic ability (a trait White athletes are stereotyped to lack), whereas Black athletes do worse when told that the task measures sports intelligence (a trait Black athletes are stereotyped to lack).

In general, stereotype threat occurs when aspects of individuals' environment subtly remind them that their behavior in that context is relevant to negative stereotypes targeted against their group. These reminders of group stereotypes can be as simple as merely knowing that the task is diagnostic of an ability that one's group is stereotyped to lack. But stereotype threat can also be experienced after only a very simple reminder that one belongs to a stigmatized group. For example, being the only woman taking a math test, being asked to indicate one's race, or even watching stereotypical television commercials before a test have all been shown to impair performance. Finally, it is important to note the performance decrements are exhibited only on tasks that are complex or require the active manipulation of large amounts of information. If a task is relatively easy, one's motivation to disconfirm the stereotype leads to better overall performance, or *stereotype reactance*.

Recent theory suggests that stereotype threat is not a unitary phenomenon but instead can take multiple forms. For some, threat is created by a fear that they could confirm a stereotype in their own eyes, whereas others might be more concerned about confirming the stereotype held by other people, either those who are similarly stereotyped or those who are part of the non-stigmatized majority. In addition, the target of the threat can be either oneself or one's personal identity (I don't want to be seen stereotypically) or one's social identity (I don't want my group to be seen stereotypically). This conceptual analysis results in several distinct forms of stereotype threat, each with some unique properties, but all of which lead to underperformance compared with one's true ability.

Who Is Most Susceptible to Stereotype Threat?

Several individual difference variables make some individuals more susceptible to stereotype threat effects on their performance. For example, although individuals need not endorse the stereotype to experience stereotype threat, research has shown that women who buy into gender stereotypes about men's superior math skills are more susceptible than other women to stereotype threat effects on their math performance. In addition, individuals who are most invested in doing well in a given domain are the ones who will be most susceptible to the threat that their performance could confirm a negative stereotype. Likewise, individuals who are strongly identified with their group, and perhaps have the most invested in maintaining a positive image of that social identity, also experience stereotype threat more strongly. It is not surprising that individuals high in stigma consciousness, those who are chronically aware of being viewed through the lens of stereotypes, are more susceptible than others to the effects of stereotype threat on their performance.

In addition to these factors that increase susceptibility to stereotype threat, several other individual difference variables related to more general coping abilities have been shown to moderate stereotype threat effects on performance. For example, situations of stereotype threat are thought to force individuals to consciously monitor their behavior with respect to the context. Thus, those who are already highly practiced at such self-monitoring processes are better able than others to cope with the effects of stereotype threat. In addition, having a sense of humor is generally associated with more successful coping, and research suggests that it also buffers individuals from the experience of stereotype threat. However, individuals with an internal locus of control, who are used to feeling that they have the ability to control their outcomes, do not fare as well in situations of stereotype threat.

What Processes Underlie the Effects of Stereotype Threat on Performance?

Considerable progress has been made in identifying the physiological, affective, and cognitive processes that combine to explain why stereotype threat impairs performance. Situations of stereotype threat elicit a physiological stress response. This heightened state of stress arousal is paired with greater vigilance to the situation in an effort to consciously monitor one's behavior for signs that one is confirming the stereotype. Because of this focus on detecting failure, individuals are more likely to interpret aspects of their experience, such as errors they make or even their own level of arousal, as indicating poor performance, leading to more negative thoughts and heightened feelings of anxiety. However, because they are especially threatened by feeling anxious when performing under the burden of negative stereotypes, individuals try to suppress or avoid these anxious thoughts and feelings.

Three of these elements—increased physiological stress, conscious monitoring of behavior, and active suppression of thoughts and feelings—are likely to cause impairments in working memory efficiency. Working memory refers to our ability to mentally manipulate information. It involves focusing attention on a central task while inhibiting irrelevant information or distractions, a skill that is central to performance on tasks such as reading comprehension, memorization, spatial rotation, and math calculations. Thus, situations of stereotype threat affect the same working memory resources often needed for successful performance on a range of mental tasks. Research also shows that stereotype threat impairs performance on well-learned motor tasks by increasing conscious attention to performing a sequence of physical behaviors, when relying on well-learned and automated muscle movements would lead to better performance.

How Can Stereotype Threat Be Reduced?

Research into the basic parameters of stereotype threat has led to important discoveries of ways in which stereotype threat effects can be reduced. First, it is already clear that situations that minimize reminders of negative stereotypes diminish group differences in performance. For example, the race and gender gap in test performance decreases when a set of verbal or math problems is described as a laboratory exercise that is not diagnostic of any ability. However, in many testing contexts, it is hard to deny that one's performance will be interpreted as an indicator of inherent skill. If this alone can elicit stereotype threat, what other interventions can be employed?

Reducing reminders of group membership is another way to minimize stereotype threat effects on performance. In a recent reanalysis of a field experiment of students taking an advanced placement calculus exam, researchers found that having students indicate their gender after instead of just before the test led to a 33% reduction in the gender gap in test scores (although the same manipulation did not have a significant effect for minority tests takers). An alternative to downplaying one's group membership is to highlight the existence of positive role models or group members who disconfirm the stereotype. Similarly, highlighting other positive characteristics of the group or one's own self-concept can also minimize the sting of the negative stereotype and lead to improved performance.

Whereas the above strategies reduce stereotype threat by counteracting negative features of the environment with the presence of more positive features, other interventions work to combat stereotype threat by changing how people think about the negative features that are present in the situation. For example, if stereotype threat occurs, in part, because people interpret their behavior in a more negative way, then manipulations designed to change those interpretations should reduce stereotype threat. Indeed, instructing individuals to interpret their anxiety in a more benign manner or as a normal part of the academic experience can circumvent some of the processes of emotion regulation that absorb cognitive resources and impair performance. In fact, research suggests that when individuals are taught about stereotype threat and the effects it can have in creating anxiety and impairing performance, they are more likely to report that their anxiety was caused by factors that are external to them and perform better as a result. Thus, educating people about the phenomenon could be a simple way of helping to combat its effects.

Toni Schmader

See also Collective Self; Gender and Behavior; Looking-Glass Self; Minority Coping Strategies; Minority Groups in Society; Self-Fulfilling Prophecy; Self-Stereotyping; Stereotyping; Stigma

Further Readings

Schmader, T., Johns, M., & Forbes, C. (2008). An integrated process model of stereotype threat effects on performance. *Psychological Review, 115,* 336–356.

Shapiro, J., & Neuberg, S. (2007). From stereotype threat to stereotype threats: Implications of a multi-threat framework for causes, moderators, mediators, consequences, and interventions. *Personality and Social Psychology Review*, 11, 107–130.

Steele, C. M. (1992, April). Race and the schooling of Black Americans. *The Atlantic Monthly*, pp. 68–78.

Steele, C. M., & Aronson, J. (1995). Stereotype threat and the intellectual test performance of African Americans. *Journal of Personality and Social Psychology*, 69, 797–811.

Steele, C. M., Spencer, S. J., & Aronson, J. (2002). Contending with group image: The psychology of stereotype and social identity threat. In M. Zanna (Ed.), *Advances in experimental social psychology* (Vol. 34, pp. 379–440). New York: Academic Press.

STEREOTYPING

Stereotypes are the characteristics that are believed to be true of a particular social group and its members. They are generally traits (Blacks are athletic; women are emotional) but can potentially include other attributes (___ are likely to be lawyers; ___ are likely to be on welfare). Stereotypes may be positive in valence (Italians are romantic; Asians are good in math), but most are negative. Stereotypes represent the cognitive component of intergroup beliefs and are related to the affective component (prejudice) and the behavioral component (discrimination) of intergroup relations. Stereotypes often predict, and serve as a rationalization for, both prejudice and discrimination. As trait dimensions, stereotype beliefs fall into the basic dimensions used to judge people more generally. For instance, a large part of the variance in stereotype beliefs is captured by the important underlying dimensions of warmth and competence, and the beliefs about many social groups are captured by these two factors.

Stereotypes have been studied extensively by social psychologists, in part because they represent a form of person perception more generally, in part because they can be used to understand how social information is mentally encoded, represented, and activated, and in part because they have significant societal outcomes.

Stereotypes are held by individuals, but because there is general consensus on beliefs across individuals in a culture or society, they can also be conceptualized as a cultural- or societal-level phenomenon. Stereotypes are part of the culture itself and are represented and expressed in the media, in everyday conversation, and in humor. Stereotypes are in large part social norms—they represent our underlying theories about the world of social groups and group relations—our cultural beliefs about the fundamental essence of social groups.

Stereotypes develop from the process of social categorization, which is the assignment of individuals to groups based on culturally important or otherwise salient characteristics. The most common categorizations, and thus the most common basis for stereotypes, arise from the categories of sex, race, age, and sexual orientation. When we categorize another person, we move away from individual person-based judgments to group-based judgments.

The application of a stereotype to a target person is known as *stereotyping*; it frequently occurs in an unconscious, automatic way, often without the knowledge of the person doing the stereotyping. Once developed, stereotypes become available in memory and highly cognitively accessible. They pop into mind easily and quickly when we encounter a member of the stereotyped group, and they are difficult to suppress. In fact, attempting to suppress stereotypes can make them even more highly accessible, leading to more stereotyping. The mere presence of a member of the particular social group is enough to activate the stereotype beliefs, and applying the activated beliefs—stereotyping—can inform social judgments and influence interactions between individuals in a pervasive way, on a daily basis.

Outcomes of Stereotypes

Holding stereotypes and applying them to social judgments may in some cases be informative, functional, and mentally efficient, particularly if there is some truth to stereotypes. If stereotypes are in part accurate, then stereotyping increases one's ability to predict the behavior of others. Stereotyping may also be self-protective because in dangerous situations, one can make quick judgments about possible outgroup members who may pose a threat. These quick judgments are also mentally efficient because they free up cognitive resources for other things. Instead of our evaluating each new individual as a unique person, stereotyping allows us to quickly retrieve and apply information about the new individual's group, thereby allowing a likely summary judgment of the individual himself or herself.

Stereotyping is more likely to occur when one has little motivation or capacity to individuate others or when one is tired, distracted, or cognitively busy. When we do not have much interest in the other or when we have power over the other, thinking about the other person as an individual (individuation) is not necessary, and instead we will rely on stereotypes. Alternatively, when we know the other well or when we are dependent on the other for outcomes, individuation is likely to occur without the use of stereotypes.

Stereotypes have important societal implications because they create a variety of social difficulties and problems for those who are stereotyped. For one, because stereotype beliefs are frequently overgeneralized, they have the potential to be unfair to those who are judged. Stereotypes may lead individuals to act as if characteristics believed to be true of a social group are true of every member of the group, when this cannot be the case. Not all members of the category possess the stereotyped characteristics, and assuming that they do—and particularly acting as if they do—is unfair to those who are categorized and stereotyped. Furthermore, stereotypes create anxiety and produce cognitive load during interactions. As a result, substantial effort on the part of those in interaction is required, which inhibits and reduces the quality of the social interaction.

Stereotypes also influence task performance. For instance, because Asian students are aware of the stereotype that Asians are good at math, reminding them of this fact before they take a difficult math test can improve their performance on the test. On the other hand, sometimes these beliefs are negative, and they create negative *self-fulfilling prophecies* (*stereotype threat*) such that one may perform more poorly due to knowledge about the stereotypes. Thinking about negative stereotypes that are relevant to a task that one is performing creates stereotype threat—performance decrements that are caused by the knowledge of cultural stereotypes.

Stereotypes as Mental Representations

Information that is encountered on a daily basis must be categorized and stored so that it is easily retrievable and can be used in future situations. At the individual level, social information about groups is stored in memory as cognitive representations of the groups, or stereotypes. In this sense, stereotypes allow one to make inferences about social targets, to "fill in the blanks" regarding information that is ambiguous or unknown about the social target, to interpret events that are uncertain, and to help encode new information about a social group. Several models have been used to understand the cognitive structure of stereotypes, how the social information contained stereotypes becomes activated, and how stereotypes are applied during social judgment.

Most broadly, stereotypes can be considered as schemas that contain a general set of information about a group. Individuals acquire this information through direct personal experience or through indirect cultural experiences. For instance, an individual may learn that Blacks have dark skin, or that immigrants speak English as a second language. These general characteristics will be stored in schemas about the groups and will subsequently inform the stereotypes of the groups.

Stereotypes have also been considered as *prototypes*, which are more specific group representations. They are developed through the integration of all attributes that are observed and learned about over time in many different contexts and social group members. Thus prototypes represent the average of group attributes and contain the most "typical" characteristics of the group. After multiple experiences with lawyers, one may consider the typical lawyer to be extroverted, hardworking, and argumentative. During encounters, lawyers will be judged on their "goodness-of-fit" with the prototypical lawyer, such that lawyers whose characteristics seem to be similar to those of the typical lawyer will be assimilated into the cognitive category *lawyer*, whereas lawyers whose characteristics appear to be less similar to those of the typical lawyer will be thought of as an exception and will not be assimilated into the cognitive category *lawyer*.

Within each group representation, there may be several specific exemplars that come to mind as good examples of a social group. These exemplars are most likely memories of specific group members the individual has encountered. Exemplars allow the individual to store more detailed information about the social group that may not necessarily be represented by the averaging of group characteristics. For instance, when thinking of the group *politicians*, an individual may think of George Bush or Bill Clinton. Both exemplars are good category fits, but they are quite different from one another. In certain contexts, the individual characteristics of George Bush or Bill Clinton may provide useful additional information that would not be provided by simply thinking of the most typical characteristics of politicians.

These different models of the cognitive representation of stereotypes allow researchers to understand the various ways in which stereotypes develop, function, and change. Each of these conceptual approaches allows slightly different predictions to be made about the activation and application of stereotypes. It is important to remember, however, that although stereotypes are stored as cognitive representations, they are not entirely rigid. The particular categories that are activated, as well as the particular stereotypes that are applied, vary across social context and often depend on the individual's processing goals.

Measuring Stereotypes and Stereotyping

Stereotypes are assessed through a variety of techniques. The most common approaches are self-report methods, which include thought listings, Likert-type scales (e.g., How true is this trait of the group?), and probability or percentage estimate measures (e.g., What proportion of the group possesses the trait?). However, because self-report methods are likely to be influenced by self-promotion demand characteristics, a variety of nonreactive, indirect, or unobtrusive measures have also been used. Methods that measure the specific words or characteristics that become activated after exposure to members of different categories have been used to assess group attitudes with more validity. A variety of reaction-time measures, including the Implicit Association Test (IAT), have also been used to assess associations between category labels and stereotypes of the category. Research using the IAT has shown that, based on

very large samples, most people associate stereotypes with many social groups. However, implicit measures of stereotyping such as the IAT are generally uncorrelated or only slightly correlated with responses on more explicit measures.

Recent developments in the field of social cognitive neuroscience have generated several techniques to measure neural activity in response to various social stimuli. *Functional magnetic resonance imaging* (fMRI) has become an increasingly valuable tool because it quickly produces precise images of specific brain structures. Other methods include using electrodes to measure *evoked potentials*, which are the changes in electrical activity immediately after exposure to particular stimuli. Research using neuroimaging methods has found that the medial prefrontal cortex responds to social stimuli in general. More specifically, the amygdala is an area of the brain that is involved with social categorization. In addition to becoming activated during emotional experiences, it becomes activated in response to outgroup members and social targets that are stereotyped as threatening. The anterior cingulate, a region of the brain that detects conflict, is activated when stereotypes are used, signaling the awareness of bias, and the lateral prefrontal cortex becomes activated when stereotypes are inhibited.

Accuracy

It is generally assumed that stereotypes contain some kernel of truth, and most research suggests that this is the case, although some stereotypes are more accurate than others. There are observed correlations between stereotypes ascribed to outgroups and the traits that members of those groups ascribe to themselves, as well as correlations between perceptions of stereotypes and actual observed group behavior. However, it is difficult to determine whether group traits inform the stereotype or whether the stereotype informs group traits.

In some cases, stereotypes may reflect the average roles of different groups. For instance, the stereotypes that women are nurturant and that men are dominant may occur in part because, on average and across many cultures, men are more likely to have high-status occupations, such as doctor or lawyer, whereas women are more likely to have low-status occupations, such as homemakers and child care workers. In this sense, the stereotypes are at least partly "true" for many of the members of the social categories, in terms of their actual behaviors in these roles. Consistent with this idea is the fact that stereotypes can change as a result of changes in social contexts. When individuals from a social group perform behaviors that are inconsistent with existing stereotypes, or are in different contexts, beliefs about the social group may change as well.

In many cases, however, behaviors of group members are also determined by the stereotypes of their group because stereotypes can become self-fulfilling prophecies. Expectations that outgroup members possess certain traits often lead to the perception and even the expression of the trait in the outgroup. For example, during a hiring process, if an interviewer expects a Black interviewee to be aggressive because of a stereotype about Black people, the interviewer may unintentionally phrase questions in a way that elicits aggressive responses, thus confirming the interviewer's initial belief about the social group's aggressiveness. Stereotype-based self-fulfilling prophecies are ubiquitous—even teachers' expectations about their students can influence the students' school performance

Stereotype Development

At a basic level, individuals like similar others, perhaps because, over the long course of evolution, those who were similar were more likely to be helpful and benign, whereas those who were different were more likely to be threatening. Stereotypes are formed through a variety of cognitive and affective processes. As discussed earlier, stereotypes develop through the organization of social stimuli into various categories that contain both general and specific information about the social groups. In some cases, these categories develop out of relatively accurate perceptions of everyday behaviors, but in other cases, they develop from misperceptions of behaviors. These misperceptions can be driven by preexisting expectations or by processing errors. For instance, *distinctiveness-based illusory correlations* occur when a perceiver assumes a relationship between minorities and negative behaviors after exposure to one or

some minorities behaving negatively. Because of set size effects, infrequently performed and negative behaviors tend to be particularly salient. As both minorities and negative behaviors are infrequent and therefore salient, an individual may incorrectly perceive a relationship between them when they occur together. The result is that negative stereotypes easily develop about minority groups.

Individuals also learn useful social categories and stereotypes through social processes such as everyday discourse and exposure to the media, just as they learn any other social norm. Indeed, individually held stereotypes are generally very similar to the stereotypes held by others in the same social contexts. Individuals use stereotypes when they perceive, on the basis of social norms, that it is appropriate to do so, and they refrain from using stereotypes when it is perceived as inappropriate. Stereotyping is so normal and natural that children learn stereotypes as early as 3 or 4 years of age, and their stereotypes remain quite rigid until around the age of 10. There is only a small relationship between the stereotypes of children and those of their parents, however, possibly because children's unique experiences with various social groups are more likely to inform the way they categorize social stimuli than are their parents' attitudes.

Stereotype Maintenance and Change

Because stereotyping and social categorization are basic human processes that provide some benefits for those who hold them, stereotypes are easy to develop but difficult to change. New, potentially contradictory information is discarded without influencing the existing category, whereas ambiguous information regarding the stereotype is frequently distorted to fit the existing beliefs. Furthermore, confirmation biases lead people to seek out information and ask questions about others in ways that confirm and thus reinforce their existing beliefs. Individuals pay less attention to, and are less likely to remember, information that disconfirms their existing stereotypes.

Although it is difficult, stereotype change is possible. One approach is to attempt to change the beliefs themselves. This is perhaps the most common approach, but perhaps also the most difficult, because expectancies tend to support themselves in virtually every possible way. An alternative but related approach is to attempt to change the perceived variability of stereotyped groups such that the perceiver believes that the stereotypes, although perhaps true of some group members, are far from true for every group member and thus not very diagnostic for use in social judgment.

Changing beliefs occurs in part through education, as those with more education express fewer stereotypes, and in part through increased social interactions with outgroup members. Indeed, positive intergroup contact has been found to change stereotypes in many settings, including schools, work environments, the military, and businesses. However, this approach is not a panacea. Negative intergroup contact makes beliefs more resistant to change, whereas positive intergroup opportunities are limited, and the conditions required for positive contact situations are difficult to achieve.

Furthermore, contact with individual outgroup members, even if successful at the individual level, does not always change attitudes about the group as a whole. Beliefs about individual outgroup members change much more quickly than beliefs about outgroups as a whole because the individual outgroup members are *subtyped* into lower levels of group membership if they do not match expectations about the outgroup as a whole. Thus it is possible to know many individual outgroup members to whom stereotypes are not applied and yet nevertheless apply stereotypes to the outgroup as a whole. Generalization of stereotype-discrepant information to the whole outgroup is more likely when individual outgroup members behave in ways that confirm some existing stereotypes and yet disconfirm others such that, because the individual does seem representative of the group on some dimensions, the stereotype-discrepant information is more difficult to ignore.

There are several different approaches to changing beliefs that avoid the issue of generalization. One successful approach that has created long-term changes is to convince individuals that their prejudiced beliefs are nonnormative and that others do not hold stereotypes. Another approach is to allow the beliefs to remain intact but help people avoid applying them to individuals, thus preventing the stereotyping process. This approach is also difficult because stereotyping is very well practiced and because it often occurs out of awareness and is difficult to stop. However, some social situations, including repeated practice in denying one's beliefs, awareness of one's moral hypocrisy when one stereotypes, and the presence of positive, stereotype-disconfirming exemplars, reduce the extent to which individuals apply stereotypes to outgroup members.

Stereotyping may also be reduced by changing social categorization processes such that outgroup members are recategorized as part of the ingroup. This recategorization process allows the members of different groups to be able to perceive themselves as members of a common group, to see each other as more similar, and to make friends with each other. Through fostering perceptions of shared identities, encouraging meaningful contact that defies group boundaries, and highlighting similarities on dimensions unrelated to group distinctions, the ingroup and an outgroup can begin to reduce negative beliefs and promote positive ones.

Finally, on a macro level, legal remedies can be successful in decreasing the use of stereotypes. When individuals are forced to individuate rather than categorize, learning about others as individuals may completely overwhelm the influence that their group membership would previously have had. Over long periods of time, legal remedies can also help change social climates so that stereotyping becomes less socially acceptable and so that increased opportunities for some social groups change social roles so that some stereotypes inevitably become obsolete.

Charles Stangor and Julia D. O'Brien

See also Categorization; Children: Stereotypes and Prejudice; Common Ingroup Identity Model; Illusory Correlation; Implicit Association Test (IAT); Intergroup Contact Theory; Perceived Group Variability; Prejudice; Self-Fulfilling Prophecy; Stereotype Threat; Subtyping

Further Readings

Blair, I. V. (2002). The malleability of automatic stereotypes and prejudice. *Personality and Social Psychology Review, 6*(3), 242–261.

Eagly, A. H., & Steffen, V. J. (1984). Gender stereotypes stem from the distribution of women and men into social roles. *Journal of Personality and Social Psychology, 46,* 735–754.

Fiske, S. T. (1998). Stereotyping, prejudice and discrimination. In D. T. Gilbert, S. T. Fiske, & G. Lindzey (Eds.), *Handbook of social psychology* (4th ed., Vol. 2, pp. 357–414). New York: McGraw-Hill.

Jussim, L., Lee, Y., & McCauley, R. (1995). *Accuracy and inaccuracy in stereotyping.* Washington, DC: American Psychological Association.

Rothbart, M., & John, O. P. (1985). Social categorization and behavioral episodes: A cognitive analysis of the effects of intergroup contact. *Journal of Social Issues, 41,* 81–104.

Smith, E. R., & Queller, S. (2004). Mental representations. In M. B. Brewer & M. Hewstone (Eds.), *Social cognition* (pp. 5–27). Malden, MA: Blackwell.

Spears, R., Oakes, P. J., Ellemers, N., & Haslam, S. A. (1997). *The social psychology of stereotyping and group life.* Malden, MA: Blackwell.

Stangor, C. (2000). *Stereotypes and prejudice: Essential readings.* New York: Psychology Press.

Steele, C. M., & Aronson, J. (1995). Stereotype threat and the intellectual performance of African Americans. *Journal of Personality and Social Psychology, 69,* 797–811.

STIGMA

Stigma refers to a characteristic or attribute that is associated with negative generalized inferences about the bearer. Psychological research on stigma often has focused on race and ethnicity, gender, sexual orientation, obesity, and disability. However, there is no definitive list of what does or does not constitute a stigma, only the idea that stigma involves a characteristic that is devalued across most social contexts. In addition, the characteristics that mark individuals' identities as undesirable vary across time and place.

The term *stigma* can be traced back to the Greeks, who cut or burned individuals' bodies to "brand" them as traitors, criminals, or other social misfits. In the classic Greek sense, stigmas referred to actual physical marks inscribed on the bodies of devalued members of society as visible indicators that they should be avoided or treated unfavorably. Sociologist Erving Goffman's classic 1963 monograph, *Stigma: Notes on the Management of Spoiled Identity*, is widely credited with introducing the concept of stigma to the social sciences. Goffman extended the notion of stigma to other, less obvious signs that might still designate the bearer as spoiled, flawed, and less than fully human in the eyes of other society members. He distinguished three types of stigma: "abominations of the body" (e.g., physical deformities), "blemishes of individual character" (e.g., mental disorders, addictions), and "tribal identities" (e.g., race, religion).

Much of the research on stigma in psychology focuses on the perspective of the stigmatizer. In contrast, research in sociology often focuses on the target's experience. This entry first describes the ways in which stigma has been conceptualized and classified. It then summarizes key research findings with regard to (a) the perspective of the stigmatizer (why individuals stigmatize others), (b) the perspective of the target (the consequences of being stigmatized), and (c) characteristics of social interactions between stigmatizer and target.

Conceptualizations and Classifications of Stigma

Recent psychological definitions of stigma have emphasized three fundamental components: (1) recognition of a person's difference from others based on some distinguishing characteristic or mark, (2) consequent devaluation of the person, and (3) subsequent (de)valuation of the person across most contexts. Typically, a stigmatized identity activates negative stereotypes and interpersonal rejection and ultimately produces social discrimination and economic disadvantage. As such, stigma is a more encompassing construct than deviance, prejudice, or discrimination, involving perceptions of societal-level deviance (a negative status) and elements of prejudice (negative attitudes and impressions of worth) and discrimination.

One aspect of most definitions of stigma is an acknowledgment of its dynamic nature, or the fact that it is embedded and evolving within social interactions and contexts. Hence what is deemed a stigma by one stigmatizer and target may not be viewed as such by others at a different time or in another place. For instance, White women, particularly those holding a strong ideology of blame, stigmatize obesity, whereas Black women do not. In addition, a stigma (e.g., homosexuality) may be activated in one setting (e.g., a Southern Baptist church) but not in another (a San Francisco bookstore), and some environments (e.g., buildings without elevators) may increase the salience of a stigma (e.g., certain physical disabilities) in ways that other environments do not. Thus, researchers often argue that societal-level stigmas involve those characteristics that are devalued across most contexts.

Researchers have classified how stigmas differ from each other. In one influential typology, E. E. Jones and his colleagues identified six such dimensions on which stigmas may vary: (1) concealability (whether a stigmatizing condition can be hidden from others), (2) course (the extent to which the condition changes over time), (3) disruptiveness (the extent to which the condition interferes with social interactions), (4) aesthetic qualities (the extent to which the condition makes the individual ugly to others), (5) origin (the extent to which the individual is responsible for the stigmatizing condition), and (6) peril (the extent to which the condition poses a danger to others). In subsequent empirical investigations, concealability, origin (controllability), and peril have emerged as most important in determining attitudes toward stigmas. The reason that peril has this effect is perhaps obvious, but concealability and origin deserve discussion.

The visibility (concealability) of a stigma has been argued to be one of the most important dimensions of stigma because if the stigma is visible, perceivers are more likely to view the individual primarily in terms of the stigma rather than as a whole person who may have some undesirable characteristics. Visible stigmas include race, gender, obesity, and many physical disabilities. Concealable stigmas include sexual orientation, religion, physical disabilities that are early in their course (e.g., cancer, AIDS), and histories of psychiatric disorders, drug abuse, or criminal background. Visible stigmas are often more damaging because individuals with such stigmas cannot hide their stigmatized identity to avoid the prejudice and harassment that their stigma may engender. However, individuals with concealable stigmas may become consumed by efforts to keep the stigma hidden and may lose the ability to make social comparisons with and receive social support from similar others.

The origin (controllability) of a stigma has been shown to influence outcomes significantly. For example, those who perceive homosexuality or obesity as an individual choice are more likely to stigmatize than are those who attribute such conditions to biological causes beyond an individual's control. Furthermore, physical disabilities caused by an accident are stigmatized more when the target was the cause of the accident (e.g., was driving drunk) than when another party was the cause (e.g., the target was hit by a drunk driver). When there is ambiguity as to the cause, evidence suggests that stigmatized individuals can reduce negative treatment by using environmental cues that signal an external cause for their stigma (i.e., an obese woman will be treated more positively if she carries a diet soda and discusses her exercise regimen than if she carries a fattening beverage and discusses her lack of desire to exercise).

Why Stigmatize?

While the particular conditions that are stigmatized will vary dramatically between societies, social stigma of some form is universal. The universality of stigma would seem to suggest that stigmatizing others serves some functional value to the individuals who stigmatize. Two broad reasons that stigmatization occurs involve (1) justification processes and (2) protective functions.

Justification processes focus on legitimizing the unequal societal and economic statuses of different groups (system justification theory) or of different individuals (belief in a just world). Under *system justification theory*, individuals from groups of higher status stigmatize groups of lower status in order to make their advantaged, privileged status seem fair. Research in the United States has shown that individuals who strongly endorse the belief that individuals who work hard will succeed in society are more likely to stigmatize economically disadvantaged groups.

Negative attitudes toward different disadvantaged groups tend to be related. For instance, those who believe being overweight results from a lack of willpower also tend to believe that the poor are responsible for their own poverty. In a similar way, belief in a just world, or the view that people get what they deserve, may serve to legitimate stigmatization of individuals in poverty or low-status positions.

Protective functions of rejecting stigmatized people are postulated by both sociobiological theory and the more culturally driven *terror management theory*. According to the former theory, evolutionary evidence suggests that interdependent group (societal) living was adaptive for human survival and gene transmission. Therefore, humans stigmatize others who are seen as unable (e.g., individuals with disabilities) or unwilling (e.g., individuals of outgroup ethnicities or religions) to contribute to the ingroup. Terror management theory posits that humans experience existential anxiety over their own inevitable mortality and their inability to prevent a premature and unexpected death. To buffer against this anxiety, individuals subscribe to a cultural worldview that imposes order and meaning on an otherwise random and senseless world. According to this framework, individuals with physical disabilities or deformities are stigmatized because they remind us that we might possibly experience suffering and will inevitably experience death. Terror management theory also suggests that individuals who deviate from societal norms for reasons unrelated to physical impairment (e.g., religion, cultural background) are stigmatized because their difference makes salient the lack of a social consensus regarding one's worldview. That is, the existence of discrepant worldviews makes the dominant worldview seem arbitrary and calls into question one's standards for judging what is true and valuable. Research has shown that reminding individuals of their own death makes them more rejecting of several groups that violate dominant cultural norms, including prostitutes, those who express views against their country, and outgroup members generally.

Consequences of Stigma

In general, stigmatized individuals are aware that their identity is seen negatively in society, with this awareness well established by adolescence. This consciousness has been shown across groups as disparate as ethnic minorities; women; people who are mentally, developmentally, or visually impaired; overweight individuals; and gay men and lesbians. One might assume that, because groups are aware of their stigmatized status, the self-esteem of stigmatized group members would be lower than that of nonstigmatized group members. Yet for many stigmatized groups this is untrue. For example, Blacks do not have lower self-esteem than Whites. However, overweight individuals and gay men and lesbians do tend to have lower self-esteem than their respective counterparts.

One possible reason for this discrepancy concerns the relationship between group identification and self-esteem, which is typically positive. Because ethnic and religious minorities often identity strongly with their groups, their self-esteem would be expected to be relatively high. However, individuals with physical or mental disabilities may not identity with their groups, because they do not wish to identify with others on the basis of what society considers a "limiting" condition. Moreover, some gay men and lesbians may not identify with their groups (at least across contexts) because they wish to remain "closeted."

Marred Interactions

Essential to understanding stigma is clarifying what happens in interactions between stigmatized and nonstigmatized people. Although there is relatively little research on this question, some interesting findings have emerged. For example, in interacting with stigmatized targets, nonstigmatized individuals often show a mismatch between their verbal and nonverbal behavior. A classic study showed that when participants interviewed a physically disabled applicant, they took more time deciding what questions to ask, terminated the interview sooner, and stayed farther away from the applicant than when they interviewed a nondisabled applicant. At the same time, however, participants were more likely to distort their personal opinions in a direction consistent with those thought to be held by the disabled applicant and were more likely to report positive impressions of the disabled applicant, compared with the nondisabled applicant.

As another example, White individuals have been shown to make verbal attempts to appear nondiscriminatory and helpful to Black interactants, even though their nonverbal behaviors are often discriminatory and unhelpful. One explanation for this mismatch is that the White individuals focused the majority of their attention on their verbal behaviors, which are easier to monitor and control than are nonverbal behaviors. However, and perhaps because of this difference in controllability, stigmatized targets are more likely to attend to nonverbal than to verbal behaviors of their nonstigmatized partners.

Certainly, nonstigmatized people are responsible for many of the behaviors they emit in the presence of stigmatized targets. This has been clearly shown in studies in which targets are unaware of their stigma (e.g., when they are unknowingly labeled as "gay" by words printed on their baseball cap) and hence could not have elicited the behaviors they receive. However, in some cases targets' awareness of their stigmatized status (and their resulting behaviors) can influence others' behavior toward them. For example, there is evidence that being aware that one will be stigmatized leads targets to alter their behavior in ways that worsen discrimination against them. A series of experimental studies has shown that targets led to believe that perceivers viewed them as mentally ill (even though perceivers were actually unaware of their mental health status) received more rejection than did targets who were not led to hold that belief. Beliefs about potentially being stigmatized may also lead targets to exhibit performance deficits, a phenomenon known as *stereotype threat*.

In some cases, stigmatized individuals behave in ways designed to elicit favorable treatment from nonstigmatized others. For instance, research conducted in the 1970s and 1980s showed that women's behavior became more consistent with traditional gender roles in interactions with sexist men. Women who expected to interact with a male job interviewer with sexist attitudes (compared with expecting to interact with a nonsexist man) expressed more traditional gender role attitudes and arrived wearing more makeup and accessories. Furthermore, studies have shown that when overweight women were led to believe that their interaction partner was aware of their stigma (i.e., because he could see them), they behaved in a more friendly fashion than when they did not think he was aware.

Remediation

Additional research has documented strategies that stigmatized targets may adopt if they wish to decrease discrimination. Chief among these is to verbally acknowledge the stigma ("As you can see, I use a wheelchair"). Studies have shown that such acknowledgment can increase the favorability of nonstigmatized people's attitudes and behaviors toward those with stigmas such as physical disability, obesity, and stuttering—provided that the stigma is visible. Acknowledgment may work because it causes potential stigmatizers to assume that someone who acknowledges his or her stigma will attribute any negative behavior on their part to discrimination.

A good deal of work on remediation of stigmatization has been based on the *contact hypothesis*, which assumes that reducing prejudice between groups is best achieved by bringing them together in structured situations. In a recent meta-analysis of more than 500 studies on the contact hypothesis, it was found that increased contact between stigmatized and nonstigmatized people was associated with decreased prejudice on the part of nonstigmatized people.

Bringing nonstigmatized and stigmatized people into interaction can be difficult, because nonstigmatized people often avoid interaction with stigmatized people and vice versa. However, the two groups tend to make different attributions for this state of affairs, typically blaming the other group. For instance, research on race relations shows that both Black and White individuals believe that their ingroup wants to have more contact with the outgroup than the outgroup wants to have with them. Yet in some situations, contact is inevitable (e.g., random assignment of first-year college roommates), and in such cases there is evidence that one person's positive interaction with members of another group can cause others to follow suit. For instance, when Black and White students were shown a dining hall scenario in which members of the two groups sat separately, their reported fear of race-based rejection was reduced when they imagined that their best friend enjoyed socializing with the outgroup members. Thus, there is evidence that, in some cases, intergroup relations can be improved by the behavior of individuals.

Michelle Hebl and Laura Barron

See also Ageism; Anti-Semitism; Deviance; Discrimination; Homophobia; Prejudice; Racism; Sexism; Weightism

Further Readings

Crocker, J., Major, B., & Steele, C. (1998). Social stigma. In D. T. Gilbert, S. T. Fiske, & G. Lindzey (Eds.), *Handbook of social psychology* (4th ed., Vol. 2, pp. 504–553). Boston: McGraw-Hill.

Goffman, E. (1963). *Stigma: Notes on the management of spoiled identity.* Englewood Cliffs, NJ: Prentice Hall.

Heatherton, T. F., Kleck, R. E., Hebl, M. R., & Hull, J. G. (2000). *The social psychology of stigma.* New York: Guilford.

Hebl, M. R., & Dovidio, J. F. (2005). Promoting the "social" in the examination of social stigmas. *Personality and Social Psychology Review, 9,* 156–182.

Jones, E. E., Farina, A., Hastorf, A. H., Markus, H., Miller, D. T., & Scott, R. A. (1984). *Social stigma: The psychology of marked relationships.* New York: Freeman.

Shelton, N., Dovidio, J. F., Hebl, M., & Richeson, J. (2008). Misunderstandings in interracial interactions. In S. Demoulin, J. P. Leyens, & J. F. Dovidio (Eds.), *Intergroup misunderstandings: Impact of divergent social realities* (pp. 21–38). New York: Psychology Press.

SUBJECTIVE GROUP DYNAMICS

Subjective group dynamics arise when people respond to deviant individuals within groups in a context involving comparisons between their ingroup and an outgroup. People spend a lot of time in small groups such as teams, committees, work groups, and social groups of friends. Social psychology shows that the opinions held by other people within such groups can easily affect the way members make judgments and decisions, how well they perform tasks, and how they form attitudes and opinions. The dynamics within these groups can have powerful effects on the way people share resources, who they vote for or against, and what choices they make. But these dynamics change when the groups are being compared with other groups.

Background

Research on subjective group dynamics has its roots in several areas of sociology and social psychology. In sociology, Emile Durkheim theorized that *deviance* is an important part of the way society defines its norms and rules. If people did not break rules, and if others did not enforce rules, it would be difficult to know exactly where the boundaries and guidelines for behavior were. Social psychologists such as Muzafer Sherif, Solomon Asch, and Leon Festinger showed that people make judgments, even about physical stimuli, using the opinions of others as reference points. Reaching agreement about the physical and social world allows people to feel confident about the validity of their judgments. Research on small groups has consistently shown that people who dissent within a group are liable to be marginalized, criticized, and ultimately ignored.

Much of the emphasis in research until the 1980s was on how individuals influenced one another or how people within a specific small group could influence one another. An alternative general perspective was offered by Henri Tajfel's *social identity* approach, which made the important point that people are motivated to ensure that their groups are distinctive from other groups and that they are evaluated positively relative to other groups. This desire to have a positive social identity means that people may face a problem when they discover deviant members of their groups because those members potentially reduce the extent to which all members fit in the same social category. Criticism or derogation of an ingroup member might imply criticism of the whole group, and this would damage social identity.

The Black Sheep Effect

José Marques, Vincent Yzerbyt, and Jacques-Philippe Leyens examined this question by asking Belgian students to evaluate either Belgian or North African students who showed either likable or unlikable behavior. The students were more negative to the unlikable ingroup (Belgian) students than to unlikable outgroup (North African) students, but more positive to the likable ingroup than to likable outgroup students. The more extreme derogation of an ingroup deviant (compared with ingroup normative members) than of an outgroup deviant (relative to outgroup normative members) is known as the *black sheep effect.*

Experiments investigating how people evaluate group members in intergroup situations (i.e., when their own and another group are being compared, are competing, or are in conflict) have repeatedly shown a black sheep effect. These experiments typically ask people to evaluate members of their own group or members of another group. Most of these members conform to the norm of their respective group, whereas one or a small minority deviates from the norm. The groups in these experiments are sometimes real groups, such as same-gender groups, psychology students, or people from a particular country or region. In other experiments the groups are *minimal groups* that the participants learn they belong to after taking a test.

The black sheep effect is important because it shows that people do not simply evaluate ingroup members more positively than outgroup members. Instead, people pay close attention to differences among individuals within their own and other groups. Their evaluations of these individuals are a vehicle for establishing the extent to which the norms of each group are valued more highly.

Subjective Group Dynamics

Marques, Dario Páez, and Dominic Abrams proposed a model of subjective group dynamics. A key aspect of the model is that if people are motivated to differentiate between groups (intergroup differentiation), this differentiation may be accompanied by careful differentiation among people within those groups. In fact, when people detect a deviant, people who care more about the differences between groups are more likely to differentiate among people within groups too. So the black sheep effect is a way in which people sustain the subjective validity of positive intergroup differentiation. This principle of subjective group dynamics contrasts strongly with traditional theories about social categorization, which hold that the more that people perceive differences between groups, the less they perceive differences within those groups.

Marques and colleagues theorized that there should be several factors that would affect how much people differentiate deviants from other members and how strong the black sheep effect is. First, the effect is likely only when particular types of norms are violated. Robert Cialdini distinguished between descriptive and prescriptive norms. Descriptively, men are taller than women and speak with deeper voices, but some men are shorter or have higher voices than most women. Prescriptively, hotels have washrooms that are designated for use by men and women. Only men should use those designated for men. The subjective group dynamics model argues that some norms are prescriptively relevant for social identity, and it is when these prescriptive norms are transgressed that members react strongly to the deviant. When intergroup differences are salient, deviant group members elicit a prescriptive focus that is psychologically equivalent to pressures to uniformity that arise in face-to-face groups. People are motivated to establish validity for ingroup norms, and they do this psychologically by disapproving of ingroup deviants.

It follows that subjective group dynamics should be affected by the relevance or salience of that norm. One experiment reduced the black sheep effect by having participants focus only on the individual people without emphasizing the groups to which they belonged. Another experiment increased the effect by making it clear to participants that the norm was important for the group. When adults and children believe their evaluations will be seen by other ingroup members, they respond more extremely to deviant group members, presumably because they want to be seen to have upheld the norm.

A number of studies with adults and with children show that subjective group dynamics are also affected by how strongly people identify with their group. People who identify more with their group also derogate ingroup deviants more strongly, and derogating deviants can also reinforce a positive image of their group as a whole and strengthen their ingroup identity.

Subjective group dynamics are thought to occur because people care about the validity of their positive evaluation of the ingroup compared with outgroups. One consequence is that people may be much more concerned about a deviant opinion if the ingroup's consensus is not very clear. Experiments have shown that people are more tolerant of a deviant member who strongly disagrees with others when the others hold an identical opinion than when some hold the opinion more strongly than others do. Similarly, the black sheep effect is weaker when the status of an ingroup is clearly better than an outgroup's than when there is uncertainty about the status differences.

Derogation of deviant members does not necessarily mean that people want to expel those members. For example, they may try to persuade deviants to shift position (conform) or try to resocialize them to be more committed group members. In addition, some deviant members may be tolerated because they contribute to the groups in other ways. For example, Dominic Abrams, Georgina Randsley de Moura, and colleagues showed that deviant members who are about to take on a leadership role are derogated less than deviants who are nonleaders, ex-leaders, or current leaders.

The developmental bases of subjective group dynamics have recently been investigated. A series of studies by Dominic Abrams, Adam Rutland, and colleagues asked children to evaluate ingroup and outgroup members (from teams, schools, or national categories). The members either showed complete loyalty to their group or showed positive but divided loyalty to both the ingroup and outgroup. Younger children (below the age of about 7 years) generally preferred ingroup members over outgroup members, whereas older children paid closer attention to whether the members showed loyalty to the ingroup. Older children were more likely to evaluate disloyal outgroup members positively and disloyal ingroup members negatively. Older children's evaluations of the group members were associated with how they expected peers to evaluate those members. Children who were better at taking different social perspectives and children who had belonged to a larger number of different social groups were more likely to anticipate that ingroup and outgroups would react differently to deviant members of each group. These findings suggest that subjective group dynamics have a basis in both cognitive ability, such as *perspective taking* and *categorization*, and in social experience, such as being in face-to-face groups.

Dominic Abrams

See also Black Sheep Effect; Deviance; Norms; Opinion Deviance; Ostracism; Social Identity Theory

Further Readings

Abrams, D., Randsley de Moura, G., & Hutchison, P. (2008). Innovation credit: When can leaders oppose their groups? *Journal of Personality and Social Psychology, 95,* 662–678.

Abrams, D., & Rutland, A. (2008). The development of subjective group dynamics. In S. R. Levy & M. Killen (Eds.), *Intergroup attitudes and relations in childhood through adulthood* (pp. 47–65). Oxford, UK: Oxford University Press.

Abrams, D., Rutland, A., & Cameron, L. (2003). The development of subjective group dynamics: Children's judgments of normative and deviant in-group and out-group individuals. *Child Development, 74,* 1840–1856.

Hutchison, P., Abrams, D., Gutierrez, R., & Viki, T. (2008). Getting rid of the bad ones: The relationship between group identification, deviant derogation and identity maintenance. *Journal of Experimental Social Psychology, 44,* 874–881.

Marques, J. M., Abrams, D., Páez, D., & Hogg, M. A. (2001). Social categorization, social identification, and rejection of deviant group members. In M. A. Hogg & S. Tindale (Eds.), *Blackwell handbook of social psychology: Vol 3. Group processes* (pp. 400–424). Oxford, UK: Blackwell.

Marques, J. M., Yzerbyt, V. Y., & Leyens, J.-P. (1988). The black sheep effect: Judgmental extremity towards ingroup members as a function of group identification. *European Journal of Social Psychology, 18,* 1–16.

SUBTYPING

The term *subtyping* refers to creating narrower, more specific mental categories, such as businesswoman or homemaker, within a broader social category, such as women. For example, common elderly subtypes include kind grandmothers, frequent travelers, and curmudgeons. Forming subtypes within a broad category provides more differentiated expectations and evaluations about group members but can also protect an existing general stereotype from exceptions that disconfirm it.

The term *subtyping* has been used in slightly different ways in two research streams. The first shows that as people become familiar with a group, they perceive distinctions and create multiple subtypes of members who are similar to each other in ways that differentiate them from other members, thus capturing the variability within a group. In this entry, *subtyping* refers to this form of subcategory formation. The second stream of research shows that people protect an existing general stereotype by relegating counterstereotypic members to an exceptions-to-the-rule subtype seen as unrepresentative of a group. The term *exception subtyping* refers to this type of subcategory formation. For example, a White manager might preserve his stereotype that Black males are unsuccessful by relegating highly admired Black males, such as Barack Obama, Colin Powell, or Tiger Woods, to an "exceptional Black professionals" subtype that he views as atypical, keeping his general stereotype intact.

Research on subtyping is important for understanding (a) the nature of social categorization; (b) how people differentiate social categories into subtypes as they become more familiar with varied group members; (c) how people form exception subtypes to accommodate group members who disconfirm their stereotypes, making stereotypes hard to change; and (d) how to develop strategies for reducing stereotype bias and improving intergroup relations. These topics are discussed in this entry.

The Nature of Subtypes in Social Categorization

Building on basic categorization research, Marilynn Brewer, Shelley Taylor, and colleagues showed that people categorize others in terms of subtypes rather than exclusively in terms of broad social categories. Gender, age, and ethnicity are major bases for social categorization, providing visually prominent and socially important cues. Research has identified common subtypes within each of these broad categories. For example, people perceive female subtypes such as businesswomen, homemakers, and feminists; younger people perceive elderly subtypes such as grandmothers, elder statesmen, and inactive seniors; and Whites perceive Black subtypes such as activists, athletes, and streetwise Blacks. Some subtypes cut across ingroup–outgroup boundaries, which can reduce intergroup bias by narrowing the perceived gap between ingroups and outgroups. For example, for a White executive, a Black executives subtype is a racial outgroup but an occupational ingroup.

The features associated with a subtype may overlap or differ from those of the broader category. *Warmth* and *competence* are two primary dimensions that often differentiate subtypes. For example, like the broader category of women, the homemaker subtype is seen as high in warmth but low in competence, whereas the businesswoman subtype is seen as high in competence but low in warmth. Some subtypes are more strongly associated with the broader category than others (e.g., businesswomen and homemakers are both strongly associated with the category of women). Emotions toward a category (such as poor people) may differ by subtype (poor-but-honest elicits pity, but poor-and-exploiting elicits contempt). Subtypes and their features can be inaccurate, can be based on socially prescribed roles, and can be formed by and influence behavior toward individual members without our conscious intent or awareness.

Greater Familiarity Leads to More Differentiated Subtypes

One stream of subtyping research asks, What leads people to perceive more differentiated subtypes within a category? First, forming subtypes can be socially useful because subtypes provide richer descriptive information about potential group members, enabling people to make distinctions that reflect the variability within broad categories. Suppose you are meeting a female president of a corporation. Having a female-executives subtype provides a more differentiated and potentially useful basis for anticipating her behavior than would relying on a general stereotype for women.

Two other factors also influence subtype formation: familiarity and ingroup-versus-outgroup status. Patricia Linville, Gregory Fischer, and colleagues showed that those with greater familiarity and experience with a group develop more subtypes reflecting greater differentiation and variability among group members. For example, among both college students and the elderly, those with more contact with the other age group perceived more subtypes, more variability, and more complex subtypes involving a mix of positive and negative characteristics (e.g., older frequent travelers are active but complaining, jocks are athletic but not intellectual, nerds are smart but unsociable). Similarly, White students with Black friends perceived more as well as more complex Black student subtypes than did White students without Black friends, and people with more years of business experience perceived more complex business subtypes (e.g., fast-trackers, visionary leaders, number-crunchers). People are usually more familiar with their ingroups. As this suggests, both young and older people perceived more as well as more complex subtypes for their age ingroup. Charles Judd, Bernadette Park, and colleagues also found that students perceived more ingroup subtypes (e.g., in their own fraternities and college majors), resulting in greater perceived ingroup variability.

Exception Subtyping: A Barrier to Stereotype Change

A second stream of subtyping research demonstrates that people use subtyping to protect their stereotypes against disconfirming information. By relegating counterstereotypic individuals to exceptions-to-the-rule subtypes, we can discount them as unrepresentative of the group and avoid revising our general stereotype. For example, subtyping 75-year-old Boston Marathon runners as exceptional older athletes preserves one's general stereotype that the elderly are fragile and inactive.

A classic experiment by Renee Weber and Jennifer Crocker compared three models of how people respond to counterstereotypic information: Do people change their stereotype dramatically after a few powerful disconfirming instances (*conversion*), change gradually with accumulating evidence (*bookkeeping*), or avoid change by isolating discrepant instances as atypical exceptions (*subtyping*)? People read behavioral descriptions of group members that were either consistent or inconsistent with an overall group stereotype. Stereotype change was greater when stereotype-inconsistent behaviors were dispersed over many group members than when the same number of inconsistent behaviors was concentrated in a few members. This favors exception subtyping because concentrating counterstereotypic information in a few highly atypical members allows one to relegate them to an exceptions subtype and discount them as unrepresentative of the larger group.

Bernadette Park, Charles Judd, Myron Rothbart, and colleagues showed that information-processing goals influence how subtypes are formed. After reading a general description of a group and behavioral descriptions of individual members, people received instructions to encourage either subgrouping (sorting individuals into groups of members who are similar in some way and different from other members), or exception subtyping (sorting individuals into those who fit with the group and those who do not). People receiving exception-subtyping instructions perceived less variability and made more stereotypic judgments about the group as a whole.

Because exception subtyping is an obstacle to stereotype change, it is important to know what conditions promote it. Research shows that exception subtyping is more likely when counterstereotypic information is concentrated in a few members rather than dispersed over many; when counterstereotypic individuals are perceived as highly atypical of the group; when the perceiver's goal is to judge members as fitting or not fitting the group; and when counterstereotypic members share some common characteristic that helps explain their departure from the general stereotype. Suppose John meets several accountants who go rock climbing, violating his stereotype that accountants are risk averse. It is easier for John to relegate these rock-climbing accountants to an exception subtype if they are few in number, atypical of his accountant stereotype in other respects (e.g., disorganized), and all come from Colorado, a commonality that helps explain why they rock climb.

Implications for Counteracting Stereotype Bias and Improving Intergroup Relations

Differentiating multiple subtypes within a group leads people to perceive greater variability among group members, which counteracts stereotypic thinking. On the other hand, exception subtyping discounts counterstereotypic group members, which preserves existing stereotypes. Fortunately, our growing understanding of exception subtyping suggests strategies for preventing it and thus promoting stereotype change. To be effective, intergroup contact should (a) provide exposure to a variety of group members in a variety of contexts, (b) provide exposure to stereotype-inconsistent information that is associated with otherwise typical members and is widely distributed across many members rather than concentrated in a few, and (c) create opportunities for forming subtypes that cut across ingroups and outgroups, thus narrowing the gap between them. Such situations may allow the cognitive and social benefits of subtype categorization while overcoming the costs of stereotyping.

Patricia W. Linville and Gregory W. Fischer

See also Categorization; Cross-Categorization; Ethnicity; Outgroup Homogeneity Effect; Perceived Group Variability; Prejudice; Racism; Stereotyping

Further Readings

Brewer, M. B., Dull, V., & Lui, L. (1981). Perceptions of the elderly: Stereotypes as prototypes. *Journal of Personality and Social Psychology, 41,* 656–670.

Fiske, S. T., Cuddy, A. S. T., Glick, P., & Xu, J. (2002). A model of (often mixed) stereotype content: Competence and warmth respectively follow from perceived status and competition. *Journal of Personality and Social Psychology, 82,* 878–902.

Linville, P. W., Fischer, G. W., & Yoon, C. (1996). Perceived covariation among the features of ingroup and outgroup members: The outgroup covariation effect. *Journal of Personality and Social Psychology, 70,* 421–436.

Park, B., Wolsko, C., & Judd, C. M. (2001). Measurement of subtyping in stereotype change. *Journal of Experimental Social Psychology, 37,* 325–332.

Taylor, S. E. (1981). A categorization approach to stereotyping. In D. L. Hamilton (Ed.), *Cognitive processes in stereotyping and intergroup behavior* (pp. 88–114). Hillsdale, NJ: Erlbaum.

Weber, R., & Crocker, J. (1983). Cognitive processes in the revision of stereotypic beliefs. *Journal of Personality and Social Psychology, 45,* 961–977.

SUCKER EFFECT

The *sucker effect* is a type of group motivation loss or social loafing effect—an instance in which a person works less hard as a member of group than as a comparable individual performer. The sucker effect occurs when people perceive that they are doing more than their fair share of the group's work; one way to reduce the injustice of such a situation is to reduce their own level of effort.

For example, suppose you are working on a three-person lab project in your chemistry course. Suppose that you see that you are doing much more of the work on the project than your two lab partners. If everyone in the group receives the same grade based on the quality of the final lab report, your extra work will not result in your receiving a higher grade than your partners do. Under such conditions, you may well feel exploited by your partners, or, in more colloquial terms, that you are "playing the sucker." You may well reason, "If my partners are not willing to do their fair share of the group's work, then neither will I," and therefore you will lower your own level of effort to match theirs.

Conceptual and Empirical Origins of the Sucker Effect

The sucker effect was first demonstrated experimentally in a study by Norbert Kerr in 1983. Experimental participants were first asked to do their best at a fatiguing physical task—pumping as much air as they could in 30 seconds with a small rubber bulb. They received feedback indicating that they had done well, succeeding on every one of four practice trials. Participants in an individual-control condition then did nine more trials. They received 25 cents for every trial on which they succeeded; the criterion for success was their lowest practice trial score.

Other participants also performed the task for nine more trials, but they were told that they would work in a two-person team. The air-pumping task would have disjunctive demands—that is, the group would succeed on a trial as long as either member of the dyad succeeded. When the group succeeded on a trial, each member of the dyad would receive 25 cents. In the experimental condition that interests us most, participants were told that their partner was nearly as capable as they were (the partner had succeeded on three of the four practice trials). During the following nine trials, the participants in this condition received accurate feedback on their own performance, but they received bogus feedback on their partner's performance. Specifically, after an initial success on Trial 1, their partner failed on every subsequent trial. When confronted with a capable partner who appeared to be slacking off and letting them do the group's work—yet who was getting the same cash reward—the participants reduced their efforts (relative to the individual controls). Even when such reductions in effort meant they would not earn as much money, participants appeared to prefer such failure to the inequity of "playing the sucker" and carrying a lazy partner.

Subsequent research has shown that there are reliable individual differences in the magnitude of this effect (e.g., males show a larger effect than females; those who believe that people ought to be rewarded equitably for their work or that hard work is a virtue show a larger effect than those who do not).

There is often a close parallel between the dilemma facing group members when deciding how hard to work and when confronting *social dilemmas*. The latter are situations in which an uncooperative choice appears more desirable from the individual member's perspective, yet everyone in the group would be better off making a different, cooperative choice. Many real-world situations pose such social dilemmas (e.g., choosing between using a lot or a little water during a drought).

A simple experimental game, the *prisoner's dilemma game*, is often used to study behavior in such situations. The sucker effect derives its name from the name of one of the outcomes of the prisoner's dilemma game—one receives the smallest, sucker's payoff when one makes a cooperative choice at the same time one's partner makes an uncooperative choice (and receives a large payoff). Unsurprisingly, much research on social dilemmas shows that group members will not long accept receiving the sucker's payoff—if their partner will not cooperate, neither will they. Similarly, the sucker effect shows that group members will not long accept acting cooperatively (working hard on the group's behalf) so that their uncooperative (and lazy) fellow group members can reap the rewards of group success without doing their fair share of the group's work.

Of course, it can sometimes be hard to define just what a fair share is. Does fairness require that every group member do the same work, regardless of their capabilities? We usually would not expect someone who was not as capable to perform at the same level as someone who was very capable; rather, we would make allowances for differences in group member ability. This was demonstrated in the 1983 experiment discussed earlier.

In another condition of that study, participants were told that their dyad partner was not very capable (namely, that their partner had succeeded on only one of the four initial practice trials). These participants then received the same performance feedback as those in the sucker condition—that is, their partner succeeded on Trial 1, and then failed on every trial thereafter. However, participants did not reduce their effort significantly in this condition. People appear willing to carry the load for a group member who cannot do so (i.e., who is doing the best he or she can), but not for a group member who can but will not do so (i.e., who is just lazy).

It is also important to remember that reducing one's own effort is not the only possible way to deal with an unfair group work load. For example, one might reduce the quality of one's work (rather than the quantity), one might subjectively exaggerate one's rewards (I work harder, but I enjoy the work more), or one might simply leave the group.

The Sucker Effect and Other Group Motivation Phenomena

The sucker effect may be contrasted with two closely related group motivation loss effects. The first is *free riding*. Free riding occurs when you believe that you can enjoy the rewards of group success without working hard. For example, in another condition of the 1983 study, participants were led to believe that their capable partner was succeeding on every trial. Because they could apparently get the cash payoff without working hard, they too reduced their efforts, free riding on their hard-working partners. The tables were turned, though, in the sucker condition—the participants were led to suspect that their partners were free riding on their efforts, and the unfairness of the situation led them to match the low effort of their partners.

Sometimes, however, one will do more than one's share, even if doing so is seen as unfair. Research on the social compensation effect has shown that if the payoff for group success is sufficiently high, and there is no other way of ensuring the group's success except to work exceptionally hard, group members will (reluctantly) do so. So, to return to our earlier example of the three-person lab group, suppose that you are a premedical student and that your grade in your chemistry course will be very important in your application to medical school. Further, suppose your two lab partners are taking the course as an elective and their only concern is getting a passing grade. Under such conditions, the only way you may be able to ensure the high grade you desire in the course is to compensate for the low effort of your partners—that is, to do not only your share of the lab assignments, but your partners' shares, too.

The sucker effect shows that, unless there are compelling reasons to do so, people are reluctant to contribute more than what seems to be their fair share of the group's work. This illustrates that choosing how hard to work in a group is more than a simple calculation of personal costs and benefits. It also involves considerations of social fairness and justice.

Norbert L. Kerr

See also Free Riding; Group Motivation; Prisoner's Dilemma; Justice; Social Compensation; Social Dilemmas; Social Loafing

Further Readings

Abele, S., & Diehl, M. (2008). Finding teammates who are not prone to sucker and free-rider effects: The Protestant work ethic as a moderator of motivation losses in group performance. *Group Processes & Intergroup Relations, 11*(1), 39–54.

Kerr, N. L. (1983). Motivation losses in task-performing groups: A social dilemma analysis. *Journal of Personality and Social Psychology, 45,* 819–828.

Kerr, N. L. (1986). Motivational choices in task groups: A paradigm for social dilemma research. In H. Wilke, D. Messick, & C. Rutte (Eds.), *Experimental social dilemmas* (pp. 1–27). Frankfurt am Main, Germany: Lang GmbH.

SUPPORT GROUPS

When people experience traumas, crises, or catastrophes, when they encounter medical or interpersonal difficulties that they cannot cope with by themselves, or if they simply need to find a sympathetic audience who will listen to their problems, they often turn to support groups: groups of people who meet to exchange social support about a problem or situation that they all have experienced. Support groups, which are also known as *self-help groups*, exist for nearly every major medical, psychological, or stress-related problem. Each one is likely to be unique in some respects, but most such groups are practical in focus and interpersonal in method, for they usually strive to provide members with both emotional support and useful information. Support groups are usually organized and regulated by the members themselves, yet members often report benefits from participation that rival the gains of members of more formal and traditional treatment methods.

Features of Support Groups

In times of trouble, such as illness, divorce, loss, or crisis, people tend to join with others rather than cope alone. During their first semester in college, students may seek out social networks of peers and friends as they deal with new and stressful experiences. When people first learn they are suffering from some serious illness, they often turn to friends and family members for information, advice, and a sympathetic audience. When people feel stressed and burned out by work-related pressures, they often cope by joining gripe sessions with coworkers.

Families, friends, and professional caregivers such as physicians and therapists are excellent sources of help and information in stressful, difficult circumstances, but some individuals' social networks may be too worn, too fragile, or too inexperienced to provide them with the solace they require. Sometimes, too, individuals may not wish to reveal their problems and their needs to their intimates and would prefer to unburden themselves with others who are knowledgeable but more objective and therefore less likely to judge them harshly.

Support groups are based on this natural tendency to seek reassurance and help through membership in a group. The most fundamental feature of such groups is reflected in their name: They support group members as they cope with their specific problem or illness, as well as other difficulties that can be traced back to their basic problem. Given the pragmatic orientation of self-help groups, much of this support takes the form of direct advice about the problem. More experienced members of the group may provide information, directions, advice, and suggestions regarding treatment or palliatives, demonstrate how to carry out the procedures recommended by medical authorities, or give general interpretations about symptoms that are often misunderstood or clear up uncertainties about remedies. But support groups also provide emotional support to members. They may encourage members to persevere and praise them for each achievement related to their problem. They allow members to express their fears and misgivings and so provide a receptive audience that responds positively rather than judgmentally. They respond to members in an emotionally positive and motivating way, rather than dispassionately or negatively. Support groups include the individual within the boundaries of the group, and this basic inclusion process minimizes new members' worries, tensions, and loneliness while increasing their sense of self-worth and efficacy.

How do support groups help their members, given that they usually have no formally designated leaders, no professionally trained staff, and no facility or budget? Although no two groups adopt identical procedures and structures, the hallmarks of a support group approach include focusing on a specific problem, encouraging members to form personal relations with one another, and stressing mutuality in helping. Support groups are also likely to remain independent of other sources of support that the members might be receiving, and they usually adopt an overarching perspective or worldview that provides a context for understanding the problem the group is designed to redress. These typical features of support groups are examined in more detail in the rest of this entry.

Support for a Specific Problem

Support group members may differ from one another in terms of age, sex, race, and wealth, but they share one important similarity: They are all coping with the same kind of problem. Unlike general therapeutic groups or social groups, support groups usually deal with one specific type of medical, psychological, stress-related, or social problem. So long as the population of an area is sufficiently large, support groups form for people diagnosed with physical illnesses such as heart disease and AIDS; individuals who care for those suffering chronic disease, illness, and disability; those who are addicted to alcohol or other substances; people who are grieving for someone lost to death; individuals struggling to cope with a major life change, such as unemployment, divorce, or retirement; and individuals advocating for social and political change.

Support groups are, therefore, usually communities of similar sufferers. Members are all alike in terms of their experiences and needs, and so they are peers who are all "in the same boat." This common qualification not only increases the credibility of others in group but also reduces each member's sense of uniqueness and victimization. Lone individuals may blame themselves for their problem or feel that they have been unfairly singled out to suffer, but once surrounded by others who are similarly afflicted, they realize that that their feelings and experiences are relatively common ones.

Relationships

Support groups tend to be personally and interpersonally involving. Even though individuals' identities are often masked within such groups (e.g., Alcoholics Anonymous), members nonetheless establish personal relationships with one another. Members are expected to engage in relatively high levels of self-disclosure, so that each person's unique experiences, background, and personal qualities are known by others in the group. Because this exchange of personal information is mutual, members learn to trust and rely on one another. Members are also expected to be respectful of one another and their needs and to treat people fairly. Yet because support groups take a very personal interest in their members, members are singled out for praise and commendation when they succeed in some way, but also criticized and urged to change if they fail.

Communalism

Most support groups develop a strong sense of community and sharing within the group. Each member of the group is valued as a member of the community and is cared for by the group in a personal way. Like most groups, support groups develop a degree of structure in which some members tend to be more influential than others. In support groups, however, status is based on experience with the problem rather than other socially valued individual qualities such as educational background, wealth, or ethnicity. Most support groups include veteran individuals who have knowledge and experience with both the problem and the means of dealing with the problem, and these individuals serve as role models for others. It is expected, however, that the exchange of help among members will be mutual. Members of the group draw support and encouragement from the group, and they are expected to provide support and encouragement to others within the group. Each person, then, is both a provider and a recipient of help and support.

Autonomy

Most support groups are self-governing, with members rather than experts or mental health professionals determining activities. A physician in consultation with a patient suffering from a chronic illness, a psychologist seeing a client suffering from substance abuse and addiction, or a social worker helping a grieving family cope with the loss of a child may direct individuals to join a support group that is maintained by a hospital or community social service agency. But in most cases, support groups are autonomous groups that set their own standards and practices. Some local groups may be aligned with national organizations that mandate specific procedures for all their chapters, but even this standardization does not eliminate the emphasis on the local group's control of its methods.

Because support groups are autonomous, they often operate outside of, and even in opposition to, traditional health care delivery systems. People have long turned to groups for support in times of trouble, but the number of such groups and their diversity increased during the late 1960s and 1970s. The political and social changes of that era prompted people to question more openly the wisdom of traditional methods of treatment and to seek alternatives. Support groups provide this alternative, for members are qualified as experts not by training but by common experience, and because they receive no compensation for the success of their intervention, they can be trusted to share information openly. Support groups, then,

are sometimes viewed as a radical alternative to health care systems that are considered to be bureaucratic, impersonal, and ineffective.

Perspective

Support groups' independence from more traditional approaches is also manifested in their adoption of a novel perspective with regards to their problem domain. A grief group may adopt fervently a particular model of the stages of grieving and base its interventions and recommendations on that perspective. A support group for alcoholics may maintain that recovery is never permanent, and so one must abstain from all forms of alcohol to overcome the addiction. A group for parents of children with severe immune-system deficiencies may recommend using novel methods of treatment that are rarely recognized as therapeutic by professionals. These perspectives may not be complex, nor are they always explicitly recognized by members, but in many cases the group's perspective on its affliction may become the centerpiece of the group's discussions, with new members urged to adopt the group's worldview as a means of coping effectively with the problem.

Varieties of Support Groups

Because support groups tend to operate alongside traditional health care organizations and are coordinated by volunteers rather than professionals, statistics on their number and popularity are incomplete. Even conservative estimates, however, indicate that the number of support groups is increasing rapidly, with as many as 10 million currently operating in the United States alone. A representative sample would include groups that focus on mental and physical health (including weight loss and rehabilitation), family and life-transition support, advocacy, and addiction and recovery.

Mental and Physical Health Groups

Individuals dealing with mental and physical health issues, including psychological disorders, physical illness, and recovery from injury, generally require the services of professionals to diagnose the source of their problems and carry out treatment. Support groups, however, can supplement the traditional services rendered by the health care community. In the supportive environment of a group of peers, members can learn about the procedures they must endure from people who have themselves experienced the procedures. Because members can remain in the group as long as they find it to be of value, such groups are well suited for problems that involve long-term recovery and adjustment, such as cancer, amputations, and stroke. Examples of such groups include the Cancer Aftercare and Rehabilitation Society, the National Peer Network of the Amputee Coalition of America, and Recovery, Inc. (a self-help mental health group).

One relatively common type of support group focuses on helping members achieve a change in their health-related behaviors such as food intake. Take Off Pounds Sensibly (TOPS), for example, is a worldwide organization that facilitates the formation of local clubs whose members are seeking ways to control their weight. TOPS meetings involve a private weigh-in, presentations designed to provide information about weight control, and supportive interaction that serves to motivate members to follow recommended dietary restrictions.

Family and Life Transition Support

Many of the difficulties people face in their lives are traumatic and stressful, yet they are not typically considered to be the kinds of problems that require the intervention of a health care professional. An individual who is divorcing, for example, may experience a range of negative psychological reactions to the experience, and by seeking out others who are going through this life transition, the individual may cope more effectively. Similarly, bereavement and grief groups help people adjust to the death of a family member or friend and adjust to life after the loss. Support groups can also help a family deal with a particular type of chronic problem, as when a family member is diagnosed with AIDS; an older family member begins to display symptoms of Alzheimer's; or a parent must learn to help a child with a learning disability, physical limitation, or psychological disorder. Examples include In Touch, for parents of children with mental handicaps; Parents Without Partners; and the Alzheimer's Disease Support and Information Group.

Advocacy

A number of support groups mix commitment to a specific social issue with support provided to individuals who are pursuing social change. Gay, lesbian, bisexual, and transgendered individuals may, for example, meet regularly to share information or discuss experiences of unfair treatment and ways to secure the privileges they are due as citizens (e.g., the Gay Activists' Alliance). Mothers Against Drunk Driving is a political movement, but it also provides support for members who have lost family members in automobile accidents involving alcohol.

Addictions

A number of support groups, including Alcoholics Anonymous (AA), Narcotics Anonymous, and Gamblers Anonymous, help members gain control over intemperate behaviors and maladaptive dependencies. Many of these groups help members work through various aspects of their addiction by following the 12-step program developed initially by Bill Wilson, the founder of AA. Wilson, a confirmed alcoholic, relapsed many times before he had a profound, mystical experience that forced him to recognize his own powerlessness over his alcoholism but also his oneness with the universe. After his experience, he worked closely with members of the Oxford Group, a group that was oriented toward spiritual growth and that stressed the importance of self-understanding, recognition of one's character flaws, acceptance of responsibility for one's wrongdoings, and restoration of harmony in one's relationships with others. Integrating his own experiences with the practices of that group, Wilson developed a group-based procedure aimed at alcoholics.

AA is a support group in which members give one another advice, encouragement, help, and guidance as they struggle with abstinence. AA makes use of peer influence, mediated through face-to-face interactions, structured group sessions, and testimonials by group members to help new members learn and assimilate the group's approach to controlling their drinking. AA recommends a series of stages, or steps, to take in dealing with addiction, and that general approach has been adopted by a number of other anti-addiction groups. These steps recommend admitting one's powerlessness over alcohol; surrendering one's fate to a greater power; taking an inventory of personal strengths, weaknesses, and moral failings; and helping others fight their addiction. The AA philosophy considers alcoholism to be an illness that can never be cured, so the only solution is complete abstinence from alcohol consumption. Members are known to one another only by their first names in order to emphasize that they are all equals in the quest to remain sober. Even though AA is now an international organization and is more elaborately structured than most support groups, change is still achieved through local chapters of alcoholics who meet regularly to review their success in maintaining their sobriety.

Online Support Groups

Support groups, by tradition, meet face to face at designated locations, usually following a regular schedule and agenda. Increasingly, however, individuals have begun using the Internet as a means of meeting their needs for social and informational support. Some support groups use the Internet primarily to post information about the particular problem they address, as well as to refer interested individuals to local meetings. Others, however, create virtual support groups with members communicating with each other via e-mail, message boards, forums, and real-time chat protocols. No matter what problem an individual faces, an online group that can provide self-care information, support, and referral services likely exists somewhere on the Internet.

Advantages and Limitations

Many practicing professionals are uncertain of the value of support groups because they are unregulated and unsupervised. Because their membership changes over time, their procedures and results tend to be variable—very advantageous when the group includes individuals who are committed, experienced, and helpful but less effective when the attendance fluctuates and the preconditions for social support are not met. In some cases, too, groups may actually add to members' level of stress by stirring up conflicts, increasing responsibilities, and exposing members to criticism. Because

the groups may rely on personal experiences and assumptions rather than on research to guide their recommendations, they may provide members with misinformation.

Overall, however, support groups are more frequently therapeutic than harmful. Support groups are quite cost-effective because they do not require salaried personnel and members usually pay very little for the services they provide. Groups may charge dues or small fees to cover basic operating costs, but these charges are minimal compared with other treatment procedures. In addition, research suggests that while the consequences of participation are difficult to document, individuals who take part in such groups generally report that they gain substantially from the experience. AA, for example, is generally rated by members as the most effective treatment they have experienced for dealing with a drinking problem, even in comparison with more medically sophisticated interventions. Although the benefits of participation in a support group do not emerge in all studies, many find that people who become committed members of a cohesive, well-organized group of peers experience fewer of the physical and psychological effects of stress and report overall gains in life-satisfaction and mental health.

Donelson R. Forsyth

See also Common-Identity/Common-Bond Groups; Computer-Mediated Communication; Families; Group Cohesiveness; Identification and Commitment; Sensitivity Training Groups; Social Networks; Therapy Groups

Further Readings

Flores, P. J. (1997). *Group psychotherapy with addicted populations: An integration of twelve-step and psychodynamic theory.* Binghamton, NY: Haworth Press.

Levy, L. H. (2000). Self-help groups. In J. Rappaport & E. Seidman (Eds.), *Handbook of community psychology* (pp. 591–613). Dordrecht, the Netherlands: Kluwer Academic.

Lieberman, M. A. (1993). Self-help groups. In H. I. Kaplan & M. J. Sadock (Eds.), *Comprehensive group psychotherapy* (3rd ed., pp. 292–304). Baltimore: Williams & Wilkins.

Survey Methods

Survey research is a type of field research that involves the use of a questionnaire to collect information from a sample of respondents. When the sample of survey respondents has been carefully selected, information collected from the sample can be used to draw inferences about the larger population from which the sample was drawn. The power of survey research, therefore, lies in the precision and efficiency with which the characteristics and attributes of a large population can be estimated via a set of measures collected from a small, scientifically selected subset of the population. The set of techniques that survey researchers use to gather data is known as survey methods. This entry examines some key elements underlying the validity and usefulness of surveys: survey design, sampling, response rate, questionnaire design, survey modes, and evaluation issues.

Survey Design

Surveys may take a variety of forms, depending on the aims of the research. Most surveys can be categorized as cross-sectional, repeated cross-sectional, or panel surveys. And across these basic designs, some surveys incorporate experimental manipulations into their design.

The most common design is a *cross-sectional survey*, in which data are collected from a sample of respondents at one point in time. Cross-sectional surveys offer a "snapshot" of the population, revealing the currently prevailing opinions, preferences, or other characteristics.

Instead of a static glimpse of a population, researchers may be interested in capturing over-time dynamics. In such cases, researchers sometimes turn to a *repeated cross-sectional survey* design. In repeated cross-sectional surveys, the same questionnaire is administered at two or more points in time to independent samples drawn from the same population. Such surveys provide information about aggregate-level shifts over time. For example, survey researchers periodically ask representative samples of U.S. adults about their approval of the way the nation's president is handling his job. By comparing responses to this question across time, survey researchers can track systematic trends in overall presidential approval and identify associations between historical or social events and approval ratings.

Of course, repeated cross-sectional surveys can detect changes only at the aggregate level. In the case of presidential approval, for example, cross-sectional surveys will detect change only if, on average, individuals' approval ratings changed in the same direction. If subsets of the population changed in opposite directions (e.g., Democrats became more disapproving while Republicans became more approving to equal degrees), these changes would cancel out at the aggregate.

To more precisely capture the dynamics within a population, survey researchers sometimes turn to *panel survey* designs. Panel surveys (also referred to as *longitudinal surveys*) involve the collection of data from the same participants at several points in time. Panel surveys provide information about individual-level change, enabling researchers to go beyond overall levels of change to explore rates of change among subsets of respondents, among other things.

Cross-sectional, repeated cross-sectional, and panel surveys can all provide important information about the attributes of a population and associations among these attributes. And with the use of sophisticated statistical procedures, researchers can use survey data to test hypotheses about the causal relations among variables. For stronger causal inferences, however, survey researchers have increasingly begun to embed experimental manipulations into surveys. By randomly assigning survey respondents to different versions of a questionnaire, researchers can more directly test causal hypotheses.

For example, scholars interested in the impact of race on social policy judgments have sometimes presented survey respondents with a hypothetical scenario involving a potential recipient of public assistance, and they have experimentally manipulated the race of the recipient (and in some cases other characteristics as well). By comparing respondents' support for public assistance for the target individual across experimental conditions, scholars can draw inferences about the impact of race or other factors on policy judgments. And they can examine the magnitude of these effects across various subgroups within their sample, exploring the possibility that race or other characteristics of a target have a larger impact on support for public assistance for some respondents than for others. This approach enables researchers to combine the unique strengths of survey research with the well-established advantages of laboratory experimentation, yielding powerful tests of causal processes.

Sampling

We have suggested that the strength of survey research lies in the ability to draw inferences about a large population based on information collected from a small subset of the population. The validity of these inferences, however, depends critically on the process by which the subset of survey respondents is selected. Sampling refers to this process.

At the most general level, there are two types of sampling procedures: *probability sampling* and *nonprobability sampling*. Probability sampling involves selecting respondents from the population at random such that every member of the population has an opportunity to potentially be included in the sample. In the simplest case, every member of the population would have an equal chance of being selected for inclusion in the sample. When a sample has been selected from the population through the use of probability sampling techniques, survey researchers can be confident that their sample is representative of the larger population from which the sample was drawn. Further, they can use statistical procedures to estimate just how precisely their sample represents the larger population (sometimes referred to as a *margin of error*).

Nonprobability sampling procedures are those in which members of a survey sample are not drawn randomly from the population. For example, some surveys are conducted on an *opt-in* basis whereby individuals choose to take part in a survey by calling a toll-free number to voice their opinion on an issue or by following a link on a Web page to complete a questionnaire on a particular topic. Other surveys are conducted with *samples of convenience*. Shoppers at a particular store might be approached and asked to complete a brief questionnaire, for example, or people may be stopped on the street and asked for their opinion on a particular topic. When samples have been selected in these ways, they cannot be assumed to be representative of any particular population. As a result, it is extremely unwise to generalize the results of such surveys beyond the particular individuals who took part in the survey.

Response Rate

Probability sampling procedures are necessary to ensure representative samples, but they are not sufficient for doing so. Even when probability sampling procedures have been carefully implemented, not all the individuals selected for inclusion in the sample will agree to participate in a survey. The proportion of selected members of a sample who actually take part in the survey is referred to as the *response rate*.

If a survey has used a probability sampling technique and has a high response rate, we can be confident that the sample of survey participants is representative of the larger population from which it was drawn. But as the response rate drops, there is an increasing chance that the subset of people who participated in the survey were different in meaningful ways from those who refused to do so. For example, those who participated in the survey may have been especially interested in the topic, or they may have had especially extreme attitudes that they wished to express. To the extent that people who refuse to participate in a survey differ systematically from those who agree to participate, *sample representativeness* is compromised. For this reason, a high response rate is desirable.

Questionnaire Design

The results of a survey can vary dramatically with changes in question format, question wording, and question order. When one is conducting or interpreting a survey, therefore, one must pay careful attention to these design elements.

Survey questions fall into two broad categories: *open-ended* and *closed-ended* questions. An open-ended question allows respondents to answer in their own words, and as a result, questions of this sort can capture the richness and complexity of people's views. Because the responses are idiosyncratic, however, it can be difficult to compare open-ended responses across individuals or groups. Quantifying responses for analysis requires researchers to develop and implement a *content coding scheme*, a process that can be time-consuming and labor intensive. Open-ended questions also take more time and effort for respondents to answer, potentially contributing to respondent fatigue.

Much more common in survey research are closed-ended questions, which require participants to select their response from a set of predetermined answers. For example, survey respondents are routinely asked to identify the most important issue facing the country and are provided with a list of response options from which to choose (e.g., the economy, health care, education, crime, the environment).

Although they offer many advantages, closed-ended questions have their drawbacks as well. Most obviously, responses will be powerfully influenced by the response options that are presented, which can yield a distorted portrait of public opinion. For example, closed-ended questions about the most important problem facing the country can obscure the importance of issues that are not explicitly offered as response options. In addition, participants may be influenced by the order in which responses are provided (with the first and the last options being more likely than middle options to be selected).

Regardless of whether they are posed in an open- or a closed-ended format, all survey questions must be worded clearly so that the precise meaning of each question is understood in the same way by all respondents. Vague or ambiguous question wording can result in poor data quality, which makes it difficult to tell whether different responses reflect substantive differences across participants or are instead due to differences in participants' interpretation of the question. To maximize clarity, questions should use simple language and avoid technical terms whenever possible.

Researchers and consumers of survey research should also be wary of *double-barreled questions*— questions that ask two or more questions at the same time. Consider the question, Do you think that parents and teachers should teach middle school students about birth control options? Although it is framed as a single yes-or-no question, it in fact comprises two questions (should parents teach middle school students about birth control options, and should teachers do so). Because respondents are required to answer two questions with a single response, double-barreled questions are inherently ambiguous.

Finally, the particular words that are used in a survey question can sometimes affect responses. For example, substituting the phrase *assistance for the poor* for the more politically charged term *welfare* dramatically increases public support for assistance programs. And individuals are much more likely to say that a controversial behavior should *not be allowed* than to say that this same behavior should be *forbidden*. Thus, seemingly equivalent question wordings can sometime elicit quite different responses. It is not always possible to anticipate the impact of particular wording choices, but careful attention should be paid to the precise language of survey questions and response options.

The order in which participants encounter the questions in a survey can also influence their answers. Questions that come early in a survey may bias the way respondents answer later questions. For example, if respondents are asked to report their gender before they are asked to report their attitudes toward feminism, they may answer the feminism questions differently than they would if asked to report gender later in the survey. When interpreting survey data, therefore, it is important to consider the answers to each question in the context of the entire survey.

Survey Modes

Survey mode refers to the means by which data are collected from respondents. Some surveys are conducted via *face-to-face interviews*, during which a trained interviewer records an individual's answers on a paper questionnaire or a laptop computer. Other surveys are conducted over the *telephone*. This typically involves questionnaires that are administered by trained interviewers with the help of computer-assisted telephone interviewing software, which guides the interviewer through the correct series of questions and allows him or her to enter participants' responses into the computer. Still other surveys are conducted via *self-administered questionnaires*, which respondents complete on their own using a paper-and-pencil format, on laptops, or over the Internet.

A good survey will use a mode that is appropriate to respondents' literacy and computer skills. For example, self-administered surveys are best suited to populations that are comfortable reading and following written instructions. The optimal mode of data collection also depends on the content of the survey. When a survey asks about sensitive topics, self-administered questionnaires are often preferable because they provide respondents with a greater sense of privacy, which may make them more comfortable about providing candid responses.

Evaluating Survey Data

Surveys are very common, and their quality varies markedly. When one is evaluating survey data, it is wise to consider the who, what, and how of the research methodology. Answers to *who* questions will be related to sampling: Who participated in the study? Who are the researchers trying to draw inferences about? The validity of these inferences rests on the degree to which the sample is representative of the larger population from which it was drawn, so it is important to consider the potential threats to representativeness.

Answers to *what* questions will center on the content of the survey, including the types of questions asked, the precise ways in which the questions were worded, and the order in which questions were posed to respondents. As we have seen, these design features can powerfully shape the results of a survey.

Answers to *how* questions will concern various procedural details. Were the survey design and mode of data collection appropriate, given the aims of the research, the population being studied, and the topic of the survey? What conclusions are being draw about causal relationships, and are they justified by the survey's design? Careful attention to these basic methodological elements will help ensure that appropriate inferences are drawn from the survey data that we encounter every day.

Katie M. Bowen and Penny S. Visser

See also Experimentation; Research Methods and Issues

Further Readings

Dillman, D. A. (2007). *Mail and Internet surveys: The tailored design.* New York: Wiley.

Kalton, G. (1983). *Introduction to survey sampling.* Beverly Hills, CA: Sage.

Krosnick, J. A., & Fabrigar, L. R. (in press). *The handbook of questionnaire design.* New York: Oxford University Press.

Lavrakas, P. J. (1993). *Telephone survey methods: Sampling, selection, and supervision.* Newbury Park, CA: Sage.

Visser, P. S., Krosnick, J. A., & Lavrakas, P. J. (2000). Survey research. In C. M. Judd & H. Reis (Eds.), *Research methods in social psychology.* New York: Cambridge University Press.

Weisberg, H., Krosnick, J. A., & Bowen, B. (1996). *Introduction to survey research, polling, and data analysis.* Thousand Oaks, CA: Sage.

SYMBOLIC INTERACTIONISM

Symbolic interactionism is a sociological perspective that views human conduct as a meaningful product of situated social interaction among self-conscious individuals. The perspective is rooted in the philosophy of *pragmatism*, especially as it was developed by George Herbert Mead, who taught at the University of Chicago in the early 20th century, and whose student, Herbert Blumer, named the perspective *symbolic interactionism*. This research seeks to portray social behavior from the perspective of participants by closely studying the concrete situations in which they form what is labeled "conduct." Symbolic interactionists examine how people define situations and act on the basis of those definitions, as well as how the self is shaped by group membership and by the real and imagined boundaries between groups. Symbolic interactionists have investigated such topics as race and ethnic group relations, the formation of subcultures, life in communities and urban neighborhoods, and collective behavior. To understand this perspective, we must examine the nature of meaning, the situated formation of conduct, the self, and the method of participant observation.

The Nature of Meaning

Symbolic interactionists believe that human beings are symbolic creatures for whom linguistic symbols are the principal basis for constructing, experiencing, and acting meaningfully in their worlds. A *symbol* is anything—a word, an image, a gesture—that stands for something else. National flags symbolize patriotic attitudes and feelings; certain hand gestures or facial expressions signify the user's contempt or disdain for another; derogatory words for outgroup members serve to demarcate and attach emotional significance to boundaries between "them" and "us." Symbols shared by the members of a society, a community, or a group have a critical characteristic: They arouse shared responses in members. The person who invokes a symbol responds to it with thoughts, feelings, and actions that resemble those of others who see or hear it. Symbols thus prepare people to take action: An announcement in a public place that a fire has broken out arouses in all who are present the motivation to escape; derogatory words lay a shared basis for thoughts and feelings and ultimately actions toward others.

Meaning is a social and not merely an individual phenomenon. It is the individual, of course, who learns and uses the meanings provided by the language of his or her community. Yet to use a word is to bring into public view a part of the individual's state of mind at a particular time. To speak of *fire*, for example, is to indicate to others that one believes there is danger and is prepared to act on it, that the others should define the situation and act in a similar way, and that collectively they are seeking escape or rescue from a dangerous situation. To invoke a racial or ethnic stereotype in a conversation is to invite the other to view the member of a racial or ethnic outgroup in the same way as the speaker, and implicitly (though not necessarily immediately) to act toward the outgroup member on the basis of that attitude. Meanings thus shape both the individual's conduct and that of others. Each culture embraces a variety of meanings and thus influences conduct in a variety of directions—altruism as well as selfishness, cooperation as well as conflict, tolerance of outsiders as well as hatred for them.

Situated Conduct

Human conduct is situated. People form their conduct as they interact with others, use and hear symbols, define the situation in which they find themselves, and construct lines of conduct for themselves and influence the conduct of others. Conduct cannot be explained merely by pointing to a set of "variables" with which particular forms of behavior are statistically associated. Such variables—whether they are demographic characteristics such as age, education, place of residence, group membership, or personal attitudes and beliefs as expressed in interviews or questionnaires—provide only an imperfect glimpse of the genesis of conduct. To explain why some members of an outgroup engage in a riot and others do not, or why some ingroup members seem to expect and to provoke such behavior, we must examine the situation as it unfolds.

We gain some understanding of the events by learning whether riot participants are more likely to be young or old or economically advantaged or disadvantaged, but the conduct of individuals arises in a situation and not simply and reflexively out of circumstances and characteristics they share with others. What events occurred to spark a riot? How were those events defined? Who did the defining? How did battles with the police or looting of stores become seen as legitimate responses to previous discrimination, and who saw them that way?

Likewise, to grasp how the attitudes and actions of one group toward another become more positive over time, we must examine the concrete situations in which the members of one social group interact with those of another. What are the situations that bring ingroup and outgroup members together, and what happens in their interaction that transforms attitudes and behavior?

The Self

Symbolic interactionism emphasizes the self-conscious nature of human conduct. The symbolic nature of the human species is the chief basis for the human experience of self. Humans live in a world of named objects and are capable of acting toward themselves as objects, much as they act toward any object. Individuals have names, just as other objects—houses, chairs, cars—have names. To name something—whether it is a new Lexus or a newborn infant that is called by such relational names as *son* or *daughter*, as well as by an individual name, *Jacob*—is to assign it a place in the social world and to invoke shared ways of acting toward it. A new luxury car invokes shared ideas about social standing or wealth; a new infant invokes shared ideas about how girls and boys should be treated or about an ancestral Jacob, whose qualities it is hoped will be shared by his namesake. Cars do not hear or use their names, but people do. Jacob learns his name, and along with it, as socialization proceeds, he learns his "meaning" in the eyes of others. He learns the attitudes they hold, the expectations they have of him, the ways they are prepared to act toward him. In thus becoming an object he can himself name, think about, develop feelings about, and act toward, he acquires a self.

The self is an important object in every human encounter or action. This is not to say that humans are motivated by any single goal such as a quest for self-esteem. *Self-esteem*, which we may define as a person's emotional responses to self, is an important facet of human existence, but it is a part of a complex of thoughts, feelings, and actions toward the self rather than the most important motivation for conduct. Rather, to make the self central to human conduct and social interaction is to say that in forming their conduct, people take themselves into account as a part of the situation in which they find themselves. They imagine how they appear to others and how their impending actions will affect how others see them. About to utter an ethnic slur, an individual may reflect on whether it will lead others to view him or her less favorably, and perhaps as a defensive strategy, the individual may disclaim any prejudiced intent even while making a prejudiced remark. Plans of action are constrained by the individual's view of his or her capabilities and limitations: Why work hard in school if it is likely I won't be rewarded for the effort or if I am unlikely to succeed? And when individuals find themselves defined in ways they do not like as a result of their actions, they seek to repair damage to the conceptions others have of them by excusing or justifying their conduct.

Identity

The concept of identity is central to the symbolic interactionist analysis of the self and is particularly important for the study of intergroup relations. *Identity* refers to the individual's location in social life, and it is established by the thoughts, feelings, and actions of others as well as those of the individual. A person has an identity—as a parent or a child, as a Black or a White, as a Roman Catholic or a Lutheran, as a friend or an enemy, as brilliant or intellectually slow—when the individual's announcements of identity correspond with the placements made by others.

Every act announces an identity of one kind or another. Approaching a sales clerk in a store with a confident sense that one expects his or her attention is an announcement of one's identity as a customer. The executive who disdainfully ignores a janitor or other service worker announces an identity of "superior" and assigns the other the place of "subordinate." When the clerk attends to the customer, he or she places the other in the customer identity. When the service worker avoids eye contact and attends only to the work at hand rather than to the executive, he or she places the other in the claimed position.

The individual's construction of an identity is therefore inherently a social process. Over time, people announce and are placed in a variety of identities: familial, occupational, educational, age related, political, ethnic, religious, and the like. Some of these identities acquire a more central place in the self than others—the individual may be chiefly identified by others and identify himself or herself as a professor, for example, or a Black, or a woman. People also construct personal identities for themselves that reflect their particular life histories or accomplishments and not only their group memberships and social roles. Some people—for example, Apple Computer CEO Steve Jobs—develop such distinctive personal identities that their names alone establish their place in the social world. Their personal identities nonetheless depend as much on their placement by others as on their own actions.

Identity is important because it provides a key basis for motivation and action. We see the world from the vantage points of our various identities. As Catholics or Jews, Blacks, Whites, or Hispanics, or as Steve Jobs, we define our circumstances and opportunities for action on the basis of our identities. Our actions within the groups to which we belong and our relationship to the members of other groups are shaped by how we see ourselves as members and nonmembers.

Announcements and placements do not always agree. Fellow members of one's ethnic group may be more interested in placing one among them and eliciting identification with the group than one is in announcing a group affiliation and identifying with it. An individual's identification with a group may be met with indifference or rejection by group members. In such circumstances we cannot really say that the individual "has" the group identity. Nonetheless, identity is a motivating element in his or her conduct, whether it promotes an effort to resist the group's pressures or to overcome its resistance.

Participant Observation

To study any social activity using the symbolic interactionist perspective requires the researcher to grasp the meanings that are central to it, and doing so requires a close, hands-on relationship with the social world under investigation. Participant observation is therefore a central interactionist method. Participation for a time within while also observing a social world, such as that of the neighborhood gang or of the ethnically homogeneous retirement community, is a means of learning what issues are important to members, how they define themselves and others, and what motivates their conduct. In addition to participant observation, symbolic interactionists use interviews, direct observations, historical records, and other written materials to round out their picture of a given social world.

John P. Hewitt

See also Collective Movements and Protest; Looking-Glass Self; Multiple Identities; Reference Groups; Roles; Self-Esteem; Social Identity Theory

Further Readings

Blumer, H. (1969). *Symbolic interactionism: Perspective and methods*. Englewood Cliffs, NJ: Prentice Hall.

Hewitt, J. P. (2007). *Self and society: A symbolic interactionist social psychology* (10th ed.). Boston: Allyn & Bacon.

Mead, G. H. (1964). *On social psychology* (A. L. Strauss, Ed.). Chicago: University of Chicago Press.

Reynolds, L. T., & Hermann-Kinney, N. J. (Eds.). (2003). *Handbook of symbolic interactionism*. Walnut Creek, CA: AltaMira Press.

Williams, N., & Correa, M. (2003). Race and ethnic relations. In L. T. Reynolds & N. J. Hermann-Kinney (Eds.), *Handbook of symbolic interactionism* (pp. 743–760). Walnut Creek, CA: AltaMira Press.

SYMBOLIC RACISM

Racial conflicts have plagued the United States from its very beginnings, driven in particular by racial prejudice against Blacks. In the period since the civil rights era of the 1960s, old forms of racial prejudice have nearly vanished, to be replaced by newer forms. The most politically powerful is *symbolic racism*. It is defined as a blend of anti-Black affect with traditional values, accompanied by the acceptance of formal racial equality. It applies a more general *symbolic politics theory* to the racial context, emphasizing the early acquisition of major sociopolitical attitudes and the symbolic meaning of political rhetoric, rather than interest-based politics. This entry briefly describes the theory of symbolic racism, the empirical evidence that sustains it, and competing points of view.

Background

At the end of World War II, Blacks were still second-class citizens, denied the pursuit of the American dream in all spheres of life—socially, economically, and politically. Since then, the Southern system of institutionalized *Jim Crow segregation* has been eliminated, as has most formal racial discrimination elsewhere. *Old-fashioned racism*, embodying beliefs in the biological inferiority of Blacks and support for formal discrimination and segregation, has greatly diminished and indeed has nearly disappeared from public discourse. However, Blacks continue to experience substantial disadvantages in most domains of life. Proponents of Blacks' interests have therefore continued to push for greater racial equality.

These efforts have often met with substantial White reaction, including the Republican *Southern strategy* of the 1960s, opposition to court-ordered busing in the 1970s and more recently to affirmative action, support for the use of Confederate symbols in state flags, opposition to Black political candidates, and, more indirectly, appeals for harsher crime and welfare policies.

Symbolic racism (also known as *racial resentment*) has been proposed as one explanation for Whites' political reactions, taking over the role once played by old-fashioned, or Jim Crow, racism. Symbolic racism centers around the belief that

Blacks violate traditional U.S. values, especially individualism. Perceptions that Blacks violate other values (including, for example, morality, self-restraint, and family traditionalism) have been less studied but may be important for understanding the range of values invoked in symbolic racism.

The Current Theory

Symbolic racism is usually described as a coherent belief system expressed in terms of four specific themes: that Blacks no longer face much prejudice or discrimination, that Blacks' failure to progress results from their unwillingness to work hard enough, that Blacks make excessive demands, and that Blacks have gotten more than they deserve. It is typically measured in telephone or face-to-face surveys or with computer-based or paper-and-pencil questionnaires.

The theory of symbolic racism poses five central propositions:

1. Symbolic racism has largely replaced old-fashioned racism; only a tiny minority of Whites still accept the latter whereas they are about evenly divided about the beliefs contained in symbolic racism.

2. Symbolic racism now influences Whites' political attitudes much more strongly than does old-fashioned racism.

3. The origins of symbolic racism lie in a blend of early-acquired negative feelings about Blacks and traditional values.

4. Whites' opposition to racially targeted policies and Black candidates is more influenced by symbolic racism than by realistic threats posed by Blacks to Whites.

5. Symbolic racism has political effects independent of those of ostensibly racially neutral predispositions such as ideological conservatism.

The term *racism* therefore reflects the centrality of antipathy toward Blacks. The term *symbolic* highlights both that symbolic racism is rooted in abstract moral values rather than in concrete self-interest or personal experiences and that it targets Blacks as an abstract collectivity rather than as specific individuals.

Much research shows that symbolic racism powerfully influences attitudes of White people in the United States toward racially relevant policies such as busing for school integration or affirmative action, as well as less explicitly race-targeted policies that disproportionately affect Blacks, such as welfare and crime policies. It has also been shown to promote opposition to Black candidates such as Jesse Jackson or Barack Obama, as well as support for ethnocentric White candidates such as Pat Buchanan or former Ku Klux Klan leader David Duke. The use of subtle racial appeals in political campaigns, such as the attention to Black murderer and rapist Willie Horton during the 1988 presidential campaign and the militant Black minister Jeremiah Wright in 2008, also enhances its political force. Symbolic racism also has played a pivotal role in the realignment to the Republican party of the once solidly Democratic vote of White Southerners—it is more common, and more strongly influences voting choices, among White Southerners than among other people in the United States.

There are two distinctively different ways to think about the origins of any belief system. One is its grounding in more fundamental psychological constructs, such as values, personality predispositions, or social identities. In this sense the origins of symbolic racism are described as lying in a blend of anti-Black affect and traditional values. But its origins can also be described in terms of a developmental or life-history process. Most childhood attitudes toward social groups are primitive and cognitively rudimentary. But they may develop more fully in adolescence with increasing exposure to prepackaged belief systems such as symbolic racism. Research shows that symbolic racism usually develops in adolescence, earlier than many other sociopolitical beliefs.

Distinctions, Challenges, and Future Directions

Other forms of contemporary racism are defined somewhat differently. *Modern racism* and *aversive racism* are conceptualized as reflecting an ambivalence between egalitarian cognition and anti-Black affect. *Racial ambivalence* reflects an ambivalence between egalitarianism and individualism.

Much research has been devoted to distinguishing the political influence of symbolic racism from that of personal interests. Symbolic racism is partially rooted in abstract beliefs about Blacks' violations of traditional values, beliefs acquired early in life from parents, peers, and the media. Interest-based preferences, in contrast, presumably arise from adults' calculations of their own interests, such as Whites' opposition to affirmative action because they believe it will prevent their getting desirable jobs. Considerable research shows that symbolic racism influences racially relevant political attitudes regardless of a person's own interests, just as self-interest usually plays a secondary role in public opinion more generally.

Group-based interests are another matter. Perhaps White people in the United States often oppose race-based policies such as affirmative action to protect the threatened interests of Whites as a whole, regardless of their own narrow self-interest. However, research has shown that symbolic racism strongly predicts Whites' racial policy preferences above and beyond the effects of variables relevant to group interest, such as White group identification, perceived common fate with other Whites, perceived collective threat to Whites, or competition from Blacks about valued resources, all of which themselves tend to have weak effects. The political effects of symbolic racism seem to be quite separate from Whites' desires to protect their self- or group-based interests.

Symbolic racism can also be distinguished from *conservative ideology*. The two are related, but they independently contribute opposition to racially targeted policies and Black candidates. Put another way, symbolic racism strongly promotes such opposition among both ideological liberals and conservatives. Of course some ideological conservatives may oppose race-based policies without subscribing to symbolic racism, but that seems to be the exception rather than the rule. This remains an important controversy, however, and political conservatives do not regard it as settled.

The symbolic racism claim is an important one. It asserts that the politics of race are not merely "politics as usual" but instead are significantly influenced by the underlying racial prejudice held by many racial conservatives and that ostensibly race-neutral conservative rhetoric often disguises underlying racial animosity. These controversies are of more than mere academic relevance. They go to the substantive core of longest-running and most difficult social problem facing the United States. If the symbolic racism claim is right, much remedial work of a variety of kinds needs to be done on the White side of the racial divide. If it is wrong, and racial conservatives' views about the optimal relative balance of governments and markets in modern societies are largely free of underlying racial prejudice, much obligation would be placed on Blacks to adapt to a society in which they no longer are being treated much less fairly than their fellow citizens.

The theory of symbolic racism was developed in the particular U.S. context of continuing White resistance to full racial equality in the post–civil rights era. It has since been applied to other cases of group prejudice, including attitudes toward women, the obese, or (in Europe) immigrants.

David O. Sears

See also Aversive Racism; Modern Forms of Prejudice; Modern Racism; Modern Sexism; Prejudice; Racial Ambivalence Theory

Further Readings

Hutchings, V. L., & Valentino, N. A. (2004). The centrality of race in American politics. *Annual Review of Political Science, 7*, 383–408.

Sears, D. O. (1993). Symbolic politics: A socio-psychological theory. In S. Iyengar & W. J. McGuire (Eds.), *Explorations in political psychology* (pp. 113–149). Durham, NC: Duke University Press.

Sears, D. O., & Henry, P. J. (2005). Over thirty years later: A contemporary look at symbolic racism. In M. Zanna (Ed.), *Advances in experimental social psychology* (Vol. 37, pp. 95–150). San Diego, CA: Elsevier.

Sears, D. O., Sidanius, J., & Bobo, L. (Eds.). (2000). *Racialized politics: The debate about racism in America*. Chicago: University of Chicago Press.

SYMLOG

The acronym SYMLOG stands for a *SY*stem for the *M*ultiple *L*evel *O*bservation of *G*roups. The SYMLOG system was developed by Robert F. Bales and his colleagues and was first published in book form in 1979. At its most basic level,

SYMLOG is a method for quantitatively and graphically describing the behavior or personality of groups or group members across a three-dimensional conceptual space defined by the factors of *dominance, friendliness,* and *acceptance of authority.* The resulting descriptions can be used for a variety of purposes, including to provide feedback on group functioning, to assess the effects of an intervention, or to describe organizational values. This entry describes both the scoring and presentation of results in the SYMLOG system.

The SYMLOG system grew out of earlier work by Bales that used his *interaction process analysis* system, which was a systematic framework for making observations important to Bales's theoretical ideas concerning group problem solving. In that earlier work, Bales proposed that a group moves through a particular sequence of phases as it moves from the beginning to the completion of a task: (a) orientation (gathering information and clarifying the task), (b) evaluation (assessing that information), and (c) control (deciding what to do).

In SYMLOG, those phases reemerge as dimensions that capture important distinctions in interpersonal and group dynamics: dominance versus submissiveness, friendliness versus unfriendliness, and acceptance versus nonacceptance of authority. In the SYMLOG system, these three dimensions form a cube that constitutes the SYMLOG space. The dimensions of the cube have directional labels that correspond to each pole of these bipolar dimensions. *Upward* and *downward* correspond to dominance and submissiveness, respectively. *Positive* and *negative* correspond to friendliness and unfriendliness, respectively. *Forward* and *backward* correspond to acceptance and nonacceptance of authority, respectively. Each dimension also has a neutral middle position, resulting in a 3 × 3 × 3 cube, with each cell in the cube described by singly (e.g., U, P, F), doubly (e.g., NB, UP, DP), or triply (e.g., DNB, UPB, UNF) designated coordinates. The interior cell of the cube is left undesignated.

The *SYMLOG rating form* consists of 26 items that correspond to each of the 26 labeled cells of the cube. Each entity being assessed (e.g., a person or an organization) is rated on a 3-point scale on each of the 26 items. The 3-point scale represents a frequency rating of the behavior, and the scale values are typically labeled as *rarely* = 0, *sometimes* = 1,

and *often* = 2. The 26 items are each briefly defined with specific behaviors or adjectives. Ratings can then be made by untrained coders or by members of an interacting group who rate each other's behavior retrospectively on each of the 26 descriptive items.

The scores are then tallied and arranged to produce a location for each coder's perception of each group member in the three-dimensional space, thereby producing a graphical representation of interpersonal relations and group dynamics. The results of those ratings can then be graphically displayed by means of one of a number of representations described later in this entry.

A summary location for each of the three dimensions can also be calculated by adding together all the items that contain one end of the dimension and subtracting from it the sum of all the items that contain the opposite end of the dimension. For example, a location on the friendliness-versus-unfriendliness dimension can be determined by summing together the nine items that contain an F descriptor (e.g., F, PF, DNF) and subtracting from that sum the sum of the nine items that contain a B descriptor (e.g., B, UB, DNB). SYMLOG can also be used for act-by-act coding of verbal content (as with the *interaction process analysis*), although this application is rare.

The specific content of the SYMLOG rating forms varies, such that different behaviors or adjectives may be used to describe each of the 26 cells. For instance, the SYMLOG General Behavior Rating Form assesses each of the 26 cells using specific corresponding behaviors. For example, U is assessed by means of the behaviors *active, dominant,* and *talks a lot,* whereas PF is assessed by means of the behavior *works cooperatively with others.* On the other hand, the Value Rating Form assesses each of the 26 cells by means of general values that might underlie each description. For example, on this form U is assessed by means of the underlying value of *material success and power,* whereas PF is assessed using the underlying value of *altruism, idealism, cooperation.*

Other possible rating forms include the Specific Behavior Rating Form, in which the 26 cells are described with more specific behaviors than on the General Rating Form (e.g., active, entertaining, depressed), and the Individual and Organizational Values Rating Form, in which the 26 cells are described by means of underlying values that are central (e.g., efficiency, protecting less able members, conservative). The level at which the dimensions are assessed can also vary and can range from ratings of the self to ratings of other group members to ratings of the group as a whole and to ratings of the organization as a whole.

Presenting the Results

The results of the SYMLOG rating form are generally presented by means of a graphical representation—most commonly in the form of a horizontal bar graph across the 26 items or in terms of a field diagram. The horizontal bar graph is perhaps the most intuitive form of representation. Each of the 26 items to be assessed is listed down one side of the graph. Frequency ratings or averaged frequency ratings for each of those items are then presented as histograms to the side. These bar graphs can be used quite flexibly. For example, the ratings of each of two group members can be compared by comparing the bar graphs displaying the group's averaged assessments of each member's behavior.

Similarly, one could compare the dominant organizational values of two organizations by comparing bar graphs displaying average ratings of these values for each organization. Researchers can also include on the bar graph indications of a norm or an *optimum location* for effective behavior or effective teamwork on each of the 26 cells derived from survey research conducted by Bales and others to aid in the interpretation of individual scores.

The more common way of graphically presenting SYMLOG ratings is the *SYMLOG field diagram*. Essentially, the field diagram is a strategy for displaying ratings of the three dimensions of the SYMLOG space on a two-dimensional surface. Two of the dimensions—forward versus backward and positive versus negative—define a two-dimensional grid. The third dimension—upward versus downward—is indicated by the size of the circle that represents the group member or other entity represented on the grid.

For example, a researcher might want to represent ratings for each member of a group on a single field diagram. The researcher must first determine each group member's location on each of the three dimensions, using the subtraction method described above. The researcher then represents each group member on the grid by first locating the group member's coordinates on the forward–backward and positive–negative grid and then adjusting the size of the image used to mark those coordinates according to the member's location rating on the upward–downward dimension, with a larger circle indicating more dominance.

Note that by using difference scores to represent values on each dimension, researchers lose information concerning the magnitude of ratings on each pole of the dimension. Bar graphs retain this more specific information and can be used if necessary to aid in the interpretation of the field diagram. In addition, it is common to expand the pattern of the field diagram so that it fills up the available diagram space. It is therefore important to be aware of the expansion multiplier used when one is trying to compare the overall patterns of two or more diagrams.

Bales also recommends that the field diagram be used to help define the main forces of tension and balance within a group and between group members. In examining a field diagram, one can see various clusters of group members and separations between group members. A number of strategies exist for determining the polarizing and unifying aspects of group dynamics that create such clusters, including both statistical calculations and the use of a more subjective transparent overlay that is placed over the field diagram in order to identify subgroups within the larger group. The overlay consists of two large circles tangent to one another.

The *line of polarization* is drawn through the centers of those circles and identifies differences among clusters of group members. The *line of balance* is drawn at right angles to the line of polarization and marks the dividing line between the two polarized clusters. By examining the position of group members relative to the lines of polarization and balance, researchers can identify reference groups, opposition groups, and more specific group member roles, such as *scapegoat* and *mediator*.

Thus, the field diagram provides a graphical representation of the underlying structure of the group or organization. Feedback in the form of the bar graphs or field diagrams can be given to individuals to help them understand how their behavior is viewed by others in the group. The group as a whole can also be given group-level feedback in order to help its members understand the underlying dynamics that are affecting group behavior and contributing to effective or ineffective group performance.

Janice R. Kelly

See also Group Structure; Interaction Process Analysis; Social Networks

Further Readings

Bales, R. F. (1950). *Interaction process analysis: A method for the study of small groups.* Cambridge, MA: Addison-Wesley.

Bales, R. F., & Cohen, S. P. (with Williamson, S. A.). (1979). *SYMLOG: A system for the multiple level observation of groups.* New York: Free Press.

Hare, A. P., Sjovold, E., Baker, H. G., & Powers, J. (2005). *Analysis of social interaction systems: SYMLOG research and applications.* Lanham, MD: University Press of America.

Polley, R. B., Hare, A. P., & Stone, P. J. (1988). *The SYMLOG practitioner: Applications of small group research.* New York: Praeger.

SYSTEM JUSTIFICATION THEORY

System justification theory was initially proposed by John T. Jost and Mahzarin R. Banaji in 1994 to explain how and why people tolerate unjust and exploitative social arrangements rather than doing everything they can to change the status quo and thereby create a better, more just system. The need for such an explanation arises from historical observations revealing numerous instances of people not merely passively accepting—but sometimes even actively justifying and rationalizing—social systems that are seen as extremely unjust by outsiders, often in retrospect.

For example, the caste system in India has survived largely intact for 3,000 years, and the institution of slavery lasted for more than 400 years in Europe and the Americas. Colonialism was also practiced for centuries and still is in some places (as is slavery), and the apartheid system in South Africa lasted for almost 50 years. According to system justification theory, social systems such as these are supported and maintained at least in part because of processes of motivated social cognition that lead people to consciously and unconsciously defend, bolster, and rationalize aspects of the societal status quo. System justification is accomplished by individuals and groups through the use of stereotypes, social judgments and evaluations, legitimizing beliefs, and more formal ideologies such as political conservatism and religious fundamentalism.

System justification theory may be distinguished from other sociological and psychological perspectives that emphasize self-interest, identity politics, and the thirst for justice as primary or ubiquitous motives. These other perspectives assume that people are quick to anger in the face of injustice and exploitation, and they suggest that protest, rebellion, and moral outrage on the part of the disadvantaged should be commonplace. However, rebellion in social, economic, and political domains occurs more rarely than one would expect, and the sense of injustice is surprisingly difficult to awaken. Moral outrage is frequently directed at those who dare to challenge the system rather than those who are responsible for its failings. What needs to be explained, then, is the surprising extent to which people, including members of disadvantaged groups, acquiesce in the face of an unjust status quo.

Ego, Group, and System Justification Motives

A unique prediction of system justification theory is that people are motivated to defend, bolster, and rationalize their own self-interest and the basis of their self-esteem (*ego justification*), the interests and esteem of their own group (*group justification*), and also the social systems that affect them (*system justification*). The result of this last motive is a general inclination to see the status quo as good, fair, legitimate, and desirable. System justification theory does not suggest that people always perceive the status quo as completely fair and just; as with other motives (including ego and group justification motives), the strength of the system justification motive is expected to vary considerably across individuals, groups, and situations.

The theory suggests merely that people are prone to exaggerate their system's virtues, to downplay its vices, and to see existing social arrangements as more favorable and just than they actually are. Social systems to which people become psychologically attached can range in size and scope from relationship dyads and families to formal and informal status hierarchies to social, economic, or political institutions and organizations, or even to entire societies.

According to system justification theory, the three motives of ego, group, and system justification are generally consonant, complementary, and mutually reinforcing for those who occupy a relatively advantaged position in the social system. For those who are disadvantaged, however, these three motives are often in conflict or contradiction with one another, and different individuals may make different "choices" about how to resolve these conflicts. Accordingly, several studies show that the more members of disadvantaged groups (e.g., Blacks) subscribe to system-justifying beliefs, such as the belief that inequality in society is fair and necessary, the more they suffer in terms of self-esteem and neuroticism and the more ambivalent they feel toward fellow ingroup members.

Furthermore, these negative consequences are more likely to arise for those members of disadvantaged groups who are relatively highly identified with their own group, presumably because the conflict between group and system justification motives is more acute for such individuals. Distancing from (or dis-identifying with) one's own group is another way of resolving the conflict between group and system justification motives.

System Justification on the Part of the Disadvantaged

Because ego, group, and system justification motives are in opposition for those who are disadvantaged by the status quo, such individuals are on average less likely than those who are advantaged to see the existing system as fair and legitimate. However, under some circumstances—such as when the salience of individual or collective self-interest is very low—members of disadvantaged groups can be the most ardent supporters of the status quo. For example, survey studies in the United States reveal that extremely low-income respondents are more likely, rather than less likely, to believe that income inequality is legitimate and necessary than are medium- or high-income respondents.

Similarly, a study of the social and political attitudes of severely disadvantaged indigenous children in Bolivia revealed that they were significantly more likely to approve of the Hispanic-run government, more likely to endorse the suppression of speeches against the government, and less likely to be cynical or distrusting of the government than were children from other ethnic groups that were more advantaged. These results, which are difficult to explain from the standpoint of other prominent theories in sociology and psychology, suggest that nearly everyone holds at least some system-justifying attitudes and that, paradoxically, it is sometimes those who are the worst off who are the strongest defenders of the system.

It is possible, of course, that members of disadvantaged groups feel strong social pressure to exaggerate their support for the status quo in public and that they privately hold attitudes that are far more critical of the existing social system. However, a large number of studies using implicit measures that reduce opportunities for impression management, such as the Implicit Association Test, suggest that it is extremely common for members of disadvantaged groups to internalize relatively favorable attitudes toward members of more advantaged outgroups and the social system as a whole.

For example, substantial proportions of members of disadvantaged groups—including dark-skinned Morenos in Chile, poor people and the obese, university students randomly assigned to low-status rather than high-status residential colleges, gays and lesbians, Latinos and Asians, and even Blacks, who reject the legitimacy of racial inequality at an explicit level—exhibit implicit biases in favor of more advantaged outgroup members. Furthermore, the extent to which members of disadvantaged groups exhibit implicit outgroup favoritism is predicted by their scores on measures of system justification and political conservatism.

The Palliative Function of System Justification

It has been theorized that system justification serves a set of relatively proximal epistemic, existential, and relational functions that help people manage uncertainty and threat and smooth out social relationships. System-justifying belief systems are reassuring because they enable people to cope with and feel better about the societal status quo and their place in it. Along these lines, John T. Jost and Orsolya Hunyady suggested that system justification serves the palliative function of reducing negative affect and increasing positive affect. This idea bears some resemblance to Karl Marx's notion that religion is the "opiate of the masses," or the "illusory happiness of the people."

Several studies reveal that giving people the opportunity to justify the system does indeed lead them to feel better and more satisfied and to report feeling more positive and fewer negative emotions. Furthermore, chronically high system justifiers, such as political conservatives, are happier (as measured in terms of subjective well-being) than are chronically low system-justifiers, such as liberals, leftists, and others who are more troubled by the degree of social and economic inequality in our society.

The hedonic benefits of system justification, however, come at a cost in terms of decreased potential for social change and the remediation of inequality. Research shows that system-justifying ideologies, whether measured or manipulated through a mindset-priming technique, do indeed serve to reduce emotional distress—including negative affect in general and guilt in particular—but they also reduce moral outrage. This last consequence is particularly important because moral outrage motivates people to engage in helping behavior and to support social change. Thus, the reduction in moral outrage makes people less inclined to help those who are disadvantaged, measured in terms of research participants' degree of support for and willingness to volunteer for or donate to a soup kitchen, a crisis hotline, and tutoring or job training programs for the underprivileged.

How Do We Know It Is Motivated?

Some scholars recognize that attitudes and behaviors are commonly system justifying in their consequences but question the notion that people are motivated to see the societal status quo as fair, legitimate, and desirable. There are at least five lines of empirical evidence suggesting that system justification is a motivated, goal-directed process.

First, studies show that the endorsement of system-justifying attitudes is correlated with individual differences in self-deception and ideological motivation. Second, laboratory experiments in which exposure to system threat is manipulated reveal that most people respond defensively on behalf of the system, using stereotypes and evaluative judgments to rationalize inequalities between social groups. Third, research demonstrates that system justification leads people to engage in selective, biased information processing in favor of system-serving conclusions, such as the conclusion that the U.S. economic system is highly meritocratic. Fourth, system justification exhibits several other properties of goal pursuit, including *equifinality* (the fact that there are multiple, functionally interchangeable means of reaching the system justification goal) and *multifinality* (the fact that the system justification goal satisfies multiple needs, including epistemic, existential, and relational needs). Fifth, studies indicate that the desire to make the system look good and fair inspires behavioral efforts in terms of task persistence and performance. For all these reasons, it seems as if the guiding theoretical assumption of system justification theory, namely that people are motivated to defend, bolster, and justify the status quo, is on relatively solid empirical ground.

A motivational approach to system justification may ultimately help explain when people will (and will not) engage in social change. Because a goal systems framework allows for the operation of competing goals—such as ego justification or group justification, goals for novelty or accuracy, or the desire for retribution and other justice-related motives—it can help clarify the circumstances under which people will challenge or criticize the system. Such an approach will enable us to better understand the processes that give rise to widespread defection from the motivational clutches of system justification.

When justifying the system no longer satisfies epistemic, existential, or relational needs—either because the status quo itself offers no stability or certainty or because it is regarded as a source of threat rather than reassurance, or because it has become counternormative to stick with the old regime when a new one is gaining in popularity—then the system justification goal will finally be abandoned. Once a new system or regime acquires an aura of inevitability, system justification motives should lead people to engage in rationalization processes that will bolster the new system at the expense of the old one.

John T. Jost

See also Collective Movements and Protest; Ideology; Protestant Work Ethic; Social Dominance Theory; Social Identity Theory; Uncertainty-Identity Theory

Further Readings

Jost, J. T., & Banaji, M. R. (1994). The role of stereotyping in system-justification and the production of false consciousness. *British Journal of Social Psychology, 33,* 1–27.

Jost, J. T., Banaji, M. R., & Nosek, B. A. (2004). A decade of system justification theory: Accumulated evidence of conscious and unconscious bolstering of the status quo. *Political Psychology, 25,* 881–919.

Jost, J. T., Glaser, J., Kruglanski, A. W., & Sulloway, F. (2003). Political conservatism as motivated social cognition. *Psychological Bulletin, 129,* 339–375.

Jost, J. T., & Hunyady, O. (2002). The psychology of system justification and the palliative function of ideology. *European Review of Social Psychology, 13,* 111–153.

Jost, J. T., Liviatan, I., van der Toorn, J., Ledgerwood, A., Mandisodza, A., & Nosek, B.A. (in press). System justification: How do we know it's motivated? In A. C. Kay et al. (Eds.), *The psychology of justice and legitimacy: The Ontario Symposium* (Vol. 11). Hillsdale, NJ: Erlbaum.

Jost, J. T., Pelham, B. W., Sheldon, O., & Sullivan, B. N. (2003). Social inequality and the reduction of ideological dissonance on behalf of the system: Evidence of enhanced system justification among the disadvantaged. *European Journal of Social Psychology, 33,* 13–36.

Kay, A. C., Jost, J. T., Mandisodza, A. N., Sherman, S. J., Petrocelli, J. V., & Johnson, A. L. (2007). Panglossian ideology in the service of system justification: How complementary stereotypes help us to rationalize inequality. In M. Zanna (Ed.), *Advances in experimental social psychology* (Vol. 39, pp. 305–358). San Diego, CA: Academic Press/ Elsevier.

Wakslak, C., Jost, J. T., Tyler, T. R., & Chen, E. (2007). Moral outrage mediates the dampening effect of system justification on support for redistributive social policies. *Psychological Science, 18,* 267–274.

SYSTEM THEORY

System theories are concerned with the relationships among *elements* (such as individuals) within *systems* (e.g., a group). *General systems theory* was popularized by Karl Ludwig von Bertalanffy as an interdisciplinary framework, or metatheory, aimed at describing the fundamental principles of systems of all kinds, from cells and organisms to societies and from biological and ecological to social systems. Several other metatheories, such as cybernetics and information theory, the theory of complex adaptive systems, and dynamical systems theory, are also system theories. The most important concepts from these theories for group psychology are briefly presented below.

One main assumption of system theories is that the system itself (e.g., a group) has, or develops, properties that cannot be fully described, explained, or predicted by observing the behavior of elements of the system (e.g., the group members). Recall Aristotle's claim that the whole is something besides (or more than) its parts. Moreover, the properties of the elements within a system (e.g., group members' behavior) can be understood only when one knows something about the system as a whole. Given that groups are complex, composed of individuals, and embedded in contexts, a system theory perspective seems especially appropriate for the study of groups.

Core Assumptions of System Theories

Biological and social systems are open systems that interact (exchange information, material, or energy) with their environment and thus are influenced by and influence their context. They are hierarchically organized: A system is composed of subsystems and is embedded into suprasystems. A subsystem in a group might be a single group member or a clique of members, and the group's suprasystem might be an organization in which the group is embedded. System theorists assume that all the concepts they have identified can be observed at different system levels.

Systems, such as groups, have a tendency toward self-organization, which means that they develop structures or functions "by themselves," without pressure or influence from an outside agent. Examples of self-organization include growth and development processes. The local dynamics in a system, that is, the interactions among system components (e.g., group members), produce what are called *order parameters* at the system level. These parameters influence the behavior of system elements and thus become what are called the *global dynamics* of the system. For instance, group members establish rules during their interactions (*local dynamics*). These rules then become a given for the group as a whole (global dynamics) and thereby influence the behavior of group members.

Systems change over time. System theorists assume that open systems tend to move toward higher organization and more differentiation and specialization, but they also move toward higher *centralization*, because they can import energy and thus resist *entropy* (a state of disorder) for a time. Centralization means that some components have greater influence on the system than do others. An example is the development of leadership structures in groups. *Complexity theory* investigates patterns of changes over time in systems and describes whether and under what conditions a system evolves to one or several stable states. These stable states are called *attractors*. Often, the trajectories of different system states over time toward attractors are estimated on the basis of mathematical formulae and plotted in a so-called *phase space* (a graphical representation of predicted behavior).

Temporal changes in systems are seldom linear but occur instead in an abrupt and nonlinear way. The system may be stable for a time, even under considerable pressure to change, but eventually a small event, which would not normally influence the system, can have a dramatic effect. Given the complex interplay of different influences in most systems, it is difficult to predict when such a dramatic change occurs. Rapid, large changes in systems are described by *catastrophe theories*, which depict changes as surfaces or curves and describe abrupt changes from one state to another as bifurcation or phase transitions. Below the bifurcation point, the system is stable, but above that point, there is a short phase of instability, and, after a massive change, the system again attains stability.

A system is self-regulating and thus adapts to changes as it pursues goals. Feedback loops are a central element of this regulation: The output of a system's actions serves as an input into the system, and the system readjusts its behavior when it seems to be deviating from the chosen, or prescribed, course. In following this course, many systems move toward an end state, and so their movement seems purposeful. Goal orientations are especially important for human and social systems. There are usually many possible ways to achieve a goal; this is described as *equifinality*.

System Theories in Group Research

System theories have influenced group research in different ways. In a few studies, researchers have applied mathematical concepts from system theories to their data. The next section presents an example of such an application. Some researchers have formulated theories about groups on the basis of system thinking. Two such theories are summarized briefly. Furthermore, system theories have influenced many different aspects of group research, and some examples of that influence are also described.

Formal Analyses of Group Processes

Although the propositions in most system theories have been formulated as mathematical concepts, only a few researchers have analyzed group processes using the resulting mathematical models. Some have even questioned whether doing so is useful, because the high precision and the large number of data points required for such analyses are difficult to achieve. In addition, the results of such analyses are often difficult to interpret. However, an interesting example of group process analyses based on dynamic system theory is the work of Losada and his colleagues. They analyzed trajectories in phase space for teams that showed different temporal patterns (e.g., positive and negative emotional exchanges among group members). The researchers found that high-performing groups occupied a clearly larger phase space before entering a stable state, whereas low-performing groups rapidly moved toward an attractor. This indicates that high-performing groups display a greater variety of behaviors, which may help them adapt better to changing demands. One can expect more analyses like these in the future as new technology allows researchers to collect more fine-grained data on group processes.

Theoretical Frameworks Based on System Theories

Probably the most extensive and integrative theoretical framework that incorporates dynamical systems and complexity theory is that published by Arrow, McGrath, and Berdahl in 2000. They see groups as open systems that are complex, dynamic, and adaptive. Besides local dynamics and global dynamics, Arrow and her colleagues have emphasized the importance of contextual dynamics. *Contextual dynamics* require the adaptation of a group to changes in its environment. An interesting and novel aspect of this theory is the assumption that some elements of a group (e.g., group structure) go beyond its members. Rather, a group's elements also include its *tasks* (or *intentions* or *projects*) and the resources and technologies (called *tools*) that are available to it. The interplay among members, tasks, and tools (the local dynamics) forms the overall coordination network. Group behavior must respond to the three main functions of groups, namely fulfilling member's needs, maintaining the structure and integrity of the group as a system, and achieving group projects. The main activities of a group are communication (information processing and the generation of meaning), conflict management, and the coordination of member behavior.

Another important aspect of this theory is its emphasis on different temporal changes in groups. The theory does not assume predictable, consecutive stages of development in groups. Instead, it uses complexity theory and the concept of attractors to explain different possible change trajectories in group behavior. For example, groups can (rapidly) move toward a stable state, but they sometimes oscillate between different attractors and thus show multiple stable states. Arrow, McGrath, and Berdahl assume that group-level patterns can emerge independently from the particularities of individual members' behavior. Identifying regularities, or patterns, in a group thus requires studying the group as a whole, rather than trying to predict group-level variables on the basis of individual behavior. Furthermore, such studies should be carried out over time.

Contextual variables (e.g., the organization in which a group is embedded) also influence group behavior because the group must adapt to changing conditions. The influence of contextual factors is often nonlinear. This means that large changes may not always have big effects, whereas small changes at specific times may alter the group in dramatic ways. This makes the identification of critical times for external influence as important as the identification and evaluation of the influence itself. A discussion of critical times for external influences can be found in Hackman and Wageman's *team coaching model*. Their model claims that motivational coaching should be provided at the beginning, strategic coaching at the midpoint, and educational coaching at the end of a group's task.

Another system-based group theory is DeSanctis and Poole's *adaptive structuration theory*. It is based on structuration theory, which was proposed by the sociologist Giddens. Adaptive structuration theory attempts to explain how groups and their members structure each other, and it helps explain why one often observes very different outcomes and interaction processes in groups with very similar features.

Generally stated, a group's structures (rules, regulations, and resources) guide its members' interactions, but member behavior also reproduces, constitutes, adapts to, and changes those structures and thus alters the group. On one hand, individuals in groups act according to social structures, for example the rules and regulations that govern their behavior. Often, these social structures are adopted from general rules (e.g., the majority rule for decision). Sometimes, new structures are created or adapted (e.g., to the group's task or technology) and influenced by available resources. On the other hand, when members respond to group structures, they also create and reproduce them. This is called the *duality of structures*: The behavior of group members is governed by the rules and regulations in the group (the structures), but these structures also emerge and are influenced by the interactions. Thus, group members influence the group's structures.

Topics in Group Research Influenced by, or Compatible With, System Theories

The ideas of many group theorists, such as Kurt Lewin, are compatible with a system theories approach. But most group researchers have studied either the influence of groups on individual behavior or the influence of individual behavior on group outcomes. More recently, new research questions have been inspired by the systems perspective, which may help overcome what Lewin (1947) once called a taboo on studying group-level phenomena. Such a taboo is evident in Allport's claim that all group-level phenomena can and should be explained by individual factors. Allport denied that groups exist apart from their members.

Examples of recent concepts from the groups literature that seem compatible with a system theories perspective include *shared mental models*, *socially shared cognitions*, *group reflexivity*, and *transactive memory systems*. These concepts refer to group-level phenomena and describe the processes involved as functionally analogous to similar processes within the individual. In other words, they suggest that groups can be viewed as (larger and more complex) information processing systems. Other examples involve temporal changes in groups: For example, the *group socialization theory* proposed in 1982 by Moreland and Levine describes role transitions, which mark qualitative shifts in the relationship between the group and the individual. Between role transitions, that relationship usually changes in a more continuous, incremental fashion. Group development theories, such as that proposed by Worchel, Coutant-Sassic, and Grossman, describe group development as a cyclical activity that is influenced by the relationships among group members, the group as a whole, and its context. And Gersick's *punctuated equilibrium model* of project group development suggests that group development involves long periods of relative inertia, separated by sudden transitions associated with special events, such as the midpoint of the group's work. These transitions are likely to involve large, nonlinear changes in the group. During its midpoint transition, for example, a group will often radically change its work strategies and direction. Afterward, another period of relative stability begins. Gersick's approach is compatible with a system dynamics perspective and helps identify the critical points at which it may be easiest to change a group.

Conclusion

The serious use of system theories implies an extension of traditional paradigms of experimental and analytical research on groups because these paradigms often cannot adequately assess the complex social dynamics the system theories have proposed. Instead of studying single, cause–effect relationships, system theories are interested in the complex interplay of elements, features of the whole system and its contexts, and changes over time. System theories assume that precise predictions of system states are difficult or even impossible to make, but the assumptions of system theories can still serve as valuable heuristics to draw attention toward important phenomena that would be otherwise overlooked. Empirical investigations based on system theories are difficult. Arrow and her colleagues have suggested three research strategies compatible with a system perspective:

1. Comparative case studies that investigate groups over time may help scholars understand the interplay of and the recursive influence between multiple levels of a system.

2. More naturalistic studies, including simulations based on realistic situations, allow researchers to analyze at least part of the complexity associated with real groups.

3. Computer simulation studies allow researchers to apply mathematical functions to data on groups or to translate verbal theories into computational models and then run computational simulation studies. The results of those studies can then be compared with real-life observations.

Ultimately, system theories are metatheories. Their application to group research requires the translation of general concepts to more specific phenomena and new or adapted research strategies, whose development is still under way.

Franziska Tschan

See also Dynamical Systems Approach; Group Composition; Group Development; Group Socialization; Lewin, Kurt; Shared Mental Models; Socially Shared Cognition; Social Networks; Teams; Transactive Memory Systems

Further Readings

Arrow, H., McGrath, J. E., & Berdahl, J. L. (2000). *Small groups as complex systems: Formation, coordination, development, and adaptation.* London: Sage.

DeSanctis, G., & Poole, M. S. (1994). Capturing the complexity in advanced technology use: Adaptive structuration theory. *Organization Science, 5,* 121–147.

Gersick, C. J. G. (1989). Marking time: Predictable transition in task groups. *Academy of Management Journal, 32,* 274–309.

Lewin, K. (1947). Frontiers of group dynamics: Concept, method, and reality in social science; social equilibra and social change. *Human Relations, 1,* 5–41.

Losada, M., & Heaphy, E. (2004). The role of positivity and connectivity in the performance of business teams: A nonlinear dynamics model. *American Behavioral Scientist, 47,* 740–765.

Moreland, R. L., & Levine, J. M. (1982). Socialization in small groups: Temporal changes in individual–group relations. In L. Berkowitz (Ed.), *Advances in experimental social psychology* (Vol. 15, pp. 137–192). New York: Academic Press.

Vallacher, R. R., & Nowak, A. (2004). *Dynamical systems in social psychology.* San Diego, CA: Academic Press.

Worchel, S., Coutant-Sassic, D., & Grossman, M. (1992). A developmental approach to group dynamics: A model and illustrative research. In S. Worchel, W. Wood, & J. A. Simpson (Eds.), *Group process and productivity* (pp. 181–202). Newbury Park, CA: Sage.

Tajfel, Henri (1919–1982)

Henri Tajfel is best known for developing the concept of *social identity*, a central construct in what later became known as *social identity theory*. His earliest work in psychology was largely experimental and dealt with social perception and stereotyping. Later, he turned his attention to the study of intergroup relations, and it was in this context that social identity theory was formulated. He is also remembered in Europe for the time and energy that he gave to establishing a European style of social psychology, one that recognized the social, political, and historical context within which social behavior takes place.

Tajfel's Personal and Intellectual History

Born into a Jewish family in Poland, Henri Tajfel was a student at the Sorbonne in France when Germany invaded Poland in September 1939. A fluent French speaker, he served in the French army, was captured by the invading German forces in 1940, and spent the rest of the conflict as a prisoner of war. His survival depended on his assuming a French identity and concealing his Polish–Jewish heritage. Years later, he had difficulty understanding the Polish language on a return visit to his native country, a reminder that he had come to think and speak as a Frenchman.

The war's end revealed that all his family and most of his friends had been killed. While still in France, he spent his time for several years helping European refugees to rehabilitate and be repatriated or else resettled in other countries. These events left profound psychological marks on Tajfel and provided him with important intellectual signposts for his later research and writing dealing with discrimination against minorities and how identity is shaped by ethnic and national group membership. In his own wartime experience, he observed that had his Polish–Jewish identity been revealed, his fate would have been determined by his social category—a certain death, no matter what other personal qualities his might have had.

He married and with his wife, Anne, moved to England in 1951. As an undergraduate student at Birkbeck College, London, he won a scholarship for an essay on a topic close to his heart, prejudice. He graduated in 1954, worked as a research assistant at the University of Durham, and later became a lecturer in social psychology at Oxford. In 1967, he was appointed to a chair in social psychology at Bristol University, a post that he held until his death.

Tajfel's Research Contributions

Tajfel's earliest published research was on *social perception*, based on what was termed the *New Look* in perception and stimulated by Jerome Bruner at Harvard University. What was new was an emphasis on perception as an active rather than a reactive process. People's mental processes often organize everyday stimuli according to those values or need states that are current or salient at that moment. For example, a meat eater who was very hungry might mistake a blurred photographic image of a red flower for a juicy steak.

Perceptual Accentuation

Tajfel absorbed such ideas into his work on perceptual *accentuation*. In one study, the stimuli were eight lines that differed in length by a constant percentage increment. He showed that a simple manipulation in an experimental condition caused the eight lines to be categorized into two groups of four, and their estimated lengths were different from those judged in a control condition. In the experimental condition, the four shorter lines were labeled A and the four longer lines are labeled B, whereas in the control condition, the A and B labels were random. In the experimental condition, therefore, length was correlated with the labels, and the lines were perceived to be in two categories or groups, a shorter one and a longer one. Further, there was an accentuation effect: The A lines were judged a little shorter and the B lines a little longer than they really were. The concept of accentuation fit with Tajfel's thinking about social stereotypes. Members of ethnic groups are (mis)perceived to fit more closely to stereotypes commonly held about them.

An important development in his thinking was revealed in a 1970 paper in which he explored the concept of *social categorization* as a basis for intergroup discrimination. Unlike Muzafer Sherif's *realistic group conflict theory*, which argued that intergroup conflict derives from mutually incompatible goals, Tajfel proposed that the simple act of becoming a group member was sufficient to precipitate discrimination against members of an available comparison outgroup. Intergroup conflict was now seen as an outcome of people being socially categorized rather than the result of competition for tangible rewards. It is an irony of Sherif's work that in his famous studies of intergroup discrimination carried out in boys' summer camps, there was evidence that the mere separation of children into groups led quickly to outgroup negative stereotyping. In Tajfel's view, *social categorization* rather than intergroup competition was the key to incipient prejudice.

Social Identity and Intergroup Relations

His most famous work was theoretical and followed next. His concept of social identity became the central ingredient in a new theory of intergroup behavior. The main ideas were first published in French in 1972, followed by an English version in 1974 and later amplified as social identity theory with John Turner in 1979. The concepts invoked were the following:

Social categorization: Social categorization is a cognitive tool. It is the social classification of people as members of social groups. It is a more powerful determinant of intergroup discrimination than are individual-level variables, such as personality characteristics, which might be shared by group members. The key to understanding outgroup prejudice is that individuals know that they are members of discrete categories, that is, groups.

Social comparison: Intergroup comparison is a group-level concept that is analogous to Leon Festinger's individual-level concept, also called social comparison. Both concepts serve to define the self, but in Festinger's case, the inferences arise from interpersonal comparisons. For example, Jim concludes he is fast because he usually wins footraces against other individuals. In Tajfel's case, social comparison is an intergroup concept, and the inferences are based on group membership. For example, Jane decides she is advantaged by her ethnicity because it confers higher status when she makes comparisons with other salient ethnic groups.

Social identity: This is a crucial aspect of identity. It is part of the self-concept that derives from people knowing that they members of one or more social groups, such as political or religious groups. An individual strives to achieve positive self-definition, an outcome based on comparisons that advantage the ingroup over salient outgroups.

Social change: This concept is thought by some commentators to be the most innovative of Tajfel's contributions to social identity theory. Social change is a significant perceived alteration in the relationship between large social groups, such as national, religious, and ethnic groups. Whereas *social mobility* is a change in self-definition when an individual moves into a new group, social change applies to a transformation of social identity for an entire social group. Social change is the process by which people actively seek positive social identities in response to being defined negatively in a world of social inequality.

Tajfel drew widely on theory and examples from history, literature, sociology, politics, and economics in elaborating these ideas and went to considerable lengths to link social identity theory to large-scale social structures and to ideology. Unlike many theorists in social psychology, Tajfel made a deliberate connection with collective movements and political action.

Although Tajfel conducted and encouraged others to undertake experimental research, his goal was more ambitious and was explicitly pitted against *reductionism* in theory. He was mindful of the scope and magnitude of North American social psychology and what it had achieved in defining the discipline in the 20th century. However, he was convinced that a European perspective could offer something different and valuable. He argued that North American social psychologists were mostly reductionist, even myopic, in their pursuit of psychological laws that reside in the individual. In contrast, Europe's political history of disputes and wars, and the stunning, horrific experience of the Holocaust, pointed to the need for theoretical constructs that were embedded in the social group.

Tajfel demonstrated his beliefs and values in his professional as well as research activities. According to many, Tajfel did more than any other person in helping to develop a distinctively European form of social psychology, one that stressed that people should be studied as members of groups. Tajfel's efforts, and those of his colleagues, are recognized today in the European Association of Experimental Social Psychologists and the *European Journal of Social Psychology*. In the decades following his death, his main ideas won wide acceptance in social psychology. They currently permeate research and teaching in many countries around the world, including the United States.

Graham M. Vaughan

See also Ethnocentrism; Ingroup Allocation Bias; Minimal Group Effect; Norms; Realistic Group Conflict Theory; Reference Groups; Social Identity Theory

Further Readings

Cohen, D. (1977). *Psychologists on psychology: Modern innovators talk about their work*. Oxford, UK: Taplinger.

Tajfel, H. (Ed.). (1978). *Differentiation between social groups: Studies in the social psychology of intergroup relations*. London: Academic Press.

Tajfel, H. (1981). *Human groups and social categories: Studies in social psychology*. Cambridge, UK: Cambridge University Press.

Tajfel, H., & Turner, J. C. (1979). An integrative theory of intergroup conflict. In W. G. Austin & S. Worchel (Eds.), *The social psychology of intergroup relations* (pp. 33–47). Monterey, CA: Brooks/Cole.

TEAM BUILDING

The term *team building* is used to refer both to team formation and efforts to advance group development within existing teams. Team building is important because the use of team-based structures is ubiquitous in today's organizations, making practices related to the formation, design, and development of work teams vital to both group and organizational success.

Team Formation

Despite its importance, research on building teams has lagged behind other work on teamwork in organizations. This is in part because most research on teamwork starts with the assumption that the team already exists. (Some exceptions to this view exist, such as work on group development and engineering models of team building.) At the most basic level, building a work team involves specification of the work to be done, selection of members based on the skills and knowledge required to complete that work, and use of effective techniques for recruiting members who will contribute to team effectiveness.

One important dimension of work with implications for building teams is *interdependence*, which concerns the extent to which a task can be completed by people working separately versus together. Work with low interdependence can be completed either by an individual without any assistance from others or by a number of individuals working independently and then coming together for a final product. Work with high interdependence requires members of a team to work closely together, share and integrate their knowledge and skills, and generate a collective product or output in which the input of particular members may be difficult to discern.

Once the team's task is understood, the next key challenge is identifying the "right" people for the team. A critical goal is to align individuals' knowledge and skills with the requirements of the team's work. Building a team with the necessary skills and knowledge seems straightforward, but this is not always the case. For example, in some organizations, chemical engineering skills may correlate with gender or organizational department. As a result, assigning an individual on the basis of such skills may introduce conflict into a team (e.g., because other team members do not appreciate the value of his or her skills) that has negative consequences for group processes and outcomes. Moreover, certain skills and knowledge may exist in only a small number of individuals, and these people may not have the time or the motivation for a particular team assignment.

In addition to alignment between members' knowledge and skills, on one hand, and task requirements of the team, on the other hand, it is important to consider the dispersion of knowledge and skills across members of the team. This form of alignment concerns the extent to which the team members have similar or different knowledge and skills and, in the latter case, complementary or noncomplementary knowledge and skills. When team members have different and noncomplementary knowledge and skills, they are highly specialized. Such specialization may make recognition of expertise easier but coordination of effort more difficult. Alternatively, similar knowledge and skills or different but complementary knowledge and skills can result in easier coordination but may come at the cost of insufficient expertise in particular areas. In addition, certain kinds of knowledge and skill diversity may reduce internal cohesion but at the same time provide more external ties for

a team. Research suggests the need for caution in drawing simple conclusions about knowledge and skill alignment as uniformly harmful or helpful. Therefore, managers must be aware of the potential advantages and disadvantages of various kinds of alignment among team members.

Finally, the selection of members for a team involves a choice about how to recruit the people with the right knowledge and skills. Team members can be recruited from the social network of the manager forming the team or identified through more impersonal channels, such as organizational databases. Of course, the choice of recruiting channel may be constrained by the need for specific knowledge or skills available through only one channel. The means used to recruit members when forming the team have implications for team performance. Members with social ties to each other may speed the development of internal cohesion and superior knowledge utilization, but they can also produce flawed decisions if close ties produce a team whose members favor harmony over critical judgment. Furthermore, if a premium is placed on selecting team members from an existing social network, knowledge and skill alignment may be compromised in favor of personal relationships among the team members. This could disadvantage a team's ability to effectively complete its task. Alternatively, the manager in charge of forming the team may use organizational databases, human resources recruiting techniques, or other "impersonal" means of identifying team members. Although this approach may be useful in some ways, it may miss opportunities to leverage existing knowledge structures among individuals who have prior experience with one another.

Team-Building Programs

Once teams are formed, managers may engage team members in *team-building* programs focused on group development. Team building involves some type of planned intervention, ranging from short-term to long-duration activities, designed to enhance process effectiveness and reduce problems through setting group goals and supporting interpersonal relations, problem solving, and role clarification. Although the concept of team building was introduced some 30 years ago, research on formal team building is rather limited, and the work that has been done indicates that team-building programs have a mixed impact on team performance. For example, in a meta-analysis of 11 empirical studies of team building, Eduardo Salas and his colleagues found that team-building programs have a positive, but weak, effect on subjective measures of performance (e.g., team members' self-reports of their effectiveness) and no effect on objective measures of performance (e.g., productivity).

Providing contradictory evidence, a meta-analysis by Daniel Svyantek and colleagues revealed that team-building interventions have positive effects on both subjective and objective measures of team performance. Moreover, they noted that this relationship is affected by several characteristics of the team-building effort and the organizational context. In particular, interventions initiated by people outside the work group (e.g., higher level management) have a greater (positive) impact than those initiated internally; supervisor support increases the effectiveness of the team building; and team building focused on corrective action has a stronger effect on performance than team building designed as a preventive measure. Furthermore, team-building efforts led by external consultants are more effective than efforts led by internal consultants, with team building producing the most positive outcomes when led by a combination of internal and external consultants. Finally, team building focused on group change (e.g., improving group problem-solving processes) is more effective than team building focused on individual changes (e.g., role definition for individuals in the group).

It is worthwhile to note that a very popular form of team-building intervention involves outdoor challenges or experiential training, such as ropes courses and wilderness trips. To date, no research evidence supports a performance benefit or specific return on investment in the form of improved productivity for teams that participate in outdoor team-building interventions.

Conclusion

In sum, managers engaged in team formation must pay careful attention to defining the team's task, identifying potential members with the right knowledge and skills, and using effective means for recruiting these people. Although there is fervent support for team-building interventions in some quarters and anecdotal evidence that such interventions improve team productivity, solid research has yet to unequivocally support these views. The research record suggests that if managers wish to implement formal team-building interventions, these interventions ought to focus on role clarification and be of short to moderate duration. It has been suggested that the lack of positive effects of team building on productivity is due to problems in transferring learning from the team-building experience to the actual work environment. Therefore, special attention must be paid to how the experiences in the program relate to the work completed by the team and what specific efforts will be made to reinforce the learning in the program when the team is back on the job.

Mary E. Zellmer-Bruhn

See also Diversity; Group Composition; Group Development; Group Formation; Group Task; Interdependence Theory; Social Networks; Team Performance Assessment; Teams

Further Readings

Beer, M. (1976). The technology of organization development. In M. D. Dunnette (Ed.), *Handbook of industrial and organizational psychology* (pp. 937–994). Chicago: Rand McNally.

Jackson, S. (1991). Team composition in organizations. In S. Worchel, W. Wood, & J. Simpson (Eds.), *Group process and productivity* (pp. 138–176). London: Sage.

Moreland, R. (1987). The formation of small groups. In C. Hendrick (Ed.), *Review of personality and social psychology* (Vol. 8, pp. 80–110). Newbury Park, CA: Sage.

Salas, E., Rozell, D., Mullen, B., & Driskell, J. E. (1999). The effect of teambuilding on performance: An integration. *Small Group Research, 30*(3), 309–329.

Svyantek, D. J., Goodman, S. A, Benz, L. L., & Gard, J. A. (1999). The relationship between organizational characteristics and team building success. *Journal of Business and Psychology, 14*(2), 265–283.

Wageman, R. (1999). The meaning of interdependence. In M. Turner (Ed.), *Groups at work: Theory and research* (pp. 197–218). Hillsdale, NJ: Erlbaum.

Team Negotiation

In many negotiations, one individual sits down at the table to represent his or her own interests. This is also true in multiparty negotiations in which three, four, or even more individuals are negotiating to resolve their own interests. *Team negotiations* are different, however, because more than one individual represents each side. Team negotiations can become exceptionally complex because individuals must negotiate and resolve their interests and positions *within* each team, as well as *between* each team.

Advantages and Disadvantages of Teams

Is a team negotiation, that is, two groups negotiating against each other, likely to produce a better outcome than two individuals coming to the table? The *discontinuity effect* proposes that intergroup interaction will be more competitive than interindividual interaction, primarily because groups generate both more fear and more greed than individuals do. However, the vast majority of the evidence for this effect comes from contexts that are relatively information poor (e.g., prisoner dilemma games) when compared with most negotiation contexts.

By contrast, researchers studying richer bargaining contexts have consistently found that having even one team at the bargaining table increases the cooperativeness, and hence the integrativeness, of joint agreements—in other words, all parties are better off when one of them is a team. This so-called *team effect* seems to occur because teams stimulate the discussion of more information than do individuals. This information exchange leads to greater accuracy about both parties' interests and priorities, enabling trade-offs on issues that increase overall profitability.

Thus, we know that teams increase *integrative* (or *win–win*) outcomes, but are teams always at an advantage compared with their solo counterparts? In other words, do teams do better on the *distributive (win–lose)* dimension? Not necessarily. Although one of the advantages to teams is the ability to split roles within the team, such as the famous *good cop– bad cop* technique, research has shown that this ability does not always lead to better performance for the team. This is because one of the major issues teams must contend with is how to manage the division of labor within the team itself.

Consider this example: One member of a negotiation team has strong analytic skills, another has vast technical and industry knowledge, and a third has strong relationship-building skills. These ingredients should add up to a formidable team. But if members disagree about the key issues—such as what the bottom line is or when to make concessions—then they are unlikely to take advantage of their differing skills. Clearly, teams can be an effective presence at the negotiating table but only if they are able to uncover, leverage, and efficiently coordinate their diverse abilities.

Managing a Team Negotiation

Thus, the greatest challenge for a team is to manage its internal negotiation before, as well as during, negotiation with an opponent team. A negotiating team's preparation phase should include three components: (1) a substantive discussion of the negotiation, (2) a skills assessment of team members and the assignment of team roles, and (3) a plan for the negotiation process.

Discuss the Negotiation's Substance

Before entering into the negotiation, team members must agree about the basics of the negotiation's substance, striving for as much agreement as possible. Basic negotiation principles come into play here—it is basically a prenegotiation or even a negotiation that is embedded within the larger negotiation. Before meeting their opponents, the team members must agree on their *best alternative to a negotiated agreement* (BATNA). The BATNA is basically what the team will do if it does not reach an agreement with the other team. The team members must also decide on their *reservation point*, or the worst outcome that they will agree to before walking away, and their *aspiration level*, or the best outcome that they can imagine. The team members can use these critical limits to think through their priorities, the issues on which they might be willing to consider trade-offs, and their underlying assumptions. Research has shown that negotiators who set specific limits and focus on their aspirations outperform those that set "do your best" limits and focus on reservation points.

The team must also consider what it knows about the other team(s). The team should do its best to estimate its opponent's priorities, BATNA, reservation point, and aspiration level. A team can be superior to a solo negotiator here because each team member may have different expertise, knowledge, and experience, which can be integrated to arrive at accurate estimates. The team might also need to engage in research before the actual negotiation begins, and a division of labor is often easier with more people to do the work.

Assess Skills and Roles

In addition to assessing the negotiation's substance, a team must determine how to take advantage of the diverse skills among its members. In some cases, the team's composition is determined by an outside manager or superordinate authority, but in other cases, there is an opportunity for members to make sure that there is a match between the needs of the team and their composition. In either case, the first step should be an assessment of what skills, knowledge, and abilities are required. The next step is to match skills with essential roles.

Most teams elect one person as the team's *chief negotiator*. The chief negotiator must be articulate, not easily rattled, and able to follow the team's predetermined negotiation plan. Other important roles include a team member who can record and analyze data, keeping track of offers and counteroffers. This individual should also be able to interpret the data and their implications for the team. Finally, the team might want someone who can attend to and interpret the other side's private reactions to offers. Research has shown that only a small amount of information is conveyed through actual words. Much more is communicated through tone of voice, posture, stance, and body language.

Plan the Negotiation Process

The substance of the negotiation and the diversity of roles come together in the third step as the team makes decisions about the central process features of the negotiation. What opening offer should it make? When should it make the first concession? For example, a substantial amount of research now shows that making the first offer allows negotiators to set an anchor for the negotiation, and when they do so with a focus on their aspiration levels, they do better than negotiators who concede the first offer to the other party.

One process feature is unique to the team: the *recess*, or *caucus*. Teams should take advantage of opportunities to break away from the other side, whether to raise new issues, do a reality check, or resolve internal disputes. The team leader may ask one member of the team to focus on the emotions of the other team or report on that team's reaction to a recent offer or ask the team member keeping track of the numbers to analyze and assess new data. Any differences within the team should always be handled in a recess, outside of the other side's earshot. The team leader should ultimately resolve any arguments about concessions or trade-offs.

The team can also call a caucus for strategic reasons, such as signaling a willingness to abandon the negotiation. Caucuses can also slow down talks that are moving too fast, giving both sides time to consider options and make offers. Teams can communicate with each other electronically via laptops or handheld computers, or they can simply pass notes on slips of paper.

When to Use a Team

As noted above, teams have assets as well as liabilities, and therefore the key task is to maximize the assets and minimize the liabilities. One way to do that is to use a team when it will be most beneficial. Research has shown that teams are particularly beneficial in situations in which the task is complex, requiring a diverse set of knowledge, abilities, or expertise, or the problem has great potential for creative, integrative solutions. Teams are also beneficial in situations in which one party wants to display its strength to the other, teams are expected to be used (e.g., in certain international settings), diverse constituencies must be represented (such as in union negotiations), or either party wishes to signal that the negotiation is extremely important (as in a merger or acquisition). Another factor to consider is whether there is time to organize and coordinate a team effort.

Elizabeth Mannix

See also Cooperation and Competition; Group
    Performance; Group Problem Solving and
    Decision Making; Negotiation and Bargaining;
    Socially Shared Cognition; Teams; Transactive
    Memory Systems

Further Readings

Brodt, S., & Thompson, L. (2001). Negotiating teams: A
    levels of analysis approach. *Group Dynamics: Theory,
    Research and Practice, 5*(3), 208–219.

Liang, D. W., Moreland, R. L., & Argote, L. (1995).
    Group versus individual training and group
    performance: The mediating role of transactive
    memory. *Personality and Social Psychology Bulletin,
    21*, 384–393.

Mannix, E. (2005). Strength in numbers: Negotiating as a
    team. *Negotiation: Negotiation and Decision-Making
    Strategies That Deliver Results, 8*(5), 1–4.

Sell, J., Lovaglia, M., Mannix, E., Samuelson, C., &
    Wilson, R. (2004). Investigating conflict, power, and
    status within and among groups. *Small Group
    Research, 35*(1), 44–72.

Wildschut, T., Pinter, B., Vevea, J., Schopler, J., & Insko, C.
    (2003). Beyond the group mind: A quantitative review
    of the interindividual–intergroup discontinuity effect.
    Psychological Bulletin, 129(5), 698–722.

TEAM PERFORMANCE ASSESSMENT

Teams are a hallmark of modern societies. They
are most evident in organizations, especially work
organizations. The effective performance of teams
is closely linked to the accomplishment of goals
for both the members involved and the organizations in which they operate. Thus, the nature of
team performance and the issues involved in the
assessment of team performance are central to an
organization's success.

Approaches to *team performance assessment* are
quite varied, and they should be. Both the appropriate definition of team performance and the best
way to measure (assess) it will depend on a variety
of factors. Thus, those interested in assessing a
team should become fairly knowledgeable about
the context involved. This entry examines team performance assessment from a context-dependent, or
contingent, perspective.

Is It a Team?

Although all social collectives share certain properties, a team is generally considered to be distinct
from other groups in that a team has a history and
a future and exists to perform a function for some
larger entity (e.g., a company, military unit, or
school). In addition, most teams involve members
who are recruited for specific positions and have
specific duties or roles that they must fulfill. In most
teams, individual responsibilities can be executed
only in concert with other team members. That is,
there is task or workflow interdependence. While
the issues associated with the assessment of *group*
performance and *team* performance are similar in
many ways, this entry focuses on the latter.

Purposes of Team Performance Assessment

There are many purposes for conducting a team
performance assessment, including establishing
training needs; guiding the redesign of training
programs, equipment, or work processes; improving performance levels; and shaping compensation
awards. Moreover, the kind of setting in which
assessment is to take place will affect the appropriateness of particular assessment measures and
methods.

Parameters of Team Assessment

What to Measure

A team usually operates in some larger organizational context. Just as team members have personal assignments within the team, so the team as
a whole has a function within this larger system.
Accordingly, many writers make use of the *Input-
Process-Output* rubric to organize thinking about
the features of a team that will influence performance and therefore affect the ways that one goes
about defining and assessing performance.

Inputs include such things as the type of people
involved (number and skills of members), team
resources available (money and equipment), the
nature of the "raw" materials to be used, team
structure (communication channels, distribution of
authority), team history (levels of past performance,
past relationships among members), and team mission (time urgency, novelty, and difficulty). Processes

involve patterns and sequences of individual-level thinking and feelings, on one hand, and team-related activities associated with such things as managing relationships, coordinating work flow and communications, and using influence tactics, on the other. Outcomes usually refer to levels of individual performance within the team, degree of mission accomplishment by the team, positive or negative changes in capacity (over time) to function well as a team, and levels of stakeholder satisfaction. Degree of satisfaction with outcomes is usually related to the needs, goals, and expectations of the stakeholder. Stakeholders interested in team performance can include the team members themselves, the team leader, clients, customers, and (in the case of a sports team) an audience.

Current thinking is that a complete team assessment should also provide information regarding the contribution of the various factors that are thought to drive team performance. Typically this requires an examination of the activities of individual team members, the team leader, key team-member dyads (e.g., pilot and copilot), and the team as a whole. For example, the team may perform poorly because of one unprepared member, poor team leadership, or team-level problems with communication. Although the preferred approach to assessment will depend on its purpose, most experts on team assessment emphasize the need to examine both processes (individual or team) and outcomes (individual or team) in order to gain an adequate perspective on the nature and causes of high or low performance.

The mission or type of the team will strongly affect the key inputs, processes, and outcomes to assess. Most typologies of teams include variants of the following: production, project, service, command and control, action, advisory, or management. This list conveys some notion of the kinds of people (with attendant skills) required as input for effective team performance.

Where to Measure

Team performance can be exhibited in a number of venues, such as a training situation, the actual workplace, or a setting created for assessment purposes (e.g., a simulation). The choice of setting should relate to the purpose of assessment. That is, the purpose may be to improve team member skills, to measure the "typical" performance of the team, or to discover the team's capacity for maximum performance or performance under stress. The choice of setting should also relate to the function that the assessment information will play (e.g., remediation, compensation, or certification).

How to Measure

Many methods are useful to the assessment of team performance, but the feasible set will depend on the purpose, the foci, and the setting. Typically, obtaining valid assessments of processes represents the greatest challenge. Processes by their very nature are emergent, in that they unfold over time. They are also ephemeral in that they usually do not leave any signs or artifacts. Individual processes of interest include the way someone attends to, selects, stores, and retrieves information.

Under some circumstances, getting a good measure of the pattern of decisions or choices made by each of the team members or the way that members handle emotions (e.g., relative to success or failure) may also represent important process information. At the team level, processes are reflected in interactions and activities by and among team members. In this case, measures need to be crafted and used to assess the number and patterns of communications among members, interpersonal influence, decisions made, work flow, and so on.

Measuring Processes

When team performance is defined as effective individual or team processes, the assessment is traditionally done by using techniques such as ratings by skilled observers, postperformance reports of team members, content analysis of video recordings of individual and team-level activities, or the pattern of choices or decisions captured by computer work stations. Each of these approaches has both advantages and liabilities.

Current thinking is that team-level processes (e.g., patterns of member activities) result in what are called *proximal* outcomes. These are transitory or recurrent states of a team that are produced by team dynamics. Once these states are created, they become a characteristic of a team. It is important to note that, as a team property, they will have an impact on future team processes and often on the eventual performance level of the team (called *distal outcomes* or *outputs*). Concepts such as *team cohesion*, *team shared cognition*, *team potency*, *team trust*, and *team climate* have been used to describe such emergent states. As a generalization, teams that can be described (rated) as highly cohesive, possessing a supportive climate, or having members with shared goals and high levels of trust are thought to be effective. To put it another way, such teams are poised to demonstrate high performance, subject to resources and authority.

Measuring Outcomes

When team performance is defined as desired individual or team outcomes, valid assessment can be equally challenging. In operational settings, performance may be estimated by examining outcomes such as level, speed, or efficiency of work goal attainment for either the members or the team as a whole. Such outcome information is often found in operational records. However, before one selects such metrics, it is important to control for or rule out factors that could contaminate the measure and thus reduce its validity. For example, high mortality rates of a hospital team may be an artifact of the way cases get assigned to teams, such that truly effective teams get the worst cases. Blindly accepting mortality rate as a metric without adjustments would be inappropriate. Ratings by supervisors, analysts, or customers are commonly used to obtain assessments of outcome quality. An outcome of importance in some contexts is a measurable improvement in team member skills or a more positive attitude by members relative to such things as their desire to stay in the team or their feelings of individual or collective efficacy. These too are frequently assessed via ratings based on member behaviors or activities during or after a team performance episode. Such ratings can also be obtained from members directly.

Stakeholder satisfaction is increasingly being used as an indicator of team performance because many teams exist to provide service to others. Levels of satisfaction can be estimated by customer surveys, unsolicited customer comments, or levels of repeat business garnered by the team. Because each of these indicators may be imperfect or incomplete, many organizations make use of more than one measurement tool to assess stakeholder satisfaction.

The level of team performance may take time to become manifest. For example, the objective may be to assess the performance of a top management team of a large work organization after a change of CEO. The nature of work at the level of the CEO and the interplay among members of the *top management team* are complex and poorly understood. However, it is believed that it takes time for a new CEO to staff a strong top management team. Once team members are in place, the CEO must build a well-functioning team and create and then implement strategy.

Even if all this is done expeditiously, it still may take months to see the impact of strategy on such outcomes as market share, return on investment, or stock price. Yet these are the kind of measures to which the typical CEO and top management team will be held accountable. Clearly the scores obtained from an assessment of the performance of a top management team depend greatly on when that assessment takes place.

Interteam Relationships

In many contexts, the quality of interteam relationships is important to the assessment of team performance. Examples include project teams that must function within a larger program, production teams that combine outputs from other teams, teams that are part of a supply chain, or military units that must function effectively with units in a battle situation. In such cases, teams are interdependent relative to inputs or outcomes. Moreover, in business today, there are team member clusters and whole teams that are separated geographically but connected via technology (virtual global teams). These present a special challenge for team performance assessment.

In summary, the assessment of team performance must be guided by a deep knowledge of team dynamics, the team mission, and the context in which the team functions. The appropriate approach will also be contingent on the goal or purpose of assessment.

Richard Klimoski

See also Group Cohesiveness; Group Development; Group Performance; Group Potency; Shared Mental Models; Team Building; Team Reflexivity; Teams

Further Readings

Cannon-Bowers, J. A., & Salas, E. (1997). A framework for developing team performance measures in training. In M. T. Brannick, E. Salas, & C. Prince (Eds.), *Team performance assessment and measurement* (pp. 45–62). Mahwah, NJ: Erlbaum.

Gessner, T. L., Langkamer, K. L., & Klimoski, R. J. (2007). Research designs for assessing group learning. In V. Sessa & M. London (Eds.), *Work group learning* (pp. 391–420). Mahwah, NJ: Erlbaum.

Klimoski, R. J. & Kiechel Koles, K. L. (2001). The chief executive officer and the top management team interface. In S. L. Zaccaro & R. J. Klimoski (Eds.), *The nature of organizational leadership* (pp. 219–269). San Francisco: Jossey-Bass.

Kozlowski, S. W. J., & Bell, B. S. (2003). Work groups and teams in organizations. In W. C. Borman, D. R. Ilgen, & R. J. Klimoski (Eds.), *Handbook of psychology: Industrial and organizational psychology* (Vol. 12, pp. 333–376). Hoboken, NJ: Wiley.

Marks, M. A., Zaccaro, S. J., & Mathieu, J. E. (2000). A temporally based framework and taxonomy of team processes. *Academy of Management Review, 26,* 356–376.

McGrath, J. E. (1984). *Groups: Interaction and performance.* Englewood Cliffs, NJ: Prentice Hall.

Sundstrom, E., DeMeuse, K. P., & Futrell, D. (1990). Work teams: Applications and effectiveness. *American Psychologist, 45,* 120–143.

TEAM REFLEXIVITY

With the increasing relevance of teamwork in organizations, the quest for the factors that enhance team effectiveness has grown exponentially. *Team reflexivity* is one of the factors that has been identified as a possible key variable in explaining the effectiveness of work teams. Team reflexivity can be defined as the extent to which team members collectively reflect on the team's objectives, strategies, and processes, as well as their wider organizations and environments, and adapt accordingly.

Conceptualization

The concept of team reflexivity was initially developed by Michael West, but other scholars, such as Michaela Schippers and Carsten de Dreu, have also contributed significantly to its understanding. It is conceptualized as a process involving three stages or components: *reflection, planning,* and *action* or *adaptation.* The three stages are of equal importance.

The first stage, *team reflection,* refers to a team's joint exploration of work-related issues and includes behaviors such as questioning, planning, exploratory learning, analysis, reviewing past events with self-awareness, and coming to terms over time with the new awareness. Reflection levels are assumed to vary in depth. Shallow reflection consists of thinking about issues closely related to the task at hand. An illustrative question at this level is, Do people think we communicate information about patients well within this team? Moderate reflection is characterized by a more critical approach toward tasks. An illustrative question at this level is, Let's think about some alternatives in terms of how we could best improve our product design processes. Finally, deep reflection involves rethinking the norms and values of the team or organization, as illustrated in a statement such as, "So we agree that our communication about patients is hampered by professional divisions within the team."

The second stage, *planning,* refers to the activities that enable reflections to change into action or adaptation. Planning involves four dimensions: *detail* (the extent to which a plan is worked out in detail before action as opposed to being worked out only during action), *inclusiveness of potential problems* (the extent to which a team develops alternative plans in case of inadvertent circumstance), *a priori hierarchical ordering of plans* (the extent to which plans are broken up into subplans before actions are commenced), and *time scale* (the extent to which both short- and long-term plans are drawn). Planning is important because it creates a perceptual readiness for, and guides team members' attention toward, relevant opportunities for action and means to accomplish the team's goal.

The third stage, *action* or *adaptation,* concerns the goal-directed behaviors relevant for achieving the desired changes in team objectives, strategies, processes, organizations, or environments previously identified by the team during the stage of reflection. The action component of reflexivity can be assessed in four dimensions: *magnitude* (the scale of an action or change initiated by the team), *novelty* (how new the action or change is for the team, organization, or other stakeholders), *radicalness* (the amount of change in the status quo that the action or change represents), and *effectiveness* (the extent to which the action or change achieves the intended team goals).

Typically, reflexive teams show more detailed planning, pay more attention to long-term consequences, and have a larger inventory of environmental cues to which they respond. In contrast, a nonreflexive team shows little awareness of the team's objectives, its strategies, and the environment in which it operates. Nonreflexive teams tend to rely on the use of habitual routines. In other words, they tend to repeatedly exhibit a similar pattern of behavior in a given situation without explicitly discussing it or by selecting it over other possible courses of action. This lack of exploration of alternative hypotheses ultimately leads to stagnation, lack of innovation, and inability to adapt to a changing environment.

Factors That Trigger Team Reflexivity

Team reflexivity is unlikely to arise naturally. Reflection often involves recognizing a discrepancy between actual and desired circumstances, which can generate anxiety and uncertainty. Moreover, reflection might demand change in action, and individuals and organizations are naturally resistant to change. In the face of these factors, teams tend not to engage in reflexivity in a voluntary fashion.

In contrast with other, more stable team characteristics that are difficult to modify (such as membership), managers can actively promote team reflexivity and consequently increase the level of team effectiveness. Indeed, several factors have been suggested to trigger team reflexivity.

Leadership style is one such factor. In order to foster reflexivity, leaders should adopt a style that creates the conditions for experimentation and risk taking and that develops shared commitment to reflecting on and questioning routine practices. Leaders can concentrate their efforts on longer-term goals, emphasize a vision, inspire team members to pursue the vision, coach followers to take responsibility for their development, and encourage team members to reflect on errors. *Team member changes* also provide an opportunity for reflection as they imply a rearrangement of work processes and enable an exchange of perspectives between the newcomer and the team. *Errors and failures* can be used as a tool for learning because they offer valuable feedback and have the potential to stimulate teams to reflect on the processes or assumptions that led to them. *Successes* constitute an equally important trigger for reflection. Although teams tend not to look back on their work when they are successful, analyzing what they did well and how they did it offers important learning. Other factors that can trigger team reflexivity are cooperative conflict management; difficulties over time allocations; difficulties in synchronizing the work of the different team members; and interruptions, such as crises, obstacles, and organizational changes.

Interventions conducted by West and his colleagues to promote team reflexivity suggest that these concepts are readily grasped by teams and that levels of reflexivity rapidly increase, with sustained reflexivity up to 12 months after interventions begin. Moreover, reflexivity has also been successfully manipulated in experimental studies, suggesting that in applied settings managers should be able to induce reflexivity.

Studying reflexivity demands methodologies that can gauge the depth and richness of the process. Most research on team reflexivity has been conducted by means of questionnaires. Other methodological approaches that have potential for advancing understanding of reflexivity are critical incident techniques, observation of team meetings, focus groups, and longitudinal interventions.

Impact on Team Effectiveness

Recent research in both experimental and field settings has found evidence for the positive effects of team reflexivity. These effects were observed in samples comprising management, production, and service teams from a variety of sectors, including banking, government, health care, the chemical industry, and research and development. In these studies, the impact of team reflexivity was particularly powerful when the environment was uncertain and teams had complex tasks that required nonroutine activities.

Overall, team reflexivity has been found to be positively related to desirable outcomes such as systematic information processing, creativity, innovation, performance, and organizational citizenship behavior. Furthermore, reflexivity has been found to moderate the impact of other team characteristics on team performance. For instance, diversity in terms of goal orientation is positively associated with team performance only when teams are highly reflexive. In addition, cooperative outcome interdependence is related to more intensive information sharing, increased learning, and higher team effectiveness only when team reflexivity is high.

Although the mechanisms by which reflexivity affects performance have been specified theoretically, there is little empirical research examining them. One of the few relevant studies reported that reflexivity increased team effectiveness by enhancing communication and implementation of strategies, as well as similarity of mental models.

Conclusion

Team reflexivity is a useful concept for both understanding and promoting team effectiveness. This is partly because many teams are not naturally reflexive. The capacity to reflect on behavior is unique to humans and is useful in many contexts. In the complex setting of interdependent teamwork, reflexivity offers a powerful means of improving the effectiveness of the team.

Michael A. West and Claudia A. Sacramento

See also Group Learning; Group Motivation; Group Performance; Group Problem Solving and Decision Making; Shared Mental Models; Teams

Further Readings

De Dreu, C. (2007). Cooperative outcome interdependence, task reflexivity, and team effectiveness: A motivated information processing perspective. *Journal of Applied Psychology, 92*(3), 628–638.

Gurtner, A., Tschan, F., Sernmer, N. K., & Nagele, C. (2007). Getting groups to develop good strategies: Effects of reflexivity interventions on team process, team performance, and shared mental models. *Organizational Behavior and Human Decision Processes, 102*(2), 127–142.

Tjosvold, D., Tang, M. M. L., & West, M. (2004). Reflexivity for team innovation in China: The contribution of goal interdependence. *Group & Organization Management, 29*(5), 540–559.

West, M. A. (2000). Reflexivity, revolution, and innovation in work teams. In M. M. Beyerlein, D. A. Johnson, & S. T. Beyerlein (Eds.), *Product development teams: Advances in interdisciplinary studies of work teams* (pp. 1–29). Stamford, CT: JAI Press.

TEAMS

Teams are social entities that come together to perform complex, dynamic, and critical tasks that are beyond the capabilities of an individual. Teams are now part of every aspect of organizational life. They are prevalent in government, the military, health care, aviation and space, the corporate world, the oil industry, and manufacturing, to name just a few settings. Teams are deployed to solve organizational effectiveness problems, to deal with life-or-death situations, to create new products, to resolve world conflicts as peace keepers, to put out wildfires, and to rescue people during natural disasters.

Indeed, teams are an integral part of our society. Nonetheless, questions remain about teams: What are teams? How are they different from groups? What is teamwork? What do we know about team dynamics? What do effective teams do? These questions are answered in this entry.

Some Definitions

Some important definitions are needed to understand team dynamics in organizations. First, a *team* can be defined as a set of two or more individuals who adaptively, episodically, and dynamically interact interdependently through specified roles and responsibilities as they work toward shared and valued goals. Team member interdependency (i.e., task interdependency) is a critical feature of a team and distinguishes a group of individuals from a team. Although this distinction might seem academic, it highlights that teams and groups are not the same. Teams and groups have different organizational and leadership structure, goals, communication requirements, life spans, and task intensity. Team members usually have a past and a future together. In contrast, group members (e.g., people who participate on juries, councils, task forces, brainstorming groups) usually have limited time together and nothing to tie them together other than a particular task at one particular time.

In addition, because they contain specific roles, teams can often be characterized as having distributed expertise. That is, team members often have different specializations in which teammates hold different information about the task and possess different knowledge and skills. In fact, it is this diversity of expertise that creates the synergy for teams to complete work outside the scope of any one individual's capabilities. And the dynamics of effective teamwork are necessary to realize this synergy.

What is teamwork? *Teamwork* is the dynamic, simultaneous, and recursive enactment of behavioral, attitudinal, and cognitive mechanisms (in the form of team processes) that affect moment-to-moment actions and performance outcomes. Teamwork, then, is a set of interrelated, adaptable, and flexible cognitions, behaviors, and attitudes needed to achieve desired team goals. One can argue that teams "think," "do," and "feel" as they perform and execute their interdependent tasks. These cognitions, behaviors, and attitudes represent the team-level competencies (i.e., the knowledge, skills, and attitudes, or KSAs) that members need in order to execute effective team functions and achieve performance greater than that predicted by the combined efforts of the individual team members.

To be clear, it is useful to think of competencies within a team as belonging to one of two types: teamwork and *task work*. Task work competencies are KSAs used to accomplish individual task performance—the application of these skills does not require interdependent interaction within the team. Teamwork competencies, in contrast, are the KSAs necessary for members to function within an interdependent team. They occur only at the team level. Therefore, team members must possess not only individual-level expertise relevant to their own individual tasks but also expertise in the social-cognitive dynamics of teamwork. Teamwork is the *process* of enacting these teamwork competencies.

What is team performance? *Team performance* is a multilevel process that arises as team members enact their individual behaviors *and* individual- and team-level teamwork processes. Team performance can be contrasted with the definition of teamwork provided above, which focused on the enactment of teamwork processes alone. Therefore, teamwork is nested within team performance. Team performance is the combination of both individual performance and teamwork processes.

What is team effectiveness? *Team effectiveness* is an evaluation of the outcomes of team performance relative to some criteria. It is a judgment of how well the results of performance meet some set of relatively objective measures (e.g., metrics of productivity) or subjective standards (e.g., supervisor or observer ratings). These standards, to be meaningful, should be aligned with the goals of the team and organization.

Research Theories and Results

What contributes to teamwork? Interest in teams has led to a plethora of theoretical models of teamwork and team performance. Eduardo Salas and colleagues recently reviewed almost 140 studies from various disciplines that model aspects of teamwork or team performance. This proliferation of models is indicative of the widespread fascination with teams and teamwork. But what do all these models tell us about teamwork and team performance?

Most models include *inputs* (e.g., task structure, member characteristics), *processes* (e.g., coordination, communication), and *outputs* (e.g., member satisfaction, team performance), which together are known as IPOs. Although the IPO perspective has become the preferred way to model teams, some theorists add system theory constructs. For example, Joseph McGrath adds the notion of *dynamic change* in his model of time, interaction, and performance. And Daniel Ilgen and colleagues extend the IPO framework to include emergent states and feedback loops. Such perspectives propose a less linear framework that takes into account the dynamic nature of team functioning.

What contributes to teamwork, however, are five factors supported or "glued" by three others. Salas and colleagues have proposed that there is a "Big Five" in teamwork. They argue that, across domains, team goals, tasks, and structures, there are five core components of teamwork (as long as team members have high task interdependence). The *core teamwork components* are team leadership, adaptability, mutual performance monitoring, backup or supportive behavior, and team orientation. The importance of each component may vary across contexts or domains, but each of the Big Five in some form is essential for any type of teamwork. In addition, Salas and colleagues have identified three *collaborating mechanisms*: shared mental models, closed-loop communication, and mutual trust. These collaborating mechanisms are necessary because they facilitate the enactment of the Big Five.

Key Components

Team leadership has substantial implications for the effectiveness of teams and organizations at large. The functional approach to leadership characterizes it as promoting coordinated, adaptive team performance by facilitating goal clarification and attainment. Leaders solve collective problems through four general types of actions. They search for and structure information, they use information in problem solving and sense-making, they manage human capital resources, and they manage material resources. Kimberly Smith-Jentsch and colleagues have identified two specific team leadership behaviors that contribute to expert team performance. First, team leaders provide guidance and suggestions on improvements. This facilitates team learning and development, which lead to higher levels of future performance. Second, team leaders identify team- and individual-level priorities to ensure that the aspects of the team and individual tasks that are most critical for team outcomes are given the most attention.

Adaptability underlies many team functions and behaviors and can be defined as the team's ability to change (shift) team-based processes in response to demands from the environment in a manner that results in effective team functioning. Adaptability is an essential component of teamwork, especially for teams operating under dynamic, stressful, and time-critical conditions. Until recently, only a small amount of research dealt with temporal aspects of team adaptation and performance. This neglect is beginning to be addressed.

For example, C. Shawn Burke and colleagues have proposed a model of team adaptation. At the core of this model is *adaptive team performance*, which is characterized as an emergent phenomenon based on the unfolding of a recursive cycle of performance. It occurs when one or more team members functionally redirect (change) current cognitive or behavioral actions or structures to meet expected or emerging demands. Burke argues that adaptive team performance is achieved as the team passes through four phases. The first phase consists of *situation assessment*, during which team members scan the environment, recognize cue patterns, and build a coherent understanding of their present situation. The second phase is *plan formulation*, during which team members collectively generate and decide on a course of action. The third phase is *plan execution*, which is achieved via the team coordination mechanisms (behavioral actions) that are in place. The fourth and final phase is *team learning*, during which the team evaluates the effectiveness of its performance and makes appropriate corrections. The results of this team learning feed into future team performance episodes (i.e., pass through the adaptive cycle).

Mutual performance monitoring is how team members keep track of their teammates' work while carrying out their own. They do this to ensure that everything is going as expected and that they are following procedures correctly. It involves team members being aware of their surroundings, an essential component of teamwork. A team must develop a strong habit of mutual performance monitoring, as well as attitudes that define it as critical to high performance. For mutual performance monitoring to be successful, team members must develop a shared understanding of their task, mission, and equipment. Such an understanding is essential in order to detect deviations from normal or expected conditions. Knowing *what should be* happening is a necessary condition for obtaining useful information from observations of *what is* happening at any one time.

Backup behavior (or supporting behavior) happens when team members step in to help one another. It is defined as a discretionary behavior enacted when there is recognition by potential backup providers that there is a workload demand distribution problem in their team. As noted above, mutual performance monitoring is a necessary condition for backup behavior, and backup behavior is necessary to transform mutual performance monitoring into performance gains. Backup behavior can involve either physical or verbal (or other communicative) assistance.

Backup behavior supports effective team functioning in three key ways. First, it allows team members to receive timely and precise feedback so that team performance processes can be adjusted. Second, it allows team members to provide assistance during task performance. Third, as already noted, it allows teams to dynamically adjust their performance strategies and processes when an imbalance in the workload distribution is detected. This creates an adaptive capacity to correct errors and shift performance strategies.

Team orientation is more than an individual's disposition to work in a team rather than alone. It is the propensity to value and use task inputs from teammates. These preferences and patterns of behavior are essential for effective teamwork. For example, when teams experience increasing levels of stress (e.g., time pressure), team members can succumb to intentional narrowing, in which they shift their focus away from the team and toward their individual tasks. This causes them to become less likely to accept input or feedback from others on their team. A strong team orientation can mitigate this tendency.

Collaborating Mechanisms

The five core components of teamwork discussed above are facilitated by three core collaborating mechanisms: shared mental models, closed-loop communication, and mutual trust. They do this by ensuring that information is exchanged, distributed, and processed in an appropriate and timely manner.

Shared mental models are organized knowledge structures that facilitate execution of interdependent team processes. An individual-level mental model is a knowledge structure that helps to integrate information and comprehend some phenomenon of interest. Expanded to the team level, a shared mental model is a knowledge structure that is shared across the members of the team. This "sharedness" allows team members to interpret information in a similar manner and thereby facilitates effective team function. Team members who hold shared mental representations are better able to develop similar causal explanations of a situation and similar inferences about possible states of the situation in the near future. Also, holding shared mental models enables implicit coordination (e.g., passing information without its having been requested), that is, communicating without overtly doing so.

Closed-loop communication is a specific pattern of communication that enables effective teamwork. In general, communication is information exchange between a sender and a receiver, with both knowing that the information was received. Communication is the means by which team members translate individual-level understanding into the team-level dynamic representations that guide coordinated actions. Effective teams are able to shift between implicit and explicit coordination when environmental demands change. When effective teams engage in explicit coordination, they use closed-loop communication. Three features define closed-loop communication: (1) a message that is initiated by the sender; (2) the receipt, interpretation, and acknowledgment of that message by the intended receiver; and (3) a follow-up by the sender, ensuring that the message was received and appropriately interpreted. This pattern of communication helps ensure that all team members are operating under the same goals and understanding of the situation.

Smith-Jentsch and colleagues have identified four specific teamwork behaviors contributing to good team communication. First, team members should use the proper phraseology. Teams that speak with a specialized communication terminology (e.g., military or health care teams) are able to pass large amounts of information quickly. Second, team members should provide complete and timely reports of the information they hold. Third, team members should minimize unneeded communications (e.g., chatter) by focusing only on the essentials of interaction necessary for team functioning. Fourth, to minimize the chance of misinterpretation, team members should make sure that their communications are clear and audible.

Mutual trust in the context of teams is members' shared perception that the team is motivated and able to protect the interests of its members. Mutual trust concerns the team's motivation and ability to resolve conflicts so that members feel accountability and ownership for team results. Without mutual trust, resources of the team (e.g., attention and communication) may be squandered on unnecessary surveillance of members to ensure that they are performing adequately. Mutual trust also underlies team processes and outcomes, such as members' willingness to disseminate information, members' contributions, members' participation, and the quality of the team's performance.

What Do Effective Teams Do?

Research has identified a number of behaviors and cognitions that distinguish high-performing from lower performing teams. High-performance teams hold shared mental models; they self-correct and adapt as they perform; they have clear roles and responsibilities; they have shared vision; they engage in a cycle of prebriefing, performing, and debriefing; their members trust one another; they have a sense of teamwork; and they optimize resources. In sum, high-performing teams are not just a collection of the "best players"—having the best person in each position does not guarantee team success. To succeed, teams need teamwork.

Eduardo Salas

See also Group Composition; Group Development; Group Learning; Group Performance; Group Structure; Shared Mental Models; Team Building; Team Performance Assessment; Team Reflexivity; Trust; Work Teams

Further Readings

Driskell, J. E., Goodwin, G. F., Salas, E., & O'Shea, P. G. (2006). What makes a good team player? *Group Dynamics: Theory, Research and Practice, 10,* 249–271.

Ilgen, D. R., Hollenbeck, J. R., Johnson, M., & Jundt, D. (2005). Teams in organizations: From input-process-output models to IMOI models. *Annual Review of Psychology, 56,* 517–543.

McGrath, J. E. (1984). *Groups: Interaction and performance.* Englewood Cliffs, NJ: Prentice Hall.

Salas, E., Sims, D. E., & Burke, C. S. (2005). Is there a "Big Five" in teamwork? *Small Group Research, 36,* 555–599.

Salas, E., Stagl, K. D., Burke, C. S., & Goodwin, G. F. (2007). Fostering team effectiveness in organizations: Toward an integrative theoretical framework of team performance. In W. Spaulding & J. Flowers (Eds.), *Modeling complex systems: Motivation, cognition and social processes* (pp. 185–243). Lincoln: University of Nebraska Press.

TERRITORIALITY

Territoriality, or territorial behavior, is related to occupation or ownership and control of a geographical area. A *territory* is a spatial unit that is defended from encroachment. In contrast to *personal space,* conceived by the anthropologist Edward T. Hall as an area or "bubble" that moves with a person, a territory is a region that is fixed. Topics of interest to social psychologists are how different kinds of territories affect social behavior and the consequences of territorial invasion. This entry examines the background of the idea of territoriality and some relevant research.

Background

Within the social sciences, the concept of territory has long been of interest to geographers and to sociologists who studied how street gangs mark out their home turf. The significance of territoriality for social psychologists, however, arose predominantly from theory developed in *ethology*—the study of animals in their natural environments. The ornithologist Henry Howard noted in 1920 that birds defined and used small spaces, which he called *territories.* How animals come to occupy and then defend a territory attracted the attention of the ethologists Konrad Lorenz and Nikolaas Tinbergen. They found that territoriality occurs mostly *within* an animal species. It is instinctive and is associated with mating, rearing of the young, and protecting access to food sources. In both social and environmental psychology, territoriality is not confined to individuals but also occurs for groups.

In territorial species, territorial behavior is linked to aggression in the defense of space. Members of a species spread out and divide the available living space, establish a territory, and defend it against intruders of their own species. Attacks against an invading conspecific can occur, but these are often minimized by the use of *boundary marking*—Bears mark trees with their claws, dogs urinate, cats spray and also leave their scent by rubbing against objects, and birds sing. If an intruder persists, an aggression display signals what could follow and may head off an actual attack. Within some species, such as primates, a territory underpins the social structure of the group and provides a context for dominance hierarchies that control access to resources by group members.

The combined thrust of arguments in the ethological and psychological literature is that territoriality serves two functions: It regulates social interaction, and it defines identity. Both functions have been explored in social-psychological research. With respect to social interaction, defining a territory eases contact between people by reducing conflict and miscommunication. It involves individualizing a place with a marking device that serves as a boundary and communicates ownership. Claiming a territory can also communicate identity, either for oneself or for one's group.

The environmental psychologist Irwin Altman viewed territorial behavior as a mechanism that controls social interaction. He argued that human territoriality has several components:

- It regulates interaction by defining self–other boundaries. (This notion overlaps with the concept of *privacy*, that is, how we control access to the self or to our group.)
- It involves personalization, or marking, of a geographical area.
- It communicates real or implied ownership by its users or inhabitants.

Kinds of Territories

Altman distinguished between primary, secondary, and public territories, noting that these vary in terms of how central they are to the lives of individuals or to the activities of groups to which they belong. Different kinds of territories also vary in terms of their duration of possession or ownership, ranging from transient to long-term occupancy.

Primary Territories

A primary territory is owned and most often used exclusively. Ownership is invested in an individual or a group, and this is clearly identifiable to others. A home is an example of a primary territory and is used often permanently by a primary group, such as a family. This kind of territory is the most central to the concept of *privacy,* as defined above. As a primary territory, someone's house is therefore the most clearly marked. It is likely to have fences or hedges as its boundaries. It may have a gate and almost certainly a lockable front door and a bell for visitors. Of all territories, it is the one that is most actively defended when invaded. Generally, the use of defensive force is accepted in the face of home invasion.

Within a primary territory, members of a primary group usually differentiate between areas in terms of how they may be used. The kitchen is likely to be communal, whereas the bathroom is declared off limits to most other group members for short periods of time. In the family home, growing children stake their claim to their bedrooms by mounting photos of friends, posters of pop stars, and trophies on the walls. In time, children may also expect their parents to knock before entering. Likewise, in shared spaces such as an open-plan office or a student dormitory, the use of decorations stamps one's personal identity on a specific zone and enhances the perception of personal control.

According to Altman, primary territories are powerful privacy-regulation mechanisms. In Western culture at least, they are usually treated in a sacrosanct way and can be entered only with the owner's permission. The degree to which an individual personalizes a primary territory indicates how attached that person is to that space. For example, university students who decorate their rooms in residence halls are more likely to identify with the hall and the university and to extend their studies there beyond their freshman year. Violation of a primary territory is a threat to a person's identity, and a failure to regulate one's privacy can lead to a loss of self-esteem. Examples of people who have little or no primary territory are prisoners, psychiatric hospital patients, and the homeless.

Secondary Territories

A secondary territory is less psychologically central and less exclusive than a primary territory. Secondary territories may have a limited degree of ownership, such as clubrooms by club members or the foyer of an apartment building by its inhabitants. Such territories may even function as "homes" in certain cases. For example, regular frequenters of a neighborhood bar may regard the bar as their shared domain and feel that they can control who may use the space, even to the point of trying to deny entry to strangers. Intruders can be subjected to hostile looks and insulting or mocking statements. Regulars at a bar can also treat it as an office, taking phone calls, storing funds with the bartender, and receiving mail.

Some researchers have included temporary interactional areas as a special kind of secondary territory. An example is the way a small cluster of people occupies a circle of floor space at a party. Altman, however, has argued that such a shared area is better classified as a *group personal space*, an enlarged and shared version of Hall's personal bubble—a "transparent membrane" that can shift with the people who are inside it. Because secondary territories are usually semipublic, conflict is possible over their location, their boundaries, and even their existence. The less clear the rules governing the use of a secondary territory, the more likely it will be encroached.

Public Territories

A public territory is one that everybody can enter and occupy from time to time. Occupancy, therefore, is temporary and usually not exclusive. For example, just because an individual has arrived first at the beach does not mean that other people can be prevented from swimming. Public territories can be exclusive for the time of occupancy, such as a seat in a restaurant or a telephone booth, but people have no rights over them once they leave. Occupancy of a public territory does not imply complete freedom of action. Behavior is typically constrained by community norms, sometimes defined in posted rules, such as the ban on alcoholic beverages in certain parks.

Territorial Invasion

A territorial encroachment involves an unacceptable breach of a personal or group boundary. Violation of a boundary means that the level of achieved privacy is less than the level of desired privacy. Like animals, people use territorial markers to deter encroachment on their territories. For example, a home owner might use fences, hedges, or signs (e.g., "Beware of dog"). And a worker in a shared office might use personal items, such as calendars, desk ornaments, or photos. At the group level, people living in a particular residential area might indicate that their neighborhood is off limits to burglars by forming citizen patrols or creating a gated community that only residents can enter. In such cases, the creation of a defensible space contributes to the stability of the social system.

The reaction to a territorial invasion varies with the type of territory. Primary territories, such as homes, usually involve legal ownership, so an emergency call to the police might serve to deal with a home invasion. Intrusions into secondary territories, where ownership is not always obvious, are more difficult to address. Marking one's space in a public territory can deter encroachment, although the success of the strategy depends on the number of occupants seeking space. In a study by Robert Sommer, when few people were using a library and density was therefore low, almost any marker, such as a paperback book or even an old newspaper (although not litter), was an effective way of protecting reading space when a person left the room. However, when many people were using the library and density was high, a personal marker such as a coat was much more effective.

Conclusion

Both individuals and groups are embedded in social environments. Although these environments provide benefits, they also generate costs. Territoriality is a means of reducing these costs by buffering individuals and groups from unwanted interactions. Given the striking similarities in how various species of animals create and defend territories, it is not surprising that territoriality has elicited a good deal of theoretical and empirical attention from researchers from various disciplines.

Graham M. Vaughan

See also Crowding; Group Boundaries; Norms

Further Readings

Altman, I. (1975). *The environment and social behavior: Privacy, personal space, territory and crowding.* Monterey, CA: Brooks/Cole.

Ardrey, R. (1966). *The territorial imperative.* New York: Atheneum.

Hall, E. T. (1966). *The hidden dimension.* New York: Doubleday.

Newman, O. (1972). *Defensible space.* New York: Macmillan.

Sommer, R. (1969). *Personal space: The behavioral basis of design.* Englewood Cliffs, NJ: Prentice Hall.

Tinbergen, N. (1968). On war and peace in animals and man: An ethologist's approach to the biology of aggression. *Science, 160,* 1411–1418.

TERRORISM

There are more than 100 different definitions of terrorism. One possible reason for this lack of consensus is that the pejorative connotation of the terrorism label motivates individuals to set it apart from forms of aggression they wish to condone. That is, because terrorism is considered heinous and illegitimate, those considered terrorists by others often reject such a label because they see their cause as righteous and justified. This is embodied in the often-heard assertion that one person's terrorist is another person's freedom fighter. One common element in the different definitions of terrorism represents its core: Terrorism is the strategic use of fear to advance one's political objectives. This definition, however, creates a situation wherein the use of fear by organized states in order to break the morale of a targeted population will fall under the label of (*state*) *terrorism*. For that reason, perhaps, most definitions used by terrorism researchers restrict terrorism to nonstate actors.

Terrorism Throughout History

Terrorism is not a new phenomenon. Documented incidents of terrorism, loosely defined, date back to the ancient world. During the 1st century CE, Jews rebelling against Roman occupation wandered through crowded streets, using daggers to indiscriminately kill not only Romans but their Jewish brethren as well. In 1605, Guy Fawkes infamously attempted to blow up King James, the King's council, and the English Parliament as part of the ultimately foiled Gunpowder Plot. During the 20th century, terrorism was successfully employed in Russia, China, Cuba, and Iran by revolutionaries looking to overthrow their governments. Although these examples offer only a small sampling of the countless numbers of terrorist acts that litter the pages of human history, their diverse nature illustrates that terrorists need not share any common goals but merely an ideological conviction legitimizing fear and violence as a means to their desired end.

During the past 40 years, the number of countries reporting terrorist incidents has steadily grown, with the countries of Israel, Iraq, Pakistan, and Colombia reporting the greatest number of incidents. During this same period, terrorists have also increasingly targeted persons, in addition to structures and other forms of property.

Terrorists show considerable creativity in the tactics they use in their attacks. Seven tactics—bombings (including suicide bombings), assassinations, armed assaults, kidnappings, arson, hijackings, and hostage incidents—account for the overwhelming majority of all terrorist incidents in recent history. Nonetheless, the way these and other tactics have been used (e.g., the conversion of commercial aircraft into missiles, the use of sophisticated improvised explosive device technology, the use of poisonous gas in public places) attests to considerable ingenuity and adaptability of terrorist activities to situational conditions.

The Psychology of Terrorism

Though terrorism has manifold aspects, fundamental questions about terrorism are sociopsychological in nature. These questions concern individuals' motivations for joining a terrorist organization, recruitment modes and means of persuasion, the inculcation of belief systems that justify terrorism and portray it as efficient and honorable, and organizational decision making regarding its use.

More generally, each of these questions belongs to one of three levels of psychological analysis. The individual level pertains to psychological factors that operate on the terrorist as a person, the group level pertains to interpersonal psychological phenomena that arise in group settings, and the organizational level pertains to factors regarding the structure and functioning of terrorist organizations.

The Individual Level

Because the atrocities that terrorists perpetrate violate fundamental norms of human conduct, terrorism was thought to represent a form of psychopathology. However, the systematic quest for a terrorist psychopathology or for a unique terrorist personality has yielded little empirical support. The majority of research has pointed to the "normality" of individuals involved in terrorist acts.

The search for situational "root causes" of terrorism, such as socioeconomic status, age, education, relative deprivation, religion, foreign occupation, or poverty, has also proven disappointing. The primary hindrance is the conceptual problem of specificity: Although many people share the same oppressive environments, only a small number consider joining a terrorist organization. Thus, none of these environmental factors can be considered the necessary and sufficient condition for, or *the* cause of, terrorism. This does not imply that personality traits or environmental conditions are irrelevant to terrorism. Rather, they are best regarded as contributing factors to terrorism in that they may enhance an individual's support for, or involvement in, a terrorist act or organization, under specific circumstances.

In recent years, a number of different theories on terrorists' motivations have been proffered. Some have emphasized a singular motivation, such as the quest for emotional and social support, resistance to foreign occupation, or religion. In contrast to this emphasis on a single crucial motivation, other theories have listed a potpourri, or cocktail, of motives (e.g., honor, dedication to the leader, humiliation, modernization, pain and personal loss, group pressure, vengeance) that might propel individuals toward terrorism.

A reasonable step in dealing with such heterogeneity is to reduce it by aggregating the diverse motives for becoming a terrorist into more general, motivational categories. Several authors have hinted at such a taxonomy, based on a partition between ideological reasons and personal causes for engaging in terrorism. For instance, alienated individuals' quest for social and emotional support stems from their personal experience, as do pain, trauma, and redemption of lost honor, often listed as motives. In contrast, liberation of one's land or carrying out of God's will pertains to ideological factors that transcend individual actors' life circumstances. A terrorism-justifying ideology identifies a culprit (e.g., the West, Israel, infidels) presumed responsible for the discrepancy between the extant and desired state (defining the grievance) and portrays violence against that culprit (e.g., jihad, terrorism) as an effective means for redressing the grievance and moving toward the desired state.

Beyond personal causes and ideological reasons, a third motivational category pertinent to suicidal attacks involves a sense of social duty and obligation, whether internalized or induced by social pressure. This is exemplified in the case of World War II Japanese kamikaze pilots, but it is also highly relevant to present-day terrorism.

Suicide terrorism is an extreme form of terrorism in which terrorists claim their own life along with those of their victims, thus becoming "martyrs" for an ideological cause. Although a wide variety of specific factors have been suggested as possible motives of suicide bombers, it is possible that a quest for personal significance serves as an overarching motivational category responsible for suicidal terrorism. This explanation posits that suicide missions are seen by those who undertake them as means of gaining or restoring significance or as preventing the loss of significance.

The Group Level

Violence, in general, and the killing of innocents, more specifically, fall outside the norms of most civilized societies. Because it is difficult to sustain deviance on one's own, terrorism is typically carried out in the context of groups whose ideologies or shared realities lend terrorism an aura of legitimacy. Several sociopsychological aspects of terrorism require analysis at the group level. These include recruitment to the group, construction and maintenance of the group's shared beliefs, and the mechanism of public commitment.

Recruitment to terrorist groups can occur through networking (introduction to the group through a family member, friend, romantic partner, or other acquaintance), institutions (e.g., churches and mosques, religious schools) whose climates and/or explicit objectives concern ideological indoctrination, or self-recruitment (e.g., through the Internet). These bottom-up (e.g., networking, the Internet) and top-down (e.g., religious institution) recruitment processes are intertwined. The personal relations provide the motivational impetus for adopting the ideology and its social validation, whereas the Internet messages furnish the ideological arguments themselves and inflame the motivation to accept those arguments.

Another important group-level process inherent in terrorist activity is the creation of an *ensconced culture*. Typically, a terrorist group exists within a larger society with which it may have varying degrees of worldview overlap. In some cases, the perspectives, values, and objectives held by the terrorist group have little in common with those of the larger society. In other cases, the overlap is substantial, and the terrorist group is seen as acting on behalf of the larger society. Because of the nearly inevitable exposure of the embedded terrorist group to views emanating from the larger society, the latter may impact the terrorists' opinions. Thus, terrorist groups whose ideologies are divergent from the societal worldviews often feel the need to protect their ideological premises from contrary external influences. This is often accomplished via reduction of members' contact with outside sources and the creation of a unique culture wherein the terrorism-justifying ideology is repeatedly highlighted.

Because defection from a terrorist group may be demoralizing as well as dangerous (potentially involving the provision of important intelligence to the enemies), terrorist organizations often use tactics of *public commitment* and *social pressure* to ensure members' loyalty. For instance, an important element of the group process brought to bear on the suicidal bomber in training is the creation of a psychological point of no return, which few individuals can overcome. Often, the candidate is made to prepare his or her will and write last letters to family and friends and is then videotaped bidding everybody farewell and encouraging others to follow his or her example. This places an extraordinary amount of pressure on the individual to carry out the deed as planned, thus helping ensure the group's success.

The Organizational Level

The organizational level of analysis is of considerable importance for understanding terrorism. Terrorist groups vary immensely in degree and type of organization that characterize them. Some organizations revolve around a single leader. Others are less autocratic and leader centered.

Based on considerable intuitive appreciation of various psychological principles (of recruitment, indoctrination, training, etc.), terrorist organizations have been able to create a veritable assembly line for the production of devoted foot soldiers prepared to go so far as to sacrifice their own lives for the cause. It is the organizations that then decide when and where to deploy these operatives in ways that best serve the organizations' political agendas.

Because beyond a certain minimal size, terrorist organizations require infrastructure, space for training, and funding, the organizational level of analysis may reveal major vulnerabilities of terrorist organizations, hence affording an opening for launching significant counterterrorism efforts exploiting those vulnerabilities.

Conclusion

Violent and deadly acts of terrorism perpetrated by both large, multinational organizations (e.g., al-Qaeda) and single individuals acting on their own (e.g., Ted Kaczynski) are capable of undermining the sense of security in the international system as a whole. Hence, a solid understanding of terrorism at macro, micro, and middling levels of analysis is of critical importance. This entry has discussed psychological phenomena proposed to underlie, and thus help explain, various facets of terrorism at the individual, group, and organization levels, with the aim of offering insight into the general psychology of terrorism across its manifold manifestations.

Arie W. Kruglanski and Anna C. Sheveland

See also Ideology; Intergroup Violence

Further Readings

Crenshaw, M. (2007). Explaining suicide terrorism: A review essay. *Security Studies, 16,* 133–162.

Hoffman, B. (2006). *Inside terrorism*. New York: Columbia University Press.

Kruglanski, A. W., Chen, X., Dechesne, M., Fishman, S., & Orehek, E. (2009). Fully committed: Suicide bombers' motivation and the quest for personal significance. *Political Psychology, 30*(3), 331–357.

Kruglanski, A. W., Crenshaw, M., Post, G., & Victoroff, J. (2008). What should this fight be called? Metaphors of counterterrorism and their implications. *Psychological Science in the Public Interest, 8*, 97–133.

Kruglanski, A. W., & Fishman, S. (2006). The psychology of terrorism: "Syndrome" versus "tool" perspectives. *Terrorism and Political Violence, 18*, 193–215.

Rapoport, D. C. (2004). Modern terror: The four waves. In A. K. Cronin & J. M. Ludes (Eds.), *Attacking terrorism: Elements of a grand strategy* (pp. 46–73). Washington, DC: Georgetown University Press.

Sageman, M. (2004). *Understanding terror networks.* Philadelphia: University of Pennsylvania Press.

Victoroff, J. (2005). The mind of the terrorist: A review and critique of psychological approaches. *Journal of Conflict Resolution, 49*, 3–42.

Victoroff, J., & Kruglanski, A. W. (2009). *Psychology of terrorism: Classic and contemporary perspectives.* New York: Psychology Press.

TERROR MANAGEMENT THEORY

All humans view life through a culturally based worldview. According to *terror management theory*, a central function of these worldviews is to imbue existence with meaning and our lives with enduring significance to obscure the terrifying possibility that existence is a brief episode punctuated with oblivion upon death. Groups serve a central role in perpetuating these worldviews, and conflict is often fueled by the threat that other groups' worldviews pose to sustaining faith in the validity of one's own worldview.

Building on Ernest Becker's existential psychoanalytic writings, Sheldon Solomon, Jeff Greenberg, and Tom Pyszczynski formulated terror management theory and initiated research to assess the theory. A large body of published experiments from many countries has supported the theory. One central finding is that reminding people of their own mortality generally increases identification with their cultural group and derogation of others who criticize or violate the group's norms. This research demonstrates that concerns about mortality contribute to many aspects of human behavior, including conformity, obedience, self-esteem striving, nationalism, dogmatism, intergroup conflict, stereotyping, political decision making, and terrorism. This entry summarizes the theory's basic propositions, describes supporting evidence, and discusses the implications for intergroup relations.

Basic Propositions

Like other animals, humans have a host of biological systems that serve to perpetuate their survival. For humans, survival is enhanced by the evolved human brain, which has the capacity to experience symbolic thought, to think about the past and the future, and to be aware of oneself. However, these same capabilities also make humans aware that eventually these systems will fail, and they will die. This knowledge of mortality in a creature designed for survival creates an ever-present potential for anxiety, or terror.

To manage this potential for terror, humans must view themselves as more than animals fated to obliteration. Cultural worldviews facilitate this denial by portraying life as meaningful and humans as beings of enduring significance who will live on literally or symbolically beyond death. Literal immortality is provided by the concept of a soul that transcends death through an afterlife. Symbolic immortality is provided by viewing the self as continuing on through offspring, legacies, group identifications, and valued achievements: "I will die, but my group, achievements, influence, memory will live on."

Each culture provides a meaning-imbuing story of where life came from, what its purposes are, and how, through one's valued deeds and roles, one will endure beyond one's physical death. Various religious, educational, political, and entertainment institutions, symbols, and rituals promote faith in this meaningful and security-providing cultural worldview. By sustaining faith in one's cultural worldview and living up to the standards of value prescribed by that worldview (i.e., maintaining self-esteem), individuals can believe they are more than just material animals fated to obliteration and thereby manage their potential terror.

Along with explaining the function of cultural worldviews and self-esteem, the theory explains how meaning and self-worth become the individual's psychological security base. Newborns are completely helpless and dependent on their parents for survival. Thus, parental love and protection constitute the initial basis of security. The many fears of the child, the dark, strangers, big dogs, monsters, and so forth are quelled by the protection of the seemingly omnipotent parents.

From the beginning, parents instill the culture's values and beliefs into their children, including what it means to be good and what it means to be bad. As children develop, parents put demands on them to be good: to behave in certain ways and not in others. When children follow these standards of value, they are comforted and rewarded. When they do not, love is withdrawn, or they are punished. Thus, children come to associate being good with feeling secure and being bad with feeling anxious. Children internalize these standards so they can regulate their own behavior to try to sustain the parental love and protection.

Thus self-esteem, the sense that they are good, buffers children from anxiety. When children feel good, they bask in the omnipotent love and protection of their parents, and everything is right in their world. However, with cognitive development, they become increasingly aware of more powerful threats, especially the ultimate threat to existence, death, and realize the limits of the parents. Children's basis of psychological security, therefore, must be transferred to something greater than the parents, namely, the cultural constructs the parents have instilled in them throughout childhood, including deities (e.g., Jesus), authorities (e.g., the president), and groups (e.g., the United States). From then on, being valued in the eyes of the larger culture rather than the parents is the basis of psychological security. Through this developmental process, the individual's worldview and sense of self-worth provide security in the face of the threats posed by reality that culminate in the knowledge of mortality.

Empirical Evidence

Terror management theory fits what we know about cultural worldviews, social influence, and the need for self-esteem. Beliefs and rituals concerning death transcendence have been an important component of virtually all known cultures, from the ancient Sumerians, Egyptians, and Chinese to tribes throughout the globe and to modern Christian, Hindu, and Islamic cultures. History has been greatly influenced by the spread of and clashes among groups with different afterlife beliefs. Psychological research documents the human proneness to conformity and obedience to cultural dictates, the relationship between self-esteem and good mental health, and the many ways people pursue and defend their self-esteem.

Terror management research has focused primarily on two broad hypotheses. First, faith in one's worldview and self-esteem should buffer anxiety and protect one from death-related concerns. Research has supported this hypothesis in a number of ways. For example, giving people a boost to their self-esteem reduces their anxiety in response to the prospect of receiving electric shocks, and threats to an individual's worldview or self-esteem arouse anxiety and bring thoughts of death closer to consciousness.

The second broad hypothesis is that when people are reminded of their mortality (known as *mortality salience*), they will intensify their efforts to sustain faith in their worldview and strive harder to demonstrate their self-worth. Mortality salience has been induced in a variety of ways, including asking people to write briefly about their own death, filling out a death anxiety questionnaire, interviewing them near a cemetery, or exposing them to the word *dead* on a computer screen flashed so quickly that the participants are not aware they are seeing the word. Most of the studies compare the effects of mortality salience with the effects of making salient other aversive potential future events, such as being in intense pain, taking an upcoming exam, giving a speech in public, being socially excluded, or feeling uncertain.

These studies show that mortality salience leads to negative reactions to those who violate the morals of or criticize one's worldview and positive reactions to those who uphold the morals of or praise one's worldview. For example, mortality salience led municipal court judges to increase recommended bond for a fictional prostitute from $50 to $455. On the other hand, mortality salience also increased people's recommendations for how much reward should be given to a hero.

Mortality salience also leads people to distance themselves from reminders of their similarities to other animals and their material, and therefore mortal, nature. In addition, mortality salience leads people to strive harder to display attributes on which they base their self-esteem. For example, people reminded of mortality drive more boldly if they base their self-esteem partly on driving ability and display more physical strength if they base their self-worth partly on physical strength. Mortality salience also generally increases people's identification with their nation and other valued groups but reduces such identification when these groups are depicted in a negative light.

Implications for Intergroup Relations

The theory's fundamental implication for understanding intergroup relations is that groups who espouse a worldview different from one's own call the validity of one's own worldview into question and thereby threaten one's psychological security. From the terror management perspective, this psychological threat is a fundamental cause of prejudice and intergroup conflict. To cope with this threat, people react to other cultural groups in one of three primary ways. First, they often derogate such groups, such as by dismissing them as "ignorant savages." Second, they often try to assimilate such different others into their own worldview, for example through missionary activity. Third, threatening groups are often aggressed against. What better way to assert the superiority of one's own way of life than by derogating, converting, dominating, or annihilating those with an alternative worldview?

In support of these ideas, mortality salience increases preference for aspects of one's own culture and those who validate it and decreases liking for aspects of other cultures and people who criticize one's own culture. For example, mortality salience increased Christians' liking of a fellow Christian and dislike of a Jew, and it increased Germans' preferences for German over foreign products. Mortality salience also increased individuals' aggression against someone who criticized their political party.

Terror management theory posits two additional mechanisms that contribute to prejudice and conflict. First, because worldviews prescribe specific stereotypes of minority group members, when the need for worldview validation is strong, people will prefer individuals who conform to rather than violate cultural stereotypes of the minority group. For example, in a control condition, White people in the United States preferred a counterstereotypic studious, conservatively dressed Black male over a stereotypic Black male in hip-hop garb who expressed a strong interest in basketball and had violent tendencies. However, after mortality salience, U.S. Whites preferred the stereotypic U.S. Black over the counterstereotypic one.

Finally, worldviews that provide the most satisfying sense of significance are those that portray one's group as representing all that is good in a heroic battle to triumph over evil. Therefore, when the need for terror management is strong, people will be drawn to leaders and ideologies that promote such a "we are great and we must defeat those who are evil" worldview.

When judging hypothetical gubernatorial candidates, reminders of mortality increased preference for a charismatic leader who emphasized the greatness of one's own state and nation. Similarly, before the 2004 U.S. presidential election, mortality salience increased preference for Republican president George W. Bush, who emphasized a need for a heroic triumph over evildoers, over Democratic candidate John Kerry. Mortality salience also directly increases support for eradication of the evil other. Mortality salience increased Iranians' support for suicide bombings against the United States and U.S. conservatives' support for extremely lethal military actions in the Middle East.

Terror management theory and research suggest two ways to reduce the inclination toward intergroup hostility. First, if individuals could develop more individualized ways to ameliorate their fear of death, they would be less reliant on defending their particular worldview. Second, if people invested in worldviews that were more flexible and that highly valued tolerance of different others, they would be less threatened and less prone to negativity toward them.

Jeff Greenberg

See also Collective Self; Culture; Intergroup Anxiety; Intergroup Violence; Nationalism and Patriotism; Prejudice; Self-Esteem; Stereotyping; Terrorism

Further Readings

Goldenberg, J., Pyszczynski, T., Greenberg, J., & Solomon, S. (2000). Fleeing the body: A terror management perspective on the problem of human corporeality. *Personality and Social Psychology Review, 4,* 200–218.

Greenberg, J., Solomon, S., & Arndt, J. (2007). A basic but uniquely human motivation: Terror management. In J. Shah & W. Gardner (Eds.), *Handbook of motivation science* (pp. 114–134). New York: Guilford.

Pyszczynski, T., Greenberg, J., & Solomon, S. (1999). A dual process model of defense against conscious and unconscious death-related thoughts: An extension of terror management theory. *Psychological Review, 106,* 835–845.

Pyszczynski, T., Solomon, S., & Greenberg, J. (2003). *In the wake of September 11: The psychology of terror.* Washington, DC: American Psychological Association.

Schimel, J., Simon, L., Greenberg, J., Pyszczynski, T., Solomon, S., Waxmonsky, J., et al. (1999). Stereotyping and terror management: Evidence that mortality salience increases stereotypic thinking and preferences. *Journal of Personality and Social Psychology, 77,* 905–926.

Solomon, S., Greenberg, J., & Pyszczynski, T. (1991). A terror management theory of social behavior: On the psychological functions of self-esteem and cultural worldviews. In M. P. Zanna (Ed.), *Advances in experimental social psychology* (Vol. 24, pp. 93–159). San Diego, CA: Academic Press.

THERAPY GROUPS

Therapy groups are designed to promote the health and adjustment of their members. Initially used when the demand for services outstripped available health care providers, therapists discovered that group approaches offered unique benefits over more individualistic therapies. Some of these benefits include a reduced sense of isolation and uniqueness, mutual support, exposure to positive models, and the opportunity to develop coping skills by interacting with others. Therapists now use groups to address a variety of psychological and physical maladies, and their methods are as varied as those used in individual approaches. Even though the idea of having people suffering from problems gather together seemed radical at first, researchers have confirmed the value of group methods for helping people reach their therapeutic goals.

History

People have long recognized the curative potential of groups. Down through the ages, palliative and curative practices, including religious rites intended to purify and heal members of the community and treatments for those suffering from both physical and psychological problems, have been conducted in groups rather than in solitude. The restorative power of groups was rediscovered by practitioners in the early years of the 20th century when they brought together, for treatment and instruction, patients who suffered the same malady. At first, such grouping was done to save time and money. Working with a group of people was more efficient than treating each one individually. In time, however, practitioners realized that their patients were benefiting from the groups themselves, in that they supported each other, shared nontechnical information about their illnesses and treatment, and seemed to appreciate the opportunity to express themselves to attentive and sympathetic listeners. Whereas group therapy was once used only as a last resort when the number of patients outstripped the available therapists, group approaches became the treatment of choice for a variety of psychological problems, particularly those that originate from difficulties in making and maintaining strong interpersonal relationships with other people or limitations in self-regulation. Their effectiveness led practitioners to recognize that, in many cases, it is easier to change individuals when they are gathered into a group than to change individuals one at a time.

Group psychotherapy is currently used to treat many types of psychiatric problems, including addictions, thought disorders, depression, eating disorders, posttraumatic stress disorder, personality disorders, and some forms of psychosis. Group therapy is, however, a treatment for individuals rather than intact groups that are behaving in a dysfunctional way. Group therapists are mindful of the interpersonal processes that operate within the group and often deal with the group as a whole, but they do not treat groups per se. They make use of the group milieu and its interpersonal dynamics to promote the adjustment of the individuals in it.

Types of Therapy

Many groups have therapeutic purposes. In support groups, members who are suffering from some illness or share in common a troubling experience provide one another encouragement and hope. Some groups guide members who are recovering from an addiction. When individuals wish to strengthen and broaden their personal or social skills, they often join educational and training groups. Even groups of friends, relatives, or colleagues from work, by sharing an experience and offering one another support, can be considered therapeutic for their members. Traditionally, however, therapy groups are ones that are organized and led by a mental health professional and whose members are individuals suffering from a diagnosed psychological or medical problem.

Group therapists are similar in that they treat their patients in groups, but they differ in their general approach to treatment and conception of groups themselves. When the group is led by a therapist who uses psychoanalytic methods, then the focus of treatment is on each individual's anxieties and his or her reliance on defense mechanisms to cope with these anxieties. As in individual psychoanalysis, the therapist encourages members to speak freely with each other about troubling issues, and by interpreting these associations and interactions, patients gain insight into their difficulties.

Not all therapies, however, involve the search for hidden motives, conflicts, and repressed tensions. Cognitive behavioral therapy groups, for example, focus on the specific behaviors or thoughts that are considered troubling and use principles derived from learning theory to deal with these problems. These therapies were initially developed as one-on-one therapies, but they have been used with great success in groups. They assume that individuals who wish to change must learn a new set of thoughts and behaviors and unlearn those that are dysfunctional and disturbing. Cognitive behavior therapy groups therefore stress modeling desired behavior, learning sessions in which members practice the behaviors they wish to learn, and feedback to group members about their progress toward their goals.

In the more humanistic, interpersonally focused group therapies, leaders take advantage of the group's dynamics to help members learn about themselves, their personal and existential concerns, and how they are perceived by other people. Some group therapists rely on relatively structured activities and role-playing methods to give members the opportunity to reexperience previous life events and explore the interpersonal roots of their emotional reactions. The therapists may also make use of *psychodrama*, in which group members are asked to take on roles that are defined in advance for the session or to develop their parts spontaneously as the activity progresses. Interpersonal group therapy, more than other approaches, explicitly focuses on the processes that occur within the therapy group itself. Members are encouraged to develop meaningful relations with one another, and then their reactions to one another are explored so that members can better understand how they respond to others interpersonally, and also how others perceive them.

Treatment Factors

Traditional, one-on-one therapies are thought to be based on a set of common, curative factors. Research suggests that most therapies, despite using various techniques, help patients by providing an alliance between the patient and the therapist, by giving the patient the opportunity to review previous problems, and by working through any emotions the patient may have about prior experiences. Similarly, despite their varying focuses and methods, all group therapies are thought to take advantage of common group-level processes to facilitate the attainment of treatment goals.

These group-level treatment factors that yield therapeutically positive gains for members include social and personal comparison, interpersonal learning, and mutual support among members. Groups prompt people to engage in social comparison—they can compare their own experiences with those of others in the group—and these comparisons can be both inspiring and reassuring. When group members discuss their problems openly in the group, these disclosures increase trust and reduce members' feelings that they are "odd" or "unusual." Groups, because they include multiple individuals rather than just a single therapist, also provide members with more extensive opportunities to learn from others. The members can also learn by observing the other members of the group, so they need not be directly involved in the discussion to gain a benefit. Groups, when cohesive, also provide members with the social support they need to overcome the negative effects of stress, and they even satisfy members' needs for interpersonal intimacy. In some cases, members find they can disclose more private, and sometimes troubling, information about themselves to other people rather than to therapists, and in doing so they learn to experience a sense of trust and commitment. When group members vent strong emotions, the resulting catharsis may reduce their stress. Group members also benefit from increased self-confidence produced by helping others and by gaining insight about their personal qualities from other group members.

Effectiveness

Joining a group and remaining active in it often improve a person's adjustment and well-being, and therapy groups are no exception. Group therapy has been shown to be an effective method for helping individuals change their thoughts, emotions, and actions. Individuals are sometimes more reluctant to take part in group psychotherapy than in individual therapy, and this bias may prevent them from profiting from a highly effective mode of treatment. Reviews of clinical trials that have compared the effectiveness of various types of psychological treatments conclude that group therapy is as effective as individual methods, at least for certain types of disorders. Specifically, individuals experiencing mood disorders (anxiety, depression) respond better to group therapy than individuals experiencing other types of disorders (e.g., thought and dissociative disorders). Group therapy has been shown to work well with children, adolescents, and adults and with both inpatient and outpatient populations.

Researchers continue to study ways to improve the effectiveness of therapy groups. Some factors, including pretraining members so they know what to expect in treatment and including two therapists rather than just one in each group, are associated with enhanced outcomes. Moreover, as in individual therapy, members of groups sometimes terminate their participation before reaching their

therapeutic goals. Those who drop out of treatment tend to be skeptical about group approaches and are more likely to also report having problems with substance abuse issues. In some rare cases, individuals are significantly harmed by the group treatment, particularly when the group becomes too critical of its members. Such responses are rare, however, for most individuals respond positively when presented the opportunity to work in a group to achieve mental health goals.

Donelson R. Forsyth

See also Sensitivity Training Groups; Social Comparison Theory; Support Groups

Further Readings

Forsyth, D. R., & Corazzini, J. G. (2000). Groups as change agents. In C. R. Snyder & R. E. Ingram (Eds.), *Handbook of psychological change: Psychotherapy processes and practices for the 21st century* (pp. 309–336). New York: Wiley.

Yalom, I. D., & Leszca, M. (2005). *The theory and practice of group psychotherapy*. New York: Basic Books.

TOKENISM

Tokenism occurs when only a small percentage of a disadvantaged group is permitted membership in a specific setting, with those individuals referred to as *tokens* (e.g., a token female firefighter in an otherwise all-male department). Tokenism implies that there are external restrictions that prevent the entry of greater numbers of group members who would otherwise be qualified. Tokenism is also characterized by a specific constellation of negative psychological and emotional consequences for the tokens. Thus, although there may be situations in which a high-status group has an insignificant presence (e.g., White students at a historically Black college), the term *tokenism* is usually reserved for situations in which the tokens are from a lower-status group.

From a systems perspective, tokenism is contrasted with a social system that is completely open to all qualified individuals (a *meritocracy*), and tokenism is also contrasted with a system that is completely closed to members of a particular group (e.g., a caste system). Because a token system is neither fully open nor fully closed, there is ambiguity about the circumstances under which members are permitted entry. This ambiguity is problematic for disadvantaged groups because it can undermine efforts to change the system.

History and Background

Rosabeth Moss Kanter introduced the concept of tokenism into the sociological and psychological lexicon in 1977 with the argument that the relative proportions of group members in a situation have a critical effect on group dynamics. Kanter was especially interested in groups in which men greatly outnumbered women because large numbers of women were finding themselves in such a situation as they joined traditionally male organizations during the feminist revolution. Kanter described specific consequences of tokenism that she believed were due to the visibility or salience of the tokens, including social isolation and increased stereotyping. Although much research has provided support for Kanter's analysis, the effects of tokenism appear to depend greatly on the wider social context and the social status of the tokens. For example, female engineers are much more likely to suffer negative consequences as tokens than male nurses are.

Research on tokenism has also expanded to provide a better understanding of the psychological impact on tokens. A classic series of studies by Charles Lord and Delia Saenz showed that tokens may suffer cognitive and behavioral deficits due to preoccupation with self-presentation, even when they are not treated differently from others. This idea has been further developed in research on *stereotype threat*. Finally, as described later in this entry, research on tokenism has expanded to include system-level analysis, such as how tokenism undermines social change.

Consequences of Tokenism

Research on tokenism has traditionally focused on the tokens. However, there are others who are affected, both directly (e.g., the majority group members in the token setting) and indirectly (e.g., the minority group members who have been left behind). Tokenism also has consequences for broader social change.

Majority Group (Dominants)

Most research on tokenism focuses on the negative consequences of the situation for the individual tokens, yet the "action" is often located in the majority group. By definition, tokens differ from dominants, but dominants also tend to exaggerate these differences and engage in greater stereotyping and negative evaluations of the tokens, due to the tokens' visibility and appearance as "representatives" of their group. For example, dominants tend to confuse who said what among token members of their group and to view token members' behavior as consistent with stereotypes. Such stereotyping may be even more exaggerated if it allows dominants to preserve their status through familiar forms of interaction (e.g., a male manager treating an equal-status female colleague as he would a secretary). These behaviors create artificial boundaries between the groups, further isolating the tokens and preventing them from full membership and equal status in the organization.

Tokens

Tokens must contend with multiple handicaps. They are usually assigned to lower-status roles—with lower pay and benefits—and they have to cope with being stereotyped and negatively evaluated on the basis of their group membership. Tokens can fight these stereotypic role assignments, but if they do, they may then be labeled as disagreeable or militant. In contrast, if tokens accept the stereotypic roles assigned to them, this passivity can limit their ability to demonstrate competencies. Tokens must also manage the heightened self-focus and accompanying anxiety that come with being the focus of attention. They are likely to feel self-conscious about their actions, worry about *impression management*, and feel pressured to work harder in order to stand out for their achievements rather than just their group status. A token's performance may thus suffer because such pressure and anxiety consume cognitive resources that could otherwise be devoted to relevant tasks (cf. *stereotype threat*). The studies by Lord and Saenz, for example, showed that individuals randomly assigned to a token position in a group displayed significantly worse memory for what was said during group interaction than did individuals assigned to nontoken positions.

Finally, tokens have to manage potentially competing social identities. Tokens who are able to overcome obstacles and avoid social rejection—perhaps by assimilating to dominant norms—risk being isolated from their original group. At the same time, they may never be fully accepted by the dominant group and thus risk being left without real support from either group.

Social System

One of the most effective strategies for making a token system more open and egalitarian is *collective action*. Stephen C. Wright argues that tokenism may maintain and even enhance social hierarchy more than if the system were completely closed, because tokenism undermines perceptions of injustice and group identity and suggests that individual-level action is effective. Wright points out that everyone in the system—the tokens, the remaining disadvantaged group members, and the dominant majority—can be invested in viewing the system as just fine.

For the individual tokens, the system *has* permitted them some measure of success, and thus they may be motivated to preserve it. The lone female state senator, for example, is unlikely to charge that the system that placed her there is unfair. Moreover, her need to adhere to the norms and values of the organization may further undermine her identity with women who do not share her advantage.

The dominant majority is similarly invested in maintaining the system. Its members have material advantages to preserve, but, unlike a fully closed system, the presence of tokens serves to assuage any guilt the dominants may have about the fairness of the current system and the degree to which they deserve their advantaged positions. If disadvantaged group members *can* advance, the lack of advancement by others can be attributed to their own failings.

Perhaps most surprising is the finding that disadvantaged group members who are not themselves tokens also go along with tokenism. These individuals have the most to gain through social change, and they ought to be motivated to see the system as unfair. However, research shows that this is often not the case. Whereas disadvantaged

group members do attempt to change a *fully closed system*, in which no one from their group is permitted to advance, they rarely do so in a token system. Instead, the accomplishments of the tokens are taken as proof that the system is fair and that individual-level achievement is possible. Because a token system is not actually open to all who are qualified, however, many disadvantaged group members will fail to advance despite their best efforts. Such failure leads to resentment (often against those who have achieved, further eroding the group cohesion that is necessary for social change), anger, stress, and depression. Moreover, by accepting the system as fair, disadvantaged group members are likely to attribute their low status to personal failings rather than to system-level barriers, further reducing the chances of their engaging in social change.

Remediating the Negative Effects of Tokenism

Tokenism provides advantages for at least some disadvantaged group members, but there are considerable drawbacks, including psychological stress and worsened performance among tokens and the material exclusion of many other disadvantaged group members. Solutions to the problems created by tokenism range from organizational change to individual coping strategies.

Organizational change is perhaps the most obvious solution. The problems of tokenism would presumably disappear if organizations simply increased the number of disadvantaged group members in their ranks. As discussed above, however, tokenism is not easy to dismantle. Even if a significant increase were allowed in the number of disadvantaged group members permitted entry, the outcome may not be all positive. There may simply not be enough disadvantaged group members available to eliminate the effects of tokenism, and a large increase in the number of disadvantaged group members in a particular setting could result in perceptions of threat on the part of the dominant group, greater and more active hostility, and the loss of important mentors and allies for the new members.

Research conducted by Janice Yoder suggests a different organizational approach for avoiding some of the negative effects of tokenism: Enhance the status and legitimacy of the tokens. Yoder found that token women in a simulated organizational setting perceived less performance pressure and anxiety if they had higher status (e.g., were older or more educated) than the male members of the group. Similarly, token women who received advanced training *and* were explicitly labeled as "experts" were able to successfully influence the male-dominated groups, whereas token women without such legitimacy were not.

Individual tokens may also be able to avoid some of the negative psychological effects of tokenism by using certain cognitive strategies. For example, Saenz and Lord showed that tokens who thought of themselves as "judges" (i.e., focused on evaluating the majority group members) showed better cognitive performance than did tokens who either believed they were the targets of evaluation or were told nothing (controls). This benefit was observed even when the majority members were unaware that they were being judged, suggesting that the strategy might be effective in the absence of social validation by others. Individual-level strategies that have been shown to be effective in overcoming stereotype threat, such as a brief self-affirmation, may also be effective in combating the negative effects of tokenism.

Conclusion

Although research on tokenism initially focused on the issues facing women in male-dominated careers, its principles have allowed insight into broader facets of intergroup interaction and the extension of research on tokenism into a variety of domains, including race, religion, and sexual orientation. Tokenism research has further informed the study of social systems by providing an explanation for how attitudes develop to favor system stability rather than change. In this respect, knowledge of tokenism highlights the importance of remaining vigilant even after low-status individuals appear to have achieved membership in high-status groups. As research progresses on tokenism, it is likely that its focus will shift from identifying its negative impacts to finding ways to reduce them. It may be impossible to balance group ratios completely, but there are ways to ensure that token members suffer fewer consequences of being in the minority.

Irene V. Blair and J. Allegra Smith

See also Categorization; Collective Movements and Protest; Minority Groups in Society; Stereotype Threat; Stigma; System Justification Theory

Further Readings

Jost, J. T., & Major, B. (Eds.). (2001). *The psychology of legitimacy: Emerging perspectives on ideology, justice, and intergroup relations.* New York: Cambridge University Press.

Kanter, R. M. (1977). *Men and women of the corporation.* New York: Basic Books.

Saenz, D. S., & Lord, C. G. (1989). Reversing roles: A cognitive strategy for undoing memory deficits associated with token status. *Journal of Personality and Social Psychology, 56,* 698–708.

van Zomeren, M., Postmes, T., & Spears, R. (2008). Toward an integrative social identity model of collective action: A quantitative research synthesis of three socio-psychological perspectives. *Psychological Bulletin, 134,* 504–535.

Wright, S. C. (2001). Restricted intergroup boundaries: Tokenism, ambiguity, and the tolerance of injustice. In J. T. Jost & B. Major (Eds.), *The psychology of legitimacy: Emerging perspectives on ideology, justice, and intergroup relations* (pp. 223–254). New York: Cambridge University Press.

Yoder, J. D. (2002). 2001 Division 35 presidential address: Context matters: Understanding tokenism processes and their impact on women's work. *Psychology of Women Quarterly, 26,* 1–8.

Transactional Leadership Theories

The hallmark of the transactional leadership theories is the idea of *equitable exchange.* Every day, individuals engage in an exchange process whereby one valued benefit, resource, or commodity is exchanged for another. A mechanic fixes a car for monetary compensation, a student completes a thesis to receive a degree, or a supervisor praises an employee for securing a lucrative contract. The transactional approach characterizes effective leadership as a reciprocal and mutually beneficial process of give and take between leaders and followers. Leaders manage valued resources (e.g., information, support, consideration) and provide rewards or punishments to assist followers to achieve goals. In return, followers reciprocate with loyalty and compliance to the leader's requests while bestowing status on the leader.

Historical Background

Early studies of leadership did not consider the role of exchange in leader–follower relationships. Instead, attempts were made to unearth a successful profile of a leader in terms of personality traits. In 1948, Ralph Stogdill conducted an influential review of traits research and concluded that traits alone could not fully explain the leadership phenomenon. Thereafter, the traits approach lost momentum and other approaches to leadership soon emerged. By the 1950s, social scientists began to explore new territories to explain the important role of leadership in groups.

Using what is called the behavioral approach, researchers at Ohio State University and the University of Michigan studied effective leader behaviors. Their studies helped initiate the development of the *contingency approach*, which jointly considers leadership behaviors and *situational factors* to explain effective leadership. Around the same period, the *transactional approach* was developed to explain leadership in terms of the transactions between leaders and followers as a means of bidirectional influence. The transactional approach is evident in a variety of leadership theories developed before the 1980s. It also later became a theory of leadership in its own right.

Early Transactional Approaches: Idiosyncrasy Credit

One of the first transactional theories of leadership, the concept of *idiosyncrasy credit*, was put forth by the social psychologist Edwin Hollander in 1958. Drawing on *social exchange theory*, Hollander held that group members are bonded in a relationship in which they give and receive credit from one another. Each group member accrues credits to the extent that his or her behavior conforms to group norms and positively contributes to the group. As a result of earned credits, group members gain trust, status, and influence potential in the group. Leaders are assumed to possess a relatively large account of accrued credits. In

return, their credits give them leeway to diverge from group norms. This leeway is referred to as idiosyncrasy credit. Leaders are expected to spend some of their idiosyncrasy credit to bring about change and innovation in the group that may be contrary to the status quo. The leadership position, however, still requires successful fulfillment of role obligations and conformity to group expectations. As such, leaders should ideally use their idiosyncrasy credit wisely, that is, to bring about change while still demonstrating successful performance. Otherwise, they may bankrupt their accrued credit and jeopardize their leadership position.

A number of studies support the idea that initial conformity can increase the influence potential of group members. In an experiment by Hollander in 1960, five engineering students and a confederate were brought together to work on a problem-solving task. The confederate's conformity to group norms and demonstration of competence early in the experiment were translated into greater group acceptance of his recommended solutions in later stages of the experiment. Having amassed idiosyncrasy credit at the beginning of the experiment, the confederate was able to exert influence when he displayed nonconforming behavior (e.g., interrupting people) later on. Subsequent research has generally supported the concept of idiosyncrasy credit.

Leader-Member Exchange Theory

Another important transactional approach to leadership effectiveness, the *vertical dyad linkage model*, was proposed by George Graen and colleagues in 1973. In 1982, it was renamed and expanded into leader-member exchange (LMX) theory. LMX theory emphasizes the quality of the relationship between leaders and followers as a central predictor of leadership effectiveness in organizations. The quality of this relationship depends on the nature of social (e.g., esteem) and material (e.g., compensation) exchanges and the level of compatibility (e.g., personal traits, background, skills) between leaders and followers.

In low-quality exchange relationships, exchanges between the leader and the subordinate follow the terms set forth in the employment contract. That is, they are materially based. For example, the leader provides only the necessary resources and guidance for the follower to get the job done. The follower, in turn, exerts sufficient effort to do the job in order to maintain employment and receive compensation. High-quality exchange relationships involve close relationships and performance beyond the call of duty. The leader and the follower engage in reciprocal interpersonal exchanges that surpass the terms of the employment contract. The relationship is built on mutual positive regard, trust, loyalty, and dependability. For instance, followers may take on additional duties or provide extra assistance to the leader that are not called for in their job description. In return, leaders may provide additional support, information, mentoring, esteem, or resources to the subordinate.

LMX theory has received substantial empirical support in predicting leadership effectiveness. High-exchange relationships between leaders and followers are associated with a number of important positive organizational outcomes, including better performance, increased job satisfaction, lower turnover, increased innovation, follower empowerment, and more organizational citizenship behavior.

Several scholars, however, have noted limitations of LMX theory and research. Some limitations involve the potentially questionable content validity of the LMX scale and the need for more extensive theory building that includes consideration of the self-concept and the wider social context (e.g., group processes) in which leader-member relations are embedded. For example, the *social identity* perspective suggests that leadership effectiveness is tied to the extent that the group (team or organization) is salient in the mind of followers. When the group is highly salient, research shows that leadership effectiveness is more strongly related to a depersonalized leadership style than to an interpersonal (dyadic) one. This suggests that high LMX relationships between leaders and followers may be more important when personal identities are salient.

Transactional and Transformational Leadership

In 1978, political scientist James MacGregor Burns wrote a book, *Leadership*, in which he presented an in-depth analysis of several political leaders, ranging from Franklin D. Roosevelt to Gandhi.

This classic work stimulated renewed interest in leadership and is often credited with helping spur the *new leadership paradigm*, which aims to demystify transformational and other "extraordinary" forms of leadership.

Burns argued that true leadership is commensurate with *moral leadership*, which is built on a foundation of moral values. Moral leadership comes in two forms, *transactional* and *transforming*, which are at opposite ends of a continuum. Both transactional and transforming leadership involve exchanges between the leader and the follower, but they differ regarding what is being exchanged and what values guide the leader. Burns also held that transactional leaders are more commonplace than are transformational leaders. Transactional leaders engage followers in instrumental exchanges that satisfy the self-interests of both the leader and the followers. Furthermore, such leaders are guided by modal values such as honesty, responsibility, and fairness. In contrast, being grounded in transcendent values such as equality, liberty, and justice, transforming leaders motivate followers to transcend their self-interests and to pursue higher-order morality. The leader–follower relationship in this case involves mutual motivation to work together to achieve some collective good. Therefore, an instrumental exchange does not take place between a transformational leader and followers. Instead, a mutual consciousness-raising process emerges from this relationship.

In 1985, Bernard Bass extended Burns's ideas into a theory of transformational leadership. Contrary to Burns, Bass did not address the moral concerns in the earlier versions of the theory but instead placed emphasis on the behaviors that characterize transformational versus transactional leaders. In the most recent version of the theory, transformational leadership behaviors include (a) motivating followers by articulating enticing visions that evoke follower emotion (inspirational motivation); (b) challenging followers to be innovative and to view issues from new vantage points (intellectual stimulation); (c) encouraging follower identification with the leader, role modeling, and evoking perceptions of charisma (idealized influence); and (d) paying attention to followers, being in tune with their needs, and providing them with support and mentoring (individualized consideration).

Drawing from earlier research on contingent reinforcement, Bass specified that transactional behaviors include *contingent rewards* and *management by exception*. Contingent rewards include leader behaviors that clarify the rewards that followers receive when designated objectives and tasks are successfully completed. For example, the manager of a car dealership may attempt to motivate salespeople by creating an incentive such that any employee who sells at least six cars per week will receive double commissions for that week. Research shows that contingent rewards (both material and social) help reduce role ambiguity, clarify the task or goal at hand, increase follower satisfaction, and contribute to better performance.

Management by exception involves leadership behaviors that actively or passively seek to correct or punish poor performance or problematic follower behavior. In active management by exception, the leader actively attends to followers' performance to ensure that it meets the necessary rules and standards. If errors, oversights, or violations are evident, the leader engages in corrective behavior or negative reinforcement to rapidly remedy the situation. Research suggests that active management by exception is related to higher ratings of the leader than is passive management by exception, which involves less direct monitoring of followers. In passive management by exception, leaders intervene to provide correction or punishment only when there is an obvious mistake or problem that requires attention.

The Multifactor Leadership Questionnaire (MLQ) was developed to measure both transactional and transformational leadership behaviors. Because of criticisms regarding its validity, the MLQ has undergone a number of revisions, but concerns are still voiced about its utility. One concern is that various transformational behaviors tend to be correlated with transactional behaviors. This is problematic because transformational and transactional leadership styles are theorized to represent two distinct types of leadership.

Considerable empirical research has been conducted on transformational versus transactional leaders in a variety of settings and countries. Various meta-analyses suggest that transformational leadership is more effective than transactional leadership in increasing followers' performance and satisfaction. However, research also suggests that leaders who interchangeably adopt a transformational and an active transactional style (e.g., contingent rewards) tend to receive the highest effectiveness ratings. This suggests that leadership aiming to realize a vision of a new and improved reality for the collective is vital, but some active transactional behaviors are necessary to accomplish this feat.

Even during radical transformation, not all parts of the status quo require transformation. Transactional leadership behaviors may help sustain some sense of stability during change while clarifying followers' role expectancies, signaling appropriate behaviors, and providing rewards to reinforce positive behavior and performance. As Bass and colleagues implied in 2003, the next step may be helping leaders develop a wider repertoire of behaviors that include both transformational and transactional styles to optimize successful navigation in the often turbulent waters of change.

Viviane Seyranian

See also Charismatic Leadership; Contingency Theories of Leadership; Great Person Theory of Leadership; Idiosyncrasy Credit; Interactionist Theories of Leadership; Leader-Member Exchange (LMX) Theory; Leadership; Path–Goal Theory of Leadership; Personality Theories of Leadership; Social Identity Theory of Leadership; Transformational Leadership Theories; Vertical Dyad Linkage Model

Further Readings

Bass, B. M. (1985). *Leadership and performance beyond expectations*. New York: Free Press.

Bass, B. M. (1990). *Bass and Stogdill's handbook of leadership*. New York: Free Press.

Bass, B. M. (2003). Predicting unit performance by assessing transformational and transactional leadership. *Journal of Applied Psychology, 88*, 207–218.

Burns, M. J. (1978). *Leadership*. New York: Harper & Row.

Graen, G. B., & Uhl-Bien, M. (1995). Relationship-based approach to leadership: Development of leader-member exchange (LMX) theory of leadership over 25 years: Applying a multi-level multi-domain perspective. *Leadership Quarterly, 6*, 219–247.

Hogg, M. A., Martin, R., Epitropaki, O., Mankad, A., Alici Svensson, A., & Weeden, K. (2005). Effective leadership in salient groups: Revisiting leader-member exchange theory from the perspective of the social identity theory of leadership. *Personality and Social Psychology Bulletin, 31,* 991–1004.

Hollander, E. P. (1958). Conformity, status, and idiosyncrasy credit. *Psychological Review, 65,* 117–127.

Lowe, K. B., Kroeck, K. G., & Sivasubramaniam, N. (1996). Effectiveness correlates of transformation and transactional leadership: A meta-analytic review of the MLQ literature. *Leadership Quarterly, 7,* 385–425.

TRANSACTIVE MEMORY SYSTEMS

A *transactive memory system* is a group-level memory system that often develops in close relationships and work teams. It involves the division of responsibility among group members with respect to the encoding, storage, retrieval, and communication of information from different knowledge areas and a shared awareness among group members about each member's knowledge responsibilities (or "who knows what"). For example, in a family, one parent may be responsible for knowing when the bills are due and what is needed at the grocery store, and the other may be responsible for knowing the children's schedules and how to fix things around the house. Or in a new product development team, one member may be responsible for all information related to prototype development while another member may be responsible for all information related to marketing and advertising.

Transactive memory systems enable people in relationships and groups to share information more efficiently and effectively. They can reduce the memory load for each individual in the system while providing each individual with access to a larger pool of information collectively. When individuals need information in another's area of expertise, they can simply ask the person responsible rather than taking the time and energy for locating and learning the information themselves. As a result of their developed transactive memory system, members of experienced groups often perform their tasks more effectively and make better decisions than newly formed groups do. Evidence of transactive memory systems has been documented in a wide variety of relationships and groups, including married couples, dating couples, families, friends, coworkers, and project teams in both organizational and laboratory settings. This entry describes transactive memory systems, discusses how they develop and what makes them work, and summarizes their outcomes

Characteristics of Transactive Memory Systems

The term *transactive memory systems* was coined by Daniel Wegner in a paper published in 1985. Since that initial paper, researchers in psychology, management, communication, and other fields have worked on identifying the antecedents, processes, and consequences of transactive memory systems. Research on transactive memory systems borrows heavily from what is known about the memory processes of individuals and applies it to groups. At a minimum, a transactive memory system can be defined in terms of two components: the organized store of knowledge in the memory systems of the individual members and the knowledge exchanges that occur between members.

A directory-sharing computer network has been used as a metaphor for illustrating the three key processes of transactive memory systems. The first process is *directory updating,* whereby individuals develop a working directory or map of who knows what and update it as they obtain new information about the knowledge and expertise of group members. The second process is *information allocation,* in which new information that enters the group is communicated to the person whose expertise will facilitate its storage. The third process *is retrieval coordination,* which involves devising an efficient and effective strategy for retrieving needed information, based on the person expected to have it.

In terms of content, transactive memory systems contain both differentiated and integrated knowledge. *Differentiated knowledge* represents the specialized and unique knowledge held by each individual in the system, whereas *integrated knowledge* represents the knowledge that individuals hold in common. Integrated knowledge, such as shared directories, routines, and procedures, is especially useful for coordination.

Development of Transactive Memory Systems

Unlike the literal way that computer networks update directories and locate, store, and retrieve information, transactive memory systems among humans are often flawed. Transactive memory systems vary in terms of their *accuracy* (the degree to which individuals' perceptions about other members' expertise are accurate), *sharedness* (the degree to which individuals have a shared representation of who knows what in the group), and *validation* (the degree to which individuals accept responsibility for different knowledge areas and participate in the system). Transactive memory systems will be most effective when knowledge assignments are based on group members' actual abilities, when all group members have similar representations of the group's transactive memory system, and when members actively participate in the system.

One necessary requirement for the development of a transactive memory system is *cognitive interdependence*. That is, individuals must perceive that their outcomes are dependent on the knowledge of other people in their relationships or groups and that others' outcomes are dependent on their knowledge. Cognitive interdependence is what motivates the development of the transactive memory system and often develops in close interpersonal relationships, in which people share responsibilities, engage in conversations about many different topics, and make joint decisions. It can also arise as a result of a reward system or the structure of a group task, as is the case in work teams.

Transactive memory systems develop as individuals learn about the knowledge of other group members and begin to delegate and assume responsibility for different knowledge areas. Individuals can become linked to knowledge areas based on relative expertise (the best cook is likely to become the person in charge of knowing what is in the refrigerator), by negotiated agreements (one person agrees to keep track of car maintenance if the other will keep track of bill payment due dates), or through circumstance (the person who answered the phone when a new client calls becomes the "new client" expert). In newly formed groups, individuals often rely on stereotypes based on personal characteristics (such as gender, ethnicity, organizational role) to infer what others know. In

some cases, such as in diverse work teams, these initial assumptions can become self-fulfilling prophecies. Individuals can be assigned knowledge areas that are consistent with social stereotypes even though those areas do not reflect their actual expertise, and they eventually become experts as a result of those assignments.

Researchers have created and validated a scale with three key indicators for measuring the degree of development of a transactive memory system in work teams. The first indicator is *memory specialization*, the tendency for groups to delegate responsibility and to specialize in different aspects of the task. The second is *credibility*, beliefs about the reliability of members' expertise. The third is task *coordination*: the ability of team members to coordinate their work efficiently based on their knowledge of who knows what in the group. The greater the presence of each indicator, the more developed the transactive memory system and the more valuable the transactive memory system for efficiently coordinating the actions of group members.

Transactive memory systems usually develop informally and implicitly through interpersonal interaction rather than by formal design. Members can learn informally about one another's expertise through interactions and shared experiences working together, thus identifying likely experts in different areas. Informal interactions and shared experiences working together provide opportunities for team members to hear about members' background and credentials, to observe members' skills in action, to indicate their interests and preferences, to coordinate who does what, and to evaluate the willingness of team members to participate in the transactive memory system. Team training can also facilitate the development of a transactive memory system. Those systems set up by formal design (such as a listing of staff members' responsibilities in an office procedures handbook) are either validated or modified over time as group members learn more about one another, so the informal transactive memory system may not correspond directly to the formal system.

New technologies are being developed to help people locate and retrieve information from experts, facilitating the development of new and expanding existing transactive memory systems. *Social networking sites* such as LinkedIn.com can help people identify experts both inside and outside their social networks. *Intranets* (Web sites designed for internal use in organizations) can help employees learn about the expertise and knowledge of others in their organization. Some features that intranets might include are expert directories, postings of formal job descriptions and/or responsibilities, search engines for information and expertise, expertise inference systems (capture and analysis of activities such as who attended meetings on a particular topic, who participated in which forum, etc.), and *communityware*, tools that generate visual representations of knowledge and communication networks based on information voluntarily shared by individuals. There is some debate among scholars about whether social networking technologies and other formally based systems can facilitate the development of transactive memory independently of group structures and incentives that promote cognitive interdependence among individuals.

Outcomes of Transactive Memory Systems

For many reasons, groups that have a developed transactive memory system perform better than groups that do not. Groups with transactive memory systems are more likely to assign tasks to individuals who can perform those tasks best and are better equipped to anticipate rather than to simply respond to group members' actions. When individuals have responsibility for only a portion of the group's knowledge, they may be able to accumulate a more extensive and deeper understanding in their area of specialization. Individuals who know about one another's knowledge may be able to obtain better and more accurate information because they know the right person to ask. When group members have experience communicating with one another, they may know how to ask for information so that the request is understood and how to cue members having difficulty retrieving information in ways that facilitate its accessibility. They may also be less likely to fall prey to an overly confident and persuasive but inaccurate group member.

Transactive memory systems can lead to improved group performance in situations in which groups must process a large amount of information quickly or on group tasks that require expertise from many different knowledge domains.

However, there may be situations in which too much specialization may impede group performance, such as when assigned experts are unavailable, unable, or unwilling to contribute their knowledge. Even when specialization leads to better outcomes, some redundancy may be useful. It helps members to communicate more effectively, it can encourage group members to be more accountable to one another, and it can provide a cushion for transitions in relationships when, for example, the designated expert leaves the group.

Andrea B. Hollingshead

See also Group Learning; Group Mind; Group Performance; Shared Mental Models; Socially Shared Cognition; Social Representations; Teams

Further Readings

Brandon, D. P., & Hollingshead, A. B. (2004). Transactive memory systems in organizations: Matching tasks, expertise, and people. *Organization Science, 15,* 633–644.

Hollingshead, A. B. (1998). Retrieval processes in transactive memory systems. *Journal of Personality and Social Psychology, 74,* 659–671.

Lewis, K. (2003). Measuring transactive memory systems in the field: Scale development and validation. *Journal of Applied Psychology, 88,* 587–604.

Moreland, R. L. (1999). Transactive memory: Learning who knows what in work groups and organizations. In L. Thompson, D. Messick, & J. Levine (Eds.), *Shared cognition in organizations: The management of knowledge* (pp. 3–31). Mahwah, NJ: Erlbaum.

Wegner, D. M. (1995). A computer network model of human transactive memory. *Social Cognition, 13,* 319–339.

Wegner, D. M., Giuliano, T., & Hertel, P. T. (1985). Cognitive interdependence in close relationships. In W. J. Ickes (Ed.), *Compatible and incompatible relationships* (pp. 253–276). New York: Springer-Verlag.

Transformational Leadership Theories

Transformational leadership theory suggests that leaders transform their followers' values, priorities, and goals and inspire followers to perform beyond expectations and to transcend their narrow self-interests for the good of the larger group, organization, and mission. Transformational leaders articulate compelling visions that stress the meaning, importance, and value of goals, as well as of the strategies designed to achieve them. Transformational leaders thus build followers' confidence and broaden their needs to assist them in achieving higher potential, ultimately developing followers into leaders. Research suggests that transformational leadership is positively associated with trust, job attitudes, and a broad range of individual performance outcomes.

Although 20 years of research suggests that transformational leadership is strongly related to followers' attitudes and performance, this research also indicates that such leadership plays an important role in shaping, inspiring, and directing group goals and processes. Transformational leaders enhance group members' confidence, motivation, and performance by asserting the importance of the group's mission and its capabilities to achieve synergistic outcomes, while supporting followers in aligning their individual goals with collective goals. Research has also shown that transformational leadership builds group cohesiveness, identification, efficacy, and climates that positively influence group outcomes. This entry reviews the history of this research, describes key dimensions of transformational leaders, and discusses evidence related to their impact.

Background and History

For much of the 20th century, leadership scholars studied exchange-based, or transactional, leadership behavior, which involves reinforcing followers' behaviors and providing direction and support. In 1978, James Burns introduced the notion of transforming leadership. In the mid-1980s, partly inspired by Bernard Bass, researchers began to shift their attention to leadership models that emphasize visionary messages, inspirational appeals, ideological and moral values, intellectual stimulation, and individualized consideration. Burns initially posited that transactional and transformational leadership represent opposite ends of a continuum and differ in terms of what leaders and followers offer one another.

Transactional leadership focuses on the proper exchange of resources between a leader and his or her followers. Transformational leadership, in contrast, emphasizes meaning and purpose to develop and fulfill deeper existential needs that go beyond a simple relationship of quid pro quo. Although Burns suggested that leaders engage in either transactional or transformational leadership, Bass posited that effective leaders engage in both types of leadership behavior.

Transformational leadership augments, or supplements, the effect of transactional leadership. Stated differently, transactional leadership can be effective, but transformational leadership will improve leadership effectiveness, achieving performance beyond expectations. Transformational leaders establish goals and objectives with the developmental objective of changing followers into individual leaders or into a collective leadership group, such as self-directed teams.

The focus on follower development distinguishes transformational leadership from transactional leadership. Transforming followers into leaders not only empowers associates but also enhances their capability to deal effectively with ambiguity, develops their competence to handle more intellectually stimulating tasks, and gives them the opportunity to assume some of the leader's responsibilities. Although transactional leadership may yield short-term extrinsic benefits, transformational leadership produces longer-term intrinsic rewards. In other words, transformational leadership significantly adds to transactional leadership effectiveness, thus building higher individual, group, and organizational potential. Subsequent empirical research supported these hypotheses, suggesting that more effective leaders engage in exchange-related, as well as inspirational, motivational, and developmental, behaviors.

Transformational Leadership Dimensions

Transformational leaders exhibit four types of behaviors: *idealized influence, inspirational motivation, intellectual stimulation,* and *individualized consideration.* A leader who exhibits idealized influence increases followers' respect, pride, trust, and admiration for the leader's high ethical standards and conduct. Such leaders enhance followers' trust through their commitment to overcome challenges, their willingness to sacrifice their personal self-interest, and their prior successes.

Inspirational motivation refers to leaders' articulation of shared goals and communication of a compelling vision of what is possible and how it can be achieved. Transformational leaders inspire followers by setting high standards, expressing optimism about attaining them, and infusing meaning into the daily tasks.

Intellectually stimulating leaders challenge followers to think critically; solve problems creatively; and challenge their own values, beliefs, and assumptions, as well as those of their leaders, when appropriate. Such leaders motivate followers to more fully engage in their job, which causes the followers to achieve higher levels of performance and experience greater job satisfaction and commitment.

Finally, leaders who exhibit individualized consideration recognize and satisfy followers' unique needs. They encourage followers, through coaching and mentoring, to reach their maximum potential, and they enhance followers' ability to respond to individual, group, and organizational challenges.

The accumulated research indicates that leaders who are rated higher on the four transformational leadership components generate higher levels of group confidence, effort, and work performance.

Group Cohesiveness

Social identity theory suggests that group characteristics can become self-defining over time. One aspect of group cohesiveness is the tendency for individual members to incorporate the group's vision, mission, and goals as self-referential. Research suggests that transformational leadership is positively related to this component of group cohesiveness. Transformational leaders can influence group cohesiveness through several behaviors.

First, transformational leaders influence and facilitate group cohesiveness by emphasizing the importance of sacrificing for the benefit of the group and demonstrating high ethical standards. Appealing to these higher-order needs enables followers to transcend self-interest and pursue collective group interests. Furthermore, transformational leaders are able to link followers' individual identities to their group's collective identity by appealing emotionally to socially desirable behaviors, such as

making personal sacrifices in the short term for the common good in the long term.

Second, transformational leaders build group cohesiveness through encouraging and enabling followers to take greater responsibility for their own development as well as their group's development. Empowering followers in this way helps them share information with each other and therefore improves group information processing.

Finally, transformational leaders increase group cohesiveness by stressing the followers' involvement and membership in the group and by distinguishing the ingroup from outgroups. Social identity theory suggests that when ingroups and outgroups are prominent, people identify with their ingroup and perceive more positive attributes of the ingroup and more negative attributes of outgroups.

Group Identification

As suggested above, group identification refers to a feeling of psychological belongingness to a particular group. It conveys a sense of being a part of something, because one's self-definition is tied to membership in particular groups. There is considerable evidence that work group identification can impact work behavior, because identification promotes positive responses toward ingroup members. A strong group identity also spurs group members to obtain greater expertise in their jobs. Consequently, group members engage in more active job-relevant learning to the extent that they possess strong relationships with others in their group.

Research shows that transformational leadership is related to group identification in at least two ways. First, because transformational leaders are proactive, change oriented, and inspiring, they create identification among group members and therefore extract extra effort from the members toward the mission of the group. Second, transformational leaders increase group members' sense of self-worth by emphasizing the importance of each individual's contribution to the group, encouraging each member to internalize a "collective" frame of mind. This also increases members' efforts for the group as a whole.

Group Efficacy

In 1986, Albert Bandura, in the process of developing *social cognitive theory*, developed the notion of group efficacy. Group efficacy is a construct that refers to an individual's evaluation of his or her group's capability to effectively perform job-related tasks. A group with high efficacy believes that it can perform well on a task, whereas a group with low efficacy thinks that it will fail. Numerous studies indicate that group (as well as individual) efficacy is positively related to a number of positive outcomes (e.g., effort, organizational commitment, and job satisfaction).

Research suggests that transformational leadership is an important antecedent of group efficacy. Transformational leaders provide followers with opportunities to appreciate the group's accomplishments and members' contributions when they make the group mission salient, stress shared values, and connect followers' individual interests to the group's interests. As individuals become more aware of and confident in the group's capabilities, group efficacy increases. Thus, transformational leaders can directly influence collective efficacy and, as a result, indirectly influence important group-level outcomes.

Service Climate

Climate refers to the environment and atmosphere in which employees work. In a recent study, Hui Liao and Aichia Chuang drew a distinction between individual- and work unit–level transformational leadership. The former refers to leadership behavior as perceived by an individual. The latter refers to leadership behavior as perceived by an entire group. Hence, work unit–level transformational leadership is perceived similarly by different group members. Work unit–level transformational leadership aspires to achieve group- and organizational-level outcomes by transforming the climate into one that is more positive and promotion oriented.

Service climate represents employees' shared perception of the organizational context's practices, policies, and procedures as they relate to customer service. Research suggests that service climates are malleable, and work unit–level transformational leadership has a major role in shaping perceptions of the climate. Transformational leaders who provide a compelling customer service vision arouse excitement and hope about securing and deepening customer loyalty. They also serve as role models for employees and challenge followers to create new ways to serve customers. Recent research indicates that transformational leaders who influence the service climate motivate followers to deliver high-quality service.

In sum, a considerable body of evidence demonstrates the positive impact of transformational leadership on outcomes at the individual, group, and organizational levels. Moreover, across cultures, when people describe their ideal leader, they typically describe a transformational leader.

Fred O. Walumbwa, Bruce J. Avolio,
and Chad Hartnell

See also Charismatic Leadership; Contingency Theories of Leadership; Great Person Theory of Leadership; Interactionist Theories of Leadership; Leader-Member Exchange (LMX) Theory; Leadership; Path–Goal Theory of Leadership; Personality Theories of Leadership; Social Identity Theory of Leadership; Transactional Leadership Theories; Vertical Dyad Linkage Model

Further Readings

Avolio, B. J. (2005). *Leadership development in balance: Made/born.* Mahwah, NJ: Erlbaum.

Avolio, B. J., & Yammarino, F. J. (Eds.). (2003). *Transformational and charismatic leadership: The road ahead.* New York: Elsevier.

Bandura, A. (1986). *Social foundations of thought and action: A social cognitive view.* Englewood Cliffs, NJ: Prentice Hall.

Bass, B. M. (1998). *Transformational leadership: Industrial, military, and educational impact.* Mahwah, NJ: Erlbaum.

TRUST

Researchers have long recognized the central and beneficial role that trust plays in effective intragroup processes and in facilitating constructive intergroup relations. Trust has been shown, for example, to facilitate the sharing of information within groups and to contribute to more cooperative interaction between groups.

Conceptualizing Trust

Although recognizing the benefits of trust, social scientists have also noted that trust is a psychologically and socially complex construct. Reflecting this psychological and social complexity, a concise and universally accepted definition of trust remains elusive even to this day. As a consequence, the term *trust* is used in a variety of distinct, and not always compatible, ways by different researchers. At one end of the definitional spectrum are formulations that highlight the ethical and moral facets of trust. For example, one scholar characterized trust in terms of people's expectations regarding ethically justifiable behaviors, on the assumption their decisions were based on ethical principles. Conceptions at the other end of the spectrum, in contrast, emphasize the purely expectation-based and calculative dimensions of trust. For example, some researchers have defined trust simply as "anticipated cooperation," arguing that the issue is not moral at all.

Despite such divergence, most trust theorists do agree that—whatever else its essential features—trust is fundamentally a cognitive state. When conceptualized as a cognitive state, trust has been defined in terms of several interrelated properties. Most important, trust entails a state of perceived vulnerability or risk that is derived from individuals' uncertainty regarding the motives, intentions, and prospective actions of others on whom they depend. For example, researchers have often characterized trust in terms of risky actions predicated on confident expectations that others involved in a relationship will act competently and with benign motives.

From this definition, the question logically arises: What are the bases for such confident expectation?

Bases of Trust

Considerable research has focused on identifying the bases or antecedents of trust within and between groups. Early work in this area focused on identifying individual differences with respect to the propensity to trust. To explain the origins of such differences, researchers proposed that people extrapolate from their early trust-related experiences to build up generalized beliefs and expectations about other people and, in particular, their trustworthiness in particular social situations. As these trust-related expectancies are generalized from one social agent to another, according to this view people acquire a sort of diffuse expectancy

about the trustworthiness of others. Over time, this diffuse expectancy can even come to assume the form of a relatively stable personality characteristic or disposition.

Other research on the development of trust has shown that one's perceptions of others' trustworthiness and one's willingness to engage in trusting behavior when interacting with them are largely history-dependent processes. According to such models, trust between two or more interdependent actors increases or decreases as a function of their cumulative interactions. These interaction histories presumably give individuals information that is useful in assessing others' trust-related dispositions, intentions, and motives. This information, in turn, provides a basis for drawing inferences regarding others' trustworthiness and reliability—information that will be useful when making predictions about their future behavior.

Appreciating both the importance of information regarding others' trustworthiness and the difficulty in obtaining such information, scholars have noted that third parties can sometimes function as important conduits of trust because of their ability to diffuse trust-relevant information to other parties. In effect, they become trust brokers. One recent study of exchange relations among firms in the New York apparel industry provides evidence of this constructive third-party role in the development and diffusion of trust. This study found that third parties acted as important go-betweens in new relationships, enabling individuals to essentially roll over their expectations from well-established relationships to others in which adequate knowledge or history was not yet available. In explaining how this worked, the researchers who conducted this study argued that such go-betweens help transfer positive expectations and opportunities from existing embedded relationships to newly formed ones, thereby furnishing a foundation for trust.

With respect to trust within and between groups, trust based on social category—defined as trust predicated on information regarding a trustee's membership in a particular social category—may be an important form of both intragroup and intergroup trust. For at least two reasons, membership in a salient social category can provide a basis for such presumptive trust. First, shared membership in a given category can serve as a basis for defining the boundaries of a low-risk form of interpersonal trust. By so doing, such information eliminates the need for more personalized, individuating knowledge. Second, because of the cognitive consequences of categorization, individuals tend to attribute positive characteristics such as honesty, cooperativeness, reliability, and trustworthiness to other ingroup members.

Benefits of Trust

In addition to exploring the bases of trust, researchers have been keen to document more fully its benefits within and between groups. Indeed, the ascension of trust as a major focus of recent research during the past two decades has reflected in no small measure accumulating evidence of the substantial and varied benefits, both individual and collective, that accrue when trust is in place. These myriad benefits of trust have been discussed primarily on three levels: (1) trust as a mechanism for reducing transaction costs within and between groups; (2) trust as a means for increasing spontaneous sociability, cooperation, and coordination within and between groups; and (3) trust as a mechanism for facilitating appropriate (i.e., adaptive) forms of deference to group authorities or leaders.

In the absence of personalized knowledge about others, or adequate grounds for conferring trust on them presumptively, either trust within and between groups must be individually negotiated or substitutes for trust must be located. Even when effective, such remedies are often inefficient and costly. Recognition of this problem has led a number of theorists to focus on the role of trust in reducing the costs of both intra- and interorganizational transactions. For example, as noted above, trusted third parties can serve as useful conduits for establishing trustworthiness of social actors about which one knows relatively little.

One of the most important manifestations of trust as a form of social capital is the spontaneous sociability such trust engenders. When operationalized in behavioral terms, spontaneous sociability refers to the myriad forms of cooperative, altruistic, and extrarole behavior that members of a social community engage in that enhance collective well-being and further the attainment of collective goals. Within group contexts, spontaneous sociability

assumes many forms. Group members are expected, for example, to contribute their time and attention toward the achievement of collective goals, they are expected to share useful information with other organizational members, and they are expected to exercise responsible restraint when using valuable but limited organizational resources.

Another important stream of research has examined the relationship between trust and various forms of voluntary deference within and between groups, especially those embedded in hierarchical relationships. From the standpoint of those in positions of authority, trust is crucial for a variety of reasons. First, if group leaders or authorities had to continually explain and justify their actions, their ability to effectively manage would be greatly diminished. Second, because of the costs and impracticality of monitoring performance, authorities cannot detect and punish every failure to cooperate, nor can they recognize and reward every cooperative act. As a result, efficient group performance depends on individuals' feelings of obligation toward the group, their willingness to comply with its directives and regulations, and their willingness to voluntarily defer to group leaders. In addition, when conflict arises, trust is important because it influences acceptance of dispute resolution procedures and outcomes. Research has shown that individuals are more likely to accept outcomes, even if unfavorable, when individuals trust an authority's motives and intentions.

Other researchers have investigated the influence of procedural variables on attributions regarding group leaders' trustworthiness. Procedures are important because they communicate information, not only about authorities' motivations and intentions to behave in a trustworthy fashion, but also about their ability to do so, a factor characterized as *procedural competence*. In support of this general argument, evidence indicates that procedures that are structurally and procedurally fair tend to increase trust, whereas the absence of such procedures tends to elicit low levels of trust.

In the context of group processes and intergroup relations, the future of trust research seems bright indeed. Trust theorists have been interested in elaborating on the institutional bases of trust and the role culture plays in the development and maintenance of trust. Another recent and important extension includes examination of cross-cultural variations in the bases and consequences of trust. For example, studies have compared the construal of trust and its antecedents in the United States and Japan.

Roderick M. Kramer

See also Cooperation and Competition; Distributive Justice; Justice; Leadership; Negotiation and Bargaining; Organizations; Procedural Justice

Further Readings

Brewer, M. B. (1981). Ethnocentrism and its role in interpersonal trust. In M. B. Brewer & B. Collins (Eds.), *Scientific inquiry in the social sciences* (pp. 345–359). San Francisco: Jossey-Bass.

Cook, K. S. (2001). *Trust in society*. New York: Russell Sage.

Hardin, R. (2002). *Trust and trustworthiness*. New York: Russell Sage.

Insko, C. A., & Schopler, J. (1997). Differential distrust of groups and individuals. In C. Sedikides, J. Schopler, & C. Insko (Eds.), *Intergroup cognition and intergroup behavior* (pp. 75–108). Mahwah, NJ: Erlbaum.

Kramer, R. M., & Cook, K. S. (2004). *Trust and distrust in organizations: Dilemmas and approaches*. New York: Russell Sage.

Sztompka, P. (1999). *Trust: A sociological theory*. New York: Cambridge University Press.

ULTIMATE ATTRIBUTION ERROR

The *ultimate attribution error* refers to a psychological phenomenon in which individuals explain the behaviors of people in groups by attributing those behaviors to the influence of dispositional or situational forces. The dispositional or situational nature of the attribution depends on the positive or negative valence of the behavior and on whether the individuals so observed are members of the observer's ingroup or another group. Individuals making the ultimate attribution error tend to overemphasize broad *dispositional* explanations, or explanations based on innate group characteristics (e.g., ethnicity or gender) when explaining the negative (antisocial, undesirable) behaviors of members of groups they do not belong to. Conversely, positive (prosocial, desirable) behaviors of outgroup members are often attributed to exceptionality, luck, effort, special advantage, or other mutable *situational* forces.

Background and History

The Fundamental Attribution Error

One way in which we can make sense of the world around us is to determine why other people act the way they do. Is a behavior we observe merely a function of the observed individual's personality traits (dispositional factors)? Or is he or she being influenced to act by something in the environment (situational factors)? Or both? For example, if the barista at the coffee shop fails to smile at us, should we conclude that she is antisocial by nature, or will we notice that she also looks tired and infer that she might have stayed out too late the night before?

Attribution researchers have determined that when we attempt to explain someone else's behavior, we typically tend to underestimate the impact of the situation and overestimate the impact of personal characteristics such as traits and attitudes. This phenomenon has been dubbed the *fundamental attribution error* (also called the *correspondence bias* or the *overattribution effect*). In one classic experiment investigating the fundamental attribution error, Edward Jones and Victor Harris had university students read opinion essays supporting or criticizing Cuba's then leader, Fidel Castro. When students were told that the position taken had been chosen by the author, they quite reasonably assumed that the essay content reflected the author's true opinion. However, when they were told that the position taken had been assigned by a third party, students still inferred that the author of the essay had either pro- or anti-Castro leanings, in accordance with the position taken in the essay. In other words, when explaining the reason the author of the essay wrote what he or she did, individuals participating in this experiment overemphasized the influence of the author's personal attitudes about Castro and discounted the situational influence of being told what to write by a third party. A large body of work following the Jones and Harris study supports this general finding, making it one of the most robust phenomena studied by behavioral researchers.

Extrapolating From the Individual to the Group: The Ultimate Attribution Error

In the fundamental attribution error, we tend to ascribe the behavior of other individuals to innate personal characteristics such as traits or attitudes and overlook the impact of situational factors. In some cases, the attributions made by others will be negative for an observed individual (e.g., "he's poor because he's lazy"). In other cases, an individual may benefit from a positive dispositional attribution (e.g., "the quiz show contestant knew all the answers because she is intelligent"). But what happens when people's behavior can be potentially attributed to a dispositional characteristic of a *group* they are a member of, and the attribution may reflect on dispositional characteristics of a group the observer is a member of?

In the ultimate attribution error, we tend to primarily ascribe dispositional explanations to *negative* behaviors (e.g., antisocial or undesirable) of outgroup members, and situational explanations to *positive* behaviors (e.g., prosocial or desirable). In other words, outgroup members are viewed as wholly responsible for negative behaviors and simultaneously not responsible for positive ones. Thomas Pettigrew has suggested that the reason for this view lies in the desire to protect currently held stereotypes about members of other groups and maintain the perception that one's ingroup is inherently superior to outgroups.

An outgroup member performing a negative act supports a negative stereotype about that group that we may already hold and confirms our tendency to ascribe dispositional attributions to the behaviors of others. So for instance in the case of race, ethnicity, or gender, this dispositional attribution may take the form of assumptions about genetic characteristics of members of that group. Attributing behaviors of members of that group to genetic characteristics may in turn support a currently held stereotypical perception of the group as a whole and allow an individual to favorably compare his or her ingroup to members of an outgroup (e.g., "Unlike Whites, Blacks are violent by nature, which is why that Black man mugged me").

However, when an outgroup member behaves in a positive way that is inconsistent with an overall negative view of the outgroup, it violates preconceived, stereotypical notions about innate differences between ingroup and outgroup members (e.g., "Everyone knows women aren't as good as men at sports, so how could I have been beaten at tennis by that girl?"). An ingroup member exposed to this dilemma must find a way to reconcile his or her natural tendency to make dispositional attributions about the behavior of others with the desire to maintain positive differentiation between his or her own ingroup and members of an outgroup.

One way to resolve this discrepancy is to change one's view about an entire outgroup. Research indicates that this does happen, but only under specified situational conditions, such as repeated positive contact with multiple members of an outgroup. In many instances, a typical observer does not have information about the behavior of outgroup members over time. In this case, individuals will likely assume that an isolated positive act by a member of an outgroup can be explained by forces such as luck, special advantage, being an "exceptional member" of a group (including having particularly high motivation or putting in extra effort), being influenced by members of the ingroup, and so forth, which do not indicate anything dispositional about the outgroup as a whole. Positive acts may also be *reframed* by observers so as to indicate the presence of a negative disposition (e.g., behaviors indicating intelligence are described as *cunning*, ambition becomes *being pushy*, high ability in women is framed as *unfeminine*).

Although research on the ultimate attribution error is relatively scarce when compared with the large body of work investigating its cousin, the fundamental attribution error, several studies support Pettigrew's assertions. Birt Duncan, for example, found that White participants were more likely to interpret a shove as both more violent and indicative of personal attributes (e.g., aggression, dishonesty, immorality) when it came from a Black person than when it came from a White person. Another study, by Donald Taylor and Vaishna Jaggi, found that Hindu participants tended to make dispositional attributions for negative behavior when an observed individual was Muslim (outgroup member) and displayed the opposite pattern when an observed individual was Hindu (ingroup member). Similarly, a meta-analysis by Janet Swim and Lawrence Sanna found that in experiments involving traditionally masculine tasks, participants were more likely to attribute male than female successes to ability, and male failures were more likely than female failures to be attributed to bad luck or lack of effort.

Conclusion

The ultimate attribution error can in some ways be said to be at the heart of the continuation of prejudice against racial, ethnic, or other groups in a particular culture. The practice of explaining away individuals' successes and simultaneously holding their shortcomings against them and their identity as a group member sets up an attributional double standard from which it can be very difficult for members of stigmatized or stereotyped groups to break free. Thus, it is important for behavioral researchers studying stereotyping and prejudice and individuals who attempt to mitigate the effects of stereotyping and prejudice via public policy to take into account the influence of misattribution of behavior at the intergroup level.

Kira M. Alexander

See also Attribution Biases; Discrimination; Essentialism; Intergroup Contact Theory; Linguistic Intergroup Bias (LIB); Prejudice; Racism; Sexism; Stereotyping

Further Readings

Duncan, B. L. (1976). Differential social perception and attribution of intergroup violence: Testing the lower limits of stereotyping of Blacks. *Journal of Personality and Social Psychology, 34,* 590–598.

Jones, E. E., & Harris, V. A. (1967). The attribution of attitudes. *Journal of Experimental Social Psychology, 3,* 1–24.

Pettigrew, T. F. (1979). The ultimate attribution error: Extending Allport's cognitive analysis of prejudice. *Personality and Social Psychology Bulletin, 5,* 461–476.

Swim, J. K., & Sanna, L. J. (1996). He's skilled, she's lucky: A meta-analysis of observers' attributions for women's and men's successes and failures. *Personality and Social Psychology Bulletin, 22,* 507–519.

Taylor, D. M., & Jaggi, V. (1974). Ethnocentrism and causal attribution in a south Indian context. *Journal of Cross-Cultural Psychology, 5,* 162–171.

UNCERTAINTY-IDENTITY THEORY

Uncertainty-identity theory, developed by Michael Hogg in 2000 and elaborated more extensively in 2007, argues that people are motivated to reduce feelings of uncertainty, particularly about themselves and about their perceptions, attitudes, and behaviors that reflect most directly on self. One way to satisfy this motivation is to identify with a group (a team, an organization, a religion, an ethnicity, a nation, etc.)—a process that not only defines and locates oneself in the social world but also prescribes how one should behave and how one should interact with others.

Uncertainty-identity theory is grounded in *social identity theory* and invokes social cognitive and social interactive processes associated with social identity to explain how uncertainty motivates group identification and how identification reduces uncertainty. Uncertainty-identity theory can be considered a motivational elaboration of social identity theory. This entry describes the main features of uncertainty-identity theory and discusses the properties of groups, and thus the types of groups, that may best satisfy the uncertainty reduction motive. One implication of this analysis is an understanding of the way in which acute and chronic uncertainty may lead to group extremism: zealotry, fanaticism, ideological orthodoxy, xenophobia, dehumanization, collective violence, and so forth.

Uncertainty and the Need to Reduce Uncertainty

Feeling uncertain about our perceptions, attitudes, values, or feelings motivates us to address the uncertainty. Uncertainty can be an exhilarating challenge to be confronted and resolved, making us feel edgy and alive, but it can also be anxiety provoking and stressful, making us feel impotent and unable to predict or control our world and what will happen to us in it. Although we strive to resolve, manage, or avoid feeling uncertain, we do not do this all the time; some uncertainties we simply do not care much about, and therefore we do not bother to dedicate our stretched cognitive resources to them. We expend cognitive energy resolving only those uncertainties that are important or matter to us in a particular context.

One factor that imparts motivational impetus to feeling uncertain is self-relevance. We are particularly motivated to reduce uncertainty if we feel uncertain about things that reflect on or are relevant to self or if we are uncertain about self per se—about our identity, who we are, how we relate to others, and how we are socially located. Ultimately, we like to know who we are, how to behave, and what to think, as well as who others are, how they might behave, and what they might think.

Although we are, therefore, in the business of reducing self-uncertainty, there will always be some degree of uncertainty (we cannot ever attain absolute certainty); uncertainty-identity theory is about reducing uncertainty rather than achieving certainty. It is also important to bear in mind that individuals and groups may sometimes embark on courses of action that in the short term increase uncertainty, such as when the individual or group is confident that the experience of short-term uncertainty is necessary in order to resolve more enduring contradictions and uncertainties that have arisen.

Social Identity and Uncertainty Reduction

Feelings of uncertainty can be resolved in many different ways. However, self-uncertainty and self-relevant uncertainty are particularly efficiently reduced by the process of psychologically identifying with a group: *group identification.*

According to social identity theory, and more specifically *self-categorization theory*, people cognitively represent social groups as *prototypes.* A prototype is a fuzzy set of attributes that defines the group and distinguishes it from other groups in a specific context. In describing members' perceptions, beliefs, attitudes, values, feelings, and behaviors, a prototype accentuates similarities among members within the same group and accentuates differences between groups (a phenomenon called *metacontrast*). The prototype of a group we belong to, the ingroup, tends to be *prescriptive* in designating how we *ought* to behave as a group member.

When we categorize someone as a group member, we assign the specific group's attributes to that person. We view that person through the lens of the prototype of that group, seeing him or her not as a unique individual but as a more or less prototypical group member—a process called *depersonalization.*

When we categorize others, ingroup or outgroup members, we stereotype them and have expectations of what they think and feel and how they will behave. When we categorize ourselves, self-categorization, the same process occurs: We assign prescriptive ingroup attributes to ourselves; we autostereotype, conform to group norms, and transform our self-conception.

In this way, group identification very effectively reduces self-related uncertainty. It provides us with a sense of who we are that prescribes what we should think, feel, and do. Because self-categorization is inextricably linked to categorization of others, it also reduces uncertainty about how others will behave and what course social interaction will take. Group identification also provides consensual validation of our worldview and sense of self, which further reduces uncertainty. This is because people in a group tend to have a shared prototype of "us" and a shared prototype of "them," and therefore our expectations about the prototype-based behavior of others tend to be confirmed, and our fellow group members agree with our perceptions, beliefs, attitudes, and values and approve of how we behave.

Identification can effectively reduce and protect us from uncertainty, and so uncertainty can motivate group identification. We identify with groups in order to reduce or protect ourselves from uncertainty. We may "join" existing groups as new members, create and identify with entirely new groups, or identify more strongly with existing groups to which we already belong. Empirical studies have provided solid support for this motivational analysis of the relationship between uncertainty and group identification.

Group Attributes Best Suited to Reduce Self-Uncertainty

Not all groups are equally well equipped to reduce self-uncertainty. One property of a group that improves its ability to reduce uncertainty is *entitativity.* A high-entitativity group is clearly structured with clear boundaries, it is internally relatively homogeneous, and its members have a sense of common goals and shared fate. Such groups may also be subject to *essentialism*—a tendency for people to see the group's attributes as fixed and unchanging because they reflect, for example, invariant personality or genetically grounded attributes of the group's members.

An unclearly structured, low-entitativity group, which has indistinct boundaries, ambiguous membership criteria, limited shared goals, and little agreement on group attributes, will do a poor job of reducing or fending off self-uncertainty. In contrast, a clearly structured, high-entitativity group with sharp boundaries, unambiguous membership criteria, highly shared goals, and consensus on group attributes will do an excellent job.

Identification reduces uncertainty because it provides a clear sense of self that makes social interaction predictable and because self is governed by a prototype that prescribes cognition, affect, and behavior. Prototypes that are simple, clear, unambiguous, prescriptive, focused, and consensual are more effective than those that are vague, ambiguous, unfocused, and *dissensual*. Clear prototypes are more likely to be grounded in high- than low-entitativity groups. A number of studies have shown that under uncertainty, people prefer to identify with high- rather than low-entitativity groups.

Uncertainty, Social Identity, and the Psychology of Extremism

When self-uncertainty is acute and enduring (e.g., in times of economic collapse, cultural disintegration, civil war, terrorism, or large-scale natural disasters or in the face of unemployment, bereavement, divorce, relocation, or adolescence), the motivation to reduce uncertainty effectively is strengthened. Under these circumstances, people will identify strongly. They will have a strong sense of belonging and a strong feeling of attachment to the group, and their sense of self will be comprehensively defined by the group; they could be described as zealots, fanatics, or true believers.

Furthermore, people will seek to identify with groups that are not merely entitative but extreme. Relatively, these are groups that have some combination of the following attributes: They are homogeneous in their attitudes, values, and membership; they have inflexible customs and carefully policed boundaries; they have orthodox and ideological belief systems; they are intolerant and suspicious of outsiders and of internal dissent and criticism; they are rigidly and hierarchically structured, often with strong autocratic leadership; and they are ethnocentric and narcissistic. These *extremist* attributes are particularly effective at providing a clearly directive and unambiguous sense of who you are and how you should behave.

There is a well-documented association between societal uncertainty and various forms of extremism, such as genocide, cults, ultranationalism, blind patriotism, religious fundamentalism, terrorism, ideological thinking, fanaticism, and being a "true believer." Uncertainty-identity theory specifies a psychological mechanism that converts uncertainty into extremism or *totalism*. Under certain circumstances, uncertainty-induced identification underpins zealotry, fanaticism, ideological orthodoxy, xenophobia, dehumanization, collective violence, and so forth.

There is now some evidence that even liberal-minded Westerners can be more inclined toward being a part of and identifying with these kinds of groups when they feel self-uncertain.

Michael A. Hogg

See also Entitativity; Ideology; Self-Categorization Theory; Social Identity Theory

Further Readings

Hogg, M. A. (2000). Subjective uncertainty reduction through self-categorization: A motivational theory of social identity processes. *European Review of Social Psychology, 11,* 223–255.

Hogg, M. A. (2006). Social identity theory. In P. J. Burke (Ed.), *Contemporary social psychological theories* (pp. 111–136). Palo Alto, CA: Stanford University Press.

Hogg, M. A. (2007). Uncertainty-identity theory. In M. P. Zanna (Ed.), *Advances in experimental social psychology* (Vol. 39, pp. 69–126). San Diego, CA: Academic Press.

Hogg, M. A. (in press). Uncertainty-identity theory. In P. A. M. van Lange, A. W. Kruglanski, & E. T. Higgins (Eds.), *Handbook of social psychological theories*. Thousand Oaks, CA: Sage.

VERTICAL DYAD LINKAGE MODEL

The *vertical dyad linkage* (VDL) *model* is a framework for understanding workplace leadership that focuses on the interactions between the leader (manager) and his or her subordinates. The name of the model reflects its focus on two people (a *dyad*) and the facts that the position of the leader is above that of the subordinate in terms of authority in the organization (*vertical*) and that there is interrelated behavior between them (*linkage*). The basic premise of VDL is that leaders develop separate exchange relationships with each subordinate. This premise challenges the dominant perspective in many behavioral and situational leadership models that leaders should adopt the same leadership style for all group members (sometimes referred to as *average leadership style*). This entry looks at the basic features of the VDL model, the different kinds of possible relationships, and the most recent evolution of the idea.

Development of VDL Relationships

VDL proposes that leaders develop differentiated relationships with their subordinates based on the types of exchanges that develop between them. The model does not focus on leadership style but on the way relationships develop between the leader and subordinates and how this affects the exchanges that occur between them.

According to the VDL model, the relationship between the leader and the subordinate develops over time through a number of stages based on a role-making process. The positions of leader and subordinate are associated with specific role-assigned behavior (e.g., leaders are expected to make major decisions, and subordinates are expected to implement them). Leaders generally take a significant role in the development of the relationship with their subordinates because leaders typically have the legitimate authority, invested in them by their organization, to negotiate exchanges. In addition, leaders who are admired and liked by their subordinates can have informal power over them, and this can determine the types of exchanges that occur.

It is proposed that the relationship between the leader and the subordinate develops through three stages. The first stage (*stranger*) is an initial testing phase, in which the leader and the subordinate evaluate each other's motives and beliefs and the potential value of resources each has to offer. For the leader, these resources might include the ability to increase remuneration or grant promotion or the allocation of interesting and rewarding work. For the subordinate, these resources might include being a loyal and trusted worker, supporting the leader, and being a good team member. During this stage, the role expectation between the leader and the subordinate is established. Some leader–subordinate relationships do not develop beyond this first stage.

If the relationship proceeds to the second stage (*acquaintance*), then mutual trust and loyalty develop between the leader and the subordinate. The leader takes into consideration the subordinate's needs and ambitions and tries to satisfy them within the workplace. Finally, the two may enter a third stage (*mature partnership*), in which the exchanges become based on mutual commitment to the goals and objectives of the work group. The leader and the subordinate work closely together, and the level of mutual influence between the two is very high.

High- and Low-Quality Relationships

VDL theory proposes that leaders do not develop the same type of exchange relationships with all their subordinates. In many cases, leaders develop two main types of relationships, high- and low-quality exchange relationships, sometimes referred to as ingroup and outgroup relationships, respectively.

Leaders develop high-quality exchange relationships with those subordinates whom they trust and who in return show them loyalty, and these subordinates can function as lieutenants and advisers to the leader. These high-quality exchange relationships can be extremely beneficial to both the subordinate (in terms of receiving valued rewards) and the leader (in terms of support, commitment, and help). In order to sustain these types of relationships, the leader needs to maintain an interest in the needs and goals of the subordinate to ensure that the subordinate receives the benefits expected.

On the other hand, low-quality exchange relationships are not characterized by these positive features. In low-quality situations, the relationship between the leader and the subordinate is based on the formal working contract in that the subordinate is expected to fulfill set duties and work requirements. If subordinates meet these expectations, then they will receive the benefits (such as salary), but the relationship is not designed to motivate the subordinate beyond this level, nor is it concerned with the subordinate's personal needs for development.

Research has shown that people in high-quality exchange relationships with their leader report much higher rates of job satisfaction and commitment to the organization and lower levels of job stress than those who report having a low-quality relationship with their leader. In addition, those with a high-quality exchange relationship with their leader tend to display better work performance than do people with a low-quality exchange relationship.

Research has identified many reasons that a leader might develop exchange relationships of different quality with his or her subordinates. One reason might be managing a very large group of people (many leaders are responsible for very large groups of subordinates). Because leaders do not have enough time to develop good-quality exchanges with all their subordinates, there is a tendency to subgroup the subordinates into good- or poor-quality exchange relationships. Such a strategy might be cost-effective for the leader time-wise, but this advantage has to be weighed against having poor-quality exchange relationships with other members of the work group, who may underperform.

Another reason might be personal compatibility between the leader and the subordinate. The more similar the subordinate is to the leader, on a range of work and nonwork factors, the greater is the likelihood that a high-quality exchange relationship will develop. Research in the relationships area shows that similarity leads to attraction, and this also applies to the relationship between a leader and his or her subordinate. In this situation, the similarity between the leader and the subordinate may lead to their liking each other, which can result in the development of high-quality exchanges between them.

Recent Developments

Recent versions of VDL emphasize that leaders should not form high-quality exchange relationships with just a few of their subordinates but should try to develop positive relationships with all their subordinates. This advice recognizes that conflict can occur among subordinates if they feel that the leader treats some members of the work group more favorably than others—especially if such favorability is based on the leader's personal preference rather than on work performance criteria.

Research into VDL has developed to take a broader view of leadership in order to examine how leaders manage groups of subordinates, and this research has been the forerunner for the establishment of the *leader-member exchange theory* of leadership.

Robin Martin

See also Charismatic Leadership; Contingency Theories of Leadership; Great Person Theory of Leadership; Interactionist Theories of Leadership; Leader-Member Exchange (LMX) Theory; Leadership; Path–Goal Theory of Leadership; Personality Theories of Leadership; Social Identity Theory of Leadership; Transactional Leadership Theories; Transformational Leadership Theories

Further Readings

Danserau, F., Jr., Graen, G., & Haga, W. J. (1975). A vertical dyad linkage approach to leadership within formal organizations: A longitudinal investigation of the role making process. *Organizational Behavior and Human Performance, 13,* 46–78.

Graen, G. B., & Uhl-Bien, M. (1995). Relationship-based approaches to leadership: Development of leader-member exchange (LMX) theory of leadership over 25 years: Applying a multi-level multi-domain perspective. *Leadership Quarterly, 6,* 219–247.

VIRTUAL/INTERNET GROUPS

The development and adoption of network-based collaboration tools and services have allowed the formation of virtual groups, or groups that exist primarily via technology-mediated interaction. The evolution of virtual groups has followed the evolution of the Internet, from groups defined by electronic mailing lists in the 1980s to the contemporary use of social networking sites, such as Facebook. Virtual groups differ in important ways from traditional groups, and these differences are the focus of practical and theoretical interest. From a practical perspective, virtual groups allow organizations to build work teams that are geographically dispersed, which can make it easier to combine far-flung expertise. In theoretical terms, virtual groups challenge many assumptions about group process, such as the importance of physical proximity and face-to-face communication for group formation and maintenance.

The emergence of virtual groups is tied closely to the emergence of key enabling technologies, in which succeeding stages of technology development have supported more elaborate forms of virtual groups. This progression can be thought of in terms of the increasing "richness" of virtual group communication, or the expanded capacity for communication and connection. Using the richness metaphor, the time line of virtual groups can be roughly bracketed into an early phase, oriented around text-based communication (1960s to 1980s); a middle phase, oriented around *groupware* (1980s to 1990s); and the current phase, oriented around social computing (1990s to 2000s).

Text-Based Virtual Groups

The creation of the first computer networks (e.g., ARPAnet) in the 1960s led to the introduction of network-based tools, of which the most significant was electronic mail (e-mail). E-mail allows text-based communication that can be stored and forwarded by computers, meaning that messages are delivered just as easily to a single recipient as to a list of recipients (e.g., an electronic mailing list). Similarly, messages can be delivered to local or distributed addresses with equal effort. Mailing lists were quickly adopted as mechanisms for both formal and informal communication. For example, the computer language Common Lisp was an initial successful instance of work accomplished almost completely via mailing list discussions. During a span of 30 months in the early 1980s, the Common Lisp team exchanged thousands of messages among dozens of contributors all over the world and demonstrated that complex tasks could be coordinated and executed via electronic interaction.

At the same time as work groups discovered the advantages of mailing lists for coordinating and accomplishing activity, non-work groups also adopted mailing lists. For instance, in a 1990 paper, Tom Finholt and Lee Sproull documented the first purely social uses of mailing lists in the context of groups devoted to particular interests (e.g., cooking or movies), as well as groups that existed as virtual extensions or counterparts to traditional groups (e.g., coworkers who go to bars together or members of a sports team). In the case of interest groups, mailing lists allowed those with rare interests (e.g., playing the Japanese strategy game *go*) to identify similarly oriented others, unconstrained by time or place. In the case of extensions to traditional groups, mailing lists allowed members to expand socializing beyond occasions for face-to-face gatherings.

Groupware

Instances of group activity supported via electronic communication created demand for tools to enable a broader spectrum of group interaction. For instance, rather than sharing text through e-mail, users wanted to edit the text in real time. Starting in the mid-1980s, researchers in academia and corporate labs began to develop prototype applications to support synchronous and asynchronous activity at a distance, called *groupware*. Research on groupware formed the core of a new research area, called *computer-supported cooperative work*.

Some early instances of groupware focused on shared writing tools and shared whiteboards. By the 1990s, commercial applications of these technologies, such as Microsoft NetMeeting, were available, as well as open-source versions, such as Virtual Network Computer. Typically, these applications allowed remote users to share a common desktop, enabling joint viewing and manipulation of documents, images, and other application interfaces. Communication occurred via text-based chat windows. Successful interaction via these tools required a number of technology and interface innovations, such as mechanisms to avoid simultaneous work on the same section of a text and the use of user-specific telepointers to represent focus of attention (because remote users cannot see gaze direction). For example, in a 1999 paper, Gloria Mark and colleagues showed how design teams at Boeing were able to use NetMeeting to increase common ground in long-distance collaboration by creating a shared visual reference when talking about design changes. Contemporary versions of synchronous groupware, called *data conferencing tools* (e.g., WebEx), have become ubiquitous in corporate environments and have added capabilities, such as video and audio.

Another important early line of research on groupware focused on asynchronous applications, such as systems that combined shared secure file spaces, threaded discussion lists, and e-mail repositories. By the 1990s, commercial applications of these technologies, such as Lotus Notes, were in wide use. A primary advantage of asynchronous groupware was the controlled group access to the system, such that distributed group members could upload work in progress with the expectation that only other group members would see these materials. The use of shared file spaces also allowed groups to see what members were working on, with corresponding benefits in terms of reduced coordination overhead. Systems like Notes did introduce certain difficulties. For example, Wanda Orlikowski found that use of Notes in one professional organization was very sensitive to incentive structures. For example, a goal of installation was to encourage employees to share more of their individual work-related information, with the expectation that doing so would accelerate the conversion of personal knowledge into community knowledge (so that employees could better benefit from the wisdom and experience of their coworkers). However, in practice, employees withheld contributions, both because contributions were not classified as billable activity and because employees thought managers were using Notes contributions to monitor performance. Similarly, in a 1994 study of an asynchronous groupware system for biologists, called the Worm Community System (WCS), Susan Leigh Star and Karen Ruhleder found that junior scientists, particularly postdocs, were reluctant to deposit data in the WCS. Part of their concern reflected fears that availability of their data within the WCS could lead a more senior researcher to analyze the data and hence anticipate, or scoop, the postdocs' discoveries.

Social Computing

The arrival of the World Wide Web in the mid-1990s dramatically expanded use of computer networks for social activity. Initially, much of this expansion involved the introduction of conventional applications and services, such as e-mail, to new populations of users or the appropriation of synchronous groupware technologies for entertainment, such as online games (e.g., *Everquest* and more recently *World of Warcraft*). Recently, a host of new uses of the Web have emerged, collectively termed *social computing*. These emerging services take advantage of the Web's capacity to link and store information, particularly with respect to social relationships. The best known instances of social computing include social networking sites (e.g., Facebook), recommender systems (e.g., Digg), and user-contributed content sites (e.g., Wikipedia).

Social networking sites, begun as tools for users to catalog their friendships, have become infrastructures for supporting a diverse array of social processes. Facebook, for example, is a means for maintaining a running commentary, with one's friends, about events, opinions, and affiliations. This commentary is enriched by combining features of the social networking site with other services, such as photo sharing (e.g., via Flickr), video sharing (e.g., via YouTube), or game playing (e.g., Scrabbulous). LinkedIn, a networking site oriented toward career development and business opportunities, has become a way for prospective employers to identify and assess job candidates, effectively replacing such traditional features of job search as the distribution of cover letters and resumes.

Recommender systems, originally developed as tools for users to express their opinions about favorite movies and books, have become sophisticated mechanisms for mining and extracting aggregate opinions. For instance, in the news site Digg, stories are elevated to the top of the queue based on how many times users have "digged" a story, effectively transferring traditional editorial functions of story selection to consumers as opposed to a select group of editors. Aggregate recommendations can also be used to tailor selections of movies or books based on preferences of viewers or readers with similar tastes. An active area of research concerns efforts to make recommender systems resistant to manipulation, such as reducing the influence of software agents that might cast votes for a book or movie to boost its popularity artificially.

A final notable form of social computing is the emergence of user-contributed content sites, such as Wikipedia. These sites coordinate and collect the efforts of thousands of users to produce resources (an encyclopedia in the case of Wikipedia) that can be more comprehensive and up-to-date than some traditional counterparts. For example, in the case of Wikipedia, contributors concerned with a particular topic will monitor that topic and then immediately update or correct entries. Active areas of research on user-contributed content include efforts to understand motivation and incentive structures for contributors. Specifically, much of the effort to create Wikipedia and similar sites comes from the voluntary efforts of contributors, whose reasons for this effort reflect the contributors' altruistic impulses as well as more instrumental goals (e.g., contributors to open-source software projects increase their visibility to prospective employers).

The Coming Era of Virtual Organizations

The experience with virtual groups during the past two decades has produced calls, for example from Jonathon Cummings and colleagues in 2008, for the creation and study of *virtual organizations*. Initially considered largely in the context of global scientific collaborations, such as the community of researchers who use the Large Hadron Collider at the European Organization for Nuclear Research, virtual organizations are envisioned as ways to transparently share resources across institutional and geographic boundaries. For example, a typical application involves identification and allocation of computational and data resources for large-scale computations. Traditionally, sharing these resources might involve explicit negotiations among resource owners, such as contracts and other agreements. By contrast, within a virtual organization, these complex social arrangements are delegated to software called *middleware*, which automatically negotiates resource access and use according to authentication and authorization schemes. In some sense, virtual organization schemes take the work of trust formation and maintenance and move it from the realm of managers and decision makers to the realm of software and system developers. There may be significant advantages to the virtual organization approach. For instance, middleware may reduce bias in resource allocation and create new opportunities for groups and organizations that might otherwise have no access. However, embedding important social processes within software also carries risk. Notably, decisions made under software control may be invisible or unintelligible to those affected, much as recent operation of the financial sector (e.g., software-controlled hedge funds) has been obscured, with important consequences in terms of reduced accountability and monitoring.

Thomas A. Finholt

See also Collaboration Technology; Communication Networks; Teams

Further Readings

Cummings, J., Finholt, T. A., Foster, I., Kesselman, C., & Lawrence, K. (2008). *Beyond being there: A blueprint for advancing the design, development and evaluation of virtual organizations*. Retrieved April 5, 2009, from: http://www.ci.uchicago.edu/events/VirtOrg2008/VO_report.pdf

Finholt, T. A., & Sproull, L. S. (1990). Electronic groups at work. *Organization Science, 1,* 41–64.

Mark, G., Poltrock, S., & Grudin, J. (1999). Meeting at the desktop: An empirical study of virtually collocated teams. In *Proceedings of the Sixth Conference on European Computer-Supported Cooperative Work* (pp. 159–178). Norwell, MA: Kluwer Academic.

Nov, O. (2007). What motivates Wikipedians? *Communications of the ACM, 50,* 60–64.

Orlikowski, W. (1992). Learning from Notes: Organizational issues in groupware implementation. In *Proceedings of the 1992 ACM Conference on Computer-Supported Cooperative Work* (pp. 362–369). New York: ACM Press.

Resnick, P., & Varian, H. (1997). Recommender systems. *Communications of the ACM, 40,* 56–58.

Star, S. L., & Ruhleder, K. (1994). Steps toward an ecology of infrastructure: Complex problems in design and access for large-scale collaborative systems. In *Proceedings of the 1994 ACM Conference on Computer-Supported Cooperative Work* (pp. 253–264). New York: ACM Press.

Steele, G. L. (1984). *Common Lisp: The language* (1st ed.). Newton, MA: Digital Press.

WEIGHTISM

Weightism involves negative attitudes and discriminatory behavior toward people on the basis of their weight. Although in the developing world there is some bias against thin people, the most common form of weightism is bias against people who are heavier than average. When this bias is an attitude, it is sometimes called *antifat prejudice*. This entry looks at the origins of weightism, compares it with other kinds of prejudice and discrimination, and discusses its consequences and potential remedies.

Origins of Weight-Based Bias

Social norms regarding weight suggest that there is an ideal body type that individuals should strive to attain. Although there is variability in the ideal body type across cultures, most cultures endorse a lean, thin ideal. Because heavyweight individuals do not fit this ideal, they are often viewed and treated negatively.

Heavyweight people are often seen as less reproductively fit than average-weight people. From an evolutionary perspective, heavyweight people are seen as unhealthy and less likely to produce healthy offspring. There is no evidence, however, that any but the most morbidly obese are less capable of successful reproduction.

Heavyweight people are often seen as responsible for their condition. In Western countries, people believe that becoming heavy is a result of overeating and a lack of exercise, and thus fatness is avoidable. In addition, because weight is perceived to be connected to self-control, being heavy is perceived to be reversible. Heavyweight individuals are thus considered responsible for their fate—they have brought this condition on themselves, and if they only worked hard enough, they could return to "normality."

This perception of control over weight is not consistent with the vast array of data showing that dieting rarely works (and when it does, the effects are usually temporary), that exercise programs are hard to stick with and do not directly contribute large amounts to weight loss, and that by far the greatest contributors to weight are genetic and physiological factors rather than self-control.

Comparing Weightism With Other Prejudices

Antifat prejudice is like other prejudices in that it involves negative feelings toward people in a group (based on category status rather than individual characteristics) and stereotypes about the group, and it affects the major life areas of friendships, romance, employment, education, and health. As with other prejudices, people who hold antifat prejudice find justifications for their attitude by endorsing negative stereotypes and holding people responsible for their condition. For example, people with negative feelings toward fat people emphasize the role of personal responsibility, the potential success of diet and exercise programs, and the value of self-denial.

Heavyweight people are underrepresented in television programs, movies, and advertising. Rather than being presented as protagonists, heavyweight individuals are more likely to be portrayed as secondary characters. When they appear in the media, heavyweight people are often in the role of clowns, fools, villains, or people who are damaged in some way.

Heavyweight people have more difficulty than others in navigating important social institutions. They are less likely to go to college, particularly elite colleges, and they receive less support from their parents when they do, despite equal interest, grades, and test scores.

Heavyweight people are less likely to seek medical care for their problems, whether weight related or not, perhaps because they fear humiliating or depersonalizing treatment when they go to the doctor. The evidence suggests that they are right: Physicians, medical residents, nurses, and other health care workers hold antifat attitudes and stereotypes. Physicians express more negative emotions, recommend fewer procedures, show less personal desire to help, and spend less time with heavyweight patients. Some health programs explicitly do not cover obesity or other weight-related issues.

Heavyweight people can have trouble negotiating the physical environment. Public accommodations are often not built with them in mind—seating, transportation, bathrooms, automobile seat belts, and doorways are often developed with leaner users in mind (although more recent laws, notably the Americans with Disabilities Act, have increased accessibility in many public accommodations). The range of clothing available for heavyweight people can be quite limited, and the higher ends of the fashion industry aim primarily at a very lean silhouette; the latest fashions are rarely designed with heavyweight people in mind.

Although weightism is similar to other prejudices, there are some important differences. Unlike other discriminated-against groups, heavyweight people do not identify strongly with their group. Perhaps because weight is seen as an issue of personal responsibility, and perhaps because overweight is a category that people believe they can escape, heavyweight people do not see their weight as part of a group membership. They do not seek fellowship with other heavyweight people, and, surprisingly, they do not show ingroup bias—fat people are every bit as antifat, on average, as thin and average-weight people. Perhaps as a result, heavyweight people do not tend to engage in advocacy or join groups promoting social change. Although activism is relatively rare for many stigmatized groups, the rate of activism for heavyweight people, particularly given their prevalence in modern society, is surprisingly low.

Consequences of Weight-Based Discrimination

The negative consequences of excess weight appear early in life. Although most children experience some teasing, heavyweight children experience significantly more than average. Individuals who are discriminated against on the basis of their weight show an increased likelihood of depression as well as suicidal thoughts and attempts. Heavyweight people may also suffer decrements in self-esteem and feelings of self-efficacy, particularly if they feel responsible for their weight.

Women are more likely than men to be victims of antifat bias. Women are more likely than men to develop friendships with people of similar weight (and height). Women are more likely to be judged by their physiques in general and by their weight in particular. A woman's attractiveness is more affected by her weight than is a man's, and women's self-approval and self-esteem are more strongly linked to their weight and body image. Many of the biases demonstrated against heavyweight people in the literature seem to be more serious for women than for men (e.g., discrimination in hiring, education, and dating preference).

The bias against heavyweight people, and particularly women, is also found in marriage. Heavyweight people, and particularly heavyweight women, begin dating later in life and marry later than their leaner counterparts. On average, they also date and marry less desirable partners. Fortunately, once heavyweight people are in stable dating relationships or marriages, they report the same levels of commitment and satisfaction as lean couples do.

Heavyweight people are more likely than leaner individuals to avoid public exposure and social situations. Heavyweight people seem to have slightly fewer friends than lean people have. They are also more likely to live alone and to report being lonely, and they are less likely to be well integrated into the groups and informal friendship networks that can offer social rewards and life opportunities. Heavyweight people often work hard to compensate for some of these social disadvantages, developing social skills and nurturing friendships.

There has been a long history of investigation of the mental health of heavyweight people. When body image and body esteem are set aside (the heavyweight are more negative in both), there are few if any differences in the psychological functioning or health of heavyweight people compared with the rest of the population. When differences are occasionally found in research, they seem to be connected to the negative treatment to which heavyweight people are exposed.

Reducing Weight-Based Prejudice and Discrimination

Antifat bias has been reduced through education about the causes of obesity. These efforts are only occasionally successful in shifting explanations for fatness from internal causes and personal responsibility to causes outside the individual's control (e.g., genetics, physiology, *in utero* nutritional environment). When successful, however, change in attribution for weight leads to a change in the overt expression of antipathy for heavyweight people. As with other discriminated-against groups, increased positive interpersonal contact between heavyweight and nonheavyweight individuals should also lead to a decrease in bias. Finally, increasing empathy for heavyweight individuals, perhaps through perspective taking, may also reduce negative attitudes.

In summary, antifat bias is pervasive and often seen as justified by those who endorse it. It is widespread and affects all the major arenas of life. Unlike other forms of prejudice, antifat bias is equally endorsed by members of the group, and thus group membership and identity offer little comfort or buffer against discrimination. Heavyweight people often do not identify with their group and hence do not work for social change or improvement in heavyweight people's lives. In practice, movement out of the group is relatively rare and often temporary.

Christian S. Crandall and Nia L. Phillips

See also Ageism; Ambivalent Sexism; Discrimination; Modern Forms of Prejudice; Ostracism; Prejudice; Self-Esteem; Stigma

Further Readings

Brownell, K. D., Puhl, R. M., Schwartz, M. B., & Rudd, L. (Eds.). (2005). *Weight bias: Nature, consequences and remedies*. New York: Guilford.

Crandall, C. S. (1994). Prejudice against fat people: Ideology and self-interest. *Journal of Personality and Social Psychology, 66,* 882–894.

Pearce, M. J., Boergers, J., & Prinstein, M. J. (2002). Adolescent obesity, overt and relational peer victimization, and romantic relationships. *Obesity Research, 10,* 386–393.

Puhl, R., & Brownell, K. D. (2001). Bias, discrimination, and obesity. *Obesity Research, 9,* 788–805.

WORK TEAMS

Work teams are composed of two or more individuals who (a) perform organizationally relevant tasks, (b) share one or more common goals, (c) interact socially, (d) exhibit interdependencies in task workflows, (e) manage and maintain group boundaries, and (f) are embedded in a broader organizational context that constrains the team and influences exchanges with other units in the organization. During the past two decades, strategic, technological, and economic forces have driven a shift from work organized around individual jobs to team-based structures. Teams serve as the basic building blocks of modern organizations and represent a critical means by which work is accomplished in today's world. Therefore, significant research during the past few decades has been focused on understanding work team effectiveness. This entry looks at the history of this research and what it says about team types, team composition, team development, team processes, and team effectiveness.

History and Background

The idea of people working together in teams is certainly not new. Yet for much of the 20th century, the concept of work in large organizations was primarily centered on individual jobs. During the past two decades, however, there has been an evolution in the design of work, shifting from individual jobs in functionalized structures to teams embedded in more complex workflow arrangements. This shift is the result of numerous forces, including increased globalization, consolidation, and technological innovation. To compete in this environment, organizations need access to diverse skills and experiences, they need to remain flexible and adaptive, and they must be able to operate effectively across geographical and cultural boundaries. Teams enable these characteristics. For example, an organization can use cross-functional teams to bring together individuals with diverse talents to solve a problem or create a new product and can use virtual teams to connect individuals who may be distributed around the globe. Unfortunately, the transition to team-based work structures has not always been a smooth one. Teams are frequently unsuccessful, as evidenced by the fact that failures in team functioning are commonly cited as a primary cause of air crashes, medical errors, military catastrophes, and industrial disasters.

The combined promise and peril of work teams has captured the attention of researchers and has led to a growing number of theories, empirical studies, and literature reviews on the topic of work team effectiveness. For many years, team research focused on the study of small interpersonal groups in social psychology, but during the past two decades, it has become increasingly centered in the fields of organizational psychology and organizational behavior, representing the growing interest in work teams. Most theoretical frameworks for understanding team effectiveness follow the input → process → output (IPO) logic proposed by Joseph McGrath in 1964. Inputs represent the resources (e.g., characteristics of individual members, organizational resources) that can contribute to team effectiveness and constraints (e.g., task requirements, workflow interdependencies) that have to be managed or resolved for a team to be effective. Processes represent the psychological mechanisms that allow team members to combine their talents and resources to resolve the constraints and achieve success. Outputs represent internal and external aspects of team performance and the impact of the experience on team members (e.g., team member satisfaction).

In a 2005 review, Daniel Ilgen, John Hollenbeck, Michael Johnson, and Dustin Jundt proposed an alternative to the traditional IPO framework, a model they term input–mediator–output–input (IMOI). The IMOI model reflects the fact that there are a broad range of factors, beyond just processes, that mediate the effects of team inputs on outcomes, and it acknowledges the potential for a cyclical feedback loop in which outputs, such as team performance, serve as inputs to future team processes. The following sections review several of the inputs, processes and other mediators, and outputs that have been studied frequently in the research on work team effectiveness.

Work Team Types

Work teams come in a variety of different forms, and new forms are regularly invented to deal with emerging organizational needs (e.g., virtual teams). The diversity of team forms presents a challenge for understanding team effectiveness, as many factors that influence team functioning vary across different types of teams. General typologies distinguish a broad range of teams, often based on functional differences. For example, general team types include production teams, service teams, and management teams. Some researchers have identified more specific types of teams, including crews, top management teams, transnational teams, and virtual teams. The value of such typologies stems from the underlying dimensions that distinguish team types, because these dimensions highlight the varying contingencies that determine the effectiveness of different types of teams.

In a 2003 review, Steve Kozlowski and Bradford Bell suggested that the following dimensions can be used to characterize the constraints faced by different team forms: (a) the external environment or organizational context with respect to its dynamics and degree of required coupling; (b) team boundary permeability and spanning; (c) team member diversity and collocation, or spatial distribution; (d) internal coupling requirements; (e) workflow interdependencies, with their implications for goal, role, process, and performance demands; and (f) temporal characteristics that determine the nature of performance episodes, or cycles, and the team life cycle.

Team Composition

As noted earlier, one of the resources that work teams use to manage these constraints and achieve success is the characteristics of their individual members. Although research on team composition has examined many different characteristics of teams and their members, a general conclusion that cuts across this literature is that the effects of team composition depend on the nature of a team's task. For example, studies examining the effect of team size on effectiveness have failed to reach consensus on an "optimal" size for different types of teams. Rather, it appears that the appropriate team size depends on the task and the environment in which a team operates. Larger teams may be able to leverage their resources to facilitate performance on more complex tasks, but smaller teams may find it easier to coordinate the activities necessary to tackle less complex tasks.

There also exist very few consistent findings regarding the effects of diversity on team performance. Whereas some studies have found that greater levels of heterogeneity or diversity can improve performance, other studies have reported negative results for diversity or have shown diversity to have no significant effects. In a 2005 review of this literature, Elizabeth Mannix and Margaret Neale noted that the effects of diversity depend largely on whether teams are able to capitalize on the benefits of increased information and perspectives while mitigating the disruptive effects of their differences on team processes, such as cohesion. Further, the information-processing and problem-solving benefits of diverse teams are most likely to translate into enhanced effectiveness when the team's task is cognitively complex or requires multiple perspectives. Although these findings suggest that the effects of team composition are complex, a better understanding of these contingencies can help organizations select and construct effective teams.

Team Development

Team development applies not only to the formation of new teams but also to the process of socializing newcomers to existing teams that naturally experience outflows and inflows of new members during their life span. Much of the research in this area assumes the formation of a brand-new team with no prior history. The classic stage model proposed by Bruce Tuckman in 1965, for example, describes a sequential series of developmental stages: forming, storming, norming, and performing. This model was based on clinical and therapy groups, which had no prior history, no broader context, and an unstructured task. As a result, the model emphasizes the interpersonal processes that teams must manage to achieve their goals.

In contrast, existing teams possess a relatively stable set of shared norms and role expectations and a distinct group climate that have emerged during the course of the team's life span. The inflow of a new member presents a potential challenge to this stability, and thus teams seek to assimilate newcomers, and newcomers, for their part, endeavor to adapt while seeking accommodation by the group. Unfortunately, much of the research in this area has focused on the socialization of individuals into the organization and has paid very little attention to the role of the work group or team in the socialization process. However, there is some evidence that work group members are helpful socialization agents, much more so than formal socialization practices, and play an important role in newcomers' learning, understanding, and adjusting.

Team Processes and Performance

At the core of all models of team effectiveness are the process mechanisms through which team inputs are translated into team performance and other outcomes. The literature on team processes is voluminous, and there exists little convergence on a core set of processes or broader mediators. In their 2003 review, Kozlowski and Bell classified team processes into cognitive, affective-motivational, and behavioral mechanisms in an attempt to organize this research. Cognitive mechanisms, such as *team mental models*, *transactive memory*, and *team learning*, capture the collective task-relevant perceptions, knowledge, and information of team members.

A common theme of much of the work in this area is that team performance is enhanced when members share a common understanding of the task environment, its goal–role–strategy requirements, and perceptions of the broader organizational climate. However, other research suggests that success depends on a team's ability to access the unique informational resources held by members. Transactive memory systems, for example, allow different members of a team to process and store information related to their expertise. The result is that team members can rely on their teammates' expertise, enabling the team to access a larger pool of task-relevant information and avoid wasting cognitive effort.

Affective and motivational processes are also important to team effectiveness. For example, *group cohesion*, or team members' shared commitment or attraction to the group, the task, and one another, has been shown to positively predict team performance. *Team efficacy*, or the shared belief in a group's collective capacity to organize and execute courses of action required to produce given levels of goal attainment, has also been shown to relate positively to team performance. In contrast, both interpersonal and task conflict within a team have been shown to undermine team effectiveness. It is important to note that the positive or negative effect of each of these affective-motivational processes has been shown to be stronger when a team's tasks entail higher levels of interdependence.

Behavioral team processes, such as coordination, communication, and cooperation, focus on what team members do to combine individual effort and action to accomplish team objectives. These three processes are related in that communication serves as a means to enable coordination and cooperation. Coordination and cooperation are related concepts, but coordination involves a temporal component that is not an essential part of cooperation. For example, complex tasks typically require high levels of interdependence, temporal pacing, and synchronicity. Under these conditions, effective performance requires coordinated action, not simply discretionary cooperation.

Enhancing the Effectiveness of Work Teams

Given the growing importance of work teams in today's organizations, there exists considerable interest in designing, selecting, training, and leading teams to be effective. However, this is also an area in which practice has significantly outpaced research, leading to interventions being developed in the absence of a solid scientific foundation. In a recent 2006 article, Kozlowski and Ilgen identified those areas of the team effectiveness literature that have well-developed theoretical and empirical foundations and used the findings from these areas to identify interventions that can improve

team effectiveness. For example, the evidence has consistently supported the use of several training techniques, such as cross-training, simulation-based training, and crew resource management, for enhancing team processes and performance.

Leadership is also a potentially critical lever for enhancing team effectiveness. A variety of leader approaches, such as *transformational* and *transactional leadership*, have received consistent research support, although there is a need to extend theory and research in this area to the team context. Research on other topics, such as group composition and team development, holds considerable promise for helping organizations select and develop effective teams, but continued work is needed to develop scientifically grounded tools and applications.

Bradford S. Bell and Steve W. J. Kozlowski

See also Diversity; Group Composition; Group Development; Group Learning; Group Performance; Team Building; Team Performance Assessment; Team Reflexivity; Transactive Memory Systems

Further Readings

Bell, B. S., & Kozlowski, S. W. J. (2002). A typology of virtual teams: Implications for effective leadership. *Group & Organization Management, 27*(1), 14–49.

Ilgen, D. R., Hollenbeck, J. R., Johnson, M., & Jundt, D. (2005). Teams in organizations: From input-process-output models to IMOI models. *Annual Review of Psychology, 56,* 517–543.

Kozlowski, S. W. J., & Bell, B. S. (2003). Work groups and teams in organizations. In W. C. Borman, D. R. Ilgen, & R. J. Klimoski (Eds.), *Handbook of psychology: Vol. 12. Industrial and organizational psychology* (pp. 333–375). New York: John Wiley.

Kozlowski, S. W. J., & Ilgen, D. R. (2006). Enhancing the effectiveness of work groups and teams. *Psychological Science in the Public Interest, 7*(3), 77–124.

Mannix, E., & Neale, M. A. (2005). What differences make a difference? The promise and reality of diverse teams in organizations. *Psychological Science in the Public Interest, 6,* 31–55.

McGrath, J. E. (1964). *Social psychology: A brief introduction.* New York: Holt, Rinehart & Winston.

Tuckman, B. W. (1965). Developmental sequence in small groups. *Psychological Bulletin, 63,* 384–399.

Xenophobia

The term *xenophobia* derives from the Greek *xenos* (foreigner or stranger) and *phobos* (fear or aversion) and is generally used to describe fear of, contempt for, or aversion to foreigners and, more broadly, people, values, customs, beliefs, and even artifacts differing from those of one's own culture.

Xenophobia is related to several social science concepts describing different kinds of antipathy to others. These include *prejudice* (dislike of others, who may differ in almost any way, but which mostly refers to intergroup differences), *racism* (dislike of others seen as racially different; racism is usually associated with an ideology of superiority over those others), *stigmatization* (devaluation or dislike of others seen as deviating from socially desirable standards or norms), and *ethnocentrism* (dislike of ethnically or culturally different others; ethnocentrism is associated with a strong sense of ingroup preference and superiority). Of these, xenophobia is most similar to ethnocentrism, if the term *ethnic* is broadly interpreted, but it may not necessarily involve the implication of strong ingroup preference. If the concept of prejudice, which is the broadest noted here, is interpreted widely, xenophobia can be viewed as a kind of prejudice directed against persons seen as strangers or foreigners. This entry begins by examining the impact of xenophobia on immigrants and relates that topic to ethnocentrism, then looks at the bases of xenophobia at intergroup, individual, and cultural or societal levels.

Xenophobic Reactions to Immigrants

In contrast to the vast research literatures on prejudice and racism, there has been little research on xenophobia. The term is most frequently used in reference to negative reactions to immigrants. One area of recent research has been the upsurge in anti-immigrant xenophobia in western Europe during the past half century. Thomas Pettigrew reviewed this research for the *Annual Review of Sociology* in 1998 and described four major reactions to "new minorities" in western Europe.

One reaction was pervasively hostile attitudes or prejudice expressed either blatantly and overtly or in more subtle and covert forms. A second was discrimination, which could also be either direct, creating inequality through differential treatment and access to employment and housing, or indirect, as when inability to gain citizenship restricts opportunities, thereby perpetuating inequality. A third was political opposition, with the formation of far-right anti-immigrant political parties openly propagating racist and xenophobic policies and shifting the entire political spectrum on the issue to the right. Finally, there was increased anti-immigrant and antiforeigner violence, sometimes associated with far-right political activity but also seen in sporting contexts and individual *hate crimes*.

It is interesting to note that recent ecological studies of xenophobic violence and hate crimes have not supported early findings on lynching in the United States, which had suggested a link with economic hardship or unemployment. Instead, these studies, notably by Donald Green and his colleagues, have indicated that xenophobic violence is particularly likely when social groups feel that they are confronted by growing numbers of outsiders with different social practices in a way that seems to challenge the groups' more favorable, established position in the social hierarchy.

Extent of Xenophobia and Ethnocentrism

The idea that anti-immigrant hostility may be a direct response to the arrival of new migrants, as appears to have happened in western Europe, seems overly simplistic. Host people living in the areas most affected by new immigrants and who have most contact with them tend to be most favorable to them, whereas those living in areas least affected by new immigrants and having least contact with them are most unfavorable to them.

This observation also contradicts the idea proposed by some evolutionary theories that hostility to outsiders had survival value for early human groups and therefore became an evolved adaptive response that was universal and genetically transmitted, underlying most forms of prejudice. These theories have cited many examples of strangers or outsiders being killed, attacked, avoided, or rejected by tribes or communities they encountered. The historical record, however, provides equally numerous examples of cultural outsiders or strangers being welcomed and greeted with interest, curiosity, and sometimes even veneration.

Ethnographic and cross-cultural studies of ethnocentrism, such as a classic series of studies conducted among East African tribes by Donald Campbell and Marilynn Brewer in the mid-20th century, have also shown that attitudes to outgroups and outsiders were not universally negative but varied widely, sometimes being negative, sometimes positive, and sometimes varying markedly by situation or context. Surveys of attitudes toward foreigners among East German youth during the 1990s, when antiforeigner attacks in East Germany were causing concern, also showed that these attitudes were organized along two independent dimensions, with one comprising "good," or liked, foreigners (English, Swedes, North Americans, French) and the other "bad," or disliked, foreigners (Turks, Poles, Jews, Gypsies).

These considerations raise the question of why foreigners or strangers are sometimes viewed with hostility and dislike and sometimes not. Social scientific theory and research suggest answers to this question at three different levels: intergroup processes, individual differences, and societal or cultural group.

Intergroup Bases of Xenophobia

The observation that dislike of certain outsiders and foreigners, but not others, may be widely shared or consensual in a society suggests that some kind of real or anticipated intergroup processes may be causing the antipathy for those particular outgroups but not for others. Three kinds of intergroup processes seem to be particularly conducive to intergroup dislike.

First, there is *intergroup threat*, whereby members of a group who perceive outsiders or foreigners as posing a threat to their resources (*real threat*) or values or identity (*symbolic threat*) will dislike them. Second, there is *intergroup competition*, whereby outsiders or outgroups seen as competing either over real resources, such as territory, or over relative prestige and superiority will be disliked. And third, there is *intergroup inequality*, whereby outsiders or foreigners seen as lower in status, prestige, or power will tend to be devalued and derogated.

Individual Bases of Xenophobia

Dislike and rejection of outgroups and foreigners can also be an individual phenomenon, and it is well documented that reactions to foreigners may vary widely within societies or cultures, with some people responding with hostility and others not. Research has also shown that individuals' prejudiced attitudes tend to be generalized over outgroups, with some people being generally prejudiced and others generally tolerant. This suggests that some stable characteristics of individuals cause them to be either generally prejudiced or tolerant.

Research findings show that two social attitude dimensions are strongly related to generalized prejudice in individuals. One is labeled *right wing authoritarianism* (RWA) and is broadly equivalent to *social conservatism*, as opposed to *liberalism*. The other is labeled *social dominance orientation* (SDO) and comprises attitudes supporting social inequality, or *hierarchy*, as opposed to *egalitarianism*.

RWA and SDO seem to be social attitudinal expressions of basic social values, with RWA expressing values of collective security (valuing social order, cohesion, stability, conformity, and tradition) and SDO expressing values of power, dominance, and superiority over others. In any particular society, therefore, persons high in RWA and SDO would be the most ethnocentric and xenophobic, and persons low in RWA and SDO the least.

Cultural or Societal Bases of Xenophobia

Finally, cross-cultural research has shown that dislike and rejection of outgroups and foreigners can also be a societal or cultural phenomenon, with certain cultures or societies responding collectively with greater xenophobia to outsiders than others do. For example, Michael Bond investigated cultural values across 22 cultures and found that they were clearly differentiated along a cultural value dimension with one pole characterized by generalized tolerance for others and openness to outside influences and the other pole characterized by cultural inwardness, traditionalism, ethnocentric superiority, and generalized dislike of outsiders.

However, there has been little research on what causes societies or cultures to be ethnocentric or xenophobic. An anthropologist, Marc Ross, found that more ethnocentric and xenophobic preindustrial cultures were characterized by relatively harsh, punitive, and unaffectionate childhood socialization practices, which he speculated may have created a psychological disposition for people in those cultures to view outsiders with suspicion and hostility.

Another approach extends the individual difference perspective noted above by suggesting that certain social environmental influences on societies (high levels of threat and danger or of inequality and competition) may cause social attitudes such as RWA and SDO to become dominant ideologies and culturally normative in these societies. Such societies would then tend to be collectively ethnocentric and xenophobic in their normative attitudes and reactions to outsiders.

John Duckitt

See also Assimilation and Acculturation; Discrimination; Ethnocentrism; Hate Crimes; Islamophobia; Prejudice; Racism; Right Wing Authoritarianism; Social Dominance Theory

Further Readings

Bond, M. (1988). Finding universal dimensions of individual variation in multi-cultural studies of values: The Rokeach and Chinese value surveys. *Journal of Personality and Social Psychology, 55,* 1009–1015.

Brewer, M., & Campbell, D. (1976). *Ethnocentrism and intergroup attitudes: East African evidence.* New York: Sage.

Duckitt, J. (2003). Prejudice and intergroup hostility. In D. Sears, L. Huddy, & R. Jervis (Eds.), *Oxford handbook of political psychology* (pp. 559–600). Oxford, UK: Oxford University Press.

Green, D., Abelson, R., & Garnett, M. (1999). The distinctive political views of hate-crime perpetrators and White supremacists. In D. Prentice & D. Miller (Eds.), *Cultural divides: Understanding and overcoming group conflict* (pp. 429–464). New York: Russell Sage.

Pettigrew, T. (1998). Reactions to the new minorities of Western Europe. *Annual Review of Sociology, 24,* 77–103.

Ross, M. (1993). *The culture of conflict.* New Haven, CT: Yale University Press.

Watts, M. (1996). Political xenophobia in the transition from socialism: Threat, racism, and ideology among East German youth. *Political Psychology, 17,* 97–126.

Index

Entry titles and entry page numbers are in **bold.**

AA. *See* Alcoholics Anonymous (AA)
ABCs of role entry, 2:714–715
Abelson, Robert, **1:**138
Abilities, social comparison theory and, **2:**762–763
Abrahamson, Eric, **1:**271
Abrams, Dominic, **1:**56, **1:**210, **2:**688, **2:**866–867
Abstraction-based models, **2:**638
Abu Ghraib, Iraq, **1:**54, **2:**839
Accentuation phenomenon, **1:**363
Acceptance criteria (AC), **1:**378
Acceptance threat, **2:**800
Accommodation, **1:**378, **1:**379
Acculturation. *See* **Assimilation and acculturation**
Action research, 1:1–6, 2:535
    common elements in, **1:**4–5
    differences from traditional social science research, **1:**2–4
    history and forms of, **1:**1–2
Action verbs (AV), **2:**536
Actor control (AC), **1:**463
Adams, Henry, **1:**409
Adams, J. Stacey, **1:**218
Adaptability, of teams, **2:**911
Adaptive structuration theory, **2:**893
Addictions, support groups and, **2:**875–876
Additive rule, **1:**324
Adler, Alfred, **1:**350
Adorno, Theodor, **1:**22
    The Authoritarian Personality, **1:**45–46, **1:**47, **1:**419,
        1:445, **2:**656, **2:**706
    dogmatism and, **1:**225–226
    hate crimes and, **1:**396
    status and, **2:**842
Aesop, **1:**317
Affect control theory, 1:6–8
    cultural sentiments, **1:**6–7
    interaction, **1:**7
    mathematical foundation of, **1:**7–8
Affective empathy, **1:**476
Affect theory of social exchange, **2:**789
Affirmative action, 1:8–13, 1:224
    diversity in higher education and, **1:**11
    history of, **1:**8–9

intergroup relations and, **1:**11–12
    workplace composition and, **1:**10–11
African National Congress (ANC), **1:**27
Afrikaners, **1:**25–26
Ageism, 1:13–15
    discrimination against aging people, **1:**215–216
    forms of, **1:**13–14
    internalization of, **1:**14–15
    motivation for, **1:**14
    pervasiveness of, **1:**15
    reducing, **1:**15
Agentic behaviors, **1:**297
    gender roles and, **1:**301
    minority groups in society and, **2:**563–564
    roles and, **2:**713
    sexism and, **2:**744–749
Aggression, **1:**440
Agreeableness, **2:**639–640
Ahmadinejad, Mahmoud, **1:**408
Ainsworth, Mary, **1:**38, **1:**276
Air Florida, **2:**751
Akert, Robin, **1:**212
Albanese, Robert, **1:**288
Alcoholics Anonymous (AA), **2:**873, **2:**875–876
Aliens Act of 1905, **1:**256
Allen, Natalie, **1:**412, **1:**424
Allport, Floyd, **1:**16, **1:**170
Allport, Gordon, 1:15–17, 1:212, **1:**445, **2:**558, **2:**571,
        2:573, **2:**655
    on categorization, **1:**68–69
    extended contact effect and, **1:**265
    intergroup contact theory and, **1:**468–473
    jigsaw classroom technique and, **1:**491
    on prejudice, **2:**657–658
    on rumor, **2:**719–720
    on stereotyping, **1:**291
    work of, **1:**16–17
Altemeyer, Robert, **1:**47, **1:**226, **1:**419, **2:**706–707, **2:**842
Altman, Irwin, **2:**914–915
Alvaro, Eusebio, **2:**529
Alzheimer's Disease Support and Information Group, **2:**875
Amazon, **1:**97–98

Ambassador activities, 1:58
Ambivalence amplification, 2:675–676
Ambivalent racism theory, 2:573
Ambivalent sexism, 1:17–19, 2:579
 components of, 1:17–18
 consequences of, 1:19
 measuring, 1:19
 sources of, 1:18
American Arbitration Association, 2:550
American Bar Association, 2:550
American Cancer Society, 1:132
American Civil Liberties Union (ACLU), 1:86
American Civil War, 2:757–758
American Dilemma, An (Myrdal), 2:571
American Heart Association, 1:132
American Jewish Committee, 1:45
American Psychological Association, 1:16, 1:40,
 1:264, 1:286
American Revolution, 2:757
American Sociological Association, 2:833
American Sociological Society, 2:833
American Soldier, The (Stouffer), 2:685, 2:694
Americans with Disabilities Act, 1:84, 2:954
Amnesty International, 1:86
Amputee Coalition of America, 2:875
Anchoring, 2:824–825
Ancona, Deborah, 1:327, 1:333–334, 2:786
Anderson, Elijah, 1:229
Anderson, Judith, 1:271
Anderson, Norman, 1:29
Androgyny, social representations and, 2:824
Animals, crowding and, 1:166–167
Annual Review of Sociology, 2:959
Anomie, 1:206–207
Anthony, Carmelo, 2:836
Anti-Christ, 1:24
Anticonformity, 1:141
 anticonformists and, 1:21
 background and historical overview, 1:20
 by overconformity, 1:21
 theories of, 1:20–21
Antifat prejudice, 2:953
Anti-immigration rhetoric, eugenics and, 1:257
Antinorm effect, 1:210
Anti-Semitism, 1:22–25
 implications of, 1:24–25
 new anti-Semitism, 1:23–24
 psychological foundations, 1:22–23
Apartheid, 1:25–28
 "grand apartheid" and "petty apartheid," 1:26–27
 historical and theoretical context, 1:25–26
 ingroup allocation bias and, 1:447
 opposition to and demise of, 1:27
Apollo 13, 1:375
Appropriateness model, 2:779
Arbitration, 2:551
Arendt, Hannah, 1:53
Argumentation, 2:607
Argyle, Michael, 1:20

Aristotle, 1:113, 1:217, 1:404, 2:891
Aronoff, Joel, 1:357
Aronson, Elliot, 1:94, 1:212, 1:224, 1:491–493, 2:546
Aronson, Joshua, 2:853
ARPAnet, 1:96–97, 2:949
Arrow, H., 2:893
Arrow, Holly, 1:327
Artest, Ron, 2:836
Arthur, Michael, 1:153
Asch, Solomon, 1:28–30, 1:140–144, 1:209, 1:351, 2:566,
 2:685, 2:688, 2:754
 impression formation and, 1:28–29
 informational influence and, 1:443
 legacy of, 1:30
 social impact theory and, 2:805
 social influence and, 1:29–30
 subjective group dynamics and, 2:865
Ashforth, Blake, 2:714, 2:716
Assigned competence, 2:848
Assimilation and acculturation, 1:30–37, 2:720
 acculturation, uni-dimensional to bi-dimensional models,
  1:31–32
 acculturation and deculturation, 1:31
 conclusions and implications of, 1:36–37
 ethnicity and, 1:246
 group socialization and, 1:378
 immigration and, 1:428–429
 interactive acculturation model, 1:32–33
 studies of host community acculturation orientations,
  1:33–34
 studies of immigrant acculturation orientations, 1:35–36
Association for Psychological Science, 1:40
 See also American Psychological Association
Attachment theory, 1:37–39
 families and, 1:278
 individual difference features of, 1:38–39
 need for belonging and, 2:595
Attempted influence, 2:618
Attending to, group memory and, 1:347
Attenuation effect, 2:847
Attitudes Toward Women Scale, 1:39–42
 background and historical overview, 1:40
 change over time, 1:41
 limitations and new directions of, 1:41
 significance of, 1:40
Attribution biases, 1:42–45
 attribution theory, 1:42
 ideology and, 1:418
 individual, 1:42–43
 intergroup, 1:43–44
 intergroup, reducing, 1:44
Audience groups, 2:686
Audio recording, for research, 2:702
Aum Shinrikyo, 1:174
Auschwitz, 1:24, 1:53
Austin, Texas, 1:491
Authoritarian personality, 1:45–48, 2:842
 authoritarianism and culture, 1:48
 criticisms of authoritarian personality theory, 1:46–47

dogmatism and, 1:225
evidence of, 1:45–46
hate crimes and, 1:396–397
historical and theoretical context, 1:45
intergroup violence and, 1:479–480
Islamophobia and, 1:486
realistic group conflict theory and, 2:683
responses to criticisms of, 1:47–48
right wing authoritarianism and, 2:705–706
social dominance theory and, 2:781–782
Authoritarian Personality, The (Adorno,
    Frenkel-Brunswik, Levinson, Sanford),
    1:45, 1:47, 1:419, 1:445, 2:656, 2:706
Authoritative parents, 1:277
Authority structures, performance and, 1:357–358
Autokinetic effect, 1:178, 1:209, 1:443
Autonomy
    job characteristic theory (JCT) and, 1:495
    support groups and, 2:874
Average leadership style, 2:947
Aversive racism, 1:48–51, 2:572, 2:884
    combating, 1:50–51
    nature of the attitudes, 1:48–50
Avolio, Bruce, 1:458
Axelrod, Robert, 2:662–663
Axis Rule in Occupied Europe (Lemkin), 1:304

Back, Kurt, 2:742
Backup behavior, of teams, 2:911–912
Balance theory, 1:93–94
Bales, Robert Freed, 2:712, 2:826, 2:840, 2:885–887
    dynamical systems approach and, 1:232
    group development and, 1:325
    group structure and, 1:383
    interaction process analysis and, 1:460
    language and intergroup relations, 2:514
Ball-tossing paradigm, 2:629
Banaji, Mahzarin R., 2:888
Banality of evil, 1:53–55
Bandura, Albert, 1:189, 1:368–369, 2:935–936
Banks, Curtis, 2:837
Bannister, Roger, 2:791
Barabasi, Albert-Laszlo, 1:129
Barnes-Farrell, Janet, 2:851
Bar-Tal, Daniel, 1:189
Bartel, Caroline, 1:334
Bartlett, F. C., 2:754
Baseline homophily, 1:404
Basic expectation assumption, 2:847
Bass, Bernard, 2:929–930
Baumeister, Roy, 1:316, 1:439, 1:441, 2:834
Baumrind, Diana, 1:277
Bavelas, Alex, 1:128, 1:382–383
Bay of Pigs, Cuba, 1:374, 1:390
Bazerman, Max, 2:605
Beagle Channel, 2:550
Beccaria, Cesare, 2:774
Beck, John, 2:744
Becker, Ernest, 2:919

Becker, Howard, 1:207
Begin, Menachem, 1:159
Begue, Laurent, 1:505–506
Behavioral asymmetry, 2:760
Behavioral decision approach, 2:605–606
Behavioral empathy, 1:476
Behavioral interaction model, 2:556–557
"Being there"/"being beyond there" technology, 1:97
Belief-Pattern Scale for Measuring Attitudes Toward
    Feminism, 1:40
Bell, Bradford, 2:956–957
*Bell Curve: Intelligence and Class Structure in American
    Life, The* (Herrnstein, Murray), 1:256
Bell Labs, 1:204
Bem, Daryl, 1:131
Benedict, Ruth, 2:769
Benevolent ageism, 1:14
Benne, Kenneth, 2:742
Bennington College, 2:684–686
Bennis, Warren, 1:325
Bentham, Jeremy, 2:774
Berdahl, J. L., 2:893
Berger, Joseph, 1:383, 2:840, 2:844, 2:847
Berkowitz, Leonard, 1:291–292, 1:377n, 1:397
Berlin Wall, 1:472
Bernd, Simon, 1:118
Berry, John, 1:31, 1:35, 2:583
Bertuzzi, Todd, 2:836
Best alternative to a negotiated agreement (BATNA), 2:902
Bicultural identity patterns, 2:586
Biddle, Bruce, 2:711
Big Five (personality factors), 2:639–640
Biko, Steve, 1:27
Billig, Michael, 1:157, 2:555, 2:656
Binet, Alfred, 1:255
Bion, Wilfred, 2:728
Biosocial model, 1:303
Bishop, George, 1:362
Black Power, 1:27, 1:112
Black sheep effect, 1:55–57, 2:620
    deviance and, 1:210
    empirical evidence of, 1:56–57
    social identity and ingroup favoritism, 1:56
    subjective group dynamics and, 1:56, 2:865–866
Blake, Robert, 1:152, 1:154
Blanchard, Ken, 1:154
Blascovich, James, 2:793
Blatant sexist behaviors, 2:578
Blau, Peter, 2:652, 2:787, 2:790
Blumer, Herbert, 1:103, 1:366–367, 2:542, 2:880
Boadicea (British queen), 2:804
*Board of Education of Oklahoma City Public Schools
    v. Dowell,* 1:200
Boas, Franz, 2:769
Bobo, Lawrence, 1:367, 2:682
Body image, 1:271–272
Boer Wars, 1:25
Bonacich, Phillip, 2:787
Bond, Michael, 1:144, 2:961

Borderwork, 1:297

Bordia, Prashant, 2:721

Boston Marathon, 2:869

Bottom-up approach, to group task, 1:386–387

Boundary spanning, 1:57–59, 1:314

Bounded rationality, 2:605–606

Bourhis, Richard, 1:32, 1:252, 2:511

Bowers, Kenneth, 1:457

Bowlby, John, 1:37–39, 1:276, 2:595

Bow tie structure, 2:818, 2:818 (figure)

Boyd, Robert, 2:807

Boy Scouts, 2:683

Bradac, Jim, 2:513

Bradford, Leland, 2:742

Brainstorming, 1:59–63
  enhancement of, 1:62–63
  historical overview of, 1:59–61
  illusion of group effectivity and, 1:423–424
  models of, 1:61–62
  process gain and loss, 2:669

Branch Davidians, 1:174

Brauer, Markus, 1:362

Brawley, Lawrence, 1:316

Bray, Steven, 2:836

Brazil, 2:756

Brehm, Jack, 1:20

Brewer, Marilynn, 2:620, 2:730, 2:868, 2:960
  decategorization and, 1:185–187
  homophily and, 1:406
  intergroup contact theory and, 1:470
  looking-glass self and, 2:544
  multiple identities and, 2:586–587

Brian's Song, 1:319

Bristol, England, 1:248

Britain, 2:574

British North America, 2:756–757

Broederbond, 1:27

Bronfenbrenner, Urie, 1:333

Browder v. Gayle, 1:87

Brown, John, 2:758

Brown, Roger, 2:656, 2:840

Brown, Rupert, 1:187, 1:470, 2:587

Brown, Vincent, 1:61–62

Brown Power, 1:112

Brown v. Board of Education, 1:76, 1:84, 1:87–89, 1:111, 1:199, 1:491

Bruner, Jerome, 1:68, 2:897

Buchanan, James, 2:758

Buchanan, Pat, 2:884

Bulgaria, 1:308

Burden of proof assumption, 2:846–847

Burger, Warren E., 2:550

Burke, C. Shawn, 2:911–912

Burlingame, Gary, 1:233

Burns, James McGregor, 1:312, 2:517–518, 2:929, 2:934

Burt, Ronald, 2:819

Bush, George W., 1:208, 2:858, 2:921

Butera, Fabrizio, 2:793

Bystander effect, 1:63–65
  decision making and, 1:64
  diffusion of responsibility and, 1:64–65
  informational social influence and, 1:64
  Kitty Genovese and bystander intervention, 1:63–64
  modern forms of prejudice, 2:572
  pluralistic ignorance and, 2:645
  social compensation and, 2:767

Cacioppo, John, 2:793

California Supreme Court, 2:550

Calvin, John, 2:672

Cambridge University, England, 1:16

Campbell, Donald, 1:70, 1:178–179, 2:681, 2:960

Canada, 2:594
  ethnolinguistic vitality and, 1:254
  language and intergroup relations, 2:513
  modern forms of prejudice and, 2:574
  multiculturalism and, 2:582–583
  racial ambivalence theory and, 2:676

Cancer Aftercare and Rehabilitation Society, 2:875

Cannon-Bowers, Jan, 2:751

CANOE (personality model), 2:639–640

Cantona, Eric, 2:836

Cantril, Hadley, 2:754

Carli, Linda, 1:144

Carlsmith, J. Merrill, 1:94

Carlyle, Thomas, 1:312

Carnegie, Andrew, 2:768

Carnevale, Peter, 2:551

Carron, Albert, 1:316–318

Carter, Jimmy, 1:159

Cartwright, Dorwin, 1:209, 1:383

Castro, Fidel, 2:941

Catastrophe theories, 2:891

Categorization, 1:67–72
  category learning, formation, use, 1:69–71
  discrimination and, 1:213
  ethnocentrism and, 1:248
  functions of, 1:68–69
  group boundaries and, 1:315
  ongoing debates about, 1:71–72
  process of, 1:67–68
  self-categorization theory and, 2:729
  structures of, 1:69
  subtyping and, 2:868

Categorization threat, 2:800

Ceiling effects, 1:41

Cellular automata, 1:234

Centers for Disease Control, 1:102

Central Intelligence Agency, 1:149

Centrality, 2:819

Chagall, Marc, 1:20

Chaiken, Shelly, 1:418

Challenger (space shuttle), 1:390

Chang, Artemis, 1:327

Charismatic leadership, 1:72–74
  defined, 1:72–73
  historical illustration of, 1:73

limitations of and problems of, 1:73–74
personality theories of leadership and, 2:641
romance of leadership, 2:719
social identity theory of leadership and, 2:803
transformational leadership and, 2:522
Charismatic relationship model, interactionist theory and, 1:458
Chatman, Jennifer, 1:411–412, 1:458
Cheaters, punishing, 1:259
Chechnya, 1:390
Chemers, Martin, 2:828
Chen, Xin, 2:569
Chesapeake Bay, 1:166
Children: stereotypes and prejudice, 1:75–78
explicit judgments about social exclusion, 1:77–78
implicit biases in children, 1:75–76
implicit prejudice in children, 1:76
origins of prejudice and, 1:75
self-presentation and explicit prejudice, 1:76–77
Children's groups, 1:79–83
historical overview of, 1:79
peer group acceptance and individual differences, 1:80–82
peer group in development and, 1:79–80
social groups, 1:82–83
Chippewa Indians, 1:367
Choice homophily, 1:404
Christian Church, 2:566
Christie, Richard, 1:46, 1:48
Chuang, Aichia, 2:936
Church of England, 2:726–727
Cialdini, Robert, 1:130–131, 2:866
Cisco's Telepresence, 1:98
City College of New York, 1:204, 1:284
Civil Rights Acts, 1:84–88
of 1964, 2:550, 2:750
of 1968, 1:395
Civil rights legislation, 1:83–86
controversies of, 1:84–85
effects of, 1:85–86
historical overview of, 1:84
monitoring activities of, 1:86
Civil rights movement, 1:86–89
aftermath and ongoing struggles of, 1:88–89
background and context, 1:87
historical overview, 1:87–88
related efforts, 1:89
Clark, Kenneth, 1:111
Clarke, Steve, 1:151
Clash of Civilization, The (Huntington), 1:486
Class conflict, 2:760
Class consciousness, 2:760
Classical view, of categories, 1:69
Climate, 2:936
Clinton, Bill, 1:72, 2:858
Cliques, 1:89–90
gender differences and, 1:90
related constructs, 1:90
as social hierarchies, 1:90

Closed-ended questions, 2:878
Clustering, social impact theory, 2:807
Coalitions, 1:91–93
coalition formation, 1:340
coalition games, 1:91
dynamic theories of coalition formation, 1:92
empirical support and theoretical limitations of, 1:92–93
static theories of coalition formation, 1:91–92
Code switching, ethnolinguistic vitality and, 1:253–254
Coding scheme, 2:699, 2:703–704
Cognitive consistency, 1:93–96
application to groups, 1:95
balance theory and, 1:93–94
cognitive dissonance and, 1:94–95
intergroup processes and, 1:95–96
Cognitive dissonance, 1:94–95
Festinger on, 1:286–287
Holocaust and, 1:402
Cognitive elaboration perspective, 1:162
Cognitive empathy, 1:476
Cognitive interdependence, 2:932
Cognitive models of brainstorming, 1:61–62
Cognitive priming, 2:649
Cognitive role theory, 2:710–711
Cognitive social structures, 2:820
Cohen, Bernard, 2:844
Cohen, Dov, 1:181–182
Cohen, Elizabeth, 2:848
Coie, John, 1:80
Cold War, 1:208, 1:309
Collaboration technology, 1:96–98
"being beyond there" technology and, 1:97–98
"being there" technology and, 1:97
new directions in, 1:98
Collective action
collective action and, 1:110–111
emergent norm theory and, 1:237
feminism and, 1:283
Collective Effort Model, 1:352
Collective guilt, 1:98–101
causes of, 1:99–100
genocide and, 1:308
reducing, 1:100–101
Collective induction, 1:101–103
collective vs. individual induction, 1:101–102
processes of, 1:102
for research, 1:101
simultaneous collective and individual induction, 1:102
Collective induction, group potency and, 1:373
Collective movements and protest, 1:103–110
historical overview of, 1:103–104
new evidence and ideas about, 1:104–106
recent directions in, 1:107–109
standard agenda for, 1:106–107
Collective responsibility, 1:240
Collective self, 1:110–112
collective action and, 1:110–111
self-esteem and ethnicity, 1:111–112
two kinds of self and, 1:110

Collective Self-Esteem Scale, 2:732
Collectivism/individualism, 1:112–117
  historical overview of, 1:112–113
  varieties of collectivism, 1:113–115
  varieties of individualism, 1:115–116
Colorado Avalanche, 2:836
Columbia (space shuttle), 1:390
Columbia University Teachers College, 1:204
Columbine High School, 1:440
Columbus, Christopher, 2:582
Commitment
  relational cohesion theory and, 2:689
  social exchange in networks and groups, 2:789
Committee on the Selection and Training of
    Aircraft Pilots, 1:284
Common-bond groups. *See* **Common-identity/
  common-bond groups**
Common-identity/common-bond groups, 1:117–119
  differences between, 1:117–119
  historical overview of, 1:117
Common ingroup identity model, 1:119–122,
    1:186, 2:588
  empirical support for, 1:121–122
  functional relations, categorization, bias, 1:120–121
  social categorization and bias, 1:120
  social categorization and recategorization, 1:120
Common knowledge effect, 1:123–125
  decision making and, 1:123
  fostering better decisions and, 1:124–125
  theoretical explanation for, 1:123–124
Common Lisp, 2:949
Common pool resource (CPR), 1:125
Commons dilemma, 1:125–127, 1:156
  cooperation and competition, 1:156–157
  factors promoting conservation in, 1:125–127
  social dilemmas and, 2:778
Communal behaviors, 1:297
  gender roles and, 1:301
  normative influence and, 2:607
  roles and, 2:713
  sexism and, 2:744–749
  support groups and, 2:873–874
Communication networks, 1:127–130
  classic research on, 1:128
  communication processes and social representations,
    2:825–826
  computer-mediated communication,
    1:133–136
  performance and, 1:357
  recent advances in, 1:128–129
  study of, 1:128
  teams and communication, 2:912–913
Communist Manifesto, The (Marx), 1:489
Communist Party, 1:47
Community Relations Service,
    U.S. Department of Justice, 2:550
Communityware, 2:933
Comparative reference groups, 2:685
Complexity theory, 2:891

Compliance, 1:130–133
  as change in public behavior, 1:130–131
  in response to a request, 1:131–132
Computer-mediated communication, 1:133–137
  to broaden social networks, 1:136
  CMC technologies, 1:133–134
  deindividuation and, 1:194
  effects of, on conversational processes, 1:134–135
Computer simulation, 1:137–139
  mate selection and, 1:137–138
  modeling of group process, 1:138–139
  models in social psychology, 1:138
Conflict Resolution Center, 2:550
Conflict theory, 1:118, 1:204
Conformity, 1:139–145
  classic studies of, 1:139–140
  definitional and measurement issues of, 1:140–141
  deviation and, 1:208–209
  motivational bases of, 1:141–143
  role of individual differences, 1:143–144
  social impact theory and, 2:805–806
  social support and conformity reduction, 1:143
Congress of Racial Equality, 1:88
Conjunctive group tasks, 2:507
Connecticut State Teachers College, 2:742
Connell, R. W., 1:409
Conscientiousness, 2:639
Conscious Loving and Living, 2:744
Conservatism, 1:145–148
Consolidation, social impact theory, 2:807
Conspiracy theories, 1:148–151, 2:721–722
  explanations for, 1:150–151
  related phenomena, 1:148–149
  research on, 1:149–150
  scapegoating and, 2:725
Constantine, Emperor, 2:528
Constitutional Convention, 2:758
Contact hypothesis, 1:16–17, 1:202
  jigsaw classroom technique and, 1:491
  realistic group conflict theory and, 2:683
Containment and manipulation, 2:578
Contemptuous prejudice, 1:307
Contextual dynamics, 2:893
Contingency theories of leadership, 1:151–155, 2:521,
    2:828, 2:928
  contingency theory of leadership effectiveness, 1:152–153
  historical overview, 1:151–152
  mediation and, 2:551
  normative decision model, 1:153–154
  path-goal theory, 1:153
  path-goal theory of leadership as, 2:635
  situational leadership theory, 1:154
Contingent rewards, 2:930
Continuing diversity, social impact theory, 2:807
Continuum of benevolence, 1:308
Continuum of destructiveness, 1:306
Contractual mediation, 2:550
Control, 1:6, 1:463
Convergent outcomes, 2:644

Conversation
    computer-mediated communication and, 1:134–135
    dominance hierarchies and, 1:228–229
Conversion, 1:130
Cook, Karen, 2:653, 2:787–790
Cooley, Charles Horton, 1:110, 2:541–543
Cooper, Joel, 1:214
Cooperation and competition, 1:155–160
    defined, 1:155
    evolution and genetics, 1:155–154
    game theory and rational choice, 1:156
    interdependence and realistic conflict, 1:157
    minimal groups and social identity, 1:157–158
    negotiation and, 1:159
    social dilemmas, 1:156–157
    superordinate goals and social harmony, 1:158–159
Cooperative interaction, 1:205
Cooperative learning, 1:160–163
    future of, 1:163
    theoretical perspectives on, 1:161–163
Coordinator activities, 1:58
Copper, Carolyn, 1:317–318
Core-periphery structure, 2:818, 2:818 (figure)
Correlation, social impact theory, 2:807
Correspondence bias, 2:941
Coser, Lewis, 2:728
Costly signaling, 2:778
Cottrell, Catherine, 1:260–261
Coutant-Sassic, D., 2:894
Covariation of interest, 1:463
Covert sexist behaviors, 2:578
Crano, William, 2:529, 2:569
Crazes, 1:269
Crocker, Jennifer, 2:869
Crosby, Faye, 2:696
Cross-categorization, 1:44, 1:163–166
    countering negative stereotypes, 1:164–165
    modeling complex intergroup relations, 1:164
Crowding, 1:166–169
    models of, 1:167–168
    practical implications of, 1:168
    research approaches to, 1:166–167
Crowds, 1:169–173
    broadening relevance of crowd psychology, 1:172
    classic crowd theory, 1:169–170
    crowd dynamics and social change, 1:171–172
    deindividuation, 1:191
    normative theories of, 1:170–171
"Crude law" of interpersonal relations, 1:206
Crutchfield, Richard, 1:20
Csikszentmihalyi, Mihaly, 2:828
Cuban Missile Crisis, 1:375
Cults, 1:173–176
    defined, 1:173–174
    leadership and structure, 1:174
    socialization in, 1:174–176
Culture, 1:176–181
    cultural racism, 2:677, 2:679–680
    cultural sentiments and affect control theory, 1:6–7

cultural transmission and small group processes, 1:177–178
    esconced culture and terrorism, 2:918
    evolutionary psychology and, 1:261
    gender and behavior, 1:298
    groups and cultures, 1:176–177
    implicit prejudice and, 1:438
    in large populatons and groups, 1:178–180
    parenting styles and, 1:277
    recent trends in psychology and, 1:180
    See also Multiculturalism
Culture clash, 2:552
Culture of honor, 1:181–183
    development in, 1:182
    mechanisms of persistence and change, 1:182–183
    overview of, 1:181–182
    related concepts, 1:183
    violence and, 1:182
Culture's Consequences (Hofstede), 1:113, 1:179
Cummings, Jonathon, 2:951
Curious spectators, 1:236
Cusp models, 1:233
Cyberball paradigm, 2:629–630
Cyert, Richard, 2:623

Darfur, Sudan, 1:305
Darley, John, 1:64–65, 1:262–264
Darwin, Charles, 1:155, 1:255, 2:768–770
Darwinism, social Darwinism vs., 2:770
Data collection, for research, 2:701–702
D'Augelli, Anthony, 1:216
Davenport, Charles, 1:255, 1:257
Davies, James C., 1:489–490
Dawkins, Richard, 1:155
Decategorization, 1:185–188, 2:588
    critiques and limitations of, 1:187
    empirical evidence of, 1:187
    generalization process in decategorized contact, 1:186–187
    three aspects of: individuation, differentiation, personalization, 1:185–186
de Dreu, Carsten, 2:907
Defense of Marriage Act (DOMA), 1:454
Deflection studies, 1:332
Degree of completeness of information, 1:463
Dehumanization/infrahumanization, 1:188–190
    dehumanization, defined, 1:188
    genocide and, 1:306
    infrahumanization, defined, 1:189–190
    intergroup violence and, 1:480
    theories of, 1:189
Deindividuation, 1:190–195
    accountability and, 1:191–193
    computer-mediated communication and, 1:194
    genocide and, 1:306
    group norms and, 1:193–194
    historical overview and analyses of crowd behavior, 1:191
    social identity model of deindividuation effects and, 2:794

Delphi technique, 1:195–197
   advantages and limitations, 1:196–197
   origin of, 1:195–196
Democratic Party, 2:758
Demographics
   ethnolinguistic vitality and, 1:252
   group composition and, 1:320
Denny, Reginald, 1:397
Denver Nuggets, 2:836
Dependent variables, defined, 1:262
Depersonalization, 1:197–199, 2:687
   defined, 1:197–198
   examples of, 1:198–199
   identification and commitment, 1:413–414
   self-categorization theory and, 2:729
   social identity model of deindividuation effects and, 2:794
   social identity theory of leadership, 2:802
Deprovincialization, 1:470
DeSanctis, G., 2:893
Descriptive action verbs (DAV), 2:536, 2:538
Descriptive roles, 2:608–609
Desegregation, 1:199–204
   consequences for achievement, 1:200–202
   consequences for intergroup relations, 1:202–203
   historical overview and policy changes, 1:199–200
Detroit Pistons, 2:836
Deutsch, Morton, 1:142, 1:155, 1:157, 1:204–206, 1:218, 1:444, 1:502
   on cooperation and competition, 1:204–205
   insights of, 1:206
   opinion deviance and, 2:617
   reference groups and, 2:685
   on Trucking Game, 1:205
Deviance, 1:206–211
   deviant groups, defined, 1:210–211
   opinion deviance, 2:617–620
   psychological perspectives on, 1:208–211
   reaction to deviant group members, 1:209–210
   social deviance and, 2:774–776
   sociological perspectives on, 1:206–208
   subjective group dynamics and, 2:865
Devine, Patricia, 2:573
DeWall, C. Nathan, 1:441
Dickens, Charles, 1:293
Dickson, Markus, 1:458–459
Diehl, Michael, 1:60, 2:851
Diener, Edward, 1:192, 1:211
Differentiated knowledge, 2:931
Differentiation, 1:185–186
Diffuse status characteristics, 2:522, 2:845
Diffusion of responsibility, 1:307
DiFonzo, Nicholas, 2:721
Digg, 2:950–251
DiMaggio, Paul, 1:455
Dion, Kenneth L., 1:317, 1:329
Direct exchange, 2:787
Direct observation process, 2:701
Directory updating, 2:931
Discontinuity effect, 2:902

Discourse-based learning process, in action research, 1:4–5
Discrimination, 1:211–217
   blatant, 1:212
   examples of contemporary discrimination, 1:214–217
   feminism and, 1:282
   subtle, 1:212–214
   toward immigrants, 1:431
   See also Prejudice
Disengaged parents, 1:277
Disengagement, 2:563
Dishion, Thomas, 1:83
Distinctiveness-based illusory correlation, 1:425–426
Distraction-conflict theory, 2:792–793
Distributed groups, 1:96
Distributive fairness judgments, 2:693
Distributive justice, 1:217–219, 1:501–502, 2:664
District of Columbia, 2:758
Divergence criteria (DC), 1:378, 1:379
Divergent outcomes, 2:644
Diversity, 1:219–225
   diversities within, 1:220
   education and training, 1:224–225
   group performance vs. dynamics, 1:221–222
   policies, 1:222–224
Dodds, Peter, 1:270
Dodge, Kenneth, 1:81
Doe v. Belleville, 2:750
Dogmatism, 1:225–227
   historical overview of, 1:225–226
   implications of, 1:226–227
   origins of, 1:226
   related constructs, 1:226
Doherty, Mary, 1:459
Dollard, John, 1:290–291, 1:396, 2:655
Domain-specific self-esteem, 2:732
Dominance hierarchies, 1:227–229
   allocating ranks, 1:227–228
   conversation and, 1:228–229
   need for power and, 2:600–601
   testosterone and, 1:229
Doob, Leonard, 1:290, 2:754
Dorr's Rebellion of 1842, 1:489
Double-barreled questions, 2:879
Dovidio, John, 1:198, 1:470, 2:676, 2:846
Downing, Leslie, 1:193
Drescher, Stuart, 1:316
Drive, social facilitation and, 2:792
Drug abuse, social representations and, 2:826
Dual concern theory, 2:604–605
Duality of structures, 2:893
Dual-process theory of social influence, 1:442–443
Duckitt, John, 1:47–48, 2:783
Duke, David, 2:884
Dunbar, Robin, 1:128, 2:720–721
Durkheim, Émile, 1:104, 1:113, 1:179, 1:206, 2:865
   deviance and, 1:209
   group structure and, 1:381, 1:382, 2:581
   social representations and, 2:823

Dyads, 1:229–231
    categorizing, 1:229–230
    context of, for understanding social phenomena, 1:231
    dyadic-level and individual-level variables, 1:230
    interdependence between individuals and, 1:230
    special considerations for, 1:230–231
Dynamical systems approach, 1:231–234
    chaos and complexity in therapeutic groups, 1:233
    continuous/discontinuous change in accident rates,
        1:232–233
    historical overview, 1:232
    methods, 1:232
    self-organization in group formation, 1:233–234
Dynamic social impact theory, 2:807–808
Dynamogenic Factors in Pacemaking and Competition,
    The (Triplett), 1:381
Dysfunction, within family system, 1:278

Eagly, Alice, 1:144, 1:297, 1:300, 1:303, 1:418, 2:713
Earley, Christopher, 2:665
Ebaugh, Helen Rose Fuchs, 2:715–716
Economic game theory, 2:778
Education Amendments of 1972, 2:750
Egocentrism, 1:251
Egoistic deprivation, 1:501
Ego justification, 2:888
Egypt, 2:602
Eichmann, Adolf, 1:53, 1:403
Eichmann in Jerusalem (Arendt), 1:53
Eisenberger, Naomi, 1:441
Eisenhower, Dwight, 1:223
Elaborated social identity model (ESIM), 1:171–172
Elderspeak, 1:216
Elites, 2:562, 2:782
Elliott, Jane, 2:543
Emancipation Proclamation, 1:84, 2:758
Embedding knowledge, group learning and, 1:345
Emergent mediation, 2:550
Emergent norm theory (ENT), 1:170–171, 1:235–238,
    1:236–237
Emerson, Ralph Waldo, 2:542
Emerson, Richard M., 1:383, 2:653–654, 2:787–789
Emotion
    collective action and, 1:108
    emotion equations and affect control theory, 1:7–8
    emotion-focused minority coping strategies, 2:559–560
    inclusion/exclusion and, 1:442
    intergroup emotions theory, 1:473–475
    interpersonal power and, 2:650
    relational cohesion theory and, 2:690
    sociology of emotions, 2:542–543
Emotional intelligence, 2:641
Empathy, 2:543
Employment settings. See Workplace
Encoding information, group memory and, 1:347
Encyclopedia of Social Sciences, 2:728
Endorsement, 2:525
Engels, Friedrich, 1:418
Enlightenment, 2:774

Entitativity, 1:238–241, 2:638, 2:729
    perceived, 1:238–239
    perceived, and perceived similarity, 1:240
    perceived, consequences, 1:239–240
Entry criterion (EC), 1:377
Envious prejudice, 1:307, 1:402
Epistemic motives, conservatism and, 1:146
Equal division norm, 2:611
Equal Employment Opportunity Commission (EEOC), 1:86
Equal excess theory, 1:92
Equifinality, 2:890, 2:892
Equipment models, 2:752
Equitable exchange, 2:927
Equity norm, 2:611
Equity theory, 1:218
Error correction, group memory and, 1:346–347
Escalation of commitment, 1:241–243
    background and causes, 1:241–243
    importance of, 1:241
Esperanto, 1:253
Essay on the Principle of Population, An (Malthus), 2:768
Essentialism, 1:243–245, 2:944
    defined, 1:243–244
    implications of, 1:244–245
    importance of, 1:245
Eternal Jew, The, 1:402
Ethics
    experimentation and, 1:264
    obedience to authority and, 2:615–616
Ethics (Aristotle), 1:217
Ethnic cleansing, 1:305
Ethnicity, 1:245–247
    collective self and, 1:111–112
    definition and comparison, 1:245–246
    extended contact effect and, 1:266–267
    significance for identity, 1:246–247
    stereotype threat and, 2:853–854
Ethnocentrism, 1:247–252
    historical overview, 1:248
    ingroup bias and, 1:248–250
    realistic conflict theory and, 2:755
    self-categorization theory and, 2:730
    theories of, 1:250–252
Ethnolinguistic identity theory, 1:252
Ethnolinguistic vitality, 1:252–255
    future directions, 1:254
    language and intergroup relations, 1:252–253
    language attitudes and, 1:254
    multilingualism and, 1:253–254
Ethnophaulisms, 2:512, 2:761
Eugenics, 1:255–258
    contemporary importance, 1:256–257
    historical overview, 1:255–256
    social Darwinism and, 2:769
European Association of Experimental Social
    Psychology, 2:580, 2:899
European Journal of Social Psychology, 2:899
European Laboratory of Social Psychology, 2:581
European Organization for Nuclear Research, 2:951

European social psychology, 2:580
European Union, 1:108, 1:159, 2:564, 2:583
Evaluation apprehension, 1:60
Evaluation groups, 2:686
Evaluation potential perspective, 2:809
Evaluation theory, 2:792
Evaluative structures, performance and, 1:358
Evans, Charles, 1:317
Evans, Martin, 1:153
Everquest (game), 2:950
Evolution, cooperation/competition and,
    1:155–154
Evolutionary psychology, 1:258–262
    basic assumptions of, 1:258–259
    intergroup processes and, 1:260–261
    intragroup processes and, 1:259–260
    social dominance theory and, 2:782
Exception subtyping, 2:869
Exclusion
    group boundaries and, 1:315
    opinion deviance and, 2:618–620
    See also **Inclusion/exclusion**
Exemplar-based models, 2:638
Exemplar view, of categories, 1:69
Existential motives, conservatism and, 1:146–147
Exit criteria, group socialization and, 1:379
Expectancy-based illusory correlation, 1:426–427
Expectancy theory, 2:767
    path-goal theory of leadership and, 2:635
    social loafing and, 2:810
Expectation states theory. *See* **Status characteristics/**
    expectation states theory
Expected utility theory, social dilemmas and, 2:778
Experimentation, 1:262–265
    ethics and, 1:264
    historical overview, 1:262–263
    types of experiments, 1:263–264
Expert groups, jigsaw classroom technique and, 1:492
Explanandum/explanans, 1:351
Explicit coordination, 2:670
Explicit measures, 2:732
Extended contact effect, 1:265–267
    implications of, 1:267
    supporting evidence for, 1:265–266
    underlying processes of, 1:266–267
External representation, 1:58
External validity, defined, 1:263
Extraversion, 2:640
Extremism, 2:945
Eysenck, Hans, 1:47, 1:208

Facebook, 1:97, 1:136, 1:269, 2:949–951
Facesaving function of mediation, 2:551
Face-to-face interviews, 2:879
Factionalism, 2:727–728
Factions, 2:725
Fads and fashions, 1:269–272
    body image and, 1:271–272
    historical overview, 1:269–270

    organizational fashions, 1:271
    social influence and, 1:270–271
Fair Housing Act of 1968, 1:84, 1:88
Fairness
    common-identity *vs.* common-bond groups, 1:117–118
    ethnocentrism and, 1:248–249
Fairness heuristic theory, 2:665
Fairness norms, 2:611
Fair process effect, 2:664
"Faithfulness gene," 2:825
False consciousness, 2:760
False consensus effect, 1:272–275
    explanations of, 1:273
    historical overview, 1:272–273
    implications of, 1:274
    related constructs, 1:273–274
False uniqueness bias, 1:273
Families, 1:275–278
    family as system, 1:278
    family socialization processes, 1:276–278
    family support groups, 2:875
Farr, Rob, 2:530
Faultlines, 1:220, 1:278–281
    defined, 1:279
    examples and implications, 1:280
    recent research on, 1:280–281
Fawkes, Guy, 2:916
Feather, Norman, 1:418
Federal Bureau of Investigation, 1:216
Federalist Papers, 1:483
Fédération Internationale de Football Association World
    Cup, 2:836
Federico, Christopher, 1:47
Feldman, Stanley, 1:47
Female gangs, 1:294
Feminism, 1:281–284
    historical overview, 1:281
    relevance to intergroup relations, 1:281–284
    social dominance theory and, 2:782
Festinger, Leon, 1:94, 1:130, 1:191, 1:284–287,
    2:762, 2:865, 2:898
    background, 1:284
    on cognitive dissonance, 1:286–287
    deviance and, 1:209
    ethnocentrism and, 1:251
    group cohesiveness and, 1:316
    group mind and, 1:351
    group polarization and, 1:364
    informational influence and, 1:443
    opinion deviance and informal social
        communication, 2:617
    on social comparison, 1:285–286
    social comparison theory and, 2:762
    social comparison theory and relative
        deprivation, 2:695, 2:697
    on social pressures in informal groups, 1:284–285
Fichte, Johann Gottlieb, 1:349
Fiedler, Fred, 1:152–154, 1:358, 1:387, 2:521, 2:828
Fiedler, Klaus, 2:515, 2:538

Field experimentation, 1:263–264
Field theory, 2:533, 2:534
Filtering, 1:58
Finholt, Tom, 2:949
First Principles (Spencer), 2:768
Fischer, Gregory, 2:868
Fisher, Roger, 2:602
Fiske, Susan T., 1:17–19, 1:29, 1:189,
    2:647–648, 2:658, 2:843
Fission, 2:726
Fixed-pie assumption, 2:605–606
Flickr, 2:951
Florida International University, 2:836
Focus theory of normative conduct, 2:610–611
Folger, Robert, 2:664
Folkman, Susan, 1:167
Folkways (Sumner), 1:248
Follett, Mary Parker, 2:602
Followers/followership, 2:718–719
Forbes, Hugh, 1:472
Ford, Henry, 2:624
Ford Motor Company, 1:390
Forgiveness, genocide and, 1:308
Fortune 500, 2:799
Fourteenth Amendment, 1:200
Frankfurt/Berkeley School, 1:45
Frankfurt School, 1:22, 2:656
Fraternal deprivation, 1:501, 2:695
Freeman, Linton, 1:384
Freeman v. Pitts, 1:200
Free riding, 1:287–289
    historical overview, 1:287–288
    process gain and loss and, 2:670
    related processes, 1:289
    research findings, 1:288–289
    social dilemmas and, 2:778
    sucker effect and, 2:871
Free-Soilers, 2:758
Free Soil Republican party, 2:758
Freezing, 2:598, 2:742
French, John, 2:647
French Canadians. *See* Canada
Frenkel-Brunswik, Elsa, 1:45, 1:419, 2:706
Freud, Sigmund, 1:21, 1:191, 1:208, 1:409, 2:566, 2:583
    ethnocentrism and, 1:250
    need for belonging and, 2:595
    scapegoating theory and, 2:723–724
Friedkin, Noah, 2:787
Fromm, Erich, 1:208, 2:705
Frustration-aggression hypothesis, 1:289–292, 2:683
    applications to intergroup relations, 1:290–291
    background and assumptions, 1:290
    criticism and modifications, 1:291–292
    hate crimes and, 1:396
    scapegoating and, 2:724
Frustration and Aggression (Dollard, Doob, Miller, Mowrer,
    Sears), 1:290
Fugitive Slave Law, 2:758
Fuhriman, Addie, 1:233

Full ingroup-outgroup designs, 2:636
Functional magnetic resonance imaging (fMRI), 2:858
Fundamental attribution error, 1:135, 2:941–942
    conspiracy theories and, 1:150
    obedience to authority and, 2:614
Fundamental Interpersonal Relations Orientation, 1:325

Gacaca (tribunals), 1:481
Gaertner, Samuel, 1:198, 1:470, 2:660, 2:676
Galbraith, John Kenneth, 2:764
Galileo, 2:566
Galinsky, Maeda, 1:326
Galton, Francis, 1:255, 2:768
Gamblers Anonymous, 2:875
Game theory, 1:156, 2:661
Gandhi, Mohandas, 1:73–74
Gangs, 1:293–296
    composition of, 1:294
    crime and, 1:294–295
    historical overview, 1:293
    institutionalization of, 1:296
    methods of studying, 1:293–294
    victimization and, 1:295
Gardner, William, 1:458
Garfinkel, Harold, 2:715
Garrett, James, 2:672
Gatekeeping and monitoring, 1:277
Gay Activists' Alliance, 2:875
Gays. *See* Homosexuality
Gender and behavior, 1:296–300
    locations of gender differences in behavior, 1:298–299
    perspectives on, 1:296–298
Gender roles, 1:300–304
    concept of, 1:300–301
    conformity and, 1:144
    deviation from, 1:301–302
    as diffuse status characteristic, 2:845
    discrimination and, 1:215
    essentialist beliefs and, 1:244–245
    female gangs, 1:294
    homophily and, 1:405–406
    impact on individuals and society, 1:303–304
    interpersonal power and, 2:649–650
    need for power and, 2:600
    origins of, 1:302–303
    self-concept and, 1:302
    sexism and, 2:744–749
    social dominance theory and, 2:784
    stereotype threat and, 2:853–854
    weight-based discrimination and, 2:954
Generalized exchange, 2:788
General systems theory, 2:891
Genetics
    cooperation/competition and, 1:155–154
    Moscovici on genetic model of minority influence, 2:580
Genocide, 1:304–309
    bystanders and supporters of, 1:307
    collective guilt and forgiveness, 1:308
    conditions leading to, 1:305–306

defined, **1**:305
    group emotions and, **1**:335–336
    heroes and resisters, **1**:307–308
    perpetrators of, **1**:306
    scapegoating and, **2**:724–725
    victims of, **1**:306–307
Genovese, Kitty, **1**:63–65
Genzlinger, Neil, **1**:53
Geography, collective action and, **1**:107
Gerard, Harold, **1**:142, **1**:444, **2**:617, **2**:685
German Crusade, **1**:22
Germinal (Zola), **1**:191
Gersick, Connie J. G., **1**:327, **1**:329, **2**:894
Gestalt, **1**:16, **1**:28, **2**:533, **2**:754
Get-acquainted paradigm, **2**:630
GI Joe, **1**:271
Giles, Howard, **1**:252, **2**:511–513
Gill, Diane, **1**:318
Glasgow Gang Observed, A (Patrick), **1**:294
Glass ceiling, **2**:749
Glass escalator, **2**:749
Glick, Peter, **1**:17–19, **2**:724–725
Global self-esteem, **2**:732, **2**:830
Goal-setting theory
    path-goal theory of leadership and, **2**:635
    social dilemmas and, **2**:779
Goertzel, Ted, **1**:47
Goethals, George, **1**:272–273
Goffman, Erving, **1**:408, **2**:543, **2**:558, **2**:710, **2**:861
Golden Panthers, **2**:836
Golden Rule, **2**:764
Golec, Agnieszka, **2**:599
Goleman, Daniel, **2**:641
Google, **1**:97, **1**:363
Goths, **1**:271, **1**:363
Graduated reciprocation in tension reduction (GRIT), 1:159,
    1:309–311
    applications of, **1**:310–311
    principles of, **1**:309–310
Graen, George, **2**:517–519, **2**:928
Granfield, Robert, **2**:715
Graves, James, **2**:708
Great Depression, **1**:290, **2**:735
Great Life Foundation, **2**:744
Great person theory of leadership, 1:311–313, 2:639
    critiques of, **1**:312–313
    historical overview, **1**:311–312
Great Wall of China, **1**:472
Green, Donald, **2**:959
Greenberg, Jeff, **2**:919
Green Line of Cyprus, **1**:472
Grey, Jim, **1**:98
Groff, Brad, **2**:792
Grossman, M., **2**:894
Grotenberg, Hanneke, **1**:222
Group boundaries, 1:313–316
    meaning seaking and, **1**:314
    origins and functions of, **1**:313–314
    permeability, **1**:313–314

strategic identity expression and, **1**:314–315
    threats of inclusion/exclusion, **1**:315
Group cohesiveness, 1:162, 1:316–320, 2:643
    development of, **1**:317
    ingroup relationships, **1**:317–319
    negative consequences of high levels of, **1**:319–320
    power-dependence theory and, **2**:653–654
    transformational leadership theories and, **2**:935
    of work teams, **2**:958
Group composition, 1:320–324
    as cause, **1**:322–324
    as consequence, **1**:321–322
    as context, **1**:322
    performance and, **1**:356–357
Group Decision Support Systems, **2**:702
Group development, 1:325–328
    group formation and, **1**:341–342
    group-level theories, **1**:325–326
    group socialization and, **1**:375
    multi-level theories, **1**:326–328
Group dissolution, 1:328–330
Group distinctiveness threat, **2**:800
Group diversity, **1**:221–222
    group cohesion and, **1**:319
    personnel turnover and, **2**:643
Group ecology, 1:330–335
    performance and, **1**:358–359
    physical environments and, **1**:331–332
    social environments and, **1**:332–334
    temporal environments and, **1**:334
    work environment and organizations,
        2:625–626
Group emotions, 1:335–339
    emotions based on identification with group,
        1:336–338
    historical overview, **1**:335–336
    in individual encounters with outgroup members, **1**:336
    related topics and new directions, **1**:338–339
Group formation, 1:339–342
    acting group formation, **1**:339–340
    formation as stage of group development, **1**:341–342
    self-organization of new standing groups, **1**:340–341
Group-generalized exchange, **2**:788
Group identification
    culture and, **1**:177
    self-esteem and, **2**:734
    transformational leadership theories and, **2**:935
    uncertainty-identity theory and, **2**:944
Group justification, **2**:888
Group learning, 1:342–346
    consequences, **1**:345
    learning process and, **1**:344–345
    research on, **1**:342–344
Group memory, 1:346–349
    group potency and, **1**:372
    shared mental models, **1**:348–349
    stages of group memory performance, **1**:347–348
    superior group performance and, **1**:346–347
    transactive memory, **1**:348

Group mind, 1:169, 1:349–351
  critique of, 1:350–351
  historical and philosophical overview, 1:349–350
  socially structured field in individual and, 1:351
Group Mind, The (McDougall), 1:350
Group motivation, 1:351–354
  historical overview, 1:352
  motivation gains, 1:353
  motivation losses, 1:352–353
  study of, 1:352
Group norms
  common-identity vs. common-bond groups,
    1:118–119
  deindividuation and, 1:193–194
  group cohesion and, 1:318–319
Group performance, 1:354–360
  actual vs. potential group productivity, 1:359–360
  diversity and, 1:221–222
  factors affecting, 1:356–359
  group task and, 1:387
  individual vs. group performance, 1:354–356
Group polarization, 1:361–365
  case of "risky shift" and, 1:361–362
  explaining, 1:364–365
  group problem solving and, 1:374
  group task and, 1:386
  juries and, 1:498
  opinions and, 1:362–364
  pluralistic ignorance and, 2:645
  referent informational influence theory and, 2:688
Group position theory, 1:365–368
  limitations of, 1:367
  related theories, 1:367
  research on, 1:367
  theory of, 1:366–367
Group potency, 1:368–370
  applications of, 1:370
  background, 1:368–369
  correlates of, 1:369–370
  factors affecting, 1:369
Group problem solving and decision making,
    1:370–375
  bystander effect and, 1:64
  common knowledge effect and, 1:123–125
  decision issue of Holocaust and, 1:401–402
  effective group decision making, 1:346
  escalation of commitment and, 1:241
  group memory and, 1:346
  group potency and, 1:373–375
  need for closure and, 2:598
  process gain and loss and, 2:669
  social decision schemes and, 2:773–777
Group relative deprivation, 2:695
Groups: Interaction and Performance (McGrath), 1:385
Group size, 1:320
Group socialization, 1:178, 1:375–380, 1:438, 2:894
  basic processes of, 1:376
  model of, 1:377 (figure)
  passage through group, 1:376–380

Group status threat, 2:800
Group structure, 1:381–385
  historical overview and background, 1:381–382
  in intergroup contexts, 1:384–385
  in intragroup contexts, 1:382–384
  performance and, 1:357
Group task, 1:385–390
  bottom-up approach, 1:386–387
  McGrath's Group Task Circumplex, 1:385–386, 1:388,
    1:389 (figure)
  top-down approach, 1:387–389
Group therapy, sociometric choice and, 2:832–833
Groupthink, 1:390–393
  group problem solving and, 1:374–375
  homophily and, 1:406
  methods for overcoming, 1:392
  pluralistic ignorance and, 2:645
  recent developments in, 1:391–392
  research on, 1:390–391
Group threat theory, 1:202
Group value model, 2:523
Growth need strength (GNS), 1:495
Gruenenthal Chemie, 1:390
Gruenfeld, Deborah, 2:647–648
Grutter v. Bollinger, 1:200
Guard activities, 1:58
Guastello, Stephen, 1:233
Guimond, Serge, 2:765
Guinote, Ana, 2:650
Gunn, Lawanna, 2:545
Gunpowder Plot, 2:916
Gurr, Ted R., 1:490, 2:696
Guzzo, Richard, 1:369

Hackman, Richard, 1:368, 1:387, 1:494
Hadrian's Wall, 1:472
Hafer, Carolyn, 1:505–506
Hagan, John, 1:295
Hagedorn, John, 1:296
Hahn, Eugene, 1:41
Hall, Edward T., 2:913, 2:915
Halloween, 1:192
Hamilton, Alexander, 1:483
Hamilton, T. E., 1:138
Hamilton, William, 2:769
Handbook of Research Methods in Social and Personality
    Psychology (Hastie, Stasser), 1:138
Handbook of Social Psychology (Abelson), 1:138
Haney, Craig, 2:837
Hanges, Paul, 1:458–459
Hanley, John, 2:744
Happiness, social comparison theory and, 2:764–765
Harary, Frank, 1:383
Hardin, Garrett, 1:125–126
Hardy, James, 1:319
Harkins, Stephen, 2:709, 2:810
Harlow, Harry, 1:79, 1:276
Harper's Ferry, West Virginia, 2:758
Harris, Lasana, 1:189

Harris, Victor, 2:941
Harrison, Douglas, 1:220
Hart, Claire, 2:545
Harvard Project on Negotiation, 2:602
Harvard University, 1:16
Harwood Manufacturing Company, 2:625
Haslam, Alexander, 2:659
Haslam, Nick, 1:190
Hastie, Reid, 1:138, 2:807
Hate crimes, 1:395–398
    historical overview and modern targets of, 1:395–396
    theoretical approaches to, 1:396–398
    xenophobia and, 2:959
Hate speech, 2:512
Hawthorne studies, 2:625
Hazan, Cynthia, 1:38
Heaven's Gate, 1:174
Hebl, Michelle, 1:216
Hecht, Tracy, 1:424
Hegel, Georg Wilhelm Friedrich, 1:349
Heider, Fritz, 1:42, 1:93, 1:382–383
Heise, David, 1:6
Helmreich, Robert, 1:39–40
Hendricks, Gay, 2:744
Hendricks, Kathlyn, 2:744
Henrich, C. C., 1:90
Herder, Johann Gottfried, 1:349
Hereditary Genius (Dalton), 2:769
Heredity in Relation to Eugenics (Davenport), 1:255
Herek, Gregory, 1:216
Herrnstein, Richard J., 1:256
Hersey, Paul, 1:154
Herzberg, Frederick, 1:494
Heteronormativity, 1:407
Heterosexism, 1:407
Heuristic reasoning, juries and, 1:500
Hewstone, Miles, 1:187, 1:470, 2:587, 2:825
Hidden profile task, 1:123, 1:398–400
    causes of poor performance, 1:399
    limitations of, 1:400
    remedies, 1:399–400
    socially shared cognition and, 2:813
    task illustration, 1:398–399
Higham, T. M., 2:720
High social dominance orientation, 2:563
Hill, Gayle, 1:355
"Hinglish," 1:253–254
Hinz, Verlin, 1:221
Hirschi, Travis, 1:207
Hirschman, Albert, 2:728
Hitler, Adolf, 1:21, 1:55, 1:74, 1:400.
    See also **Holocaust**
Hobbes, Thomas, 1:113, 1:155
Hochschild, Arlie Russell, 1:299, 2:543
Hoffman, L. Richard, 1:221
Hofstadter, Richard, 1:150, 2:769
Hofstede, Geert, 1:113, 1:179
Hogg, Michael, 1:47, 1:197, 1:316, 2:523, 2:687, 2:730, 2:801, 2:943

Hollander, Edwin, 1:210, 1:313, 1:420–422, 2:517–518, 2:521, 2:619, 2:928
Hollenbeck, John, 2:956
Holocaust, 1:22, 1:24, 1:255, 1:305, 1:400–403, 2:655, 2:899
    anticonformity and, 1:21
    anti-Semitism and, 1:22–25
    bystander issues and, 1:403
    decision issue and, 1:401–402
    genocide and, 1:308
    group emotions and, 1:335–336
    historical overview of, 1:400–401
    multiculturalism and, 2:582
    obedience to authority and, 2:616
    perpetrator issues and, 1:402–403
    prejudice and, 2:655–656
    scapegoating, 2:723
    scapegoating and, 2:725
    social psychological perspectives of, 1:401
Homans, George, 1:383, 2:517, 2:652, 2:787
"Home advantage," sports teams and, 2:836
Homophily, 1:404–407
    bases and patterns of, 1:405–406
    consequences of, 1:406
    types of, 1:404–405
Homophobia, 1:407–410
    historical overview, 1:407–408
    importance of, 1:409–410
    social distance and, 1:408–409
Homosexuality
    discrimination against, 1:216–217
    essentialism and, 1:245
    homophobia and, 1:407–410
    prejudice and, 2:655–656
Hook, Sidney, 1:309
Horton, Willie, 2:884
Host Community Acculturation Scale (HCAS), 1:32
Hostile environment, sexual harassment and, 2:750
House, Robert, 1:153, 2:635
Household labor, 1:299
Hovland, Carl, 1:396, 2:566
Howard, Henry, 2:913
How To Think Like a Social Scientist (Pettigrew), 2:530
Hugo, Victor, 1:191
Huguet, Pascal, 2:793
Hulin, Charles, 1:138
Human Behavior and Evolution Society, 2:769
Human Legacy, The (Festinger), 1:287
Human relations training, 2:742
Hummert, Mary Lee, 2:512
Huntington, Samuel, 1:486
Hunyady, Orsolya, 2:890
Hurricane Katrina, 2:721
Hurting stalemate, 2:551
Hussein, Saddam, 1:149, 2:562
Hutus, 1:306, 1:480–481, 2:725
Hyman, Herbert, 2:684–685
Hypothesis, defined, 1:262

IAT. *See* Implicit Association Test (IAT)
ICCCR. *See* International Center for Cooperation and
    Conflict Resolution (ICCCR)
Identification and commitment, 1:411–415, 2:686
    common ingroup identity and intergroup violence, 1:481
    cultivating commitment among group members,
        1:414–415
    cultivating normative commitment through social control,
        1:412–413
    dimension models of commitment, 1:411–412
    ethnicity and, 1:246
    fashion and, 1:270–271
    feminism and, 1:281–282
    gender and behavior, 1:296–297
    group benefit from members' normative commitment
        and, 1:413
    group emotions and, 1:336–337
    group identification, 1:413–414
    intergroup emotions theory and, 1:475
    leaders as entrepreneurs of, 2:803–804
    national, 1:430–431
    personal identity, 2:798
    person identities, 1:416
    social/personal, and ethnocentrism, 1:251–252
    social psychology of schism and, 2:726
    symbolic interactionism and, 2:882
Identity control theory, 1:415–417
    bases of identity and, 1:416
    control of perceptions and, 1:416
    emotions and, 1:417
    identity change and, 1:417
    identity verification and, 1:416
    meaning and, 1:415–416
    multiple identities and, 1:416–417
Identity threat, 2:800
Identity verification, 1:416
Ideology, 1:147, 1:417–420
    features of, 1:418
    importance of, 1:420
    politics and, 1:418–420
Idiosyncrasy credit, 1:420–422, 2:518, 2:521, 2:619
    related research, 1:421–422
    theoretical origins and, 1:421
Iellatchitch, Alexandre, 1:451
Ilgen, Daniel, 1:138, 2:910, 2:956, 2:958
Illusion of group effectivity, 1:422–425
    brainstorming and, 1:423–424
    implications of, 1:424
    romance of teams and, 1:424
Illusory correlation, 1:425–427
    distinctiveness-based illusory correlation, 1:425–426
    expectancy-based illusory correlation, 1:426–427
Immigrant Acculturation Scale (IAS), 1:35
Immigration, 1:427–432
    acculturation and, 1:428–429
    attitudes toward immigrants and immigration in host
        society, 1:429–431
    discrimination toward immigrants, 1:431
    push and pull factors of, 1:428

    reciprocal relations between immigrants and members of
        host society, 1:431
    See also Xenophobia
Implicit Association Test (IAT), 1:49, 1:75, 1:432–435,
    1:438, 2:574, 2:577, 2:659, 2:858, 2:889
    construct and predictive validity of, 1:434
    defined, 1:432–433
    discoveries about intergroup cognition, 1:433
    evidence about bias, 1:433–434
Implicit coordination
    process gain and loss and, 2:670
    shared mental models and, 2:751
Implicit leadership theories (ILT), 2:515–516
Implicit measures, self-esteem and, 2:732
Implicit prejudice, 1:435–439
    critique of, 1:437–438
    manifestations, 1:436
    measuring, 1:436–437
    origins and prevalence, 1:435–436
Impression formation
    affect control theory and, 1:7–8
    Asch on, 1:28–29
    common-identity *vs.* common-bond groups, 1:119
    social comparison theory and, 2:762–763
Inbreeding homophily, 1:404–405
Inclusion/exclusion, 1:439–442
    belonging to groups as fundamental need, 1:439
    group boundaries and, 1:315
    inclusion of the group in the self, 1:266–267
    inside/outside laboratory, 1:439–440
    negative consequences of exclusion, 1:440–441
    opinion deviance and, 2:618–620
    positive consequences of exclusion, 1:441–442
Independence, anticonformity and, 1:20
Independent variables, defined, 1:262
Index of agreeement, 1:318
Indiana Pacers, 2:836
Indirect exchange, 2:787–788
Indirect measurement, 2:732
Indirect reciprocity, 2:778
Individual and His Religion, The (Allport), 1:16
Individual mobility, 2:799
Individuals, 1:429
    collective induction *vs.* individual induction, 1:101–102
    conformity and, 1:143–144
    deviation and, 1:208
    group emotions and, 1:336
    impact of gender roles on, 1:303–304
    individualism, 1:33
    individual racism, 2:677–679
    individual representations, 2:823
    intraindividual levels of analysis, 2:531 (figure), 2:532
    juries as, 1:497–498
    loyalty to, and relationships, 2:545
    multiple identities and, 2:585–587
    performance of, *vs.* group performance, 1:354–356
    personal spaces of, 1:332
    satisfaction and group cohesion, 1:318
    social decision schemes and, 2:771–773, 2:772 (tables)

socially structure field in, and group mind, **1**:351
social networks and, **2**:819
terrorism at individual level, **2**:917
ultimate attribution error and, **2**:942–943
See also **Collectivism/individualism;** Individuation
Individuation
common ingroup identity and intergroup violence, **1**:481
decategorization and, **1**:185–186
Induced homophily, **1**:404
Inequity theory, **1**:218
Informal social communication theory, **2**:617
Informational influence, 1:130, 1:442–445
conformity and, **1**:141–142, **1**:142
debate and controversy, **1**:444
group polarization and, **1**:364
historical overview and background, **1**:444
juries and, **1**:498
normative influence and, **2**:606–607
opinion deviance and, **2**:617–618
reference informational influence theory and, **2**:687
Information allocation, **2**:931
Informational social influence, **1**:269, **1**:270
Information pooling, **1**:346
Information processing, **1**:58
entitativity and, **1**:239
interactionist theory and, **1**:458–459
need for closure and, **2**:598
Information retrieval, group memory and, **1**:347–348
Information sharing
process gain and loss and, **2**:669–670
rumor and, **2**:720–721
Information storage, group memory and, **1**:347
Ingham, Alan, **2**:708–709, **2**:808
Ingham, Richard, **1**:352
Ingham project, **2**:708–709
Inglehart, Ronald, **1**:113
Ingroup allocation bias, 1:445–448
discrimination in minimal groups, **1**:445–446
historical overview, **1**:445
resource allocations using Tajfel matrices, **1**:446–448
Initiation rites, 1:448–451
description, **1**:448–449
explaining impact of, **1**:449–450
group characteristics and, **1**:450–451
Innovation, 1:451–454
basic distinctions, **1**:451–452
determinants of team innovation, **1**:452
major findings in, **1**:452–454
Input-mediator-output-input (IMOI), **2**:956
Input-process-output (IPO), **2**:956
Inquiries Into Human Faculty and Its Development (Galton), **2**:769
Insko, Chester, **1**:157, **1**:159
Institutionalized bias, 1:454–456
Institutional racism, **2**:677, **2**:679
Institutional support, ethnolinguistic vitality and, **1**:252
Integrated knowledge, **2**:931
Integrated threat theory of prejudice, **1**:429

Integration
ethnicity and, **1**:246
integrationism, **1**:32
Integrative agreements, **2**:602–606
Integrity, **2**:641
Intellective tasks, group potency and, **1**:371
Intelligence
leadership and, **2**:640
leadership and emotional intelligence, **2**:641
self-fulfilling prophecy and, **2**:736–737
INTERACT, **1**:8
Interaction groups, **2**:686
Interactionist theories of leadership, 1:456–459
interactionist models of leadership, **1**:458–459
interactionist perspective, **1**:457
interactionist perspective and leadership, **1**:457–458
person-situation debate, **1**:457
Interaction process analysis, 1:383, 1:459–462
analysis of group processes using, **1**:461
content and coding of, **1**:460
development of, and its extensions, **1**:460–461
evaluation of, **1**:461
Interdependence theory, 1:462–465
cooperation and competition, **1**:157
interdependence structure, **1**:463
power and, **2**:648
social dilemmas and, **2**:778–779
team building and, **2**:899–900
transformation of situations, **1**:463–464
Interglobal level of analysis, **2**:530, **2**:531 (figure)
Intergroup anxiety, 1:336, 1:465–468
causes of, **1**:465–466
consequences of, **1**:466–467
directions for future research, **1**:467–468
reducing, and improving intergroup relations, **1**:467
Intergroup contact theory, 1:468–473, 2:587
critique of, **1**:472
explanatory models, **1**:470
future directions of, **1**:472
generalization of effects, **1**:470
group structure, **1**:384–385
historical overview and background, **1**:468–469
interindividual-intergroup discontinuity and, **1**:485
policy implications of, **1**:473
prejudice and, **1**:469–470
when/how contact effects occur, **1**:471
Intergroup discrimination, self-esteem and, **2**:732–733
Intergroup emotions theory, 1:337, 1:473–475
evidence supporting, **1**:474–475
focused *vs.* general emotions, **1**:474
historical overview, **1**:473
key themes of, **1**:475
Intergroup empathy, 1:475–478
practical and policy implications, **1**:477
research findings, **1**:476–477
types of, **1**:476
Intergroup leadership, **2**:804
Intergroup level of analysis, **2**:531–532, **2**:531 (figure)
Intergroup power, **2**:648, **2**:651

Intergroup relations
  cognitive consistency and, 1:95–96
  cross-categorization and, 1:164
  desegregation and, 1:202
  ethnolinguistic vitality and, 1:252–253
  evolutionary psychology, 1:260–261
  feminism and, 1:281–284
  frustration-aggression hypothesis and, 1:290–291
  hate crimes and, 1:397–398
  intergroup anxiety and, 1:467
  self-fulfilling prophecy and, 2:735–737
  sociometer model and, 2:830–831
  subtyping and, 2:869–870
  xenophobia and, 2:960
Intergroup status. See Status
Intergroup violence, 1:478–482
  background and origins, 1:478–479
  factors promoting, 1:479–480
  strategies for promoting intergroup
      harmony, 1:480–482
Interindividual-intergroup discontinuity, 1:482–446
  generality of effect, 1:484
  historical overview, 1:483
  intergroup cooperation and, 1:485
  laboratory evidence, 1:483–484
  mechanisms producing effect, 1:484–485
  nonlaboratory evidence, 1:484
Interindividual levels of analysis, 2:531 (figure), 2:532
Internalization, 1:130
Internal validity, defined, 1:263
Internal working model, 1:276
International Center for Cooperation and Conflict
      Resolution (ICCCR), 1:204, 1:206
International Committee of the Red Cross, 2:550
International Monetary Fund, 1:108
Internet. See Virtual/Internet groups
Interpersonal power, 2:649–651
Interpositional knowledge training, 2:753
Interpretive action verbs (IAV), 2:536, 2:538–539
Interpretive reliability, 2:704
Intersocietal level of analysis, 2:531, 2:531 (figure)
Intimacy groups, 1:238–239
Intimate relationships, 1:298
In Touch, 2:875
Intraglobal level of analysis, 2:530, 2:531 (figure)
Intragroup (ingroup) processes, 2:532
  evolutionary psychology and, 1:259–260
  group cohesiveness and, 1:317–319
  group structure, 1:382–384
  multiculturalism and, 2:583–584
  See also Categorization
Intragroup status. See Status
Intraindividual levels of analysis,
      2:531 (figure), 2:532
Intranets, 2:933
Intrasocietal level of analysis,
      2:531, 2:531 (figure)
Invasion studies, 1:332
Iron law of oligarchy, 2:818

Islamophobia, 1:486–487
  historical overview, 1:486
  prevention and reduction of, 1:487
  psychological causes of, 1:486–487
Isozaki, Mititoshi, 1:362
Israel, realistic group conflict theory and, 2:682
Italian Communist Party, 2:726–727

Jackson, Jesse, 2:884
Jacobs, Robert, 1:178
Jaggi, Vaishna, 2:942
Jago, Arthur, 1:153–154
Jahoda, Gustave, 1:193
Jahoda, Marie, 1:46
James, King, 2:916
James, William, 1:350, 1:384, 2:517,
      2:541, 2:731–732
Janicik, Gregory, 1:334
Janis, Irving, 1:319, 1:374, 1:390, 1:392
Jay, John, 1:483
J-curve hypothesis, 1:489–491
  historical overview and background, 1:489–490
  relative deprivation theory, 1:490
  weaknesses of research on, 1:490–491
Jealousy, 1:318
Jefferson, Thomas, 1:29
Jefferson County, Kentucky, 1:200
Jensen, Mary Ann, 1:325–326, 1:329
Jermier, John, 1:153
JFK, 1:150
Jigsaw classroom technique, 1:491–493
Jim Crow, 1:27, 1:455, 2:883
Job characteristic theory (JCT), 1:494–495
Job design, 1:493–495
  early work on, 1:494
  job characteristic theory (JCT), 1:494–495
  Job Diagnostic Survey (JDS), 1:495
Jobs, Steve, 2:882
Johns Hopkins University, 1:161
Johnson, Lyndon B., 1:8, 1:149
Johnson, Mark, 2:840
Johnson, Michael, 2:956
Johnson, Robert, 1:193
Johnson-Laird, Philip, 2:751
Joint control (JC), 1:463
Jones, E. E., 2:862
Jones, Edward, 2:941
Jones, James, 1:74, 2:546, 2:641, 2:677, 2:679
Jones, Ned, 2:676
Jones, Richard, 2:716
Jost, John T., 1:111, 1:147, 1:418, 1:419–420,
      2:599, 2:888, 2:890
Journal of Applied Behavioral Science, 2:742
Journal of Experimental Social
      Psychology, 1:138
Judd, Charles, 2:869
Judgmental issues
  juries and, 1:498
  normative influence and, 2:606–607

Judgmental tasks
    group potency and, 1:371
    group task and, 1:387
Julian, James, 1:421
Jundt, Dustin, 2:956
Jung, Carl Gustav, 1:350
Juries, 1:496–500
    as groups, 1:498–500
    as individuals, 1:497–498
    mock jury decisions and group potency, 1:373–374
    problems of studying, 1:496–497
    socially shared cognition and, 2:813
Justice, 1:500–504
    distributive, 1:501–502
    procedural, 1:502–503
    retributive, 1:503–504
    roots of justice research, 1:501
Just world hypotheses, 1:307, 1:504–506
    historical overview and background, 1:505–506
    importance of, 1:506
    status and, 2:843
Just World Scale, 1:505

Kaczynski, Ted, 2:918
Kalick, S. M., 1:138
Kameda, Tatsuya, 2:807
Kamphoff, Cindra, 1:318
Kandinsky, Wassily, 2:555–556, 2:658
Kanfer, Ruth, 2:665
Kansas-Nebraska Act of 1854, 2:758
Kanter, Rosabeth Moss, 1:299, 1:414, 2:925
Karau, Steven, 1:334, 2:809
Kashima, Yoshihisa, 2:721
Katz, Irwin, 2:675–676
Keating, Caroline, 1:450
Keech, Mrs., 1:286
Kelley, Harold H., 1:42, 1:462, 2:517, 2:603, 2:648, 2:652,
    2:685–686, 2:695, 2:787
Kelly, Janice R., 1:334, 2:785–786
Kelman, Herbert, 1:130, 1:412
Keltner, Dacher, 2:647–648
Kennedy, John F., 1:8, 1:74, 1:88, 1:149–150,
    1:310–311, 1:375
Kenny, David, 2:821–822
Kent State, 1:390
Kerr, Norbert, 1:208, 1:288–289, 2:870
Kerr, Steve, 1:153
Kerry, John, 2:921
Keynoting, 1:235–236
Keyton, Joann, 1:329
Khmer Rouge, 1:305
Killian, Lewis, 1:170, 1:235–237
Kimmel, Michael S., 1:409
Kinder, Don, 2:676
King, Martin Luther, Jr., 1:73–74, 1:85, 1:87–88, 2:543
King, Rodney, 1:397
Kinsey, Alfred, 2:647
Kirkpatrick, Clifford, 1:40
Kitayama, Shinobu, 1:113, 1:179

Kitt, Alice, 2:685
Klee, Paul, 2:555–556, 2:658
Kline, Wendy, 1:256
Knapp, Robert, 1:148
Knowledge
    group learning and, 1:345
    job characteristic theory (JCT) and, 1:495
    knowledge, skills, and abilities (KSAs), 1:452–453, 2:910
    scientific knowledge in action research, 1:5
Köhler, Otto, 1:353, 2:507–508, 2:709
Köhler effect, 2:507–509
    causes of, 2:508
    free riding and, 1:289
    group motivation and, 1:353
    historical overview, 2:507–508
    process gain and loss, 2:671
    research on, 2:508–509
Kollock, Peter, 2:789–790
Kolowski, Steve, 1:459
Korean War, 1:390
Koresh, David, 2:641
Kozlowski, Steve, 2:956–958
Kramer, Bernard, 1:291
Kramer, Roderick, 2:544
Krantz, James, 1:329
Krauss, Robert, 1:205
Kravitz, David, 2:708
Kressel, Ken, 2:551
Kristallnacht, 1:401
Kruglanski, Arie, 1:48, 2:597–598
Kuhn, Thomas, 2:533
Ku Klux Klan, 1:87, 1:192–194, 1:397, 2:583, 2:884
Kula ring, 2:788

Labeling, 1:207–208
Labeling equations, 1:7–8
Laboratory experimentation, 1:263
Lack of authorization, 2:526
Lacoursier, Roy, 1:326
Lag sequential analysis, 2:700
Lakoff, George, 2:840
Lambert, Wallace E., 1:254, 2:513, 2:583
Language. *See* **Ethnolinguistic vitality; Language and
    intergroup relations; Linguistic category model (LCM);
    Linguistic intergroup bias (LIB)**
Language and intergroup relations, 2:511–515
    management of social distance and, 2:511–512
    power and, 2:513–515
    prejudice and, 2:512–513
Large Group Awareness Training, 2:744
Large Hadron Collider, 2:951
Larson, James, 2:851
Larsson, Knut, 2:791
Lasswell, Harold, 2:728
Latané, Bibb, 1:64–65, 1:128–129, 1:139, 1:233–234,
    1:262–264, 2:709, 2:805–810
Lau, Dora, 1:220
Lauderdale, Patrick, 2:619
Laughlin, Patrick, 1:357, 1:387, 2:773

LaVoie, Lawrence, 2:821
Lawler, Edward, 2:654, 2:787–789
Lazarus, Richard, 1:167
Lea, Martin, 2:795
Leader categorization theory, 2:515–517, 2:522
Leader-member exchange (LMX) theory, 2:517–519, 2:521–522
   Graen team's work, 2:518–519
   historical overview, 2:517–518
   transactional leadership and, 2:928–929
Leadership, 2:520–524
   contingency theories of, 1:151–154, 2:520–521
   defined, 2:520
   effectiveness of leaders, 2:520
   group task and, 1:386
   innovation and, 1:453–454
   interactionist theories of, 1:456–459
   leader-member exchange (LMX) theory, 2:517–519
   in organizations, 2:626–627
   path-goal theory of, 2:635–637
   perceptions, schemas, stereotypes, 2:522
   personality theories of, 2:639–641
   romance of, 2:717–719
   social identity and, 2:522–523
   social identity theory of leadership, 2:801–804
   task-oriented *vs.* relationship-oriented leadership styles, 2:827–828
   team reflexivity and, 2:908
   of teams, 2:911
   transactional, 2:521–522
   transformational, 2:522
   trust and group value model, 2:523–524
Leadership (Burns), 2:929
Leadership Quarterly, 1:457
Leary, Mark, 1:316, 1:439, 2:596, 2:829, 2:834
Least Preferred Coworker Scale (LPC), 2:521, 2:828
Leavitt, Harold J., 1:128, 1:382–383
Le Bon, Gustave, 1:169–171, 1:191, 1:211, 1:235, 1:312, 1:350, 1:483
Lefebvre, Henri, 1:171
Legitimation, 2:524–527
   consequences of, 2:526–527
   emergence of, 2:525–526
Lemaine, Gerard, 1:111
Lemert, Edwin, 1:207
Lemkin, Raphael, 1:304–305
Leniency bias, 1:373
Leniency contract, 2:527–530
   elements of, 2:528–529
   related research, 2:529–530
   theoretical context, 2:528
Lenin, Vladimir, 1:29
Lenski, Gerhard, 1:46
Lerner, Melvin, 1:218, 1:505
Lesbians. *See* Homosexuality
Level of dependence, 1:463
Levels of analysis, 2:530–533
   multiple levels, 2:530–532, 2:531 (figure)
   relations among levels, 2:532–533

Leviathan (Hobbes), 1:155
Levine, John M., 1:178, 1:314, 1:376–378, 2:544, 2:618, 2:714, 2:894
   group composition and, 1:323–324
   group development and, 1:323–324, 1:324–328
   group dissolution and, 1:329
LeVine, Robert, 2:681
Levinger, George, 2:708
Levinson, Daniel J., 1:45–46, 2:706
Lévi-Strauss, Claude, 2:653, 2:787
Lévy-Bruhl, Lucien, 2:823
Lewicki, Roy, 1:448–449
Lewin, Kurt, 1:1–2, 1:117, 1:204, 1:232, 2:533–535, 2:754, 2:806, 2:894
   action research of, 2:535
   as empiricist, 2:534–535
   Festinger and, 1:284–287
   group cohesion and, 1:320
   group mind and, 1:351
   group performance, 1:355
   interactionist theories of leadership and, 1:457
   interaction process analysis, 1:460
   levels of analysis and, 2:532
   Lewin's field theory, 2:533, 2:534
   Lewin's paradigm shift in social psychology, 2:533–534
   sensitivity training groups and, 2:742
   on social class, 2:764
   socioemotional and task behavior, 2:827
Lewin, Miriam, 2:534
Leyens, Jacques-Philippe, 1:189–190, 2:865
Liao, Hui, 2:936
Libertarians, 2:562
Lieberman, Matthew, 1:441
Life-alone prognosis paradigm, 2:630
Lifespace, 1:457, 2:534
LifeSpring, 2:744
"Lightbulb" theory, 2:806
Lightdale, Jenifer R., 1:117
Likud Party, 1:34
Liminality, 2:713
Lincoln, Abraham, 1:84, 2:758
Lind, E. Allan, 2:665
Linguistic category model (LCM), 2:535–538
   features and applications, 2:537–538
   linguistic intergroup bias (LIB) and, 2:537, 2:538–539
   model of, 2:536–537
   using language to describe people, 2:536
Linguistic expectancy bias (LEB), 2:540
Linguistic intergroup bias (LIB), 2:538–541
   interaction of speaker goals and recipient inferences, 2:540
   linguistic category model and, 2:537, 2:538–539
   measuring, 2:539
   underlying mechanisms, 2:539–540
LinkedIn.com, 2:932, 2:951
Linton, Ralph, 2:710
Linux, 2:624
Linville, Patricia, 2:676, 2:868
Lippitt, Ronald, 2:742

Little Engine That Could, The, 2:672
Little Rock, Arkansas, 1:20, 1:87
Liverpool, Scotland, 2:757
Locke, John, 1:113
Locomotion function of consensus, 2:617–618
Log linear analysis, 2:700
Lohr, Bethany, 1:409
Lombroso, Cesare, 2:774
Long Walk to Freedom (Mandela), 1:480
Looking-glass self, 2:541–544
Lord, Charles, 2:925, 2:927
Lord, Robert, 1:313, 1:458–459, 2:522
Lorenz, Konrad, 2:913
Lorenzi-Cioldi, Fabio, 2:823
Losada, M., 2:892
"Lose-switch" strategy, 2:663
Lotus Notes, 2:950
Lowe, Charles, 2:851
Loyalty, 2:544–547
    dilemmas, 2:546
    to groups, 2:544–545
    to principles, 2:545
    related constructs, 2:545–546
    to relationships and individuals, 2:545
Luther, Martin, 2:672
Lykken, David, 1:363

Maass, Ann, 2:515
Maccoby, Eleanor, 1:80, 1:362
Machiavelli, Niccolò, 1:418
Mackie, Diane, 1:473
MacKinnon, Catherine, 2:749
Macro role transitions, 2:714–716
Macrostructural theory, 1:202
Madison, James, 1:483
Mafia, 1:149, 1:182
Maintenance-oriented behavior
    group socialization and, 1:378
    process consultation and, 2:667–668
Maison des sciences de l'homme, Paris, 2:581
Malignant ageism, 1:14
Malinowski, Bronislaw, 2:653, 2:787–788
Malthus, Thomas, 2:768
Management by exception, 2:930
Manchester United, 2:836
Mandela, Nelson, 1:27, 1:422, 1:480, 2:522
Mannix, Elizabeth, 1:319, 2:957
Maori, 1:112
Mao Zedong, 1:419
Mapping, 1:58
Marathon groups, sensitivity training groups and, 2:743
March, James, 2:623–624
March on Washington, 1:88
Mark, Gloria, 2:950
Markov chain analysis, 2:700
Markovsky, Barry, 2:787–788
Marks, Gary, 1:273
Markus, Hazel, 1:113, 1:179
Marques, José, 1:55–56, 1:210, 2:865–866

Marshall, Thurgood, 1:87
Martin, Barbara, 2:708
Marx, Karl, 1:21, 1:113, 1:235, 1:418, 2:760–761
    emergent norm theory and, 1:235
    ideology and, 1:418
    J-curve hypothesis and, 1:489
    motivation and, 2:890–891
    on social class, 2:760
    social dominance theory and, 2:782
    system justification theory and, 2:890
Maslow, Abraham, 1:291, 2:595
Massachusetts Institute of Technology, 1:204, 1:284
Mate selection, computer simulation and, 1:137–138
Mauss, Marcel, 2:653, 2:787
Maximum differentiation, 1:447, 2:555
Maximum ingroup profit, 1:446, 2:555
Maximum joint profit, 2:555
Mayrhofer, Wolfgang, 1:451
McCarthy, John, 1:104–105
McCauley, Clark, 1:363
McConahay, John, 2:575
McDougall, William, 1:191, 1:350–351
McGrath, Joseph E., 1:220, 1:327, 1:385–386, 1:388–389n,
    2:785, 2:893, 2:910, 2:956
McGrath's Group Task Circumplex, 1:385–386, 1:388,
    1:389 (figure)
McHoskey, John, 1:150
McLeod, Poppy, 1:221
McPhail, Clark, 1:236
Mead, George Herbert, 1:110, 2:542, 2:711, 2:811, 2:880
Mead, Magararet, 2:769
Meaning seeking, 1:314
Mechanical Turk, 1:97–98
Mediation, 2:549–552
    contingent effectiveness of, 2:551
    cooperation and competition, 1:159
    historical overview and background, 2:549–550
    study of, 2:550–551
    team negotiation, **2:902–904**
    Trucking Game, 1:205
Medieval English (language), 2:840
Medin, Douglas, 1:70
Meindl, James, 1:313, 1:358, 2:520, 2:523, 2:717–719
Member characteristics, group potency and, 1:371
Member-group-context dynamics, group development and,
    1:327–328
Member-group relations, group development and,
    1:326–327
Mental health support groups, 2:874–875
Merari, Ariel, 1:364
Mere exposure effect, 1:425, 1:470
Mergers, 2:552–554
Meritor Savings Bank v. Vinson, 2:750
Merten, Don, 1:449
Merton, Robert K., 1:207, 2:683, 2:695
Mesh, social entrainment and, 2:785–786
Mesopotamia, 2:549
Messé, Lawrence, 1:357

Messick, David, 2:517–518
Messner, Steven, 1:363
Metaphors We Live By (Lakoff, Johnson), 2:840
Meyer, David, 1:105, 1:108
Meyer, John, 1:412
Miami Hurricanes, 2:836
Microprocesses, collective action and, 1:108
Micro role transitions, 2:716
Microsoft NetMeeting, 2:950
Middleware, 2:951
Mikulincer, Mario, 1:38
Milgram, Stanley, 1:30, 1:53–54, 1:129, 2:754
    obedience studies of, 1:306
    obedience to authority and, 2:613–616
    social impact theory and, 2:805–806
    status and, 2:841
Mill, John Stuart, 1:281, 1:312
Miller, Dale T., 1:117
Miller, Neal, 1:290, 1:396
Miller, Norman, 1:185–187, 1:273, 1:470
Milling, 1:235
Mills, C. Wright, 2:543
Mills, Judson, 1:94, 2:546
Milosevic, Slobodan, 2:522
Minimal group effect, 2:555–557
    debate about, 2:556–557
    historical overview and background, 2:555–556
Minimal group paradigm (MGP), 2:555–557, 2:651
    group cohesiveness and, 1:317
    ingroup allocation bias and, 1:446
    subjective group dynamics and, 2:866
Minimal group studies, 2:797
Minimum outgroup benefit, 1:447
Minimum power theory, 1:92
Minority coping strategies, 2:557–561
    coping with stressors, 2:558
    emotion-focused, 2:559–560
    problem-focused, 2:558–559
Minority groups in society, 2:562–566
    discrimination against ethnic minorities, 1:214–215
    genocide and, 1:306–307
    minorities as deviants, 1:209
    minorities as targets and dominant groups' reactions,
        2:562–563
    minority and dominant group perspectives, 2:563
    optimal distinctiveness and, 2:621–622
    social change strategies and, 2:564
Minority influence, 2:566–570
    background, 2:566
    change brought about by, 2:570
    minority group, defined, 2:567
    research on, 2:567–570
Mirels, Herbert, 2:672
Mischel, Walter, 1:457
Misérables, Les (Hugo), 1:191
MIT Center for Group Dynamics, 2:535
Mixed-motive conflict, 2:661
Mock jury decisions, 1:373–374
Model Standards of Conduct for Mediators, 2:550

Modern forms of prejudice, 2:570–575
    conceptualizations of, 2:571–574
    historical overview and background, 2:571
    measuring, 2:574
Modern racism, 2:572, 2:575–577, 2:884
    Modern Racism Scale, 2:576
    nature and origins of, 2:575–576
    relations to other forms of racism, 2:577
    theoretical criticisms, 2:576
Modern sexism, 2:577–580
    ambivalent sexism, 2:579
    integration and implications, 2:579
    Modern Sexism Scale, 1:41, 2:579
    modern sexist behaviors, 2:578
    modern sexist beliefs, 2:578–579
Moede, Walther, 2:708
Molm, Linda, 2:654, 2:787, 2:789–790
Momentus, 2:744
Mondrian, Piet, 2:763
Monin, Benoit, 1:274
Monroe, Marilyn, 1:271
Montgomery, Alabama, 1:87
Montgomery Improvement Association, 1:87–88
Moore, Steve, 2:836
Moral leadership, 2:929
Moreland, Richard, 1:178, 1:314, 1:376–378, 2:714, 2:894
    group composition and, 1:323–324
    group development and, 1:324–328
    group dissolution and, 1:329
Moreno, Jacob L., 1:80, 1:382, 2:711, 2:831–833
Morrison, Elizabeth, 2:714
Mortality salience, 2:920–921
Moscovici, Serge, 1:30, 1:209, 1:362, 1:423, 2:566–568,
        2:580–582, 2:619, 2:823–825
    social representations, 2:581
    theory of minority influence, 2:580–581
Mothers Against Drunk Driving, 2:875
Motivation
    cooperative learning and, 1:161–162
    social dilemmas and, 2:779–780
    social identity theory and, 2:798–799
Motivation losses
    process gain and loss and, 2:670–671
    Ringelmann effect and, 2:709
    See also Social loafing
Mouton, Jane, 1:152, 1:154
Mowrer, O. H., 1:290
MSN Messenger, 1:97
Mudrack, Peter, 1:316
Mugny, Gabriel, 2:619
"Muhammad Ali" effect, 1:273–274
Mullen, Brian, 1:192, 1:317–318, 2:512
Muller, Dominique, 2:793
Multiculturalism, 1:429, 2:582–585
    cultural free market, 2:582–583
    heritage-culture retention, 2:583
    ingroup affiliation and outgroup bias,
        2:583–584
    ingroup confidence and outgroup acceptance, 2:583

minority/majority endorsement of, and intergroup attitudes, 2:584
policy issues, 2:584
See also **Culture**
Multifactor Leadership Questionnaire, 2:522, 2:930
Multifinality, 2:890
Multilingualism, 1:253–254
Multiple abilities, 2:848
Multiple identities, 2:585–587
    identity control theory and, 1:416–417
    intergroup tolerance and, 2:587
    social identity complexity, 2:585–586
Multi-valued games, 1:91
Munsterberg, Hugo, 1:496
Murnighan, J. Keith, 1:220
Murphy, Gardner, 2:754
Murray, Charles, 1:256
Mute procedure, 2:664
Mutual intergroup differentiation model, 2:587–590
    background of, 2:588
    evidence supporting, 2:588–589
    recent developments in, 2:589
Mutuality of dependence, 1:463
Mutual performance monitoring, of teams, 2:911
Mutual reciprocity and affect sharing, 1:277
Mutual trust, teams and, 2:912–913
Myers, David, 1:362
My Lai, Vietnam, 1:54
Myrdal, Gunnar, 2:571
MySpace, 1:136

NAACP, 1:87–88
Nail, Paul, 1:130
Napoleon, 1:349
Narcotics Anonymous, 2:875
Nash, John, 2:603, 2:605
Nash equilibrium, 2:603–604
Nashville, Tennessee, 1:200
National Academy of Education, 1:201
National Academy of Sciences, 1:286
National Aeronautics and Space Administration, 1:390
National Center for Educational Statistics, 1:201
National Hockey League, 2:834, 2:836
Nationalism and patriotism, 2:591–595
    consequences of, 2:592–594
    distinguishing, 2:591–592
    functions of, 2:592
    implications of, 2:594–595
    national identification as social identity, 2:594
National Peer Network, 2:875
National Research Council, 1:364
National Training Laboratory for Group Development, 2:535
Natural kind, defined, 1:243
Nature of Prejudice, The (Allport), 1:16–17, 1:445, 1:469, 1:491, 2:558, 2:571, 2:657
Navajo Indians, 1:21
Nazi Germany. *See* Holocaust
Nazis, 2:725

Ndembu, 2:726
Neale, Margaret, 1:319, 2:605, 2:957
Need for belonging, 2:595–597
    background and psychological bases, 2:595–596
    group processes, 2:596–597
Need for closure, 2:597–599
    historical overview and background, 2:597–598
    Need for Closure Scale (NFCS), 2:598
    research areas, 2:598–599
    study of, 2:598
Need for power, 2:599–601
Need for specific closure, 2:598
Negative intergroup contact theory, 1:471–472
Negative reference groups, 2:685
Negative stereotypes, 1:164–165
Negotiated exchange, 2:787
Negotiation and bargaining, 1:58, 2:601–606
    integrative agreements, 2:602–606
    negotiation, defined, 2:601–602
    team negotiation, 2:902–903
    See also **Mediation**
Negy, Charles, 2:583
Nemeth, Charlan, 2:568
Neosexism Scale, 2:579
Neosexist beliefs, 2:578–579
Netflix, 1:98
the Netherlands, 1:127, 1:269, 2:574
Network-generalized exchange, 2:788
Neuberg, Steven, 1:29, 1:260–261
Neuroticism, 2:640
Newcomb, Theodore, 2:684–686
New institutionalism, 1:455
New leadership paradigm, 2:929
New social movement (NSM) theory, 1:105–106
New York Knicks, 2:836
New York Times, 1:63
New Zealand, 1:112, 2:594
Ng, Sik Hung, 2:513–514
Nicholson, Nigel, 2:714
Nichomachean Ethics (Aristotle), 1:113
Nietzsche, Friedrich, 1:312
Nijstad, Bernard, 1:60–61
Nippert-Eng, Christena, 2:716
Nisbett, Richard, 1:179, 1:181–182
Nixon, Richard, 2:518
Nobel Prize, 2:842
Nonconformity, 1:20
Nonconscious measurement, 2:732
Nonprobability sampling, 2:878
Normative decision model, 1:153–154
Normative influence, 1:130, 1:269, 1:270, 2:606–608
    argumentation and, 2:607
    conditions promoting, 2:606–607
    conformity and, 1:142
    consequences of, 2:607–608
    group polarization and, 1:364–365
    informational influence and, 1:443
    juries and, 1:498
    leadership and, 2:521

opinion deviance and, 2:617–618
reference informational influence theory and, 2:687
Norm of reciprocity, 2:611
Norms, 2:608–612
    characteristics of, 2:611–612
    deviation and, 1:208–209
    group potency and, 1:371
    personal, 2:610
    reference groups and, 2:686
    roles of, in social behavior, 2:610–611
    social, 2:608–610
    social psychology of schism and, 2:726
    sports teams and, 2:834
Northern Ireland, 1:472
Norton, Michael, 1:274
Nowak, Andrzej, 2:807
Nuremberg Race Laws of 1935, 1:400, 1:447

Oakes, Penelope, 2:659
Obama, Barack, 1:85, 2:868, 2:884
Obedience to authority, 2:613–616
    background of, 2:613–614
    ethical concerns, 2:615–616
    explaining effect of, 2:614–615
    implications of, 2:616
Objectification, 2:824–825
O'Bryan, K. G., 2:583
Observable power and prestige order, 2:847
Oesterreich, Detlef, 1:47
Ohio State University, 1:151–152, 2:626, 2:928
Oklahoma City, Oklahoma, 1:200
Oldham, Greg, 1:494
Oliver Twist (Dickens), 1:293
Olson, Mancur, 1:106, 1:288
Olympic Games, 2:836
Oncale v. Sundowner Offshore Services, 2:750
O'Neal, Jermaine, 2:836
Online support groups, 2:876
On the Origin of Species (Darwin), 2:768
Open-ended questions, 2:878
Openness, 2:640
Opinion deviance, 2:616–620
    consensus in small groups, 2:617
    group uniformity and, 2:618
    inclusive/exclusive reactions to deviants, 2:618–620
    social comparison theory and, 2:762–763
    social reality, group locomotion, group influence, 2:617–618
    See also Deviance
Opotow, Susan, 1:189
Optimal distinctiveness, 2:620–623, 2:730
    defined, 2:620–621
    implications, 2:621–622
Optimal identity, 2:621
O'Reilly, Charles, 1:411–412
Organizational development groups, 2:742
Organizational fashions, 1:271
Organization of African Unity, 2:550
Organization of American States, 2:550

Organizations, 2:623–628
    control and coordination of member contributions, 2:624–625
    defined, 2:623
    interaction with environment, 2:625–626
    leadership and, 2:626–627
    person-organization fit and turnover, 2:643
    selection and training of members, 2:623–624
    trends in, 2:627–628
Organized gangs, 1:294
Orlikowski, Wanda, 2:950
Orpheus Chamber Orchestra, 2:626
Orthodox Catholic Church, 2:727
Osborn, Alex, 1:59–60
Osgood, Charles, 1:6, 1:159, 1:309–310
Ostracism, 2:628–631
    methods to experimentally induce, 2:629–630
    responses to, 2:630–631
Ostrom, Elinor, 1:127
Ostrom, Thomas, 1:138
Oswald, Andrew, 2:842
Oswald, Lee Harvey, 1:149–150
Ottoman Empire, 1:306–307, 1:395
Outgroup favoritism, 1:447, 2:583–584
Outgroup homogeneity effect, 2:631–633
    background research, 2:631–632
    causes and consequences of, 2:632–633
    group emotions and, 1:336
Overattribution effect, 2:941
Overconformity, 1:21
Oxford Group, 2:875
Oyserman, Daphna, 1:113

Pace, social entrainment and, 2:786
Páez, Dario, 1:56, 2:866
Pagerank, 1:97
Parallel empathy, 1:476, 2:543
Paranoid style, 1:150
Parenting style, 1:278–279
Parents Involved in Community Schools v. Seattle School District No. 1, 1:89, 1:200
Parents Without Partners, 2:875
Pareto, Vilfredo, 1:288
Paris Commune of 1871, 1:191
Parity-fairness, 2:555
Park, Bernadette, 2:869
Parks, Rosa, 1:87
Parsons, Talcott, 1:460, 2:710
Partner control (PC), 1:463
Passive voice transformation, 2:514
Pathfinder (statistical package), 2:752
Path-goal theory of leadership, 2:521, 2:635–636
    contingency theories of leadership and, 1:153
    leadership styles and, 2:635–636
Patrick, James, 1:294
Patriot Act, 1:85
Patriotism. *See* **Nationalism and patriotism**
Pattern and Growth in Personality (Allport), 1:16
Paulus, Paul, 1:61–62

Pearl Harbor, 1:390

Peckham, Vaughn, 2:708

Peer group
  children's groups and development of, 1:79–80
  children's groups and individual differences, 1:80–82

People's Temple, 1:174, 2:546

Peplau, Anne, 1:505

Perceived group variability, 2:636–639
  effects of, 2:638
  measuring, 2:637
  theories of, 2:637–638

Perceiver effect, 2:821–822

Perceptual accentuation, 2:898

Performance expectations, language and, 2:514

Permeability, 1:58

Permissive parents, 1:277

Permutation, 2:514

Perseverance, leadership and, 2:640

Pershing, Jana, 1:449

Personal attraction, 1:316

Personal deprivation, 2:695

Personal growth movement, 2:744

Personality: A Psychological Interpretation (Allport), 1:16

Personality and Assessment (Mischel), 1:457

Personality theories of leadership, 2:520–523, 2:639–642
  critiques of trait approach to leadership, 2:641
  emotional intelligence and, 2:641
  leadership and the Big Five, 2:639–640
  prejudice and, 2:655–656
  traits associated with leadership and, 2:640–641

Personalization, decategorization and, 1:185–186

Personal norms, 2:610

Personal Responsibility and Work Opportunity
    Reconciliation Act (PRWORA), 1:454

Personal roles, 2:610

Personal self-esteem, 2:732

Person identities, 1:416

Personnel turnover, 2:642–645
  consequences of, 2:643
  group predictors of, 2:642–643
  turnover decision process, 2:642

Person-organization fit, 2:643

Persuasion arguments theory, 1:374

Petersen, Bill, 1:47

Pettigrew, Thomas, 1:17, 1:47, 2:530, 2:583, 2:695, 2:697,
    2:942, 2:959

Pfeffer, Jeffrey, 1:331, 2:654

Pharr, Suzanne, 1:409

Phase analysis, 2:700

Physical health support groups, 2:874–875

Piaget, Jean, 2:823

Piccolo, Brian, 1:319

Piliavin, Irving, 1:263–264

Piliavin, Jane, 1:263–264

Pincus, David, 1:233

Pioneer Fund, 1:256

Place dependence, 1:332

Plato, 1:311, 1:404, 1:483

Plessy v. Ferguson, 1:87

Pluralistic ignorance, 1:64, 1:274, 1:403, 2:645–647
  consequences of, 2:647
  genocide and, 1:307
  roots of, 2:646–647
  as social phenomenon, 2:645–646

Poète Allongé (Chagall), 1:20

Political attitudes
  need for closure and, 2:598–599
  politicians and stereotyping, 2:858

Political processes
  action research and, 1:5
  collective action and, 1:105
  conservatism and, 1:146–147
  ideology and, 1:418–419

Poole, M. S., 2:893

Poole, Scott, 1:327

Pope, Harrison, 1:271

"Popularity," social identity theory of leadership
    and, 2:802–803

Portugal, 2:756

Positive reference groups, 2:685

Postman, Joseph Leo, 2:719–720

Postmes, Tom, 1:193, 2:795

Powell, Colin, 2:868

Powell, Walter, 1:455

Power, 2:647–652
  future directions in, 2:651–652
  intergroup, 2:648, 2:651
  interpersonal, 2:649–651
  language and, 2:513–514
  methods, 2:648–649
  need for power, 2:599–601
  power-approach theory, 2:648
  power-as-control theory, 2:648
  power-balancing operations, 2:654
  power bases, 2:647
  sexual harassment and, 2:750
  social class and, 2:759
  social dominance theory and, 2:784
  social exchange in networks and groups, 2:788–789
  theoretical background, 2:647–648

Power-dependence theory, 2:652–655
  defined, 2:652–653
  expansion beyond dyad, 2:653
  influence of, 2:654
  key concepts, 2:653–654

Pragmatism, 2:880

Prapavessis, Harry, 1:317

Pratto, Felicia, 1:367, 1:419, 2:657, 2:707, 2:782–783

Prejudice, 2:655–660
  categorization and, 2:657–658
  feminism and, 1:282
  genocide and, 1:306–307
  group position theory and, 1:365
  habit of mind and, 2:659
  hate crimes and, 1:395–398
  Holocaust and, 1:400–402
  implications, 2:659–660
  implicit, 1:435–438

intergroup contact theory and, 1:469–470
    language and, 2:512–513
    nature of, 1:16
    psychodynamic/personality factors and, 2:655–656
    realistic group conflict and, 2:656–657
    social identity and, 2:658–659
    toward immigrants, 1:429–431
    xenophobia and, 2:960
Prentice, Deborah A., 1:117–118
Prentice-Dunn, Steven, 1:192
Prescriptive roles, 2:609–610
Presley, Elvis, 2:763
Primary territories, 2:914–915
Princeton Institute for Advanced Studies, 2:603
Princeton University, 1:274
Principle of organized subsets, 2:847
Principle of social forces, 2:805
Prisoner's dilemma, 1:483–484, 2:661–664
    antecedents of cooperation, 2:661–662
    future directions in, 2:663
    historical overview, 2:661
    research and, 2:662–663
    social dilemmas and payoff matrix for, 2:777 (table)
    sucker effect and, 2:871
Privacy, territoriality and, 2:914
Private acceptance, compliance and, 1:130–131
Private conformity, public conformity *vs.*, 1:141
Private self-awareness, 1:192–193
Probability sampling, 2:878
Problem-focused minority coping strategies, 2:558–559
Procedural competence, 2:938
Procedural justice, 1:502–503, 2:664–666, 2:693
Process consultation, 2:666–668
    conducting, 2:668
    enhancement of group performance and, 2:666–667
    key behaviors and, 2:667–668
Process gain and loss, 2:669–671
    coordination gains and losses, 2:669–670
    motivation gains, 2:671
    motivation losses, 2:670–671
Production blocking, 1:60
Productive exchange, 2:788
Progress: Its Law and Causes (Spencer), 2:768
Prohibition, 2:646
Pronorm effect, 1:210
Propinquity, 2:820
Proposition 8 (California), 1:85
Protestant Ethic and the Spirit of Capitalism (Weber), 2:672
Protestant work ethic, 2:671–674
    consequences for group processes, 2:672–673
    consequences for intergroup relations, 2:673–674
    historical overview, 2:672
Prototypes, stereotypes as, 2:857
Prototype view, of categories, 1:69
Pruitt, Dean, 2:551, 2:603, 2:605
Psychic unity of humankind, 2:531
Psychodrama, 2:923
Psychological reactance, 1:20
Psychological Review, 1:420

Psychology of Interpersonal Relations, The (Heider), 1:382
Psychology of Peoples, The (Le Bon), 1:350
Psychology of Social Norms (Sherif), 2:754
Public good dilemma, 2:777
Public goods dilemma, 1:156
Public Health Service, 1:150
Public self-awareness, 1:192
Public territories, 2:915
Punctuated equilibrium model, 2:894
Punctuated equilibrium model, group development
    and, 1:327
Push/pull factors, of immigration, 1:428
Pyszczynski, Tom, 2:919

Al Qaeda, 1:149, 1:364, 2:918.
    See also **Terror management theory**
Quantity estimation, group potency and, 1:373
Questionnaire design, 2:878–879
Quid pro quo, sexual harassment and, 2:749–750

Rabbie, Jaap, 1:157
Rabbie, Jacob, 2:556
Rablen, Matthew, 2:842
Race
    affirmative action and, 1:8–12
    essentialism and, 1:244
    extended contact effect and, 1:265–267
    homophily and, 1:404
    Implicit Association Test and, 1:433
    implicit prejudice and, 1:435–438
    intergroup contact theory and, 1:469
    interracial contact and evolutionary psychology,
        1:260–261
    modern forms of prejudice and, 2:571–575
    race prejudice and group position theory, 1:365
    stereotype threat and, 2:853–854
Racial ambivalence theory, 2:675–676, 2:884
    applications and extensions, 2:676
    historical overview and background, 2:675–676
Racism, 2:677–681
    ambivalent racism, 2:573
    aversive, 1:48–51, 2:572, 2:884
    cultural, 2:679–680
    individual, 2:677–679
    institutional, 2:677, 2:679
    modern, 2:572, 2:575–577, 2:884
    scientific, 1:256
    symbolic racism, 2:572, 2:576, 2:782,
        2:883–885
Rajecki, A. W., 2:792
RAND Corporation, 1:195
Random assignment, defined, 1:263
Randsley de Moura, Georgina, 2:867
Rank, dominance hierarchies and, 1:227–228
Rational choice, 1:156, 2:778
Rau, Johannes, 2:593
Raven, Bertram, 1:390, 2:647
Rawls, John, 1:504
Reactive empathy, 1:476, 2:543

Realistic group conflict theory, 1:157, 2:681–684,
        2:753, 2:755
    cooperation and competition, 1:157
    critique of, 2:682–683
    group position theory and, 1:367
    hate crimes and, 1:397
    historical overview, background, major findings,
        2:681–682
    importance of, 2:683
    ingroup allocation bias and, 1:445
    intergroup violence and, 1:479
    prejudice and, 2:656–657
    social dominance theory and, 2:782
Real-time data collection, for research, 2:701–702
Recategorization approach, 2:588
Reciprocal altruism, 1:259, 2:611
Reciprocity, 2:788
    group socialization and, 1:376
    power-dependence theory and, 2:653
    social dilemmas and, 2:778
Recording, for research, 2:701–702
Recovery, Inc., 2:875
Reference groups, 2:684–687
    expansions and critique, 2:686
    historical overview, 2:684–686
    importance of, 2:686
    social comparison theory and, 2:763–764
Referent informational influence theory,
        1:444, 2:687–689, 2:731
    debate about, 2:688–689
    evidence, 2:688
    historical overview and background, 2:687–688
Reformed Protestantism, 2:672
Regents of the University of California v. Bakke, 1:9
Reich, Wilhelm, 2:705
Reicher, Stephen, 1:111, 1:170, 1:193–194, 1:198,
        1:211, 1:237
    leadership and, 2:523
    prejudice and, 2:660
    SIDE model and, 2:689, 2:795
Reid, Scott, 2:514
Relational cohesion theory, 2:689–691
    central assumptions, 2:690–691
    overview, 2:689–690
    related research, 2:691
Relational model of authority in groups, 2:523, 2:691–694
    relational model, explained, 2:693–694
    traditional approaches, 2:692–693
Relationship effect, 2:821–822
Relative deprivation, 2:694–698, 2:761
    conceptual and empirical challenges, 2:697–698
    hate crimes and, 1:397
    historical overview, 2:694–696
    J-curve hypothesis and, 1:490
    theoretical linkages, 2:696–697
Relative Deprivation and Social Justice
        (Runcimann), 2:695
Relative gratification, 2:698
Repeated cross-sectional survey design, 2:877

Report of the National Advisory Commission on Civil
        Disorders, 2:677
Republic (Plato), 1:311
Research Center for Group Dynamics, University of
        Michigan, 1:284–286
Research methods and issues, 2:698–705
    action research conducted in situ, 1:3
    action research methodologies, 1:3–4
    analyzing group process, 2:702–704
    capturing group process, 2:700–702
    overview of group process research methods, 2:699–700
    research design process, 2:700–701
Resolution of Conflict (Deutsch), 1:204
Resource dependence perspective, 2:654
Resource dilemma, 1:125
Resource mobilization, collective action and, 1:104–105
Response condition, 1:463
Response rate, to surveys, 2:878
Retaining knowledge, group learning and, 1:345
Retributive justice, 1:503–504
Retrieval coordination, 2:931
Rhode Island, 1:489
Rhythm, social entrainment and, 2:785
Rice, Robert, 1:152
Richerson, Peter, 2:807
Richmond, Anthony, 1:35
Ridgeway, Cecilia, 1:299
Right wing authoritarianism, 2:705–707, 2:960–961
    contemporary developments, 2:706–707
    theory of authoritarian personality, 2:705–706
Ringelmann, Maximilien, 1:352, 1:360, 2:708, 2:766, 2:808
Ringelmann effect, 2:708–709
    Ingham project and, 2:708–709
    later research on, 2:709
Rio de Janeiro, Brazil, 1:106
Risky shift phenomenon, 1:361–362
    group problem solving and, 1:374
    group task and, 1:386
Robbers Cave, 1:121, 1:384, 2:656, 2:681–682, 2:755
Robert's Rules of Order, 1:371
Roccas, Sonia, 2:586–587
Rockwell, Norman, 2:765
Rodin, Judith, 1:263–264
Roe v. Wade, 1:281
Rogelberg, Steven, 2:851
Rogers, Ronald, 1:192
Rojas v. Superior Court, 2:550
Rokeach, Milton, 1:46, 1:48, 1:225–226
Role clarity/ambiguity, 2:835
Role congruity theory, 2:522
Role differentiation, 2:712–713
Role entry, 2:713, 2:714–715
Role exit, 2:713, 2:715–716
Roles, 2:709–713
    gender and, 1:297
    general concepts, 2:709–710
    group potency and, 1:371
    of norms, in social behavior, 2:610–611
    processes, 2:711–713

role identity, 1:416, 2:712
role negotiation, 1:378
role-playing, 2:711
role-taking, 2:711–712
sports teams and, 2:834–835
theories about, 2:710–711
Role transitions, 2:713–717
macro role transitions, 2:714–716
micro role transitions, 2:716
Romance of leadership, 2:717–719
critique of, 2:719
implications of, 2:717–719
theory, 2:717
Romeo and Juliet effect, 1:21
Roosevelt, Franklin D., 2:929
Rosch, Eleanor, 1:69
Rosenberg Self-Esteem Scale, 2:732
Ross, Edward, 1:350
Ross, Lee, 1:272
Ross, Marc, 2:961
Rossi, Alice, 2:685
Rothbart, Myron, 2:869
Rousseau, Jean-Jacques, 1:113
Rubik's cube, 1:269
Rubin, Jeffrey, 2:605
Rubin, Lillian, 1:297
Rubin, Zick, 1:505
Ruhleder, Karen, 2:950
Rumor, 2:719–722
conspiracy theories and, 2:721–722
historical overview, 2:719–720
social functions of, 2:720–721
Runciman, Walter Gary, 1:490, 1:501, 2:695
Rusbult, Caryl, 2:545
Russell, Bertrand, 1:309
Rutland, Adam, 2:867
Rwanda, 1:305, 2:725
genocide and, 1:307
intergroup violence and, 1:480–481
Ryan, Ellen, 2:512

Sacrifice, group cohesion and, 1:317
Sadat, Anwar, 1:159
Saenz, Delia, 2:925, 2:927
Salafi Jihad, 1:364
Salancik, Gerald, 1:331, 2:654
Salas, Eduardo, 2:901, 2:910–911
Salganik, Matthew, 1:270
Salience assumption, 2:846
Sampling, 2:878
Samuelson, Paul, 1:288
Sanford, R. Nevitt, 1:45, 2:706
Sani, Fabio, 2:726
Sanna, Lawrence, 2:943
Sarri, Rosemary, 1:326
Sassenberg, Kai, 1:118
Sayers, Gale, 1:319
Sayles, Leonard R., 1:368
Scaffolding and coaching, 1:277

Scapegoating, 1:291, 2:723–725
classic scapegoating theory, 2:723–724
new approaches to, 2:724–725
prejudice and, 2:656
Schachter, Stanley, 1:209–210, 1:285, 1:287, 2:618–619
Schein, Edgar, 1:449
Schippers, Michaela, 2:907
Schisms, 2:725–728
empirical research on, 2:725–726
limitations of model, 2:727
related phenomena, 2:727–728
social psychology of, 2:726–727
Schkade, David, 1:362
Schmid, Thomas, 2:716
Schneider, Benjamin, 1:458
Schooling closer to home, 1:200
Schopler, John, 1:157, 1:159
Schutz, William, 1:325
Schwartz, Gary, 1:449
Schwartz, Shalom, 1:189
Schwarzenegger, Arnold, 1:72
Schweitzer, Albert, 1:492
Scientific racism, 1:256
Scottish Highlands, 2:759
Scout activities, 1:58
Scrabbulous, 2:951
Search for ideas in associative memory (SIAM), 1:61
Sears, David, 2:676
Sears, Robert, 1:290, 1:396
Seashore, Stanley, 1:319
Seattle, Washington, 1:199–200
Secondary anti-Semitism, 1:24
Secondary territories, 2:915
Second Intifada, 1:24
Second Life, 1:97, 1:136
Seeley, Elizabeth, 1:118
Segal, Mary, 1:363
Segregationism, 1:33
Self. See **Collective self**
Self, actual vs. ideal, 2:732
Self-administered questionnaires, 2:879
Self-categorization theory, 2:728–731
categories and prototypes, 2:729
categorization and depersonalization, 2:729
deindividuation and, 1:193
diversity and, 1:220
historical background, 2:728–729
influence in groups and, 2:731
intergroup behavior and, 2:730
motivational processes and, 2:730
psychological salience and, 2:730–731
reference informational influence theory and, 2:687
relative prototypicality and psychology of
marginalization, 2:731
self-stereotyping and, 2:740
social attraction and, 2:730
social identity theory and, 2:797
social identity theory of leadership and, 2:802
uncertainty-identity theory and, 2:944

Self-concept
  compliance and, 1:131, 1:132
  gender roles and, 1:302
  identification and commitment, 1:413–414
Self-confidence, 2:640
Self-esteem, 2:731–735
  collective self and, 1:111–112
  contingencies of self-worth, 2:734
  emerging role of implicit self-esteem, 2:733–734
  in intergroup discrimination, 2:732–733
  Protestant work ethic and, 2:672–673
  sociometer model of, 2:829
  status *vs.*, and group identification, 2:734
  symbolic interactionism and, 2:882
  system justification theory and, 2:888–889
  terror management theory and, 2:734
  types of, 2:732
Self-fulfilling prophecy, 2:735–737
  early research, 2:735–736
  limits of, 2:736–737
  stereotyping and, 2:857
Self-help groups, 2:872
Selfish gene theory, 2:778
Self-managing teams, 2:737–739
  future research, 2:738–739
  impact on outcomes, 2:738
  limitations of, 2:739
Self-reports process, 2:701
Self-serving attribution bias, 1:43
Self-stereotyping, 2:621, 2:739–741
  future directions of, 2:741
  historical overview and importance, 2:739–740
  theory and evidence, 2:740–741
Self-worth, self-esteem and, 2:734
Semin, Gun, 2:515, 2:538
Sensitivity training groups, 2:741–744
  current status, 2:744
  debate, 2:743–744
  goals and format, 2:742–743
  historical overview, 2:741–742
Sequencing, 2:847
Service climate, 2:936
Sexism, 2:744–749
  ambivalent, 1:17–19
  consequences of, 2:746–748
  sexism against men, 2:748–749
  sex stereotypes, 2:745–746
Sexual harassment, 2:749–751
  explanations for, 2:750–751
  prevalence and reporting, 2:749
  types of, 2:749–750
Sexual Harassment of Working Women
    (MacKinnon), 2:749
Shakespeare, William, 1:21
Shamir, Boas, 1:153
Shared beliefs, group cohesion and, 1:318
Shared mental models, 2:751–753
  empirical research on, 2:752–753
  future directions in research, 2:753

  group memory and, 1:348–349
  measuring, 2:752
  socially shared cognition and, 2:814
  teams and, 2:912
Sharpening, 2:720
Shaver, Phillip, 1:38
Shaw, Marjorie, 1:355
Shaw, Marvin E., 1:128, 1:387
Shea, Gregory, 1:369
Sheldon, William, 1:208
Shepard, Herbert, 1:325
Shepard, Matthew, 1:396
Sherif, Muzafer, 1:121, 1:351, 2:656–657, 2:681–683,
    2:688, 2:753–756, 2:865, 2:898
  conformity and, 1:139–144
  contributions of, 2:754–755
  cooperation and competition, 1:155, 1:157–158
  culture and, 1:178
  deviance and, 1:209
  emergent norm theory and, 1:235
  Festinger and, 1:285
  group position theory and, 1:367
  group structure and, 1:384
  hate crimes and, 1:397
  informational influence and, 1:443
  ingroup allocation bias and, 1:445
  personal/intellectual history, 2:754
Shils, Edward, 1:46
Should-Would Discrepancy Scale, 2:574
Sidanius, James, 1:48, 1:367, 1:419, 2:657, 2:707,
    2:760–761, 2:782–783
Siegal, Sidney, 2:603
Silent treatment, 2:629
Silverstein, Brett, 1:271
Similarity, entitativity and, 1:240
Similarity-attraction theory, 2:643
Similarity-selection-attraction theory, 2:643
Simmel, Georg, 1:381–382
Simmons, Carolyn, 1:505
Simon, Herbert, 2:624
Simple games, 1:91
Simpson, O. J., 1:500
Singer, Eleanor, 2:686
Situated focus theory, 2:650
Situational leadership theory, 1:154, 2:521
Skill variety, 1:494–495
Skinner, B. F., 2:787
Skvoretz, John, 2:787
Slater, Philip E., 2:712
Slavery, 2:759–762
  abolition and, 2:758
  Civil War and, 2:757–758
  early development of, 2:756–757
  in U.S., 1790-1860, 2:757–758
Slime effect, 2:841
Smelser, Neil, 1:104
Smith, Adam, 1:113
Smith, Eliot, 1:473
Smith, Peter, 1:144

Smith-Jentsch, Kimberly, 2:911
Sociability, 2:640
Social attraction, 1:316, 2:730
Social categorization, 2:798
   entitativity and, 1:239
   Tajfel and, 2:898
Social change
   feminism and, 1:283–284
   minority groups in society and, 2:564
   Tajfel and, 2:898–899
Social class, 2:762–765
   additional considerations, 2:761–762
   defined, 2:759–760
   key research findings, 2:760–761
   theories, 2:760
Social cognitive theory, 2:935–936
Social combination approach, 1:387
Social comparison theory, 2:765–769
   of affiliation, 1:251
   brainstorming and, 1:60–61
   defined, 2:762–763
   Festinger on, 1:285–286
   group problem solving and, 1:374
   happiness, well-being, and, 2:764–765
   reference groups, 2:763–764
   Tajfel and, 2:898
Social compensation, 2:509, 2:769–771
   background, 2:766
   implications, 2:767
   occurrence of, 2:766–767
Social competition, 1:253, 2:799–800
Social computing, 2:950
Social control, commitment and, 1:412–413
Social creativity, 1:253, 1:254, 2:800, 2:843
Social Darwinism, 2:771–773
   Darwinism vs., 2:770
   Galton and, 2:769
   in late 20th century, 2:769–770
   Spencer and, 2:768
Social Darwinism in American Thought (Hofstadter), 2:769
Social decision schemes, 2:773–777
   capturing decision processes, 2:773
   group composition and, 2:771
   individual preferences and, 2:771
   predicting group choices from individual
      preferences, 2:772–773
   relationships among distinguishable distributions and
      group choices, 2:771–772, 2:772 (tables)
Social deviance, 2:777–780
   contemporary understandings of, 2:774–775
   group dynamics of, 2:775–776
   historical overview and perception of, 2:774
   punishment and, 2:775
   social change and, 2:776
Social dilemmas, 1:289, 2:780–784, 2:810
   cooperation and competition, 1:156–157
   defined, 2:777–778
   implications and applications, 2:781
   payoff matrix for prisoner's dilemma game, 2:777 (table)

   solutions to, 2:779–781
   theories of, 2:778–779
Social distance, 1:408–409
Social dominance theory, 2:761, 2:785–788
   behavioral asymmetry, 2:783–784
   gender and group dominance, 2:784
   group position theory and, 1:367
   ideology and, 1:419
   Islamophobia and, 1:486
   legitimizing myths and, 2:782–783
   Marx and, 2:760
   power dynamics and, 2:784
   prejudice and, 2:657
   right wing authoritarianism and, 2:706–707
   social dominance orientation, 2:783
   social dominance theory and, 2:783
   status and, 2:842–843
   structure of group-dominance societies, 2:782
   xenophobia and, 2:960–961
Social drama, 2:726
Social entrainment, 2:788–790
   components of, 2:785–786
   related research, 2:786
Social environments, group ecology and, 1:332–334
Social exchange in networks and groups, 2:790–794
   affect and affective commitment, 2:789–790
   commitment and, 2:789
   future directions in, 2:790
   historical overview and background, 2:787
   power and, 2:788–789
   trust and, 2:790
   types of exchange, 2:787–788
Social exchange theory
   leader-member exchange (LMX) theory, 2:518
   power-dependence theory and, 2:652
   relational cohesion theory and, 2:689
Social facilitation, 1:354, 2:810
   group structure and, 1:381
   group task and, 1:386
Social facilitation, 2:794–797
   historical overview, 2:791–792
   theoretical views of, 2:792–793
Social identity model of deindividuation effects, 2:689,
      2:756–759
   background, 2:794–795
   contributions of, 2:796
   development of, 2:795–796
Social identity theory, 1:416, 2:797–801, 2:798
   cognitive processes and, 2:797–798
   common misunderstandings about, 2:801
   conformity and, 1:142
   cooperation and competition, 1:158–159
   culture and, 1:177
   deindividuation and, 1:193
   diversity and, 1:221
   forms of identity threat, 2:800
   genocide and, 1:306
   group emotions and, 1:337–338
   hate crimes and, 1:397

historical overview and background, 2:797
identification and commitment, 1:413–414
leadership and, 2:522–523
Marx and, 2:760
mergers and, 2:553
minimal group effect and, 2:556
motivation and, 2:798–799
multiple identities and, 2:585–586
mutual intergroup differentiation model
    and, 2:587–589
national identifications and, 2:594
prejudice and, 2:658–659
realistic group conflict theory and, 2:683, 2:755
reference informational influence theory and, 2:687
relative deprivation, 2:694
self-categorization theory and, 2:728, 2:729
self-esteem and, 2:732–733
social dominance theory and, 2:782
social identity theory of intergroup relations, 2:797
social identity theory of leadership and, 2:802
social mobility and, 2:815–816
sports teams and, 2:834
status and, 2:843
strategies for status improvement, 2:799–800
Tajfel and, 2:897, 2:898–899
transactional leadership and, 2:929
transformational leadership theories and, 2:935
uncertainty-identity theory and, 2:945
Social identity theory of leadership, 2:522, 2:687, 2:731,
    2:801–805
group membership, social identity, and, 2:802–803
intergroup leadership, 2:804
leaders as entrepreneus of identity, 2:803–804
Social identity threat, 2:800
Social impact theory, 2:805–808
    dynamic, 2:807–808
    limitations of, 2:806–807
    principles of, 2:805–806
    social loafing and, 2:810
    strengths of, 2:806
Social inclusion pattern, 1:164
Social influence
    Asch on, 1:28–29
    conformity and, 1:139
Social inhibition, 1:354
Social loafing, 2:808–811
    free riding and, 1:289
    group motivation and, 1:352–353
    historical overview and background,
        2:808–809
    key findings, 2:809
    Köhler effect and, 2:507–508
    process gain and loss and, 2:670–671
    related phenomena, 2:810
    Ringelmann effect and, 2:709
    social compensation and, 2:766
    social facilitation and, 2:791–792
    sucker effect and, 2:870
    theories of, 2:809–810

Socially shared cognition, 2:811–815
    development of, 2:811–812
    implications of, in groups, 2:812–814
Social mobility, 2:815–817
    ethnolinguistic vitality and, 1:253
    perception of, as possible, 2:816
    problems of, 2:816
    questions about, 2:817
    social identity and, 2:815–816
Social-motivational startegies of brainstorming, 1:61
Social networking Web sites, 2:932–933, 2:949–951
Social networks, 2:817–821
    cognitive social structures (Level 2), 2:820
    computer-mediated communication and, 1:136
    dyad (Level 2), 2:819–820
    individual actors (Level 1), 2:819
    structure of network (Level O), 2:817–818, 2:818 (figures)
Social norms, 2:608–610, 2:754
Social perception, 2:897
Social pressures in informal groups
    Festinger on, 1:284–285
Social Psychology (Allport), 1:350
Social Psychology of Groups, The (Thibaut, Kelley), 2:787
Social Psychology Quarterly, 1:382, 2:833
Social reality function, 2:617–618
Social reality testing, 1:251
Social relations model, 2:821–823
Social representations, 2:581, 2:823–826
    background, 2:823–824
    communication processes, 2:825–826
    objectification and anchoring, 2:824–825
    social dominance theory and, 2:782
    socially shared cognition and, 2:812
Social role theory, 1:144, 1:297, 1:300, 1:303, 1:418, 2:713
Social Science Research Council, 1:469
Social support, conformity and, 1:143
Social utility model, 1:93
Social value orientations, 1:464
Society of Experimental Psychology, 1:286
Society of Experimental Social Psychology, 1:286
Society of Jesus (Jesuits), 1:375
Society of Professionals in Dispute Resolution, 2:550
Sociobiology: The New Synthesis (Wilson), 2:770
Sociobiology of ethnocentrism, 1:250
Socioemotional and task behavior, 2:826–829
Socioemotional leaders, 2:712–713
Sociology of emotions, 2:542–543
Sociometer model, 2:596, 2:829–831, 2:830–831
Sociometric choice, 2:831–833
    causes and consequences, 2:832
    historical overview and future direction of, 2:833
    measurement, 2:831–832
    in use, 2:832–833
Sociometry, 1:382, 2:833
Sociotechnical systems (STS), 1:2
Solomon, Sheldon, 2:919
Some Social Factors in Perception (Sherif), 2:754
Sommer, Robert, 2:915
Son Hing, L. S., 2:676

Source credibility, status and, 2:842
South Africa, 1:25–26
    intergroup contact theory and, 1:472
    intergroup violence and, 1:480–481
    minority influence and, 2:567
Southern California Mediation Association, 2:550
Southern Christian Leadership Conference, 1:88
Southern Poverty Law Center (SPLC), 1:86
"Spanglish," 1:253–254
Spanish Inquisition, 1:22
Spears, Russell, 1:119, 1:193–194, 2:795
Specific status characteristics, 2:522, 2:845
Speech accommodation, 2:511
Speech divergence, 2:511
Spence, Janet T., 1:39–41
Spencer, Herbert, 1:312, 2:768–769
Sports teams, 2:833–837
    sports team and relationship with outgroup, 2:835–836
    sports team as ingroup, 2:834–835
Sproull, Lee, 2:949
Sroufe, Alan, 1:276
Staggenborg, Suzanne, 1:105
Stanford prison experiment, 2:711, 2:837–839
    implications, 2:838–839
    study design and findings, 2:837–838
Stanford University, 1:192, 1:272, 1:286, 2:711, 2:837
Star, Susan Leigh, 2:950
Stasser, Garold, 1:138
Stasser, Gary, 2:850–851
State action verbs (SAV), 2:536–537
State self-esteem, 2:830
State Self-Esteem Scale, 2:732
State verbs (SV), 2:536–537, 2:539
Status, 2:839–844
    consequences of intragroup status, 2:841–842
    ethnolinguistic vitality and, 1:252
    gender and behavior, 1:298
    intragroup dynamics of, 2:840–841
    roles and, 2:710
    self-esteem and, 2:734
    social identity theory and, 2:799–800
    social identity theory of leadership and, 2:802–803
    social-psychological theories of responses to intra- and intergroup status, 2:842–843
Status Characteristics and Social Interaction: An Expectation States Approach (Berger), 2:847
Status characteristics/expectation states theory, 2:522, 2:844–848
    expectation states theory, defined, 2:844–845
    interventions, 2:847–848
    sexism and, 2:745
    status characteristic, defined, 2:845–846
    status-organizing process, 2:846–847
Status construction theory, 2:848–850
    defined, 2:849–850
    evidence, 2:850
    historical overview, 2:849
Status generalization, 2:846
Status giving, 2:654

Staub, Ervin, 1:306, 2:724
Staw, Barry, 1:242
Steele, Claude, 2:853
Steiner, Ivan, 1:317, 1:351–352, 1:359–360, 1:388, 2:708
Stephan, Cookie, 2:676
Stephan, Walter, 1:47, 1:486, 2:676
Stepladder technique, 2:850–853
    evidence, 2:851–852
    future research, 2:852
Stereotype confirmation, 2:562
Stereotype consistent (SC)/stereotype inconsistent (SI), 2:515
Stereotype content model, 2:843
Stereotype reactance, 2:854
Stereotypes
    feminism and, 1:282
    gender roles and, 1:300–301
    perceived group variability and, 2:636–638
    rumor and, 2:721
    self-fulfilling prophecy and, 2:736–737
Stereotype threat, 2:562, 2:680, 2:853–856
    defined, 2:853–854
    impact on performance, 2:854–855
    reducing, 2:855
    social class and, 2:761
    stigma and, 2:864
    susceptibility to, 2:854
Stereotyping, 2:856–861
    accuracy of, 2:858–859
    entitativity and, 1:239–240
    frustration-aggression hypothesis and, 1:291
    measuring, 2:858
    optimal identity and, 2:621
    outcomes of stereotypes, 2:856–857
    self-categorization theory and, 2:729
    self-stereotyping, 2:739–741
    stereotype development, 2:859
    stereotype maintenance/change, 2:859–860
    stereotypes as mental representations, 2:857–858
Stereotyping and Social Reality (Oakes, Haslam, Turner), 2:659
Sternberg, Robert, 1:154, 1:457
Stevens, S. S., 2:805
Stigma, 2:861–863
    conceptualizations and classifications of, 2:861–862
    consequences of, 2:863
    marred interactions, 2:863–864
    reasons for, 2:862–863
    remediation, 2:864
Stigma: Notes on the Management of Spoiled Identity (Goffman), 2:558, 2:861
Stogdill, Ralph, 2:827, 2:928
Stokols, Daniel, 1:332
Stone, Oliver, 1:150
Stone, William, 1:47
Stoner, James, 1:361
Stonewall Rebellion, 1:89
Stouffer, Samuel, 2:685, 2:694–695
Strategy for Peace, 1962, 1:310
Street gangs, 1:294

Strodtbeck, Fred, **1:**325, **1:**383
Stroebe, Wolfgang, **1:**60–61, **2:**851
Structural holes, **2:**819
Structural-motivational approaches, to negotiation and bargaining, **2:**604
Student Nonviolent Coordinating Committee, **1:**88
Student Teams-Achievement Divisions (STAD), **1:**161
Subject effects, defined, **1:**263
Subjection of Women, The (Mill), **1:**281
Subjective group dynamics, 2:620, **2:**865–867
    background, **2:**865
    black sheet effect and, **2:**865–866
    defined, **2:**866–867
Substitutability effect, **1:**219
Subtle sexist behaviors, **2:**578
Subtyping, 2:638, **2:**867–870
    counteracting, and improving intergroup relations, **2:**869–870
    differentiated, **2:**868–869
    exception subtyping, **2:**869
    nature of, in social categorization, **2:**868
Sucker effect, 1:289, **2:**767, **2:**870–872
    group motivation phenomena and, **2:**871–872
    origins of, **2:**870–871
Sulloway, Frank, **1:**21
Sumner, William Graham, **1:**85, **1:**248, **1:**350
Sunstein, Cass, **1:**362
Superordinate goals, **1:**158–159
Supervisors, satisfaction with, **2:**643
Support groups, 2:872–876
    advantages and limitations, **2:**876
    features of, **2:**872–874
    varieties of, **2:**874–876
Survey methods, 2:877–880
    evaluating data, **2:**880
    questionnaire design, **2:**878–879
    response rate, **2:**878
    sampling, **2:**878
    survey design, **2:**877–878
    survey modes, **2:**879–880
Svyantek, Daniel, **2:**901
Swim, Janet, **1:**41, **2:**943
Swiss People's Party, **1:**257
Symbolic interactionism,
        2:542, **2:**710, **2:**880–883
    identity and, **2:**882–883
    nature of meaning and, **2:**880–881
    participant observation and, **2:**883
    self and, **2:**881–882
    situated conduct and, **2:**881
Symbolic racism, 2:572, **2:**576, **2:**883, **2:**883–885
    background, **2:**883–884
    current theory of, **2:**884
    future directions, **2:**884–885
    social dominance theory and, **2:**782
    Symbolic Racism 2000 Scale, **2:**576
Symbolics politics theory, **2:**883
SYMLOG, 1:460, **2:**885–888
Systematic reasoning, **1:**500

System for the Multiple Level Observation of Groups (SYMLOG). *See* **SYMLOG**
System justification theory, 2:579, **2:**761, **2:**888, **2:**888–891
    disadvantaged groups and, **2:**889
    ego, group, system justification motives, **2:**888–889
    ideology and, **1:**419–420
    Marx and, **2:**760
    motivational approach and, **2:**890–891
    palliative function of, **2:**889–890
    status and, **2:**843
    stigma and, **2:**862–863
System theory, 2:891–895
    assumptions of, **2:**891–892
    in group research, **2:**892–894
    implications, **2:**894
Szamrej, Jacek, **2:**807
Szymanski, Kate, **2:**810

Tajfel, Henri, 1:23, **1:**70, **1:**110, **1:**149, **1:**157, **1:**177, **2:**755, **2:**865, **2:**897–899
    biographical information, **2:**897
    ethnocentrism and, **1:**248–249, **1:**251
    group boundaries and, **1:**314–315
    group cohesiveness and, **1:**317
    group structure and, **1:**384
    hate crimes and, **1:**397
    ingroup allocation bias and, **1:**445–448
    minimal group effect and, **2:**555–556
    Moscovici and, **2:**580
    on prejudice, **2:**657–658
    relative deprivation and, **2:**696–697
    research of, **2:**897–899
    schisms and, **2:**726
    self-categorization theory and, **2:**728–730
    on social identity theory, **2:**797
Take Off Pounds Sensibly (TOPS), **2:**875
Take-some dilemma, **1:**125
Tarde, Gabriel, **1:**103
Target effect, **2:**821–822
Task conflict, **1:**453
Task groups, entitativity and, **1:**238–239
Task identity, job characteristic theory (JCT) and, **1:**495
Task leaders, **2:**712–713
Task models
    shared mental models and, **2:**751
    socially shared cognition and, **2:**814
Task-oriented behavior, process consultation and, **2:**667
Task work, **2:**910
Tasmania, **1:**307
Taylor, Donald M., **1:**252, **2:**583, **2:**942
Taylor, Frederick, **1:**494, **2:**624
Taylor, Shelley, **2:**658, **2:**868
Team building, 2:899–901
    programs, **2:**900–901
    team formation and, **2:**899–900
Team climate, **1:**453
Team coaching model, **2:**893
Team effectiveness, **1:**354
Team interaction model, **2:**751

Team learning. *See* **Group learning**
Team negotiation, 2:902–904
    advantages/disadvantages of teams, 2:902
    managing, 2:902–903
    timing of, 2:903
Team performance assessment, 2:904–907
    defining teams and, 2:904
    interteam relationships and, 2:906
    measuring, 2:904–906
    purpose of, 2:904
Team reflexivity, 2:907–909
    conceptualization, 2:907–908
    factors affecting, 2:908
    future directions of, 2:909
    team effectiveness and, 2:908–909
Teams, 2:909–913
    defined, 2:909–910
    determinants of team innovation, 1:452
    research, 2:910–911, 2:910–913
    self-managing teams (SMTs), 2:737–739
    shared mental models and, 2:751–752
    socially shared cognition and, 2:814
    team orientation, 2:912
    together everyone achieves more (TEAM), 1:424
    work teams, 2:955–958
Team self-correction training, 2:753
Teamwork, 2:910
Tempo, social entrainment and, 2:786
Temporal environments, group ecology and, 1:334
Territoriality, 2:913–916
    background, 2:913–914
    kinds of, 2:914–915
    territorial invasion, 2:915
Terrorism, 2:916–919
    group polarization and, 1:363–364
    psychology of, 2:916–917
    throughout history, 2:916
Terror management theory, 1:250–251, 2:919–922
    defined, 2:919–920
    empirical evidence, 2:920–921
    implications for intergroup relations, 2:921
    need for belonging and, 2:596
    self-esteem and, 2:734
    stigma and, 2:863
Testosterone, dominance hierarchies and, 1:229
Tetlock, Philip, 1:48, 1:420
T-groups, 2:742
Thatcher, Margaret, 2:803
Therapy groups, 2:922–924
    effectiveness of, 2:924
    historical overview, 2:922–923
    treatment factors, 2:923–924
    types of therapy, 2:923
Thibaut, John, 1:462, 1:502–503, 2:517, 2:648, 2:652, 2:664–665, 2:787
Third Reich. *See* **Holocaust**
Thirteenth Amendment, 2:758
Thompson, James, 2:624–625
Thorndike, Edward, 2:517

Thorne, Barrie, 1:297
Thrasher, Frederic, 1:293–294
Three Mile Island, 2:751
Tilly, Charles, 1:107
Time pressure, negotiation and bargaining, 2:604
Tinbergen, Nikolaas, 2:913
Tindale, Scott, 1:221
"Tit for tat" strategy, 2:661, 2:780
Tocqueville, Alexis de, 1:115, 1:489
Together everyone achieves more (TEAM), 1:424
Tokenism, 2:563, 2:924–927
    consequences of, 2:925–926
    historical overview, 2:925
    optimal distinctiveness and, 2:620
    remediating negative effects of, 2:926–927
Tönnies, Ferdinand, 1:114, 1:179, 1:381–382
Top-down approach, to group task, 1:387–389
Touraine, Alain, 1:105
Town Meeting (Rockwell), 2:765
Tracy, Destutt de, 1:418
Tragedy of the Commons, 1:125–126, 2:778
Training laboratory, sensitivity training groups and, 2:742
Trait-based measures, of self-esteem, 2:732
Transactional leadership theories, 2:521–522, 2:927–931
    historical overview, 2:928
    idiosyncrasy credit, 2:928
    leader-member exchange (LMX) theory, 2:518
    leader-member exchange theory, 2:928–929
    transactional and transformational leadership, 2:929–930
Transactive memory systems, 1:344, 2:644, 2:931–933
    characteristics of, 2:931
    development of, 2:932–933
    group memory and, 1:348
    group potency and, 1:372
    outcomes, 2:933
    socially shared cognition and, 2:814
Transcriptions, for research, 2:702
Transferring knowledge, group learning and, 1:345
Transformational leadership theories, 2:522, 2:933–936
    dimensions of, 2:934–935
    group cohesiveness and, 2:935
    group efficacy and, 2:935–936
    group identification and, 2:935
    historical overview, 2:934
    leader-member exchange (LMX) theory, 2:518
    service climate and, 2:936
    transactional leadership and, 2:929–930
Transnational processes, collective action and, 1:107–108
Trash talking, sports teams and, 2:835
Trends, 1:269
Triandis, Harry, 1:113, 1:179–180, 1:221
Triplett, Norman, 1:381, 2:708, 2:791, 2:793
Trivers, Robert, 2:769
Trobriand Islands, 2:788
Tropp, Linda, 1:17
Trucking Game, 1:205
Trudeau, Pierre, 2:582
Truman, Harry S, 1:84

Trust, 2:936–939
　　bases of, 2:937–938
　　benefits of, 2:938–939
　　conceptualizing, 2:936–937
　　Deutsch on, 1:204–205
　　idiosyncrasy credit and, 1:421
　　leadership and group value model, 2:523–524
　　mutual trust and teams, 2:912–913
　　social exchange in networks and groups, 2:790
　　social identity theory of leadership and, 2:803
Truth and Reconciliation Commission in
　　　South Africa, 1:481
Truth-wins model, 1:346
Tuckman, Bruce, 1:325–326, 1:329, 1:341, 2:957
Turkey, 1:306
Turner, John C., 1:197, 1:251, 1:315–318, 1:384, 1:397,
　　　1:444, 2:755, 2:898
　　minimal group effect and, 2:556
　　prejudice and, 2:658–659
　　reference groups and, 2:686–687
　　relative deprivation and, 2:696
　　schisms and, 2:726
　　self-categorization theory and, 2:728–730
　　on social identity theory, 2:797
Turner, Jonathan, 2:686
Turner, Ralph H., 1:170, 1:235–237
Turner, Victor, 2:713, 2:726
Tuskegee Institute, 1:150
Tutsis, 1:305–307, 1:480–481, 2:725
Twenge, Jean, 1:41
Twiggy, 1:271
Tyler, Tom, 1:358, 1:503, 2:517–518, 2:523, 2:664

Ultimate attribution error, 2:941–943
　　historical overview, 2:941–943
　　implications, 2:943
Uncertainty-identity theory, 2:596, 2:943–945
　　group attributes and, 2:944–945
　　need for belonging and, 2:596
　　self-categorization theory and, 2:730
　　social identity and, 2:944
　　social identity and psychology of extremism, 2:945
　　uncertainty and need to reduce uncertainty, 2:943–944
Uncertainty reduction theory, 1:251
Underestimating, false consensus effect and, 1:273–274
Unfreezing, 2:742
Unified instrumental model of group conflict, 1:429, 1:479
Uniqueness bias, 1:273–274
United Farm Workers of America, 1:89
United Nations
　　Convention on the Prevention and Punishment of the
　　　Crime of Genocide, 1:304
　　Convention Relating to the Status of Refugees, 1:428
Unitizing, 2:699
Unitizing reliability, 2:704
Units of analysis, for research, 2:702–703
University of Alabama, 1:87
University of Bristol, 2:728
University of California, Berkeley, 1:45

University of California, Davis, 1:9
University of California Regents v. Bakke, 1:200
University of Georgia, 1:9
University of Iowa, 1:284
University of Michigan, 1:9, 1:152,
　　　2:535, 2:928
　　Festinger and, 1:285
　　Law School, 1:11
　　Survey Research Center, 1:152
University of Minnesota, 1:161, 1:285–286
University of Mississippi, 1:87
University of Pennsylvania, 1:204
University of Rochester, 1:284
University of Texas Law School, 1:9
University of Warwick, 2:842
Ury, William, 2:602
U.S. Commission on Civil Rights, 1:86
U.S. Congress, 1:84
U.S. Federal Hate Crime Statistics, 1:395
U.S. Immigration Restriction Act of 1924, 1:256
U.S. Marine Corps, 2:546
U.S. Merchant Marine, 1:468–469
U.S. Navy, 1:325
U.S. Supreme Court. *See individual names of cases*
USS *Vincennes,* 2:751
Utah, 2:647
Utz, Sonja, 1:118

Vancouver Canucks, 2:836
van den Bos, Kees, 1:219, 2:665
Van Fleet, David, 1:288
van Gennep, Arnold, 1:449
Van Hiel, Alain, 1:47
van Knippenberg, Daan, 2:801
van Vugt, Mark, 2:545
Vatican, 2:550
Vaughan, Graham, 1:111
Venkatesh, Sudhir, 1:294
Verkuyten, Maykel, 2:584
Versailles Treaty
　　genocide and, 1:306
　　hate crimes and, 1:401
Vertical dyad linkage model, 2:518–519, 2:521, 2:928,
　　　2:947–949
　　development of VDL relationships, 2:947–948
　　high- and low-quality relationships, 2:948
　　recent developments in, 2:948
Veysey, Bonita, 1:363
Victimization
　　gangs and, 1:295–296
　　genocide and, 1:306–307
　　intergroup violence and, 1:480
Video recording, for research, 2:702
Vietnam War, 1:173, 1:374, 1:390
Vindication of the Rights of Women, A
　　　(Wollstonecraft), 1:281
Violence, sports teams and, 2:835–836
Violent Crime Control and Law Enforcement
　　　Act of 1994, 1:85

Virtual/Internet groups, 2:949–952
group polarization and, 1:363
groupware, 2:950
social computing, 2:950–951
text-based virtual groups, 2:949
virtual organizations and, 2:951
Virtual Network Computer, 2:950
Virtual organizations, 2:951
Voice effects, 2:664
Voice procedures, 2:664
Völkerpsychologie (Wundt), 2:581
Von Bertalanffy, Karl Ludwig, 2:891
Vonk, Roos, 2:840
Voting Rights Act, 1:84–85, 1:88
Vroom, Victor, 1:153–154, 1:457
Vygotsky, Lev, 2:811

Waal, Frans de, 2:549
Walker, Laurens, 1:502–503, 2:664–665
Waller, Mary, 1:327
Wanna-be gangs, 1:294
Ward, Colleen, 1:35
Warner, Rebecca, 2:785
Warner, W. L., 1:90
Watts, Duncan, 1:129, 1:270
Weapons Identification Task, 2:574
Weber, Christopher, 1:47
Weber, Max, 1:72, 1:288, 1:312, 2:524, 2:624, 2:672
Weber, Renee, 2:869
WebEx, 1:97, 2:950
Webner, Daniel, 2:931
Web of Science, 1:422
Webster, Donna, 2:598
Weightism, 2:953–955
comparing to other prejudices, 2:953–954
consequences of, 2:954–955
origins of, 2:953
reducing, 2:955
Weimar Republic, 1:401
Weinberg, George, 1:407
Weiner, Bernard, 1:42
Welch, Jack, 1:72
Well-being, social comparison theory and, 2:764–765
West, Candace, 1:297
West, Michael, 2:907
West Bank Wall, as intergroup contact theory, 1:472
West Indies, 2:756
Wheelan, Susan, 1:326, 1:341
White, Harrison, 1:384
Why Men Rebel (Gurr), 1:490
Whyte, Glen, 1:362
Widmeyer, Neil, 1:316
Wikipedia, 1:97, 2:624, 2:950–951
Wilder, David, 1:187
Wilkes, A., 1:314
Willer, David, 1:384, 2:787–788
Willer, Robb, 1:409
Williams, Kipling, 1:441, 2:628, 2:709, 2:809
Williams, Robin, 1:265, 1:469

Willis, Richard, 1:20–21
Wilson, Bill, 2:875
Wilson, E. O., 2:760, 2:770
Wilson, G. D., 1:145–146
Wilson, Glenn, 1:47
Wilson, John, 1:357, 2:726
Wilson, Timothy, 1:212
"Win-stay" strategy, 2:663
Winter, David, 1:47
Witte, Erich, 2:507–508
Wittgenstein, Ludwig, 1:69
Wolf, Scott, 1:464
Wollstonecraft, Mary, 1:281
Women's Political Council, 1:87
Wood, Carolyn, 2:754
Wood, Wendy, 1:303, 1:356
Woods, Tiger, 2:868
Worchel, S., 2:894
Worchel, Stephen, 1:326
Word, Carl, 1:214
Workplace
affirmative action and workplace composition, 1:10–11
diversity education and training in, 1:224–225
gender and behavior, 1:299
gender roles and, 1:303
sexism and, 2:746–747
Work teams, 2:955–958
development of, 2:957
effectiveness of, 2:958
historical overview, 2:955–956
processes and performance, 2:957–958
team composition, 2:956–957
types of, 2:956
World Bank, 1:108
WorldCom, 1:390
World knowledge tasks, group potency and, 1:372
World of Warcraft (game), 2:950
World Trade Center, 1:181, 2:531. *See also* **Terrorism**
World War I, 1:305–306, 1:401–402, 2:655, 2:725, 2:769
World War II, 1:1, 1:26, 1:43, 1:45, 1:105, 1:158, 1:304
food preference study, 2:535
genocide and, 1:308
great person theory of leadership and, 1:312
group emotions and, 1:335
group formation and, 1:339
hate crimes and, 1:400–403
idiosyncrasy credit and, 1:421
Islamophobia and, 1:486
justice and, 1:500–501
prejudice and, 2:571, 2:655
relative deprivation and, 2:694
symbolic racism and, 2:883
terrorism and, 2:917
World Wide Web, 2:950
Worm Community System, 2:950
Wright, Jeremiah, 2:884
Wright, Lester, 1:409
Wright, Robert, 1:363
Wright, Stephen C., 2:926

Wright, Stuart, 2:728
Wundt, Wilhelm, 1:350 2:581

Xenophobia, 2:959–961
    cultural/societal bases of, 2:961
    extent of, and ethnocentrism, 2:960
    individual bases of, 2:960–961
    intergroup bases of, 2:960
    Islamophobia and, 1:486
    xenophobic reactions to immigrants, 2:959–960

Yale University
    on frustration-aggression hypothesis, 1:290
    on obedience to authority, 2:613–614
Yamagishi, Toshio, 2:789–790
Yang, Huei-Chuan, 1:62
Yetton, Phillip, 1:153
Yoder, Janice, 2:926–927

YouTube, 2:951
Yzerbyt, Vincent, 2:865

Zajonc, Robert, 1:355, 1:386, 2:791–793
Zald, Meyer, 1:104–105
Zambia, 2:726
Zamenhof, Ludvic, 1:253
Zander, Alvin, 1:209
Zanna, Mark, 1:214
Zavalloni, Marisa, 1:362
Zdaniuk, Bozena, 2:544
Zeeman, E. C., 1:232
Zeifman, Debra, 1:38
Zelditch, Morris, Jr., 2:844
Zembrodt, Isabella, 2:545
Zimbardo, Philip, 1:53–54, 1:192–193, 1:197, 2:711, 2:837
Zola, Émile, 1:191
Zucker, Lynne, 1:178